Views of e-Commerce Leaders on
Global e-Commerce: Text and Cases

In *Global e-Commerce: Text and Cases* Farhoomand and Lovelock have clarified many of the mysteries that surround the e-commerce world. Perhaps more importantly, they have also identified the significant challenges that have yet to be resolved in this emerging arena. It is clear that the basic principles of business will continue to apply in the marketspace as they have done so in the past in the marketplace. The key difference is that as a result of the speed of change, the evolution of e-business demands that business practices be anchored in sound and adaptable business models. This book provides such a conceptual framework, and uses up-to-date and practical business case studies to highlight the rewards of successful implementations as well as the costs of failure.

William L. Conley
Vice President & Managing Director, Europe
FedEx Global Logistics, Inc.

In *Global e-Commerce: Text and Cases* Farhoomand and Lovelock introduce important topics that are often neglected. In addition to the standard topics in e-commerce, they devote chapters to the legal aspects, the need for trust in transactions, and the management of process. The number and extensiveness of their cases make the book particularly useful for educating professionals.

Paul Gray, Ph.D.
Editor, Communications of the Association for Information Systems
Professor and Founding Chair, Information Science, Claremont Graduate University, USA

As e-commerce is becoming a core part of the business curriculum, Farhoomand and Lovelock provide urgently needed empirically based and theoretically grounded guidance on how to succeed in the electronic marketspace. This impressive collection of cases, embedded in the theoretical fundamentals of doing business electronically, gives insights not only into organisations operating in different industries and in different countries but also into the wealth of e-commerce issues: from technology to marketing, operations to strategy, infrastructure to human relations. In *Global e-Commerce: Text and Cases*, the business model is used as a pedagogical anchor to guide the reader through the broad set of e-commerce topics. The book addresses entrepreneurs who are planning an e-commerce venture and managers who are responsible for transforming an existing organisation into an e-business. *Global e-Commerce: Text and Cases* is a valuable source of insight and knowledge. I strongly recommend it.

Stefan Klein, Ph.D.
Professor of Information Systems, University of Muenster, Germany

Global e-Commerce: Text and Cases brings together business and technology perspectives in addressing key issues involved in e-commerce. These issues will be the cornerstone of business education in coming years when e-commerce will become synonymous with commerce. The further blending of text and cases makes this book especially useful for instructional purposes.

Kenneth L. Kraemer, Ph.D.
Professor, Graduate School of Management
Director, Center for Research on Information Technology and Organizations
University of California, Irvine, USA

This book is superb in linking the conceptual frameworks of e-commerce to cases of not only well-known US companies, but also companies operating in Asia and other parts of the world. The book is particularly useful in teaching general concepts and frameworks, applying them to real-life cases, and fostering a global view of e-commerce.

Jae Kyu Lee, Ph.D.
Professor of e-Commerce,
Graduate School of Management
Korea Advanced Institute of Science and Technology
Director, International Center for Electronic Commerce (icec.net)

Global e-Commerce: Text and Cases is a practical and comprehensive guide to the Network Economy. It blends cohesive theories with empirical cases to raise fundamental questions facing today's practitioner. Using a rich international context, the book highlights the importance of infrastructure, regulatory frameworks and trust in shaping viable e-commerce models, streamlining an increasingly global value-chain, and transforming a company into an e-business. The material and cases in this book have saved me large sums in my venture into e-commerce.

Richard Leung
Chairman & CEO, E-Marketplace Limited, Hong Kong

Those of us who have been teaching e-commerce have wanted a book such as this for some time. *Global e-Commerce: Text and Cases* combines a clear explanation of e-commerce principles and technologies with substantive case studies for classroom use. It is as current as any book in this space can be. My thanks go to Ali Farhoomand and Peter Lovelock for their efforts on our behalf.

Donald J. McCubbrey, Ph.D.
Director, Center for the Study of Electronic Commerce
Daniels College of Business, University of Denver, USA

A fascinating coverage of cases and concepts. Farhoomand and Lovelock have produced a truly global text that gets to the heart of e-commerce strategy. Highly recommended.

Bob O'Keefe, Ph.D.
Editor, European Journal of Information Systems
Professor of Information Management
Brunel University, UK

Amid the plethora of recently published texts on e-commerce/e-business, *Global e-Commerce: Text and Cases* stands out by virtue of its in-depth analysis of issues and its detailed cases and learning tools. It covers the business issues in which the impact of e-commerce is most felt: from the building of a new 'business ecosystem' through the conduct of business and the management of relationships in the New Economy, to the transformation of today's enterprises. The book fills a gap that has existed for some time, providing a complete coverage for MBA and post-graduate students. One feature that will be particularly appreciated by students and teachers alike is the diversity of the cases – these are not merely the best-known US case studies, but a genuinely wide group of large and small firms operating around the world.

Paula Swatman, Ph.D.
Professor of e-Business & Director, Institute for Management
University of Koblenz-Landau, Germany

There are four aspects of *Global e-Commerce: Text and Cases* that I like. First, the book is carefully crafted. The authors have clearly worked hard to avoid hyperbole and instead provide a high-quality text that will assist educators, managers and students to better understand the world of electronic commerce. Second, the book presents a set of conceptual models that should be robust over time. Such models are essential if we are to deal effectively with the on-going, rapid change that is likely to occur in electronic-commerce phenomena. Third, the book contains rich problems and cases. Users of the book will learn about electronic commerce from the facts presented in the cases. They should also be able to develop facility with solving problems and developing strategy in a world of electronic commerce. Fourth, as someone who lives in the Asia-Pacific region and teaches a large number of students from the region, I am delighted to see so many of the cases are based on organisations within the region. Students from within the region should be able to identify readily with the organisations described in the cases. Students from outside the region will better appreciate the commonalities and differences they are likely to encounter as the world moves increasingly towards a global marketspace.

Ron Weber, Ph.D.
Professor of Information Systems, The University of Queensland, Australia

In this fascinating book, you will find out everything you need to know about global e-commerce, from the various parts of the emerging e-commerce environment and its impacts, to e-relationship building and customer trust management, to the design and implementation of e-business. Through in-depth field studies, *Global e-Commerce: Text and Cases* also includes strategies for transforming a traditional organisation into an e-business by distilling the experiences of a large number of global companies. Whether discussing the exploration of a new e-market, or the building of e-relationships and trust, or the establishment of global e-presence, the authors cover the topics under the study thoroughly and in an easy-to-read style with great detail and compelling insights. The book is truly indispensable for academics, practitioners and students who are interested in global e-commerce.

Kwok Kee Wei, Ph.D.
Senior Editor, MIS Quarterly
Professor and Head
Department of Information Systems
National University of Singapore

Successful e-business initiatives combine the best of the old and the new – sound business principles and new technology interwoven to provide innovative ways to create customer value. To make the changes required for e-business requires bold and informed firm leadership. By far the best way to develop the insight need to lead and implement e-business initiatives is through case studies of firms who have led the way. Farhoomand and Lovelock have written one of the best sets of case studies of firms implementing e-business available today. The cases are rich, compelling and provide a powerful vehicle for motivating and informing the implementation of e-business.

Peter Weill, Ph.D.
Director, Center for Information Systems Research
MIT Sloan School, USA

CONTENTS

■■■

ABOUT THE AUTHORS

Ali Farhoomand, Ph.D. is an educator, researcher and consultant. In the last 20 years he has taught in universities and taken part in executive development programmes across Asia, Australia, Europe and North America. He is the author of three books and many articles in journals such as *Communications of the ACM, Electronic Markets, Journal of Organizational Computing and Electronic Commerce, IEEE Transactions* and *MIS Quarterly*. In addition, he has consulted widely on projects related to international trade, information systems planning and e-commerce. He can be reached at ali@business. hku.hk.

Peter Lovelock, Ph.D. is a senior researcher with the Telecommunications Research Project, a telecommunications and IT think-tank for the Asian region. He is also associated with the Chinese Academy of Social Sciences, and has worked as a policy analyst at the United Nation's International Telecommunication Union (ITU) in Geneva, contributing to seven of its major research publications.

FOREWORD

■-■-■

This book is about electronic COMMERCE and the World Wide World Wide Web. No, neither of these two phrases are misprints. The strengths of Ali Farhoomand's and Peter Lovelock's book are that, first, it is about managing commerce and second, it puts Web-based commerce into its international context. This is in bold and valuable contrast to the seductive but damaging mainstream focus over the past few years on building technology – ELECTRONIC commerce – and following the business path of the US Web: e-commerce has not been worldwide in its focus and business models, just US-centric.

What may be termed the dot.com era of e-commerce is well and truly over. The search now is for the value path to do profit. Dot.com was based on myths of first mover advantage, Website 'hits' as the measure of business success, and the dot.com as the business model. This 'new' economy views basically disdained management. It ignores the realities and complexities of marketing, customer service, business processes, organisation, regulatory issues, public relations, financial management, organisation and the role of the executive.

Electronic commerce is hard work in terms of both the 'e' and 'c'. It requires a new style of management that faces up to the challenge of integrating business and technology. Historically, they have been very separate, with a wide gap – often a chasm – between them in terms of culture, language and dialogue. IT – information technology – was a separate fiefdom, run by a CIO (Chief Information Officer) that built 'systems' and 'applications' and tried to ensure 'user' involvement. The IT field talked about the need for business alignment, business management awareness and top management awareness and top management commitment. On the other side of the chasm, business executives complained of IT costs, lack of payoff and most of all its jargon.

e-Commerce succeeds only when business and technology come together as management fusion. That is very difficult to achieve with no simple answers to the many uncertainties, risks and complexities. Here is the first of this book's distinctive strengths. For students and their teachers, the rich set of cases it presents do not point to single or simple answers. They point to a business picture of e-commerce. They do not have tidy endings in many instances and often end with a question that demands a *management* focus, not a technology fix. Case 6.1 is an example. CaseTrust is a Singapore firm with explicit ambitions to become a global standard trademark. In other words, it is a wwwww player – world wide World Wide Web. The case ends by asking, "Could the Singapore scheme be directly replicated in other countries?" That is a key question that is not asked in the dot.com and US Web world, because the implicit answer is that a Website can be transferred anywhere with only minor linguistic and marketing adaptations.

Business managers have to answer such questions. They need help to do so. That is the role of cases in business education. They cannot learn, though, if the cases are the traditional national e-commerce examples. Dell, for instance, is one of the three most widely discussed e-commerce pacesetters (Cisco and amazon are the others.). Just about every book on e-commerce describes Dell – from its national US perspective. This is the very first book I have come across – and I read them all! – that discusses how Dell expanded beyond the United States. Again, the focus is on managers managing, with Michael Dell, in the forefront. He is quoted as saying in his semi-autobiography that "many people told us the direct model would fail in virtually every country we expanded into…. The message was always the same: our country is different, your business model would not work here."

Dell made it work; the discussion of how it did so in China (Case 3.1) is both instructive and mind-expanding. It is not really a case about e-commerce in China but a richly textured description of management in action and leadership for a new business context.

The Internet is global. The technology talent base is global. India is the most noted instance of how a new economy is built on new skills. Singapore preceded it in becoming the world's first IT-based nation state. Sweden and Finland are the pacesetters in mobile e-commerce. The US increasingly relies on imported talent; ten percent of all US IPOs are headed by an Indian and over half of all advanced technical degrees are earned by foreigners.

It is time for e-commerce management to go global. This is an indispensable book.

Peter Keen

Peter Keen is the founder and Chairman of Keen Innovations and has served on the faculties of Harvard, MIT and Stanford. He is the author of over 20 books that have strongly influenced the business–technology dialogue, including *From .com to .profit* (2001), *The eProcess Edge* (2000), *Electronic Commerce Relationships: Trust By Design* (1999) and *The Process Edge* (1997).

PREFACE

The proliferation of e-commerce has led to the emergence of a new business ecosystem where transactions are conducted with an increasing degree of speed, openness and transparency. The success of companies in the future will largely depend on their ability to leverage the existing technological infrastructure to find new ways of cooperating with their partners to provide customers a wide range of value-added products and services.

Global e-Commerce: Text and Cases builds theory, fundamentals and structure with a view to highlighting how traditional business methods are being transformed by the evolving business order. It combines the emerging principles and theories related to the network economy, and a context-rich, detailed set of 16 case studies to show how to use the Internet effectively to expand market reach, minimise costs and shorten production and ordering time, thus enhancing customer value and loyalty. The book is accompanied by an Instructor's Manual that includes comprehensive teaching notes to all the case studies.

The book is a useful tool for business and economics students and managers who desire to understand the following:

- ❑ How the new business ecosystem is being created.
- ❑ How to devise and implement viable business models in the marketspace.
- ❑ How to build and manage e relationships.
- ❑ How to transform an organisation into an e-business.

In *Global e-Commerce: Text and Cases* we have relied on the basic principles of economics and business and built on these fundamentals to explain the nature of forces underlying the sweeping changes driven by the network economy. We have tried, as much as possible, to steer away from the hype espoused by public media and trade publications by providing in-depth coverage of the antecedents and consequences of e-business transformation.

In addition, we have used a rich mix of fully fledged global case studies to highlight the context within which the new business order is taking shape. The cases are analytical and decision-oriented, and are written based on specific teaching objectives revolving around particular concepts and theories. They should be useful in exposing students to a generalised approach to problem-solving or decision making involving the application of analytical techniques for choice making and problem resolution. To further reinforce the application of concepts covered in the book, we have also included an up-to-date set of company vignettes to highlight a particular problem, example or method. We believe such confluence of theory and practice provides a useful framework where students will have an opportunity to first conceptualise, analyse and synthesise, and then practically apply relevant theories and concepts in a business environment.

The book consists of ten chapters organised into four modules. The first module outlines the way in which the various parts of the emerging e-commerce environment – the marketspace, infrastructure and regulatory framework – come together. Module 2 assesses the impact of e-commerce on the way in which business is conducted. It examines activities within business-to-business relations and within the mass market, or business-to-consumer relations. Module 3 describes how to build and manage relationships in the marketspace through the appropriate mix of technology, customer relationship management and trust. Module 4 examines how the success of the new business ecosystem depends on enhanced collaboration and communication not only along the firm's external business web, but also within the enterprise itself. It describes the concepts of techno-business architecture and process management and the role they play in transforming a company into an internetworked enterprise.

The material in this book is based on our in-depth field studies of over 40 global companies conducted in a span of four years. Some of the results are presented in the case studies, others have been used in formulating principles and concepts presented throughout the book. We thank the University Grants Committee and acknowledge their generous financial support for these field studies (Grants Nos. 342/108/0002 and 10100120.19979.44000.327.01).

We are also grateful to many case writers at the Centre for Asian Business Cases at The University of Hong Kong School of Business. Maria Cascales, Marissa McCauley, Eva Chang, Vanessa Clark, Minako Fukagata, Amir Hoosain, Eva Kwan, Andrew Lee and Deric Tan all worked very hard and did the field work necessary to write the cases.

We are particularly indebted to two people who made indispensable contributions to this project. Shamza Khan provided immense intellectual and scholarly input and so diligently oversaw the progress of the project. Using her marketing background she was particularly instrumental in shaping the ideas behind the chapters on e-relationship and trust in the marketspace. We miss her and wish her luck at Columbia University where she is pursuing her postgraduate studies. Last but not least, Pauline Ng, the Senior Researcher of the Centre, was our moral outpost throughout the project. She was always there to help – professionally, patiently and steadfastly. Many thanks to her for making this project come to a successful fruition.

Ali F. Farhoomand

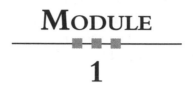

MODULE

1

Building a New Business Ecosystem

Without changing our pattern of thought, we will not be able to solve the problems we have created with our current pattern of thought.

– Albert Einstein

We are living in a time epitomised by rapid technological changes, increasing environmental complexity and uncertainty, intense global competition and growing interdependence among businesses. We are living in a time where geographical and temporal barriers are falling, where form and function are being disaggregated, where time and speed are taking centrepiece as critical business success factors.

We are in the midst of a paradigmatic shift, witnessing the emergence of a new business ecosystem governed by time-tested principles but shaped and influenced by a new set of rules. Like all other paradigmatic changes, understanding this emerging ecosystem requires certain gestalt shifts – a new way of looking at things without forgetting past practices and their role in the emerging environment.

In this module we will examine the forces shaping the marketspace. In Chapter 1 we show how in the new ecosystem the distinctions between the market, the distribution channel and the promotion channel have become blurred. We will also discuss how morphing of the market, the distribution channel and the promotion channel has in turn brought about unforeseen challenges and opportunities to businesses. The chapter ends with two cases – *Travelling Via the Web: The Changing Structure of an Industry* and *SCMP.com: Strategic Repositioning of a Newspaper* – that examine how the balance of power is changing at industry level and firm level, respectively.

Building the marketspace requires a solid infrastructural foundation. In Chapter 2 we examine what constitutes an e-commerce infrastructure and why technological convergence and integration are crucial in building such infrastructure. The chapter ends with two cases – *adM@rt.com: If You Build It, Will They Come?* and *New Technologies, New Markets: The Launch of Hongkong Telecom's Video-on-Demand* – that explore the important role that infrastructure plays in the marketplace.

Apart from the infrastructure imperative, the new business ecosystem requires a global regulatory framework, a topic that is covered in Chapter 3. More specifically, we will discuss the problems associated with taxation, privacy, consumer protection, copyright, certification, and service and content regulations in cyberspace. The case following the chapter – *Multi-jurisdictional Compliance in Cyberspace* – outlines the international implications of doing business on the Internet.

CHAPTER

1

The Marketspace

OBJECTIVES

- To study the emergence of the marketspace concept.
- To distinguish between the marketspace and the marketplace.
- To learn about the various types of marketspace.
- To distinguish between the physical value-chain and the virtual value-chain.
- To study the emergence of infomediaries.
- To recognise the importance of building sustainability in the marketspace.

Electronic business and trade in information-driven markets have led to the emergence of a new 'marketspace' concept. The marketspace embodies the transition from physically defined markets to markets based on information and governed by information. This transition is impacting upon almost all aspects of commercial activity. As a result, the emergence of the marketspace has become as important as the advent of the hierarchical physical marketplace that came before it.

To encompass the emergence of the marketspace, we have, as shown in the module introduction, borrowed the term 'ecosystem', referring to all the entities that co-exist in a particular area and the complex relationships that exist between them and their environment. We then use 'ecosystem' to describe the virtual business and economic dynamics and resulting interrelationships being forged in the marketspace and the equilibrium required for sustaining the environment. This emerging ecosystem implies business co-dependencies between producers, manufacturers, wholesalers, distributors, retailers and customers in a borderless global community and the resulting 'marketspace' within which these forces operate. Marketspace dynamics impel the resulting market consequences, which have triggered the most profound economic impact in recent business history.

In this initial chapter, we study the emergence of the marketspace as the cornerstone of the information economy – a task we shall continue throughout the book. The first section of the chapter defines the marketspace concept, examining what comprises it and the elements leading to its creation. This is followed by a comparison of the marketplace and the marketspace to determine the structural changes and examine the various *types* of marketspace. Just as there are different types of physical marketplace, from flea markets to malls, so too the virtual market comes in many forms. The next focus is the accompanying transition from a physical value-chain to a virtual value-chain. We then discuss the emergence of market makers, or information intermediaries, and their role in the virtual value-chain. Finally, the creation of environments that lead to sustainable marketspace development is examined.

THE EMERGENCE OF THE MARKETSPACE

Defining the Marketspace

The marketspace term was first popularised in a 1994 *Harvard Business Review* article.[1] Rayport and Sviokla's market*space* is distinguished from the traditional, physical market*place* by a virtual context in which buyers and sellers discover one another and then conduct business transactions. It is the working environment that arises from the complex interaction of increasingly rich and mature telecommunication-based services and tools, and the underlying information infrastructure.

The e-commerce marketspace offers substantial advantages over conventional commerce (c-commerce) conducted in conventional marketplaces.[2] Marketspaces connecting buyers and sellers are being built across many product categories, and are

---

[1] Rayport & Sviokla (1994).

[2] Bar & Murasse (1999).

creating value by facilitating more efficient trade processes. Early experiences of participants suggest that an electronic marketspace can capture savings of at least 10–20 percent on sales and those savings result in lower prices for buyers.

Given that e-commerce, by definition, relates to those portions of the business process that involve information flows, there is a perception in some quarters that e-commerce is merely an adjunct to the physical flow of goods and services in c-commerce. But there are already substantial and important marketspaces in which the goods and services are digital in nature, and in which contracts are fulfilled using the same infrastructure on which they are negotiated. These include the following (adapted from Clarke, 1997):

- ❐ Documents, including articles and books
- ❐ Data, including statistics
- ❐ Reference information, including dictionaries and encyclopaedias
- ❐ Commodities, and commodity derivatives such as futures
- ❐ Weather forecasts
- ❐ Bookings and tickets for live events
- ❐ News
- ❐ Musical performances
- ❐ Images, including structured graphics such as diagrams and musical scores, and photographs
- ❐ Video and video-with-sound, including television, video-conferencing and video-clips
- ❐ Entertainment, infotainment, edutainment and education via multimedia
- ❐ Money, and particularly foreign currencies
- ❐ Insurance
- ❐ Software
- ❐ Securities and financial derivatives, such as stock-based, interest-rate-based and index-based options
- ❐ Projected and interactive voice, including addresses, telephone conversations and teleconferencing

A majority of financial services, for example, are digital in nature, and therefore lend themselves to being supported by e-commerce. It comes as no surprise, therefore, to find that financial services have been one of the earliest adopters of the e-commerce marketspace. Indeed, c-commerce in financial services may soon be relegated to a collection of niches, and the current dominance of physical locations and analogue communications may soon be superseded by virtual locations and digital communications.

Financial Services

The costs of on-line banking and investment services are dramatically lower than traditional services [see **Figure 1**]. A few standard examples illustrate the point:

❐ A banking transaction at a traditional branch teller costs more than US$1; an Internet transaction costs 1 cent.
❐ A travel reservation may cost US$10 through an agent; it costs $2 on-line.
❐ Where stock trading can cost US$150 through a full-service broker, and $69 through a discount broker, it is less than $10 through the Internet.

Transaction costs and annual account management costs are in the order of 20 percent or less of the costs of supplying traditional services. Moreover, the operating costs of on-line services decline steeply as volumes grow.

Figure 1: The cost of banking

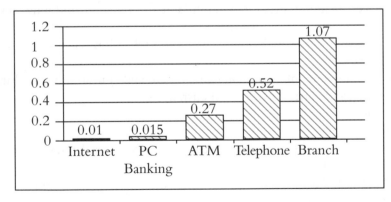

In the financial and banking market of the future, transactional revenues (of all sorts) and some asset-driven revenues (e.g., for fund management, custody and administrative services) will become severely commoditised. Primary profit sources will increasingly be liability-driven (e.g., margin lending) and the result of innovative service bundling. The most successful competitors will offer fully integrated services (i.e., brokerage, banking, pensions) through multiple channels (i.e., *both* traditional and on-line).

Source: Lovelock (1999).

Marketplace vs. Marketspace

In the transition from physical marketplace to electronic marketspace, information becomes a critical strategic resource. Apart from merely adding efficiency to a transaction, it adds value. By participating in the marketspace, tighter and increasingly dynamic links can be established between businesses, partners and customers – thereby creating and benefiting from a virtual value-chain (discussed later in the chapter).

Currently, the business environment supports both marketplace and marketspace transactions, either independently or simultaneously. Many companies continue to operate solely in the marketplace while certain businesses pursue 'pure e-commerce' or 'pure Internet' strategies, operating solely in the marketspace.[3] The majority of companies increasingly fall somewhere in between, employing a hybrid strategy that straddles the two business realms. The distinction between the two environments can be broken down into three components: context, content and infrastructure, as captured in **Table 1**.

Table 1: Marketplace vs. marketspace

Transaction characteristics	Marketplace	Marketspace
Content	Products/goods	Information
Context	Physical interaction	On-line interaction
Infrastructure	Trading lots, shopping malls, warehouses	Electronic networks (computers and communication lines)

Source: Adapted from Rayport & Sviokla (1994).

In the marketplace, a product's strength is established and managed by manipulating content, context and infrastructure through a traditional marketing mix, wherein the three elements are usually aggregated. However, in the marketspace, content, context and infrastructure can be disaggregated to create new ways of adding value, lowering costs, forging relationships with non-traditional partners, and reassessing 'ownership' issues. This is a key distinction from traditional business.[4] The corollary here is

---

[3] This is what the European Union terms 'direct e-commerce'; the entire transaction, from communication through payment to delivery, is conducted on-line. See Bar & Murasse (1998).

[4] Berryman *et al.* (1998).

that in mature marketspace environments, it is possible to mix and match content and context in ways that may at first seem unrelated to the core transaction. Consider these components in a marketspace environment:

- ❐ *Content.* The information *about* a product or service, when separated from the product or service itself, can become as critical as the actual product or service. To take one high-profile example, within on-line stock trading, stock market *information* has become a service offering every bit as commoditised as the actual trading of stocks themselves.
- ❐ *Context.* Commercial agents aim to establish and build customer loyalty. The potential for related transactions increases dramatically when a marketspace consumer becomes loyal to a particular context, due to the separation of content and context. As a result, establishing customer loyalty in the marketspace becomes even more critical than in the marketplace. Customer relationships are elaborated in Chapter 7: Internet Marketing.
- ❐ *Infrastructure.* The infrastructure allows a company to add value to its products and services, and satisfy its customers, by keeping processes virtual. Obvious examples are already well-established, such as: computer companies that allow prospective customers to search for products and services remotely, 'test drive' new components over the Internet, and specify their own configuration; software companies that offer software for downloading over the Internet for 60- or 90-day trial periods (so-called 'demonstration copies') that can then be converted to fully licensed products by obtaining a key code from a sales representative or the company's Internet site.

A TAXONOMY OF MARKETSPACE

Different types of marketspace have evolved as a result of the underlying information economy dynamics. Broadly speaking, the marketspace can be divided into those controlled by sellers, by buyers and those controlled by neutral third parties [see **Table 2**].

Seller–controlled

Marketspaces controlled by sellers are usually set up by a single vendor seeking many buyers. The aim is for the seller to retain (or create) market power in any transaction. The corporate Website set up by Cisco Systems (www.cisco.com), for example, enables buyers to configure their own routers, check lead times, prices, and order and shipping status, and confer with technical experts. By 1998, the site was already gener-

Table 2:   Types of electronic marketspace

Seller-controlled	• Information-only vendor Websites
	• Vendor Websites with on-line ordering
Buyer-controlled	• Website procurement posting
	• Purchasing agents
	• Purchasing aggregators
Neutral	• Industry/product-specific search engines
	• Information marts (structured access to vendor/ product information)
	• Business malls (multiple vendor storefronts)
	• Auction spaces

Source: Berryman *et al.* (1998), p. 153.

ating more than US$3 billion a year in sales – about 40 percent of the company's total sales.[5]

In addition, by publishing technical documentation on-line and giving customers access to ordering information, Cisco saves approximately US$270 million annually in printing expenses, configuration errors and telephone-based technical support. Its on-line marketspace has also increased customer loyalty by speeding up ordering, order status checking and response time.

Buyer-controlled

Buyer-controlled marketspaces are set up by or for one or more buyers with the aim of shifting market power and value to the buyer's side. Many involve an intermediary, but some particularly strong buyers have developed marketspaces for themselves. Japan Airlines (www.jal.co.jp),[6] a big purchaser of inflight consumable items, such as plastic rubbish bags and disposable cups, posts procurement notices on-line in order to find the most attractive suppliers.[7]

Buyer **intermediaries** act as agents or aggregators. FreeMarkets On-lin (www.freemarkets.com), a small company that helps traditional industrial firms loc

---

[5] US Department of Commerce (1998).

[6] Refer to the associated case study, "Japan Airlines: Impact of e-Ticketing".

[7] Berryman *et al.* (1998), p. 154.

a pool of competitive suppliers for semi-complex assembly parts, such as plastic injec-tion mouldings and iron castings, provides an example of such an agent. Its off-line consulting service helps refine buyer specifications and screen potential suppliers. When the best contenders have been identified, it sets up and conducts an on-line bidding session (which can last for up to three hours). This service promises buyers average price savings of 10–25 percent in addition to enhancing their purchase choice because suppliers submit bids that are customed to match buyer needs.

Aggregators combine several companies' offerings to increase the aggregator's collective buying power. TPN Register (www.tpn.geis.com), a joint venture between GE Information Services and Thomas Publishing, grew out of an initiative within GE to consolidate purchases, first within a single division (GE Lighting), then across all divisions. Finally, it expanded beyond GE to include other leading corporations in a buying consortium. The results have been a reduction in order processing time (from a week to one day for GE Lighting) and processing costs, and 10–15 percent lower prices.

Neutral

Neutral marketspaces are set up by third-party intermediaries to match many buyers to many sellers. One such intermediary, FastParts (www.fastparts.com), operates an anonymous spot market to trade overstocked electronic components. It receives notice of available stock from sellers, then matches buyers to sellers at an on-line auction. Sellers receive higher prices than they would through a traditional broker; buyers get market-driven prices that are lower than those offered by brokers' in addition to guar-d quality because FastParts inspects the products; and FastParts earns up to eight commission. Traditional brokers risk being eliminated by this process.

ever, neutral electronic marketspaces do not *necessarily* eliminate traditional ies. For example, Digital Markets established itself as an electronic inter-ade electronic components. Its aim was not to change the relationship and sellers, but to make their transactions more efficient. Its on-line es buyers' orders to their preferred distributors after checking for and suggesting substitute products. The intermediary then notifies ility and passes on delivery and pricing information from the seller. enables buyers to confirm and track their orders. For this service, ransaction fee when an order is placed. Buyers pay nothing.

MARKETSPACE THEMES

At this point, five broad themes can be discerned in the emergence of the e-commerce marketspace. It is important to recognise not only the individual themes but also their interrelationships. It is the interrelationships *between* these various e-commerce themes which are building a sustainable environment – a new business ecosystem. We elaborate on each of these themes and their interrelationships throughout the book.

1. *e-Commerce is altering the relative importance of time.* Economic and social influences within a society are a function of time; communities tend to be geographically determined because time is a determinant of proximity. However, e-commerce is changing the importance of time by allowing 24-hour communication and thus creating the ability to buy, sell and transact continuously. On the other hand, by speeding up production cycles, firms are increasingly able to operate in close coordination no matter what time zone they may be in (see Chapter 9: Process Management Through e-Business).

2. *e-Commerce is removing geographical boundaries.* e-Commerce allows individuals and companies to communicate and transact business anywhere, anytime. The removal of geographical barriers fundamentally changes the economic dynamics of doing business. e-Commerce provides opportunities and challenges for firms to *virtually* reach new markets across the globe:

   ❏ *Legal issues.* What are the taxation and multi-jurisdictional compliance issues surrounding global e-commerce?
   ❏ *Logistical issues.* How can the virtual supply-chain and physical supply-chain be managed concurrently?
   ❏ *Financial issues.* How should payment issues related to global business transactions be handled?
   ❏ *Security issues.* How can we ensure that private information stays private across a diverse array of open platforms?
   ❏ *Cultural issues.* How best can different market cultures be served under one virtual umbrella?

   The Internet is turning national markets into global markets in which companies must increasingly contend with domestic and international competitors (see Chapter 3: The Regulatory Framework, Chapter 7: Internet Marketing and Chapter 9: Process Management Through e-Business).

3. *e-Commerce is challenging traditional intermediation.* With e-commerce changing the way in which business is conducted, intermediary functions are being re-

defined and, in many cases, replaced. In certain cases, this is leading to new and closer relationships between business and consumer. In others, it is leading to opportunities for new intermediaries to emerge and provide market coordination. Such disintermediation and reintermediation has a major effect on a firm's management of competitors, supply-chains, reach and customer service (see Chapter 4: Business-to-Business e-Commerce and Chapter 5: Business-to-Consumer e-Commerce).

4. *Openness is the underlying technical and philosophical tenet of the expansion of e-commerce.* The widespread adoption of the Internet as a business platform is propelled from its non-proprietary standards and open nature; in the past decade, a huge industry has evolved to support it. In parallel, openness has emerged as a business strategy, with most successful e-commerce ventures granting business partners and consumers extraordinarily open access to inner logistics, databases and personnel. This has necessitated a change in organisational structure, interactivity and channels for knowledge diffusion in the workplace. At the same time, it has led to a shift in the role of consumers, who are increasingly implicated as partners in product design and creation. This customer involvement will cause fundamental economic and social transformations ranging from increased transparency and competition to potential invasion of privacy and spamming (see Chapter 2: The Infrastructure, Chapter 6: Trust in the Market-space and Chapter 10: Metamorphosis: The Internetworked Enterprise).

5. *e-Commerce is having a catalytic effect.* e-Commerce is accelerating many of the fundamental regulatory and economic changes already underway, such as the globalisation of economic activities and the demand for knowledge-based labour. Likewise, e-commerce is increasingly acting as a catalyst in bringing about change in many industries such as banking, travel and retail. In turn, this causes change at an enterprise level, compelling reorganisation, restructuring and new management attitudes (these topics are covered throughout the book).

BUILDING THE VIRTUAL VALUE-CHAIN

The value-chain is a model that describes the series of value-adding activities in a company's business processes, from inbound logistics and production through to sales and marketing [see **Figure 2**]. By analysing the stages of a value-chain, managers can redesign their internal and external processes to improve efficiency and effectiveness. Traditional business strategy has focused on the creation of value through the se-

Figure 2: Physical value-chain

quence of value-adding steps that comprise the chain.[8] In this established mode of thinking, information is a support function to the central value-adding process, and strategic management is focused on value-chain *integration*. Indeed, according to Porter, 'competitive advantage is increasingly a function of how well a company can manage this entire system'.[9]

However, in the marketspace, information is a source of value in itself. Therefore, information management within the value-chain has two direct consequences. First, it allows for disintermediation because stages within the value-chain are bypassed [see **Figure 3**]; information technology allows the producer to reach the consumer directly (Figure 3, Variant 3).

Secondly, information becomes a variable in the value-adding process and the value-chain's linearity comes under challenge. The linear business process becomes a

Figure 3: Value-added chains in the shirt industry

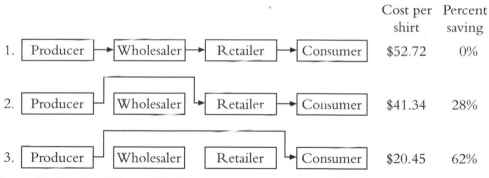

					Cost per shirt	Percent saving
1.	Producer →	Wholesaler →	Retailer →	Consumer	$52.72	0%
2.	Producer	Wholesaler	Retailer →	Consumer	$41.34	28%
3.	Producer	Wholesaler	Retailer	Consumer	$20.45	62%

Source: Benjamin & Wigand (1995), p. 67.

---

[8] Sviokla (1998) notes that 'McKinsey & Company was one of the first proponents of the value-chain concept, as was Joe Bower of the Harvard Business School'. Michael Porter performed the most comprehensive explication of the value-chain concept in his book *Competitive Advantage* (1990).

[9] Porter (1990), pp. 42–43.

matrix of potential inputs and outputs that can be accessed and distributed through a wide variety of channels [see **Figure 4**].

Creating value in the virtual value-chain involves five modular activities: gathering, organising, selecting, synthesising and distributing information. Each of these five activities allows the development of new customer relationships.

The value-adding transition from a physical to a virtual value-chain can be broken into the following three stages:

1. To manage physical operations more effectively.
2. To create a parallel value-chain.
3. To use the information for new customer relationships.

In the first stage, companies acquire an ability to manage physical operations more effectively as a result of an integrated value-chain (represented by the top bold line in Figure 4). Managers use large-scale information technology systems to coordinate activities in physical value-chains. In the second stage, companies create a parallel value-chain (the bottom bold line in Figure 4) by substituting physical activities for virtual ones. This could consist, for example, of streamlining supply logistics, or consolidating customer support services on the Web. Finally, businesses use this information as a resource to establish *new* customer relationships. At this stage, managers draw on the virtual value-chain's information flow to deliver value to customers in new ways. In effect, adding the virtual value-chain creates a matrix that allows companies to benefit from new markets and new relationships by applying the generic value-adding information to each activity in the virtual value-chain. In Module 3, we describe how the virtual value-chain can be managed to improve organisational performance. Another

Figure 4: Building the virtual value matrix

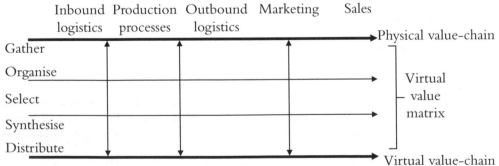

Source: Adapted from Rayport & Sviokla (1994).

result of linear value-chain disaggregation is that the info-centric value-chain becomes customer-centric rather than producer-centric [**Figure 5**]. This signals the further movement away from a production-oriented physical economy.

Figure 5:   Customer-centred value-chain

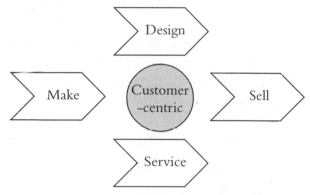

Source: Sviokla & Quinn (1997), p. 36.

VerticalNet: A B2B Infomediary

VerticalNet® (www.verticalnet.com) began as WaterOnline.com in 1995. From an Internet content player to the e-commerce technology firm of today, VerticalNet has 56 industry-specific, on-line, B2B communities grouped into 14 industry sectors, 10 of which were acquired by VerticalNet, and have raised over US$300 million. Its mission is two-fold: (1) build and manage dynamic, industry-focused Internet communities and environments where business can be performed faster and in a more efficient manner and (2) provide the foremost on-line information resources, communication vehicles, and e-commerce channels for industrial, professional and technology-based businesses within the VerticalNet communities.

VerticalNet aggregates suppliers and builds communities of interest. It is an on-line marketplace for the communities' buyers and sellers: buyers source and compare complex products on-line and sellers participate in e-commerce without developing a costly infrastructure. VerticalNet trading communities enable buyers and sellers worldwide to exchange information and execute on-line transactions. Communities also benefit from other capabilities at VerticalNet, such as auctions, catalogues, bookstores and career services, among others.

To host a storefront, VerticalNet charges an annual fee of US$6,000. It has over 3,300 storefronts. The average transaction value for storefronts is in excess of US$25,000, with half of the sales coming from firms who have never done business with that company before. VerticalNet has created joint ventures globally: VerticalNet Europe, VerticalNet Japan Kabushiki Kaisha, VerticalNet Metropolis★ (Africa), and VerticalNet UK. Almost 40 percent of VerticalNet traffic come from outside the US. Becoming a portal on VerticalNet requires the industry to meet certain criteria: US$8 billion or more in domestic revenue, with at least 2,000 vendors, 30,000 buyers and strong cross-border data flow, and companies must have a high penetration rate of Internet-connected PCs.

Sources: Callahan (2000); Hellweg (1999); *Upside* (2000); VerticalNet (2000); Wilson (2000).

General Motors' TradeXchange: A Virtual Marketplace for Automakers and Suppliers

As the world's largest vehicle manufacturer, General Motors (www.generalmotors.com) spends about US$87 billion annually in buying parts and equipment from its 30,000 suppliers worldwide. By the end of 2000, purchasing activities were to be conducted on-line through the TradeXchange, a B2B virtual marketplace for automakers and its suppliers to buy and sell goods. TradeXchange operates on Commerce One's MarketSite global trading platform and allows for three different types of business transactions: an on-line catalogue, a bid-quote process, or an on-line auction. GM can buy from its suppliers, and suppliers can transact business among each other. TradeXchange has the ability to provide information simultaneously to the multiple tiers, eliminating waste, overtime and excess inventory, while improving quality for GM and its suppliers. By using TradeXchange, GM could save as much as US$500 million in a year as the cost involved in processing and managing a purchase order via the Internet is about US$10; conventional supply-chain routes costs about US$100. With its automated order processing, it could help suppliers significantly streamline purchasing operations that could lead to lower operational costs. "Suppliers have a single connection to the TradeXchange, not multiple connections. They provide their content once, and it becomes visible to the entire trading community. That's a powerful model that can be used to help facilitate indirect procurement," says Doug Maulbetsch, GM's chief information officer.

Source: Krizner (2000).

MARKETSPACE LOGISTICS

As the value matrix in Figure 4 illustrates, many processes in a typical selling and procurement system can be streamlined in the transition from marketplace to marketspace. From product development to account information management on the selling side, and from assembling manufacturing specifications to tracking vendors' performance on the procurement side, electronic marketspaces have a measurable impact. Consider the following examples of marketspace logistics:

1. *Cost reduction through improved process efficiency.* In early marketspaces, companies focused on reducing costs, for example, the costs associated with publishing and distributing printed documents, by using the Web to make promotional materials available on-line. Digital Equipment Corporation (DEC) estimated that putting its promotional materials on its Website saved the company US$4.5 million annually in catalogue and mailing costs (prior to being bought by Compaq).

2. *Improved reach.* As e-commerce eliminates barriers of time and distance, businesses can tap resources in dispersed locations and perform functions, such as software development, wherever the most skilled and cost-effective talent resides, rather than because of the proximity to management or resource locations. Equally, business system processes can be outsourced to the most cost-effective providers. With the emergence of distributed, low-cost networks (i.e., the Internet), communicating between enterprises is cheaper than developing or maintaining certain skills in-house. Similarly, time differences have become less compelling, and in many cases the creation of an electronic marketspace has facilitated 24-hour business practices.

3. *The unbundling of business systems.* The disaggregation of what were traditionally integrated business structures has allowed companies to focus on the most competitive aspect of their business – their core competency. Vertical integration entails significant cross-functional coordination, often resulting in high costs and meaning that companies will seek to find ways to promote the disaggregation of vertically related businesses.[10] e-Commerce has accelerated this dynamic by enabling firms to enjoy the benefits of traditional vertical integration (e.g., economies of scale and scope) without requiring 100 percent ownership of related businesses. For example, with news and information content readily available on-line, local newspapers can package together material relevant to

---

[10] Galbraith & Lawler (1993).

their particular geographic market, concentrating their resources on local news while accessing networked sources for national and international news.

4. *Price reductions.* Due to greater market reach, the lower costs associated with e-commerce have led to greater product, market and international competition, especially in services. This, in turn, results in greater price competition. An associated effect will be that e-commerce will potentially change price structures.[11] A dramatic increase in the use of price discrimination (e.g., different prices charged for the same product at different times), such as is associated with customised products, market segmentation and auctions, can be expected as the ease of changing prices increases (see Chapter 9: Process Management Through e-Business).

While these changes will generally improve economic efficiency, they raise certain concerns. For example, a more general use of variable pricing, greater price competition, and price volatility could affect consumer expectations – and this could result in consumer hostility. Although consumers are accustomed to paying different prices for products such as cars, they may feel less comfortable with differentiated pricing for smaller common purchases. Changes in price structure also affect the ability to measure changes in prices and inflation accurately.

However, a major threat in the transition from marketplace to marketspace is that nimble new entrants may reduce revenue streams by recognising the *emerging* value proposition while existing players are attempting to re-engineer their business. For example, competitive interests could focus on the most valuable components of the newspaper business (classifieds, advertising) and specifically target it independently of the information package. To this end, examples are already apparent of non-related businesses *giving away* classified advertising as a means of driving traffic to their Website.

FROM DISINTERMEDIATION TO REINTERMEDIATION: THE EMERGENCE OF 'INFOMEDIARIES'

The emergence of information intermediaries is a direct consequence of the creation of the electronic marketspace. While e-commerce can dramatically reduce certain production and logistics costs, it does not really offer the 'friction-free' environment many

---

[11] See Chapters 2 and 3 of Varian & Shapiro (1999).

once believed it would, eliminating the middleman and allowing direct producer-to-customer interaction. Rather, owing to new costs associated with establishing trust and reducing the risks inherent in this type of activity (see Chapter 6: Trust in the Marketspace), e-commerce requires *new* intermediaries. Indeed, widespread 'disintermediation' is unlikely to be more pronounced than what occurred in earlier info-centric clusters, such as through direct mail, telephone, newspapers, TV and radio.[12] Rather than eliminating intermediaries, it is more likely that e-commerce will serve to restructure and redefine their role.

What we find then is that the electronic marketspace is providing what are really two intermediation opportunities:

- ❑ New entrants have the opportunity to *disintermediate* existing relationships. The likes of Travelocity, InsWeb and Charles Schwab are reaching out directly to their customers and eliminating the retailers and other channel intermediaries.
- ❑ Established players have the opportunity to reinvent (or *reintermediate*) existing markets. UPS and DHL, for example, are capitalising on the growth in Internet retailing.

Both opportunities result from the emergence of information as a critical strategic resource. Information intermediaries – or *infomediaries* – can be defined as '*a business whose sole or main source of revenue derives from capturing consumer information and developing detailed profiles of individual customers for use by selected third-party vendors.*'[13]

According to Hagel and Rayport (1997), a bargaining process is destined to ensue in which companies negotiate with customers to gain access to information about them. The sheer volume of, and accessibility into, such information will create the need for infomediaries who can handle negotiations and payments and add value in the way they process customer information for analysis and commercial exploitation.[14]

Two basic types of vendor-oriented intermediary have already appeared on-line:

- ❑ *Audience brokers* capture information about users across multiple Websites to help advertisers reach the most appropriate audiences. A leading example is

---

[12] Disintermediation is the elimination or displacement of market intermediaries, enabling direct trade between buyers and consumers without agents (Crowston & Wigand, 1999).

[13] Hagel & Rayport (1997), p. 13.

[14] Another dimension of information management will be around privacy issues. We explore this theme in Chapter 6: Trust in the Marketspace.

DoubleClick (www.doubleclick.net). While they may position themselves as media buyers, their primary value lies in their ability to find the best audiences for advertisers.

❑ *Lead generators* aggregate potential customers according to their profiles, preferences and other criteria, translate this data into specific product and service needs, and then direct these customers to vendors who meet those needs. A prime example is Auto-By-Tel (www.edmunds.com) which provides a network of 2,200 car dealers with consumer requests in exclusive sales territories in return for a fee per lead.

SUSTAINABILITY

The gathering momentum of open and interactive networks is creating a virtuous cycle of growth. Network economies of scale and scope mean that the community of networked users – businesses and individuals alike – is benefiting from increasing returns. Continuing advances in network infrastructures and computing devices are allowing Website designers, Web hosts and ancillary support businesses to supply the overlay technologies and services that enable the proliferation of electronic marketspaces. Together, these independent – and interdependent – developments are accelerating the expansion of e-commerce.

In its earlier phases, e-commerce was the preserve of large companies that could afford to build or lease the necessary proprietary networks. Applications were mostly limited to EDI (electronic data interchange) and EFT (electronic funds transfer). The computer systems required were generally mainframes, with complex, purpose-specific software and massive systems integration requirements. Today, however, all that is required is a PC and a phone line to take advantage of the growing number of public and private networks that use standard protocols such as Transmission Control Protocol/Internet Protocol (TCP/IP) (see Chapter 2: The Infrastructure).

New marketspace businesses have the opportunity to benefit from similar increasing return dynamics as the fax machine did through the 1980s. Once a critical mass of networked users is achieved, revenues quickly accelerate. Once eyeballs begin to congregate at a particular site, the incentive for other sellers and consumers to locate at the same site increases exponentially.

Buyers will concentrate their spending where they find what they want and need. The infomediaries that take an early lead in attracting buyers and sellers will capture an increasing share of transactions and advertising revenue. However, the costs for these new network-oriented businesses in acquiring and retaining customers may be significantly higher. Because of the ease of information access and information comparison in a networked world, switching costs – where customers move from one vendor to another – are extremely low. Initially therefore, costs may be dramatically higher than revenues, as money is lost on every customer acquired ('customer acquisition cost'). Hence the importance of creating a sustainable business platform, wherein each new customer drives revenue per customer upwards. Where successful, the result is that eventual profit dramatically eclipses earlier losses.

Therefore, in the shift from marketplace to marketspace, a fundamental economic change is evident. Electronic intermediaries or markets that can create the content, context and infrastructure that consumers want, have the chance to develop a successful new business model. Trusted content, a viable economic scale, and compatibility with the consumer's buying habits are critical to this business model. In the following two chapters we look at the necessary infrastructure and context required. In Module 2 (Conducting Business in the Marketspace) we discuss the content in more detail.

SUMMARY

- ❑ The shift from marketplace to marketspace business represents a fundamental commercial transition. Whereas in the marketplace, a product's strength is an integrated package of content, context and infrastructure, in the marketspace, the three elements can be disaggregated to create new ways of adding value, lowering costs, forging relationships with non-traditional partners and rethinking 'ownership' issues. Because of the separation of content and context, the potential for related transactions increases dramatically in the marketspace.
- ❑ In the transition from physical marketplace to electronic marketspace, the use of information becomes a source of value in itself, rather than merely a supporting element in the value-adding process. In the marketspace, tighter and increasingly dynamic links can be established between businesses, partners and customers – thereby creating and benefiting from a virtual value-chain.
- ❑ The value-chain is moving from a production focused physical one, comprising key steps such as design, manufacturing, sales and service, towards a virtual value-chain which is info-centric and consumption focused.
- ❑ Different types of marketspace emerge, depending on their principal constituency: buyer or seller. These marketspaces are being driven in part by market makers who are able to use the network infrastructure to aggregate a wide array of information and then resell the repackaged information. These 'infomediaries' have become central in the evolving process of marketspace creation.

❐ The creation of sustainable marketspace development is dependent upon the achievement of critical mass. And for a critical mass of network users to become involved in emerging e-commerce in turn requires the sustained development of the three necessary marketspace features – infrastructure, context and content – both individually and together. Issues such as the continued development of a stable, robust and interoperable network platform that works at high speed need to be addressed; issues such as security, trust and standards need to be addressed and developed; and the development of compelling content and services will need to continue.

REFERENCES

Applegate, L.M., Holsapple, C.W., Kalakota, R., Radermacher, F.J., & Whinston, A.B. (1996), "Electronic Commerce: Building Blocks of New Business Opportunity", *Journal of Organizational Computing and Electronic Commerce*, Vol. 6, No. 1, pp. 1–10.

Armstrong, A. & Hagel, J., III (1996), "The Real Value of On-line Communities", *Harvard Business Review*, Vol. 74, Iss. 3, May–June, pp. 134–141.

Arthur, B. (1989), "Positive Feedbacks in the Economy", *Scientific American*, 26 November.

Bar, F. & Murasse, E.M. (1999), "Charting Cyberspace: A US-European-Japanese Blueprint for Electronic Commerce", in Steinberg, R. & Stokes, B. (eds), *Transatlantic Trade Cooperation in Asia: Sectors, Issues and Modalities*, Totowa, NJ: Rowman & Littlefield Publishers.

Benjamin, R., DeLong, D., & Scott-Morton, M. (1990), "Electronic Data Interchange: How Much Competitive Advantage?" *Long Range Planning*, Vol. 23, No. 1, pp. 29–40.

Benjamin, R. & Wigand, R. (1995), "Electronic Markets and Virtual Value Chains on the Information Superhighway", *Sloan Management Review*, Vol. 36, No. 2, pp. 62–72.

Berryman, K., Harrington, L., Layton-Rodin, D., & Rerolle, V. (1998), "Electronic Commerce: Three Emerging Strategies", *The McKinsey Quarterly*, No. 1, pp. 152–159.

Callahan, S. (2000), "VerticalNet: A Web Pioneer in Transition", *B to B*, Vol. 85, Iss. 5, Chicago, 8 May, pp. 1, 68.

Clarke, R. (1997), "Regulating Financial Services in the Marketspace: The Public's Interests", paper delivered at the 'Conference on Electronic Commerce: Regulating Financial Services in the Marketspace', The Wentworth Hotel, Sydney, 4–5 February, URL: http://www.anu.edu.au/, February 1998.

Clark, T.H.K. & Westland, J.C. (1999), *Global Electronic Commerce: Theory and Case Studies*, Boston, MA: MIT Press.

Cortese, A. (1996), "Here Comes the Intranet", *BusinessWeek*, 26 February, pp. 76–84.

Crowston, K. & Wigand, R.T. (1999), "Real-estate War in Cyberspace", *Electronic Markets*, Vol. 9, No. 1/2, pp. 37–44.

Galbraith, J.R. & Lawler, E.E. (1993), *Organizing for the Future: The New Logic for Managing Complex Organizations*, San Francisco, CA: Jossey–Bass Publishers.

Hagel, J., III & Armstrong, A.G. (1997), *Net Gain – Expanding Markets Through Virtual Communities*, Boston, MA: Harvard Business School Press.

Hagel, J. & Rayport, J.F. (1997), "The New Infomediaries", *The McKinsey Quarterly*, No. 4, pp. 54–70.

Harrington, L. & Reed, G. (1996), "Electronic Commerce (Finally) Comes of Age", *The McKinsey Quarterly*, No. 2, pp. 68–77.

Hellweg, E. (1999), "VerticalNet: Industrial-Strength Portal", 1 September, URL: http://www.business2.com/content/magazine/indepth/1999/09/01/16854, 24 August 2000.

Kalakota, R. & Whinston, A.B. (1996), *Frontiers of Electronic Commerce*, Reading, MA: Addison-Wesley.

Kalakota, R. & Whinston, A.B. (1997), *Electronic Commerce: A Manager's Guide*, Reading, MA: Addison-Wesley.

Kosiur, D. (1997), *Understanding Electronic Commerce: How Online Transactions Can Grow Your Business*, Redmond, WA: Microsoft Press.

Krizner, K. (2000), "TradeXchange Provides Historical Shift to GM", *Frontline Solutions*, Vol. 1, Iss. 4, Duluth, April, p. 9.

Lee, H.G. (1997), "AUCNET: Electronic Intermediary for Used-car Transactions", *EM–Electronic Markets*, Vol. 7, No. 4, pp. 24–28.

Lovelock, P. (1999), "Hong Kong as an Internet Financial Hub", Telecoms InfoTech Forum, Position Paper No. 2, September.

Malone, T.W., Yates, J., & Benjamin, I. (1987), "Electronic Markets and Electronic Hierarchies", *Communications of the ACM*, Vol. 30, No. 6, pp. 484–497.

Moore, J.F. (1996), *The Death of Competition: Leadership & Strategy in the Age of Business Ecosystems*, New York, NY: Harper–Collins.

Nash, K. (1996), "Extranet: Best of Both 'Nets'", *Computerworld*, Vol. 30, No. 33, 12 August, p. 1.

OECD (1999), *The Economic and Social Impacts of Electronic Commerce: Preliminary Findings and Research Agenda*, URL: http://www.oecd.org/, September.

Porter, M. (1990), *The Competitive Advantage of Nations*, New York, NY: Free Press.

Rebello, K. (1996), "Making Money on the Net", *BusinessWeek*, 23 September, pp. 104–118.

Rayport, J.F. & Sviokla, J.H. (1994), "Managing in the Marketspace", *Harvard Business Review*, November–December, pp. 141–150.

Sviokla, J.J. (1998), "Virtual Value and the Birth of Virtual Markets", in Bradley, S.P. & Nolan R.L. (eds), *Sense and Respond: Capturing Value in the Network Era*, Boston, MA: Harvard Business School Press.

Sviokla, J.J. & Quinn, M.F. (1997), "Marketspace Strategy and the European Information Society (Post 1998 Deregulation)", *Electronic Markets*, Vol. 7, No. 4, pp. 35–40.

Upside (2000), "VerticalNet Is Building B-to-B Communities with Functionality", Vol. 12, Iss. 8, August, p. 146.

US Department of Commerce (1998), "The Emerging Digital Economy", 15 April, Washington, DC: URL: http://www.ecommerce.gov/emerging.htm, June 2000.

Varian, H.R. & Shapiro, C. (1999), *Information Rules: A Strategic Guide to the Network Economy*, Boston, MA: Harvard Business School Press.

VerticalNet (2000), URL: http://www.verticalnet.com, 29 August.

Wilson, T. (2000), "VerticalNet Keeps Pace", *Informationweek*, Iss. 790, Manhasset, 12 June, pp. 136–138.

Zwass, V. (1996), "Electronic Commerce: Structures and Issues", *International Journal of Electronic Commerce*, Vol. 1, No. 1, pp. 3–23.

CASE

1.1

Travelling Via the Web:
The Changing Structure of an Industry*

The late 1990s witnessed the proliferation of the commercial uses of the World Wide Web (WWW) and the travel industry jumping onto the bandwagon too. Websurfers all over the world not only found travel-related information on the WWW, but also made flight, hotel or rental car reservations at such travel-related Websites. These Websites, in essence, became virtual travel agencies operating round the clock and across geographical boundaries. By mid–1998, conventional travel agencies found themselves in a situation they had never been in before – one that could escalate into a survival issue in the near future. How best could travel agencies fare in this rapidly changing environment?

THE TRAVEL INDUSTRY

Travel for religious, health, commercial, political, recreational and pleasure purposes could be traced back to the ancient Roman, Greek and Chinese civilisations. Although

---

* Andrew Lee prepared this case in conjunction with Louis Lee under the supervision of Dr. Ali Farhoomand. *Copyright © 1998 by The University of Hong Kong. Ref. 98/22C*

it was not a phenomenon of recent history, the travel industry made several break-throughs in the 19th and 20th centuries. From inter-continental railways, to trans-Atlantic vessels, to aeroplanes, each new mode of transportation revolutionised and expanded the travel industry. Throughout the 1990s, the travel industry was one of the largest industries in the world, serving and satisfying the different needs of travellers from all over the world.

Customers of the Travel Industry

To understand the needs of travellers, different methodologies had been adopted to segment and characterise them, for example, by demographics and by lifestyles. An-other common way of segmenting the travel market was by purpose. Under this scheme, travellers were distinguished as either leisure or business travellers. On average, half of the travel agencies' customers were leisure travellers, and half were business travellers.[1] While there could be overlaps and further subdivisions between the two, this distinction was well accepted because it was commonly recognised that business travellers had different needs and spending patterns. In short, the travel demands of the business market were more inelastic to price and economic conditions than those of the leisure market. This was evidenced by the 1997–98 Asian economic crisis. As a manager of one major international travel agency explained: "Let's say a manufacturer in Malaysia wants to borrow money from a bank in Hong Kong. Before the deal is struck, the bank will need to send someone down to Malaysia to check out the actual facility. When there's a business need, they'll travel."

Although the leisure market was more sensitive to economic conditions, it repre-sented a greater growth opportunity for travel agencies. When people became more affluent, they also became keener on travelling for pleasure and excitement. Leisure travellers usually did not have a good idea of the kind of vacation they wanted; nor were they aware of the details and alternative options. They required more time, assist-ance and expertise from travel agents. Leisure market bookings also realised a profit margin of ten percent or more, whereas the profit margin for the business market was around five to six percent.

---

[1] Gregory, A. (1993), *The Travel Agent: Dealer in Dreams* (Fourth Edition), Englewood Cliffs, NJ: Regents/Prentice Hall.

The Players in the Travel Industry

Unlike other distinctive industries such as the software or garment industries, the travel industry was not comprised of an integrated group of players. Rather, it represented a wide array of organisations that directly and indirectly provided travel-related services. These organisations could be grouped into three categories: direct providers, support services and tourism development [see **Exhibit 1**].[2]

Direct providers represented the layer of businesses that directly provided travel-related services to travellers. This category included airlines, hotels, water and ground transportation, restaurants, retail shops and travel agencies. They interacted most often with the travellers. Support services included organisations providing specialised services (e.g., tour organisers, travel and trade publications, hotel management companies and travel research firms) and support services (e.g., contract laundry and contract catering services). While the former lived almost entirely off the travel market, the latter did not. There were also organisations that belonged to a third category – tourism development. These were usually involved in tourism developmental issues of a long-term nature, e.g., building a resort. This category included planners, government agencies, real estate developers, financial institutions, and educational and vocational training institutions.

The Sales Distribution System of the Travel Industry

To effectively reach potential customers, service suppliers depended largely on the sales distribution system of the travel industry, which consisted of three main types of intermediaries: tour operators, specialty channellers and travel agencies (wholesale and retail). Although the customer could deal directly with the service provider or any one of the intermediaries, travel agencies were involved in the process [see **Exhibit 2**].

Tour operators organised the various service components of a package tour for leisure travellers. A typical package included an escort, transportation, meals, accommodation and sightseeing. Some tour operators also had their own escorts, buses and hotels. Others arranged for suppliers or other tour operators to provide such services.

Specialty channellers were intermediaries that focused on a special type of travel such as incentive travel,[3] meetings and conventions, and university exchange pro-

---

[2]   Gee, C.Y., Makens, J.C., & Choy, D.J.L. (1997), *The Travel Industry* (Third Edition), New York: Van Nostrand Reinhold.

[3]   Incentive travel: The use of travel as a reward for meeting or exceeding goal(s) at work.

grammes. Firms and organisations that concentrated on one of these areas could be either a company or a unit within an organisation. Their work involved dealing with consumers, and interfacing with travel agencies and tour operators. They were experienced in handling the special travel arrangements demanded of them. For example, the expertise of a university travel office was in organising exchange programmes and academic conferences, whereas the experience of a meeting and convention planner was in organising business conventions and management retreats.

Wholesale and retail travel agencies ■ A wholesale travel agency typically organised tour packages that were sold to customers through retail travel agencies. Nevertheless, the distinction was never clear-cut, especially in the eyes of the customers. Some wholesalers also assumed retail functions and sold tour packages directly to customers. Similarly, some retail agencies might package their own tours and sell them to customers. In any case, travel agencies, wholesale and retail alike, were perhaps the most important intermediary between the suppliers of travel services and their customers. To suppliers, travel agencies helped them reduce the costs of direct promotion and operation. Thus, suppliers could concentrate more on trade promotion and marketing. On the other side of the equation, customers usually had only a vague idea of what they wanted, and were unaware of the details and alternatives. Thus, customers sought advice from travel agents on travel-related matters. By understanding their needs and requirements, travel agents then offered recommendations about destinations, package tours, airlines and hotels. Therefore, the influence that travel agencies exerted over customers' choices was quite considerable.

Financially, the travel agencies and suppliers of travel services were mutually dependent. As an authorised dealer, travel agencies sold services directly to customers on behalf of service suppliers, wholesalers and tour operators. The primary source of income of most travel agencies, therefore, was derived from the commissions paid by these organisations. Among the various suppliers of travel services, airline bookings formed the largest slice of revenue of retail agencies, accounting for over 60 percent [see **Exhibit 3**].[4] In turn, travel services suppliers also relied heavily on travel agencies to sell their services [see **Exhibit 4**].

The commission rates offered by service suppliers varied across industries as well as suppliers. For instance, in the US market, cruise lines traditionally offered a higher rate than airlines. Similarly, in the airline industry, Japan Airlines offered a higher com-

---

[4] Gee, C.Y. *et al.* (1990), *Professional Travel Agency Management*, Englewood Cliffs, NJ: Prentice Hall.

mission rate (ten percent) in the US than its American rivals, which maintained an eight percent policy.[5] Commissions were only one of the several means that service suppliers employed to encourage travel agencies to sell their services. Override commissions were another common means. Typically, suppliers offered a graduated rate of overrides (a commission rate that was directly proportional to the volume of bookings). The more the travel agents sold, the higher the commission rate. Other forms of incentives included a quarterly bonus and free seats or rooms (from airlines, cruise lines or hotels).

Computer Reservation Systems – The Linkage Between Travel Agencies and Airlines

From 1976, United Airlines installed Computer Reservation Systems (CRSs) at travel agencies. Many other airlines followed suit, and from then on the use of CRSs proliferated. In the 1990s, the majority (75–80 percent) of airline bookings were made through travel agents via CRSs.[6]

Computer Reservation Systems worldwide ■ In the late 1990s, there were about a dozen major CRSs worldwide. In terms of global agency locations, European CRSs headed the list. Amadeus had become the world leader after merging with SystemOne, with a 27 percent market share, followed by Galileo and Sabre, each with 22 percent. Next came Worldspan with a ten percent market share. Abacus and Infini were the dominant CRSs in Asia, with a combined share of nine percent. Axess, with an emphasis on the Japanese local market, had a five percent market share.

To gain synergy and global competitiveness, CRSs were looking into different forms of alliances and partnerships:

- ❐ Core system integration, such as Galileo and Apollo.
- ❐ Host systems interconnection, such as Axess and Sabre.
- ❐ Partnerships with technology companies and service providers, e.g., Sabre with IBM, EDS and AT&T, as well as Amadeus with START on German Rail and Tour.

On the coalition front, Worldspan and Abacus were looking for a possible alliance with Galileo. Meanwhile, several CRSs were looking for opportunities to work with

---

[5] Small, S.H. (1998), "Rising to the Challenge", *Travel Agent*, 16 February.

[6] Flint, P. (1998), "End the CRS Oligopoly", *Air Transport World*, Vol. 35, Iss. 4, April.

the Civil Aviation Administration of China (CAAC) for the development of China CRS. Individually, Abacus decided to invest heavily in enhancing its non-air products and front-end PC workstations. Worldspan changed its strategy to more proactively address airline interests and concerns, and formed a partnership with Microsoft as the CRS behind Microsoft Expedia – a travel Website. In the meantime, Axess' main focus was still on the Japanese market and it had no plans to expand beyond Japan. Other individual efforts and developments included the following:

Amadeus, which offered very good travel products, entered Asia aggressively by setting up a regional office in Bangkok, from where it penetrated new markets, including Bhutan, Nepal, Sri Lanka, Bangladesh, Indochina, Malaysia, the Philippines and Indonesia. It already operated in Taiwan and Australia.

Galileo actively pursued sales and promotion to travel agents in order to penetrate into various markets, in particular, Asia. Its target markets included Indonesia, South Korea, Malaysia, Sri Lanka, Pakistan, Bangladesh, Thailand and Vietnam.

Sabre focused on maintaining its technological leadership. In alliance with Axess (a CRS developed by Japan Airlines), it gained market leadership in Japan. In the meantime, it also tried to strengthen its operations in the Asia-Pacific region through an alliance with Abacus and planned to expand to the Taiwan and China markets.

A bitter-sweet relationship ■ The relationship between travel agencies and service suppliers, especially airlines, was not an entirely mutually beneficial one. From the airlines' viewpoint, although a significant amount of their bookings were sold through travel agencies, it came with a cost. In fact, travel distribution costs were the third-largest controllable expense for airlines (after people and aircrafts). The revenue from sales through travel agencies typically incurred a 14 to 18 percent cost.[7] Japan Airlines, for instance, estimated that dropping the commission rate from ten percent to eight percent would translate into a US$4 to US$5 million annual saving.[8] Thus, the ability to bypass travel agencies and still reach the potential customers at a low cost was ideal. Increasingly, the WWW was seen as a promising alternative.

---

[7] Gee, C.Y. *et al.* (1990).

[8] Small, S.H. (1998), "Rising to the Challenge", *Travel Agent*, 16 February.

THE INTERNET AND WWW: IMPACT ON THE TRAVEL INDUSTRY

The travel industry was one of the earliest industries to join the Internet bandwagon. Since travel, by nature, had few geographical boundaries, the travel industry was uniquely suited to be on the Web. With 100 million Internet users around the world in 1997[9] (and this number continued to grow), there was simply no better way to reach such a global crowd than the WWW. With both existing players in the industry and outsiders trying to reap a slice of the on-line market, new travel-related Websites were springing up and rejuvenating continually. By 1997, the Web became the second most popular source of travel information in the United States.[10] People also became more likely to purchase travel-related services on-line. Forrester Research estimated that on-line travel sales would go up to US$570 million in 1998, second only to the computer industry, with estimated sales of US$700 million.[11]

Travel-related Websites

Many airlines, hotels, car rental companies, CRSs and national or municipal tourist organisations went on-line. They provided travel tips and information of all kinds, and accepted enquiries and bookings on-line. A growing number also accepted payments on-line. With abundant information available in the comfort of one's home or office, even travel agents agreed that more and more people sought travel-related information from the Web.

Depending on the nature of the hosting organisation, travel Websites could be categorised as either service suppliers, destination-related or virtual travel agencies.[12]

Service suppliers ■ In their earlier forms, the Websites of service suppliers such as airlines, hotels and car rental companies were aimed primarily at providing information. They advertised companies and allowed Websurfers to check service schedules or

---

[9] CommerceNet Research Center (1999), URL: http://www.commercenet.com/research/stats/wwstats.html, February.

[10] Kate, N.T. (1998), "Surfing for Travel", *American Demographics*, Vol. 20, Iss. 2, February, pp. 36–37.

[11] "EC", *Link-Up*, Vol. 15, Iss. 2, March/April 1998, pp. 8–10.

[12] Please refer to Appendix 2 for a list of the Websites mentioned in this section.

room rates and availability, e.g., Cathay Pacific Airways Ltd. or Hilton Hotel chains. As they evolved, many accepted reservations and payments on-line. Some sold more than just their core business. DragonAir, for example, sold travel packages on its Websites. Similarly, United Airlines allowed users to make reservations for flights, hotels and car rentals through its Websites. Taking it a step further, Japan Airlines even made its inflight merchandise available for sale.

Destinations ■ Destination marketing was an important aspect of the travel industry, and destination-related sites also appeared on the Web. Such Websites provided information and travel services related to a destination country, city or area. The information ranged from transportation, accommodation, sightseeing and dining, to local cultural and sports events. Since destination marketing was usually the responsibility of national or local tourism organisations, their Websites, like the ones by the Japan National Tourist Organisation and the London Tourist Board, embodied this flavour. France.com was a similar Website, but without the official tone. Some of these Websites advertised specific resort areas. The Websites of Bintan resorts and the Whistler resorts, for example, emphasised the outdoor activities available in these destinations. While all of these sites listed the traditional means of contact for the various service suppliers in the respective cities or countries, i.e., address, telephone or fax, some accepted on-line reservation and/or purchases, either through their own Websites or through links to the service suppliers' Websites.

Virtual travel agencies ■ The Web represented a virtual marketplace for a new breed of travel agencies to enter the travel industry – virtual travel agencies. Unlike traditional travel agencies, virtual agencies conducted their business on the Web. In addition to selling normal travel services, such as air tickets and hotel rooms, these Websites were loaded with travel tips, destination information and other value-adding services, such as maps, directions and even paging services, that would come in handy for travellers once they were on the road. Three of the largest and most well-known ones were Internet Travel Network (ITN), Travelocity and Microsoft Expedia [see **Exhibit 5**]. Founded in 1995, ITN consisted of a large network of local travel agencies around the world acting as its distribution channels for physical tickets, coupons and so on. Similarly, as the on-line customer-oriented branch of Sabre, Travelocity utilised the Sabre network of over 120,000 travel agencies globally. Both ITN and Travelocity dealt with customers directly through the Internet without local travel agencies as intermediaries. Microsoft Expedia, in contrast, embraced the concept and implementation of electronic ticketing (e-ticketing). As long as e-ticketing was available for the flights booked, customers would have the option to choose e-ticketing and received only a receipt by mail. Different airlines had different procedures for issuing boarding passes to e-ticket holders – in general travellers could get them by either using a self-service machine or by showing a picture ID at the check-in counter or boarding gate. If e-ticketing was not available, paper tickets would be mailed directly to customers and travel agencies were completely out of the picture.

Other variations of these types of Websites also existed. Condé Nast Traveler's Website, for instance, was presented as a Web version of the namesake popular travel magazine, but it also listed travel deals and packages. Regardless of the styles that any travel Websites took, they all had a common aim – to attract potential travellers from the global Internet population.

Customers of On-line Travel Services

It was estimated that the on-line travel market comprised only one percent of the total travel market in 1997. Reports and surveys also showed that the profile of those who had made travel plans on-line were different from the general public. First, the majority of on-line travel sales originated in the US. Hilton, for instance, found that 44 percent of its on-line bookings came from the US, the country contributing the highest number of on-line bookings. Japan, which had the second-largest Internet population, only contributed four percent. As far as the purpose of travel was concerned, discretionary travel topped business 59 percent to 41 percent [see **Exhibit 6**].[13] Demographically, the likely users of on-line travel services also appeared to be of a profile different from the general population. A survey by the Travel Industry Association of America showed that compared to the general public, a travel Website user in the US was more likely to be employed, educated to postgraduate level, and be a professional or manager [see **Exhibit 7**].[14] Of all the on-line travel revenue, air travel contributed 88 percent [see **Exhibit 8.**]

TRAVEL AGENCIES: DOOMED TO EXTINCTION?

Many people regarded travel Websites as new distribution channels that bypassed travel agencies. In the past, distribution channels such as 24-hour reservation hotlines and sales offices of airlines and hotels were seen as the number one threat to travel agen-

---

[13] Flint, P. (1998), "Web of Ambivalence", *Air Transport World*, Vol. 35, Iss. 4, April, pp. 31–36.
[14] Kate, N.T. (1998).

cies.[15] Travel agencies survived them, however. Despite all the hype about the on-line travel market and the viability of travel Websites, people in the travel industry, especially travel agents, were not too concerned. They believed that the value of the services that travel agencies provided to both service suppliers and travellers was not replaceable by Websites. Others, however, maintained that there was still much room for growth in the on-line travel market, as people became more comfortable shopping on-line. The two opposing schools of thought co-existed. But who would prove to be right?

Taking Sides: Travel Agencies Overcome the On-line Challenge

There were several main reasons for sceptics to believe that travel agencies would continue to be important players in the industry, in spite of the rising popularity of the Web. First, many considered that the expertise and services that travel agencies provided to both leisure and business travellers were simply not replaceable by the Internet. Discretionary or leisure travellers usually did not have a clear idea of what their vacation should include, and the advice and recommendations from travel agents were often influential in the travellers' decision-making process.

Similarly, travel agents believed that their expertise and services to corporate clients were not replaceable by any on-line offerings. In a corporate environment, travel arrangements were usually not made by the travellers themselves. Travel arrangers, whether they were the travel department or the secretaries, never risked making the bookings themselves. The fact that on average every business itinerary went through six to seven amendments further complicated the issue. The expertise and experience of the travel agents gave the corporate clients confidence and peace of mind. Time was another major concern for business travellers. Navigating through a travel Website and filling out a booking form on-line could be more time-consuming than talking it through with a travel agent over the phone, where confirmation was received instantly. Furthermore, the fare structure in the travel industry was highly complex and differed from company to company and from industry to industry. It was very difficult for the general public to understand the related implications if they made reservations on the Web.

Another selling point that travel agencies touted was their tailored service to corporate clients. Travel agencies knew their customers well. They maintained company

---

[15] Gee, C.Y., Makens, J.C., & Choy, D.J.L. (1997).

profiles and individual profiles for their corporate clients. Thus, when a booking was made, they could ensure that company travel policies were complied with, while individual preferences, such as meal and seat preferences, were also taken care of. On top of that, they provided periodic and ad-hoc MIS reports to assist corporate clients in understanding their travel history and managing their travel expenses.

In the on-line travel market, virtual travel agencies, too, had their own problems.[16] First, the on-line travel market only accounted for a meagre one percent of the entire travel market. Virtual travel agencies were competing really hard for only a tiny portion of the market. Second, because of the high CRS fees, it was estimated that the operating costs of a large site could range from US$10 to US$15 million per year. Meanwhile, airlines were capping the commission paid to on-line travel services providers to protect their own direct selling channels on the Web. In the end, only a few travel site giants would survive by a narrow profit margin. With Sabre and ITN taking up almost 50 percent of the market, this phenomenon was about to take shape.

Taking Sides: Travel Websites Take Charge

While some were sceptical about the on-line travel market, others had a lot of faith in it. Figures and estimates from around the world were showing solid growth in the number of Internet users worldwide [see **Exhibits 8**, **9** and **10**]. And even though the on-line travel market composed an insubstantial one percent of the entire travel market, it was undoubtedly growing. A report commissioned by the Travel Industry Association (TIA) in the US indicated that in 1997, people were 19 percent more likely to make reservations through the Internet than in 1996, and that one in four Internet users made travel plans or reservations on-line in 1997, up from only 11 percent in 1996.[17] The report also estimated that on-line travel sales would triple from 1996 to 1997, to US$827 million and forecast a ten-fold increase by 2002.[18] Similarly, Forrester Research, Inc. projected that Web-based electronic commerce (EC) would total US$73 billion by 2000,[19] and that travel would contribute 25 percent.[20] Even though the US market dominated the use of the Internet, the report estimated that the number of on-

[16] Flint, P. (1998), "Web of Ambivalence", *Air Transport World*.

[17] Kate, N.T. (1998).

[18] Flint, P. (1998).

[19] "EC", *Link-Up*, 1998.

[20] "Travelocity Takes off", *Computerworld*, 23 December 1996/2 January 1997, p. 30.

line households in certain European and Asia-Pacific markets would grow faster than in the US. [21] The outlook for the on-line travel market was bright.

The key reasons for people to purchase travel services on the Web were convenience and control. Travel Websites operated round the clock. Customers could access them at any time of the day. They could also take their time to look around before making a buying decision. Advances in information technology, especially the Internet, had lessened the importance of face-to-face human interaction. Even travel agents admitted that the impersonal media of human communication, e.g., e-mail and voice-mail, had become increasingly popular in the travel industry. They also realised that more and more travellers resorted to the Web for travel-related information.

Ticketless travel, an important technological advancement in the travel industry, also foreshadowed the diminishing role of travel agencies. Airlines around the world embraced the idea of ticketless travel through the implementation of e-ticketing. Travellers could purchase their e-tickets directly from the airlines, and only needed to produce a picture ID to receive their boarding passes at the check-in counter or boarding gate. For certain airlines the boarding pass issuance process was even entirely automated through the use of self-service machines. In Europe and North America, many airlines (e.g., British Airways, Northwest and United) adopted e-ticketing. On an increasing number of flights, passengers had the choice of using paper tickets or e-tickets. In the Asia-Pacific Rim, Ansett Australia implemented e-ticketing in its domestic network. Singapore Airlines and Cathay Pacific Airways were also putting the technology into trial on selected flights. By eliminating the need for a paper ticket, travellers saved the cost of replacing lost tickets and airlines saved the massive costs of issuing and distributing paper tickets[22] (estimated to be US$1 billion a year in the United States[23]). If e-ticketing was to take off in full swing globally, the role of travel agencies in the air travel distribution network would shrink even further.

In the meantime, virtual travel agencies also brought a new venture to the on-line market – an on-line travel product designed for corporate clients. Sabre Business Travel

---

[21] Travel & Tourism Intelligence (1998), "More Pointers to Increasing Use of the Internet for Travel", *Travel Industry Monitor*, No. 97, April.

[22] It cost US$1.00 to issue an e-ticket compared to the industry average of US$8.20 for a paper ticket.

[23] Parsons, T. (1998), "Taking an e-Ticket Ride", *ABCNEWS.com*, URL: http://www.abcnews.com/, 3 February.

Solutions (BTS)[24] was one such package. It maintained company policies, accepted on-line bookings and provided business reports for management purposes. In essence, it was designed to replicate, and in the long term, supersede services provided by traditional travel agencies to their corporate clients. In early 1997, Sabre BTS scored a landmark success in signing General Electric, the second-largest travel account in the United States, as its corporate client.[25]

It seemed more likely than ever that the roles of traditional travel agencies would be replaceable by the on-line offerings. Looking at the figures, Microsoft Expedia was able to pull off US$100 million in sales in its first year of operation from 1996 to 1997. Similarly, the gross revenue for Travelocity was well above US$100 million in 1997.[26] This put the big players in a position to bargain with suppliers. For instance, Microsoft Expedia negotiated a commission of US$5.00 per transaction with hotels – US$1.50 to US$2.00 higher than the other global distribution systems that hotels were using. Hotel chains gave in and signed up with Expedia.[27] It was not surprising that some people believed these on-line travel service providers would become viable competitors of traditional travel agencies by the year 2002.

TRAVEL AGENCIES: PAVING THEIR WAY

Amid this debatable threat from travel Websites, some travel agencies were actively shaping the future on and off the Web. One such travel agency was American Express. As an international travel agency, the Website of American Express was also one of the largest virtual travel agencies on the Web. Apart from providing travel services through the Internet, American Express also offered an on-line business travel reservations product jointly developed with Microsoft – the American Express Interactive or AXI.[28] Introduced in mid-1997, AXI was designed to cater to the needs of companies to

---

[24] Sabre Business Travel Solutions (1998), URL: http://www.sabrebts.com/index.html, February.

[25] "GE Chooses Sabre BTS, Carlson for New Travel System", *Travel Distribution Report*, Vol. 4, No. 22, 13 February 1997.

[26] Flint, P. (1998), "Web of Ambivalence", *Air Transport World*.

[27] Wolff, C. (1997), "Is the Travel Agent Headed for Extinction?" *Lodging Hospitality*, Vol. 53, Iss. 2, February, pp. 18–22.

[28] American Express (1998), URL: http://www.americanexpress.com/corp/latestnews/axi.shtml, February.

control and monitor travel expenses. It ensured that company travel policies were strictly adhered to and that the companies' preferred service suppliers were used whenever possible. American Express estimated that the system would save time spent on booking trips by 75 percent through the reduction of total time required to book, change and check business itineraries.

Off the Web, realising the various bypassing threats within the travel industry, travel agents in the US initiated the Genesis project in 1995.[29] Formed in November 1995 as a result of the Genesis project, the first task of the United States Travel Agent Registry (USTAR) was, in turn, to implement the project. In short, the idea of the Genesis project was to devise a travel agent-owned and -operated non-profit-making CRS that also handled ticketing and settlement. The system was designed to reinforce travel agencies as an efficient and effective distribution channel in the travel industry while reducing the cost of CRS fees for service suppliers, especially airlines, by some 30 to 40 percent. Since the announcement of the project, it had gained support from travel agents worldwide. Sister organisations to USTAR were formed in Canada, Europe and Australia to bring Genesis to the respective regions.[30] In a survey conducted in 1996 by USTAR, over 90 percent of service suppliers (including airlines, hotels, cruises, tour operators and car rental companies) expressed their support for the Genesis project. With Genesis scheduled to start beta-testing in Winter 1998, USTAR was excited about the progress and hopeful of the product launch.

TRAVEL AGENCIES IN A RAPIDLY CHANGING WORLD

Changes in the distribution system of the travel industry had been going on for many years. In the past, travel agencies were able to survive previous challenges from airlines and/or hotels, such as toll-free reservation hotlines, 24-hour service and sales offices.[31] With the turn of the millennium, information technology brought a new wave of challenges. Were there opportunities for travel agencies to surf along and prosper? Could travel agencies succeed against all odds and ride out of the challenges once again? How should they act and react in this rapidly changing environment?

---

[29] Genesis Travel Distribution System (1998), URL: http://www.ustar.com/, February.

[30] Canadian Standard Travel Agent Registry (CSTAR), European Standard Travel Agent Registry (ESTAR) and Australian Standard Travel Agent Registry (ASTAR) were formed in late 1997 and early 1998.

[31] Wolff, C. (1997).

Exhibit 1: The linking concept

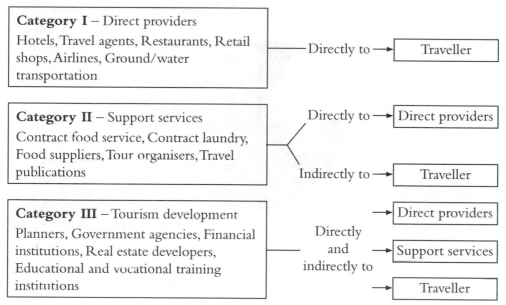

Category I – Direct providers
Hotels, Travel agents, Restaurants, Retail shops, Airlines, Ground/water transportation

———— Directly to ➞ Traveller

Category II – Support services
Contract food service, Contract laundry, Food suppliers, Tour organisers, Travel publications

Directly to ➞ Direct providers

Indirectly to ➞ Traveller

Category III – Tourism development
Planners, Government agencies, Financial institutions, Real estate developers, Educational and vocational training institutions

Directly and indirectly to

➞ Direct providers

➞ Support services

➞ Traveller

Source: Gee, C.Y., Makens, J.C., & Choy, D.J.L. (1997), *The Travel Industry* (Third Edition), New York: Van Nostrand Reinhold.

Exhibit 2: Travel industry sales distribution system

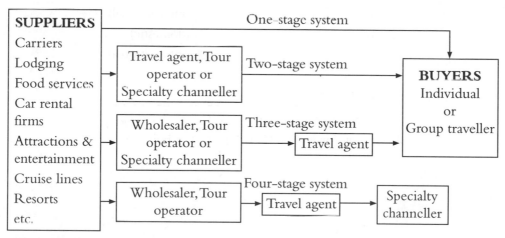

SUPPLIERS
Carriers
Lodging
Food services
Car rental firms
Attractions & entertainment
Cruise lines
Resorts
etc.

One-stage system

Travel agent, Tour operator or Specialty channeller

Two-stage system

Wholesaler, Tour operator or Specialty channeller

Three-stage system → Travel agent

Wholesaler, Tour operator

Four-stage system → Travel agent → Specialty channeller

BUYERS
Individual or Group traveller

Source: Gee, C.Y., Makens, J.C., & Choy, D.J.L. (1997), *The Travel Industry* (Third Edition), New York: Van Nostrand Reinhold.

Exhibit 3: Travel agency income

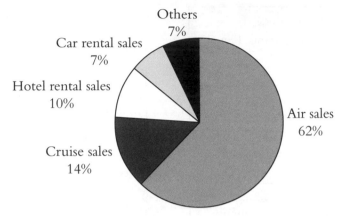

Source: Gee, C.Y. *et al.* (1990), *Professional Travel Agency Management*, Englewood Cliffs, NJ: Prentice Hall.

Exhibit 4: Supplier dependence on US travel agents

	Estimated volume booked by agents
Airlines	67% (domestic)
	80% (international)
Hotels	18% (domestic)
	79% (international)
Cruise lines	92%
Packaged tours	90%

Source: Gee, C.Y. *et al.* (1990), *Professional Travel Agency Management*, Englewood Cliffs, NJ: Prentice Hall.

Exhibit 5: Virtual travel agencies – A comparison

	Travelocity	**Microsoft Expedia**	**Internet Travel Network**
	www.travelocity.com	www.expedia.com	www.itn.com
Graphics	Good	Fair	Good
Ease of use	Good	Fair	Poor
Performance	Fair	Good	Good
Low-cost air fare search	Fair	Good	Poor
Overall grade	**A-**	**B**	**D**

Source: "Travel Sites Take Off On-line", *Computerworld*, 21 July 1997.

Exhibit 6: On-line travel market by revenue type, 1996

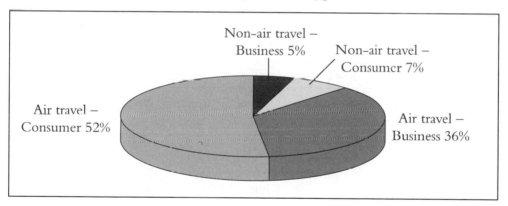

Source: Flint, P. (1998), "Web of Ambivalence", *Air Transport World*, Vol. 35, Iss. 4, April, pp. 31–36.

Exhibit 7: User profile of on-line travel services in the US

	Users	General public
Employed	91%	78% of the population
Professional or manager	52%	33% of the population
Postgraduate educated	33%	20% of all adults

Source: Kate, N. T. (1998), "Surfing for Travel", *American Demographics*, Vol. 20, Iss. 2, February, pp. 36–37.

Exhibit 8: Internet population worldwide

Region	Regional Internet pop. (mn)	Countries/ areas of Internet users	Internet pop. (mn)	Total pop. of country/ area (%)
Africa	1	South Africa	0.7	1.67
Asia–Pacific	15	Japan	8.8	6.4
		Taiwan	1.26	0.05
		Australia	1.21	4.3
		New Zealand	0.56	15.8
		Singapore	0.5	14.7
		Hong Kong	0.5	7.9
Europe	23	UK	6.0	10.25
		Germany	5.8	7.0
		Sweden	1.9	21.34
		Norway	1.4	3.42
		Finland	1.04	20.4
Middle East	0.541	Israel	0.2	3.7
Canada & USA	58	Canada	6.0	25.0
		USA	52.0	26.0
South America	2	Brazil	1.0	0.61
		Mexico	0.37	0.38
		Chile	0.2	1.3
		Argentina	0.17	0.49
		Columbia	0.12	0.32
World total	*99.54*			

Source: Adapted from CommerceNet Research Center, *Worldwide Statistics* (URL: http://www.commercenet.com/research/stats/wwstats.html).

Exhibit 9:   Demographics of Internet users

Gender: Male/female 61.3%/38.7% in April 1998 as compared with 94.9%/5.1% in October 1994.

Age:

Age	Percentage
5–15	2.1%
16–20	10.9%
21–30	30.9%
31–40	21.7%
41–50	19.0%
51+	15.4%

Education: 80.9% having at least some college experience and 50.1% having obtained at least one degree.

Occupation: 26.2% in education-related fields, followed closely by computer (22.3%) and professional (21.7%) fields.

Income:

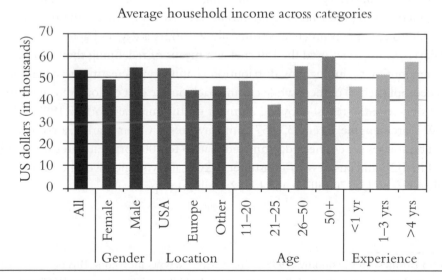

Average household income across categories

Exhibit 10: Internet population growth

Year	Population (in millions)
1995	22
1996	37.84
1997	58
1998	87.75 (projected)
1999	110.25 (projected)
2000	132.75 (projected)

Source: CommerceNet Research Center, *Worldwide Statistics* (URL: http://www.commercenet.com/research/stats/wwstats.html).

APPENDIX 1: THE INTERNET AND ELECTRONIC COMMERCE

Introduction

Before the onset of the Internet, electronic commerce (e-commerce) was usually conducted over a proprietary network connecting a group of organisations. The nature of the transaction was purely business-to-business (B2B). Nonetheless, the Internet made it possible to reach consumers electronically, 24 hours a day, and across geographical boundaries. Companies used the Internet as a means of redefining their business, creating new products, finding new distribution channels and creating new markets, and they accomplished all of these while cutting back on the cost of doing business. In fact, business became the fastest-growing segment on the Internet. In July 1998, Yahoo!, a WWW search engine, listed 333,457 company sites.[32] Open Market, a company that helped businesses get connected, estimated that 50 to 100 corporate sites were added a day.[33] The B2B and business-to-consumer (B2C) sales volumes over the Internet were calculated to be US$70 billion and US$2.4 billion respectively.[34]

---

[32] Yahoo Business and Economy (1998), URL: http://www.yahoo.com/Business/, February.

[33] "Doing Business on the Web Is New Status Symbol", *USA Today*, 20 June 1995.

[34] "EC", *Link-Up*, Vol. 15, Iss. 2, March/April 1998, pp. 8-10.

IMPACT OF ELECTRONIC COMMERCE ON THE VALUE–CHAIN

Before the advent of e-commerce, when a consumer was interested in buying a certain type of product, she would look for the various products available and compare their prices, qualities and features. At some point the search was stopped because further searching was no longer beneficial. After weighing the pros and cons, the consumer decided what to buy and where. The product was then purchased and taken home.

e-Commerce between companies enabled a wide range of seller- and customer-related activities to converge into one place, including marketing, order processing, distribution, payments and even the product development process that involved several separate firms. Not only did all these activities become easier and more convenient, but costs were reduced at the same time. With the digitisation of products, value–chain costs including inventory and packaging costs were reduced even further. Distributing these products directly and electronically to consumers also minimised the distribution costs that would otherwise have been incurred and translated into the price tag. The cycle time for order fulfilment was also reduced: digitised products could be distributed in minutes whereas shipping a product took days or weeks.

The emergence of the Web took e-commerce to new heights. Through no other medium could a company market its products globally and receive orders from around the world in such a short period of time. Web-based e-commerce provided companies with an expedient global reach that was unmatchable. The benefits arose partly from the use of the Web as a distribution channel. The Web had the potential to cut distribution costs or the cost of sales to almost zero. This was especially true for firms in publishing, information services or digital product categories.[35] Since it was possible to deliver products in digital format immediately over the Net, the need for intermediaries was reduced.[36] Moreover, buyers and sellers could access and contact each other directly, thereby eliminating some of the marketing costs and constraints associated with such interactions. Distribution channels became much more efficient (mainly due to the reduced overhead costs through such outcomes as uniformity, automation and large-scale integration of management processes). The time required to complete

---

[35] Jones, R. (1994), "Digital's World Wide Web Server: A Case Study", *Computer Networks & ISDN Systems*, Vol. 27, Iss. 2, November, pp. 297–306.

[36] Michalski, J. (1995), "People Are the Killer App", *Forbes ASAP*, 5 June, pp. 120–122.

business transactions was reduced as well, translating into a higher turnover rate for the companies.

Even for companies providing non–digitisable products or services, taking business to the Web presented a whole range of advantages as follows:

1. *Reduced costs per transaction versus other channels.* Although establishing and maintaining a Website had its costs, the price of using the Web versus other sales channels was substantially lower. For example, Federal Express' (FedEx) Website allowed customers to track their own packages at a cost to the company of US$0.10 per inquiry. When operators handled these enquiries over toll-free telephone lines, each call cost FedEx US$7.00.

2. *Full-time business and increased market access.* Time zone differences and geographical constraints obviously inhibited international business negotiations and transactions, but this was not an issue on the Web. Websurfers could look for information and send electronic mail to request further information any time they wanted. Prospective customers could locate companies that they had previously not heard of through the numerous search engines on the Web. Barnes and Noble, a United States-based book store chain, was able to receive orders from all over the world through its on-line branch.

3. *Customer information gathering.* The Web technology offered companies the opportunity to gather market intelligence and to monitor consumer choices as customers revealed their preferences in navigational and purchasing behaviour on the Web. With such information, companies could better position their products and marketing strategies, and solicit further sales from customers.

4. *Operational benefits.* Taking business to the Web also translated into a number of operational benefits for sellers. Reduced errors, time, overhead costs in information processing and costs of reaching potential suppliers electronically, and improved capabilities to submit and accept bids, were all operational benefits of using the Web.

5. *Marketing communications.* It was rarely desirable to compete solely on the basis of price. From a marketing perspective, it was the ability to differentiate one's product and service mix, and to attract customers, that made the difference. Consumers indicated that price was the least important product attribute when they considered making on-line purchases.[37] Therefore, the ability to compete

---

[37] Gupta, S. (1995), HERMES: A research project on the commercial uses of the World Wide Web.

along dimensions other than price was especially critical in categories where brands were perceived as substitutes.

SECURITY CONCERNS OF THE INTERNET

A widely discussed issue in relation to performing business transactions over the Internet was security. Even though many specialists considered it to be a matter of perception rather than reality,[38] customer perception was really what mattered. From the companies' point of view, hacking and unauthorised access, or hardware and software failures often gave rise to the following problems related to abuse, misuse and failure:

1. *Hacking and unauthorised access.* An external hacker or a fraudulent insider could gain access to confidential information, wrongfully transfer funds, destroy important data or even plant computer viruses (a program designed to create disruptions and trouble in computer systems). All these could result in significant operational disruptions and losses to a company.
2. *Hardware and software failures.* Disasters and accidents such as earthquakes or fire could cripple electronically dependent services. Similarly, undetected hardware faults or software bugs could severely disrupt daily operations.

Interruptions to the orderly transaction of business, whether they were caused by external intrusions, dishonesty, improper business practices, human mistakes or electronic system failures, could paralyse business transactions for significant periods of time. As well as the immediate loss of business and possible costs of dispute resolution, the long-term damage to credibility and goodwill were incalculable.

ELECTRONIC COMMERCE – A NEW WAY TO CONDUCT BUSINESS

Undoubtedly, e-commerce, and especially Web-based e-commerce, was revolutionising the way business transactions were conducted between businesses, and between businesses and consumers. More and more consumer products were available for purchase over the Web. Tangible products such as books and CDs were among the more popular ones on the Web, but less tangible products from service-based industries, say,

---

[38] David, K. (1995), "False Alarm: Credit Card Security: Market Forces", *Hotwired*, 23 October.

the travel industry, were also becoming readily available on the Web. Even primary/ grade school students were using the Web in class. In the foreseeable future, shopping on-line might well be part of our daily lives.

APPENDIX 2: LIST OF URLS

Company name/site name	URL
American Express Travel Services	www6.americanexpress.com/travel/index.html
Barnes and Noble	www.barnesandnoble.com
Bintan Resorts	www.bintan-resorts.com
Cathay Pacific Airways Co. Ltd. (flight schedule)	www.cathaypacific.com/schedules/
Condé Nast Traveler	www.cntraveler.com
DragonAir	www.dragonair.com
Expedia	www.expedia.com
France.com	www.france.com
Hilton Hotel (Reservations)	www.hilton.com/reservations/index.html
Internet Travel Network	www.itn.com
Japan Airlines	www.jal.co.jp
Japan National Tourist Organisation	www.jnto.go.jp
London Tourist Board	www.londontown.com
Travelocity	www.travelocity.com
United Airlines	www.ual.com
Whistler Resorts	www.whistlerblackcomb.com

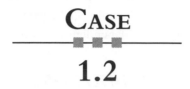

CASE

1.2

SCMP.com: Strategic Repositioning
of a Newspaper*

Prior to mid-1999, the Internet presence of our newspaper was a defensive move. Six months ago, our Board of Directors took the view to seriously develop the on-line business. We realise that if we don't spend a lot of money to establish our on-line business now, we could lose a lot of money in the future.
– Owen Jonathan, Chief Executive, *South China Morning Post* Publishers[1]

In 1996, the *South China Morning Post* (*SCMP*), a Hong Kong–based English-language news daily, established PostNet (an electronic publishing division) to experiment with the on-line medium. In mid-1999, *SCMP*'s Board of Directors observed the Internet's meteoric rise and considered PostNet's e-commerce opportunity. In order to leverage e-commerce growth, they resolved to reposition the *SCMP* from a print-based publisher to a company capable of multimedia publishing. PostNet was renamed SCMP.com.

To be successful in this endeavour, the *SCMP* had to overcome numerous prob-

---

[1] Interview with Owen Jonathan, 16 November 1999.

* Eva Y.H. Kwan prepared this case under the supervision of Dr. Ali Farhoomand. *Copyright © 2000 The University of Hong Kong. Ref. 99/51C*

lems, including the need to build a viable business model, to streamline internal workflows, to transform the mindset of the employees and to search for the 'right' strategic partners to strengthen its on-line network. In addition, the *SCMP* would be required to decide whether or not to spin off SCMP.com (or any other part of its Internet-enabled business) into an independent concern.

THE *SOUTH CHINA MORNING POST*

The South China Morning Post Publishers published the *South China Morning Post* and the *Sunday Morning Post.* TVE (Holdings) Limited, its wholly-owned subsidiary, published *Automobile, Champion,* Harper's *Bazaar, Cosmopolitan, Amoeba* and *PC Home*; TVE also produced music CDs and laser discs, operated retail stores (Daily Stop and Health Plus) and published Channel Home, a Hong Kong personal computing Website [**Exhibit 1**].[2] TVE was also a major shareholder in Post Publishing Co., which published the *Bangkok Post*, a leading English-language newspaper in Thailand.

Debuting in Hong Kong in 1903, the *SCMP* was one of the oldest newspapers in Asia. It remained Hong Kong's dominant English-language daily newspaper. The *SCMP* had established a reputation as a quality content provider; its writers and photographers regularly won a majority of awards at the Newspaper Society of Hong Kong Press Awards. In July 1999, the *SCMP* was voted the 'Best English-language Newspaper in Asia' by the Society of Publishers in Asia. The *SCMP* was the flagship publication, earning most of its profits through advertising sales.[3, 4]

Having gained the highest readership among Hong Kong's best-educated and most affluent households, the *SCMP* amassed a large base of advertisers and became the most reputable source of job advertisements in Hong Kong. The *SCMP*'s approach to enhancing its brand name was to continuously introduce new editorial products and to improve existing ones:

Quality is the key to holding and winning readers, and the advertising which follows.[5]

---

[2] Welcome to PC Home (2000), URL: http://www.channelhome.com.hk, January.

[3] In 1998, newspaper operations accounted for 63 percent of the Company's total turnover and 95 percent of its operating profit.

[4] South China Morning Post (Holdings) Ltd, 1998 Annual Report.

[5] South China Morning Post (Holdings) Ltd, 1999 Annual Report.

The *SCMP*'s circulation displayed steady growth, capturing some 90 percent of English-language local newsstand sales in Hong Kong [**Exhibit 2**].[6] Its readership rose from 225,000 in 1994 to 280,000 in 1998.[7,8] In comparison, copysale revenue generated markedly less revenue than advertising.

To enhance its Chinese news coverage, the *SCMP* established news bureaus in Beijing, Shanghai and Guangzhou and became the highest-selling English-language newspaper in China, published outside the country.[9]

The *SCMP* was a highly profitable newspaper, but it became a victim of the 1997 Asian financial turmoil [**Exhibit 3**]. The general economic downturn intensified business closures and retrenchments, which adversely affected the *SCMP*'s display advertising and classified advertising revenue. From a high of 200 pages on a Saturday, classified pages shrank to a quarter of this in late 1998.[10] Signs of recovery were evident in spring 1999. Sally Chow, assistant general manager at the *SCMP*, said, "Classified ads are up 20–30 percent from a year ago, and we are expecting things to get better."[11]

JOINING THE LEAGUE OF ELECTRONIC PUBLISHERS

In the early 1990s, electronic publishing gradually became popular in the West. In late 1995, print-based publishers and other traditional media – radio and television – increasingly claimed a piece of 'Webspace' of their own.[12] A number of Asian publishers also began to take part in this new form of publishing [**Exhibit 4**]. In 1994, the *SCMP*'s Head of Library noticed this trend and suggested the setting up of an electronic publishing division to participate in this emerging business area. The Company's Chief Executive accepted her suggestion. In 1996, the *SCMP* established PostNet as its electronic publishing division. Its initial mission was quite basic:

---

[6] South China Morning Post (Holdings) Ltd, 1997 Annual Report.

[7] South China Morning Post (Holdings) Ltd, Annual Reports: 1997, 1998 and 1999.

[8] The circulation of a newspaper referred to the number of copies sold. The readership of a newspaper referred to the number of people who read the newspaper.

[9] South China Morning Post (Holdings) Ltd, 1997 Annual Report.

[10] Most job ads were placed in the Saturday paper.

[11] Tharmaratnam, M. (1999), "Internet Boom Boosts Hongkong Job Ads", *The Business Times*, Singapore, 22 November, pp. 1–2.

[12] Peek, R. (1997), "What Is Internet Publishing?" *Information Today*, Vol. 14, Iss. 6, June, pp. 57–60.

To formulate and execute an electronic publishing strategy for the Company.[13]

When it was launched, the PostNet management was not confident about the Internet becoming a dominant electronic publishing medium. Therefore, it defined 'electronic publishing' widely to encompass 'any form of publishing that was not ink-on-paper'. PostNet intended to capitalise on the *SCMP*'s broad collection of news stories, photographs and editorials by designing content-based products delivered to users through various electronic media such as voice, fax, CD-ROM, global database hosts and the Internet.

As electronic publishing was still a relatively new concept in Asia, PostNet found there was little prior product design experience it could draw on; as a result, it adopted a trial-and-error product development approach to explore technical feasibility and market reaction to new products.

Internet-based Products

- ❐ In December 1996, the daily Internet Edition of the *SCMP* and Classified Post On-line were launched.[14]
- ❐ In June, the 1997 Handover Website was added. This Website attracted a lot of public attention; it received 6.5 million hits within the 36 hours surrounding the Handover event on 1 July 1997.
- ❐ In July 1997, the *SCMP*'s official Website, PostNet, was launched with the Countdown to History Website, reporting on Hong Kong's transition from British colonial rule to a Special Administrative Region of China.
- ❐ By mid-1999, Internet-based products offered on PostNet included the daily Internet Edition of the *SCMP*, Classified Post On-line, SCMP Careers, SCMP Archive Search, the Regional Hotel Guide, Racing Post On-line and the Meeting Point (a personal advertisements Website) [**Exhibit 5**].
- ❐ In 1997, Global Investor was launched as a subscription-based service, but it was subsequently discontinued because of difficulties in obtaining adequate content [**Exhibit 6**].

---

[13] Justice, C.S. (1998), *The Guide to Financial Technology in Asia*, Hong Kong: EFP International (HK) Limited, p. 166.

[14] The on-line edition of the *Hong Kong Standard*, the *Post*'s English-language daily rival in Hong Kong, was launched a few months ahead of the *Post*'s on-line edition.

Non-Internet Products

By mid–1999, non–Internet products offered by PostNet included:

- ❐ PostCD–ROM.
- ❐ PostSyndication.
- ❐ PostPhoto and the Meeting Point's voice service [**Exhibit 5**].
- ❐ PostFax and IVR were two non–Internet products that had been offered in the past but were discontinued.
- ❐ PostResearch was initially in the launch plan but was eventually withdrawn because PostNet was unable to prove its commercial viability [**Exhibit 6**].

By 1998, PostNet became a critically acclaimed Website. In February 1998, *Editor & Publisher*, a US journalism magazine, voted PostNet the Best Non–US Newspaper On-line Service because 'it was well-designed, easy to use and impressive in its breadth of information and services available. The news and business information were deemed particularly useful'.[15] In June 1998, the Newspaper Association of America awarded PostNet the Digital Edge Outstanding Achievement Award for Best News Presentation. These two awards were won by a Hong Kong electronic publisher for the first time.

PostNet was one of the most visited Hong Kong Websites. By April 1998, PostNet recorded over a million visits each week; by late 1998, the Internet Edition of the *SCMP* had more than 220,000 registered users, a high percentage of whom were professionals, managers and executives.[16] PostNet's SCMP Careers section regularly carried over a thousand employment advertisements and was considered one of the largest job databases in the world.[17]

'INVEST NOW OR ELSE TOO LATE'

In Asia, the number of Internet users was expected to reach 160 million by 2000 [**Exhibit 7**].[18] Driven by customer demand and business imperatives, both Internet-

---

[15] Justice, C.S. (1998), p. 166.

[16] South China Morning Post (Holdings) Ltd, 1999 Annual Report.

[17] "Website Proves Big 'Hit' with Job Seekers", *South China Morning Post*, 18 April 1998, p. 35.

[18] Informal Working Group on Financial Technology Infrastructure (December 1997), *Financial Technology Infrastructure for Hong Kong*, Hong Kong: Hong Kong Government Printer, p. 92.

based companies and traditional businesses were quickly transforming their business processes into e-commerce processes.

In five years, there won't be any Internet-specific companies because they will all be Internet companies.

— Craig Barrett, President and CEO, Intel Corporation [19]

In 1999, the Board of Directors resolved to seriously develop commercial imperatives for the *SCMP*'s on-line presence. To reflect this new focus, PostNet was renamed SCMP.com and an investment of HK$20 to 30 million was set aside to equip SCMP.com. [20, 21]

Building the SCMP.com Team

In November 1999, SCMP.com had 30 employees working in four divisions: Editorial and Research, Design, Marketing and Administration, and Technical. SCMP.com planned to increase staffing to approximately 70 during 2000. New employees would be recruited for the Finance Division, taking care of SCMP.com's financial matters; in the Editorial Division, handling content-based products; in the Technical Division, designing Webpages; and in the Marketing Division, managing advertiser relationships.

In the same month, SCMP.com announced the appointment of four senior executives: Chief Executive, Editorial Director, Chief Financial Officer and Publisher [**Exhibit 8**]. [22] One of SCMP.com's greater challenges was to attract qualified candidates with Internet exposure and experience. However, many other companies in Hong Kong were also searching for similar candidates, who were in short supply.

Enhancing the Brand Name

Building and enhancing the brand name in both print and on-line mediums were a

---

[19] Markowitz, E. (1999), "Intel CEO Pushes e-Business World", *TechWeb News*, Computer Reseller News, CMP Media, Inc., 20 July.

[20] Saunders, D. (1999), "On-line Notices No Threat", *South China Morning Post*, 9 November, p. 2.

[21] US$1 = HK$7.78

[22] "SCMP On-line Unit Makes Four Senior Appointments", *South China Morning Post*, 19 November 1999, p. 3.

major marketing effort, and the *SCMP* continuously launched new and improved editorial products.

> *We realise that at some stage, it is inevitable that readers will migrate from print to on-line medium. We want to ensure that if that migration does happen, readers will migrate with us.*

> – Owen Jonathan

The cost of entry for on-line publishers, in terms of technology investment, Website design and implementation, was low compared to marketing and branding costs. SCMP.com intended to leverage the *SCMP*'s reputable brand name to differentiate itself cost effectively from other on-line content providers.

SCMP.COM'S CHALLENGES

To Build a Viable e-Business Model

Similar to many on-line businesses, a major challenge SCMP.com faced was to build a viable business model. Owen Jonathan recognised the different nature of its print business and on-line activities. "We have been experimenting to find a business model; on-line business is very different from what we have been doing. While planning for a new business within our traditional business environment, we project expenses, revenues and payback periods. While developing the on-line business, these components of business have to be put to one side, for a while at least," he said.

The business model of an on-line content provider could include one or more revenue streams, including subscription, pay-per-view information download, advertising and e-commerce transactions. Determining an optimal mix of revenue streams was difficult. Advertising revenue and syndication sales had been SCMP.com's two largest sources of revenue, but so far, these revenue streams were unable to generate profits for SCMP.com.

Past e-commerce trends indicated that a viable business model could not be built upon advertising revenue alone; in any case, SCMP.com's on-line advertising revenue had been slow to emerge. In the US, click-through rates dropped from two percent in 1997 to less than half a percent in 1999.[23, 24] Advertisers were wary of spending their

---

[23] Click-through is the percentage of people viewing a banner ad who actually clicked on it.

[24] Tweney, D. (1999), "Net Prophet: On-line Advertising: A \$3 Billion Industry Limping on Its Last Legs", *InfoWorld*, 4 October, p. 72.

advertising dollars on on-line ads as 'the ability to gauge advertising effectiveness remained elusive'.[25]

SCMP.com was reluctant to impose subscription charges on most of its content because charges could reduce Website traffic, further restricting the opportunity to earn advertising revenue. Also, a subscription-based business model required a major overhaul of on-line readers' buying habits as a lot of information could be accessed on-line for free. For SCMP.com to increase subscription revenue, it needed to change the buying habits of its on-line audience.

Generating revenue ■ Apart from selling banner ads and corporate sponsorship of particular Website sections, SCMP.com adopted a 'print-plus' approach to generate revenue from on-line classifieds. When an advertisement was placed in the Classified SCMP print edition, it would be posted on Classified Post On-line for an additional incremental charge. Revenues from the Classified Property section came from selling 'buttons' to real estate developers and agents on the main page [**Exhibit 10**]. Through the 'print-plus' approach, advertisers were charged in incremental stages according to the amount of additional materials they wanted to post on-line.

As for generating subscription revenues from content-based products, SCMP.com had three alternative approaches:

1. To 'push' an extensive amount of information that carried advertisements to the on-line audience. On-line readers obtained the information free of charge. [**Exhibit 9** is one example of this.]
2. To 'push' the same amount of information to the on-line audience without including any advertisements. On-line users still obtained the information free of charge but they needed to provide more demographic information upon registration.
3. To offer information that was much more focused based on the specific needs of the recipients. On-line users were required to pay a subscription charge.

Jonathan strongly believed that in the age of information overload, Internet users valued an information filtering service, so SCMP.com resolved to provide a more focused approach. The challenge was to create new revenue streams using this approach to make SCMP.com viable.

Designing products ■ SCMP.com was in the process of examining all existing products for on-line commercial potential. A group of advertisers and e-commerce

---

[25] Mottl, J. (1999), "The Trouble with On-line Ads", *Internet Week*, 11 October.

parties, i.e., potential customers or companies that SCMP.com could set up strategic alliances with, was attached to each product identified during this process.

In 1999, SCMP.com launched/relaunched the following products:

❐ In May 1999, SCMP.com formed a six-member team to turn the *SCMP's* weekly supplement *Technology Post* into a daily IT news Website targeted at professionals and executives.[26] A sister Website, *Nan Hua Ke Ji*, using simplified Chinese to target a mainland audience, was also launched.[27] A link was established in SCMP.com's homepage to the Channel Home Website.[28]

❐ In June 1999, *SCMP's* Internet Edition was redesigned to enhance content depth. A 'news ticker' was introduced to update local and international news throughout the day. Hong Kong share prices and the index were updated twice a day. A *HK Quick Quotes* service was included to allow users to obtain free stock quotes – updated four times a day with a one-hour delay – for up to ten Hong Kong stocks at a time. Coverage of other Asian financial markets was also expanded.

❐ The *SCMP* embarked on a two-pronged strategy to strengthen its position as Hong Kong's leading provider of classified job advertisements. In 1999, *Careers Post*, a print job classified supplement catering to young job seekers with career development advice, was launched. The careers.SCMP.com Website was launched in autumn 1999 to replace Classified Jobs On-line.[29] careers.SCMP. com had a sophisticated search engine and provided a range of services for both job seekers and employers.

Jonathan believed that a trial-and-error approach would be used in the product design process before product offerings could be refined according to customer taste. "We realise that some of these product offerings will be successful and some will not," he said. He also felt that specialisation was important as the Internet was growing so fast. SCMP.com would be positioned as a news Website that provided rich, targeted and in-depth coverage on business, financial markets, banking and China news. Although the specific form of on-line products was to be determined, SCMP.com decided its future product offerings would be 'far more sophisticated and in-depth' than its existing offerings.

---

[26] *South China Morning Post* (2000), URL: http://www.technologypost.com/main, February.

[27] Nanhuatech.com (2000), URL: http://www.nanhuatech.com, February.

[28] Welcome to PC Home (2000), URL: http://www.channelhome.com.hk, February.

[29] *South China Morning Post* (2000), URL: http://careers.SCMP.com/home.asp, February.

While the *SCMP*'s printed edition was predominantly read by Hong Kongers *SCMP*'s Internet Edition readership varied.[30, 31] Jonathan wanted SCMP.com to design on-line products that addressed the needs of its multi-faceted readership and offer these products at prices that captured their value to readers.

Marketing issues ■ Although SCMP.com had not yet marketed itself through any channels except making references to printed *SCMP* editions, it planned to launch a marketing campaign in 2000. The 'new-and-improved' careers.SCMP.com Website would be marketed first in early 2000 as a 'one-stop shop' for job seekers and employers in Hong Kong. Other Websites in Hong Kong had employed cross-media advertising campaigns using radio, television, billboard, the print media and on-line tools to promote their Websites. The management was considering whether SCMP.com should adopt the same approach, which required a sizeable advertising budget, or to launch a more modest marketing campaign, as the *SCMP* had already possessed a strong brand name.

The *SCMP*'s established brand name and customer base meant that the marketing expenditure could be devoted to enhancing customer relationship management in addition to building a subscriber-based customer data bank. However, it was critical that SCMP.com overcome user inertia against subscription-based products and prevent subscribers from switching to competitors' products.

A fundamental feature of on-line content-based products, or information goods, was that the production cost was largely determined by 'first-copy costs'. Once the first copy of the information about the goods was produced, the cost of reproducing and delivering additional copies of the same product through a digital network was close to nothing. SCMP.com's challenge was how to price its on-line products appropriately in view of these cost characteristics to maximise the total revenue.

To Streamline Internal Coordination

Interlocking workflow and employee mindset ■ SCMP.com worked closely with a number of *SCMP* departments: Display Advertising, Classified Post, Circulation, Editorial, Library, Graphics and Design and Information Technology.[32]

---

[30] In 1998, more than 50 percent of the Website traffic originated in Hong Kong; the remainder came from the US (26.64 percent), Canada (3.5 percent) and Australia (2.93 percent).

[31] "Website Proves Big 'Hit' with Job Seekers", *South China Morning Post*, 18 April 1998, p. 35.

[32] Library and Graphics and Design were subdepartments. Library was part of the Editorial Department while Graphics and Design was part of the Display Advertising Department.

As evidenced from its product offerings, SCMP.com was not a content creator. SCMP.com utilised the *SCMP*'s existing content supplied by the Editorial Department (for the Internet Edition), the Classified Post Department (for Classified Post On-line and careers.SCMP.com) and the Library (for PostSyndication and PostPhoto).

SCMP.com collaborated with other departments on joint projects. The Regional Hotel Guide was developed at the request of the Circulation Department.[33] SCMP.com also often conducted joint presentations with sales teams from the Display Advertising Department to advertisers who might also be interested in placing on-line advertisements. Cross-departmental cooperation was therefore needed.

Allocation of revenues and costs ■ SCMP.com's costs and revenues by late 1999 were as follows:

- ❐ *Advertising revenue*: On-line advertising included banner ads and the sponsorship of specific Webpages [**Exhibits 11** and **12**].
- ❐ *Classified Post On-line and SCMP Careers*: SCMP.com's revenue came from the 'print-plus' services it offered to advertisers.
- ❐ *Other revenues*: Revenues also arose from syndication sales of *SCMP* articles and photographs, voice reply charges and the sale of electronic stamps for the Meeting Point service, subscriptions to Racing Post On-line, paid access to the SCMP Archive Search and the sale of PostCD-ROMs.
- ❐ *Operating costs*: SCMP.com had two types of operating cost − direct costs and allocated costs. Direct costs consisted of salaries, production costs for CD-ROMs, product development costs, and sales and marketing costs. A portion of the operating costs incurred by the *SCMP*'s Display Advertising Department and Information Technology Department was allocated to SCMP.com for services it received from these two departments. The allocated amounts were determined through negotiations between these departments and SCMP.com.

Joint product design constraints ■ The close working relationship between SCMP.com and other departments limited SCMP.com's flexibility in product design. The Regional Hotel Guide was a good example. Several hotels in Hong Kong that did not subscribe to the *SCMP* had expressed interest in placing advertisements in the on-

---

[33] The Circulation Department wanted to use the Regional Hotel Guide as an incentive for hotels in Hong Kong to subscribe to the *SCMP*. The *Hong Kong Standard*, the *SCMP*'s rival, was offered to hotels in Hong Kong free of charge. Hong Kong hotels that subscribed to the *SCMP* were given free listings in the Regional Hotel Guide.

line Regional Hotel Guide and banner ads on that Webpage. The Circulation Department, however, insisted that listings on the Guide be offered to *SCMP* subscribers only.

To Find the 'Right' Strategic Partners

In July 1999, *SCMP* took the first step towards enlarging its on-line network by acquiring a strategic interest in ChinaWeb Ltd., the majority owner of Homeway Co. Ltd.[34, 35] ChinaWeb Ltd. launched ChinaWeb in November 1999.[36] This bilingual Website was positioned as 'a definitive tool for the China-focused investor' featuring on-line financial and business news, stock quotations and foreign exchange data on the Greater China region. Jonathan explained why the *SCMP* took this strategic stake: "As world attention turns to Greater China and as the Internet begs the need for intelligent content, the *South China Morning Post* is well-positioned to promote understanding of this region among the global business community interested in Greater China investment."[37]

SCMP.com was also actively seeking other 'relevant' strategic partners. In order to leverage e-commerce opportunities, Jonathan felt that SCMP.com needed to create an e-commerce environment with the right content and readership to attract companies to effect transactions within that environment. First, SCMP.com needed to identify the type of e-commerce companies it would like to partner with. It could then create an appropriate e-commerce environment and articulate its relevance to potential e-commerce partners to entice them to create a partnership. Also, instead of building an e-commerce infrastructure from scratch, which was not considered one of *SCMP*'s core competencies, SCMP.com preferred to form alliances with e-commerce companies that specialised in this area.

While the Company had the financial strength to purchase strategic interests in the 'right' companies to enlarge its on-line network, it remained important to look for the right allies.

---

[34] Homeway was one of China's first Internet content providers (ICPs) and the only ICP in China to be authorised by the Chinese Securities Regulatory Commission as an on-line financial advisory company.

[35] Homeway (2000), URL: http://www.homeway.com.cn, February.

[36] ChinaWeb (2000), URL: http://www.chinaweb.com, February.

[37] "ChinaWeb.com to Fulfill Growing Demand for Greater China Business and Financial Market Insights", *Business Wire*, 30 November 1999.

TO SPIN OFF OR NOT?

Other than dealing with the issues of building a viable e-business model, streamlining internal coordination and looking for the 'right' strategic partners, Jonathan and the Board of Directors were also considering the corporate form that SCMP.com would assume. SCMP.com could exist in one of the following forms:

❐ To remain a division of the *SCMP*.
❐ To be spun off, through the launch of an initial public offering (IPO), as an independent, self-sustaining Internet venture, given a free rein to manage its own business and report its own results.

In 1999, several highly publicised IPOs were launched by a few Hong Kong-based Internet and technology companies [**Appendix 1**]. While a successful IPO would allow SCMP.com to generate positive publicity, to recoup the investment made, and to raise additional funds for expansion, the Board had to carefully evaluate the impact of such a move on the rest of the Company. After all, the working relationship between SCMP.com and the other departments was extremely close. The impact of an IPO on *SCMP*'s integrated workflow, overall profitability, employee morale and existing share-holders would have to be carefully considered.

Jonathan and the Board of Directors were certain that in order to sustain growth, the *SCMP* had to make a serious commitment to develop its on-line business. The transformation from a print-based publisher to a multimedia publisher would not be a smooth journey, however. All these outstanding issues would have to be resolved if SCMP.com wanted to be successful in the Internet arena.

APPENDIX 1: INTERNET IPOS

Initial public offerings (IPOs) allowed companies to recoup their investments and helped finance expansion. In 1999, several technology and Internet-based companies in Hong Kong and China took advantage of the market condition by launching IPOs in stock exchanges.

Technology companies that had solid performance and/or were backed by large parent companies could seek listings on the Hong Kong Stock Exchange and the Nasdaq Stock Exchange in the US to raise funds. China.com was the first Hong

Kong-based Internet company to list on the Nasdaq.[38] It raised more than US$80 million from its IPO and began trading in July 1999.[39]

i–Cable Communications, a cable television and Internet service network unit of Wharf Holdings, one of Hong Kong's largest conglomerates, raised more than HK$3.74 billion in its November 1999 IPO in both stock exchanges.[40] On 10 November 1999, Cable & Wireless HKT announced its plan to spin off its interactive activities by obtaining a dual listing for this new concern.

Internet-based companies shared some commonalities: young, loss-making and struggling to find revenue streams. Most of them did not fulfil the profitability/track record listing requirements of the Hong Kong Stock Exchange. The Growth Enterprise Market (GEM), or the so-called second board of the Hong Kong Stock Exchange, was designed to bridge this gap.

The GEM was modelled after Nasdaq, offering small- to medium-sized companies in Greater China that showed the potential for high growth, especially in technology industries, opportunities to raise funds. To obtain a listing on GEM, a company was not required to have achieved a history of years of profitability. As the companies listed on GEM were in the 'high-risk, high-growth' category, GEM was positioned as a 'buyers beware market' for informed investors.

GEM started trading on 25 November 1999 and attracted significant interest from investors. The first two companies listed on GEM were Timeless Software, a Hong Kong-based software company, and China Agrotech, a China-based fertiliser maker. Timeless Software and China Agrotech raised HK$495 million and HK$90 million respectively in their IPOs.[41] In November 1999, China.com announced its intention to spin off its wholly-owned Internet portal, hongkong.com, through a listing on the GEM.[42]

---

[38] Lo, J. (1999), "On–line Giant to Stay in Red Ink", *South China Morning Post*, 21 August, p. 3.

[39] Chan, Y. (1999), "China.com Losses Reach US$4.42m on Asia Expansion", *South China Morning Post*, 4 November, p. 4.

[40] Lo, J. (1999), "Hi–tech Fever a Healthy Prognosis as New Market Catches Imagination of Investors; Dramatic Debut as i–Cable Soars 51pc", *South China Morning Post*, 25 November, p. 1.

[41] Tharmaratnam, M. (1999), "Roaring Start for Two Technology Listings on GEM", *The Business Times*, Singapore, 26 November, p. 16.

[42] Hui, Y.M. (1999), "China.com Eyes Injection As Portal Spin-off Planned", *South China Morning Post*, 19 November, p. 3.

Appendix Table 1: Requirements comparison

	Hong Kong Stock Exchange (the main board)	Growth Enterprise Market (the second board)
Listing requirements	Company must be in operation for two years but does not need to have a record of profitability.	Company must have HK$6.5 million profits over three years and have been in business for three years.
Disclosure	Companies post financials twice a year and do not need to publish comparisons.	Twice a year, companies must compare their performance to plans announced at time of listing. Financials must be published 45 days after the end of each quarter.
Corporate governance	No such requirements.	Audit committees and compliance officers are mandatory. Investment banks must monitor companies two years after they help them list.

Source: Prasso, S., Moore, J., & Roberts, D. (1999), "A Bourse of Their Own", *Business Week*, International Editions, Asian Business, Stock Markets, No. 3644, 30 August, p. 26.

Exhibit 1: South China Morning Post (Holdings) Ltd subsidiaries and associated companies

Company	Ownership	Nature of business
SUBSIDIARIES		
South China Morning Post Finance (Cayman) Limited, Cayman Islands	100%	Investment holding
South China Morning Post Investments (Cayman) Limited, Cayman Islands	100%	Investment holding
South China Morning Post Publishers Limited	100%	Newspaper and magazine publishing
South China Morning Post (S) Pte Limited, Singapore	100%	Advertising agent
Sunny Bright Development Limited	100%	Property holding

Exhibit 1 (cont'd)

Company	Ownership	Nature of business
Sunny Success Development Limited	100%	Property holding
SCMP (1994) Limited	100%	Investment holding
West Side Assets Limited, British Virgin Islands	100%	Investment holding
Markland Investments Limited	100%	Investment holding
TVE (Holdings) Limited	100%	Investment holding
Capital Artists Limited	99.7%	Organisation and promotion of stage and film performance and record publishing
Praise Onward Development Limited	88.9%	Operation and management of kindergartens
Publications (Holdings) Limited	100%	Publishing
Retailcorp Limited	100%	Operation of retail kiosks
South Horizons Residents Club Limited	100%	Operation of recreation club
Shanghai Pacific Ice Palace Corporation, The People's Republic of China	100%	Operation of amusement centre in Shanghai
Spotlight Enterprises Limited	100%	Operation of recreation club
Sun Island English Kindergarten Limited	88.9%	Operation and management of kindergartens
Telford Recreation Club Limited	100%	Operation of recreation club
TVE International Limited	100%	Investment holding
TVE Publications Limited (formerly T.V. Week Limited)	100%	Publishing
Video-Film Production Limited	100%	Production of commercial films
Kalkeith Limited, The Commonwealth of The Bahamas	100%	Investment holding

Exhibit 1 (cont'd)

Company	Ownership	Nature of business
Coastline International Limited, The Commonwealth of The Bahamas	100%	Property holding
Lyton Investment Limited, The Commonwealth of The Bahamas	100%	Property holding
Macheer Properties Limited, British Virgin Islands	100%	Property holding
ASSOCIATED COMPANIES		
Asia Magazines, Limited	27.1%	Magazine publishing
The Post Publishing Public Company Limited, Thailand	20.3%	Newspaper and magazine publishing
New Trend International Limited, British Virgin Islands	45%	Investment holding
NIIT-TVE (Hong Kong) Limited (formerly Home PC Limited)	35%	Operation of computer training centre
Dymocks Franchise Systems	45%	Bookshop operation
Earn Active Limited	50%	In liquidation
Start Circle Limited	50%	Investment holding

Source: South China Morning Post (Holdings) Ltd, 1998 Annual Report.

Exhibit 2: *South China Morning Post* daily circulation statistics

	1999	1998	1997	1996	1995	1994
January – June	107,129	106,609	105,808	104,037	102,881	–
July – December	–	117,563	119,921	116,992	115,795	115,773

Source: South China Morning Post (Holdings) Ltd, Annual Reports: 1999, 1998, 1997 and 1996.

Exhibit 3: **South China Morning Post (Holdings) Ltd turnover classification**

(HK$'000)	1999	1998	1997	1996	1995
Publishing, printing & distribution of newspaper & other publications	1,028,370	1,574,326	1,692,667	1,280,328	1,253,845
Provision of entertainment, recreation & leisure services	161,681	181,996	218,069	69,221	–
Retailing	344,672	352,234	318,628	61,258	–
Production of commercial films	30,732	42,895	42,787	10,162	–
Gross rental revenue	83,058	84,862	80,299	23,136	12,285
Total turnover	1,648,513	2,236,313	2,352,450	1,444,105	1,266,130
Net profit attributable to shareholders	389,433	412,168	805,300	695,874	580,062

Source: South China Morning Post (Holdings) Ltd, Annual Reports: 1999, 1998, 1997, 1996 and 1995.

Exhibit 4:   Selected English-language Websites of Asian newspapers

Country/city	Website
CHINA	
China Daily On-line	http://chinadaily.com.cn
China News Services	http://www.chinanews.com
People's Daily On-line	http://peoplesdaily.com
HONG KONG	
South China Morning Post	http://www.SCMP.com
Hong Kong Standard	http://hkstandard.com
JAPAN	
The Japan Times On-line	http://www.japantimes.co.jp
Asahi Newspaper	http://www.asahi.com/english
Mainichi Shimbun	http://www.mainichi.co.jp/english
KOREA	
The Korea Herald	http://www.koreaherald.co.kr
THE PHILIPPINES	
Manila Times	http://www.manilatimes.net
SINGAPORE	
The Straits Times Interactive	http://straitstimes.asia1.com.sg
TAIWAN	
China Times Interactive	http://www.china-times.com.tw
Taiwan News	http://taipei.org
THAILAND	
Bangkok Post	http://bangkokpost.co.th

Exhibit 5: SCMP.com products

A group of Websites were housed within SCMP.com. They included the *Post*'s Internet Edition, Classified Post On-line, Your Money, SCMP Archive Search, the Regional Hotel Guide, Racing Post On-line and the Meeting Point.

Internet Edition of the *Post*

Selected full-text articles from all sections of the *Post*, including local, regional and world news, Business Post, Markets Post, Focus, Sport, Property and Technology, were featured in the Internet Edition. The Internet Edition was updated at 9:00 am every day from Monday to Saturday.

Classified Post On-line

This Website contained all advertisements printed in the Classified Post. Similar to the printed edition, Classified Post On-line was divided into four sections: Classified Property, Motor Vehicles and Boats, Business Opportunities and Notices. Classified Property was the largest section, carrying the largest number of advertisements.

SCMP Careers (careers.SCMP.com)

Originally the largest section of the Classified Post On-line, the Careers section was developed into an independent Website, offering services to both job seekers and employers. Registered users could access all the services offered to job seekers free of charge.

All the printed employment advertisements in the Classified Post were posted on SCMP Careers. A sophisticated search engine was designed to help job seekers locate the relevant jobs. Employment advertisements were searchable by keyword, SCMP reference number, industry (38 categories), job type (22 categories), industry description, academic qualifications, length of work experience and salary. Services offered to job seekers included My Career (listing of relevant jobs according to criteria preset by the job seeker), My Resume (on-line submission of resumes), Career Forum, Career Advice and Development, and a listing of employment agencies and their available vacancies.

Services for employers included Candidate Search (a matching service to locate the desirable candidates for employers based on candidate profiles provided) and Employer Profile (posting of a brief profile of the employer together with a list of available jobs). These services were available to employers for a fee.

Exhibit 5 (cont'd)

SCMP Archive Search

This was a subscription-based service. Full-text articles from the *Post* were available from 1993 onwards. These articles could be downloaded for HK$10 each.

The Regional Hotel Guide

PostNet offered this free-of-charge service to hotels that subscribed to the *Post*. A Webpage was developed for each hotel. Other than a graphic display of the hotel, details such as location of the hotel, facilities, room types and rates and reservation information were also available. The Regional Hotel Guide did not handle on-line hotel reservations. It provided links to hotels' own Websites, however. Users of the Regional Hotel Guide could post e-mail or fax requests directly to PostNet for additional information on hotels that appeared in the Guide.

Racing Post On-line

This Website offered both free and subscription-based services. Free services included news on horse races, details of upcoming races and racing results from the last racing day. For a monthly fee of HK$198, users were granted access to services such as racing tips, statistics, jockey and trainer analysis, racing databases, etc.

The Meeting Point

The Meeting Point was initially launched as a voice service. PostNet developed this voice service together with MicroVoice, a US voice marketing company. The Meeting Point Website was launched at the beginning of 1998. This Website housed all the personal advertisements printed in the *Post*'s Personals section. Advertisers, who placed their print and on-line personal advertisements free of charge, were each assigned a mailbox with a passcode. They could record a voice introduction to go with their advertisements. Each advertiser was set up to receive both e-mail and voice replies. Interested parties had to purchase a certain number of electronic stamps on-line with their credit cards and use these stamps to send in their e-mail replies to advertisers.[43] Alternatively, they could call and leave a message in the advertisers' voice mailboxes.[44]

---

[43] As at June 1999, five electronic stamps that cost US$2 were required to post one e-mail reply.

[44] An access charge of HK$10 per minute was imposed on the posting of voice replies.

Exhibit 5 (cont'd)

PostCD-ROM

PostCD-ROM was launched in the second half of 1996. It was the CD-ROM edition of the *Post* from 1993 onwards. Each PostCD-ROM contained full-text articles from an entire year of the *Post*. These CD-ROMs were used as reference materials in corporate, government and academic libraries.

PostSyndication and PostPhoto

This was the licensing of *Post* articles and photographs to publishers and information database hosts. Before PostNet was established, the syndication business was handled by the Library. A PostPhoto Website was developed to drive the sales of the *Post*'s news photographs. PostSyndication's customers included global database hosts such as Lexis-Nexis, Dow Jones News Retrieval and FT Profile.

Exhibit 6: 'Discontinued' PostNet products

PostFax

Launched in 1996, PostFax offered *Post* headlines and stories on fax. This service was discontinued due to diminished demand.

IVR

This interactive voice response audiotext service was launched in October 1996. Users of IVR called in and selected the *Post*'s editorial and advertising content they wanted to listen to. Charges were based on minutes of usage. This service was cut back substantially in 1999 due to diminished demand.

Global Investor

This subscription-based service, accessible through PostWeb, was launched in the second quarter of 1997. PostNet developed this service together with M.A.I.D., a provider of on-line business information. M.A.I.D. was also the content provider of this service.[45] Global Investor subscribers could set up on-line investment portfolios to track public companies, and had access to newswires, archived news and other research materials focused on the Asian region. This service was subsequently discontinued because of difficulties in obtaining adequate content.

---

[45] M.A.I.D. was renamed the Dialog Corporation following its takeover of Knight-Ridder Information, Inc., another on-line information provider, in 1997.

Exhibit 6 (cont'd)

Your Money

This was a weekly electronic magazine about personal finance. It was offered free of charge and was targeted at small investors in Asia. This magazine featured articles on personal financial management, weekly reviews of Asian business news, weekly summaries of stock market performances in Hong Kong and Mainland China, and reviews on foreign currency market movements.

PostResearch

PostResearch was initially planned as an information brokerage service that would utilise the resources of the *Post*'s Library to meet research needs in the marketplace. Upon further evaluation, two decisions were made. First, the Library, which was part of the Editorial Department and the holder of all the *Post* content, decided to devote all its efforts to supporting the *Post*'s journalists and editorial staff. Second, it was difficult to design an information brokerage product that had a mass appeal and yet was cost-effective to implement. Based on these decisions, PostResearch was withdrawn from the launch plan.

Exhibit 7: Internet penetration rate as at the beginning of 1999

Country/city	Percentage
Singapore	25.0
Hong Kong	12.5
Taiwan	12.0
Malaysia	6.3
China (Beijing, Shanghai & Guangzhou)	2.9
The Philippines	2.0
Thailand	1.5
Indonesia	1.2
Canada	38.0
USA	25.0
Australia	25.0
New Zealand	24.0
Germany	14.0

Source: ACNielsen (1999), "Singapore the Top Net Surfer in Asia, ACNielsen Global Study Reveals", *ACNielsen NetWatch Survey*, ACNielsen press release, 5 February.

Exhibit 8: Biographies of SCMP.com senior executives appointed in November 1999

Mr. Kuok Koon-seng, Chief Executive	Mr. Kuok was a former executive director of TVE International and a former director of Television Broadcasts. He had several years of experience in the publishing, retailing and entertainment businesses.
Mr. Ray Bashford, Editorial Director	Mr. Bashford joined the *Post* as Business Editor in 1995, after spending 10 years at the *Financial Times* in London as financial news editor. Prior to that, he had worked on newspapers in Australia.
Ms. Cheng Chai, Chief Financial Officer	Ms. Chai was a former director, mergers and acquisitions, for Merrill Lynch (Asia) in Hong Kong. Ms. Chai had 20 years of experience in the financial industry, and had worked for Schroders Asia in Hong Kong, D&C Nomura Merchants Bankers in Kuala Lumpur and Touche Ross & Co in London.
Mr. Larry Campbell, Publisher	Mr. Campbell had been in journalism for 15 years and had been involved in on-line publishing since 1993. He was Technology Editor of the *Post* from 1990 to 1996. Before joining the *Post*, he was publisher of *The Dataphile*, an on-line and print Internet magazine he founded in 1993.

Source: "SCMP On-line Unit Makes Four Senior Appointments", *South China Morning Post*, 19 November 1999, p. 3.

Exhibit 9: Index of employer profiles on the careers.SCMP.com Website

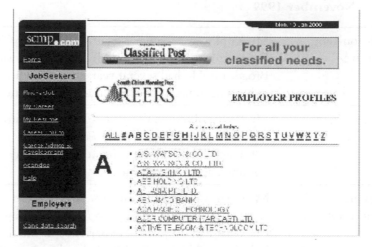

Source: SCMP Careers (careers.SCMP.com) Website (2000), URL: http://careers.scmp.com/
profile.asp?agency=N&Alphabet=C, 10 January.

Exhibit 10: 'Buttons' on the main page of Classified Property

Source: Classified Post On-line, Classified Property (2000), URL: http://www.classifiedpost.
com.hk/prop_ind_fs.html, 10 January.

Exhibit 11:   Sybase's banner ad in Technology Section of SCMP.com

Source: URL: http://www.technologypost.com/main/index.asp, 10 January.

Exhibit 12:   The Markets Update Webpage sponsored by HSBC

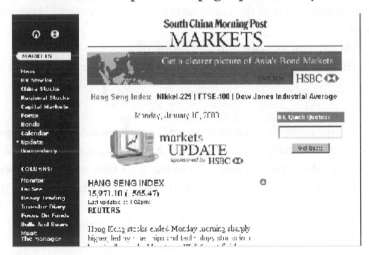

Source: URL: http://www.SCMP.com/News/Markets/Update/Update.asp, 10 January.

CHAPTER

2

The Infrastructure

OBJECTIVES

- To study the underlying infrastructure of e-commerce.
- To identify the components of the information infrastructure.
- To gain an appreciation of the issues surrounding technological convergence and integration.
- To learn about network standards and protocols.
- To study the development of emerging technologies in a historical context.

At this stage, the model that you want to start thinking about is not the bandwidth problem – that's essentially fixed – but what happens to electronic commerce when everyone is connected to the Net with a device that gives them a continuous megabyte. When every home and every office has access to that. That's a whole new level, a whole new range of possibilities.

– Eric Schmidt, CEO, Novell[1]

---

[1] Cited in Siebel & House (1999), p. 43.

E-COMMERCE INFRASTRUCTURE: CONVERGENCE AND INTEGRATION

Like traditional commerce, electronic commercial activities involve the following four basic levels:

- ❏ A *communications* infrastructure, carrying messages about prices, quantities, service or product characteristics.
- ❏ A *marketplace*, the market coordination environment in which buyers meet sellers and negotiate (this of course, encompasses *intermediaries*, allowing sellers to transact business with buyers).
- ❏ *Transaction* mechanisms to send, execute and settle orders (including payments).
- ❏ *Deliverables*, the service or merchandise being exchanged.[2]

Since their inception, electronic technologies have assisted in the entire range of commercial activities, from automated processes to electronic payments to delivery and distribution. However, with the rise of the Internet to the position of a mainstream network – global in nature and (increasingly) universally accessible – the landscape has changed radically. Why? This is because with the Internet, diverse commercial activities, previously confined to separate electronic networks or to isolated locations, can now take place over a single, integrated 'network of networks'.[3]

---

[2] Bar & Murasse (1999); Picot *et al.* (1997).

[3] The Internet is frequently described as a 'network of networks'. While this is correct, it can often confuse more than it clarifies. The official definition of the Internet was announced in a resolution of 24 October 1995, when the US Federal Networking Council, a body of Internet architects, unanimously passed a resolution defining the term 'Internet'. This definition was developed in consultation with members of the Internet and intellectual property rights communities.

Resolution: The Federal Networking Council (FNC) agrees that the following language reflects our definition of the term 'Internet'. 'Internet' refers to the global information system that :

(i) is logically linked together by a globally unique address space based on the Internet Protocol (IP) or its subsequent extensions/follow-ons;

(ii) is able to support communications using the Transmission Control Protocol/Internet Protocol (TCP/IP) suite or its subsequent extensions/follow-ons, and/or other IP-compatible protocols; and

(iii) provides, uses or makes accessible, either publicly or privately, high-level services layered on the communications and related infrastructure described herein.

Source: URL: http://www.fnc.gov/Internet_res.html

What this has meant is that, in the first phase of e-commerce development, the big winners have naturally been the suppliers of the network infrastructure. Assuming, for example, that only one-fifth of Cisco's US$6.4 billion in router sales for 1997 was attributable to the demand generated by e-commerce, this alone would have exceeded most estimates of *total* e-commerce. When Cisco first allowed customers to purchase equipment over its Website in 1996, the company generated US$100 million in sales. In 1997, sales reached over US$1 billion, and were more than US$4 billion in 1998. At the user end Dell tapped successfully into the demand for PCs and, in the space of one year, 1997, increased its on-line sales from US$1 million a day to US$6 million a day. By 1999, on-line sales represented 50 percent (i.e., approximately US$12 billion) of total sales. (There is, of course, nothing surprising in this pattern. In the US gold rush of the 1800s – to which the growth of e-commerce is often compared – the early winners were the sellers of food, clothes and pickaxes, rather than the miners themselves.)

For e-commerce to grow successfully (i.e., to become self-sustaining), there are two necessary structural aspects. The first is the physical infrastructure – in this case that means not simply the physical networks but the convergence of different media networks (voice, data and video, *or* broadcasting, communications and computing) and the integration of the networks into a single platform. The second is the superstructure – the framework of rules and regulations, accountability and enforcement [**Figure 1**]. We look at the latter in Chapter 3: The Regulatory Framework. In this chapter we examine the development of the infrastructure for e-commerce. The first section defines the concept of the information infrastructure – what exactly do we mean by the concept of an integrated e-commerce platform? The following section enlarges upon this picture of network development. We then place the emergence of the integrated network platform into historical context so as to explain the important benefits of network economics to e-commerce development (in a section which looks at the so-called trilogy of networking 'laws': Moore's Law, Metcalfe's Law and Gilder's Law). Finally, we explain why the open source movement has played a fundamental role in the on-going growth of early e-commerce and why it has been such an integral part of the infrastructural development.

Figure 1:   Generic e-commerce framework

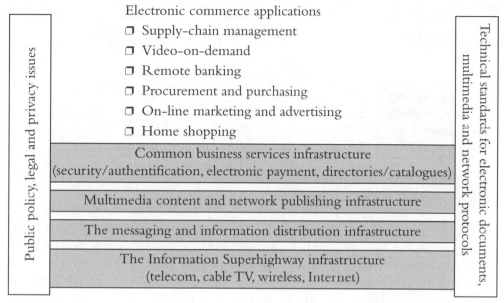

Source: Kalakota & Whinston (1996), p. 4.

INFORMATION INFRASTRUCTURE: DEFINING THE CONCEPT

Infrastructure is *the basic framework or underlying foundation*, upon which a complex structure of service provisions can be built. An information infrastructure can be regarded as the set of facilities that provide a basis for information services.

As Internet technology continued to drive convergence across what were once considered separate areas (broadcasting, communications and computing), the infrastructure to support e-commerce has emerged [see **Figure 2**]. Three major components make up this information infrastructure: consumer access equipment, media-specific networks (or local networks) and global backbone information distribution networks.

❏ Of these components, *consumer access equipment* is often ignored in the analysis of the underlying information infrastructure. But the success of Dell Computer and Nokia Corporation demonstrate that consumer equipment represents a critical category – the absence or slow development of which will signifi-

Figure 2:   Information infrastructure components

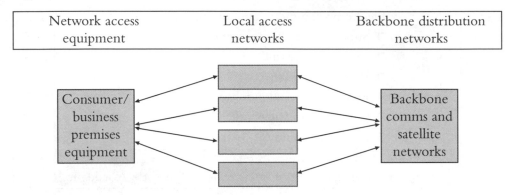

Source: Kalakota & Whinston (1996), p. 50.

cantly frustrate the growth of other segments. For instance, the technology for interactive TV has long been possible, but has not become widely available because of a lack of affordable equipment on the customer's side for access and on the provider's side for distribution.[4] Consumer access equipment providers include hardware and software vendors who provide physical devices, such as routers and switches; access devices, such as computers and set-top boxes; and software platforms, such as browsers and operating systems.

❏ *Media-specific (or local) networks* are the linkages between businesses, schools or homes and the communications backbone. In the telecommunications industry this component is often called the 'last mile'. The providers of access networks can be differentiated into four categories: telecom-based, cable TV-based, wireless-based and computer-based on-line information services (including value-added networks (VANs)).

❏ *Backbone networks* represent the infrastructure criss-crossing countries and continents, and include the fibre-optic strands, coaxial cables, radio waves, satellites, and copper wires spanning the globe. This backbone, put in place over the last four decades by the telephone, cable and satellite companies, includes such networks as long-distance telephone lines, satellite networks and the Internet [see **Table 1**]. Although the Internet uses the same hardware (leased telephone lines), the history, protocols and regulations surrounding it warrant its placement in another category.

---

[4]   Kalakota & Whinston (1996), p. 50.

Table 1: Major PSINet peer interconnect points

US		International	
CIX	Palo Alto, CA	AIX	Amsterdam, Netherlands
CIX	Herndon, VA	CERN	Geneva, Switzerland
MAE East	Washington, DC	DE-CIX	Frankfurt, Germany
Mae West	Palo Alto, CA	E-Bone	London, England
NAP	San Jose, CA	LINX	London, England
PAIX	Palo Alto, CA	MAE-Frankfurt	Frankfurt, Germany
Sprint NAP	New York, NY	MAE-Paris	Paris, France
		NSP/IXP II	Tokyo, Japan
		SFINX	Paris, France

Linking all the components of the emerging information infrastructure requires large capital investment in 'open' systems[5] (see below) and installing gateways between various networks. A final requirement is the switching hardware and software to move huge amounts of data effortlessly over such a complex network.

The information infrastructure concept is not simply a descriptor of these individual networks. Rather the concept encompasses the *integrated networking* of the platform. As we have seen in the Module introduction, the development of the information infrastructure is an area of extremely active debate because of a number of different drivers as follows:

❑ *Technological developments*, which have dramatically increased data-transmission capacity. Current technologies include fibre-optic cable, terrestrial microwave, high-orbit and low-orbit satellites, digital cellular mobile telecommunications, and so on. These all have niches in which they enjoy or have the potential for significant advantages over alternatives, but are complementary, in the sense that none is dominant in all circumstances.

❑ *Cross-segment competition* (business convergence), i.e., an increasing tendency for suppliers which used to operate in distinct market segments (in particular, local and long-distance telephony, broadcast and cable television, and data transfer) to enter into alliances and offer services directly competing with one another's offerings.

---

[5] 'Open' systems are interoperable equipment that uses common standards.

❏ *Regulatory liberalisation.* Owing to the technological and commercial change, governments have acknowledged the need for a restructuring of the various regulatory regimes governing telephone, television and data-network operators.

❏ *Strategic initiatives,* driven by leading industrialised nations, notably IT2000 in Singapore, and the Clinton/Gore Administration's National Information Infrastructure (NII) initiative in the United States [see **Table 2**].

Most importantly though, the information infrastructure that supports e-commerce has become a significant and growing part of the overall economy. A report by the US Department of Commerce estimated that while information and communication technologies (ICTs) represented only about eight percent of GDP, they contrib-

Table 2:   Asian NII programme and their estimated costs

Country	NII programme	Timeframe	Cost (US$bn)
Japan	Japan National Information Infrastructure (JNII)	National broadband infrastructure by 2010	330-550
South Korea	Korea Information Infrastructure (KII)	Broadband infrastructure installed by 2010	57.9
Singapore	IT2000	Fibre to building; full-service cable network by 2000	2.65
Malaysia	Malaysian Multimedia Super Corridor (MSC)	Fibre to the home by 2020	30
Thailand	IT 2000	Broadband access by 2002	18
Indonesia	Indonesian National Information Infrastructure (INFONAS)	Broadband infrastructure in place by 2010	na
China	China National Information Infrastructure (CNII)	Broadband network delivering over one million telephone channels and 10,000 TV channels by 2020	200

uted nearly double that to GDP growth [see **Figure 3**]. By 1998, the US ICT sector contributed a larger share to GDP than the automobile and aerospace sector combined. It is for this reason that so much effort is being devoted to getting the infrastructure right.

Figure 3:   US Information industry share of GDP and contribution to growth

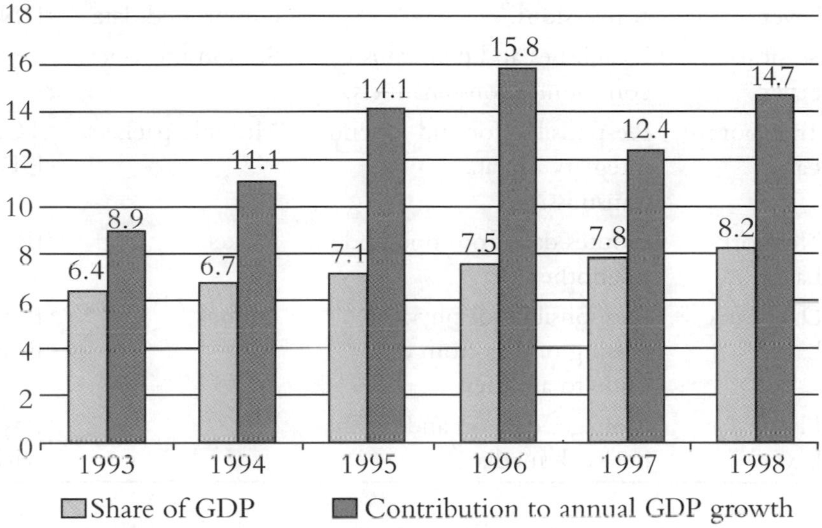

☐ Share of GDP   ■ Contribution to annual GDP growth

Source: US Department of Commerce (1998), "The Emerging Digital Economy", 15 April, Washington, DC, URL: http://www.ecommerce.gov/emerging.htm, June 2000.

NETWORK INFRASTRUCTURE

Network technologies are specified by protocols – rules that determine everything about the way a network operates. Protocols govern how applications access the network, the way data from an application is divided into packets for transmission through a cable, and which electrical signals represent data on a network cable. Protocols are essentially software instruction sets in the headers of messages transported over the networks. In an effort to standardise network protocols, the International Standards Organisation (ISO) created a 7-layer model [see **Table 3**] defining the basic network functions. This model is called the Open Systems Interface (OSI) reference model. The 7-layer OSI 'stack' is an agreed way for computers to communicate, and be understood as a grammar for machines.

Table 3: The OSI reference model

Layer	Name	Function	Information transferred	TCP/IP
7	Application Layer	Program-to-program communication.	Application messages	FTP, HTTP
6	Presentation Layer	Manages data representation conversions.[6]	Encrypted data, compressed data	SNMP, DNS
5	Session Layer	Establishes and maintains communications channels.[7]	Session messages	
4	Transport Layer	Responsible for end-to-end integrity of data transmission.	Multiple packets	TCP, UDP
3	Network Layer	Routes data from one node to another.	Packets	IP, ARP
2	Data Link Layer	Responsible for physical passing of data from one node to another.	Frames	Ethernet, PPP
1	Physical Layer	Manages data on and off the network media.	Bits	Physical wiring

The existence of layers in data communications represents a subtle and powerful method for changing how people are able to take advantage of networks. Layers provide agreements among people – and the machines that they build and program – as to who will do what, and when. As such, layers are standards. Knowledge of the existence of layers is therefore fundamental to understanding how the Internet works and why it works differently from previous signal transport media. While the Internet uses a layered-signal architecture, the founders of the Internet decided not to conform to the OSI 7-layer model. Rather Transmission Control Protocol/Internet Protocol (TCP/IP) takes the top three layers, five through seven, and combines them into one – the Application layer. (It is also useful to realise that the physical and data link layers have

---

[6] For example, the Presentation Layer would be responsible for converting from EBCDIC to ASCII.

[7] In practice, this layer is often combined with the Transport Layer.

nothing to do with TCP/IP but TCP/IP must have these layers below it in order to work. The signal must transport across something, even the air.)

The result is that the Internet is an open system where new protocols may be added by a process of consensus within the industry. The effect of these protocols can be to change how the system of signal transmission works. Protocols can be introduced without any money being spent on changing any physical object within the signal transmission system. Thus, to understand why the Internet is driving technological and business change so effectively, one needs to understand the function of layers.

Get2Net: Public Internet Access Terminals

Get2Net (www.get2net.com), a fast-growing operator of hundreds of public Internet access terminals in the US, offers business and leisure travellers free Internet access through its NetSets (stand-up Internet kiosks) or NetStations (private Internet sit-down phone booth-like cubicles) located in 75 percent of the country's busiest airports. For roadside travellers, Get2Net installed 'ruggedised' terminals at roadside travel plazas around the country. The Intel-architectured PCs are manufactured by Miltope and PGI, companies that specialise in making rugged equipment for military applications. Thus, terminals consist of 'ruggedised' hard drives, monitors and keyboards contained in tabletop models, standalone stations or private booths. By the end of 2000, over 1,000 terminals were planned to be set up around the country, and by 2003 there would be 6,000 units installed for Internet-savvy travellers.

The efforts at Get2Net show that there is an increasing interest in the open-ended opportunity of Internet business. Established in 1997, its mission is to provide fast, convenient public access to the Internet in high-traffic US travel venues. Get2Net installed the first units at Norfolk International Airport in 1997. The terminals are strategically located near airport gates, frequent flier clubs and restaurants. By mid-1999, there were already 120 units active in 19 locations mostly at airports. Its plan is to install 1,000 units in airport concept bars and grills and restaurants operated by Host Marriot Services. Get2Net hopes that their terminals will be as ubiquitous as ATM banks.

Keeping its overhead low and its reliability high (with the UNIX system), Get2Net designed its infrastructure around the Intel architecture. For stable and cost-effective network connectivity, Get2Net utilises Intel Express Routers, Hubs and Switches. A ten-person technical team from ISIS 2000 (Integrated Systems and Internet Solutions 2000, Get2Net's sister company) manages the physical network of Get2Net located in Tucson. The back-office configuration has five mission-critical servers: (1) a primary Web server running Apache; (2) a terminal management server to keep track of and monitor all user access stations; (3) a network management server to track and monitor network equipment; (4) a secure server running Apache Stronghold used for billing; and (5) a network management server. All of the servers are based on Intel architecture, except the network management server that runs Hewlett-Packard's HP OpenView Framework.

Like its back-end server, the user terminals are specialised, rugged PCs and run Linux (as opposed to Windows OS). Get2Net preferred Linux due to its stability and its ability to smoothly facilitate remote management. And because Linux is free, it helps Get2Net reduce costs. The combination of affordability and excellent reliability in deciding to use Intel in its back-end and Linux in its front-end processes, sets Get2Net apart from competitors. Both system and network reliability are critical to Get2Net. As services are offered to users free of charge, Get2Net's business model is built on advertising support.

Sources: Get2Net (2000); Planet IT (1999); *Poptronics* (2000).

A HISTORICAL LEGACY

Information-processing power has grown along with transistor density, while the cost to make a chip of given size has stayed roughly constant. Computers today have 66,000 times the processing power at the same cost as the computers of 1975; computers in 2010 will have ten million times the processing power of the computers of 1975. How does the information-processing revolution compare to other, previous waves of innovation? Stephen Cohen, Brad De Long and John Zysman have compared the past 40 years of progress in information processing with the replacement of the steam engine by the electric motor [see **Figure 4**].[8] In 1869, America's steam engines delivered 1.2 million horsepower to America's manufacturing firms. By 1939 America's electric motors delivered 45 million horsepower to America's manufacturing firms. This was roughly a 40-fold increase in mechanical power in 70 years – a five percent per year increase in muscle power.

---

[8] Cohen *et al.* (1999).

Figure 4:   Information-processing growth vs. electric-power growth

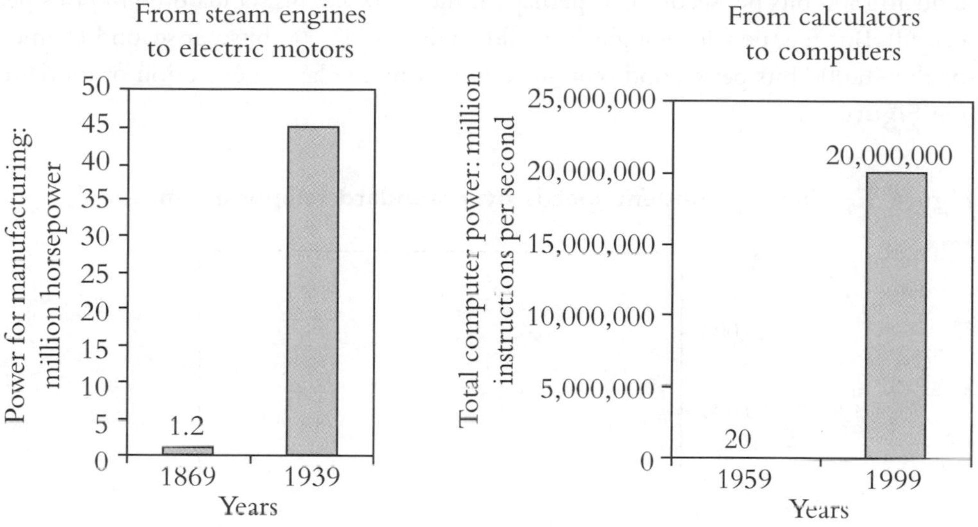

From steam engines
to electric motors

From calculators
to computers

Sources: Devine (1983); Campbell-Kelly & Aspray (1996).

At the end of the 1950s, the moment at which electronic computers had largely replaced electromechanical calculators, there were roughly 2,000 installed computers in the world – machines like Remington Rand UNIVACs, IBM 650s or 702s, or DEC PDP-1s with processing power that averaged perhaps 10,000 instructions per second. By the end of the century there were approximately 200 million active computers in the world with processing power that averaged approximately 100,000,000 instructions per second. This is a million-fold increase in 40 years – a 35 percent per year increase in information processing power.[9] In other words, the price of computers has fallen more than 10,000-fold in a single generation; the price of semiconductors has fallen even faster.

The extraordinary build-out of the network is as remarkable as has been the explosion in computing power. In the early days of networking – the 1960s and 1970s – it was thought that high-speed data communications would require special data-friendly

---

[9] A contemporary microprocessor contains about 10 million transistors. PixelFusion is on the road towards developing a single chip containing 50 million transistors, capable of doing 1.5 trillion operations per second (URL: http://www.pixelfusion.com/). Their Fuzion 150 chip will include 24 megabits of memory.

phone lines. Telephone lines would be capable of carrying data transmissions at the 103 standard (300 bits per second), or perhaps at most the V.22bis standard (2,400 bits per second). But few people thought it would attain the 53,000 bits per second claimed (or the 40,000 bits per second typically *achieved*) by the latest generation of modems [see **Figure 5**].

Figure 5:   Dial-up modem speeds over standard telephone lines

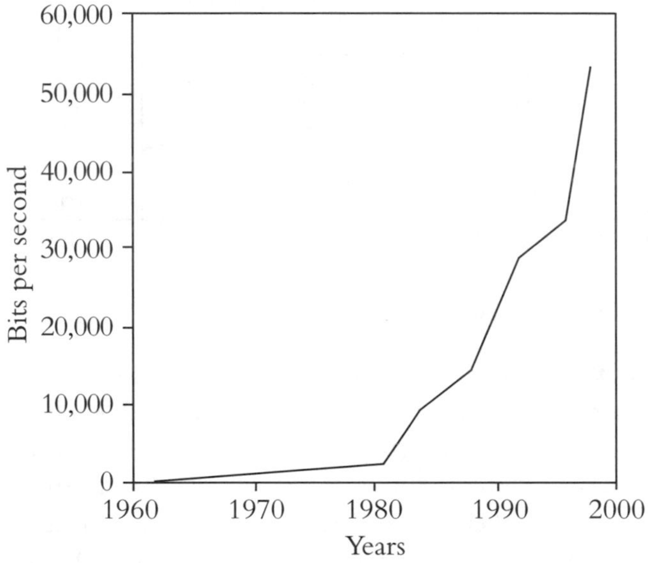

Source: Maxwell (1999).

Over the past two decades, there has been a 22-fold increase in the speed of data transmission obtained over *ordinary* telephone lines. This extraordinary 18 percent per year improvement in data transmission over plain old telephone lines[10] is not at the pace of Moore's Law, but it is still extremely rapid, particularly over a sustained timeframe. It allows everyone with a phone line today the potential to connect at speeds that 20 years ago was thought to require expensive, dedicated equipment.[11]

---

[10] Industry acronyms for distinguishing between basic voice services and the more impressive data services were, for many years: POTS (plain old telephone service) or PANS (pretty awesome new stuff).

[11] Maxwell (1999).

This wave of innovation in data communications has allowed the rapid build-out of the worldwide data network *on top of* the already existing phone network. It has thus shaved a telephone-equipment generation off the time it would have otherwise taken to wire the United States for the Internet. Worldwide, there are more than 60 million computers on the Internet. Since 1987, the Internet Software Consortium (www.isc.org) has run a semi-annual survey to count the number of 'hosts' on the Internet. By the end of 1999 the count was over 60 million – 60 million computers, all accessible one to another through the global Internet. By comparison, in October 1990 there were only 300,000 computers on the Internet. And in August 1981 there were only 213.

'Moore's Law', 'Metcalfe's Law' and 'Gilder's Law'

Underlying the spread of connectivity and of electronic intelligence is the extraordinary force of Moore's Law: the observation first made by Gordon Moore, then chairman of Intel, that every 18 months[12] it is possible to double the number of transistor circuits etched on a computer chip. This 'law' has prevailed for the past 40 years.[13] Moore's Law implies a ten-fold increase in memory and processing power every five years, a 100-fold every ten years, a 1,000-fold every 15. This is one of the most dramatic rates of sustained technical progress in history.

But as we noted above, as extraordinary as Moore's Law has proven, of even greater impact has been Metcalfe's Law. Bob Metcalfe, inventor of Ethernet, first observed that the value of a network is proportional to the square of the number of people using it. Thus, Metcalfe's Law, which is a modern version of the old law of increasing returns, says that the value of a network increases in direct proportion to the square of the number of machines that are on it. This is also known as the 'network effect'. The

---

[12] In 1965, Moore actually projected that the density of transistors on a silicon chip would double every *12 months*. He was somewhat over optimistic in his initial pronouncements, and the accepted time-span has become 18 months.

[13] Gordon Moore has been unwilling to extend his 'law' beyond 2010 because that is when current technologies will hit limits dictated by the size of the electron and the nature of silicon. After a certain microprocessor gate size – around one micron, or a billionth of an inch – you cannot get any more speed, so you reach a ceiling and Moore's Law ceases to have any effect. That will happen in another nine years, maybe a little longer. (See Moore, "Nanometers and Gigabucks – Moore on Moore's Law", *UVC Distinguished Lecture*, 1996.) By 2010, the Semetech National Semiconductor Roadmap (1994) predicts that 450 times as many transistors will reside on a chip than in 1997. However, many observers anticipate that other technologies, such as optical computing, will extend the 'law' much farther into the future.

value to any one individual of a telephone or fax machine, for instance, is proportional to the number of friends and associates who have phones or faxes. Double the number of participants, therefore, and the value to each participant is doubled, and the total value of the network is multiplied four-fold.[14] On-line classifieds, for example, are a navigation business where buyers and sellers are looking for each other. Buyers choose where to browse based on the number of advertisers, and sellers select where to advertise based on the number of browsers. Whoever establishes a clear lead becomes the first choice for buyers looking to reach the maximum number of sellers, and also for sellers seeking the maximum number of buyers. Reach then becomes a self-fulfilling prophecy. Whoever has superior share gains share.

This advance has pulled through extraordinary rates of associated innovation and has led to communications capacity exploding at a rate that now dwarfs even Moore's Law. The result has become known as 'Gilder's Law' (named after the high-tech futurologist, George Gilder) and forecasts that total bandwidth will triple every year for the next 25 years.[15] Improvements in data compression, amplification and multiplexing now permit a single fibre-optic strand to carry 25 terabits of information per second: 25 times more information than the average traffic load of the entire world's communications networks put together. In the US, communications companies are now laying fibre-optic networks at the rate of 4,000 strand miles per day. And thus the total bandwidth of US communications systems is tripling every year.

NETWORKS AND E-COMMERCE

The earliest forms of computer-based electronic commerce date from the late 1960s. In those days, they served a variety of distinct purposes, such as time sharing of mainframe computing CPU cycles (e.g., GE Information Service), packet-switched express mail delivery (e.g., Federal Express), data-transfer delivery (e.g., AT&T) or business-to-business (B2B) facsimile transmission. Businesses could acquire early e-commerce services by leasing the value-added networking services of international telephone companies, and by acquiring leased computer time and network access offered by the large in-house shops of GE, IBM, McDonnell Douglas and EDS.

---

[14] The term 'Metcalfe's Law' was coined by George Gilder in 1993 (URL: http://www.discovery.org/gilder/metcalf) though Bob Metcalfe has protested that he was merely trying to see Ethernet technology.

[15] Gilder (1997).

In the 1970s and 1980s, businesses extended their networks to reach out to customers and business partners by electronically sending and receiving purchase orders, invoices and shipping notifications. The result was a proliferation of electronic data (or document) interchange (EDI) transmitted over value-added networks (VANs). In the 1980s, vendors such as McDonnell Douglas and General Motors introduced computer-aided design (CAD), engineering and manufacturing over these communications networks, which allowed managers, engineers and users to collaborate on design and production.

The consequences of this *laissez-faire* development of e-commerce were felt throughout the 1970s and 1980s. Bewildering arrays of proprietary network architectures, computer architectures and clumsy text-based computer interfaces of proprietary software were haphazardly grouped together with vendor hardware, making e-commerce and computing both labour- and capital-intensive. None of this came cheaply. All but the largest firms were locked out of e-commerce technologies by their sheer cost and scale. In response, services bureaux grew out of the internal corporate computing operations of larger firms. They used their already substantial economies of scale to offer network and computing services of greater reliability and lower cost than even large firms could develop internally.

The traditional market for e-commerce services over the last three decades until 1990 can be encapsulated in the following five broad divisions:

1. Electronic mail, providing store-and-forward services for the B2B exchange of information. Mailbox services transferred information directly from the sender to the receiver, gateway services transferred information only as far as a corporate server.
2. Enhanced fax, providing point-to-point delivery of documents encoded as fax rather than e-mail, which usually implied that there was non-text information that needed to be encoded.
3. Electronic data interchange, providing computer-to-computer exchange of information using standardised transaction formats. These transactions typically involved purchase or sales functions.
4. Transaction processing, supporting credit, claims, payment authorisation and settlement of transactions. Transaction processing services often involved collaboration between an information transport service and an authorisation provider, such as a bank.
5. Groupware, employed within a secure, managed environment, which supported e-mail, calendering, scheduling, real-time conferencing, information sharing and workflow management.[16]

---

[16] Clarke & Westland (1999).

OPEN SYSTEM ARCHITECTURE

In contrast to the earlier proprietary e-commerce systems, the Internet's focus on networks that use non-proprietary protocols – a relatively new phenomenon – has been central. The rapid growth in Internet e-commerce is due to the following:

- ❑ The open, non-proprietary protocol (TCP/IP).
- ❑ The development of the World Wide Web which uses a standard coding system (Hypertext Markup Language – HTML) for representing data.
- ❑ The development and diffusion of browsers that provide a standard interface for accessing Websites.

Thus, although the precursor to the Internet appeared in the late 1960s, Internet e-commerce only began to take off with the arrival of the Web and graphical browsers (Mosaic, followed by Netscape) in the early 1990s.

The Internet's success through the first two phases resulted directly from the network's openness. A large variety of service and content providers could share existing infrastructure: the basic phone network. Experimentation by users and competition among providers, across the range of segments that constitute the Internet, generated a surge of self-sustaining innovation. Perhaps the most dramatic single example is the emergence and evolution of the Web, which was driven almost entirely by its users who pioneered all of the new emerging applications. The Web in turn facilitated a new round of innovation that opened into the world of Internet-based e-commerce.

This network openness and the user-driven innovation it encouraged were a distinct departure from the supply-centric, provider-dominated, traditional model. In the traditional model, a dominant carrier or broadcaster offered a limited menu of service options to subscribers; experimentation was limited to small-scale trials with the options circumscribed and dictated by the supplier. Open access to the network, by contrast, led to rich experimentation by many different participants. As we noted above, in the early days of 300-baud modems, few people thought 28.8kbps data communications would flow over ordinary voice phone lines. Even speeds of 9,600bps were seen as likely to be accomplished only with expensive, cleaned, better-than-voice lines: ISDN or some similar special service. The diversity of experimentation and the competition on a relatively open network was the key to what evolved because nobody could foresee the successful applications. Openness allowed many paths to be explored – not only those that the phone monopolies, i.e., the infrastructure owners, favoured. It is a safe bet that without *regulatory-mandated* openness, only those connections and projects that the telephone companies and monopoly franchise cable networks would have favoured would have ever been attempted. Thus, it is doubtful that without such regulatory-mandated openness the network-based new economy would have occurred.

Many of the most successful development paths have challenged the very core of the phone monopoly business, and many of the technology and business *assumptions* of the communications industry. For instance, the Internet is largely distance price insensitive, both because of the character of the emerging technologies and because of the particular regulatory settings under which they operate. Flat-fee pricing has meant the same price for one or many e-mails for sending them around the corner or around the world. But this has relied upon policy decisions requiring network incumbents to open their networks to the new entrants, and flat-rate pricing mechanisms for the Internet have resulted from policies exempting ISPs from access charges for data and cross-subsidies for data transport. (This is covered in detail in Chapter 3: The Regulatory Framework.)

Freeserve: Free Internet Service

Freeserve (www.freeserve.com) is UK's first fully featured free Internet service launched in September 1998 by Dixons, Europe's leading consumer electronics retailer. Freeserve offers users no registration or set-up fees and no monthly subscription charges to pay; what users pay for is the local rate phone call to access the service. The no-cost Internet service provider revolutionalised the use of the Internet in Britain and has attracted over 475,000 members in its first eight weeks – making Freeserve the second-biggest Internet platform in Britain, behind AOL UK. Britain has seven million plus Internet users and with Freeserve, this means more users are encouraged to log onto the Internet. Dixons distribute free discs in its stores and customers join by merely installing the disc on their computers.

According to Fletcher Research's survey of on-line users, Freeserve has increased its share of the home Internet market to 37 percent. In June 2000, Freeserve captured more than double the market share of the second-largest ISP, AOL. In April and June 2000, Freeserve launched its two high-quality and reliable unmetered access propositions, while other providers have either cancelled their unmetered access offers or have failed to fulfil their promises.

Source: Freeserve (2000).

Open Source Software

Open Source development and distribution has already had a major impact in several areas, the notable ones being the Apache Web Server, the Linux operating system, the Sendmail messaging server, the entire GNU project (e.g., Emacs and GCC), PERL, Python, TCL and X-Windows. All of these areas have achieved wide penetration in a number of venues.

In the early 1980s, Richard Stallman began a project called GNU ('GNU's Not Unix') which was meant to create a variety of free source codes, including a version of Unix. Unix had been released by AT&T earlier and had become the *de facto* standard for a new class of computers called Workstations. As part of the effort, Stallman created a licence called GPL (GNU Public Licence) that gave broad freedom to the users of GNU, with one important exception: *Users were required to donate any changes/improvements that they made to the code back to the original copyright owner (also coined 'copyleft')*. Concurrently, there was a brief movement in the DOS world when people released source code into the public domain. Public domain software came with no restrictions whatsoever. Most of the programs were small and utilitarian, rather than large-scale systems. This phenomenon seems to have died down once Microsoft Windows became the dominant operating system for PCs; the shareware movement largely replaced it. Here, the author of a program permits a user to use the product without paying an upfront fee. There are various schemes utilised to entice or force users to eventually pay if they are satisfied with the program.

In 1998, in response to the specific announcement by Netscape that it would open up the source to its browser, the term Open Source was defined and trademarked. Open Source is a wide, but still controlled definition. It attempts to define certain parameters (by virtue of its branding) so that users do not have to concern themselves too deeply with the particular nuance of a licence. A number of business models are developing around Open Source initiatives, and as more companies prove the viability of such models, Open Source will continue to drive developments such as Linux and Red Hat.

Red Hat: Provider of Open Source Internet Infrastructure

Red Hat (www.redhat.com) is the industry's largest source of custom Open Source development expertise in embedded, networked and post-PC devices. It is the technology and market leader for Open Source Internet Infrastructure solutions ranging from powerful servers to the smallest embedded devices. The Red Hat Linux operating system is the company's principal product. With the open source community under the GNU General Public Licence (GPL), Red Hat shares all of its software innovations freely. Red Hat software products are made available to users through free download from its Website, www.redhat.com, and other sites across the Internet. Abiding with the open source guidelines, Red Hat reveals the internal workings of the software in the form of the 'source code', a concept that is substantially different than other software versions like Microsoft, in which the source code is a closely-guarded secret and modification by outsiders is actually illegal.

According to the International Data Corporation (IDC), Red Hat Linux 'is by far the most popular distribution, preferred by 68.7 percent of US Linux users'. Furthermore, IDC reported that paid Linux shipments grew faster than any other server operating system: preliminary 1999 figures showed Linux shipments held 24.6 percent of the server operating system market, an increase of 15.8 percent on 1998. As of May 2000, Linux is the most popular choice for deploying public Websites, with 36 percent of all public Websites running on Linux-based operating systems, according to Netcraft, Inc. research firm.

Red Hat not only sells open source products, it also offers extensive professional services on the development and use of open source products including technical support, custom development, consulting, training, education and hardware certification. Most of the industry's leading software and hardware manufacturers, including Compaq, Computer Associates, Dell, Hewlett-Packard, IBM, Intel, Netscape, Novell, Oracle and SAP, utilise the official Red Hat Linux-based applications for their open source support infrastructure.

The uses of Red Hat Linux are extensive and include networking, software development, and desktop applications. The variety of software in Red Hat Linux enables users to install it as a server or desktop. As a server, it can be set up for use as Web server, e-mail, DNS server or news server, and can be configured for multiple sites and virtual hosting. As a desktop, Red Hat Linux enables users to have e-mail, browsers, publishing tools, calendars and Internet tools among others. Some packages include the ability to conduct easy networking with heterogeneous computer networks.

Sources: Burns (2000); *M2 Presswire* (2000); Red Hat (2000).

A combination of regulatory reform and technological innovation has enabled e-commerce to evolve as it has. Although the precursor to the Internet appeared in the late 1960s, Internet e-commerce only really began to take off with the arrival of the World Wide Web and graphical browsers in the early 1990s, the liberalisation of the telecommunication sector, and the innovations which have greatly expanded the volume and capacity of the communication networks.

As a result, barriers to engage in e-commerce have progressively fallen for both buyers and sellers. Earlier forms of e-commerce were mostly custom-made, complex, expensive and the province of large firms. Today, for a few thousand dollars, anyone can become a merchant and reach millions of consumers worldwide. What used to be B2B transactions between known parties has become a complex web of commercial activities that can involve vast numbers of individuals who may never meet.

SUMMARY

❑ The Information Superhighway infrastructure is the backbone of e-commerce; it provides the underlying foundation upon which e-commerce rests. The major components of the infrastructure are consumer access equipment, media-specific networks and global backbone information distribution networks.

❑ Protocols are rules that determine everything about the way a network operates; they govern how applications access the network and the way data from an application are divided into packets for transmission. The Internet is based on Transmission Control Protocol/Internet Protocol (TCP/IP), making it an open system where new protocols can be added by the process of consensus within the industry.

❑ The staggering rate of technological developments in the past 50 years has largely been due to the exponential growth in computing power, which has been doubling every 18 months.

❑ The power of the Internet in propelling the new economy can be explained largely in the light of the network effect; i.e., the value of a network is proportional to the square of the number of people participating in that network.

❑ We should see accelerated proliferation of e-commerce across the globe in tandem with increased bandwidth and higher Internet use.

APPENDIX 1: BUILDING THE BACKBONE

Backbones, it should be noted, are not all created equal – and many are labouring under the weight of traffic they never foresaw. A *Boardwatch Magazine* study (available on-line at URL: http://www.boardwatch.com/isp/) found, for example, that the best performing backbone in the US in 1998 was run by relatively small Savvis Communications, which had moved away from the overloaded public access lines (like MAE-West and MAE-East) to construct 'private peering' alliances with other small networks.

Increased demand on the Internet's backbone infrastructure can be expected to make the on-line experience feel as though it is getting worse before it gets better. But it *will* get better. Already, at the network level, current router technology from vendors such as Cisco Systems, Bay Networks and 3Com allow for the delivery of up to 500,000 packets per second. In design and development are the next generation of routers that will be able to deliver as much as 30 million packets per second – a 60-fold increase in throughput.

We are also seeing improvements at the server level. In the past, ISPs used T1 lines (1.5Mbps) to deliver an Internet connection into corporate networks, with T3 lines (45Mbps) serving as their national backbones. Today, technology is leapfrogging these older technologies, with many companies now using optical cables to transmit over OC-3 links (155Mbps). UUNET, for example, completed a major upgrade to its backbone connections in 1999 to OC-12 (622Mbps) capacity. Similarly, PSINet has negotiated for the rights to use a new backbone that uses OC-48 technology, operating at 2.4 billion bps – 50 times faster than a T3 line.

APPENDIX 2: HISTORY AND GROWTH OF THE INTERNET

1957
- ❐ The Union of Soviet Socialist Republics launched Sputnik, first artificial earth satellite. In the United States, the Department of Defense (DoD) formed the Advanced Research Projects Agency (ARPA) to establish US lead in science and technology applicable to the military.

1967
- ❐ First design paper on ARPANET (Advanced Research Projects Agency Network) was published.

1969
- ❐ First node connected to ARPANET at UCLA.

1973
- ❐ First international connections to the ARPANET were established at University College of London (England) and Royal Radar Establishment (Norway).
- ❐ Basic concepts for Ethernet, Internet and gateway architecture were developed.

1974

❏ Design of a Transmission Control Program (TCP) was published.

1982

❏ Number of Internet hosts surpassed 1,000. [See **Figure 6**.]

❏ Transmission Control Protocol (TCP) and Internet Protocol (IP), which form the protocol suite commonly known as TCP/IP, were adopted as standard for ARPANET. This led to one of the first definitions of an 'Internet' as a connected set of networks.

❏ Domain Name System (DNS) was introduced.

1988

❏ DoD saw TCP/IP as an interim protocol and chose to adopt Open Systems Interface (OSI).

1990

❏ ARPANET ceased to exist.

1991

❏ NSFNET backbone was upgraded to T3 (44.736 megabits per second). NSFNET traffic passed one trillion bytes per month and ten billion packets per month.

1992

❏ The Internet Society (ISOC) was chartered for promoting global information exchange through technology. ISOC members appointed a council that has responsibility for technical management and direction of the Internet.

❏ The World Wide Web (WWW) was developed by *Centre European de Recherches Nucleaires* (CERN), the European particle physics laboratory in Switzerland. WWW provides access to information files on the Internet through hypertext links and supports graphics, sound and video as well as text.

1994

❏ The Internet celebrated its 25th anniversary.

❏ Shopping malls arrived on the Internet; first cyberstation, RT-FM, broadcasted from Interop in Las Vegas; First Virtual, the first cyberbank, opened for business.

❏ NSFNET traffic exceeded ten trillion bytes per month.

1995

❏ Number of Internet hosts surpassed five million. [See Figure 6.]

❏ NSFNET backbone began to be replaced by a system of interconnected commercial network providers and US Net subsidies for research and education, funded by the National Science Foundation, were scheduled to end.

(Source: Adapted from Cronin, M.J. (ed.) (1996), *Internet Strategy Handbook: Lessons from the New Frontier of Business*, Boston, MA: Harvard Business School Press, pp. 249–255.)

Figure 6: **Growth in Internet host computers and major e-commerce developments**

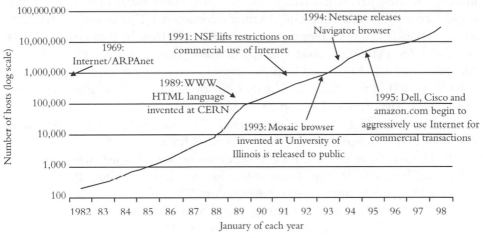

Source: OECD.

REFERENCES

Applegate, L.M., Holsapple, C.W., Kalakota, R., Radermacher, F.J., & Whinston, A.B. (1996), "Electronic Commerce: Building Blocks of New Business Opportunity", *Journal of Organizational Computing and Electronic Commerce*, Vol. 6, No. 1, pp. 1–10.

Armstrong, A. & Hagel, J., III (1996), "The Real Value of On-line Communities", *Harvard Business Review*, May–June, pp. 134–141.

Bar, F. & Murasse, E.M. (1999), "Charting Cyberspace: A US-European-Japanese Blueprint for Electronic Commerce", in Steinberg, R. & Stokes, B. (eds), *Transatlantic Trade Cooperation in Asia: Sectors, Issues and Modalities*, Totowa, NJ: Rowman & Littlefield Publishers.

Benjamin, R., DeLong, D., & Scott-Morton, M. (1990), "Electronic Data Interchange: How Much Competitive Advantage?" *Long Range Planning*, Vol. 23, No. 1, pp. 29–40.

Burns, S. (2000), "Out of the Hat", *Far Eastern Economic Review*, Vol. 163, Iss. 27, 6 July, pp. 36–37.

Campbell-Kelly, M. & Aspray, W. (1996), *Computer: A History of the Information Machine*, New York, NY: Basic Books.

Clark, T.H.K. & Westland, J.C. (1999), *Global Electronic Commerce: Theory and Case Studies*, Boston, MA: MIT Press.

Clarke, R. (1994), "Background Briefing on the Information Infrastructure", *Policy*, Vol. 10, No. 3, Spring.

Cohen, S., DeLong, J.B., & Zysman, J. (1999), "An E-conomy?" 13 December, URL: http://econ161.berkeley.edu/OpEd/virtual/technet/An_E-conomy, January 2000.

Cortese, A. (1999), "Here Comes the Intranet", *BusinessWeek*, 26 February, pp. 76–84.

Cronin, M.J. (ed.) (1996), *Internet Strategy Handbook: Lessons from the New Frontier of Business*, Boston, MA: Harvard Business School Press.

Devine, W. (1983), "From Shafts to Wires: Historical Perspectives on Electrification", *Journal of Economic History*, June, pp. 347–372.

Downes, L. & Mui, C. (1999), *Unleashing the Killer App: Digital Strategies for Market Dominance*, Boston, MA: Harvard Business School Press.

Evans, P., Thomas, S., & Wurster, T.S. (2000), *Blown to Bits: How the New Economics of Information Transforms Strategy*, Boston, MA: Harvard Business School Press.

Freeserve (2000), URL: http://www.freeserve.com, 22 August.

Get2Net (2000), URL: http://www.get2netcorp.com/, 22 August.

Gilder, G. (1997), "Fiber Keeps Its Promise", *Forbes ASAP*, February.

Hagel, J., III & Armstrong, A.G. (1997), *Net Gain – Expanding Markets Through Virtual Communities*, Boston, MA: Harvard Business School Press.

Harrington, L. & Reed, G. (1996), "Electronic Commerce (Finally) Comes of Age", *The McKinsey Quarterly*, No. 2, pp. 68–77.

Kalakota, R. & Whinston, A.B. (1996), *Frontiers of Electronic Commerce*, Reading, MA: Addison-Wesley.

Kalakota, R. & Whinston, A.B. (1997), *Electronic Commerce: A Manager's Guide*, Reading, MA: Addison-Wesley.

Kosiur, D. (1997), *Understanding Electronic Commerce: How Online Transactions Can Grow Your Business*, Redmond, WA: Microsoft Press.

M2 Presswire (2000), "Red Hat to Acquire Embedded Linux Developer WireSpeed", Coventry, 15 June, p. 1.

Malone, T.W., Yates, J., & Benjamin, I. (1987), "Electronic Markets and Electronic Hierarchies", *Communications of the ACM*, Vol. 30, No. 6, pp. 484–497.

Maxwell, K. (1999), *Residential Broadband*, New York, NY: Wiley.

Moore, J.F. (1996), *The Death of Competition: Leadership & Strategy in the Age of Business Ecosystems*, New York, NY: Harper–Collins.

Nash, K. (1996), "Extranet: Best of Both 'Nets'", *Computerworld*, Vol. 30, No. 33, 12 August, p. 1.

OECD (1999), *The Economic and Social Impacts of Electronic Commerce: Preliminary Findings and Research Agenda*, URL: http://www.oecd.org/subject/e_commerce/ebooks/009-026.pdf, September.

Picot, A. *et al.* (1999), "Organization of Electronic Markets: Contributions from the New Institutional Economics", *The Information Society*, Vol. 13, pp. 107–123.

Planet IT (1999), "Intel Architecture at Get2Net Corp", 8 July, URL: http://www.PlanetIT.com/docs/PIT19990625S0018, 22 August 2000.

Poptronics (2000), "Free Internet Access on the Go", April, p. 8.

Rebello, K. (1996), "Making Money on the Net", *BusinessWeek*, 23 September, pp. 104–118.

Red Hat (2000), URL: http://www.redhat.com, 18 August.

Sandholtz, W. (1993), "Institutions and Collective Action: The New Telecommunications in Western Europe", *World Politics*, pp. 242–270.

Siebel, T.M. & House, P. (1999), *Cyber Rules: Strategies for Excelling at e-Business*, New York, NY: Currency/Doubleday.

US Department of Commerce (1998), "The Emerging Digital Economy", 15 April, Washington, DC, URL: http://www.ecommerce.gov/emerging.htm, June 2000.

Wigand, R. (1997), "Electronic Commerce: Definition, Theory, and Context", *The Information Society*, Vol. 13, No. 1, January–March, pp. 1–16.

Zwass, V. (1996), "Electronic Commerce: Structures and Issues", *International Journal of Electronic Commerce*, Vol. 1, No. 1, pp. 3–23.

CASE

■ ■ ■

2.1

adM@rt: 'If You Build It, Will They Come?'*

At 5:00 in the morning he is already awake. He reads for about an hour, then goes across the street to do his daily exercise. At 8:00 am, he is at his office in an industrial district in Kowloon, far from the flash and modern offices in Central, Hong Kong. He spends most of the day in his office until 6:00 pm, after which he heads home to his family. By 9:30 or 10:00 in the evening, he is already in bed.

He is the founder and owner of a chain of clothing retail stores, two major publications and the first on-line shopping market in Hong Kong, yet he rarely attends social functions and charity gatherings in town with the city's *glitterati*. His picture hardly ever appears in the lifestyle or glamour pages, but his business ventures are often discussed and talked about in daily, national and even regional newspapers and magazines. He is Hong Kong's most flamboyant, outspoken, irreverent and radical businessman. He is Jimmy Lai.

Lai began a clothes-retailing revolution with Giordano stores. The Giordano chain of stores was a hit; a textbook example of how to build a successful retailing operation

---

* Marissa McCauley prepared this case in conjunction with Shamza Khan under the supervision of Dr. Ali Farhoomand. *Copyright © 2000 The University of Hong Kong. Ref. 99/62C*

in Asia. Although Lai never completed his MBA, he made a fortune out of challenging Hong Kong's establishment and embarrassing everyone from business tycoons to movie stars to nobodies. He started another revolution in Chinese-language newspapers with his *Next Magazine* and *Apple Daily* publications. He changed the 'face' of the dailies.

In 1999, Lai launched adM@rt, a HK$300[1] million home-delivery shopping service, among other things, to compete head-on with Hong Kong's oligopolistic grocery-store market.[2] His vision was to build a virtual shopping mall, rent out virtual store space to niche marketers, and deliver their goods as well as its own line of products to every household and office in Hong Kong within a few hours of receiving an order. This was an entirely new business idea, so Lai was not sure how best to go about implementing his vision. He knew that the start-up glitches would eventually be fixed. The trickier part was to map out his e-business plan so that the processes involved in adM@rt's business transaction cycle could be seamlessly integrated with the technological infrastructure he was building. It was more difficult to decide how to attract suitable tenants and prospective customers to his newly built marketspace. If he built it, would they come?

JIMMY LAI CHEE-YING

As a young and barely literate boy of 12, Lai escaped solo by boat from Guangzhou in China to Hong Kong during the Cultural Revolution. A stowaway, he worked his way from a labourer in a zipper factory to become one of Asia's leading clothing retailers with his chain of Giordano stores. He made his first fortune in clothing.

'Intelligent, hard-working and down-to-earth'. This was how people who worked for Lai described him. He goes to work in jeans and drives a basic Honda. He often invites staff home for an abalone or shark's fin meal. "He may be generous, but he dislikes extravagant people," one of his employees said.[3]

In a story run by *Asiaweek* in December 1999, Lai was described as "mellower and wiser Jimmy".[4] A veteran colleague, *Next* publisher Yeung Wai-hong, said that "the

---

[1] US$1 = HK$8

[2] adM@rt, URL: http://www.admart.com.hk, February 2000.

[3] Wan, M. (1995), "An 'Apple' a Day Keeps Communists Away", *South China Morning Post*, 25 November.

[4] Wai, Y. (1999), "A Mellower and Wiser Jimmy", *Asiaweek*, 3 December.

most obvious example of a softer Lai is in corporate meetings – the amount of profanity used to be overpowering. Now, he hardly ever swears."

Like many Hong Kong tycoons, his is a classic rags-to-riches tale. He worked in factories, as did many of his contemporaries. However, he made money in Asia by satisfying people's demands, not through mere connections or *guanxi*. His Giordano clothing company was the first Asian retailing chain where staff deliberately greeted customers with 'good morning'.

JIMMY LAI'S BUSINESS EMPIRE

Lai set up a garment factory in 1975 that would eventually become Giordano.[5] After a brief, unsuccessful attempt to market expensive apparel, he turned to casual wear in the mid-1980s. Giordano Limited was incorporated in 1980 and was made public on the Hong Kong Stock Exchange in May 1991.

Giordano was a casual clothing retailer, offering a combination of low prices, high quality and two Asian rarities – a no-nonsense exchange policy and friendly staff – Giordano took Asia's retail clothing scene by storm. The brand sold clothing that catered to everybody, with a wholesome, friendly, down-to-earth and universal brand-image. The firm achieved some of the highest sales-per-square-foot in Asia and had opened shops in ten countries in the Pacific region, including China. Giordano operated or franchised more than 670 stores in Asia, New Zealand and the Middle East.

In 1996, Lai gave up managing Giordano and sold his 27.05 percent stake to institutional investors; he made HK$1.45 billion on the deal.[6] It was believed to be due to pressure from China that Lai gave up this position.

Lai became a major supporter of pro-democracy causes in Hong Kong and China in 1989, after Chinese troops stormed Tiananmen Square and killed hundreds of pro-democracy demonstrators. Frustrated by what he read about the incident, he started *Next Magazine* as a sideline business in 1990. From then on he was highly critical of the Chinese Administration in his magazine. In a short period of time, *Next Magazine* became Hong Kong's most popular weekly, known for its racy stories and controversial commentary.

---

[5] The Italian name 'Giordano' was picked because Giordano was originally positioned as an Italian-style apparel retailer targeted at middle-class men between the ages of 30 to 50.

[6] Munish, M. (1999), "'Apple Man' Happy to Be Blunt-speaking Maverick", *South China Morning Post*, 7 November.

In one of *Next*'s weekly publications in 1994, Lai ridiculed the Chinese premier, Li Peng. In print, he called Li Peng 'son of a turtle's egg with a zero IQ'. Soon after, the Chinese authorities raided and closed the main Giordano store in Beijing for 'licensing' reasons. It was never to reopen. His reporters were banned from reporting on sessions of the Preliminary Working Committee in Beijing. He was later banned from entering China.

Relishing being a publisher, Lai launched a daily newspaper, *Apple Daily*. Since hitting the newsstands in June 1995, the daily was selling 230,000 copies. In 1996, sales topped 300,000 and industry observers agreed it was a viable business venture, even though it cost Lai HK$500,000 to publish *Apple Daily* every day despite advertising revenue. But, he shrugged off the losses, saying, "If I wanted to make money, why not play the stock market?"[7]

Apple Daily was well received and became Hong Kong's No. 2 newspaper among a dozen local Chinese publications and was called 'the last best hope for press freedom'.[8] It adopted a *USA Today* layout with sensationalist coverage of crime and celebrities. Lai attributed the paper's success to its emphasis on magazine-style consumer news, its colourful design, and its readiness to accept constructive criticism and make changes accordingly.

Setting up the paper already had its setbacks. First, Lai faced the formidable opposition of the market-leading *Oriental Daily News*, and second, Lai was an ardent anti-communist and found that *Apple Daily* was not in favour with the Chinese authorities. But unlike many of Hong Kong's publishers, Lai was not prepared to bend to government bureaucracies in order to further his business interests.

In November 1999, the daily was attacked for apparently reporting scandalous stories and publishing sensational pictures. Hong Kong's anti-corruption agency, the Independent Commission Against Corruption, took the *Apple Daily* to court, alleging that its reporters had bribed as many as 20 policemen to alert them to possible stories. They swept through Apple's offices, seizing documents and arresting eight people. No charges were laid. It was the first time that Hong Kong's authorities had demanded to search a newspaper's editorial offices.

Lai's plan to float his flagship company on the Hong Kong Stock Exchange was two years in the making. His earlier attempts in 1997 were delayed after a number of

---

[7] Wan, M. (1995), "An 'Apple' a Day Keeps Communists Away", *South China Morning Post*, 25 November.

[8] Dowling, C.G. (1997), "Red Flag Over Hong Kong", *Life*, June.

merchant banks reneged on their promise of support. Sun Hung Kai Investment Bank, the group's primary sponsor, refused to handle a public share-offering and backed out of the relationship at the last minute. Finally, he was given the go-ahead in October 1999 through a backdoor listing.

THE BIRTH OF A NEW COMPANY: ADM@RT

Lai visualised that soon the computer would be ubiquitous and that people would be more adept at using it to review and order merchandise. He conceived adM@rt as an on-line shopping service with a fleet of trucks making door-to-door deliveries. Lai wanted to transform everyday shopping in Hong Kong and change the way people buy. In late June 1999, Lai directly attacked the supermarket business giants when he launched adM@rt; the move was considered Hong Kong's most ambitious electronic commerce (e-commerce) effort to date.

Lai foresaw that the business would be a good one:

If we build a backbone for the e-commerce which is to cater to people's convenience, it would be a good business in the long term.

adM@rt's vision was to build a virtual shopping mall, rent out virtual store space to niche marketers, and deliver their goods as well as its own line of products to every household and office in Hong Kong within a few hours of receiving an order. The company was determined to meet and fulfil every need of their Website 'tenants' – design their Website, house their physical shopfront, store their merchandise, process their orders, deliver their goods and collect their cash.

To realise this vision, adM@rt had to build a superstore in a limited space, considering the number of stores and selected retailers within the shopping centre. It had to convince retailers about the concept of having a superstore, creating a critical mass of customers; everyone would benefit from the increased traffic.

The main threat was to two huge chains that dominated Hong Kong's supermarket business, Park'n Shop and Wellcome:

❑ Park'n Shop stores were owned by Li Ka-shing's Hutchison Whampoa Group, and controlled roughly 35 percent of the HK$1.4 billion market. Li was Hong Kong's richest man.
❑ Wellcome belonged to Asia's biggest grocer, Jardine Matheson-controlled Dairy

Farm, and had about 30 percent of the market. Together they controlled more than 65 percent of the city's modern food retail market.[9]

adM@rt's policies on pricing and home delivery hit all areas of retailing: Jusco stores (HK), a general merchandise store operator, Wellcome, Park'n Shop, CRC Shop, healthcare retailers Watson's and Mannings, appliance distributors Fortress and Broadway. There were concerns expressed that smaller, one-shop players could be forced out of business.

A limited price war developed and grocery prices fell 20 percent in the established stores for items that adM@rt carried. Park'n Shop and Wellcome refurbished their home-delivery service and offered goods at discount prices. Park'n Shop offered 1,500 items daily at 'the steepest discount in town'.

adM@rt's Business Model

adM@rt's business model focused on leveraging the Internet and combining it with an order fulfilment and logistics infrastructure as the backbone to its marketspace, with a view to eventually become a major regional e-commerce player.

Lai was convinced that the customers still needed to see, touch and feel the merchandise in a transaction. He believed retailers should offer a mix of e-tailing and a brick-and-mortar shopfront. The concept was to sell products, but there should also be a shop or a window to generate customer focus. Goods offered included groceries, textiles, computers, home and office furniture and mobile telephones as well as discount airline tickets and travel packages. All the items were fast-moving consumer goods (FMCG). The strategy was to limit the variety of goods available, but to sell in bulk at substantially discounted prices; delivery was free on orders over HK$300.

Critics dubbed the odd collection of goods 'Pricemart-pizza'.[10] Lai said he would continue experimenting until he could establish the right mix of on-line services.

Start-up Problems

The company's goal was to make 30,000 deliveries a day from a customer base of up to a half-million people – about 7.4 percent of Hong Kong's population. One of adM@rt's competitors discerned a problem for adM@rt: Hong Kong's size – "Any on-line EC

---

[9] "Groceries to Go", *Asiaweek*, 6 August 1999.

[10] "Nothing Risked, Nothing Gained", *Asiaweek*, 3 December 1999.

focusing only on a population such as Hong Kong is going to be in for a real disappointment."[11] Lai admitted that adM@rt's start-up was not easy.

The first few weeks of operations were marred by technical systems breakdowns, complaints about late delivery, poor quality products and repeatedly running out of stock. The company acknowledged teething problems. Wilson Chu Bun, adM@rt president and Lai's right-hand man at Giordano said:

We are learning every day how to run this business. We have made many mistakes in the last six months, but we are doing the best we can. It may take time.[12]

The major problem was that adM@rt's call centre received three times as many calls daily as it could handle, which caused the switchboards to be constantly jammed. The call centre received 45,000 to 50,000 calls a day; it had the capacity to handle only 18,000 calls. New lines and new operators were added to process the overflow.[13]

The Website broke down within days of the launch. The computer system originally designed to coordinate distribution was also used to take orders via the Internet. However, it was unable to adequately process orders, and for some time, adM@rt had to close every Tuesday to repair the chaos of the previous week.

In October 1999, Customs officials raided eight warehouses and arrested ten men for having sold fake liquor, including Bordeaux wine and Hennessy XO Cognac. Some 12,000 bottles of Bordeaux wine with fake labels were confiscated. This caused a great deal of embarrassment. adM@rt offered refunds after it had sold counterfeit wines, and Cognac said it had been duped by unscrupulous middlemen, as Hutchison Whampoa and Jardine Matheson held exclusive rights to distribute many name-brand products in the territory. Rival grocers posted gloating ads offering to sell the real thing at cut-rate prices. Park'n Shop offered to replace for free any Mouton Cadet wine bought from adM@rt.

Park'n Shop and Wellcome ran daily ads in *Apple Daily* before adM@rt opened its doors. Both supermarkets pulled all their ads and said they would not be advertising in the foreseeable future. *Apple Daily* reportedly lost about 30 percent of its ad revenue.

The company apologised to its customers through full-page advertisements fol-

---

[11] "Groceries to Go", *Asiaweek*, 6 August 1999.

[12] *Asiaweek*, 6 August 1999.

[13] Johnstone, H. (1999), "Lai Bides Time on adM@rt", *South China Morning Post*, 18 July.

lowing the setbacks of its start-up. Afterwards, orders came in by phone or fax. This created the need for more operators.

The company lost an estimated HK$130,000 a day.[14] Needing 30,000 orders a day to break even, it was reportedly achieving just 3,000 to 4,000. It also had 1,500 employees and the monthly payroll was nearly HK$6.5 million.[15] The expenses so far included 220 delivery vehicles, eight warehouses and 40 shops that were opened in off-the-beaten-track spaces that gave a retail face to the company. Six months after it was launched, the firm planned to have 120 shops, 25 warehouses, 448 vehicles and more than 3,000 employees.

With all these start-up problems, Lai lost millions in getting the business going and he forced the competition to spend a great deal in their attempts to retain market share. Lai was prepared to spend HK$40 million before it turned a profit. His goal was to reach 500,000 customers and 30,000 daily deliveries. Somehow, Hong Kong finally had competition in its supermarkets. "Our intention is to take services into people's homes so they can taste the convenience. Later, we'll sell other things," he said.[16]

ADM@RT'S STRUCTURE

Jimmy Lai was the main leader in adM@rt's organisational structure. Directly reporting to him were the officers of the three main divisions: Human Resources, Information Technology and Logistics [see **Figure 1**]. These three leading officers were instrumental in turning Lai's vision into reality.

Figure 1: adM@rt's organisational structure

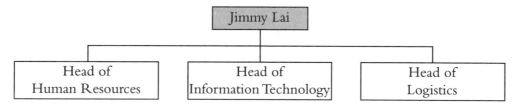

[14] "Van @ttack", *The Economist*, London, 18 September 1999.

[15] "Groceries to Go", *Asiaweek*, 6 August 1999.

[16] "Nothing Risked, Nothing Gained", *Asiaweek*, 3 December 1999.

Human Resources

The HR structure at adM@rt was different from typical Hong Kong companies in terms of dealing with employees. It was less formal, employees could openly express their opinions and there was upward mobility. The head of Human Resources, Wisteria Chung, a former Giordano employee, talked about her current job at adM@rt:

> *The big difference is that adM@rt is very new, whereas Giordano is more established. Giordano has the service culture already established and they know what they're expected to do. With adM@rt, we're still developing ways to build up the service. Our service and retail centres don't meet our own expectations and thus still need a lot of improvement. Our major role at adM@rt is to support the frontline team to provide the best service for our customers.*

Supervisors were recruited and trained in basic service, technical skills and leadership skills before adM@rt started. This first batch eventually became the core group and built up the corporate culture. Top management people such as Lai and Philippe Ravelli (CEO) met the core group and talked about different business concepts. In turn, this group led, trained and coached other groups:

- ❑ Customer service staff and delivery personnel were provided with technical skills.
- ❑ Sales staff of computer products and mobile phones were trained on basic computer skills.
- ❑ Delivery people received training on using a Palm Pilot.

Remuneration was made up of guaranteed pay and incentive options. Incentives in the form of stock options were not initially provided at adM@rt, but the company had considered using them in the future as recruitment incentives to attract senior management expertise. The turnover was said to be four percent.

To monitor the service at adM@rt, HR launched a service auditor project that involved HR team members and outsiders conducting a site visit or telephone check in any of the shops. A checklist was provided and feedback was reported back to HR. Normally the audit was based on performance concerning greetings, delivery of the service or product knowledge. The sales centres conducted surveys that provided most of the customer feedback.

However, a few months after the company was launched, HR had to downsize its workforce. They implemented a number of restructuring plans, which created uncertainty among the personnel.

Information Technology

adM@rt's order fulfilment process was based on a three-tier model as shown in **Figure 2**:

- ❑ *Channels to order.* Orders could be conducted through different means, and they could be tracked regardless of the channel because the same interface and system were used. When an order was placed on the Internet, the order time and time of expected delivery could be checked with the call centre. The logistics system coordinated delivery. Order information was downloaded to the Palm Pilot held by the delivery staff. The delivery staff could use the Palm Pilot to check details such as the merchandise to deliver, quantity, to whom, where, at what time, etc. Once the goods were delivered, they would mark it in the Palm Pilot and send the delivery status to the host centre. Customers could cancel orders, but not add to the order.
- ❑ *Processing orders.* When adM@rt launched its Website, the systems were already integrated and they were unmatched in the industry. Many other companies' systems were not integrated – there was still human intervention in the process. adM@rt's Website was relaunched, still fully integrated, after it crashed during the initial stage. The configuration was capable of 1,000 saved orders at the same time and was scalable. Actual orders made on the Web were around 200 a day. The call centre, however, received about 4,000 to 5,000 orders a day.
- ❑ *Logistics.* Palm Pilots were used as point-of-sales (POS) tools. All information from computers was downloaded to Palm Pilots and the mobile phone network was used to transmit all the data from the field back to the central data-

Figure 2:   adM@rt's order fulfilment process

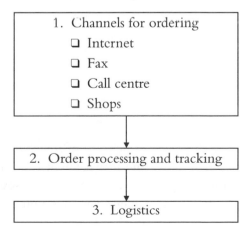

processing systems. This provided customer order status. From the warehouse, delivery staff scan the barcode to check which order belongs to whom, and when the customer receives or rejects an item, they can use the Palm Pilot as the POS and subsequently process the item. If required, this facility also enables the customer refund to be calculated.

Any plan to spin off the business' retail side would involve the integration of the ordering system using a basic structure for the integration and the design of their own data exchange model. The department built an intranet that became the main means of communication between employees. All the company information was stored in the intranet Knowledge Centre and was made available for everyone to read.

The company experienced integration problems in the start-up, thus the need to change the current system. The IT head, Terence Lee, said he would select a new system according to the following procedures:

1. Research ten or 20 vendors individually and gather information on basic system functions and features.
2. Find a system integrator or consultant to suggest industrial standards and propose a solution based on adM@rt's requirements.
3. Let users evaluate the proposed solution and come up with their own evaluation list.
4. Perform the overall construction and migration process based on the users' evaluation list.

For a department that required a structured and logical procedure to build up a system, adM@rt's IT had no set long-term plan. Terence said,

Basically we change with Jimmy's directions. And he changes every day.

Logistics

Head of logistics, Michael Chan, was responsible for building delivery. He said:

I turned Jimmy's idea into reality.

His main concern was the speed of delivery of merchandise to customers after they receive the orders. Chan joined the management team and coordinated with software providers. They met with numerous vendors and narrowed down their search to two major service providers: Alpha Anderson and Compuserve [see **Table 1**]. After lengthy evaluation, and on the advice of PriceWaterhouseCoopers, adM@rt eventually selected Alpha Anderson.

Table 1: adM@rt's comparison of the two service providers

Service provider	Software	Hardware
Alpha Anderson	Baan	IBM
Compuserve	Oracle	Compaq

Chan located and built eight warehouses based on the city's population, and based on the estimate of a few thousand orders a day with a next-day delivery time:

❑ Hong Kong: Aberdeen and Chai Wan
❑ Kowloon: Yau Tong and Hung Hom
❑ Tsuen Wan
❑ Tuen Mun
❑ Fanling
❑ Shatin

[See **Exhibit 1** showing the map of Hong Kong and the location of the adM@rt warehouses.]

A workforce of 1,200 was recruited within two months of the infrastructure being built. They were trained in using Palm Pilots with software developed by Techron for adM@rt's use.

After we spent a few months' time setting up the infrastructure, we immediately changed our ideas – we targeted to deliver on the same day. When we received the order in the morning, we delivered the merchandise in the afternoon. And when we received the order in the afternoon, we delivered it the following morning. We delivered from 15,000 up to 30,000 orders a day, selling a wide range of merchandise including grocery items, PCs, etc.

The number of warehouses doubled to 16. The size of the warehouses ranged from 10,000 to 20,000 square feet. These changes were implemented immediately to provide more loading bay facilities for vans and to shorten travel time from the warehouse to the customer location. The goal was to cut off every hour.

The inter-warehouse transfers created a lot of problems. For the third time, logistics reduced the number of warehouses to five and a number of the distribution centres were dismantled to reduce the rental charges. However, adM@rt built a big hub that was around 220,000 square feet at Asian Terminal Limited. This hub serviced everything. The whole operation mode was different: inventory was placed in the hub, and delivery was done the next day instead of the same day. All the merchandise was delivered overnight from the hub to the distribution centres. The staff of 1,200 was also downsized to about 1,000. They had 200 vans and 50 5.5-ton trucks.

Attention refocused on systems management. Since the Baan software seemed more focused on manufacturing, adM@rt considered changing the system to one that was more suitable for them.

> *We are in retail business and we get a lot of orders. We face a lot of problems. Even when the number goes up to 10,000 orders a day I feel we will still have a problem. And now we focus on e-commerce. At the moment Baan cannot interface with the Internet real time for placing an order on the Internet. So every 15 minutes we have to update the inventory again. This is the drawback.*

Merchandise goods were picked at random. There was no formula. Most of the items came from parallel importers. At most times they had to wait for the next batch. Very often they ran out of stock, and at other times they had too much stock in the warehouse. Due to the lack of support from supply agents, adM@rt did not have continuous supply. "We experienced a lot of problems because this kind of business was new in Hong Kong," Chan added.

ADM@RT: LOOKING INTO THE FUTURE

Since adM@rt launched in late June 1999, its grey and yellow delivery vans covered the city and set off a supermarket price war. Its fleet of vans operated from warehouse hubs in cheap industrial space. It exploited the parallel import market by bringing in cut-price Coca-Cola and beer, to the fury of Hong Kong's distributors. adM@rt secured 450,000 customers with average sales per order of HK$350. According to chief executive Philippe Ravelli, adM@rt handled 150,000 orders every month, but still suffered losses. "The company looks at business concepts, not numbers-based business or a revenue model."[17]

Following the takeover of the registered travel agency Citilink International Travel, adM@rt Travel was launched in December 1999. Its goal was to provide value and convenience to its customers by offering air tickets, tours and hotel bookings through adM@rt's on-line service, call centre or outlets.

Lai admitted that the company had significant troubles in the start-up period. The computer systems did not work effectively because there was no existing experience in this field. The technical department had to interface many programs and systems, causing continuous technical glitches. In addition, the eventual counter-attack by its competitors hit adM@rt hard.

After early setbacks in technology, product supply and delivery, adM@rt re-launched its Website in November 1999, in Chinese and English, with a systems configuration capable of processing 1,000 orders at one time. The possibility of introducing a new system capable of better systems integration was also being evaluated. So was the possibility of businesses being separated or spun off.

In the meantime, relationships seemed to improve slightly between China and Lai. adM@rt welcomed China's biggest H-share-listed company, Legend, to stock computers at adM@rt. Since Legend opened in 1997 in Hong Kong, it wanted to establish a strong image in the SAR before expanding across Southeast Asia. It saw adM@rt as a possible saviour.

By March 2000, Lai had invested close to HK$1 billion in setting up the Internet-based home-delivery service.[18] He was losing HK$77 million a month.[19] Lai, however, was confident:

> *We still believe e-commerce is going to be a very important business for the future, although we don't think that e-commerce will replace the traditional business, it is going to change the way we do business.*

---

[17] Tsang, D. (2000), "Focus on Concept Despite Losses, adM@rt Chief Says", *South China Morning Post*, 20 January.

[18] Lin, H.S. (1999), "adM@rt Plans Expansion of e-Commerce", *The Financial Times*, London, 16 December.

[19] Bowman, J. (1999), "Setbacks Cost Tycoon HK$77 Million Every Month", *South China Morning Post*, 1 December.

To reduce losses, adM@rt decided to break down the business by creating a separate company for the cash-intensive logistics and the door-to-door delivery business – which would essentially take on a distribution role for other businesses as well as adM@rt. The distribution company, EasyVan, would charge adM@rt and other partner companies fees for delivering their products. adM@rt would also spin off the IT system, and was having talks with a multinational company to take over the grocery supply and ordering part of the business, leaving adM@rt to focus on logistics and servicing. Travel and some B2B businesses would still be adM@rt's responsibility.

Lai's bigger plan was to build an e-Chinatown using the adM@rt and *Next Magazine* Websites as a launching pad. The sites were reported to be receiving seven million 'hits' a day; nearly three-quarters were from the overseas Chinese community.[20] Lai said site popularity would provide critical mass to start an e-commerce business selling products such as traditional Chinese medicines and Chinese tea to the large overseas Chinese community in places such as North America and Europe.

In early 2000, Lai held talks with ATV, Hong Kong's second-largest television station, seeking on-line rights to Chinese-language news and entertainment programmes. He wanted to create an Internet empire that would provide news, entertainment, shopping and other services to Chinese people around the world. His vision was to draw consumers to the already up-and-running www.nextmedia.com, which he said would eventually become a group of linked Websites providing entertainment, news and services.

Lai expressed his perception of himself and of doing business in virtual space:

I think the way I am being very unconventional in business – actually is an advantage because e-commerce is a very unconventional business. It's a business wherein you can be very daring, which has great potential yet at the same time is a great risk. e-Commerce is a kind of business that needs somebody who is as daring, open-minded and unconventional as I am.

Jimmy Lai stated his major challenge:

The challenge for us is, do we have the right model? If we have the right model, we have the right course. If we have the right course, is there enough volume for us to create critical mass for us to have economic scale. That is all unknown.

---

[20] Bowman, J. (1999).

Exhibit 1: **Location of adM@rt warehouses in Hong Kong when launched in June 1999**

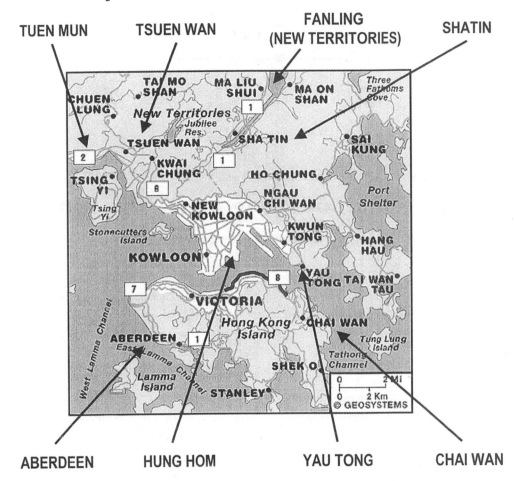

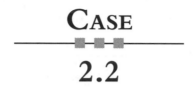

CASE

2.2

New Technologies, New Markets:
The Launch of Hong Kong Telecom's
Video-on-demand*

VOD is not a market led proposition ... An education process, therefore, has to be undergone in order to convince viewers that on-demand services are not only desirable but also indispensable.
– Luisa Riddiford, New Media Development Manager, BBC Worldwide TV

In February 1998, well over a year later than scheduled, Hong Kong Telecom's Interactive Multimedia Services (IMS) unit launched the world's first commercial video-on-demand (VOD) system. This came after years of high-profile trials and failures all around the world, costing billions of dollars and involving telecommunications carriers, cable television companies, media conglomerates, information providers, computer hardware and software vendors, consultants and systems integrators.

As a result, both Hong Kong and the Hong Kong Telecom IMS venture were thrust into the spotlight. Worldwide interest resulted not only from implementing the

---

* P. Lovelock prepared this case. *Copyright © 1998 The University of Hong Kong. Ref. 98/08C*

world's first commercial VOD system – an expensive high-technology service for which consumer demand had yet to be proven – but also for launching the first of the next generation of full-service interactive television (iTV) systems. It was widely suggested that the success or failure of the IMS venture would say a lot about the technology application's prospects elsewhere around the world. For, as was often argued by the former head of IMS, Dr. William Lo,[1] Hong Kong's environment appeared particularly suitable for the adoption of VOD. If VOD were to be unsuccessful in Hong Kong, it would not bode well for its application elsewhere – at least not without a suite of accompanying interactive services.

IMS's development, it was suggested, would tell the market much about: (i) the VOD's ability to generate consumer demand and to work as a 'market leader' for further interactive television services; (ii) the relation between customer demand and the new interactive technologies; and (iii) whether telecommunications carriers (as opposed to cable TV networks or computer companies such as Microsoft) could employ a 'first mover' strategy to dominate the future provision of broadband services. For these reasons, irrespective of whether or not VOD worked or failed in Hong Kong, the IMS venture itself could potentially have a profound influence on the development of future industry offerings – what is offered, who offers it and how.

However, as IMS took its new technology to market, none of this *post-hoc* rationalisation was of much value. In marketing the new service, the company was faced with determining whether market demand existed or whether it needed to be created. Or whether, in fact, market demand should be a secondary concern to developing the infrastructure.

INTERACTIVE TELEVISION AND VOD

> *A killer application … is a use of technology so attractive to consumers that it fuels market forces and makes an invention all but indispensable, even if it wasn't anticipated by the inventor.*
>
> – Bill Gates, 1995

Interactive television is TV that is controlled by the viewer, implying decision-

---

[1] Lo left HKT IMS in September 1998.

making capacity.[2] The core of iTV is to allow the interactivity between a service provider and a user, and it is this two-way communication with the subscriber that fundamentally changed the role of TV from a passive medium to an active one. The new services enabled by the interactivity provided for a profound change in our ability to proactively choose what we want to see and to personalise the information that we want to receive. The degree of interactivity and the quality of presentation in turn defined the technology required and the timeframe in which a full-scale commercial launch would be financially attractive. The dilemma for the service provider was to maximise the technologically provided choice (issues of bandwidth, storage capacity, etc.) so as to maximise consumer demand. (In other words, the basket of services and the degree of interactivity defined the system's requirements and determined the choice of technical components.) But consumer patterns take time to change and this change from the present broadcast mode to a future interactive mode would not be an overnight transition. As demonstrated by the launch of the IMS VOD service, the technology now existed for the rollout of iTV – albeit expensively – but the business model for services demand and revenue streams did not. Among the many eventual iTV services to be provided, VOD had been widely touted[3] and pushed as the first 'killer application' for the success of the iTV business.[4]

VOD allowed a subscriber to select a programme (such as a movie or documentary) using a remote control by browsing through a menu of titles. Once chosen, the programme would be played after a short elapsed time (typically from a few seconds to half a minute depending on the network configuration and system load). A typical VOD system allowed a subscriber to exercise VCR-like functions such as fast forward, backward, pause, stop and rewind [see **Exhibit 1**]. It was this similarity to a VCR that had driven planning assumptions on the future acceptance of VOD. In other words, if the price was right, people would prefer to watch a programme (any time) using VOD instead of waiting for broadcast at a specific time or renting a movie. It was this similarity with the VCR that had also suggested: (i) intense competition with video

---

[2] Hodge, W.W. (1995), *Interactive Television: A Comprehensive Guide for Multimedia Technologists*, McGraw-Hill: New York, p. 3.

[3] See, for example, Schwartz, E., I (1995), "People Are Supposed to Pay for This Stuff?" in *Wired*, Vol. 3, No. 7.

[4] A more recent potential 'killer app' in the iTV suite of services has been identified as home banking.

rental stores and cable television networks; and (ii) strategic relationships between large telephone companies and owners of film libraries.

Two developments, however, clouded the prospects for employing VOD as the 'killer app' business strategy in interactive television services. The first was the alarming lack of success of VOD trials all over the world through the mid-1990s. Results from the various trials – all remarkably similar [see **Exhibit 2**] – demonstrated that viewers did not appear to want what VOD developers were offering them. At least not at the sort of premium prices that would be required to sustain a viable business model. The second development to confuse VOD launch plans was the explosive, unforeseen growth of the World Wide Web.

MULTIMEDIA

> *The Internet remains the great unknown. The one factor holding back the delivery of video via the Internet is bandwidth. If this problem can be overcome … VOD could arrive immediately. If it were to arrive in such a form, then a lot of the money spent on trying to develop dedicated VOD services would appear to have been wasted … it would also suggest that telephone companies should stick to their role of developing broader bandwidth delivery mechanisms, network companies should stick to their role of working on how to send stuff along this bandwidth, and content companies should work out what consumers want delivered to their homes.*
> – Simon Cartledge, Telecom Info Technology Forum,[5] 1997

A simple value-chain for interactive television would include the content provider, service provider, network provider and subscriber [see **Exhibit 3**]. The convergence of computers, telecommunications and electronic media ('multimedia'), and the concomitant deregulation of markets had, however, blurred industrial boundaries, confusing the concepts of who sits where within this iTV value-chain.[6] Thus, while the

---

[5] The Telecommunications Information Technology Forum is part of the University of Hong Kong's Telecommunications Research Project (http://www.trp.hku.hk), September 1998.

[6] "The net effect of all the alliances that have been written up in *The Wall Street Journal* for the past three years is this: everyone is in cahoots with everyone else. Bell Atlantic is collaborating with Microsoft. Microsoft is in bed with TCI. TCI works with US West. US West has an investment in Time Warner. Time Warner is aligned with AT&T. AT&T has done deals with GTE. And so on. They visit each other's trial zones, attend the same conferences, buy the same market research." Schwartz, E., I (1995), 'People Are Supposed to Pay for This Stuff?' *Wired*, Vol. 3, No. 7, p. 191.

technical issues of iTV have largely been solved – the trials around the world have demonstrated technical feasibility – the real problem came from the high initial investment required to construct a workable network infrastructure and service platform [see **Exhibit 4**]. Indeed, the major barrier holding back the development of VOD had been the cost of rolling out the infrastructure – in particular, the 'last mile' to the subscriber – and the cost of the set-top box. By 1997, it was estimated that the equipment needed for a VOD system was still somewhere in the US$1,000–2,000 per subscriber range – significantly more than the US$200–300 required for a video cassette recorder (used on average to play two or three videos per week).

The situation was further complicated by a lack of standards in the emerging multimedia markets. Put in another way, without an agreed-upon set of standards, there would be a range of competing standards each seeking market dominance. This resulted in a lack of interoperability between networks and components (remember the problems with VHS and Beta video standards?) and high component prices, as manufacturers were unable to benefit from the economies of scale required to engage in mass production, thereby reducing costs.[7] There were a number of strategies that could be employed to minimise these problems. The service provider could create an alliance, or a consortium of vendors, so as to share the risks and returns with technology suppliers and at the same time influence the design of technical components to allow greater standardisation. Or, the service provider could pursue a non-proprietary ('open') platform, thus minimising the potential problems of early component 'lock-in' by suppliers.

However, the main issue remained on the demand side, with the unknown market response. Studies and experience both showed that subscribers were willing to pay for services or products that they valued. The questions were: at what price were they willing to buy, and could this price generate sufficient revenues to justify investment?

Admittedly, VOD was promoted as merely the first application of iTV, eventually to be only one of many such services provided via the iTV infrastructure. However, in the iTV initial phase, VOD was to be used as the key application, and much was staked on its ability to attract viewers and consumer revenue. If it failed to do so, and if consumers only came to the service slowly over an extended period of time, the iTV company faced the prospect of long-term losses before the potential of seeing decent

---

[7] One of the business justifications in being first to market is to turn just this sort of vicious circle into a virtuous cost structure by effectively setting the market standards.

returns. Even more threateningly, given rapid technological change, alternative methods of providing more accessible interactive services may well have been developed in the interim, or basic infrastructural costs may have plummetted, making it easy for late entrants to contest the lead position of the VOD provider. For Hong Kong Telecom then, by the mid-1990s, the questions regarding VOD, although complex, had come down to a simple business proposition: if they were to compete in the VOD market, could they afford not to try and gain dominance of the new market?

INTERACTIVE MULTIMEDIA SERVICES LTD. (IMS)

Hong Kong Telecom Interactive Multimedia Services Ltd. (HKT IMS) was an independent, wholly-owned subsidiary of Hong Kong Telecom, itself a member of the Cable & Wireless Federation [see **Exhibit 5**]. HKT IMS was established to take responsibility for the creation and delivery of a wide range of interactive services to the Hong Kong marketplace – primarily the residential marketplace.

IMS was established as a working unit in late 1994 under the leadership of Dr. William Lo, a former McKinsey & Co. consultant. In late 1993 Dr. Lo returned to Hong Kong from a 12-month secondment to London, working as the Executive Assistant to the Chairman and the Chief Executive of Cable & Wireless PLC. Upon his return he took up the new position as Director of Strategic Planning, focusing principally on the formulation of a corporate and regional strategy for HKT, as well as being responsible for developing HKT's broadband initiative. At this stage, VOD was already seen as pivotal to the future of HKT in the new era of interactive multimedia. In November 1995, IMS was formalised as a subsidiary business, making it the fourth major subsidiary of Hong Kong Telecom.[8] (The others were Hong Kong Telephone Company (HKTC), Hong Kong Telecom International (HKTI), and Hong Kong Telecom CSL, known simply as CSL.)

At this point in time the separation of operating business units was required by the industry regulator, OFTA (the Office of the Telecommunications Authority). This was

---

[8] In 'Waiting for VOD' (The Dataphile, 3(3): 16) Lai comments that HKT IMS is a "non-franchised subsidiary of Hong Kong Telecom", rather than a separate company, in the context of discussing PNETS (public, non-exclusive telecommunications services) charges – the fee that Internet Service Providers (ISPs) were required to pay to Hong Kong Telecom for the right to serve the customer market.

to ensure that other companies that wished to provide broadband services would be able to enter the market on a fair and equal basis, renting facilities from the incumbent, HKT, in a competitive manner. To help formalise the operational separation, IMS relocated their premises from Hong Kong Telecom Tower in Quarry Bay to a cheaper office space in Sha Tin. This, however, did not satisfy a number of industry critics, who saw the potential for continued cross-subsidisation and the pursuit of market dominance. Mueller, for example, called for the divestiture of IMS from the HKT parent body: "The creation of a free-standing, divested IMS would create a market structure more in line with the global trend towards vertical disintegration and horizontal specialisation in digital media, and thus accelerate Hong Kong's progress into the age of digital convergence. IMS would be free to buy network services from any wireless or FTNS operators, and IMS's relationship with content providers would not be affected by its market power over access."[9] Naturally, this line of attack was resisted by the company. More widely, it was pointed out that given the issues raised, if HKT was not encouraged to introduce VOD, Hong Kong was unlikely to see such development for many years. (The issue for industry regulators, therefore, was whether they should trade off industry competition for new high-technology service provision.)

In 1995, HKT began running a commercial VOD trial involving 400 households scattered across the different geographical regions of Hong Kong and the different socio-economic groups. Prior to this commercial trial, the service had been tested with HKT employees to assess whether the system itself was technically feasible and, perhaps more importantly, could be implemented using HKT's existing infrastructure. (The initial trials made use of ADSL and fibre to the building (FTTB) technologies, before eventually migrating to xDSL [see **Glossary**].) By the time of the commercial launch in late 1997, IMS had grown to more than 400 employees working across five different divisions.

---

[9] Milton M. (1998), "Why Hong Kong Telecom Should Not Get a VOD Licence", paper presented to the *Hong Kong Telecommunications Review 1997* (http://www.IIAC/papers), September.

VIDEO-ON-DEMAND IN HONG KONG – A BUSINESS SOLUTION OR A TECHNOLOGICAL BREAKTHROUGH?

We are about two years ahead of the market. The question is: do we move in now to stay ahead of the market or do we wait for costs to come down?
                                      – Kelvin Lai, HKT IMS, 4 September 1997

How were market competitors or the industry regulator to understand HKT's diversification strategy into multimedia services? For a telephone company the core competence would be its telecommunications skills in telephony, data communications and related value-added services. A new infrastructure could certainly improve operational efficiency and add cost advantages in going about the old business, but at the same time the firm must branch out into new fields – in this case these new fields included entertainment, education and interactive transactional services. Not only were there costs involved in building a new network and providing new services, there was also a steep learning curve to be traversed in the provision of new non-core services.

Phase 1: The Original Broadband Vision

The original IMS plan was to offer broadband services to the entertainment market, with the planned applications including VOD, home shopping, cross-merchandising, home banking and payment services, educational offerings, and infomercial/infotainment products of various types [see **Exhibit 6**]. Revenue for the IMS service would come from subscription fees, sales commissions and fees from business traders. By its original schedule, IMS was to provide its broadband VOD service to the residential market by July 1996.[10] In undertaking this aggressive schedule, HKT issued a Request for Proposal for a broadband network solution in March 1995. The winners – or 'technology partners' – were announced in November 1995:

- ❑ Iwatani and Fujitsu for the broadband switches and transmission technology.
- ❑ Hewlett-Packard for media servers and gateways.
- ❑ Sybase for database software.
- ❑ NEC for set-top boxes.

---

[10] Wharf Cable's exclusive cable TV licence in Hong Kong was originally supposed to expire by end of June 1996. It was later extended to 1998, thereby allowing Wharf to enjoy a monopoly in narrowcast TV but competing with broadcast TV.

- ❑ BroadVision for the support systems.
- ❑ Andersen Consulting for programme management and systems integration.

Phase 2: The Interim Narrowband Business

However, in 1996 the entire scenario changed drastically. In March 1996, HKT announced that the digital VOD project would be delayed by at least one year until mid-1997, and the focus was shifted away from VOD to the new Internet business ('Netvigator') and interactive on-line services [see **Exhibit 7**]. Netvigator, an enhanced suite of Internet offerings, was launched in early 1996, employing what was in effect the existing narrowband technology. (Within six months Netvigator became the dominant Internet Service Provider in Hong Kong with almost 40,000 subscribers, and by mid-1997, it had passed 100,000 dial-up account subscribers.[11])

Then, in March 1997, HKT announced that Sybase would not be used in the future IMS platform. In June 1996, HKT dropped Hewlett-Packard as the VOD server supplier. There were several reasons for these developments. The first was a simple issue of business 'incompatibility' and disagreements over which technological solution to adopt. (As indicated by some involved in the project, this was to be expected given the ambitious launch programme and the fluid nature of the network design program.) Somewhat more fundamentally, though, was a shift away from the earlier proprietary network design to a more open, interoperable platform. This accompanied the meteoric growth of the World Wide Web [see **Exhibit 8**] and HKT's move into the Internet service provision market. It also saw a refocus by the group towards the adoption of Java, the object-oriented networking language being permeated through its use on the Web.

Thus, whereas the first phase of development was focused on a proprietary network design (originally the IMS platform was to be set up as an IBM proprietary network), changes in the second phase (i.e., the adoption of an open operating system) mirrored developments in the networking community worldwide, as the impact of the Internet and the Web were accommodated. The original business requirements had led to the selection of a specific set of technologies and products. The subsequent change in business requirements demanded a change in components (and in some cases, ven-

---

[11] In 1996, HKT IMS established the largest 'cybermall' in Asia and in March 1997 it launched the first service of real-time Asia-Pacific stock quotations, company information and economic news in Hong Kong. The services were Hong Kong Stock Express and Asia Financial Express (AFXpress).

dors) which on the one hand met future needs (being more 'flexible' to support more services), but on the other hand delayed the project schedule and created new technological uncertainties.[12] Cumulatively, these changes were seen to cater for a more flexible adoption of services in the future, rather than just to support or to optimise, the VOD application. Implicit in this watershed was an acknowledgement by the company that VOD, by itself, would not sustain an economically viable business case.

Phase 3: The Launch of the Broadband Network

By 1997, the broadband venture had become a HK$10 billion[13] project, and the new consortium comprised the following:

- ❏ Fujitsu, providing ATM switching and local access.
- ❏ NEC, supplying the main server and set-top boxes (or 'Smart Box' hardware).
- ❏ BroadVision, supplying the electronic commerce engine.
- ❏ Iona Technologies, providing the CORBA middleware.
- ❏ Andersen Consulting, providing program management and systems integration.

Meanwhile, the infrastructure that the iTV services were finally built upon consisted of the following:

- ❏ Business and Operation Support Systems (B/OSS).
- ❏ Hardware.
- ❏ Physical Broadband ATM Network.
- ❏ Smart Box.
- ❏ Servers (MPEG video, Application data and Commerce fulfilment).
- ❏ Client Software.
- ❏ Microwave OS-9 real-time operating system.
- ❏ Java Virtual Machine.
- ❏ OrbixWeb (Common Object Request Broker Architecture (CORBA) client).
- ❏ Java Open Set-Top Environment (JOSE).
- ❏ IMS Application Framework.
- ❏ Server Software.
- ❏ Orbix 2.2 (CORBA server).

---

[12] For example, the set-top box became a simple Unix box.

[13] US$1 = HK$7.78

❑ Broadvision 1:1 Commerce Software.
❑ ObjectStore Object-Oriented Database (OODB).
❑ Tools and Utilities.
❑ Service Builder (SB authoring tool).
❑ Service Activation Manager (SAM) operations utility.

By the launch, therefore, the IMS architecture was based upon a distributed object-oriented design. The real-time environment consisted primarily of 'Smart Box' clients running Java applications, application servers and MPEG servers[14] all tied together by an ATM fibre-optic network. The centrepiece of the iTV service and the main focus of the launch phase remained VOD. However, in addition to VOD, IMS's suite of other iTV services included music-on-demand (MOD), karaoke-on-demand (KOD), home shopping and home banking – although these were all to be launched *after* the VOD service.

THE HONG KONG ADVANTAGE: A WEALTHY, 'VERTICAL' CITY

If [VOD] doesn't work in Hong Kong, it won't work anywhere.
– Dr. William Lo, 1995

Given its advantageous geography and an existing, advanced infrastructure, HKT had been hoping to hold the cost of linking homes to its iTV network to an average of US$1,200 (HK$9,360). Initial plans had customers being charged at HK$200 a month for a set-top box to decode the incoming telephone signal, and another HK$20–30 for each film they viewed.[15] Over the course of their commercial trial, IMS found that each household spent an average of HK$30–50 per week on programmes and films (billed at between HK$2 and HK$28 an item).[16] This suggested that IMS would (op-

---

[14] MPEG (Motion Picture Experts Group) is a motion picture or video standard. The acronym is derived from the US body that set the standard.

[15] To attract subscribers, the initial monthly fee upon launch was in fact only HK$100.

[16] This was compared to the HK$20–30 weekly they said they would have otherwise spent on video rentals. It costs around HK$10–25 to rent a film from one of the SAR's video rental outlets.

timistically) generate only HK$4,480 per year for each subscriber.[17] These figures help to put the 'killer application' approach in some perspective. Even without any 'churn' – the number of people who initially subscribe to a service only to then relinquish their subscription – it would take more than two years for HKT to begin to see any money from each user.

IMS was expecting to break even by its fourth year of operation, based on achieving 88,000 customers by the end of the first year and 240,000 customers (around five percent of the population) by the end of the second [see **Exhibit 9**]. (All of the middle-class estates were to be connected with fibre by the end of the first year and 80 percent of Hong Kong would be covered within three years.) But meeting this target would mean Hong Kong Telecom, through HKTC, would spend an estimated HK$2.8 billion on the basic infrastructure. In addition, IMS foresaw themselves needing to spend in excess of HK$300 million purchasing films for its new VOD service over the first three years. The VOD service would show films sourced predominantly from a joint venture between film producers, Golden Harvest Entertainment and China Star Entertainment, as Hong Kong films have been shown to be the most popular fare. The service would provide customers with a choice of between 60–80 film titles, which could be viewed at any time. Each film would have an average 'shelf life' of about two weeks, with very popular titles staying available for up to a month. Thus, turnover would be high.

A number of factors supported Dr. Lo's claims that Hong Kong was uniquely placed to attempt this experiment. Firstly, about 90 percent of residents lived in high-rise flats, which made the city comparatively easier and cheaper to connect than just about any other major metropolitan area. Even in Singapore, the average height of the high-rise residential blocks was only 20 storeys, compared to 32 for Hong Kong, making the incremental costs for HKT comparatively smaller. In addition, Hong Kong's population was broadly affluent and sophisticated: an ideal target for such entertainment services. Spending on recreation, information and entertainment in Hong Kong was more than three times that of the US on a per capita basis. (Expenditure as a percentage of GDP is 7.5 percent in Hong Kong, compared with approximately two percent in the US.) Hong Kong also has a remarkably high take-up of new technology services: the penetration of VCRs, mobile phones, pagers and Internet subscription, for example, were higher than in most other regions [see **Exhibit 10**].

---

[17] One estimate suggests that the company would need to generate revenues of more than US$40 per household per month to make an appropriate return. See Lucas, L. (1995), "William Lo and His Race to Be First", *The Financial Times*, 2 May.

All of this meant that, for IMS' VOD service to make money for HKT, a number of factors had to come into play. Firstly, the market had to exist – something that had yet to be proven, as the trials around the world had demonstrated. Secondly, network costs had to continue to fall or else the amount by which IMS was subsidising each subscriber would become too expensive. Finally, with two licences awarded initially, and potentially more to follow, IMS needed to secure a dominant position in the market.

GLOSSARY

Terms	Definition
ADSL	Asymmetric Digital Subscriber Line. A form of Digital Subscriber Line in which the bandwidth available for the downstream connection is significantly larger than for upstream. Although designed to minimise the effect of cross-talk between the upstream and downstream channels, this set-up is well suited for Web browsing and client-server applications as well as for some emerging applications such as video-on-demand. (See also xDSL.)
Broadband	A transmission medium capable of supporting a wide range of frequencies, typically from audio up to video frequencies. It can carry multiple signals by dividing the total capacity of the medium into multiple, independent bandwidth channels, where each channel operates only on a specific range of frequencies.
Broadcast	Point-to-multipoint transmission.
CORBA	Common Request Broker Architecture.
Digital compression	A technique for conserving bandwidth by reducing the bits required to represent, store or transmit data.
FTTB	Fibre to the building.
FTTH	Fibre to the home.
Hertz (Hz)	Unit of electromagnetic frequency equal to one cycle second.
HFC	Hybrid Fibre/Coaxial. Fibre-optic cable in the local loop, and coaxial cable to the home. A higher capacity alternative to ADSL, and a cost-effective alternative to FTTH.

iTV	Interactive television. A broadband (high-capacity) point-to-point transmission system that provides a subscriber with an upstream link to request a service, such as VOD, and a downstream link to transmit the service.
Java	(After the Indonesian island, a source of programming fluid.) A simple, object-oriented, distributed, architecture-neutral, general-purpose programming language developed by Sun Microsystems in 1995. Java supports programming for the Internet in the form of platform-independent Java 'applets'. Java is similar to the computing language C++, but extends C++'s object-oriented facilities with those of Objective C for dynamic method resolution.
Narrowband	A channel of radio frequencies below the level of a voice circuit 300Hz to 3,000Hz, typically using transmission speeds up to 100–200 Kbps.
NVOD	Near video-on-demand. A narrowcast service that enables a subscriber to call up a video for downloading at times set by the service provider (typically every 15 minutes, so a video lasting three hours will require 12 channels).
Server	A computer that provides some service for other computers connected to it via a network. The most common example is a file server, which has a local disk and services requests from remote clients to read and write files on that disk.
VOD	Video-on-demand. An interactive service that enables a subscriber to call up a video of choice from a menu to be downloaded at any time.
xDSL	DSL – or Digital Subscriber Line – technologies encompass technologies for the transmission of compressed digital signals along a twisted-wire pair telephone line, such as ADSL, HDSL (High bit-rate Digital Subscriber Line) or VHDSL (Very High bit-rate Digital Subscriber Line).

Exhibit 1:   IMS iTV network architecture

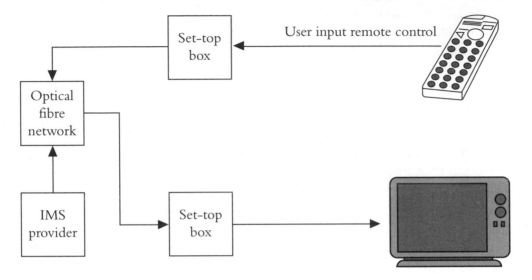

Exhibit 2: Selected iTV trials worldwide

Region	Company	Location	Launch	Users	Services	Network
United States	Bell Atlantic	New Jersey	5/1995	7,000	VOD	ADSL
	US West	Omaha	8/1995	4,000	VOD; TV listings	HFC
	Nynex	New York	1994	800		
	Time Warner	Florida	12/1994	4,000	VOD; games; home shopping	HFC
	TCI (+ Microsoft)	Washington	3/1995	2,000	VOD	HFC
	Viacom	California	1995	N/A		
Britain	BT	Colchester/Ipswich	6/1995	2,500	VOD; music; games; home shopping & banking; information	FTTH or FTTC+ADSL
	On-line Media	Cambridge	3/1995	250	VOD; home banking; music; news	FTTC + coax
Germany	Deutsche Telekom	Six cities	1/1995	6,000	VOD; home shopping; News-on-demand	FTTH; FTTC+coax
Japan	Japanese government	Kyoto	7/1994	300		FTTC
	Tokyo Cable Net. (NTT & Microsoft)	Tokyo	3/1996	400	VOD; news; KOD; home shopping	FTTC
Hong Kong	Hong Kong Telecom	Hong Kong	1995	4,000	VOD; home shopping	FTTB/ADSL
Australia	Interactive TV Australia	Adelaide	11/1994	1,500	Printed info: play-along game shows	Signals in TV programme + phone return

Exhibit 3: iTV value–chain

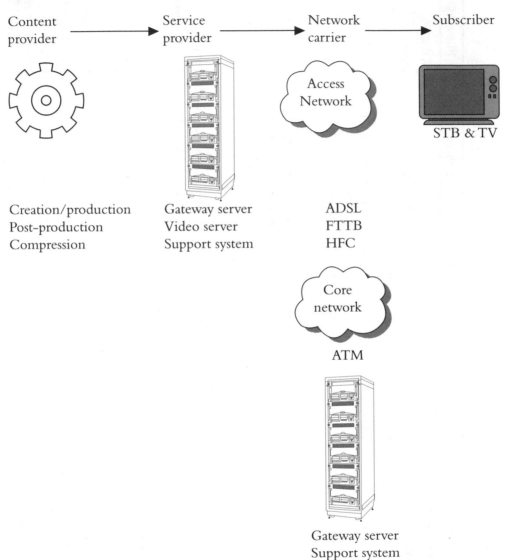

Exhibit 4:   Critical technical and cost issues

In order to make the iTV business viable, management should address the following critical technical and cost issues from a commercial point of view:

	Technical issues	Cost issues
Content provider	• Change to digital production environment • Exploitation of interactivity	• Acquisition of equipment • Compression of content • Advertising and promotion • Training and personnel
Service provider	• Support of multiple asynchronous video streams • Desired video quality of programmes • Support secure transactional service • Overall integration of network, servers, content providers and tertiary service providers • Protection of privacy	• Professional fees for consulting/integration services • Acquisition of content (royalty) • Compression of content • Cost of servers to support large number of streams, programs and high volume of transactions • Advertising and promotion • Training of personnel • Facility, operation, maintenance, etc.
Network carrier	• Leverage off new infrastructure to support other services • Minimal visits to and wiring in homes • Re-use of current infrastructure • Support of back channel	• Cost of core network to support high bandwidth • Cost of local access network to reach every subscriber • Acquisition of servers to provide gateway and support functions • Training of personnel
Subscriber	• Desired degree of interactivity • Desired quality of programmes • Early lock-in to set-top box vendor • Lack of standards • Potential early obsolescence of technology	• Facility, operation, maintenance, etc. • Acquisition of set-top boxes • Volume of subscribers

Exhibit 5: Hong Kong Telecom corporate structure

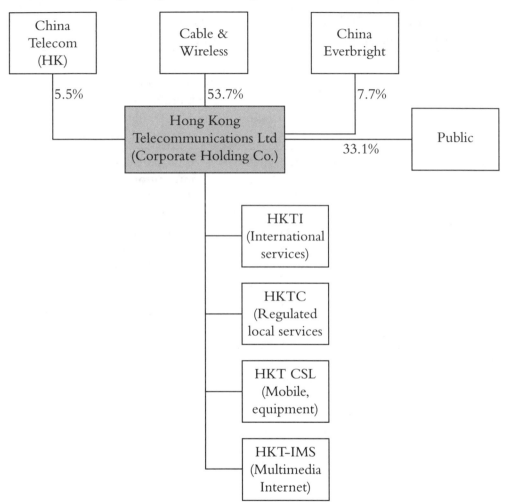

Exhibit 6:   IMS broadband services schedule (original)

1996
- Video–on–demand
- Payment services
- Cross–merchandising
- Infomercial

1997
- Home shopping
- Home banking

- Electronic Yellow Pages
- TV-on-demand

1998
- Network games
- Educational services

Exhibit 7:   Netvigator homepage (http://www.netvigator.com/)

Exhibit 8: World Wide Web growth matrix
(http://www.mids.org/market/1/htmldir/web.html)

Internet hosts and Web servers, 1981–97

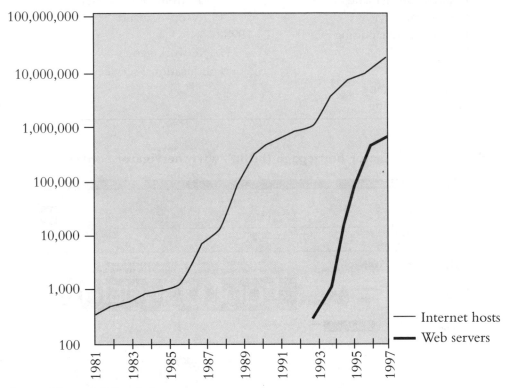

Source: Network Wizards, Inc.

Exhibit 9:   IMS' projected VOD financials

HK dollars (in mn)	FY98JF	FY99JF	FY00JF	FY01JF	FY02JF
Subscribers, year-end (thousands)	20	160	320	440	528
Subscribers, year-average (thousands)	3	90	240	380	484
Churn rate (%)	10	10	15	15	15
Total sign-up revenue	9	67	78	71	64
Total monthly revenue	5	162	432	684	871
Total movie revenue	7	270	720	912	1,162
Other revenue	1	54	144	182	232
Total revenue	23	553	1,374	1,849	2,329
Films offered per year (number)	360	360	360	360	360
Total minimum guarantee costs	(13)	(50)	(52)	(53)	(54)
Studio royalty costs (@20% of movie revenue)	(1)	(27)	(72)	(91)	(116)
Post-production costs	(0)	(15)	(25)	(29)	(34)
Total content costs	(14)	(93)	(149)	(173)	(204)
Total interconnect costs	(19)	(347)	(555)	(527)	(403)
Marketing and other costs	(50)	(150)	(175)	(250)	(250)
Employees (number)	400	800	1,200	1,500	1,600
Salary expenses	(29)	(288)	(432)	(540)	(576)
Total costs	(92)	(531)	(756)	(963)	(1,030)
EBITDA	(69)	22	619	886	1,299
Depreciation	(58)	(513)	(754)	(948)	(1,104)
Operating profit	(127)	(491)	(135)	(62)	196
Total capex per subscriber (HK$)	12,188	10,940	11,523	12,074	12,830
Revenue per subscriber (HK$)	N/A	3,457	4,295	4,203	4,412

Note: Payment to Hong Kong Telephone shown here for illustrative purposes only and not included in operating costs.

Source: Hong Kong Telecom (1997), *Jardine Fleming Research*, 1 December.

Exhibit 10: Hong Kong media development statistics

- Over 3.6 million fixed exchange lines at a penetration rate of 55 lines per 100 people
- 108 fixed domestic lines per 100 households
- Over 4.6 million telephone sets
- Over 300,000 kilometres optical fibre laid
- Over 2.1 million mobile telephone subscribers at a penetration rate of 32 percent
- Over 870,000 radio paging subscribers
- According to the Office of the Telecommunications Authority, the number of ISP in Hong Kong at the end of July 1998 was 130.[18]

---

[18] Office of the Telecommunications Authority, http://www.ofta.gov.hk/index_eng1.html

CHAPTER

3

The Regulatory Framework

OBJECTIVES

- To understand the major issues surrounding the development of a regulatory framework in the marketspace.
- To learn about the concept of jurisdiction in the marketspace.
- To gain an appreciation of the issues related to taxation, privacy, consumer protection, certification and copyright in the marketspace.
- To examine the role of the government in addressing the emerging legal and regulatory issues.

In this world nothing is certain but death and taxes.

– Benjamin Franklin

To the consternation of governments everywhere, e-commerce is challenging the validity of Benjamin Franklin's famous aphorism: taxes are no longer the certainty that they once were. The crux of the e-commerce tax problem – as with many of the emerging e-commerce regulatory problems – is one of location or, more specifically, jurisdiction. If tax is to be applied to goods sold over the Internet, where should it be applied? In the state, province or country where the on-line retailer is based *or* in the locality where the customer is based? What if the customer is paying for goods with a credit card from a bank in a third jurisdiction?

Tax, however, is just one of many emerging 'framework' issues requiring attention. A similar collision has occurred over domain names – the assignations such as '.com' which give an e-commerce company its identity. Identical trademarks can co-exist in different countries, because trademarks are geographically defined. But domain names are global and must be unique. As with taxes, intellectual property rights in copyright, trademarks and patents have been governed by the laws of nations and sovereign states, again jurisdiction-specific. While there are several international treaties that apply to member countries, by and large intellectual property laws and tax laws are domestic in nature. Intellectual property rights in copyright and trademarks, privacy and consumer protection, liability, and content and service regulation have all become potential flash points threatening to derail the development of global e-commerce.

The problem is not new. Commerce is global. Law, for the most part, is not. That has been true for hundreds of years. However, the emergence of borderless e-commerce has exacerbated the situation by crystallising a basic question: How can business be borderless when the law is not?

To reap the benefits of e-commerce, it is increasingly recognised that an acceptable level of legal certainty and uniformity must be present. Individual consumers and businesses all require an infrastructure on which they can rely in the event of dispute.

In this chapter we emphasise the importance of the emergence of an e-commerce regulatory framework. While the infrastructure necessary for global electronic commerce is already being built out at a rapid rate – as we have seen in Chapter 2: The Infrastructure – e-commerce will not take off on the basis of infrastructure alone. It needs a complementary set of conditions co-existing before 'critical mass' can be reached. In addition to the obvious – the number of people with computers, and the ease and cost of access to networks – there are a range of legal and security issues, standards issues, the provision of on-line services, along with certain financial issues, such as the number of people with credit cards and the attitude of banks towards credit card liability.

The first section of the chapter looks at the problems of locality and jurisdiction in a borderless marketspace. The next section of the chapter then outlines the issues that have emerged and which are defining business in the global marketspace. We then elaborate upon some of the regulatory solutions that are emerging.

Governments are increasingly realising that they, too, have a major role to play in the development of e-commerce, by placing their own procurement procedures and government services on-line, thereby helping to increase adoption and dissemination. But to achieve even this level of e-commerce promotion and facilitation, governments have to rethink the way that they themselves are organised and the way they respond to the economic and social needs of the community. The first reaction of policy makers to the growth of the Internet was, in essence, to do nothing. The lagging development of new laws or 'cyberlaw' for cyberspace, however, merely exacerbated the problem, and the inability to keep pace with technological developments led to uncertainty and in many instances conflict.

As a result, there has been increasing pressure on governmental agencies, industry bodies, administration agencies, standards organisations, and professional and public interest groups to come together to form uniform, universal standards that provide businesses and individuals better guidance on what they should and should not do on the Internet. They also provide a framework for dispute resolution and, eventually, security and redress. The final section of the chapter looks at the policy drivers that will promote or hinder this progress.

MARKETSPACE AND JURISDICTION

The intersection of the global multipurpose medium of the Internet, with the systems and processes designed for a physical territorial world, are resulting in the need to re-conceptualise and redefine 'markets'. Trading in the virtual marketspace is not simply a matter of 'business as usual', nor even 'business as usual, but electronically'; it requires new ways of thinking and new approaches. The collapsing of time and space, as we have seen, has meant that business can be conducted 'anytime or anywhere', affording both large and small businesses with opportunities to access global markets, opportunities that may have otherwise been constrained by time or geography. This is the upside of e-commerce. The downside is that it is often difficult to tell exactly who is responsible.

When an American woman slips and falls in a hotel in Italy, can she sue in New Jersey, just because the hotel advertises globally on the Internet? When a Christmas tree catches fire in an American home and causes a fatality, can the store where the tree was purchased sue the Hong Kong manufacturer in a US court, just because the Hong Kong company has a presence in cyberspace? In both these cases, US courts said 'no'. But the question of jurisdiction remains unresolved, both internationally and domestically. What consumer laws, contract law, privacy laws and other laws apply to e-commerce transactions? Where does a transaction take place? How will conflicts in law be determined? And who will enforce them – where?

With e-commerce more commercially developed in the US than elsewhere, it is no surprise that the US courts have taken the lead in beginning to sketch out a tentative standard for jurisdiction. They have attempted to do so by the degree of interactivity of the Website, and especially by whether a sale took place. So if a Rhode Island company maintains a purely informational Website accessed by a resident of Michigan, the company probably cannot be sued in that state. But if the company sells goods directly to the Michigan resident through the Web, then his or her home state's law would probably apply.

The question of foreign jurisdiction, however, is far murkier. According to a draft European Union e-commerce directive, the law of the consumer's home jurisdiction would apply in any case where a purchase was made through a Website. But the issue raises many problems for European and non-European companies because European privacy and consumer protection laws tend to be much tougher than most other countries. This means that non-European companies engaging in e-trade with European companies are likely to have waived their right to any legal protection, as their data protection will be comparatively lax by European requirements.

To get around such problems, companies are forced to set up either separate Websites to comply with local laws, or one megasite that meets every conceivable national and local legal requirement. Both options are costly and could potentially defeat the efficiency gains of globalised commerce.

In the physical world, businesses and individuals can potentially access and apply the most attractive laws, regulations and policies simply by identifying the most attractive location to have jurisdiction over the transaction. For example, an individual, resident in a state or nation that outlaws gambling, might travel to Macau or Las Vegas. Increasingly, it has been the case that one needs only to establish a tentative or even virtual presence to have access to such favourable conditions. For example, establishing a bank or trading account in a jurisdiction like Switzerland so as to have favourable privacy rules apply has become increasingly accessible. Similarly, simple and unburdensome incorporation laws in places like Bermuda and the Cayman Islands make it possible for companies to avail themselves of favourable commercial and corporate laws with little more than a mailing address.

Internet-mediated transactions have served to exacerbate the transience of such arrangements; but more problematically, they have served to confound pre-existing legal precedents by generating further confusion over which laws apply and which entity has jurisdiction. Two decidedly outcomes can occur as follows:

❑ *Remote access/going to a jurisdiction.* A business or individual can go to a jurisdiction remotely, i.e., without establishing any physical presence in a jurisdiction, consumers and businesses can have 'remote access' to and apply that nation's or state's laws.

❑ *Remote application/coming from a jurisdiction.* The laws, regulations and policies of the country or state apply to non-resident businesses or individuals even for Internet-mediated commerce, i.e., without establishing any physical presence in a jurisdiction, one can become subject to that nation's or state's laws.

The remote access capability of the Internet significantly extends the pre-existing opportunities for individuals and businesses to access laws, regulations and policies more favourable than those which the host nation or state would otherwise have applied. In some instances, using the Internet to go to a jurisdiction makes it possible to evade laws applicable to residents and to engage in transactions deemed illegal by the nation or state that otherwise would have had jurisdiction over the transaction. For example, one might use Internet mediation as a vehicle to evade a federal or state prohibition on gambling, to access types of pornography that would have constituted obscenity, to 'launder' money or purchase goods (alcohol, tobacco, firearms, drugs and medications) and services without proper licences, tax and duty payments, or other types of authorisations.

UK's NetBet: Duty-free Betting on the Internet

NetBet launched its Internet duty-free betting site on 19 October 1998, claiming to be the first tax-free betting service for British clients. NetBet is a subsidiary of Sportingbet.com (UK) PLC (www.sportingbet.com). It offers an on-line credit card payment facility and a betting facility for a wide variety of sporting events that include UK and European football, rugby, cricket, tennis and selected horse racing. Because NetBet is licenced by the States of Alderney in the Channel Islands, customers are not liable for UK tax. Authorities at Alderney charge a licensing fee of £50,000. They do not charge betting duty on turnover and tax company profits at a modest 20 percent. Punters benefit from Internet betting as they do not have to pay the price levied on each pound bet.

   This created anxiety within the Customs and Excise Department and the

Levy Board not due to the revenue that is fleeing them now, but because of the potential of Internet betting. According to Mark Thompson, spokesman for the Customs and Excise, their concern is "in the short term Internet betting is a very small leakage", but it could rapidly increase with the obligatory tax escaping them. Authorities are faced with the challenge of managing the unmanageable, and they are pressured to rapidly address the issue. Besides, UK has a total off-course betting market valued at £6.2 billion and growing.

In July 1999, Sportingbet.com launched its Internet betting business in North America, making it the first British company to enter the market, offering regular National Football League (NFL) and Major League Baseball (MLB) lines.

Sources: Lewell (1999); Nichols (1998); Sportingbet.com (UK) PLC (2000).

Once again we wish to emphasise our theme that what is happening here has largely been the case prior to the introduction of the Internet: businesses and individuals have exploited remote access opportunities since the beginning of international commerce. For example, ocean going shippers and cruise lines have operated under 'flags of convenience', having secured licences to operate, favourable tax treatment and possibly greater opportunities for exculpation from liability for offences that elsewhere would have triggered civil and criminal liability. The difference in the Internet era lies in the more robust and easier medium provided by the Net for the exploitation of such loopholes. Guernsey Islands requires just 20 minutes for commercial incorporation, for example.

By contrast, the remote application of a nation's laws threatens to apply extraterritorially the kinds of laws, regulations and policies that businesses and individuals seek to evade.[1] For example, the operator of a worldwide Website in the United States might not offer the level of privacy protection legislated in the European Community. In the likely event that a European Web surfer transacts commerce with this US-based site, a European court, regulator or other institution might find a violation and impose civil liability, including monetary forfeitures on any number of participants in the transaction (e.g., the Internet Service Provider and the credit card companies processing the transaction in addition to the seller of the goods or services).

Remote application of laws, regulations and policies, pose the possibility of extraterritorial jurisdiction on such diverse areas as privacy and data protection, other con-

---

[1] Swire (1998); Goldsmith (1998); Stein (1998).

sumer protection laws, professional and business licensing, labour laws, intellectual property protection, taxation and laws applicable to particular types of transactions, e.g., gambling, adult material, hate speech and defamation. In the following section, we provide an overview of some of the major regulatory flashpoints which have emerged along with e-commerce.

REGULATORY ISSUES: GLOBAL E-COMMERCE

Taxation

The crux of the taxation problem is location (or jurisdiction). If tax is applied to goods sold over the Internet, where should it be applied? In the state, province or country where the on-line retailer is based or in the place where the customer is based? What if the customer is paying for goods with a credit card from a bank in a third jurisdiction? People who buy goods in the US by mail order do not have to pay sales tax if the retailer does not have a brick-and-mortar outlet in the area in which the buyer lives. As a result, many e-tailers in the US have been exploiting this tax loophole as they do not have any brick-and-mortar outlets. Hence, many traditional retailers – both large and small – have been quite unhappy about all of this. Why should they be put at a competitive disadvantage by having to charge customers sales tax?

It is in keeping with the spirit of the Internet to support a moratorium on taxes, but state revenues will erode rapidly if no one is paying tax. It is therefore an issue that will require a resolution. The OECD has already stated that any solution must maintain the fiscal sovereignty of countries, ensure a fair sharing of the tax base between countries and avoid double taxation.

There are two principle features of tax which concern the authorities when it comes to e-commerce. The first is the emergence of digital cash that allows business transactions to remain hidden from taxation authorities. This will mean that a significant amount of business could suddenly become invisible to the current revenue base. The second tax concern is that business operations will move offshore far more readily than they have done in the past in order to take advantage of tax benefits. There are, broadly, four suggested government responses to these two emerging concerns as follows:[2]

---

[2] See Anthony Sylvester's talk at the 16 March 1999 TIF Forum on electronic commerce (URL: http://www.trp.hku.hk/tif/papers).

1. *Open up the tax havens.* While the authorities may not be able to close tax havens down *per se*, they can 'open them up' to some degree. So, for example, the Cayman Islands have been under pressure from law enforcement agencies from the US and the UK to provide greater information about transactions taking place there.

2. *Pretend that companies have never left.* Even if a company moves all of its operations offshore and only leaves behind a server and perhaps some technical contracts, then governments may well consider that those companies are still operating inside their jurisdiction for tax reasons. While this has not yet happened, it has been under discussion by both the OECD and the UK tax authorities.

3. *Maximise transactions that are already taking place.* Essentially, this requires a certain 'tweaking' of existing taxation models in order to make sure that electronic transactions are encompassed. While this may appear obvious, it is not easy to accomplish. For example, buying a CD from a music store in Los Angeles and downloading that same CD from a Website in London to a residential PC in Los Angeles may appear to involve the same transaction. But for tax authorities to make sure that tax applies in the latter case is very difficult.

4. *Formulate a new tax on electronic commerce.* In the US and the EU, there is, in fact, a three-year moratorium on any taxes on Internet commerce. However, there is also a new commission that has been set up in the US specifically to address the issue of taxation on e-commerce.[3]

Privacy and Consumer Protection

As we show in Module 2 (Conducting Business in the Marketspace) and Module 3 (Building and Managing e-Relationships), the on-line medium provides extraordinary opportunities for businesses to learn about their customers – what they like and dislike, how they shop and how they gather information. For example, data-mining techniques are now widely used to collect information about purchasing behaviour, which are then cross-referenced and compiled to generate more comprehensive consumer profiles. The loss of privacy not only undermines individuals but also corporations, as competitors are able to gain insight into what a company's next market move might be, based on certain purchasing behaviour. In addition, the Internet has provided unique opportunities for businesses to target messages to large numbers of people while tailoring the message to individual demographics and interests. As a result of

---

[3] Before the commission had even begun its work, local and municipal authorities in the US sued the commission on the basis that they were inadequately represented.

these information–gathering activities, however, privacy has become a particularly sensitive area along with consumer protection issues and the well-being of children within the Internet environment.

As with intellectual property protection and taxation, privacy and consumer protection laws are country- or region-specific. For example, the European Directive on Data Protection forbids companies from transferring personal consumer data to countries that do not share the region's privacy regulations (see below).[4]

Certification

The key issues regarding the safety of transactions are as follows:

1. The identification of the sender and recipient of a message (that he/she really is the sender/recipient and not somebody else).
2. The authentication of the message (that the message has not been changed in transit).
3. Non-repudiation (that a buyer cannot falsely claim that payment has been made and a seller that payment has not been received).
4. Encryption of the payment information (the scrambling of messages, such as credit card numbers, so that they cannot be read by unauthorised persons).

Technical progress has provided *potential* solutions in all these areas. Digital signatures and a 'message digest', for example, can verify that a message has not been altered. A digital certificate can confirm the identity of the person who sends and digitally signs a message. 'Double-blinded encryption' also allows for the payment of an 'on-line' order without the seller seeing the credit card number.

Copyright

Given the central importance of information and of ideas to the early evolution of e-commerce, establishing clear and protectible intellectual property rights is foreseen to be crucial to the efficient and equitable operation of the electronic marketspace. Yet the ease with which electronic information is reproducible and transmutable over the Internet challenges intellectual property rights in fundamental ways. For example, each time a user accesses an Internet homepage, that information is, at least temporarily, transferred to the user's computer (*cached*), ready to be copied and stored permanently

---

[4] Oakes (1999).

or incorporated into other information. Control over access to and the integrity of information that is posted on the Internet is therefore virtually impossible.

Can existing copyright regimes that were developed primarily to protect IPR for literary works be extended meaningfully to cover electronic information? How can patent protection be enforced for electronic innovations? Trademarks pose a particular problem. While trademarks are employed transnationally, trademark laws apply on a country-by-country basis. That is, trademark guarantees in one country have a limited bearing on guarantees in another. This has a major impact on e-commerce given the fact that domain names, the commercial or personal identifiers of companies on the Internet are: (a) immediately international upon registration; and (b) easily registerable in foreign countries – thereby defying national borders. As a result, protecting trademark interests on the Internet has presented a particularly thorny dilemma. Additional trademark problems have evolved out of hyperlinks, cybersquatting, framing, 'word stuffing' and linking.

❑ *Cybersquatting*, or 'domain name squatting', involves the registration of famous brands or trademark names by Internet-savvy speculators, who then offer to sell the names to the companies or individuals concerned, usually for large sums of money.

❑ *Framing* occurs when a Website becomes part of a larger 'metasite' that aggregates links and information from other sites. Metasites function as large, centralised information repositories, which make it easier and faster to use the Internet.

❑ *Word stuffing* is the use of *invisible* trademarks to lure users to their sites. Also known as the use of 'metatags', this tactic involves embedding another company's popular brand name into a Website.

❑ *Linking* is easy to do on the Internet and often increases the usefulness of a site by providing access to additional content at no extra cost. For example, if a Website is linked to a company's site without permission, that company may not know, let alone appreciate, such an association. Furthermore, there may eventually be problems of legal or commercial conflict if, for example, the link were unwittingly to a pornographic or fraudulent Website.

To address some of these issues, a draft software directive in the EU was put forward, containing a clause that would ban the caching of information protected by any form of intellectual property right. If accepted, this would put the EU in stark contrast to the US situation where the caching of information is specifically protected. The consequences for information providers and site managers would be profound if the caching of information was banned with portals coming to have quite a different dimension in the EU, than in the US or Asia.[5]

Domain Name Dispute: The Cases of Barcelona.com and Huangshan.com

There is a looming problem involving the protection of property rights in cyberspace. The recent ruling of the Geneva-based World Intellectual Property Organisation (WIPO) regarding Barcelona.com created confusion in the important aspects of cyberspace law. Another case concerns the domain name of Huangshan.com, arbitrated by eResolution, involving a Hong Kong-based company and the Huangshan district in China. The two cases involved two different and conflicting decisions from the approved arbitrators and are seemingly creating two opposing precedents for dot-com companies. ICANN established the 'uniform domain name dispute resolution procedure' to expedite proceedings and to clarify the rights of trademark holders. The rules are set for approved arbitrators to apply. The procedure requires domain owners to submit to domain name dispute resolution if the following applies: (1) domain is identical or confusingly similar to a trademark or service mark in which the complainant has rights; (2) they have no rights or legitimate interests in the domain name; and (3) their domain name is being used in bad faith.

The Barcelona City Council sued Barcelona.com, a private tourist information Website, for the domain name ownership. In August 2000, WIPO ruled in favour of the city council and stated that Barcelona.com owners have no right to their domain name, a decision that goes against the policy established by ICANN, which WIPO was supposedly enforcing. The WIPO ruling threatens a number of Websites that have invested a large sum of money for their domain names. What about sites that use names of cities but are not in any way part of a government body? Will their domain names be considered illegal? Examples of Websites with cities as domain names include:

---

[5] In Singapore, amendments to the Copyright Act in 1999 not only extended the Act into digital areas not previously covered, they also served to clarify the liability of network service providers in carrying copyright material over their networks and caching this material on a Website. See URL: http://www.biz.yahoo.com/bw/990820/dc_newsbyt_2.html.

❑   Boston.com – owned by the Boston Globe, not the city
❑   London.com – a tourist site
❑   Paris.com, Berlin.com and Madrid.com – owned by Mail.com which uses them to provide e-mail addresses
❑   Brussels.com – part of cities.com, a network of over 2,000 city Websites

On the other hand, eResolution ruled in favour of NA Global Link Ltd of Hong Kong stating that the governmental district of Huangshan in China did not have the right to seize the domain Huangshan.com. The decision seemed to be based on the RFC-1591 policy for domain names written by Internet pioneer Jon Postel – 'first come, first served' – as NA Global Link registered the name first.

Sources: ICANN (2000); Messmer (2000); Morris (2000).

Content and Service Regulation

Restrictions on content present one of the most potentially daunting legal considerations for companies doing business on the Internet. During the early 1990s and the first wave of commercialisation of the Internet, there were virtually no restrictions as to the type of content that could be posted on the Web. On-line gambling or pornographic Websites were readily accessible by all, be they children or adults. Increasingly, however, there have been calls to promulgate some form of content restriction.

In the US, the controversial Child On-line Protection Act (COPA) was put forward in an attempt to address, and restrict access to, the tens of thousands of pornographic Websites that both adults and children could easily visit.[6] COPA sought to make it a crime to publish 'any communication for commercial purposes that included any material that was harmful to minors, without restricting access to such material by minors' and was punishable by six months in jail or fines of US$50,000. However, a Philadelphia Court decision ruled the Act unconstitutional in that it violated America's First Amendment guarantee to free speech. In many ways, a more fundamental problem resulted from the interoperable and interconnected underpinnings of the Internet: who would be liable for such content?

When a similar restriction was attempted in Australia, the first response of adult content providers was to simply move their material offshore. On the Internet this can

---

[6] McCullagh (1999).

be done in a matter of minutes. Hence, the second and related problem of content control on the Internet: enforcement.

THE REGULATORY FRAMEWORK

So how do these issues all tie together? A key concern of industry is the right to intellectual property; a key concern of business is security of information; a key concern to banks and merchants is security of payments; and a key concern to customers is the privacy of personal data. Of course, these can, and do, overlap. At the centre of each of these issues is the notion of trust, and while trust is not something that can be guaranteed by law, clearly a rule of law, and a widely appreciated and accepted – and enforceable – legal framework, is fundamental to the successful establishment of trust. It underpins trust between dispersed transactors who feel confident they have the law backing them up.

Regulatory examples are slowly emerging. In 1998, the European Commission proposed a law on the use of 'electronic signatures' in on-line transactions. This would set minimum requirements on security and liability, ensuring that electronic signatures – which enable the identity of senders and the integrity of the data to be checked – are recognised throughout the European Union.[7] Similarly, the European Union Data Protection Directive which is technically enforced (although not yet operable in many countries), provides a significant legislative background to customer privacy and the protection of personal information. The level of data protection required, however, diverges significantly from the approach in the US. While the US approach has many advocates within the Internet community, it is worth bearing in mind that 81 percent of general Internet users in the US in 1998 complained that privacy was their most significant inhibitor to using e-commerce.[8]

The key difference between the EU and the US is principally one of enforcement. In America, where the philosophy is one of self-regulation, enforcement is almost entirely on the shoulders of the industry, while in Europe, enforcement is overseen by the Data Privacy Commissioners.

Even though the emphasis is towards less regulation in e-commerce, it is never-theless widely recognised that regulation and legal measures are important in e-

---

[7] The Directive is at URL: http://www.europa.eu.int/comm/dg15/en/index.htm.

[8] As cited by Anthony Sylvester at the 16 March 1999 TIF Forum on electronic commerce. See the proceedings paper at URL: http://www.trp.hku.hk/tif/papers.

commerce because they remove obstacles and generate trust. Some believe though that the European Union's Data Directive tends to extremes, potentially making routine activities illegal. For example, Palm Pilots could be illegal simply because they contain names and addresses of people who have not granted permission to store them there. This has become otherwise known as the 'laptop example', so called because American protagonists suggest that under the Directive there will be 'privacy police' at European airports stopping people to check what data they are bringing in on their laptops. The response from the European Commission is, of course, that this reaction was sensationalist; that businessmen carrying laptops or Palm Pilots across borders were not going to be stopped. Problematically though, they neither denied the basic charge nor elaborated on where the line was to be drawn.

This has further served to highlight the rapidly building need for universal laws, or laws having universal application. In 1997, the Clinton Administration entered the global debate, releasing "A Framework for Global Electronic Commerce", based on the following five principles:

- ❑ The private sector should lead.
- ❑ Governments should avoid undue restrictions on electronic commerce.
- ❑ Where governmental involvement was needed, its aim should be to support and enforce a predictable, minimalist, consistent and simple legal environment for commerce.
- ❑ Governments should recognise the unique qualities of the Internet.
- ❑ Electronic commerce over the Internet should be facilitated on a global basis.

The framework proposed a strategy through which governments and industries could work together to address the issues surrounding taxation, intellectual property protection, privacy, content restrictions and technical standards, in a way that did not inhibit the growth of the Internet as a vehicle for electronic commerce. It attempted to do this by identifying four main areas of legal and policy issues most directly affected by e-commerce as follows:

- ❑ Intellectual property rules and their relationship to commercial and antitrust law.
- ❑ Privacy rights and security concerns in cyberspace communications and transactions.
- ❑ The setting of technical standards for telecommunications and network interoperability.
- ❑ The internationalisation of e-commerce and rule making.

The framework also recognised that specific problems of e-commerce could likely involve more than one of these areas. For example, the creation of payment and settlement systems for e-commerce would raise issues of setting technical standards for security and privacy as well as for efficiency. Similarly, the revision of intellectual property rules would have important ramifications in international trade negotiations.

However, in the years since the release of the report, which called for a minimalist approach to government regulation of the Internet and e-commerce, government regulation has *increased*. This is largely due to efforts to assure users of the Internet's systemic reliability in three core areas: security, authentication and infrastructure stability. Moreover, in promoting their framework, the US government has run into conflict with other countries on issues such as the use and export of 'strong encryption' technologies.

Another example, the Guidelines for Consumer Protection in the Context of Electronic Commerce, has been evolving since the mid-1990s. The guidelines have been put forward by the Consumer Policy Committee of the OECD. They cover such areas as jurisdiction, collection of personal information and redress. And one of the key aims of the package is to deliver international guidelines to protect consumers who buy goods on the Internet so as to ensure that cross-border shopping on the Internet becomes consumer-friendly and secure. Only then, it is argued, will e-commerce have the chance to reach its full potential.

The myriad of problems faced by consumers shopping on the Internet was demonstrated by Consumers International's landmark international survey "Consumers@shopping: An International Comparative Study of Electronic Commerce", released in late 1999. For the European Union-funded study, consumer organisations in 11 countries – Australia, Belgium, Germany, Greece, Hong Kong, Japan, Norway, Spain, Sweden, the United Kingdom and the United States – ordered more than 150 items from 17 different countries and then returned most of them. The sites used were those of established traders and easy-to-find sites. The study made the following findings:

- ❏ One in ten items never arrived.
- ❏ Two buyers from the United Kingdom and Hong Kong waited over five months for refunds.
- ❏ More than half of the products ordered arrived without receipts.
- ❏ 73 percent of traders failed to give crucial contract terms.
- ❏ Over 25 percent gave no address or telephone number.
- ❏ 24 percent were unclear about the total cost of the item that was ordered.

However, a further point needs to be kept in mind. While e-commerce raises many issues regarding the application of existing regulations and issues, such as tax law, commercial codes and consumer protection, these are already receiving an increasing amount of attention. But e-commerce also calls into question the applicability of retail regulations designed for a 'brick-and-mortar' world, such as restrictions on the size of stores and of opening hours, limitations on pricing and promotions, granting of monopolies for the sale of certain products (e.g., liquor) and permit and licensing requirements. In many cases, these regulations need to be re-examined in light of the realities of e-commerce. In addition to these general commercial regulations, there are those that continue to apply to communications. For e-commerce to function properly, cheap and easy access to information and communication technologies (ICTs) is needed; conditions that increase their costs will slow the diffusion of e-commerce and place industries that use information technologies at a disadvantage. This is, of course, much more specifically a policy choice, and it is to the policy objectives that we now turn our attention.

POLICY: THE ROLE OF THE GOVERNMENT

You need governments where there is something that must be managed on behalf of the whole population. So for example, the DNS (Domain Name System) space. The whole DNS debacle was, for example, a lack of governing statute for the root of the Domain Name System.... When you have something as fundamental as that, then you have to really make sure that the government's for the people, by the people. And I hope that whatever comes out of this ICANN system eventually will do that. Then it will be very boring again. Because generally, the government's something that has to be very slow, bureaucratic, and boring, because it's not where the action is. That's just the infrastructure.

— Tim Berners-Lee

The promises held out by the Internet to the commercial and consumer communities are at once compelling and confronting – but they are perhaps even more so for governments, at least initially. Should governments intervene or not? Should they try to guide development or to let the market have free reign? Should they try and drive demand and hence uptake, because they believe it to be in the long-term interests of the community? Should they protect the citizenry (or at least, certain elements of the citizenry) from certain content?

Broadly speaking, there are three alternative approaches that governments have adopted as follows:

1. *The 'hands-off' approach.* This is the approach being adopted by US regulators.
2. *The 'supervisory guidelines' approach.* The regulator sets the standards for the industry. This is the more prescriptive approach and it is what the Europeans have been working towards.
3. *The 'due-diligence' approach.* The regulator works with industries on an individual basis, discussing how they set up Internet services to ensure that all risks are considered. This is the approach adopted in much of Asia.

While nearly everyone agrees that the development of the Internet and e-commerce will be led by businesses, with the government playing a minimalist role, it is nonetheless important to recognise that governments have played – and will continue to play – a critical role in developing technology for these activities, *and* that they have an obligation to pursue broad societal goals. Moreover, while many believe that governments should only subsidise basic research into IT technologies, historical experience (over the past three decades) has shown that most of the major IT innovations (e.g., timesharing, networking, routers, workstations, optic fibres, semiconductors (RISC, VLSI), parallel computing), many of which are more applied or developmental in nature, are the result of government-funded research or government programmes. This is also true of e-commerce. The Internet's forerunner (ARPAnet), the World Wide Web (CERN) and the browser (government centre at the University of Illinois), were developed with government support. Government procurement and demonstration projects also played an important part.

Governments have the opportunity to drive adoption rates by taking a progressive stance on e-commerce. They could also realise considerable cost savings through electronic bidding and public procurement, service provision on-line, and electronic tax collection or customs clearance. Savings could be passed on to consumers through lower costs (taxes and fees). In addition, the transparency and accountability of the public sector would improve through broader access to government data, as well as more open public procurement. For example, the International Monetary Fund (IMF) sets data dissemination standards and uses the Internet to publish the economic data sources of countries meeting these standards. This is expected to increase the transparency of public policies and government accountability towards financial markets, along with policy credibility (as errors would be quickly penalised by financial markets).

Social goods, such as government objectives of cultural diversity, and rural and regional development, could also be boosted through low cost and easy access to information on the Internet. When it comes to the mass adoption of IT, devices need to be user-friendly, reliable and cheap. By and large, these are issues which governments cannot influence directly. But governments *can* influence industry standards issues, pricing issues and innovation. Broadly speaking, there are three areas in which government policy will have a strong and pervasive influence on the development of e-commerce: the trade (and industrial development) environment; research and development; and social goals.

Trade and Industrial Policy

As we have seen, e-commerce is not only serving to increase international trade, it is blurring what is international and what is domestic commerce. This is particularly true in electronically-delivered products, many of which are services which have not yet been exposed to significant international trade but have been 'traded' through foreign direct investment or have operated on a global level only for large corporate clients. This change will come as a shock to sectors that have been sheltered by logistical or regulatory barriers. In addition, it will generate pressures to reduce differences in regulatory standards – accreditation, licensing and restrictions on activity – for newly tradable products.

Many e-commerce products benefit from non-rivalry (one person's consumption does not limit or reduce the value of the product to other consumers), network externalities (each additional user of a product increases its value to other users) and increasing returns to scale (unit costs decrease as sales increase). These factors create an environment where producers may seek to engage in practices that permit them to establish themselves as the – or part of the – *de facto* standard. At the same time that governments will want to promote widespread adoption and dissemination, they will have to be careful not to hinder innovation and competition. In the US, for example, the government is being lobbied to shorten the current period of patent protection from 20 years to just five years to promote innovation and competition.

Government-sponsored Research and Development (R&D)

Despite broad agreement that the development of global e-commerce be market-driven and industry-led, both the US and Europe have embarked on ambitious government-sponsored programmes for R&D.[9] These programmes, however, reflect different views about the appropriate size and focus of governmental involvement in R&D. Behind them are obvious desires to bolster the chances of their respective industry players in international competition.

In October 1997, the US government initiated the Next Generation Internet Initiative to fulfil the following three goals:

❑ Connect universities and national laboratories with high-speed networks up to 1,000 times faster than today's Internet.
❑ Promote experimentation with innovative networking technologies.
❑ Demonstrate new applications (see URL: http://www.ngi.gov).

The project was initially funded at US$200 million for the two years 1998–99.

In contrast to this targeted approach, the EU funds multi-year research and development initiatives under a 'framework programme' that covers all areas of research relevant to the European society. The overall budget for the Fifth Framework Programme, spanning 1998-2002, was some US$17 billion, an order of magnitude greater than that of the US programme. Of this amount, about US$4 billion was earmarked for the 'User-Friendly Information Society' programme. This was an initiative composed of four parts as follows:

❑ Systems and services for the citizen; .
❑ New methods of work and electronic commerce.
❑ Multimedia content and tools.
❑ Essential technologies and infrastructures.

---

[9] There is a fundamental philosophical difference about the role of the government in consumer protection. In Europe, governments codify regulations designed to protect consumers. Regulations afford consumers ex-ante legal protection. In the US, consumer protection is handled mostly ex-post, i.e., violations of consumer protection are handled through litigation. Tort law allows individual consumers to sue corporations directly. Compared to Europe where consumer protection is a clear objective of governmental regulation, the US government provides consumer protection by judicial enforcement of contract law. While both assert that the evolution towards e-commerce shall be 'market-driven', each has a different idea of who should be in the driver seat, suppliers or consumers. This tension resurfaces in many areas, from intellectual property to privacy protection.

Social Implications

Although still primarily an economic phenomenon, e-commerce is part of a broader process of social change, characterised by the globalisation of markets, the shift towards an economy based on knowledge and information, and the growing prominence of interconnectedness and ubiquitous access. These major societal transformations will continue far into the foreseeable future. As both a product and manifestation of such transformations, e-commerce is being shaped by, and increasingly will help to shape, the modern society as a whole especially in the areas of education, health and government services. Societal factors will merit attention from a public policy standpoint, both to establish the social conditions that allow e-commerce to reach its full economic potential and to ensure that its benefits are realised by society as a whole.

Access to the physical network will, of course, affect the adoption of e-commerce, particularly among consumers and small- and medium-sized enterprises (SMEs) located outside the urban centres of the developed world. One consistent finding across many countries is that there is a strong positive correlation between the use of IT (PC ownership, access to the Internet) and household income. Governments therefore need to look at ways to promote the development and availability of ITs and access to advanced networks, either by means of conventional telecom policy measures or through other appropriate policy instruments, if they are to raise their national competitiveness and overall economic development.

Internet penetration rates show a similar pattern. As a consequence, households with higher income have more opportunity to benefit from e-commerce than those with lower incomes. While this phenomenon is common to the introduction of most new technologies (e.g., electricity, telephone, TV), it warrants the attention of policy makers since e-commerce could provide access to a market with special properties, such as lower prices, that could particularly benefit the disadvantaged. This fuels concerns about greater inequality due to information 'haves' and 'have nots'.[10]

---

[10] There is reason to believe that the correlation between income levels and Internet usage may weaken as lower-cost and simpler alternatives to the traditional personal computer become available, although work carried out in the US between 1994 and 1997 reveals a widening gap in PC ownership between upper and lower income groups. Governments may wish to consider what policies, if any, might encourage the trend towards lower prices and thus accelerate connectivity.

SUMMARY

- ❏ e–Commerce is global, but laws are largely local. Such multi–jurisdictional paradox necessitates the development of a global regulatory framework for conducting business in the marketspace.
- ❏ There is a multitude of issues that need to be addressed, including the following:
  - • Who and how taxes should be collected for e–commerce transactions?
  - • What laws should be enacted to ensure the privacy of on–line consumers?
  - • How the integrity of on–line transactions should be ensured?
  - • How to safeguard copyrights and intellectual property rights?
  - • How to combat dysfunctional and criminal use of the Internet?
- ❏ Until now, most countries have taken a hands–off approach to legal and regulatory issues. However, the rapid increase in the commercial use of the Internet has prompted governments and international agencies to increasingly take active roles in developing regulatory frameworks and enacting laws in the cyberspace.

REFERENCES

Clausing, J. (1999), "Bill Would Make Cybersquatting a Crime", *Capital Dispatch*, URL: http://www.nytimes.com/, July.

Clausing, J. (1998), "Boy's Web Site Becomes a Domain Name Cause", *Capital Dispatch*, URL: http://www.nytimes.com/, July 1999.

Ebing, L.K. & Kreider, K.E. (1998), "Dilution Is Remedy for Internet Mark Misuse", *The National Law Journal*, URL: http://www.law.com/, July 1999.

Elgison, M.J. & Jordan, J.M., III (1997), "Trademark Cases Arise from Meta–Tags, Frames", *National Law Journal*, URL: http://www.law.com/, July 1999.

Evans, P. & Wurster, T.S. (2000), *Blown to Bits: How the New Economics of Information Transforms Strategy*, Boston, MA: Harvard Business School Press.

Goldsmith, J. (1998), "What Internet Gambling Legislation Teaches About Internet Regulation", *International Lawyer*, Vol. 1115.

Hagel, J., III & Rayport, J.F. (1997), "The New Infomediaries", *The McKinsey Quarterly*, No. 4, pp. 54–70.

ICANN (2000), URL: http://www.icann.org/general/fact-sheet.html, 18 August.

Kalakota, R. & Whinston, A.B. (1997), *Electronic Commerce: A Manager's Guide*, Reading, MA: Addison-Wesley.

Kaplan, C.S. (1999), "Court Lays Down the Law on Labels for Web Sites", *Cyber Law Journal*, URL: http://www.nytimes.com/, July.

Kobrin, S.J. (1998), "You Can't Declare Cyberspace National Territory", in Tapscott, D., Lowry, A., Ticoll, D., & Klym, N. (eds), *Blueprint to the Digital Economy: Creating Wealth in the Era of e-Business*, New York, NY: McGraw-Hill, pp. 355–370.

Legal and Policy Framework for Global Electronic Commerce: A Progress Report (1999), URL: http://www.sims.berkeley.edu/BCLT/ecom/, September.

Lewell, J. (1999), "UK Internet Betting Company Launches in USA", 7 July, URL: http://www.internetnews.com/intl-news/article/0,,6_157331,00.html, 14 November 2000.

Lynch, D.C. & Rose, M.T. (eds) (1993), *Internet System Handbook*, Reading, MA: Addison-Wesley.

Madoff, E. (1997), "Freedom to Link Under Attack: Web Community Up in Arms over Lawsuits", *The New York Law Journal*, URL: http://www.law.com/, July 1999.

McCullagh, D. (1999), "Anti-Porn Law Under Fire", *Wired News*, URL: http://www.wired.com/news, September.

Messmer, E. (2000), "Patently Unfair?" *Network World*, Vol. 17, Iss. 27, 3 July, pp. 1, 68.

Morris, J. (2000), "The Next Threat to Dot-Coms", *The Asian Wall Street Journal*, 17 August, p. 6.

Nichols, P. (1998), "The Growth of Internet Duty-Free Betting Is Hitting Revenue Where It Hurts", *The Guardian*, 24 October, p. 11.

Oakes, C. (1999), "A European's Net View of US", *Wired News*, URL: http://www.wired.com/news, September.

OECD Observer (1999), No. 208, URL: http://www.oecd.org, June 2000.

O'Rourke, M.A. (1999), "Legal Issues on the Internet", URL: http://www.dlib.org/dlib/april98/04orourke.html, July.

Porter, M.E. (1985), *Competitive Advantage: Creating and Sustaining Superior Performance*, New York, NY: Free Press.

Rector, S.D. & Fease, K.R. (1999), "Dispute Over Domain Names, Metatags; Web-based Product Sales After Brookfield Communications", *The Corporate Counselor*, Vol. 13, No. 12, p. 1, URL: http://www.lexis-nexis.com/, July.

Reuters (1999), "Britain Adds Up Net Tax Losses", *Wired News*, URL: http://www.wired.com/news, September.

Rosenberg, S. (1999), "Who Owns the *New York Times* Bestseller List?" 23 June, URL: http://www.salon.com/, August 2000.

Siebel, T.M. & House, P. (1999), *Cyber Rules: Strategies for Excelling at e-Business*, New York, NY: Currency/Doubleday.

Sportingbet.com (UK) PLC (1999), "Company Profile for Sportingbet.com (UK) PLC", 20 April, URL: http://www.ofex.co.uk/livedata/codata/sport.htm, 14 November 2000.

Stein, A.R. (1998), "The Unexceptional Problem of Jurisdiction in Cyberspace", *International Lawyer*, Vol. 1167.

Swire, P. (1998), "Of Elephants, Mice and Privacy: International Choice of Law and the Internet", *International Lawyer*, Vol. 1991.

Taggart, S. (1999a), "Aussies Bid Adieu to Web Smut", *Wired News*, 13 January 2000, URL: http://www.wired.com/news/politics/, May 2000.

Taggart, S. (1999b), "Aussie Ethics Code Still Rankles", *Wired News*, 31 August 1999, URL: http://www.wired.com/news/politics/, May 2000.

Tapscott, D., Lowry, A., Ticoll, D., & Klym, N. (1998), *Blueprint to the Digital Economy: Creating Wealth in the Era of e-Business*, New York: McGraw-Hill.

Ticketmaster Corporation v. Microsoft Corporation (No. 97-3055 DDP (C.D. Cal., filed 29/4/97)), URL: http://zeus.bna.com/e-law/docs/ticket.html, July 1999.

Waldmeir, P. (1999), "Global e-Commerce Law Comes Under the Spotlight: International Business Is Clashing with Local and National Law in the Borderless New World", *The Financial Times*, 23 December, p. 9.

World Intellectual Property Organisation (1999), "Intellectual Property", URL: http://www.wipo.org/, July.

World Internetworking Alliance (1999), "Roadmap to the Communities and Parties of the Internet", URL: http://www.wia.org/, August.

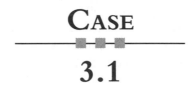

CASE

3.1

Multi-jurisdictional Compliance in Cyberspace*

Business on the Internet, or 'Internet commerce' had grown exponentially in the years following the commercialisation of the Internet in the early 1990s. On the brink of the new millennium, several challenging policy issues had arisen that fell broadly under the umbrella of 'multi-jurisdictional compliance'. These were considered a consequence of the intersection of the global, multipurpose medium of the Internet, with those systems and processes designed for the physical territorial world. Law, by definition, was jurisdictional, yet in cyberspace, it had become increasingly questionable whether laws regulating the physical marketplace could be superimposed onto this new marketspace or were altogether redundant. The collapsing of time and space had huge implications for international trade and raised a host of legal issues, such as: protecting intellectual property rights in copyright and trademarks, taxation on the Internet, privacy and consumer protection, liabilities for the acts of Internet users, and

* Vanessa N. Clark prepared this case in conjunction with P. Lovelock under the supervision of Dr. Ali Farhoomand. The Centre for Asian Business Cases also gratefully acknowledges Lisa Heath, Patent Attorney, of Sit Fung Kwong & Shum, Hong Kong, for her assistance in developing this case. *Copyright © 2000 The University of Hong Kong. Ref. 99/47C*

content and service regulation. In resolving these issues, there was a growing urgency to develop an appropriate infrastructure that would support electronic commerce endeavours. Internet stakeholder groups, such as governmental agencies, industry bodies, administration and standards organisations and professional and public interest groups, needed to urgently address the following question: What international frameworks were necessary to do business electronically?

THE INTERNET ENVIRONMENT

The Internet had its humble – but exciting – beginnings as a network known as ARPAnet, a US government experiment in packet-switched networking, in 1969. ARPA, the US Department of Defense Advanced Research Projects Agency (which later became DARPA, the Defence Advanced Research Projects Agency), initially linked researchers with remote computer centres, allowing them to share hardware and software resources such as computer disk space, databases and computers.[1] The original ARPAnet itself was later split into two networks in the early 1980s: the ARPAnet and Milnet (an unclassified military network). At first this interconnection of experimental and production networks was called the DARPA Internet but later the name was shortened to just 'the Internet'.[2] In the simplest sense, the Internet was a 'network of networks', made up of little local area networks (LANs), citywide metropolitan area networks (MANs) and huge wide area networks (WANs) connecting computers all over the world.[3]

The birth of the National Science Foundation Network (NSF) in the US, in 1986, linked researchers across the country with five supercomputer centres on NSFnet. It soon expanded to connect the mid-level and statewide academic networks that connected universities and research consortiums, and eventually NSFnet began to replace the ARPAnet for research networking. The ARPAnet was later discharged and dismantled in 1990, and since then, the Internet had become the fastest-growing global network so much so that the term 'explosive Internet growth' had become cliché.[4]

---

[1] LaQuey, T. & Ryer, J.C. (1993), *The Internet Companion: A Beginner's Guide to Global Networking*, Reading, MA: Addison-Wesley.

[2] LaQuey, T. & Ryer, J.C. (1993).

[3] LaQuey, T. & Ryer, J.C. (1993).

[4] Lynch, D.C. & Rose, M.T. (eds) (1993), *Internet System Handbook*, Reading, MA: Addison-Wesley.

Factors that contributed to this phenomenon were largely attributed to the decentralised and non-institutionalised nature of the Internet. In addition, while the Internet was largely spawned from US research and funding efforts into ARPAnet, the development of the World Wide Web (the Web) and other pivotal applications were the fruits of international collaborative global efforts. There was no equivalent or competitive other 'network of networks' of the scale of the Internet.

As the diffusion rate of the Internet had grown exponentially, stakeholder interest groups also grew in number. These ranged from governmental agencies such as WIPO and the WTO, industry bodies such as INTA and IITC, administration agencies such as IANA and ICANN, standards organisations such as ISO and W3C, and professional and public interest groups such as ISOC and WIA [see **Exhibits 1** and **2**].

COMMERCIALISATION OF THE INTERNET

The partial commercialisation and global diffusion of the Internet from 1992 to 1996 pushed the Internet to new levels of growth. The Internet merged two powerful methods of communication: information, usually contained in books, and instantaneous communication between people, usually by telephone. By bringing together information and people, the Internet ushered in an electronic, virtual world where time and space had almost no meaning.[5]

Not only was the Internet recognised for facilitating communication, research and education, it rapidly became an international medium for commerce.

Internet Commerce

On the one hand, the Internet demonstrated the potential for businesses to reach consumers. Retailers, publishers and entertainment providers flocked to the Internet and experimented with ways to create applications that would capture the imagination – and money – of users worldwide.[6] On the other hand, the Internet also demonstrated huge capabilities for businesses to transact business with one another, such as using the Internet to quickly find and exchange product and service information or conduct transactions between themselves.

---

[5] Lynch, D.C. & Rose, M.T. (eds) (1993).

[6] Kalakota, R. & Whinston, A. B. (1997), *Electronic Commerce: A Manager's Guide*, Reading, MA: Addison–Wesley, p. 34.

Early Internet commerce practices were to a large degree the equivalent of prevailing business practices and processes, but in an electronic format. For example, Webpage designs were more or less electronic versions of hard copy print-form advertisements, payment systems were still being developed so orders were settled by cheque, money order or facsimile, and customer inquiries were handled by telephoning an appropriate customer hotline.

With software innovations such as e-mail, news groups (or bulletin boards) and the Web, however, Internet commerce revolutionised the way business could be transacted. Competition between businesses to attract Internet traffic and obtain Web visibility meant that the static 'shopfront' displays gave way to interactive multimedia Webpage and Website designs. Secure payment systems and protocols were developed so that payments for products and services could be effected over the Internet and customer enquiries could be dealt with on-line as many businesses included a direct e-mail address for communication with net surfers.

Internet commerce also brought into question the notion of 'international trade'. For example, an import or export was an international or cross-border economic transaction – and such transactions assumed geographic jurisdictions and discrete borders. Yet, the Internet had no physical location and users of the Internet had no control and in general no knowledge of the path travelled by the product or information they sought or published. At issue was the idea of finite goods crossing a discrete and effective national (jurisdictional) border.[7] The ramification for governments was that if they were not in a position to control, or even track and measure, critical cross-border flows, the idea of a domestic economy or national market would lose all meaning. It would therefore become impossible to talk about international or cross-border trade and investment.

The explosion of Internet commerce was quite phenomenal. Since the early to mid-1990s, Internet growth statistics were very impressive, as were the projections associated with wealth creation and revenue generation afforded by this global multi-purpose medium. By 1999, the Internet and the Web had impacted upon and penetrated almost every industry and business in some manner or form. It had become increasingly obvious that Internet commerce heralded a new way of doing business. It

---

[7] Kobrin, S.J. (1998), "You Can't Declare Cyberspace National Territory", in Tapscott, D., Lowry, A., Ticoll, D., & Klym, N. (eds), *Blueprint to the Digital Economy: Creating Wealth in the Era of e-Business*, New York: McGraw-Hill, pp. 355–370.

was not a mere translation of 'business as usual, but using an electronic format'. Internet commerce brought about a need to reconceptualise and redefine markets.

Reconceptualising and Redefining Markets

In the 1990s, the Internet and the Web fostered the diffusion of electronic commerce. The global seamless nature of the Internet and the Web had the effect of collapsing time and space, meaning that business could be carried out irrespective of national boundaries, physical borders or time zones. This 'cyberspace', as a new virtual marketspace, was distinct from the 'traditional' physical marketplace, which had prevailed throughout the industrial revolution.

In the 'traditional' physical marketplace, business activities could be separated into discrete activities along the value-chain and arranged by function according to primary, secondary and support activities.[8] In contrast to the global multipurpose medium of the Internet, there was no such demarcation between business activities in the 'marketspace' or 'cyberspace'. Instead, business activities were becoming more and more blurred and quite often with many activities undertaken simultaneously. For example, to purchase a garment on-line, the consumer could locate the appropriate Website, such as www.gap.com, scroll through the different menus to select an item, order it and provide payment and delivery details all within a matter of minutes. This was in contrast to physically frequenting the store and making the purchase that might take anywhere from 30 minutes to a few hours.

Start-up costs in the marketplace and cyberspace also differed. Whereas the marketplace was characterised by requirements for capital investment, usually associated with office rental and human resource costs, Internet visibility could be obtained in cyberspace with access to an operating system, appropriate peripheral hardware and software. Once on-line, the opportunities for businesses and individuals to reach out to the world via cyberspace were endless.

In addition to the myriad of opportunities where the maxim 'anything goes' held true to a large extent, Internet commerce also presented many challenges. In particular, 'multi-jurisdictional compliance' had become a problem, and it was not clear if the laws used to regulate the physical marketplace still applied, or were appropriate for use in cyberspace.

---

[8] Porter, M.E. (1985), *Competitive Advantage: Creating and Sustaining Superior Performance*, New York: Free Press.

Case Example: 'McMadness' Hong Kong Style

A series of manias had swept through Hong Kong in recent years. These ranged from queuing for stamps and souvenir MTR tickets, redeeming cake or video rental coupons, to queuing for new apartments and shares in red chips. The year 1998 was no different, as the fast-food giant McDonald's Corporation (McDonald's) launched several marketing campaigns involving collectible toys.

McWinnie-the-Pooh

This promotion was scheduled to run for a five-week period in June 1998. The five 'McWinnie-the-Pooh' characters of Pooh Bear, Tiger, Pooh in Scout uniform, Eeyore and Pooh in pyjamas were priced at $18 each and available with any McDonald's purchase.[9] The campaign drew such an overwhelming response, however, with sales of one million toys in the first week alone, that the Corporation pulled television advertisements because they could not meet the demand. "People are just going crazy" is how a McDonald's spokeswoman described the queues of parents who refused to leave restaurants until managers opened new boxes of the toys, earmarked for sale later in the promotion.[10] From the sales, approximately $2.5 million dollars was to be donated to the Ronald McDonald charity house in Shatin (in Hong Kong's New Territories).

McSnoopy

The 'McSnoopy' campaign attracted an even larger following and was described by some as reaching manic proportions. 'McSnoopy' was launched on 11 September 1998 and ran for 28 days. On each day, a different 'McSnoopy' character was released at a cost of $6 with the purchase of McDonald's $17.80 Big Value Meal. The promotion was so popular that 'McSnoopy' became a social phenomenon as Hong Kong's fascination with collectible items captured world attention. Sales during the promotion were reported to be in the vicinity of $48 million, with more than 2 million 'McSnoopy' toys sold each day. This campaign was not without critics however, as hour-long queues reportedly fuelled at least two violent rows over queue jumping.[11] Health watchdogs also complained that the requirement to purchase the Big Value Meal exacerbated Hong Kong's already

---

[9] US$1 = HK$7.75

[10] Mathewson, R. (1998), "McDonald's Besieged in Winnie the Pooh Hunt", *South China Morning Post*, 19 June.

[11] Pegg, J. (1999), "McKitty Mania on the Way", *South China Morning Post*, 17 June.

poor diet among the young. Speculators were not left out in the cold either, and sales of entire 'McSnoopy' sets were soon available on the black market, as were imitations of the famous beagle. One enterprising company even went so far as to send staff to Taiwan and Thailand (where the 'McSnoopy' promotion was held earlier) in order to purchase the characters. Once available in Hong Kong, entire collections fetched $1,200 – a 700 percent mark-up on the retail price.

McKitty

'McMania' descended on Hong Kong once again, in June 1999, with the five-week McKitty promotion. Five different pairs of Sanrio's 'Hello Kitty' and her boyfriend 'Dear Daniel' were released each week at a cost of $18 each with any purchase over $15. The toy's outfits changed week by week from school uniforms to traditional Chinese dress, wedding garb, McDonald's uniforms and beachwear.[12] Round-the-block queues returned as local 'Hello Kitty' fans have led multi-billion dollar sales for Sanrio, the manufacturer of more than 15,000 'Hello Kitty' products.

Ronald's Auction House Goes On-line

Ronald Mak had long recognised the fascination Hong Kong people had with collectible items and cuddly soft toys. He himself was an eager collector of McDonald's paraphernalia and other collectible items, although many of his collections were incomplete and of personal value only. After the success of Hong Kong's 'McWinnie-the-Pooh' and 'McSnoopy' campaigns, Mak was well aware that completed sets could fetch considerable prices on the local market. It was difficult however, for hobbyists such as Mak to complete their collections, as there was no channel through which to trade or exchange items. He considered several different ways by which he could complete his own sets, which would give him an opportunity to on-sell them at a future date and perhaps for a high price. The result of his deliberations was the development of a trading Website, 'Ronald's Auction House'. At this site, Web surfers could buy, sell, exchange or auction pieces of their collections, entire sets or just discuss collection strategies and techniques on-line.

The first thing Mak did was to register the domain name 'ronaldsauctionhouse.com' on-line before approaching a Webmaster to develop

---

[12] Pegg, J. (1999).

the contents of the site.[13] On arriving at the Website, netizens were welcomed to 'Ronald's Auction House', showing 'RONALD MCDONALD' in a collage of the McDonald's colours of gold, red and white [see **Exhibit 3**]. It also showed McDonald's 'GOLDEN ARCHES logo' and contained pictures of the different collectible items Mak himself collected. These included the 'McKitty', 'McSnoopy', 'McWinnie-the-Pooh' and 'McLion-King' characters from Asia-wide promotions. Hyperlinks on the homepage provided a series of options for Web surfers to view the rest of the site, go directly to the trading pages or go to McDonald's homepage at www.mcdonalds.com by simply clicking on the 'GOLDEN ARCHES logo'. Mak was quite thorough in his approach and also asked the Webmaster to include 'MCDONALD'S' and 'RONALD MCDONALD' as metatags in the design of the homepage to increase Mak's visibility on the Internet and increase the strike rate or the number of hits to Ronald's Auction House. In the month that the Webpage was loaded on the Internet, Mak was quite surprised at the number of hits or Web traffic that frequented the site. He was also quite pleased that he had been able to complete his entire 'McSnoopy' set while helping other fans and collectors complete their own.

Big Brother's Watching: McDonald's Invisible Hand

McDonald's was an international company that had enjoyed phenomenal success both in its home country, the USA, and around the world. In fact, it was often claimed that 'MCDONALD'S' was the world's most powerful brand.[14]

The McDonald's phenomenon
Since the humble beginnings of the McDonald's empire in Des Plaines, Illinois, USA, in 1955, the popularity of the 'Big Mac' burger and the McDonald's concept had expanded exponentially. Some 44 years later, the Corporation operated more than 24,500 McDonald's restaurants in 116 countries on six continents.[15]

---

[13] 'Webmaster' was the name commonly used to refer to the person(s) who designed the Webpage(s). It was also used to refer to the person(s) who managed the Website and in some instances was a reference to the organisation responsible for domain name registration. In this case, Webmaster is used to refer to the person who designed the Webpage.

[14] McDonald's (1999), "McDonald's Reports Global Results", URL: http://www.mcdonalds.com/whatsnew/pressrelease072098.html, July.

[15] McDonald's (1999), "25 Fascinating Facts About McDonald's International", URL: http://www.mcdonalds.com/surftheworld/facts/facts.html, July.

Since international expansion began in 1967, well over 100 billion hamburgers had been sold, and more than 3.1 million kilograms of French fries were prepared every day to meet customer demand worldwide.[16] McDonald's served more than 40 million people per day, which represented nearly 15 million people annually.[17]

McDonald's had continued to post strong global results, and 1998 was no different. As at 31 December, 1998, systemwide sales increased from US$33,638.3 million in 1997 to US$35,979.5 million in 1998, an increase of seven percent. Similarly, total revenues increased by nine percent to US$12,421.4 million in 1998, up from US$11,408.8 million in 1997. Regional results were also strong, although the effects of the Asian economic crisis were mirrored in the one percent decline in Asia–Pacific results of US$5,579.4 million, down from US$5,616.0 million.[18]

The first 'golden arches' were opened in Hong Kong in January 1975. Even though that particular outlet had since closed its doors, by 1999, there were 158 restaurants in operation, or approximately one McDonald's restaurant for every 43,000 inhabitants.[19]

Value for 'McDonald's'

As one of the most valuable brands in the world, the power of the 'MCDONALD'S' brand was illustrated by the fact that while the Corporation had about half of the globally branded quick service restaurants outside the USA, it received almost two-thirds of the visits.[20] It was also undisputed that McDonald's

---

[16] McDonald's (1999).

[17] McDonald's (1999), "Investor Fact Sheet", URL: http://www.mcdonalds.com/corporate...r/reports/factsheet/factsheet.html, July.

[18] McDonald's (1999), "Press Release: McDonald's Announces Strong Global Results, 2-for-1 Stock Split Dividend Increase", URL: http//www.mcdonalds.com/whatsnew/...release/Press_Release01261999.html, July.

[19] Figures obtained by telephone from McDonald's Hong Kong Communications Department on 29 July 1999, and based on Hong Kong's population of 6,805,600 as at the end of 1998, Census and Statistics Department, URL: http://www.info.gov.hk/censtatd/eindex.htm, July 1999.

[20] McDonald's (1999), "Investor Fact Sheet", URL: http://www.mcdonalds.com/corporate...r/reports/factsheet/factsheet.html, July.

menu and many of the characters used in McDonald's promotions and market-ing campaigns were household names worldwide. And even though 'BIG MAC', 'QUARTER POUNDER', 'CHICKEN MCNUGGETS' and the 'HAPPY MEAL' had become international icons, McDonald's had on numerous occa-sions catered to local tastes. For example, 'red bean' sundae topping and 'curry and corn' hot pies were at one time available in Hong Kong, while in New Zealand the 'Kiwiburger' had become a fixed item on the menu. This meant that the Corporation's intellectual property in the name 'MCDONALDS' and all affiliated trademarks was an invaluable asset.

Protecting ALL that is 'McD'

In recent years, McDonald's had on at least 50 occasions initiated separate pro-ceedings against individuals and companies alleging trademark infringement.[21] Increasingly, McDonald's had to be vigilant in the protection of its trademarks, not only protecting the name 'MCDONALD'S' but the other 100-plus regis-tered trademarks and affiliates [see **Exhibit 4**].

The exponential growth of cyberspace and doing business via the Internet or the Web promised huge marketing opportunities for the Corporation and also provided another means by which it could communicate with its huge customer base. But it also presented new problems for the global giant: principally, how to protect its trademarks in the emerging virtual marketspace where the phrase 'anything goes' was more often the rule rather than the exception. McDonald's already had a network of volunteer informants dotted around the globe who actively reported instances of potential trademark infringement, but cyberspace

---

[21] As recently as 30 June 1999, McDonald's filed suit against rival Burger King Corp. over Burger King's use of the phrase "Burger King Big Kids Meal" which McDonald's claimed it already had rights to (see "McDonald's Sues Burger King", *Cnnfn*, URL: http://cnnfn.com/1999/07/07/news/mcdonalds, July 1999). Other suits have involved use of the name 'MCDONALD'S', 'BIG MAC' and the 'GOLDEN ARCH' device (see *McDonald's Corp. v. Joburgers Drive-Inn Restaurant (Pty) Limited and The Registrar of Trademarks*, unreported judge-ment on Grosskopf, J.A. in the Appellate Division of the Supreme Court of South Africa, case no. 547/95, dated 27 August 1996), the use of a stylised 'M', reference to 'fast-food justice' and confusion of the 'MCCLAIM' mark with 'MCDONALD'S' (see *McDonald's Corp. v. McClain*, 37 U.S.P.Q.2d 1274 (T.T.A.B. released 8 November 1995)), reference to 'MCSLEEP INN' in *Quality Inns v. McDonald's*, 695 F. Supp. 198 (D. Md. 1988) and use of 'MCDENTAL' in reference to the trading name by a group of dentists (see *McDonald's Corp. v. Druck*, No. 90-960, 26 February 1993).

was another matter altogether! McDonald's legal experts were somewhat perplexed. Who or what company could reasonably expect to 'police' the burgeoning cyberspace? Additionally, Internet law or 'cyberlaw' was still in its infancy and the institutionalisation of regulatory standards or guidelines from ICANN and WIPO still seemed a long way off.

When the first complaints relating to trademark infringement, unfair competition and dilution of trademarks began to be filed in Courts around the world, McDonald's legal experts watched with great interest. These actions covered a wide spectrum of issues such as 'cybersquatting' or 'domain name piracy' (*Panavision International v. Toeppen*, CV 96-2384 DPP (US Supreme Court),[22] and *Marks and Spencer v. One in a Million Limited*, [1998] FSR 265),[23] trademark infringement through the use of trademarks on Websites and in hyperlinks (such as *Ticketmaster Corp. v. Microsoft Corp.*, No. 97-3055 DDP (C.D. Cal., 12 April 1997)[24] and *Shetland Times Ltd. v. Wills*, Scot-Sess-Case, (24/10/96) 1 EIPLR 723 (1/11/96))[25] and the use of trademarks as metatags (such as *Playboy Enterprises Inc. v. Calvin Designer Label*, 985 F. Supp. 1218 (N. D. Cal. 1997)[26] and *Brookfield Communications Inc. v. West Coast Entertainment Corp.*, No. 98-56918 (9th Cir. 1999).[27]

The entire McDonald's empire was at risk if its hallowed trademarks became generic like Xerox, Windbreaker, Thermos and Kleenex, as they would no longer be afforded trademark protection.[28]

---

[22] *Panavision Infringement Analysis*, URL: http://cyber.law.harvard.edu/property/domain/panavision.html, July 1999.

[23] *Marks and Spencer v. One in a Million Limited and Others*, URL: http://www.nominet.org.uk/news/oiam-judgment.html, July 1999.

[24] *EPLR: Ticketmaster Corp. v. Microsoft Corp.*, URL: http://zeus.bna.com/e-law/docs/ticket.html, July 1999.

[25] *Shetland Times v. Wills*, URL: http://elj.warwick.ac.uk/elj/jilt/news/4weblink/default.htm, July 1999.

[26] *Brookfield Communications Inc. v. West Coast Entertainment Corp.*, URL: http://www.patents.com/ac/playcpt.sht, July 1999.

[27] Rector, S.D. & Fease, K.R. (1999), "Dispute Over Domain Names, Metatags; Web-based Product Sales After Brookfield Communications", *The Corporate Counselor*, Vol. 13, No. 12, p. 1, URL: http://web.lexis-nexis.com/, July.

[28] Rubenstein, B. (1994), "Knockoffs Are Generic for McDonald's General Counsel", *Corporate Legal Times*, URL: http://web.lexis-nexis.com/, July 1999.

The Case for McDonald's vs. Ronald's Auction House

One of McDonald's full-time Web investigators had just located and visited Ronald's Auction House Website and a 'cease and desist' letter had been promptly sent to Mr. Mak as the registered owner of the Website at www.ronaldsauction house.com. It called for him to remove the site from the Web immediately. Mak did not think there was anything wrong with his actions so he considered defending his Website. What should he do? On what basis could he develop an adequate defence?

Faced with the prospect that a myriad of potentially infringing activities could become commonplace in cyberspace, the Corporation had to decide how best to protect its trademarks. Were court proceedings alone the only avenue for relief? Was this sufficient given what was at stake? What else could McDonald's do?

'Multi-jurisdictional Compliance' Issues

The nature of cyberspace itself hinders the traditional development of law simply because it moves so fast; the technology has a tendency to overtake the legal issues.[29]

In the Internet environment, it was impossible to separate domestic and international issues relating to Internet commerce. But in the absence of new Internet-specific laws, the safest assumption and practice for many businesses was that the 'same old rules' that applied in the 'traditional' physical business world applied to the Internet. Although it was not possible to apply all traditional business rules to the Internet, their underlying principles were generally applicable, so that the long-standing laws that protected businesses from trademark violation and copyright infringement, for example, still had to be respected.[30]

---

[29] Handler, C.E. & Guthery, C.A. (1998), "Cyberspace Licensing: Linking, Framing, and Caching", *Cyberspace Law*, December, in Breams, C.C.M. (1999), "The Copyright Dilemma Involving On-line Service Providers: Problem Solved … for Now", *Federal Communications Law Journal*, Vol. 51, p. 846.

[30] Burrington, W., Esq. & Lavergne, E. (1999), "The Internet and the Law: Putting Your Business On-line, Not on the Line", in Ford, C.H., Muscarella, L., & Schultz, R., *Net Success*, Holbrook, MA: Adams Media Corporation, p. 147.

Given this, Internet commerce brought about several issues related to 'multi-jurisdictional compliance' in terms of the protection of intellectual property rights, taxation on the Internet, privacy and consumer protection, legal liabilities for the acts of users, and content and service regulation.

Intellectual property protection ■ Intellectual property rights in copyright, trademarks and patents were governed by the laws of nations and sovereign states, which implied jurisdiction over a physical territory. While several international treaties applied to member countries and states, by and large, intellectual property laws were domestic in nature, meaning that the laws of a state were valid only within that country. As Internet commerce had moved so quickly, it challenged this very premise and questioned whether domestic laws could be applied to the international marketspace or not. The first reaction of scholars and lawmakers upon the growth of the Internet was, in essence, to do nothing. The lagging development of new laws or 'cyberlaw' for cyberspace exacerbated the problem further, and the inability to keep pace with technological developments invariably led to uncertainty and in some instances conflict.

For example, in the area of copyright protection, with the prominence and exponential growth of the Web and the increasing ease of uploading and downloading text, graphics and software, copyright law had found itself behind the technological times.[31] But just because something was easy to do did not always necessarily mean it was legal.[32]

Protecting trademark interests on the Internet presented another dilemma. Trademarks were inextricably linked with domain names, the mechanism for identifying Internet addresses and served a dual purpose: they helped brand products and delivered potential customers to Websites.[33] But the global reach of the Internet also led to new conflicts in the trademark arena. As with copyright laws, trademark laws were regional in nature, and traditional regions did not exist on the Internet, thus presenting jurisdictional problems highlighted by the use of trademarks on Websites and in hyperlinks, cybersquatting, framing, 'word stuffing' and linking.

❑ 'Cybersquatting' or domain name squatting involved the registration of famous brands or trademark names by savvy Internet speculators, who then of-

---

[31] Breams, C.C.M. (1999), "The Copyright Dilemma Involving On-line Service Providers: Problem Solved … for Now", *Federal Communications Law Journal*, Vol. 51, pp. 823–847.

[32] Burrington, W., Esq. & Lavergne, E. (1999), p. 152.

[33] Burrington, W., Esq. & Lavergne, E. (1999), p. 147.

fered to sell the names to the companies and individuals concerned, usually for large sums of money.

❏ 'Framing' occurred when a Website became part of a larger 'metasite' that aggregated links and information from other sites. Metasites functioned as large, centralised information repositories that made it easier and faster to use the Internet.

❏ 'Word stuffing' was the use of invisible trademarks to lure users to their sites. Also known as the use of 'metatags', it involved embedding another company's popular brand name into a Website.

❏ 'Linking' was easy to do on the Internet and could increase the usefulness of a site and provide access to additional content at no extra cost. For example, if a Website linked to a company's site without permission, that company may not appreciate the association of their site with the other.

Clearly, intellectual property laws needed to change to better balance two viable policies: it needed to adjust so as to facilitate the growth of the Internet as an economic and communications tool, while at the same time not diminish the incentive to create new works or innovation in developing new products.

Taxation of the Internet ■ The potential size of the on-line marketspace (estimated to be worth more than US$300 billion of B2B commerce by the year 2002) made it an attractive target for generating tax revenues.[34] But it also raised other concerns. The lack of borders on the Internet meant that it was difficult to determine which, if any, jurisdictions could tax a business. There were also concerns that the Internet could provide avenues to avoid certain kinds of taxes. How could governments collect taxes for transactions concluded over the global and seamless Internet? For example, by the year 2001, Internet shopping in Britain was expected to cost the government up to £10 billion (US$15.89 billion) a year in lost taxes.[35, 36] Here, the problem was associated with the idea of finite goods crossing jurisdictional borders. How and at what point could taxes be collected for goods downloaded online? In Britain, value-added tax (VAT) payments from music and software bought and downloaded from the Web were expected to evade the taxman, and even larger tax losses were predicted across a huge range of products. Tax authorities would continue

---

[34] Burrington, W., Esq. & Lavergne, E. (1999), p. 161.

[35] UK£1 = HK$12.47

[36] Reuters (1999), "Britain Adds Up Net Tax Losses", *Wired News*, URL: http://www.wired.com/news, September.

to lose out where businesses were buying on-line as they were more experienced than the average private shopper and could account for their own VAT.[37] To counter this problem, different Internet watchdog groups had proposed imposing an Internet or electronic commerce tax. However, this position was not entirely satisfactory either. The Internet was still in its infancy and the imposition of new taxes on Internet-based businesses could derail an otherwise robust economic engine.

Privacy and consumer protection ∎ The on-line medium provided extraordinary opportunities for businesses to learn about their customers – what they liked, what they disliked, how they shopped and how they gathered information. In addition, the Internet and the Web provided opportunities for businesses to target messages to a large number of people while tailoring the message to individual demographics and interests. But from these information-gathering activities, privacy became a very sensitive concern, and included issues such as 'spamming' and publishing. Consumer protection issues were particularly concerned with the well-being of children in the Internet environment.

Privacy. Studies showed that privacy was the number one concern of Internet users, and also the top reason why non-users were still avoiding the Internet.[38] As with intellectual property protection and taxation, privacy and consumer protection laws were country-specific. Countries invariably adopted different approaches. On the Internet, protecting the privacy of users (whether corporate or individual), information and consumers was problematic due to the inability of a singular government or other domestic agency to regulate or police the (international) Internet. For example, the European Directive on Data Protection forbade companies from transferring personal consumer data to countries that did not share the region's privacy regulations.[39] US businesses hoping to sell to overseas customers needed to keep abreast of how online privacy laws and regulations were developing in Europe and in other parts of the world. Foreign countries often had laws and customs that protected individual privacy much more rigorously than was the case in the US.

In response to growing privacy concerns, several major Internet companies and industry trade groups, working under the aegis of the On-line Privacy Alliance, called

---

[37] Reuters (1999).

[38] Center for Democracy and Technology (1999), "CDT's Guide to On-line Privacy", URL: http://www.cdt.org/privacy/guide/, September.

[39] Oakes, C. (1999), "A European's Net View of US", *Wired News*, URL: http://www.wired.com/news, September.

for Websites to display seals to help explain their policies for the collection, use and disclosure of personal information that had been gathered on-line. As a form of industry self-regulation, there was, however, no strict requirement for companies to do so.

Spamming was the sending of unsolicited e-mail that was commercial in nature. It was evolving rapidly and presented many concerns for businesses interested in marketing. Identified as a high-growth area, the volume of unsolicited e-mail in many cases pushed useless or even fraudulent products and threatened to undermine the value of e-mail as a marketing vehicle. As spamming was capable of generating a high number of user complaints, many Internet Service Providers had employed filtering software to block spam e-mail. At another level, complaints of spamming had reached the courts (especially in the US), and typically involved the breach of contract, fraud, misrepresentation and trespass.

Publishing. One of the attractions of the Internet was the ability to publish information to a global audience at a relatively low cost. But the ease with which information could be posted and redistributed also increased the risk of claims of libel, defamation, obscenity and indecency.[40] For example, liability for defamation on the Internet had so far turned on whether one 'published' or merely 'distributed' material.[41]

Consumer protection. Companies that operated certain types of business had to consider additional industry-specific laws when they operated on the Internet, such as the concerns over children's access to on-line pornography and other inappropriate materials. Parents and educators also had concerns about the difficulty of monitoring children's on-line experiences. This prompted the development of filtering software which however had not greatly improved the situation. Industry self-regulation seemed to be a key factor in protecting children's privacy and safety, but in the absence of adherence to mandatory policies, it was more likely that parents and third-party groups (such as the US-based Recreational Software Advisory Council) would take a leading developmental role.

Legal liabilities for acts of users ■ Interoperability and interconnectivity were considered to be two of the main reasons for the huge success of the Internet. Yet these same factors also opened the Internet to large-scale abuse. As well as attracting legitimate commercial, non-profit and private endeavours, the Internet also attracted a whole range of people with less than desirable aspirations. Legal liabilities for acts of users

---

[40] Burrington, W., Esq. & Lavergne, E. (1999), p. 155.
[41] Burrington, W., Esq. & Lavergne, E. (1999), p. 155.

were not confined to the acts of technologically savvy computer hackers and virus authors or porn advocates and racist or fascist organisations and individuals only, but could also emerge from legitimate uses, such as liabilities for non-performance and breach of Internet contracts. In particular, electronic sweepstakes and on-line gambling presented unique problems.

Electronic sweepstakes were considered to be a valuable marketing device for Internet businesses as they enabled them to build audiences, capture information about their visitors and retain their visitors' loyalty. However, the question of whether or not it was legal, was not entirely clear. For example, in the US, even if a sweepstake was legal where the business was physically based, the Website could well violate other State, national or foreign laws when it was made available to others around the globe.[42] If a game was offered to users on the Internet, no matter where they lived, then potentially the game was subject to the laws of every jurisdiction in which the game was available. The issue could be reduced to the payment of 'consideration' for a chance to win a prize, as it was not clear what actually amounted to 'consideration'. In the Internet age, did purchasing a computer or paying Internet access fees constitute 'consideration'?

On-line gambling was considered to be even more problematic because gambling was more heavily regulated than sweepstakes. The crux of the gambling issue was that it was difficult to determine where an on-line bet actually took place.[43] Was it the state or country in which the bettor's computer was located, where the Internet Service Provider was located, or where the servers used by the Website were located? Was it in the foreign country where the bet was placed or all of these places? Obviously the issue was a difficult and controversial one.

Content and service regulation ■ Content restrictions created one of the most daunting legal considerations for companies doing business on the Internet. During the early 1990s and the first wave of commercialisation of the Internet, there were virtually no restrictions as to the type of content that could be posted on the Web. On-line gambling or pornographic Websites were readily accessible by all net surfers, be they children or adults. In recent times, however, there were calls to promulgate some form of content restriction. For example, in the US, the controversial Child On-line Protection Act (COPA) was to address the dire situation of tens of thousands of por-

---

[42] Burrington, W., Esq. & Lavergne, E. (1999), p. 161.

[43] Burrington, W., Esq. & Lavergne, E. (1999), p. 163.

nographic Websites that both adults and children could easily visit.[44] COPA made it a crime to publish "any communication for commercial purposes that included any material that was harmful to minors, without restricting access to such material by minors" and was punishable by six months in jail or fines of US$50,000.[45] But a Philadelphia Court decision ruled the Act unconstitutional for it violated the First Amendment's guarantees of free speech. At issue was the fact that 'there was no practicable means by which the vast majority of those who provided content over the Internet – whether profit-motivated or otherwise – could screen out minors from accessing that content, while not unduly burdening adults' access to their speech'.[46]

In a similar vein, standards or policies regulating services offered on the Internet were slow in developing. Users were not guaranteed minimum levels of service in cyberspace, whereas they were in their dealings in the physical marketplace. In the absence of such regulations, trust became one of the single most important factors when transacting on-line.

The Internet had grown at such a phenomenal rate that while Internet commerce applications flourished, there was no corresponding development of an electronic commerce infrastructure that would support developments in the new virtual marketspace of cyberspace and resolve 'multi-jurisdictional compliance' issues that transcended physical (jurisdictional) borders. Given this scenario, such issues invariably fell to governmental organisations, industry bodies, administrative agencies, standards bodies and professional or public interest groups for resolution. It also became necessary for businesses to keep abreast of the laws, not only in the state or country where the business was physically located, but also in countries all around the world.

RESOLVING 'MULTI-JURISDICTIONAL COMPLIANCE' ISSUES

Since the advent of Internet business relationships, courts, businesses and individuals alike had struggled to apply traditional jurisdictional concepts to the non-traditional transactions and business relationships found in the on-line world. That these concepts

---

[44] McCullagh, D. (1999), "Anti-Porn Law Under Fire", *Wired News*, URL: http://www.wired.coms/news, September.

[45] McCullagh, D. (1999).

[46] McCullagh, D. (1999).

were not very easy to understand or to come to grips with was exacerbated particularly when the courts could not agree on an outcome. Such confusion stemmed from the fact that the Internet was unlike other media; it was both interactive and real time. For example, the real-time aspect of the Internet allowed for much faster interaction between contracting parties, and required traditional concepts of law, such as offer and acceptance in contracts, to be rethought and redefined as electronic contracts played out over the Internet.[47]

There was increasing pressure on governmental agencies, industry bodies, administration agencies, standards organisations and professional and public interest groups to come together to form uniform, universal standards that would give businesses and individuals better guidance on what they should and should not do on the Internet [see **Exhibits 1** and **2**]. Given the duality of the Internet, the establishment of an electronic commerce infrastructure was likely to come from within two sectors: governmental organisations and private enterprise.

Governmental Organisations: Think Globally

In 1997, the Clinton Administration entered the global debate with "A Framework for Global Electronic Commerce", which was based on the following five principles:

- ❑ The private sector should lead.
- ❑ Governments should avoid undue restrictions on electronic commerce.
- ❑ Where governmental involvement was needed, its aim should be to support and enforce a predictable, minimalist, consistent and simple legal environment for commerce.
- ❑ Governments should recognise the unique qualities of the Internet.
- ❑ Electronic commerce over the Internet should be facilitated on a global basis.

The framework proposed a strategy through which governments and industries could work together to address the issues surrounding taxation, intellectual property protection, privacy, content restrictions and technical standards, in a way that did not inhibit the growth of the Internet as a vehicle for electronic commerce.

Many governmental agencies such as IETF, ITU and more recently ICANN, had also participated in working towards institutionalising Internet standards, albeit usually from technical and administrative perspectives.

---

[47] Burrington, W., Esq. & Lavergne, E. (1999), p. 164.

There was also the need for universal laws or laws having universal application to be written to take into account the fact that information could be exchanged immediately, in both directions and between parties who usually had no idea where the other person was physically located. But until international standards were established, it was likely that the area of law would change frequently and would vary from state to state (within countries) and from nation to nation.

Private Enterprise: Act Locally

Invariably, companies that had already ventured into the Internet business world had also encountered some of the uncertainties associated with doing business on the Internet. In many instances, such businesses and individuals inadvertently found themselves at the forefront of legal and policy issue development. However, in the absence of any formal framework it looked like the prospects for mining Internet 'gold' were likely to be strongest if the 'old rules' were kept in mind and businesses kept informed as new laws were written in order to be compliant with the ever-changing regulatory landscape.[48]

But how could such an infrastructure be achieved? Could uniformity and, whenever possible, industry-led, market-driven solutions be agreed upon so that all Internet users would be subject to the same universal rules? Should and could the Internet industry self-regulate and build consumer confidence and trust as the new global multipurpose medium continued to evolve. And if so, how?

For Internet watchdogs at a global level, problems brought about by the intersection of the global multipurpose medium of the Internet with systems and processes devised for the physical marketplace raised questions considered critical to the on-going development of the Internet. What international frameworks were necessary to do business electronically? Was such an infrastructure possible? At a micro level, the underlying policy question that emerged from the application of jurisdictional laws to the non-jurisdictional Internet was whether or not a person operating a Website subjected himself or herself to the laws of every state (in the case of the US) and foreign country. Were the approaches taken to date satisfactory?

---

[48] Burrington, W., Esq. & Lavergne, E. (1999).

Exhibit 1: Internet stakeholder groups

GOVERNMENTAL

ITU	International Telecommunication Union
WTO	World Trade Organisation
WIPO	World Intellectual Property Organisation
UNESCO	United Nations Educational Scientific and Cultural Organisation
OECD	Organisation for Economic Cooperation and Development
NTIA	National Telecommunication Infrastructure Administration
EU	European Union
ASEAN	Association of Southeast Asian Nations
APEC	Asia–Pacific Economic Cooperation

INDUSTRY

CIX	Commercial Internet Exchange
ISP Organisations	Internet Service Provider Organisations
AIM	Association for Interactive Media
APNG	Asia–Pacific Networking Group
IEPG	Internet Engineering Planning Group
ARIN	American Registry for Internet Numbers
ILPF	Internet Law and Policy Forum
APIA	Asia & Pacific Internet Association
ISP/C	Internet Service Providers Consortium
TEREINA	Trans-European Research and Education Networking Association
NANOG	North American Network Operators' Group
EMA	Electronic Messaging Association
ITAA	Information Technology Association of America
GIP	Global Internet Project
GIIC	Global Information Infrastructure Commission
CommerceNet	CommerceNet
Corporations	Individual Corporations
TechNet	TechNet
INTA	Internet Trademark Association

Exhibit 1 (cont'd)

IITC	Internet International Trade Council
FARN	Federation of American Research Networks
USCIB	US Council for Internet Business

ADMINISTRATIVE

APNIC	Asia-Pacific Network Information Centre
RIPE NCC	Réseaux IP Européens – Network Coordination Centre
EDNS	Enhanced Domain Name Services
IANA	Internet Assigned Number Authority
ICANN	Internet Corporation for Assigned Names and Numbers
FIRST	Forum of Incident Response and Security Teams
InterNIC	InterNIC Domain Name Registration Service
AlterNIC	AlterNIC Domain Name Registration Service
CERTs	CERT Coordination Centres
RIR	Regional Internet Registry

STANDARDS

IETF	Internet Engineering Task Force
W3C	WWW Consortium
IMC	Internet Mail Consortium
ISC	Internet Software Consortium
ITU-T	International Telecommunication Union – Telecommunication Standardisation Sector
ISO	International Standards Organisation
FSTC	Financial Services Technology Consortium
ICSC	International Computer Security Consortium

PROF./PUBLIC INTERESTS

W3CC	International WWW Conference Committee
ISOC	Internet Society
ACM	Association of Computing Machinery
DNRC	Domain Name Rights Coalition
AUI	Association des Utilisateurs d'Internet

Exhibit 1 (cont'd)

CDT	Centre for Democracy and Technology
EFF	Electronic Frontier Foundation

Source: Adapted from World Internetworking Alliance (1999), "Table of Communities and Parties to the Internet", URL: http://www.wia.org/communities.html, August.

Exhibit 2: Roadmap to the communities and parties of the Internet

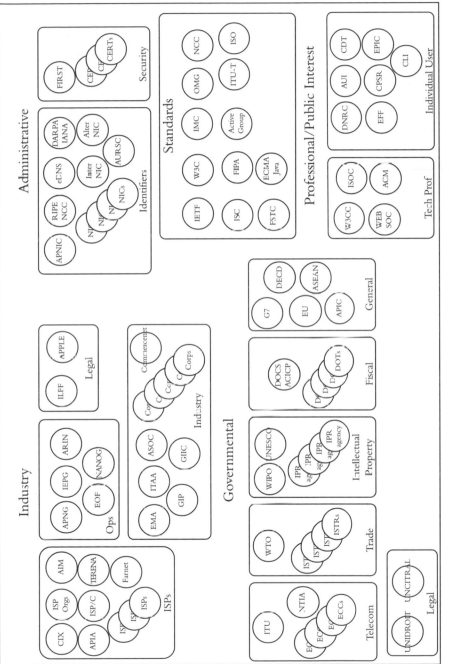

Source: World Internetworking Alliance (1999), URL: http://www.wia.org/, August.

Exhibit 3: Ronald's Auction House Website

Note: This is not an actual Website; developed for illustrative purposes only.

Exhibit 4: McDonald's trademark information

The following trademarks are owned by the McDonald's Corporation and its affiliates: McDonald's, Golden Arches, Golden Arches Logo, Single Arch Logo, McDonald's Building Design, McDonaldland and the McDonaldland character names and designs, I am Hungry character, Filet-O-Fish, Big Mac, Egg McMuffin, McDonald's All American High School Jazz Band, Good Jobs For Good People, Quarter Pounder, Chicken McNuggets, Happy Meal, MacDonald's Racing Team Design, Ronald McDonald House, Ronald McDonald House Charitics, RMHC, HACER, McPrep, Have You Had Your Break Today?, McFamily, You Deserve A Break Today, McDonald's Is Your Kind Of Place, McNuggets, You, You're The One, McDonald's Express, McDonald's Express Logo, Happy Meal Box Design, French Fry Box Design, McDonald's Earth Effort, McDonald's Earth Effort Logo, MCDirect Shares, 1-800-MC1-STCK, McRecycle USA, Hamburger University, Extra Value Meal, The House That Love Built, McGrilled Chicken Classic, Good Times Great Taste, McBurger, McRoyal, Royal, Hamburger Royal, McDonald's All American High School Basketball Team, HU, Great Breaks, What's on Your Plate, McKids, McBaby, AlwaysQuality Always Fun, McMemories, Mac Tonight, Mac Tonight Design, Speedee Logo, Ronald McDonald House Charities Logo, Ronald McDonald House Design, Healthy Growing Up, World Famous Fries, America's Favourite Fries, Alchanset, The House That Love Built Design, McKids Logo, Mac Attack, Bolshoi Mac, Super Size, Lift Kids To A Better Tomorrow, McChicken, Sausage McMuffin, McDonald's Means Opportunity, Immunise for Healthy Lives, McDonald's All Star Racing Team, McRecycle USA, McWorld, Hey, it Could Happen, My McDonald's, My Size Meal, My McDonald's Logo, Did Somebody Say McDonald's?, Did Somebody Say McDonald's? Design, Arch Deluxe, Fish Filet Deluxe, Crispy Chicken Deluxe, Grilled Chicken Deluxe, When the U.S. Wins You Win, Black History Makers Of Tomorrow, McFranchise, McDonald's Means Opportunities, Let's Get Growing America, You, Me and Ecology, McSki, Drive Thru Crew, Get Back With Big Mac, McScholar, Made For You, Chicken McGrill, PlayPlaces, Playlands, A Chance To Advance, McHappyDay, McCafe, and Twoallbeefpattiesspecialsaucelettucecheesepicklesonionsonasesameseedbun. All other trademarks are the property of the respective trademark owners.

Source: "McDonald's Trade Mark Information", *Fine Print: McDonald's Internet Site Terms and Conditions*, URL: http://www.mcdonalds.com/legal/legal.html, July 1999.

MODULE

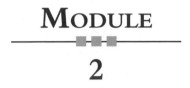

2

Conducting Business in the Marketspace

The horizon leans forward,
Offering you space to place new steps of change.

– Maya Angelou

One of the underpinnings of contemporary management, vertical integration, entails bringing together a wide range of activities involved in different aspects of a business, ranging from sourcing raw materials and production to marketing. In the past, firms reaped the benefits of vertical integration – economies of scale and scope through better control and lower transaction costs – by owning large and efficient facilities. In the new economy, however, firms are able to largely secure these benefits without owning all parts of their value-chain. Through compression of time and space, the Internet allows companies to bring together, in a most cost-effective and speedy manner, different parties involved in the production and marketing of their goods and services. In other words, the Internet allows companies to virtually integrate their business activities by disaggregating and reaggregating various parts of their value-chain to offer cheaper but at the same time more customised services and products to a larger pool of customers. Such reconfiguration of the value-chain is the centrepiece of e-commerce as it entails a fundamental rethinking of how a company defines the tasks it will perform itself and those it will outsource, how it configures its resources, and how it markets its products and services.

Because of the short history of e-commerce and thus limited experience, devising a viable business model has proven to be a sticky issue facing companies trying to conduct business in the marketspace. Many firms have taken a trial-and-error approach in developing viable business models through which they can select their customers, differentiate their products and services, create value for their customers and ultimately capture profits. Some have succeeded, but many have failed.

This module covers two major categories of business models. Chapter 4 examines B2B e-commerce. It first provides a historical overview of electronic data interchange (EDI) development. It then explores the emerging business models for B2B including infomediaries. The first case at the end of the chapter – *iSteelAsia: A B2B Exchange* – explores some of the challenges related to setting up B2B exchanges. The second case – *Dell: Selling Directly, Globally* – examines the problems associated with adopting US-style business models in other parts of the world.

Chapter 5 covers B2C e-commerce. It examines drivers of growth and provides an overview of B2C business models, including those used in banking and entertainment. The chapter concludes with a discussion of future trends in this domain. There are two cases at the end of this chapter. The first case – *Charles Schwab Inc.: Creating an International Marketspace* – looks at the challenges facing the world's largest on-line stock brokerage firm in its global expansion strategy. The second case – *Seven-Eleven Japan: Venturing into e-Tailing* – helps us to understand how traditional retailers can leverage the Internet to simultaneously extend their reach and enhance their bundle of offerings.

CHAPTER

4

Business-to-Business e-Commerce

OBJECTIVES

- To recognise the underlying role that business-to-business (B2B) e-commerce plays in transforming the economy.
- To understand the impact on e-commerce of moving from closed, proprietary systems to open systems.
- To recognise the existing B2B models and appreciate that they are still in evolution.
- To distinguish between different B2B intermediary models.

The impact of e-commerce on the economy extends far beyond the (estimated) dollar value of e-commerce activity. Businesses are using e-commerce to establish and extend competitive advantage by providing more useful information, expanding choice, developing new services, streamlining purchasing processes and lowering costs. e-Commerce is also imposing price discipline as customers gain access to a far broader variety of price and product information via the Internet than they have had before.

What we see is that doing business electronically therefore encompasses the same basic areas as 'traditional' business. Organisations are still exchanging information, marketing their products and services, buying and selling, recruiting new employees, gathering research and providing customer service, but now, to a greater extent, paper-based and face-to-face transactions are being augmented, if not replaced, by electronic means.

Nevertheless, while it is still not possible to use objectively assessable values for the size of the emerging B2B sector, the projections that are being cited by various research organisations are indicative [**Figure 1**].

Figure 1: e–Commerce projections

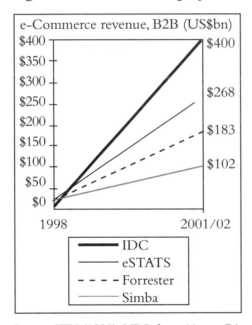 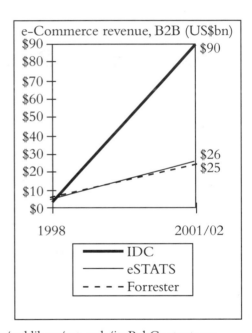

Source: ITU (1999), URL: http://www7.itu.int/publibase/cat_pub/ituPubContents.asp

Although these figures are being reassessed upwards each year (and no doubt will have been further raised by the time you read this), they are worth citing for two reasons: first, because of their absolute size; and second, because of the order of magnitude difference now being attributed to B2B e-commerce over business-to-consumer (B2C) e-commerce. In the first wave of Internet e-commerce most of the attention focused on the high-profile vendor examples, such as amazon.com, CDNow or eBay. Even when attention began focusing on the B2B realm, it was on prominent, well-established firms, such as Cisco and Dell that eliminated the 'old-economy' middlemen and sold directly to business consumers. But the real power of B2B e-commerce is taking place on a much broader scale.

Similarly, much has been written about the opportunity to gather customer data through B2C electronic networks, and thereby not only improve customer service but also begin to 'lock in' particular segments by offering them more finely targeted products and services (see Chapter 5: Business-to-Consumer e-Commerce). Much less has been said, however, about the power of networks to destabilise relationships between vendors and suppliers in B2B markets. Access to a fuller range of information about product availability and pricing can shift power away from established relationships. And, as with the B2C segment, one of the first results (in many cases) will be reduced price to the vendor.

The way that companies, such as NEC, have decided to open up their proprietary purchasing and materials databases, illustrates the point. NEC has opened its centralised purchasing control network that compares information from buyers in each division to identify the best prices and terms from each supplier.[1] The new system allows input via public networks from an unlimited number of component vendors and public databases, effectively levelling the playing field for NEC's suppliers. What this will mean, over the long term, is that traditional suppliers will no longer be able to rely on their access to buyers in order to remain the source of choice. Furthermore, for component companies that were not part of the original closed network, a whole new set of relationships becomes possible.

Indeed, B2B e-commerce is rapidly transforming from simple buy-side and sell-side solutions to a new world of electronic marketspaces which enable companies to streamline their commercial processes and reduce operational costs by linking multiple buyers and sellers via the Internet. e-Commerce enables organisations not only to exchange business documents and conduct transactions but also to collaborate on product development almost instantaneously, since electronic transactions can take place on a 24-hour, 7-day-a-week basis. As a result, product development or production cycle times can be reduced, thereby allowing companies to bring products to market much sooner than before. Additional benefits include lower purchasing costs, improved supply-chain management, improved service and new market opportunities. A Web presence can ensure improved management controls as a result of embedded business rules in the procurement system. For supply-chain companies, e-commerce technology can implement flow-through logistics that help suppliers keep companies apprised of order and shipment status while speeding the flow of goods to market. Through e-commerce, the demand for goods and services can be electronically linked to just-in-time inventory, thereby reducing inventories and, hence, space requirements.

---

[1] Harrington & Reed (1996).

Then there are the potential cost savings. Traditional electronic data interchange (EDI) has already proven to be a cost-cutting technology, particularly in reducing the overhead costs incurred in requesting or responding to Requests for Quotes (RFQs), generating, delivering, or processing purchase orders, tracking and confirming shipments, generating or processing invoices, and discounting. e-Commerce over the Internet is serving to amplify these savings. Internet access fees are far lower than those of private networks needed for EDI. Suppliers no longer require any type of proprietary interface – simple browsers provide the necessary connectivity. Suppliers can also reduce their costs through their ability to access on-line Requests for Prices (RFPs) and RFQs.

Finally, there are a growing number of electronic marketspaces that serve specific industry communities. These on-line marketspaces provide access to information about products from a variety of vendors, along with objective industry information (industry forms, research papers, newspaper and trade journal reviews, etc.). The rise of these collaborative on-line communities is fuelling the growth of on-line procurement and selling systems, as companies move to get on board with their particular industry site. The integration of on-line auctions to these sites will further increase the attractiveness of such communities.

In this chapter, we look at the evolution of e-commerce in the B2B domain from traditional EDI networks, limited by the closed nature of their proprietary interfaces, to the open systems of Internet EDI. In the following section we examine the emerging business models of B2B e-commerce. The third section looks at perhaps the most powerful sector in the emerging B2B sector – the industry intermediaries, or B2B 'hubs'. Finally, we look at some of the prospects of this transition going forward.

B2B E-COMMERCE: FROM CLOSED TO OPEN SYSTEMS

Traditional EDI

B2B e-commerce actually began in the mid-1960s with EDI inspiring a rash of predictions about the advent of the paperless office. EDI can be defined as 'the electronic transfer of commercial or administrative transactions using *agreed standards* to structure the transaction or message data'.[2] In other words, EDI allows for information in the form of structured content to be exchanged between computer systems. By the 1970s,

---

[2] As defined by the Working Party on Facilitation of International Trade Procedures, a subsidiary body of the United Nations Economic Commission for Europe. Italics added.

EDI allowed businesses to exchange documentation remotely and securely. It was fore-seen – correctly – that this would speed up transaction time and minimise transaction costs.

Through the 1970s and 1980s, large businesses extended their information net-works to reach out to businesses and trading partners so as to be able to electronically send and receive purchase orders, invoices and shipping notifications. In fact, shipping networks in particular, and the transportation industry in general, spearheaded the development of EDI through the transmission of commercial documents. Because the transportation industry requires an enormous amount of paperwork to document and track shipments, and with the same information such as the name and address of the shipper and the consignee, along with details of shipment and routings appearing repeatedly in documents such as invoices, packing lists, shipment advice and bills of lading, the application of EDI technology served to significantly minimise the number of input errors and improve the turnaround time.

However, the problem in the development of EDI was two-fold. First, even with the advent of third-party value-added network (VAN) providers, the closed nature of proprietary EDI systems resulted in a bewildering array of different network architectures, computer systems and clumsy text-based software interfaces, making e-commerce both labour- and capital-intensive. Second, the large number of networks and interfaces meant that all but the largest firms were locked out of early e-commerce technologies by the sheer scale and cost. As a result, some 20 years after its debut, EDI had failed to make significant inroads into all but the largest of multinationals and trading organisations [see **Appendix 1**].

The Emergence of Web-based EDI

Through the late 1990s, however, Web-based EDI began to emerge as the use of the Internet proliferated rapidly among business and individual users around the world. In stark contrast to the proprietary systems required with traditional EDI, Web-based EDI uses the Internet as the vehicle for information exchange, allowing companies that are not specifically EDI-enabled to still be able to exchange documents electroni-cally with those that are EDI-enabled, as well as with other companies that are not.

A company can therefore implement Web-based EDI with available software prod-ucts but *without* the necessity of an outside vendor or VAN operator. Alternatively, the company could subscribe to the services of a third-party operator that provides EDI capabilities over the Internet. Subscribers of such services can access and send EDI documents through a secure Website operated by the provider. Through the Website, a document in EDI format is converted into an HTML file so that the subscriber can view the file with their Web browser. When the subscriber wishes to send EDI documents, he/she creates the document in HTML format on the Website, and the document is then converted into the EDI format by the service provider before being sent on. Some well-known VANs such as GEIS and Harbinger have rolled out such Internet-based EDI products targeted at small- to medium-sized businesses.

Web-based EDI has several obvious advantages over traditional EDI. First, only a low level of technology is required as the ubiquitous presence of the Internet already provides accessibility, and the point-and-click interface of Web browsers makes Web-based EDI easy to use. Second, Web-based EDI is far less expensive to implement and run than traditional EDI. The cost of processing an Internet-based EDI transaction is estimated to be only one-tenth to one-half of that of a VAN-based transaction.[3] This opens EDI transactions to small- and medium-sized enterprises. Large companies that are already EDI-enabled also benefit from the emergence of Web-based EDI because their network of suppliers and customers can be vastly extended.

Obstacles for Web-based EDI

However, despite the advantages offered by Web-based EDI, the rate of adoption has still been relatively slow. This can be largely attributed to business community concerns about security and reliability of data transmission over the Internet.

Since the Internet is an open network – as opposed to the closed networks used in traditional EDI – data can potentially be intercepted and inspected by third parties. Moreover, data transmitted over the Internet may take a circuitous route, resulting in delays or data loss, depending on the volume of Internet traffic at the time of transmission. In other words, Web-based EDI does not enjoy the same level of reliability offered by traditional EDI through point-to-point networks or VANs.

Various data encryption technologies are available to keep information confidential in the open Internet environment. However, no system is foolproof and business users need to know that they will not be liable for loss before they feel comfortable adopting a new business transaction system.

Similar to traditional EDI, Web-based EDI relies on common communication protocols to exchange information. Extensible Markup Language (XML), for example, provides a flexible way to create common information formats on the World Wide

---

[3] See, for example, Knowles (1997).

Web, and Secure Electronic Transaction (SET) can be used to ensure the security of financial transactions over the Internet. However, most of the Web-based transaction standards are still in a formative stage. The lack of an accepted or institutionalised set of standards to guide and secure data transmission is a major deterrent that has so far delayed the adoption of Web-based EDI by the business community at large (see Chapter 3: The Regulatory Framework).

Where old-style EDI VANs were based on proprietary protocols and technologies for store-and-forward mailboxing, e-commerce portals are built on the Internet Protocol (IP) which underlay the Net, thereby allowing the networks to push documents along quickly using the Web's Hyper-text Transfer Protocol (HTTP) or File Transfer Protocol (FTP). Once the widespread adoption of transaction protocols occurs, it will certainly be much easier, and less expensive, for smaller firms to conduct electronic trading over the Internet than was the case with traditional EDI. Not surprisingly then, a number of the traditional VAN providers are jumping on the e-commerce portal bandwagon, hoping to pick up new business or offer a migration path.

EMERGING BUSINESS MODELS FOR B2B

Taxonomies of emerging e-commerce models are beginning to appear (see, for example, Timmers, 1998; Kalakota & Whinston, 1996; Harrington & Reed, 1996; Sawhney & Kaplan, 1999). However, as we noted above in trying to assess the size and the scope of the market, the emerging nature of the market itself makes it difficult to be defined. As a result, existing taxonomies tend to blur the line between B2B e-commerce and B2C e-commerce. However, given that the lines between these two fields *are* still very vague, it would be surprising if this were not the case.

As you will see in the following chapter, many of the advantages which accrue to B2B e-commerce 'plays' result from the same drivers as in B2C e-commerce, such as the removal of time and distance constraints. Equally, e-commerce is allowing businesses to increase the services that they offer to clients, thereby expanding the business relationship and providing more opportunity for 'lock-in' – as has been the case in the e-tail B2C sector. However, there are also significant differences. Technology is helping to create new relationships and to streamline and augment supply-chain processes. And as these changes are occurring, the role of logistics is changing (see 'Building the Virtual Value-Chain' in Chapter 1: The Marketspace).

As a result, we have divided the emerging B2B business models into two generic groups which we examine in the following two sections. First, we look at the models which bear upon the services that businesses can offer to their clients or to the expansion of the relation between business and client. Then, we examine the emergence of B2B intermediaries, or 'hubs'.

e-Procurement

e-Procurement is the electronic tendering and procurement of goods and services. With the cost of procurement estimated to be as much as one to two percent of the purchasing cost of goods,[4] the savings realised from e-procurement can be substantial.

Through e-procurement systems, businesses can access a larger number of suppliers worldwide, thereby enjoying better prices, better quality and better delivery. In this regard, e-procurement is the counterpoint to 'e-shop' in B2C e-commerce (see Chapter 5: Business-to-Consumer e-Commerce). Businesses can also use e-procurement systems to save on cost and time by providing tendering specifications on-line and receiving completed bids electronically. Further efficiencies can be gained when a company's e-procurement system permits electronic negotiation and contracting and possibly collaborative tendering, particularly where this allows a project to be broken into smaller components, permitting individual suppliers to tender for each component. Suppliers who take part in the e-procurement process also enjoy numerous benefits. They are able to access tendering opportunities around the world. Also, the cost for them to submit a tender electronically is lower. Finally, a smaller supplier may be able to gain new business opportunities by tendering for a component of a bigger project, if collaborative tendering is allowed.

> ### GE Lighting's Trading Process Network: A Web-based Procurement System
>
> Factories at GE Lighting, General Electric's lighting division, used to send hundreds of Requests for Quotes (RFQs) to its corporate sourcing department daily for low-value machine parts. It was a complex process as each RFQ was accompanied by design blueprints that had to be requested from storage, retrieved from

---

[4] Buchanan (1997).

the vault, transported on site, photocopied, folded and attached to the RFQ forms with quote sheets, put into envelopes and mailed out. Completing the bid packages of each requested item requires at least seven days. This meant that the sourcing department could only send out packages to limited suppliers.

In January 1996, GE rolled out the Trading Process Network (TPN) system, an extranet developed by GE Information Services, as a Web-based procurement system. TPN was rolled out first in GE's lighting division for buying indirect materials (those not used in GE products) and for small items such as batteries or screwdrivers. TPN allows the sourcing department to receive RFQs electronically from the factories, and send RFQs electronically via the Internet to suppliers around the world. An electronic database automatically pulls out blueprints and attaches them to the electronic RFQ forms. In a matter of two hours from the time the process is initiated, suppliers receive a notice via e-mail, fax or EDI. Automating the process of competitive bidding compresses the normal seven days into a day or two. According to GE Lighting, the TPN reduces labour costs by some 30 percent, and material costs by about 20 percent as the ability to reach a larger number of suppliers on-line has created greater competition leading to lower prices.

Sources: US Department of Commerce (1998); Waters (1998).

Collaboration Platforms

A collaboration platform provides a set of tools and an information environment to facilitate collaboration between enterprises. It may focus on a specific function, such as collaborative design and engineering, or provide project support with a virtual team of consultants. Companies that manage these platforms earn revenues from membership fees, usage charges and the selling of specialist software tools. Users of collaboration platforms can benefit from improved information flow and the shortening of product design cycles.

Virtual Communities

The value of a virtual community comes from members adding their own information into a virtual environment provided by a coordinator (or moderator). In B2B e-commerce, virtual communities are often used as an add-on to other marketing operations to build customer loyalty and to receive customer feedback. Virtual communities are also used as a means to enhance the attractiveness of other business models such as third-party marketplaces and collaboration platforms.

CheMatch.com: Chemical Trading Exchange

Launched in February 1998, www.CheMatch.com is one of the best established, most visible players in bulk chemicals e-commerce. CheMatch.com acts as an independent neutral third-party global Internet exchange for buying and selling bulk commodity chemicals, polymers and fuels. Aside from its exchange capability, CheMatch also provides an array of market formats including on-line auctions, reverse auctions and tenders to meet its members strategic sales and procurement requirements. Users can transact with confidence as CheMatch.com employs tight security standards, conducts pre-identification of trading partners and members can anonymously bid, offer and negotiate on-line. "Anonymity means that you can move within the market without moving the market," expressed Carl McCutcheon, CheMatch chairman, president and CEO. Hence, a company in need of a supply of benzene remains anonymous thus avoiding the pitfalls of moving the price against them when everybody knows they are short of supply. The high rate of successful transactions is attributed to the site's pre-identification and immediate posting of product prices.

CheMatch is targeting the 2,417 largest manufacturers and consumers of the listed commodities, of which more than 125 are already listed. DuPont, Bayer, Millennium, GE Plastics and Muehlstein are among CheMatch's strategic partners. Other partners include Stolt-Nielsen, a global transporter of bulk liquid chemicals; E-Credit, an on-line credit service; Townsend Tarnell, an information provider to the plastics industry; and PetroChemNet, the Web-based petrochemical information service. Since February 1998, CheMatch completed over US$125 million worth of transactions. In the fourth quarter of 1999 it reported over US$29 million in completed transactions, with an average transaction value exceeding US$50,000.

Sources: Boswell (2000); Chang (1999 & 2000); CheMatch.

EMERGING INFOMEDIARIES IN B2B E-COMMERCE

While e-commerce was initially expected to lead to widespread disintermediation, a new genre of intermediaries has in fact emerged in the arena of B2B e-commerce.

These 'electronic hubs', or infomediaries, have emerged by aggregating multiple buyers and sellers in a single space in which they can interact, negotiating prices and quantities. These new intermediaries are increasingly serving as electronic hubs, with the hubs focusing on specific industries (vertical hubs) or specific business processes (horizontal hubs).

Vertical Hubs

Vertical hubs serve a vertical market or industry focus. They provide extensive industry-specific content and industry-specific relationships. Vertical hubs typically start out by automating and hosting the procurement process for an industry niche, and then supplement their offerings with industry-specific content.

The characteristics of industries that lend themselves to the emergence of a vertical hub include: significant fragmentation among buyers and sellers; and inefficiency in the existing supply-chain. Emerging examples of vertical hubs suggest that to be successful, a hub will need to create a critical mass of key suppliers and buyers, demonstrate extensive and 'deep' industry knowledge and industry relationships, and establish master catalogues (along with sophisticated searching), in other words, an aggregation of resources.

The primary challenge for vertical hubs is the difficulty in diversifying and extending their business into other industry markets because their expertise and relationships will tend to be industry-specific.

Functional Hubs

Functional hubs focus on providing the same functions or automating the same business processes across different industries. Their expertise usually lies in a business process that is fairly horizontal, which means that it is scalable across vertical markets.

Functional hubs require a significant degree of process standardisation if they are to be successfully established. Again, emerging examples suggest that a successful functional hub will be required to: demonstrate process knowledge and workflow automation expertise; complement the established process automation with 'deep' content; and have the ability to customise the business process to respond to industry-specific differences.

The primary challenge for functional hubs is to deliver industry-specific content. They target functional managers who affiliate and organise their work primarily around their functional area, and not their industry.

Conceptually, these new marketspace hubs are no different from the traditional concepts of horizontal and vertical integration. They use various market-making mechanisms to mediate 'any-to-any' transactions among businesses, and they create value by aggregating buyers and sellers, creating market liquidity, and reducing transaction costs. They are looking to benefit from economies of scale and scope. The difference with these new infomediaries lies in the fact that they are not constrained by the physical limitations of their traditional counterparts.

Marketspace liquidity is created when there is a critical mass of buyers and sellers, leading to lower transaction costs. With the wealth of information that has been made available by the Web, infomediaries serve to make it easier for buyers to locate the products or services they want at the best price and the best terms, and for sellers to reach more potential customers than they could in the past. The emergence of these infomediaries signals that a greater degree of B2B e-commerce activities are taking place beyond the boundaries of individual firms.

Each of these drivers benefits from network economies (see Chapter 2: The Infrastructure), meaning that the value of the hub (and therefore the value to each participant involved) should increase with the square of the number of participants in the hub. Thus, where the value created by consumer hubs tends to increase linearly in the number of buyers; the value created by B2B hubs increases as the *square* of the number of participants.

B2B INTERMEDIARY MODELS

The new vertical and horizontal infomediary hubs can be grouped together under three generic categories: aggregators, auctions and exchanges [see **Table 1** for a summary of these]. Each of the three new activities addresses different inefficiencies, providing different solutions.

Aggregators

The aggregator, or 'catalogue model', creates value by aggregating suppliers and buyers who transact frequently for relatively small-value items across what were previously fragmented markets. The model works particularly well where occasional purchases require searching across a large number of smaller suppliers, or when most of the purchases are made with pre-qualified suppliers and according to pre-defined business rules. The model is suitable when demand is predictable and prices do not fluctuate too frequently.

Table 1:   B2B intermediary models

	Aggregator	Auction	Exchange
How it works	Demand/supply aggregation	Spatial matching	Temporary matching
How buyers benefit	Lower search and transaction costs; broader supply base	Aggregator benefits, plus better matches, better prices	Auction benefits; peak-load demand management; hedge risk in volatile markets
How sellers benefit	Broader customer access, lower transaction costs	Aggregator benefits, plus better pricing	Auction benefits; liquidate excess supply; manage volatility
Where it works best	MRO products; pre-planned purchases; fragmented supplier base	Used capital equipment; perishable capacity; hard-to-specify products	Near-commodities; high-fixed cost assets; volatile markets
How prices are set	Pre-negotiated, usually static	Most attractive bid, prices move in one direction	Marketwide bid-ask; moves up and down
Can buyers be sellers?	No	Sometimes	Yes
Key challenges	Creating master group; gaining supplier critical mass	Liquidity, misrepresentation/ fraud fulfilment	Asset specificity; off-exchange trade

e-Auctions[5]

An auction model creates value through a spatial matching of buyers and sellers. It can be used in industries or settings where one-of-a-kind, non-standard, or perishable

---

[5] e-Auctions are also discussed in Chapter 5: Business-to-Consumer e-Commerce.

products or services need to be bought or sold among businesses that may have quite different perceptions of value for the various products or services. Products, such as capital equipment, used goods and hard-to-find products, can be successfully auctioned off. e-Auctions are effectively an electronic implementation of the traditional bidding mechanism. They are usually integrated with contracting, payments and delivery processes. Revenue from selling the technology platform and transaction fees are the two main sources of income for auction providers. Benefits for suppliers and buyers include increased efficiency, timesavings and global sourcing. As selling costs are lower, it becomes feasible to auction small quantities of low-value goods. e-Auctions also allow suppliers to reduce surplus stock, better utilise production capacity and lower sales overhead costs. Buyers concomitantly benefit from reduced purchasing costs.

Rebound.com: Surplus and Auction Cybermarket

Rebound.com is turning 'excess inventory into opportunity' as it hosts on-line auctions to help companies dispose of surplus consumer goods from production overruns, cancelled orders and trade deals that went bad. Rebound specialises in selling excess stocks from Asia. Since its launch on 6 March 2000, 14 deals have already been completed, including a test phase before the launch date, with an average transaction size of US$389,000 (HK$5 million). Rebound charges between four to eight percent commission depending on the size of the transaction. Companies can list stocks on the Website free of charge and the lists of products being offered to Rebound includes VCRs, stainless steel cooking utensils, frozen chicken wings, toys, clothes, umbrellas, walkmans, etc. The amount of the products listed on the site was already worth HK$100 million before the launch date and they expect the figure to increase to HK$500 million in six months. Sellers are screened by a Rebound country representative to validate the company and its business. Once screening is done and Rebound declares approval, the seller may post an auction on-line. Rebound automatically informs buyers via e-mail about the availability of the products. Rebound applies seal-bid auctions, a bid-asked format and an aggregation model as the means of selling its merchandise. With an additional fee, Rebound offers customers to connect to an inspection company, insurance and logistics providers to facilitate the completion of the transaction.

    As an example, a Philippine-based distributor of educational products for children, Phoenix Learning Journey informed Rebound about the 70,000 electronic learning games that its American company had in store in a warehouse in China. Rebound's Canada office was able to identify a buyer from Britain. Rebound was able to turn an excess inventory into cash, helping Phoenix get rid of its excess stock.

Based in Hong Kong, Rebound estimated that in 1998 over HK$90 billion worth of excess consumables were produced globally; about two-thirds came from Asia and North America. Marybeth Dee, co-founder and President of Rebound, expressed that the excess inventory business "does well on the upside and in a downside market."

Sources: Cottril (2000); *DSN Retailing Today* (2000); Rebound; Slater (2000).

Exchange

An exchange model creates value through a temporal matching of supply and demand. It facilitates real-time, bid-ask matching processes, assists marketwide price determination and often provides a settlement and clearing mechanism. The exchange model is suitable for near-commodity items that may have several attributes but are easy to specify. Exchanges create significant value in markets where demand and prices are volatile by giving businesses a means to manage excess supply and peak-load demand. Like stock exchanges, on-line exchanges provide vetted players with a trading venue defined by clear rules, industrywide pricing, and open market information. An on-line industry spot market can operate at a fraction of physical-world cost.

eLabsEurope.com: Medical Supplies Auction Site

Founded in September 1999, eLabsEurope (www.elabseurope.com) is an on-line platform for the European life science industry and has revolutionised the way in which laboratory products are procured and scientific information is exchanged in Europe. Scientists can select from more than 200,000 products from about 122 leading manufacturers and order the products on-line. All the cumbersome administrative processes involved in ordering from a catalogue – filling out and signing order forms and the entire invoicing processes – are done electronically and are likewise handled by eLabsEurope.

eLabsEurope is targeting the Euros 8 to 10 billion European laboratory supplies market – universities, research institutes and companies in biotechnology and pharmaceutical industries. Its aim is to simplify the lives of scientists by meeting their informational, planning and purchasing needs. The services available are: (1) Marketplace – a one-stop shop to search for and purchase laboratory supplies; (2) Auctions – in addition to being a channel to buy and sell laboratory equipment and supplies, it is also a cost-effective way for buyers to experience unique buying opportunities; and (3) MyLab – an up-to-date section on the latest news and advances in the industry.

eLabsEurope on-line auction site is the first of its kind to go live and allows laboratories and suppliers the opportunity to auction on-line their surplus inventory, consumables that are nearing their expiry date, used, unused or refurbished equipment, demonstration models and discontinued or end-of-life cycle products. The auction service also enables users to sell or buy goods at prices determined in a dynamic and efficient way, a process that facilitates instantaneous selling and buying. The auction page is divided into three main areas: The Seller Auction, where a seller offers its goods and prospective buyers bid; Reverse Auction, where a buyer posts wanted items and sellers offer their products for a given price; Classified Auctions, where sellers offer their goods at a set price.

Small- and mid-sized laboratories and universities benefit as it enables them to purchase equipment at a marginal cost. With eLabsEurope, academic institutions would be able to potentially upgrade laboratory equipment at a more affordable price. According to a market survey conducted by Forrester Research and Bain and Co. Consultants, by the year 2004 trading auctions will constitute 20 to 40 percent of the entire e-business market.

Sources: eLabsEurope; *M2 Presswire* (2000a & b).

A further type of the exchange intermediary is the barter model. The barter model creates value by matching two parties that possess reciprocal assets within an asset class or across asset classes. Bartering has traditionally been practised in inflationary economies to minimise currency risks. It is now used by businesses to achieve cost savings and efficiencies as well as to improve cash flow. Companies barter manufacturing capacity, services and high-transportation cost assets, such as paper or steel, over the Web. On-line bartering sites have been established in various parts of the world.

The first method to emerge for mediating transactions between buyers and sellers was the aggregator model, which works best for small-ticket items and in markets where prices do not fluctuate too frequently. Then came the auction model, which appears to work best for hard-to-find, used, or otherwise unsaleable products. The exchange model came third as digital engines were created to enable real-time matching of bid and ask processes for commodity goods. (The stock and commodities exchanges are obvious precedents in the physical world.)

One of the most positive aspects of these models is the level of embededness that is involved. With B2B, customer acquisition is still time-consuming and comparatively expensive – supplier catalogues have to be loaded on-line, business processes need to be understood, business rules need to be defined, and the hub's systems need to be integrated with those of its buyers and sellers. Customer switching costs and customer retention rates are therefore correspondingly higher for hubs; once they embed themselves into the business processes of buyers and sellers, the barriers to competition can be significant. This potentially makes them much more powerful propositions over the long term than their counterparts in B2C.

SUMMARY

❑ Traditional EDI is conceptually sound. It brings promises of secure data transfer, cost savings through the minimisation of input errors and more productive use of human resources, better management of working capital, improved customer service, increased sales opportunities and a paperless office.

❑ Unfortunately, for many businesses, EDI via point-to-point networks or VANs is far too costly to implement. Apart from cost, traditional EDI is also associated with complex implementation, high maintenance and a lack of common standards. As a result, EDI has never caught on to the extent that was first envisioned.

❑ However, B2B e-commerce has been invigorated with the advent of the Internet. Access to the global marketplace allows businesses to open up new sales venues and sourcing opportunities. With Web-based EDI (virtual private networks, intranets and extranets), businesses are given the unprecedented option of creating the desired level of connectivity among themselves through public communications links at a price they can afford.

❑ If structured properly, inter- and intra company communication links can remove barriers among an organisation's own employees and between an organisation and its trading partners. A free flow of the most up-to-date information within these communication hubs enables members of the same hub to react to the changing market conditions in unison. It is therefore desirable for large companies to take the initiative to form communication hubs and for smaller businesses to ensure that they are on the vital spokes of these hubs.

❑ Businesses need to realise that in order to survive in this new business era, they must go beyond firm boundaries. Infomediaries that successfully break down firm barriers and bring efficiency to the marketplace are able to make handsome profits.

❑ In order to break down inter-firm barriers, B2B communication hubs should aim at integrating suppliers and customers along the supply-chain deep into their business processes, achieving levels of transparency and openness among all involved parties higher than those which could be achieved in the physical marketplace.

APPENDIX 1: SLOW ADOPTION OF EDI

The rate of adoption of EDI by business communities around the world has remained low. EDI is estimated to be used by about 338,000 companies around the world and accounts for only two to three percent of the total data exchanged between businesses in the US.[6] Most of the EDI users are large companies, such as the Fortune 1000 or Global 2000 companies.[7] And of those companies that have implemented EDI, most of them fail to implement it across the full range of business functions within their organisations. They also do not implement EDI down to the second or third tier of subcontractors.[8]

The high costs of implementing EDI and the complicated implementation process are the two major deterrents that keep EDI from becoming a popular business tool. Costs of using EDI include both the initial start-up costs and on-going costs to process transactions and to maintain the system.

The initial start-up costs of EDI include the following:

❑ Consultancy fees on system requirements and the choice of standards and communication links.
❑ Project plan development.
❑ Translation software development or acquisition.
❑ Interface software development.
❑ Communications software development or acquisition.
❑ Hardware (PC, modem, leased line, etc.) acquisition or upgrade.
❑ VAN or point-to-point network set-up costs.
❑ Training and education for technical staff, management staff and end users.
❑ EDI communication standards education and documentation.

---

[6] Rockwell (1999).
[7] Millman (1998).
[8] Kilbane (1999).

On-going costs are incurred for the following:

❑ Transmission of EDI data.
❑ Addition of EDI documents.
❑ Software modifications.
❑ Maintenance of EDI expertise on continually evolving EDI standards.
❑ Rollout of new trading partners.

The price of EDI software is between US$5,000 for PC-based systems and US$250,000 for mainframe applications.[9] The cost of VAN access alone can add up to a substantial amount. A start-up fee is charged when a company connects to a VAN. From then on, the company has to pay a fixed monthly fee and a processing charge for each transaction based on the size of the message. Most VANs charge for both sending and receiving data. It is not uncommon for large corporations to incur in excess of US$100,000 per year on VAN access.[10]

An EDI implementation process is complex. A typical EDI implementation between a large vendor and one of its suppliers can take three months.[11] In addition, companies using EDI must stay current on EDI standard developments that vary by industry and are in continual negotiation and flux. As there are numerous EDI document standards, medium or small suppliers who have to accommodate the requests of their large customers often need to deal with several EDI standards. This further complicates the implementation process and drives up the cost as multiple translation software is needed.[12]

The implementation of EDI requires detailed bilateral agreement on the technical details between the parties involved. EDI links in short-term business partnerships are rarely realised due to the high costs of establishing such an agreement. EDI links with many partners are also rarely realised because the negotiation and agreement between partners are not easily manageable. As set-up costs are high, it is difficult to justify the costs of investment if only a small number of suppliers are linked up. Many companies therefore choose not to participate in EDI.

Because of the high costs and complexity involved, it is not surprising that large companies that process high volumes of transactions and have abundant financial and

---

[9] Wilde (1997).

[10] Werner (1999).

[11] Buerger (1995).

[12] Barrett & Hogenson (1998).

personnel resources comprise the majority of EDI users. Smaller businesses adopt EDI largely because of the coercive pressure from their powerful customers. This also explains why most of the EDI links in place are hub–and–spoke arrangements with a big customer in the centre and branch out to a large number of suppliers.

APPENDIX 2: EDI STANDARDS

An EDI message is highly structured. It consists of one or more data segments and is referred to as a transaction set. A data element represents a singular fact, such as price, product model number, and so on. An entire string of data elements forms a data segment. One or more data segments, framed by a header and a trailer, form a transaction set. A transaction set consists of what would usually be contained in a typical business document.[13]

An EDI document standard specifies the syntax upon which EDI messages are built, the message design rules and the directories (i.e., the types of messages supported and the building blocks of messages: data segments, data elements and codes). To be able to create, transmit and receive EDI messages, trading parties have to adopt the same EDI document standard.

Early users of EDI used proprietary communication protocols. The lack of a common standard, however, imposed severe constraints on the size of EDI communities and thus the effectiveness of practising EDI. To address this problem, a number of government bodies and industry organisations embarked on setting cross-industry and industry-specific EDI document standards.

In 1978, the American Credit Research Foundation and the Transportation Data Coordinating Committee (TDCC) in the US formed the Accredited Standards Committee (ASC), a subcommittee of the American National Standards Institute (ANSI), and began to formalise a set of cross-industry EDI document standards.[14] The ANSI ASC X12 standard, approved by the ANSI in 1985, was the outcome of this effort.

The European initiative of setting an EDI standard was undertaken by the UN Working Party on Facilitation of International Trade Procedures. The result was the UN/EDIFACT (United Nations Electronic Data Interchange for Administration, Commerce and Transport) standard. This standard was approved by the International

---

[13] See URL: http://www.whatis.com.

[14] See Kimberley (1991), p. 103.

Standards Organisation (ISO) in 1987. UN/EDIFACT is the only international EDI communications protocol in the world. Since their codification, ANSI ASC X12 and UN/EDIFACT have established more than 200 transaction sets, or document types, to handle a broad spectrum of business data requirements.

Other than these two standards, a number of proprietary and national EDI standards are also being used in different parts of the world. This means that EDI-enabled companies that have a large number of trading partners often need to implement multiple EDI document standards to facilitate the transmission of documents along the supply-chain.

REFERENCES

Barrett, M. & Hogenson, A. (1998), "Why and How to Become EDI Enabled", *Transportation & Distribution*, Vol. 39, Iss. 8, August, pp. 67–70.

Boswell, C. (2000), "Rolling Out the Strategies of Chemical Dot-Coms", *Chemical Market Reporter*, Vol. 257, Iss. 16, 17 April, pp. 17–19.

Buchanan, L. (1997), "Procurative Powers", *WebMaster Magazine*, URL: http://www.cio.com/archive/Webbusiness/050197_procurement_content.html, June 2000.

Buerger, D. J. (1995), "Electronic Commerce Needs Better EDI Before It Hits Prime Time", *Network World*, Vol. 12, Iss. 43, 23 October, p. 69.

Chang, J. (1999), "Chemdex to Go Public As First in Life Sciences e-Commerce", *Chemical Market Reporter*, Vol. 255, Iss. 25, 21 June, pp. 1, 7.

Chang, J. (2000), "Global Chem Industry Enters Age of Electronic Commerce", *Chemical Market Reporter*, Vol. 257, Iss. 2, 10 January, pp. 1, 16.

CheMatch (2000), "The First and Only Anonymous Interactive Trading System for Commodity Chemicals, Polymers and Fuel Products", URL: http://www.chematch.com/AboutUs/CompanyOverview.htm, 21 August.

Cottril, K. (2000), "Waste Not, Want Not", *Traffic World*, Vol. 262, Iss. 2, 10 April, p. 19.

Davies, J. (1999), "The B-to-B Boom: B2B Commerce: The Next Frontier – Infomediaries on the Move", *Business 2.0*, September, URL: http://www.business2.com/articles/1999/09/content/analystview.html, June 2000.

DSN Retailing Today (2000), "B2B Marketplace Still Seeks Formula for On-line Surplus Sales", Vol. 39, Iss. 10, 22 May, pp. 15–16.

eLabsEurope (2000), URL: http://www.elabseurope.com/en/, 24 August.

Forrester Research (1998), "More Than $1 Trillion in Internet Commerce Depends on Business-Government Collaboration" (press release), 7 December, URL: http://www.forrester.com/, August 1999.

Harrington, L. & Reed, G. (1996), "Electronic Commerce (Finally) Comes of Age", *McKinsey Quarterly*, No. 2, pp. 68–77.

International Telecommunication Union (1999), URL: http://www7.itu.int/publibase/ cat_pub/ituPubContents.asp, June 2000.

Kalakota R. & Whinston A.B. (1996), *Frontiers of Electronic Commerce*, Reading, MA: Addison-Wesley, pp. 333–401.

Kilbane, D. (1999), "International Groups Making Progress on X12/EDIFACT interoperability", *Automatic I. D. News*, Vol. 15, Iss. 3, pp. 34–35.

Kimberley, P. (1991), *Electronic Data Interchange*, New York, NY: McGraw-Hill, Inc.

Knowles, A. (1997), "EDI Experiments with the Net", *Software Magazine*, Vol. 17, Iss. 1, pp. 108–110.

M2 Presswire (2000a), "eLabsEurope Launches Pan-European Auction Page", 23 May, p. 1.

M2 Presswire (2000b), "eLabsEurope: Revolution in the Lab World", 20 April, p. 1.

Mitchel, A. (1999), "Internet Zoo Spawns New Business Models", *Marketing Week*, Vol. 21, Iss. 45, 12 January, pp. 24–25.

Millman, H. (1998), "A Brief History of EDI", *InfoWorld*, Vol. 20, Iss. 14, 6 April, p. 83.

Patel, J. (1999), "Where Buyers, Sellers Meet – Electronic Marketplaces Are Changing the Way Businesses Trade with One Another", *Information Week, Behind the News, IT Impact*, 28 June, p. 120.

Rebound (2000), "About Us", URL: http://www.rebound.com/menuAbout Rebound.msp, 24 August.

Rockwell, B. (1999), "Understanding the Evolution to EC on the Internet", *EDI Forum: The Journal of Electronic Commerce*, Vol. 12, No. 1, pp. 80–89.

Sawhney, M. & Kaplan, S. (1999), "The B-to-B Boom – Let's Get Vertical", *Business 2.0*, September, URL: http://www.business2.com/articles/1999/09/content/ models.html, June 2000.

Slater, J. (2000), "Cyber Surplus", *Far Eastern Economic Review*, Vol. 163, Iss. 13, 30 March, p. 44.

The Economist (1999), "Survey: Business and the Internet: The Rise of the Infomediary", Vol. 351, Iss. 8125, 26 June, pp. B21–B24.

The Economist (1999), "Survey: Business and the Internet: You'll Never Walk Alone", Vol. 351, Iss. 8125, 26 June, pp. B11–B21.

Timmers, P. (1998), "Business Models for Electronic Markets", *EM-Electronic Markets*, Vol. 8, No. 2.

Tucker, M.J. (1997), "EDI and the Net: A Profitable Partnering", *Datamation*, Vol. 43, Iss. 4, pp. 62–69.

Tuten, D.A. (1997), "Internet EDI: How the Internet Is Shaping the Future of Electronic Commerce", *EDI Forum: The Journal of Electronic Commerce*, Vol. 10, No. 4, pp. 38–43.

US Department of Commerce (1998), "The Emerging Digital Economy", 15 April, Washington, DC, URL: http://www.ecommerce.gov/emerging.htm, June 2000.

Waters, R. (1998), "Richard Waters Finds the Group Has Learned a Lesson on Purchasing from Suppliers Via the Internet", *The Financial Times*, London, 3 November, p. 17.

Watkins–Castillo S. & Ferguson, D.M. (1999), "Key e-Business Best Practices and Trends", *EDI Forum: The Journal of Electronic Commerce*, Vol. 12, No. 1, pp. 15–23.

Werner, T. (1999), "EDI Meets the Internet", *Transportation & Distribution*, Vol. 40, Iss. 6, pp. 36–44.

Wilde, C. (1997), "New Life for EDI?" *Information Week*, 17 March, Iss. 622.

CASE

■ ■ ■

4.1

iSteelAsia.com: A B2B Exchange*

On 29 August 2000, iSteelAsia.com, the operator of the first Asia–Pacific-focused steel-trading portal, announced that it had entered into a non-legally binding agreement with the London-based international steel trader Stemcor Holdings Limited. The agreement stipulated that iSteelAsia could acquire an equity interest in Stemcor. In return, Stemcor guaranteed a minimum steel-trading tonnage through iSteelAsia's portal, with a view to placing a significant portion of its transactions through the portal after a certain period of time. Following the announcement, an Internet analyst at a European-based brokerage cautioned that the acquisition posed a threat to the attractiveness of the portal and might deter existing users from continuing to use it. Investors reacted to iSteelAsia's announcement by immediately selling off its shares, causing a drop in the price.[1] Were they trying to indicate to the directors of iSteelAsia that its business strategy was flawed? Concerned that the acquisition could adversely affect the operations of the portal, the directors held a meeting to decide whether or not they should proceed with it.

---

[1] Ng, E. & Leung P. (2000), "Portal Courting Steel Trader in Bid to Boost Volume", *South China Morning Post*, 31 August.

* K.K. Tan prepared this case from public sources under the supervision of Dr. Ali Farhoomand. *Copyright © 2000 The University of Hong Kong. Ref. 00/91C*

THE STEEL INDUSTRY

Steel products were usually categorised as either long products or flat products. Long products were mainly for construction use while flat products were mainly used as raw materials in the manufacture of end products such as automobiles, refrigerators and computer casings.

After petro-chemicals, the steel industry was the second-largest industry in the world. Annual global steel business was estimated at US$700 billion, of which 45 percent (US$300 billion) was captured by Asia. Despite its importance as a major contributor to the global economy, the industry was plagued by various inefficiencies, such as a fragmented supply-chain, a lack of information transparency, complex transportation logistics and unnecessarily high inventory levels [see **Appendix 1**]. According to industry players, these problems were more apparent in Asia.

On-line Steel Trading

In 1998, steel-related companies began establishing on-line trading portals to counter the inefficiencies in the steel-trading industry. In the US, the number of steel-trading portals had grown to dozens in a period of just over one year. These portals offered buyers and sellers an opportunity to trade in a more efficient and effective manner, helping them to achieve low transactional costs and better inventory control. Two of the better-known portals were MetalSite.com and e-STEEL.com.

MetalSite, established by three major US steel companies in 1998, was the first metal exchange on the Internet. During its first year of operation, it offered industry-related information and concentrated its activities on helping members to dispose of their excess stock of metals, including steel. Competition was introduced into the scenario with the launch of e-STEEL's portal in September 1999. Barely two hours after its launch, a prime steel deal was negotiated and closed via the portal, representing the first time such a deal was executed entirely via an Internet-enabled on-line exchange. Michael Levin, the Chairman and CEO of e-STEEL, claimed that the portal was a neutral exchange as none of its equity owners were involved in steel-trading activities.

The trend of establishing steel-related portals was apparent in Europe and Asia as well. In February 2000, Steelscreen AB, a Swedish company, launched its steel-trading portal. Its goal was to turn the portal into the leading marketplace for metal products in Europe. As part of its efforts to achieve this objective, it opened several offices in other European countries such as the UK and Germany to market its presence and the services of the portal. In Asia, iSteelAsia was the pioneer in bringing steel trading with an Asian focus to the Internet with the launch of its on-line steel-trading portal in December 1999. The high media coverage accorded to the iSteelAsia portal prompted several other Asian metal traders to establish their own portals. These included WorldMetal.com, launched in March 2000 by the Hong Kong-based WellNet Holdings and Asia-steel.com, launched in May 2000 by a steel trader. An article in a Hong Kong daily commented that WorldMetal was the only portal that was global in scope, trading in both ferrous and non-ferrous metals.[2,3] Asia-steel, which claimed to be 'the world's largest and fastest-growing B2B exchange',[4] targeted the region outside Japan and expected to capture US$1 billion worth of trades by December 2000. In one of its press releases, it claimed that none of its professional management was engaged in steel-trading activities. As such, it prided itself on its neutrality and impartiality.

Strategic alliances ■ The aforementioned portals had a strong common factor. Since their launch, they had actively forged alliances with strategic partners to cement their presence in other countries and to expand their repertoire of services.

During its second year of operation, MetalSite incorporated a range of e-commerce integration capabilities by allying with strategic partners such as CompuSoft Canada Inc. and Cohesia Corporation. Both these companies offered e-commerce applications that enhanced and expanded the functionality of MetalSite's portal. It further planned to offer its members a fully networked value-chain by signing agreements with strategic partners for value-added services such as logistics and credit services. In August 2000, it formed a joint venture with three Japanese companies to offer on-line trading to the Japanese metals marketplace. These three companies, namely Itochu Corporation, Marubeni Corporation and Sumitomo Corporation, together accounted for a substantial share of the Japanese steel market, which was the third-largest steel marketplace in the world. Not limiting its foreign ventures to Japan, MetalSite planned to construct other regional sites in Europe and Latin America, using the same strategy.

e-STEEL pursued a similar strategy as well by forming partnerships with several leading technology and information companies to leverage on their expertise. Examples included Maxager Technology Incorporate, which offered the only sell-side B2B solution that allowed participants in on-line auctions and exchanges to determine

---

[2] 'Ferrous' means containing or relating to iron.

[3] *Wen Wei Po* (2000).

[4] URL: http://www.asia-steel.com, 15 August 2000.

their maximum bid without making a loss, and 33MetalProducing, which provided timely information on domestic and global trends in metal production. In February 2000, it entered into an agreement with two Japanese trading companies, Mitsui & Company and Mitsubishi Corporation, to form a joint venture aimed at penetrating the Japanese steel market. The two Japanese companies had strong relationships with the local steel industry and were expected to help e-STEEL establish a formidable presence in the Japanese steel market.

Steelscreen AB was also active in forging a series of strategic alliances to enable users of the portal to have access to various services, such as credit insurance, trade finance, foreign exchange and material inspection. Fredrik Norén, in charge of Strategic Partnerships at Steelscreen AB, revealed intentions to partner with the market leaders for each service and to ensure that they could provide the pan-European coverage that Steelscreen aimed for.

WellNet partnered with three technical partners and 20 industry players to form WorldMetal, and claimed that the portal was the world's first professional 'one-stop' on-line metals-trading platform to offer comprehensive on-line trading and information services to the global ferrous and non-ferrous metal manufacturers, consumers and trading houses. This was achieved by signing alliances with several technology and information companies. Since its launch, WorldMetal had actively pursued its plan of launching e-commerce metal portals in other Asian countries. As of September 2000, it had established two on-line metal-trading portals, one in China (ChinaSteel.com.cn) and one in South Korea (SteelnMetal.com), with another being developed in Russia (Rusmetal.com). These portals were established by partnering with indigenous companies. (ChinaSteel was established in partnership with Minmetals Development Co. Ltd., a subsidiary of China Minmetals Group. SteelnMetal was the result of a joint venture between WorldMetal and Hyundai Corporation, South Korea's largest conglomerate.)

Asia-steel partnered with leading experts to provide members with a comprehensive trading platform. For example, it partnered with Timeless Software Limited, a Hong Kong-listed information technology company, to provide a secure and stable trading platform for its members. The portal also provided members with an extensive technical library and metal news through its partnership with authoritative steel news providers such as Metal Bulletin London, Reuters News, World Metal China and PENAVICO (also known as China Ocean Shipping Agency).

DEVELOPMENT OF ISTEELASIA.COM

iSteelAsia was conceived by Mr. Andrew C.F. Yao [see **Exhibit 1**] in June 1999. During a trip to New York City in April that year, he came across Priceline.com while researching on-line airfares.[5] Impressed with its successful listing and growth (Priceline went public at a capitalisation valued at more than that of all the airlines combined), he decided to introduce Internet-based steel trading to the Asian steel industry, which had been suffering from the ill effects of excess production capacity for the past few years.

Due to his role as the Chairman of the Van Shung Chong Group (VSC Group), a leading Hong Kong-listed distributor and processor of construction and industrial materials, Yao had considerable experience in and knowledge of the steel industry.[6] With the e-commerce expertise of the iMerchants Group (iM Group) and the information know-how of Reuters, as well as the participation of more than 20 international steel traders [see **Exhibit 2**], he established iSteelAsia in November 1999, and headed it as Chairman and Chief Executive Officer.[7]

In December 1999, amid much media attention, iSteelAsia launched the first Asia-Pacific-focused vertical portal, or vortal, for the steel industry. In an interview with *Information @ge Hong Kong* conducted in February 2000, Yao commented:

> *I know the industry very well, it's the second-largest industry in the world after petro-chemicals, and it's an industry famous for its operational inefficiencies and middlemen which makes it perfect for the Web.*[8]

In an earlier interview with *Dow Jones Newswires*, Yao commented that there was

---

[5] Priceline.com was a US-based on-line service that traded excess capacity in airline tickets.

[6] Van Shung Chong Holdings Limited was a leading distributor of construction and industrial materials, contributing to the building and infrastructure development as well as the manufacturing industries in Hong Kong and China. Founded in 1961, it was the first, and as at September 1999, the largest, importer and stockholder of steel rebars in Hong Kong. (Rebars were bars or rods of steel made to various specifications in respect of their chemical compositions, dimensions and mechanical properties.)

[7] Founded in 1996, iMerchants Ltd. was a leader in providing e-commerce solutions to businesses in Hong Kong and Asia.

[8] *Information @ge Hong Kong* (2000), "Information @ge Interviews iSteelAsia.com's Founder and CEO, Andrew C.F. Yao", 10 February.

"so much inefficiency" and "so many layers" of exchange created by steel traders.[9] As such, he stressed that it was important to establish a vortal where members could interact directly with each other and therefore eliminate the unnecessary layers of intermediaries.

> *Steel is usually sold three or four times before reaching end users. In places like China, it's five or six times. In Japan, it's eight or nine times.... A lot of times, traders aren't really creating value.*[10]
>
> — Andrew Yao, Chairman and CEO, iSteelAsia.com

Furthermore, the Asian steel-trading industry had an annual turnover of US$300 billion, representing 45 percent of the global steel turnover. This made it an attractive and lucrative prospect for vertical portals.

The rapid advancement and improvement of technologies to facilitate B2B transactions translated to lower operational costs for companies that used the Internet to conduct business. Yao knew that this appealed to companies in the steel industry as profit margins were being squeezed, especially after the economic crisis that plagued the Asian region in 1997. (Prior to 1997, for example, a trader could make commissions of up to three percent per tonne of steel. After the crisis, the commission dropped to one percent.) In addition, most Asian steel companies had not switched to using, or had not fully embraced, the Internet to conduct their trading, due to either lack of expertise or lack of funds. Recognising this, Yao knew that iSteelAsia had a vast market it could tap into.

Furthermore, prior to the establishment of iSteelAsia, existing steel portals were found to be inadequate for Asian steel-trading companies. They catered mainly to the North American or European steel markets; none was focused on the Asia–Pacific region. In addition, they focused on either trading steel or the dissemination of information, but not both. As such, Yao concluded that there was a demand for a portal that provided information and facilities relevant to Asian steel companies.

Anticipating that he needed funds to finance the development of the vortal, Yao listed iSteelAsia on the Growth Enterprise Market of the Stock Exchange of Hong

---

[9] Shen, H. (1999), "iSteelAsia.com Set to Boost Trade Efficiency", *Dow Jones Newswires*, Singapore, 9 December.

[10] Shen, H. (1999).

Kong through a placement exercise in April 2000.[11] The issue price was HK$1.08, bringing in proceeds estimated at HK$88.4 million. The capital was to finance the start-up of iSteelAsia and other activities [see **Table 1**].

Table 1:   Budgeted expenditure

Activities	Budgeted expenditure (HK$ million)
• Acquiring interests in value-added information and service providers as well as on funding start-up and operating costs.	31.0
• Conducting market research to formulate, revamp and refine its business strategy.	15.5
• Conducting marketing and promotional activities to build a strong brand name.	26.4
• Acquiring content for the Website.	15.5

Source: Dao Heng Securities (2000), "iSteelAsia.com (8080)", *CN-Markets – Brokerage Research Hub*, 19 April.

Business

Upon its establishment, iSteelAsia took over the traditionally based steel-trading operations of the VSC Group in southern China and Macau. This trading operation was originally set up by the VSC Group in 1994 in response to the establishment of a large number of manufacturers of consumer steel products and electronic appliances in the province of Guangdong in the People's Republic of China (PRC). It supplied both construction steel and industrial steel products, purchased from the VSC Group at cost plus transportation and warehousing expenses, to customers in Southern China and Macau. These customers included factories, project-based companies and stockists (shops that sold steel). It also provided value-added services by assisting customers with the transportation of goods to end users in China. The directors believed that this traditional steel-trading operation provided an alternative solution for customers who

---

[11] GEM was an alternative stock market operated by The Stock Exchange of Hong Kong Limited.

were not yet prepared to migrate to on-line steel trading. The traditional trading operation contributed approximately 97 percent of iSteelAsia's turnover for the quarter ended 30 June 2000.

In December 1999, iSteelAsia launched its steel-trading portal. The portal was formed as an Internet-based trading platform to address the inefficiencies and problems inherent in the supply-chain of the steel industry. It acted as an electronic marketplace (e-marketplace) to match the needs of both the buyers and sellers of steel. Yao envisioned it as a cohesive community of steel industry-related players, with a fair and open exchange of information and interaction, enabling members of the community to dispose of excess inventories or to source required steel products at true market prices. He also promoted the portal as a centrally accessible standard format for trading that expanded the marketplace for both buyers and sellers while reducing transaction costs.

The portal offered several core services and value-added services that were similar to the services normally done in a traditional steel-trading environment; the difference was that these services were done via the Internet instead of via the conventional methods of phone, fax and face-to-face. These services enabled the Company to facilitate e-commerce, display focused information related to the industry with a comprehensive and updated news archive, and foster a community spirit among the users of the portal, who were classified as either visitors, individual members, corporate members or founding members. (Membership was free.) Different categories of users of iSteelAsia were accorded different functions and benefits [see **Exhibit 3**]. The services offered were categorised under 'On-line Trading Centre', 'Industry Info' and 'The Steel Talk' [see **Exhibit 4**].

Members wishing to trade were required to access the On-line Trading Centre. A corporate member wanting to make an on-line purchase had to first complete an on-line form specifying his or her request with details such as product category, quantity required and closing date. Optional information specifying other terms and conditions, such as delivery date, could be supplied as well. iSteelAsia would then e-mail the details of the request to qualified members, along with invitations to offer a quote. Offers were then routed by iSteelAsia to the response list of the buyer, whereupon the buyer decided which offer to accept. Upon acceptance of the offer, the identities of both the buyer and the seller were revealed by iSteelAsia, and the seller paid a specified commission to iSteelAsia, regardless of whether or not the transaction was completed. corporate members wishing to sell their products went through a similar process.

The mechanism of trading in the portal was aimed at promoting it as a neutral platform, without dominance by any one steel mill or trader. Yao stressed that neutrality was a key factor in the success of the portal, adding that if any one steel mill dominated the portal, the other parties would not participate in it.

> *We'll put whoever has the best price and the best deal on the first page, regardless of who they are.*[12]
>
> — Andrew Yao, Chairman and CEO, iSteelAsia.com

Yao also aimed to promote the portal as a one-stop steel-trading centre, allowing members to conduct their transaction from sourcing to payment and transportation directly through the portal. To enhance this role, he actively marketed iSteelAsia to prominent service providers such as ABN-AMRO Bank, Reuters and Houlder Insurance Brokers. As a result, members of the portal were provided with referrals to a wide range of relevant third-party value-added services, such as shipping, insurance and financial services. According to iSteelAsia's Placement Prospectus, more relevant services would be added in the future, including third-party surveyors.

Business Strategies

In its Placement Prospectus, the directors of iSteelAsia identified several business strategies [see **Exhibit 5**].

1. Emphasising customer relationship management, aiming to better serve the Members and to identify their needs.
2. Building a strong brand name by promoting the services through customer-focused initiatives.
3. Forging relationships with strategic partners to expand value-added services such as shipping and insurance.
4. Establishing country-specific Websites for Asia's domestic steel markets through joint ventures with local partners.

Promotional and Expansionary Activities

Upon the launch of the portal, the chairman and other senior management members voiced their confidence in it, aiming for a cumulative transaction value of US$5 billion through the portal by the year 2002. This was to be achieved mainly through promotional activities and strategic alliances in targeted markets.

---

[12] Feng, C.H. (2000), "Man of Steel: Andrew Yao Shows His Metal on the Internet", *Asian Business*, May, p. 35.

The initial target markets for iSteelAsia were Hong Kong and the PRC. As part of its efforts to promote the portal in the PRC market, the management team participated actively in various trade shows and conferences. For example, in May 2000, Yao and several senior management members participated in the international Steel 2000 Conference, the 7th International Metallurgical Exhibition and the 2nd International Mining Exhibition. (All of these events were held in Beijing.) During the 7th International Metallurgical Exhibition alone, over 300 new corporate and individual members registered with iSteelAsia. Apart from the PRC, iSteelAsia also concentrated its marketing efforts on other countries to promote its portal. These included Korea, India and the Philippines. After May 2000, it actively promoted on-line steel trading in the Philippines and in June 2000, it hosted a Steel Trading Conference there. By July 2000, it had signed up more than 80 of the 100 major steel players in the country. Its participation in these and other events significantly boosted its membership to more than 2,000 by the end of August 2000.

Efforts at increasing the volume of transactions through its portal were not limited to public relations events. iSteelAsia actively forged alliances with foreign steel companies in various countries to promote its presence and boost the trading volume through its portal. In March 2000, it signed Memoranda of Understanding (MOUs) with several leading Korean Internet, steel and financial corporations to cement its presence in Korea. In the same month, it signed another MOU with Steelscreen.com (Steelscreen), a leading Internet trading site for metal products in Europe. Under the terms and conditions of the MOU, both iSteelAsia and Steelscreen planned to work together to enhance inter-regional interaction. In July 2000, it entered into an MOU with Kawasho Corporation, a leading Japanese steel and general trading conglomerate, to market iSteelAsia's presence in Asia. These efforts were expected to help boost the trading volume and the long-term profitability of the vortal.

iSteelAsia was also keen on building a brand name that others would associate with reliability, effectiveness and efficiency in steel trading. For example, to promote the reliability of its site, it partnered with well-known technology players such as iMerchants and Scient.[13] When choosing the providers of third-party services, iSteelAsia opted for partners that were reliable and reputable in their respective fields, for example, ABN-AMRO Bank, Dao Heng Bank and COSCO Shipping. These efforts were

---

[13] iMerchants, founded in 1996, was a leader in providing electronic commerce solutions to businesses in Hong Kong and Asia. Scient was a leading e-business systems innovator, having provided e-business strategy and technology services to Global 1000 and start-ups.

aimed at ensuring minimal interruptions to the operation of the portal and boosting the confidence of users in the reliability and security of the portal. (Since its launch, iSteelAsia had enjoyed a rise in the value of transactions conducted via its portal [see **Table 2**].)

Table 2: Volume of transactions through iSteelAsia.com trading portal

	Jan 2000	Feb 2000	Mar 2000	Jan–June 2000 (cumulative)
Volume (US$ thousands)	1,000	3,000	33,000	82,000

Earnings Results

On 10 August 2000, iSteelAsia reported an 81 percent increase in turnover for the quarter ended June 2000, amounting to HK$56.1 million. It incurred expenses amounting to HK$36 million, used on brand building, major enhancements to the Website, platform development and operation of the on-line steel-trading business. The directors viewed the spending as investments to pave the way for future long-term sustainable profitability. A large amount was spent on developing the platform and business strategy via the engagement of iMerchants, Scient and McKinsey & Company, all of them renowned in their respective fields. An amount of HK$8.3 million was spent on promoting the name of iSteelAsia.com, i.e., brand building. As a result of these efforts, iSteelAsia captured the business of a large number of steel industry players as well as the attention of international IT research groups and journals.

> If I was going to put my money somewhere, it would be in the areas of B2B trading portals and what we call 'market breakers', which are new on-line ventures specifically aimed at destroying other industries' profit margins – something along the lines of iSteelAsia.com, which must be one of the better domain names.[14]
> – Joseph Sweeney, Asia-Pacific Research Director, Gartner Group

However, these expenses reduced iSteelAsia's gross profit of HK$2.5 million to a

---

[14] iSteelAsia.com (2000), "First Quarter Results for the Three Months Ended 30th June 2000", 10 August.

net loss of more than HK$33 million. In addition, the *South China Morning Post* reported that most of the turnover was derived from off-line steel trading, which generated HK$54.63 million.[15] On-line transactions yielded a commission income of HK$1.47 million only. In the same article, the paper reported that the directors refused to comment on the level of future investments and declined to forecast when the Company was expected to post a net profit.

> *A lot of people believe digital marketplaces are the right thing to do. But they're greatly underestimating the effort it takes to build a successful one. It takes a lot of work.*
> — Kevin Costello, Managing Director,
> Arthur Andersen's Digital Markets Practice[16]

THE PROPOSED STEMCOR ACQUISITION

On 29 August 2000, iSteelAsia announced that it had entered into a non-legally binding 'head of terms' agreement with Stemcor Holdings Limited (Stemcor), a London-based international steel trader, to acquire an equity interest in Stemcor. Founded in 1951, Stemcor was principally engaged in international steel trading. It operated six major trading centres, in London, Dusseldorf, Johannesburg, New York, Singapore and Sydney, with 35 offices around the world. (In countries where no offices were established, the Stemcor Group was represented by appointed agents.) Its philosophy was to work through small, self-contained offices, each with their own management team with clearly defined areas of responsibility, but committed to common objectives, shared values and a unified group strategy. These offices integrated the personal touch of small business units with the benefits of a large group, providing an effective international communications network and bringing together buyers and sellers from different parts of the world. This strategy facilitated the development of close relations with customers, suppliers and service providers. This was of paramount importance to Stemcor as the bulk of its business came from back-to-back trading (buying steel to meet the needs of customers and subsequently arranging the physical transfer of steel from producers to end users as efficiently as possible). Stemcor also operated as a global provider

---

[15] Leung, P. (2000), "iSteelAsia in the Red to Tune of $33.35m", *South China Morning Post*, 11 August.

[16] Iwata, E. (2000), "Despite the Hype, B2B Marketplaces Struggle: Many Barricades Hamper Revolution in Corporate Purchasing", *USA Today*, 10 May.

of specialist services to the steel and metal industries in areas such as marketing, procurement, shipping, engineering and trade finance. In 1999, Stemcor reported a net profit of HK$20.32 million on a turnover of 4.4 million tonnes valued at HK$9.09 billion. (In 1998, it reported a loss of HK$40.1 million on a turnover of 3.5 million tonnes worth HK$8.8 billion.) Trade in Asian countries was about 50 percent of Stemcor's turnover, while the majority of the balance involved the European and US markets.

Under the agreement, iSteelAsia proposed to acquire a strategic interest in Stemcor and the remaining balance of the equity interest in Stemcor at a consideration to be determined. The agreement also included a put option for iSteelAsia to sell its stake back to Stemcor. In return, iSteelAsia was to provide state-of-the-art e-commerce technology and expertise to help transform Stemcor's off-line transaction models. At the same time, Stemcor committed to transact a minimum level of steel trading through the iSteelAsia portal, with a view to placing a significant portion of its volume through the portal after a certain period of time.

Following the announcement, an Internet analyst at a European-based brokerage said that iSteelAsia's move was typical of the present trend of Internet companies acquiring stakes in traditional firms.[17] However, he added that the acquisition might turn off iSteelAsia's existing customers as the portal was supposed to be a neutral exchange. Ms. Drina Yue, the Chief Operating Officer of iSteelAsia.com, dismissed such concerns by emphasising that Stemcor was itself an independent trader linking a large number of buyers and sellers. On 30 August 2000, the share price of iSteelAsia dropped by 5.3 percent to 53 cents, half of its issue price.

A BUSINESS DECISION

In the announcement, iSteelAsia reminded shareholders that it was not obliged to enter into a formal binding agreement with Stemcor. However, the reaction of shareholders towards the proposed acquisition was apparent; the share price fell immediately after iSteelAsia made the announcement. The directors were expected to arrive at a decision regarding the proposed Stemcor acquisition by the end of 2000. Should they, or should they not, pursue the acquisition? The directors would need to consider

---

[17] Ng, E. & Leung, P. (2000), "Portal Courting Steel Trader in Bid to Boost Volume", *South China Morning Post*, 31 August.

a variety of factors. For example, would the benefits of the acquisition offset the perceived threat it might have on the existing strengths and attractiveness of iSteelAsia? In an interview with *asiamoney* in May 2000, Yue claimed that one of the factors that was preventing global steel companies from entering and capturing Hong Kong's nascent steel market was that they could not offer a neutral trading environment, a feature of the vortal that was repeatedly emphasised by the senior management of iSteelAsia. A decision on the Stemcor acquisition was bound to raise questions about whether the strengths of the vortal would be threatened. On the other hand, could it afford to bypass any opportunity to increase its volume of transactions? The directors had to weigh their decision carefully as it could affect the future direction and profitability of iSteelAsia.

APPENDIX 1: THE ASIAN STEEL TRADE

The steel industry was one of the largest and oldest commodities markets in Asia. Annual Asian steel business was estimated at US$300 billion, accounting for a 45 percent share of the global steel business [see **Table 3**]. However, despite its importance as a major contributor to the global economy, the industry was plagued by various inefficiencies.

Table 3:   Apparent steel consumption, 1992 to 1998 (million metric tonnes finished steel products)

Regions	1995	1996	1997	1998
Europe	158.9	146.8	163.0	171.0
Former USSR	36.3	31.0	29.4	29.6
NAFTA	118.4	128.2	137.3	144.3
Central and South America	25.4	26.6	28.8	27.9
Africa	13.6	13.6	14.6	15.2
Middle East	11.8	13.3	13.3	11.4
Asia (including Australia and New Zealand)	291.1	301.8	312.2	291.2
Total	*655.5*	*661.3*	*698.6*	*690.6*

Source: International Iron & Steel Institute (2000), URL: http://www.worldsteel.org/trends_indicators/figures_21.html, 25 May.

Fragmented Supply-chain

Numerous parties were involved in the steel supply-chain. At the top of the chain were mining companies providing the basic raw materials in steel-making (iron ore and coking coal). This was followed by steel mills that produced pig iron as well as low-margin, semi-finished products and higher-margin, finished steel products, and then come traders who specialised in buying and selling the finished steel products. Transportation companies made a business out of delivering the products to end users such as construction companies, automobile manufacturers, etc. (those that utilised the finished steel products in their manufacturing processes).

The sheer number of parties involved in the supply-chain bred a complex web of trading relationships [see **Figure 1**]. Ms. Drina Yue, the Chief Operating Officer of iSteelAsia.com, claimed that only 20 percent of the global turnover was accounted for by the top ten global steel producers.[18] The balance was accounted for by various steel producers around the world. She added that the market was very fragmented in Asia. Due to this, the processes of sourcing and procuring were usually lengthy and time-consuming. For example, the process of getting a quotation alone would consume a lot of time: to make a comparison between prices, a purchasing executive in a manufacturing company would have to contact a dozen, or perhaps more, suppliers.

Figure 1: Steel supply-chain

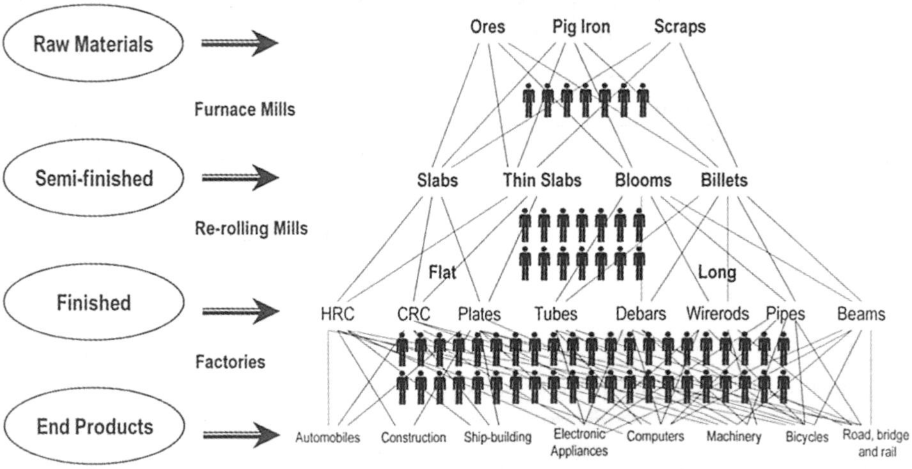

Source: iSteelAsia.com Placement Prospectus, 14 April 2000, p. 49.

---

[18] "Steely-eyed in Fantasyland", *asiamoney*, May 2000, p. 16.

Labour-intensive Negotiations

Negotiations and transactions were usually executed via telephones, faxes and telexes. These were labour-intensive and risky in terms of accuracy. For example, a purchase order made over the telephone would go through several layers of human interference before it was finally made out in a written form, leaving room for human error. This was made more error-prone as the languages used in Asia were as many and as varied as the cultures found, leading to situations in which both the purchaser and seller negotiated in a language foreign to them (usually English). In such situations, accuracy was dependent on the negotiators' prowess in the English language.

Difficult for Smaller Players to Reduce Supply-chain Costs

As in most industries, small players in the steel industry usually faced higher cost margins on their purchasing compared to their larger counterparts. Major players, being bulk purchasers, could usually obtain favourable discounts from third parties such as surveyors, financial institutions and insurance companies. Smaller players usually had to deal at standard rates.

High Inventory Levels

Steel traders tended to maintain high inventory levels to cater to unexpected demand because they lacked the necessary information to make informed decisions in relation to their customers' production schedules and purchase orders. This meant that they incurred storage space costs and tied up their working capital.

Lack of Information Transparency in Asia

Information relating to the steel industry was mostly provided by non-Asian publications or information providers. There was a lack of information focused on the steel trade in Asia. This could seriously hamper the ability of Asian steel traders to make informed decisions, especially in relation to intra-Asian trade, leading to a significant deviation from true market prices.

Transportation Logistics

One of the factors involved in the steel trade was the actual transportation and storage of steel. Often, steel was transported in bulk, and needed expert transportation to handle it. Arranging and choosing the right transportation were often complex as a large number of companies handled such logistics, each with different delivery schedules. Buyers and sellers had to expend a lot of time and effort to contact these companies in order to determine shipping schedules, available space and prices, so as to better handle their own production schedules and output.

Foregone Business Opportunities

No steel industry player could claim to have contacted all potential business partners in a done deal, or claim to have negotiated the best deal possible. This was due to the lack of communication channels to search for potential business partners. There were hundreds of steel traders in the Asia-Pacific region alone. Contacting all of them for quotes and negotiations would require a lot of time and effort. In practice, most companies usually just contacted the partners which they had dealt with, or a few potential partners. This meant that they lost the opportunity to deal with business partners who could potentially offer better prices and terms.

Disposing of Surplus Stock

One of the problems faced in the steel industry was the building up of surplus stock. The practice of disposing of surplus stock quickly did not ensure that the seller received a fair price. It also led to a major problem in the industry. The practice of dumping surplus stock in other countries irked the local steel traders as steel prices were artificially driven below their actual market price.

Exhibit 1: Biography of Andrew Yao Cho Fai

Mr. Yao was one of the key drivers behind the establishment of iSteelAsia.com and is currently serving as the founder, chairman and CEO of the company.

Mr. Yao brings to iSteelAsia.com extensive experience in the steel-trading business. He was the chairman of Van Shung Chong Holdings Limited, a Hong Kong-listed distributor and processor of construction and industrial materials. Under his direction, Van Shung Chong expanded its market share in construction steel in Hong Kong from 10 percent in 1992 to 66.6 percent in 1999. Since the company went public in 1994, profit grew almost four times in six years. Also, the company has forged strategic joint ventures in China, including a coil service centre in Guangdong with Baosteel of China and Mitsui of Japan.

Exhibit 1 (cont'd)

In addition, Mr. Yao was a pioneer in introducing to Hong Kong the 'cut and bend' services that automated the cutting and bending of rebars off-site.

Before joining Van Shung Chong, he was a strategic consultant at Matsushita Electric Industrial Co. Ltd. in Tokyo and a founder who helped start up Citisteel Inc., (a.k.a. Phoenix Steel Corporation) the mini-mill of China International Trust and Investment Corp. in the US.

He obtained a B.Sc. degree in finance from the University of California, Berkeley, and a MBA from the Harvard University Graduate School of Business Administration. Mr. Yao sits on the boards of various business and construction industry associations including the Hong Kong Housing Society and Federation of Hong Kong Industries and President of Harvard Business School Association in Hong Kong.

Source: iSteelAsia.com (2000), URL: http://www.isteelasia.com/manage_eng.html, 31 May.

Exhibit 2:   Prominent founding members

1. Van Shung Chong Holdings (Hong Kong)
    A member of the VSC Group.
2. Shougang Concord International Enterprises Company Ltd. (Hong Kong)
    A Hong Kong-based listed steel trader and a member of the Beijing Shougang group of companies.
3. Amsteel Mills Sdn. Bhd.
    Operator of a steel mill in Malaysia.
4. ICDAS Celik Enerji Tersane ve Ulasim Sanayi A.S.
    Operator of a steel mill in Turkey for more than 25 years.
5. Scaw Metals Limited
    Operator of a steel mill in South Africa since 1937 and a member of the Anglo-American Industrial group of companies.
6. CCC Steel GmbH
    A large international steel-trading joint venture established between Coutinho Caro & Co., Hamburg, Germany and Grupo Villacero, Monterrey, Mexico.
7. Stemcor (SEA) Pte Ltd.
    A Singapore-based steel trader and a member of the UK's Stemcor group of companies.

Exhibit 2 (cont'd)

8. SK Global Company

   A member of one of Korea's business conglomerates. It was established in 1953 and operated through 50 branches with business in more than 100 countries. It traded a wide range of products, including steel and chemical products.

9. CMC (Australia) Pty. Ltd.

   The Sydney-based trading and marketing subsidiary of the Commercial Metals Company that was established in 1915 and had its head office in Dallas, Texas.

10. Hanwa Co., Ltd.

    A Japanese trading house that was established in 1947 and provided its steel customers with logistical support and warehousing services.

Source: Dao Heng Securities (2000), "iSteelAsia.com (8080)", *CN-Markets – Brokerage Research Hub*, 19 April.

Exhibit 3:   Membership functions and benefits

Identity	Functional accessibility	Posting privileges	Registration requirements	Other benefits
Visitors	*The Steel Talk* and *Industry Info*	Nil	Not required	Nil
Individual members	*The Steel Talk* and *Industry Info*	*The Steel Talk*	Personal registration (on-line)	Nil
Corporate members	All	*On-line Procurement*, *On-line Auction* and *The Steel Talk*	Company registration, verification	Under review
Founding members	All	*On-line Procurement*, *On-line Auction* and *The Steel Talk*	By invitation only	Revenue options

Source: iSteelAsia.com Placement Prospectus, April 2000, p. 66.

Exhibit 4:   The products and services of iSteelAsia.com's portal

On-line Trading Centre

iSteelAsia modelled its business to benefit from the value of business conducted through its portal. Commissions [see **Table 5**] were charged on deals agreed between both sellers and buyers, regardless of whether the transactions were actually executed. The commissions earned represented the main revenue stream of iSteelAsia. Negotiations and agreements were done via the On-line Trading Centre, which included four services: *On-line Procurement, On-line Auction, Activity Highlights* and *Transactions Status*. The first two were the core services that allowed a member to buy or sell products through the exchange, whereas the latter two showed summaries of the activities of the members.

Table 5:   iSteelAsia.com commission rates

	SELLER		BUYER
	Flat products, specialities	Long products, raw materials	All products
On line procurement	0.60–1.00%	0.10–1.00%	Free
On-line auction	0.90–1.50%	0.15–1.50%	Free

Source: iSteelAsia.com Placement Prospectus, p. 66.

On-line procurement enabled a corporate member to effect an on-line purchase of the products required in three stages. Prior to reaching an agreement, the identities of the buyers and the sellers were not revealed.

1. In the first stage, the buyer filled an on-line form specifying his or her request. Details to be supplied included product category, quantity required and closing date. Optional information specifying other terms and conditions, such as delivery date, could be supplied as well. After matching the fields with its database, iSteelAsia would e-mail invitations to qualified members to offer a quote.
2. The second stage involved the sellers checking the details of the request and offering a quote while specifying any discrepancies between the offer and the request. The offers were then routed by iSteelAsia to the response list of the buyer.

Exhibit 4 (cont'd)

3. In the final step, the buyer decided which offer to accept. Upon acceptance of the successful offer, the identities of both the buyer and the seller were revealed by iSteelAsia. The seller paid a commission of between 0.10 percent and one percent of the agreed transaction value to iSteelAsia.com, regardless of whether or not the transaction was completed.

On-line auction allowed a corporate member to effect an on-line auction of its products, again in three steps. The identities of the sellers and the buyers were not revealed before they reached an agreement.

1. The seller filled an on-line form specifying the details of the product, as well as specifying the bidding duration and reserve price, if any. Optional information could be specified as well, such as restricting certain buyers. iSteelAsia then matched the specifications with the database of registered members. Qualified buyers were sent invitations via e-mail to place a bid for the product.
2. In the second stage, the buyers, after checking the particulars of the auction, would post bids to iSteelAsia, while specifying any discrepancy between the offer and the bid, and any additional terms and conditions.
3. The final stage involved the seller deciding whether to accept the bids. Again, similar to *On-line Procurement*, the identity of the parties was revealed only when the bid (not necessarily the highest) was accepted, whereupon iSteelAsia received a commission of between 0.15 percent and 1.5 percent of the agreed price, regardless of whether the transaction was completed.

This process of trading was usually referred to as the aggregation and matching method as it brought a large number of buyers and sellers together and matched their requirements. The process was also structured to promote the portal as a neutral trading platform, which the directors identified as one of the key attractions of the portal. As stated by the chairman of the Company, "We'll put whoever has the best prices and the best deal on the first page, regardless of who they are."[19]

---

[19] Feng, C.H. (2000), "Man of Steel: Andrew Yao Shows His Metal on the Internet", *Asian Business*, May, p. 35.

Exhibit 4 (cont'd)

Industry Information

This section was organised especially to provide members and visitors with access to a comprehensive array of information related to the steel industry, or information that could affect the global movement of steel. The information was provided by Reuters, a leading information provider. Subsections included *Hyperlinks Library*, *Industry Calendar*, *Industry News*, *Industry Reports* and *Industry Standards*. The information contained within this section allowed members to trade on an informed basis.

The Steel Talk

This section acted as a forum, allowing members (both corporate and individual) to express their views and concerns, or to share ideas and chat with other members about relevant subjects in the steel industry. It was aimed at promoting a community spirit among the members.

Value-added Services

iSteelAsia aimed at promoting itself as a one-stop steel-trading centre. To enhance this role, it provided referrals to third-party value-added services such as shipping, insurance and financial services, with more services to be added in the future. According to its Placement Prospectus, these value-added services would be provided by third-party surveyors, banks, shipping companies, insurance companies and content providers.

Several companies had teamed up with iSteelAsia to offer these services. These included ABN-AMRO Bank, Reuters and Houlder Insurance Brokers, all internationally known in their respective industries. The Company was also in the midst of talks with various other companies, such as Inspectorate, a division of the British Standards Institution group, and SGS Mineral Services of Switzerland. It also planned to negotiate with other sources to enrich the portal, aiming to create a one-stop centre for trading in steel by providing all the services necessary to carry out a steel-trading process from start to end.

Exhibit 5: iSteelAsia.com business strategies

Emphasis on Customer Relationship Management

As an intermediary in the supply-chain for the steel industry, the provision of quality services to facilitate the sourcing and procurement of steel products among its customers is the essence of the Group's business. Accordingly, the Group has prioritised customer relationship management as its overriding objective. The directors believe in the importance of understanding the customer's needs and of devising solutions and facilitating access to services to meet those needs. To further expand the operation of the Group, branch offices are to be established and local expertise is to be recruited to build on customer relationships with steel mills, traders, processing centres and end users in the area. A customer relationship management team is to be formed to serve Members and to identify their needs. An international management consultant has been engaged to advise the Group in relation to, among other things, customer relationship management for the steel industry.

Build a Strong Brand Name

The Group will continue to build a strong brand name by promoting its services through customer-focused initiatives. The traditional trading operation will work closely with its customers to provide the specialised services and solutions they demand. Furthermore, the Group will continue to encourage its existing customers to utilise the iSteelAsia.com trading platform to conduct their steel-trading activities. iSteelAsia.com is being marketed at roadshows, presentations and in the media as a creditable, reliable, secure and neutral marketplace. Established steel industry enterprises are being invited to become founding members to build a strong brand name. In addition, the Group intends to engage Scient to assist iSteelAsia.com to develop its e-business.

Forge Relationships with Strategic Partners to Expand Value-added Services

The directors intend to enrich the content of iSteelAsia.com by forming alliances with quality content providers and by sourcing research reports from steel industry analysts. Furthermore, additional value-added services, including the provision of payment status tracking services, on-line B2B banking facilities, shipping information and shipment booking, third-party surveying services, cargo insurance and logistic support services, may be offered through the iSteelAsia.com Website. The directors also intend to enhance the user interface to improve process efficiencies and reduce the costs of manual order processing.

Exhibit 5 (cont'd)

Establish Country-specific Websites for Asia's Domestic Steel Markets

The directors intend to leverage off the achievement of iSteelAsia.com in being the first Asia–Pacific–focused vertical portal to be launched for the steel industry by adapting its concept and technology to countries in the Asia–Pacific region to establish country–specific Websites that cater for domestic steel trade. The Group's strategy is to establish joint ventures with local partners to develop and operate such sites to seek an active management role in such joint ventures.

Source: iSteelAsia.com Placement Prospectus, 14 April 2000, p. 59.

CASE

■■■

4.2

Dell: Selling Directly, Globally*

I believe we have the right business model for the Internet age.
— Michael Dell, CEO, Dell Computer Corporation[1]

Dell Computer Corporation was into its 15th year of operation and had expanded from a US$6.2 million US-based business in 1985 to a US$21.7 billion international business in 1999. In 1999 it ranked second in both the US and the worldwide PC market. Its success was founded on the direct business-to-customer (B2C) model, which revolutionised the PC industry, at first in the US and then in over 170 countries around the world. The Company had been setting the standards for pricing and performance worldwide, despite analysts repeatedly saying, "This is an American concept. It cannot work here!" Then in 1996, Dell again rocked the PC industry by making its

---

[1] "Dell Paves the Way for a New Level of Direct Economics and Customer Benefits", 14 April 1997, URL: http://www.dell.com/corporate/media/newsreleases/97/9704/14.htm, August 1999.

* Pauline Ng prepared this case in conjunction with P. Lovelock under the supervision of Dr. Ali Farhoomand. *Copyright © 2000 The University of Hong Kong. Ref 99/53C*

direct approach even more direct through the Internet. Dell On-line seemed a natural progression for Dell. In the first quarter of 1997, Dell reported daily on-line sales of US$1 million. For the month of August 1999, daily on-line sales had reached US$30 million, translating to US$11 billion per annum. By the end of 2000, Dell targeted to conduct half of its business in each region on-line.

However, despite its remarkable growth and global expansion, there were still many regions Dell needed to break into to ensure its future position in the ranks, notably in China. Analysts predicted that China would soon become the second-largest PC market after the US, generating revenues of US$25 billion by 2002. In September 1999, Dell ranked number seven in China's PC market. The Company had ambitions to achieve approximately ten percent of its global sales through the China market by 2002, which would secure the number two ranking in China. The China market would thus account for 50 percent of regional sales by 2002. Fifty percent of sales were also to be achieved through the Internet. Was this timescale realistic? Was the market mature enough to handle its business on-line direct? Aaron Loke, Director of Marketing, was contemplating the expansion strategy for Dell to pursue in China. Could the 'American model' work in China?

DELL DIRECT

From Glory to Glory

I definitely felt that I was diving into something pretty major without knowing most of the details.... But I did know one thing. I knew what I wanted to do: build better computers than IBM, and become number one in the industry.

– Michael Dell[2]

In 1983, at the age of 18 and with US$1,000, Michael Dell realised his life ambition and started out selling upgraded PCs and add-on components from his dormitory room at the University of Texas, Austin. This dorm-room business officially became Dell Computer Corporation in May 1984. With the rapid growth of the Company, Dell went public in June 1988. Ten years on, Dell was ranked number two and the fastest growing among all major computer systems companies worldwide, with more than 26,000 employees around the globe [see **Exhibit 1**]. Michael Dell earned the

---

[2] Dell, M. & Fredman, C. (1999), *Direct from Dell: Strategies That Revolutionized an Industry*, London: HarperCollins Publishers, p. 11.

reputation of being the youngest CEO ever of a Fortune 500 company. Furthermore, he was named one of *BusinessWeek*'s 'Top 25 Managers of the Year' in 1997, 'Entrepreneur of the Year' by *Inc.* magazine, 'Man of the Year' by *PC Magazine* and 'CEO of the Year' by *Financial World*. The success of Michael Dell and the Dell Computer Corporation was founded on the direct B2C model [see **Exhibit 2**].

The Direct Model

The Company was founded on a simple concept: that by selling personal computers directly to customers, Dell could best understand their needs and provide the most effective computing solutions to meet those needs. Dell sold directly to customers, dealt directly with suppliers and communicated directly with employees, all without the unnecessary interference of intermediaries. To the customer, whether a regular consumer or a multinational corporation, Dell was their single point of contact and accountability.

Dealing directly with customers meant that Dell knew exactly what its customers wanted. While IBM's PC was an open box designed to allow for expansion, reconfiguration and continual upgrading, Dell chose to build PCs to order. Dell was the first PC manufacturer to offer free installation of applications software as a standard service option. By using patented technology, it installed network cards to customers' proprietary, in-house applications, right on the manufacturing line. Thus, Dell claimed that it offered its customers more powerful, more richly configured systems for their money than competitors. Rather than pursuing technology for technology's sake, customers got only what they wanted. Many PC manufacturers had fallen into the trap of guessing what their customers might want.

Dealing directly with suppliers was essential for the successful application of Dell's direct model. Just-in-time inventory control created advantages that had an immediate impact on customers. Inventory costs were kept to a minimum, new technological breakthroughs (e.g., faster chips, bigger disk drives) could be delivered to customers within a week as opposed to two months, and obsolete and dated stock holdings were minimised. The threat of being caught in a transition to a next-generation product with an inventory of obsolete stock was a perpetual problem in the industry, but one that the direct model could avoid. Dell was able to pass along to its customers the savings from reductions in system component costs quickly because it maintained very low inventories. This was of paramount importance in the PC industry as the rate of development of new technology dictated PC prices. Dealing directly with a few main suppliers on a global basis reinforced Dell's competitive advantage. Michael Dell's reasoning was that through closer contact with customers and with more information about customer needs, there was less need for massive amounts of inventory.

There were three golden rules at Dell: disdain inventory, always listen to the customers and never sell indirectly. The formula worked well for Dell. Its build-to-order manufacturing operation for the US was located in Texas, for Europe in Limerick (Ireland), for Asia–Pacific in Penang (Malaysia) and for China in Xiamen.

Growth and Expansion Beyond the US

Our success was, in fact, something of a crisis point.

– Michael Dell[3]

Rapid growth and expansion were necessary if the Company was to survive. The Company started out targeting the small- to medium-sized businesses in the US market. While its competitors were aiming at the top end of the market (i.e., the large corporations), Dell chose to lead a price/performance revolution from the bottom up, bringing new technology at affordable prices to the widest possible group of customers. The strategy worked well in the US. By the end of 1986, Dell had achieved US$60 million in sales. Michael Dell was concerned about the next step for his Company because staying small would make them vulnerable to the consolidation that was taking place in the PC industry. In the fall of 1986, he called together the executives of the Company and held a brainstorming meeting. Three key realisations materialised that were to map the course that Dell was to take:

1. Dell had to target large companies if the business was to grow.
2. To do this, they had to offer the best support in the industry.
3. Despite the fact the Company was only two-and-a-half years old, it needed to expand globally and to grow beyond the US.

Many people told us the direct model would fail in virtually every country we expanded into … The message was always the same: Our country is different, your business model won't work here.

– Michael Dell[4]

---

[3] Dell, M. & Fredman, C. (1999), p. 26.
[4] Dell, M. & Fredman, C. (1999), p. 28.

In June 1987, Dell ventured out of the US for the first time and started business in the UK. Journalists and analysts speculated that Dell's direct model might work in the US, but not in Europe. However, 11 more international operations opened over the period 1987 to 1991. By 1994, Dell had international subsidiaries in 14 countries, and sold and supported its products in more than 100 additional markets through partnering agreements with technology distributors. In 1995, construction began on the Asia-Pacific Customer Centre (APCC) in Penang, Malaysia. In the first half of 1995, Dell opened offices in six countries in the region. Malaysia became the hub of a comprehensive Asia-Pacific management, sales and marketing network that included Australia, China, Hong Kong, India, Indonesia, Korea, Malaysia, New Zealand, the Philippines, Singapore, Taiwan and Thailand. The intention was to begin on a selected basis and to extend out from country to country over time. In 1998, the Xiamen manufacturing and service centre (China Customer Centre) was opened. The regional headquarters of Dell Asia Pacific remained in Hong Kong. In 1998, Dell operated sales offices in 33 countries and served customers in more than 170 countries and territories around the world.

Results That Spoke for Themselves

Dell Computer Corporation defies gravity. Whether you measure its growth in sales, profits, market share, or stock price, the Company is simply weightless.
                                                            — *Business Week*, 2 November 1998

Dell went through extremely rapid growth throughout the Company's history [see **Exhibit 3**]. Its build-to-order, direct-sales approach allowed it to far outpace industry growth rates. In 1995, a company press release reported that Dell's stock value had appreciated by more than 700 percent since the Company's first public offering in 1988.[5] In the same year, *Fortune* magazine ranked Dell for 'best investment' with an 81.2 percent 'total return to investors' over the previous year. By December 1997, Dell had overtaken IBM and became the second-largest supplier of desktop PCs world-wide, with a 9.7 percent share of the market and a 10–15 percent price advantage over its major competitors who distributed their products through indirect channels.[6] [See

---

[5] "Be Quick and Focused; Global Markets Surging Ahead, Dell CEO Says", 27 January 1995, URL: http:www.dell.com/corporate/media/newsreleases/95/9501/27.htm, August 1999.

[6] US Department of Commerce (1998), "The Emerging Digital Economy", 15 April, URL: http://www.ecommerce.gov/emerging.htm, August 1999.

Exhibit 1.] Between 1988 to 1998 the Company's stock value increased by 36,000 percent. In the same period, it had grown from a US$159 million company to a US$18 billion company.[7]

By February 1998, the Company reported a sales increase in Europe of 61 percent in the fourth quarter of the 1998 financial year, bringing sales close to US$1 billion. Sales from Asia-Pacific increased by 79 percent in the 1998 financial year compared to the previous year, an increase that was more than in any other Dell regional business, albeit from a small base. In August 1999, the Company announced that it was number one in PC shipments within the UK. [See **Exhibit 4** for a breakdown of revenue by geographic region.]

For the quarter ended 31 July 1999, the Company reported revenue of US$21.7 billion. It became the number one PC vendor to businesses in the US. Dell again led industry growth in unit shipments, revenue and earnings. Shipments increased by 55 percent, two times higher than analysts' estimates of total industry growth. Dell's operating income was 11.3 percent of revenue and operating expenses declined by nearly one percentage point. Return on investment was 260 percent, four times higher than that of Dell's nearest major competitor. At quarter-end, Dell held six days of inventory. [See **Exhibit 5** for details of Dell's achievements.]

Selective Expansion

Dell had applied an expansion strategy that involved selective introduction of the direct model, country by country. The strategy followed the same pattern in each country: in the first instance, Dell would make use of distributors (e.g., currently in India). The benefits of the direct model over the indirect model (such as reduced costs and increased attention to customer experience and satisfaction) were obviously lost. The decision to apply the direct model depended on the 'readiness' of the country/region and would rest on a number of factors, including the following:

❑ The size of the market, current and potential.
❑ The availability of resources, especially a sales force that was capable of applying the direct-sales model: the PC industry was dominated by vendors selling through indirect channels. The skills set required for relating to customers' needs and translating those needs into customised products and services was not readily available.

---

[7] Dell, M. & Fredman, C. (1999), p. 225.

❑ Sufficient management resources at the local level: senior management required knowledge of the behaviour of the local market, the training potential and needs of the local labour force, as well as other cultural, physical and political limitations that had to be overcome.

❑ Local acceptance of Dell's direct model: potential customers who had not heard of the Dell brand would find it difficult to pick up the telephone and order Dell PCs without having seen one. This applied even more so in countries/ regions where the cost of a PC was two or three times an individual's monthly salary. From Dell's experience, customer trust had to be earned. This would initially entail significant resources mobilised to ensure face-to-face contact with potential customers. However, once trust was established through product and service satisfaction, customers were happy to make repeat orders through the telephone.

❑ Suppliers' ability to deliver parts at short notice: Dell's direct model was dependent to a large extent on just-in-time inventory management.

❑ Adequate arrangements with carriers to ensure the timely delivery of orders: Dell's average order-to-delivery time was six days. Dell had made arrangements with authorised carriers (American, Airborne, Conway, Eagle, First Air, FedEx, RPS, UPS and Watkins) to expedite deliveries around the globe. DHL, FedEx and Bax Global were used extensively in the Asia-Pacific region.

❑ Operating costs.

Timing for entry to new markets was therefore essential given all the factors that had to be considered. However, the underlying motivating force at Dell was that, given the right timing and the readiness of the market, all countries/regions in the world would accept the direct model for selling PCs. The PC had become a commodity and the globalisation of the PC market would, in the future, be comparable to purchasing a can of Coca-Cola or a pizza. In the past, major barriers for Dell have included government regulations, the lack of human resources, inadequate telecommunications and transportation infrastructures, and the unavailability or inaccessibility of parts.

While planning for global expansion, the impact of the Internet explosion rippled through Dell.

WWW.DELL.COM

Dell, the Company, seems to have been born and evolved with an anticipation of the Internet age.

– Andrew S. Grove, Chairman, Intel Corporation

Our PC consumer shipments grew more than 100 percent in the quarter [ended 31 July 1999], and about one-half of those sales were generated on-line, through www.dell.com.

– Michael Dell[8]

Very early on, Dell saw the advantages of the Internet and exploited them before others in the industry. For Dell, this new technology presented a medium through which it could get even closer to its customers and enhance its direct-sales approach. It was a logical extension to the direct model, making it even more direct.

In June 1994, Dell launched www.dell.com. This was phase one of Dell's plan to link with its customers through the Net. The site presented customers with simple product and price lists, almost like an on-line catalogue.

Since July 1996, Dell customers could configure and order a computer directly through Dell's Website. This was phase two of Dell's plan. Within a year, daily sales over the Net totalled over US$3 million [see **Exhibit 6**]. Dell was the first computer company to provide a comprehensive on-line purchasing tool.

Phase three included providing on-line technical support, order status information and on-line downloading of software. Dell's electronic commerce strategy was beginning to take shape [see **Exhibit 7** for the sitemap of www.dell.com]. It was developed to work seamlessly with the Company's existing systems, providing real-time pricing and order status. Its goal was to make the internal operations of the Company agile enough to respond to the ever-increasing and ever-changing needs of customers. On average, in 1998, Dell responded to over 120,000 technical support queries a week through its Website. Interestingly, 90 percent of sales through the Net were placed by small businesses and consumers. Corporate customers chose to use the Website for gathering product information, order status and technical help rather than to place orders.

For Dell, the benefits of the Internet were enormous. Eighty percent of the consumers and half of the small businesses who purchased on Dell's Website were first-time buyers. Undoubtedly, www.dell.com brought in additional revenues. Providing product information, pricing and technical support on-line helped to lower sales and marketing costs. Basic customer service and technical support functions provided through

---

[8] Dell Computer Corporation (1999), "Internet Benefits to Customers, Company Expanding; On-line Sales Reach $30 Million Per Day", URL: http://www.dell.com/corporate/media/newsreleases/99/9908/17.htm, September.

the Internet helped to lower service and support costs. Dell estimated that 20,000 customers who would check their order status on-line would present savings for Dell of between US$6,000 to US$10,000 per week, and 30,000 software requests that could be downloaded on-line would save Dell US$150,000 per week.[9]

By mid-1998, all Dell customers had individual files of their system configurations on-line. Customers were able to take advantage of the very latest technology and immediate component price reductions. In addition, it offered 24 hours on-line service and support. It removed inter-company boundaries and achieved speed-to-market in ways that were not possible before. In April 1997, Dell established a new joint-venture leasing company called Dell Financial Services, which provided a range of flexible leasing options directly to Dell customers in the US and eventually worldwide. Its Internet offerings included more than 6,500 products from its DellWare catalogue.

Dell's application of Internet technology to its direct model created a fully integrated value-chain. It allowed a three-way 'information partnership' with suppliers and customers by treating each player as a collaborator to improve efficiency across the entire supply- and demand-chain, thus sharing the benefits. For example, at Dell's manufacturing site in Ireland, after orders were received via the Web and call centres, Dell would relay to its suppliers details of the components required, all the components were then delivered to the site, and complete computers would be shipped out, all within a few hours.

Customisation

The Internet also provided great potential for enhancing customer relations and opened up new selling possibilities. Through its Website, Dell refined the services tailored to its customer segments. Dell offered capabilities, service and content tailored to the needs of its customers, including large commercial accounts, government, educational institutions, small/medium businesses and home buyers. To attract the corporate clientele, Dell created customised 'Premier Pages' that allowed them to make purchases from the company's own intranet. Microsoft was one company that made use of its customised Premier Page. Typically, the company would receive its configured systems in about four days from the day of order. The on-line paperless purchase orders and electronic invoicing capabilities saved Microsoft an estimated US$1 million in procurement costs in the first year alone. Another large company estimated that it had saved US$2 mil-

---

[9] US Department of Commerce (1999).

lion in technical support costs and another estimated 15 percent savings from Internet procurement efficiencies. Later on, the Company introduced 'My Dell' Webpages that were customised pages for home and small business consumers.

Realising the Full Potential of the Internet

In August 1999, the Company reported sales of more than US$30 million in products each day over the Net. The Website attracted more than 25 million visitors per quarter and had unique Webpages for 44 countries in 21 languages. The Company had more than 27,000 customer-specific Premier Pages within www.dell.com. In June 1999, 70 percent of Dell's Internet sales came through Premier Pages. By the end of 2000, Dell anticipated that half of its total business (sales, service and support) would be conducted on-line. The Internet had the potential to change the face of the PC industry. Dell aimed to assume a leadership position in Internet commerce, defining the Internet business model as an extension of the direct model rather than simply an adjunct to some reseller relationship.

> *... we enjoy the advantage of continuing to refine our model while others retrofit theirs.*
> – Michael Dell[10]

E-SUPPORT DIRECT

> *Our industry has generally neglected the customer. I want to take the customer experience to a whole new level.*
> – Michael Dell[11]

> *Service is the new competitive battlefield in the information technology industry ... The largest global enterprise customers are demanding more – and better – service and support from systems vendors.*
> – Michael Dell[12]

---

[10] Dell Computer Corporation (1997), "Dell Paves the Way for a New Level of Direct Economics and Customer Benefits", 14 April, URL: http://www.dell.com/corporate/media/newsreleases/97/9704/14.htm, August 1999.

[11] "What Does No. 1 Do for an Encore?" *Newsweek*, 2 November 1998.

[12] Dell Computer Corporation (1998), "Dell Joins with Unisys and Wand Global to Expand Service Offering for Global Customers", 11 May, URL: http://www.dell.com/corporate/media/newsreleases/98/9805/11.htm, August 1999.

e-Support Direct was the fourth phase of Dell's electronic commerce strategy. The Internet improved the speed and flow of information at much lower costs. It was the natural tool for Dell to deliver the ultimate in customer experience, the direct-service model. In the early years of the industry it was driven by technological break-throughs. As competition gathered pace, price became an increasingly significant driver of demand in the marketplace. For Dell, price and time to the market had become the huge differentiators. However, Michael Dell foresaw that building a business solely on pricing was not a sustainable advantage. Maintaining customer loyalty became a primary focus. This marked Dell's gradual evolution from a simple box-mover to a fully fledged service provider, yielding the powers of the Internet to build on the competitive advantages of the direct model.

In 1998, Dell announced that it intended to focus on creating a new direct-service model for building the business of the future. In August 1999, Dell unveiled e-Support Direct. The plan involved creating computing environments where a PC or server would be capable of maintaining itself. e-Support would provide tailored services designed to achieve higher levels of system uptime, streamline the customer support process and decrease the total cost of system ownership.

Just as Dell had revolutionised the PC industry with its direct model and with www.dell.com, Dell intended to use the Internet to revolutionise the customer support experience. Internet-enabled support was to provide customised capability to easily automate and speed up the support process. These included Dell On-line Knowledge Base, Ask Dudley, Resolution Assistant and HelpTech. Support information was unique to each system and could be found at support.dell.com [see **Exhibits 8A–8C** for details of e-Support services].

Dell was named one of 1999's Ten Best Web Support Sites by the Association of Support Professionals, a national body that examined industry support trends. Dell was the only PC vendor to win the award. In the same year, Dell was also awarded an 'A' in Web Support by the CNET Editor's Choice for Service and Support. The Company also announced that it was leading the industry by resolving 80 percent of technical support issues without despatching service technicians, much higher than the industry average of 27 percent.

Within the industry, there was growing consensus that the focus of business was shifting beyond the box-selling mentality.

The old model of making PCs is no longer viable.

– Mr. Anderson, IDC[13]

Global expansion through the Internet, however, had its limitations. This was especially true for regions where Internet usage was still low in terms of population density.

THE SECOND-LARGEST PC MARKET IN THE WORLD

If we're not in what will soon be the second-biggest PC market in the world, then how can Dell possibly be a global player?

– John Legere, President, Dell Asia Pacific[14]

The PC market in the Mainland had seen rapid growth. [See **Exhibit 9** for growth of China's computer industry between 1990–96.] In 1996, PC vendors sold 2.1 million desktop PCs, notebooks and servers in China, an increase of nearly 40 percent from the previous year. The total value of the market in 1996 was US$3.34 billion, an increase of over 20 percent from the previous year. In three years' time, it was estimated that China's market size would be around 10 million PCs. The major Chinese PC makers, such as Legend, Founder and Great Wall, ranked within the top ten in terms of PC shipments. All PC vendors competing in China sold through distributors who carried many brands. For example, Compaq had engaged 21 distributors at one point during 1996.

In June 1998, the Market Information Centre (MIC) reported its prediction that by the year 2000, Mainland China's annual PC production would reach 7.6 million, making it the third-largest in the world after the US and Japan. Furthermore, if Japan's economic slump continued, China could take second place in global PC production. If PC shipments in China continued to grow at 30 percent per annum (as it had between 1996–99), China's PC market would surpass Japan's by 2004. Not even the Asian financial crisis had slowed down this growth. As at June 1999, China was the fifth-largest PC market behind the US, Japan, Germany and Britain.

---

[13] Ong, C. (1999), "Crunch Time for Resellers As Direct PC Selling Grows", *South China Morning Post*, 20 April.

[14] Chowdhury, N. (1999), "Dell Cracks China", *Fortune*, 21 June.

However, China and her PC market were characterised by a number of factors as follows:

- ❏ Retail buyers only accounted for ten percent of sales.[15]
- ❏ The price of a PC was the equivalent of two years of a person's savings.[16]
- ❏ Chinese managers were becoming more and more tech-savvy on their own.
- ❏ The problem of software piracy in China was rife: Microsoft estimated that 95 percent of the software used in Chinese corporations was stolen.
- ❏ China's nationalistic politics made US companies in China vulnerable to the ups and downs of Sino-American relations.
- ❏ The Chinese government made no secret of the fact that national PC vendors would be promoted.
- ❏ There remained the tensions between the immense economic opportunities in China and the constraints on business activity, including the shortage of skilled labour and the immature legal and institutional frameworks.
- ❏ In 1995, *PCWeek On-line* reported in an article that "…building close and trusting relationships is critical to succeeding in China."[17] However, five years on, times had changed and many foreign companies in China were succeeding without having the connections.
- ❏ The government required users of the Internet to register with the police when opening an account, and there was widespread belief that user activity was monitored by the government. Many commentators predicted that one of the key obstacles to future growth of Internet usage in China was the issue of government control.
- ❏ The credit payment system: China's Ninth Five-Year Plan made it a priority to establish a series of 'Golden' projects, one of which was the 'Golden Card'. This project was aimed at developing a nationwide credit card network that would also provide debit and electronic purse facilities in China. It was reported in 1997 that the smart cards were scheduled to be operational before the end of 2002, and that 250–300 million cards would be in use by then.[18] China had

---

[15] Chowdhury, N. (1999).

[16] Chowdhury, N. (1999).

[17] Hamm, S. (1995), "Sound the Gong", *PCWeek On-line*, URL: http://www.zdnet.com/~pcweek/inside/0724/tgong.html, September 1999.

[18] Tse, S. & Tsang, P. (last update 2 July 1997), "Internet and WWW in China: All the Right Connections", AUG 95 & Asia-Pacific World Wide Web '95 Conference & Exhibition, URL: http://www.csu.edu.au/special/conference/apwww95/papers95/stse/stse.html, September 1999.

embarked on the largest smart bank card in the world. Having said that, it seemed unlikely that the smart card would be readily issued to the average citizen, but mainly to corporate bodies and people of high social standing.

❑ On the Internet front, Chinese Internet usage was proliferating. Between 1997 and 1998, according to IDC, the number of Internet users increased by 71 percent to more than two million users.

❑ Analysts predicted that China would contribute the largest Internet growth in the first part of the 21st century.[19]

DELL IN CHINA

Dell Takes the Direct Model to China

In February 1998, Dell announced its intention to expand into the world's most populous country, China. Reporters and analysts told the Company that the western concept would not work in China. China's regulation was that if goods were not manufactured in China they could not be sold directly in the Mainland. Hence, in August, a new 135,000 square-foot facility was opened and a China Customer Centre (CCC) was established to produce, sell and provide service and technical support. The intention was to place the Company closer to its customers in markets that presented long-term potential. In the previous three years, Dell's business in the Chinese market had grown steadily and sales of computer systems were through distributors.

Xiamen was chosen for its ideal location, halfway between Hong Kong and Shanghai on China's southeastern coast in Fujian Province. It was one of China's first four Special Economic Zones established in 1981. Xiamen was a rapidly growing city with a vigorous economy and a fully modern infrastructure. It boasted of excellent highway connections to major cities in China and an efficient domestic airport. Furthermore, it had a number of reputable universities and over 20 percent of Xiamen's population were graduates of higher education. The telecommunications network in Xiamen was excellent, providing over 1,000 telephone lines to the CCC. Through negotiations with the government, two power grids supplied electricity directly to the CCC.

The CCC mirrored the manufacturing and professional functions found at the Asia-Pacific Customer Centre (APCC) in Penang. The CCC allowed Dell to pass on the benefits of the direct model to its customers in China, including cutting out the

---

[19] Tse, S. & Tsang, P. (last update 2 July 1999).

costs of the distributors, being able to make-to-order within three to four days and providing upgraded systems to customers within a week. An order could be off the production line within two days. Most deliveries, using contracted carriers, were by road. Furthermore, 70 percent of Dell's parts were supplied from within the Mainland through manufacturers who had global agreements with Dell. Quality was therefore not sacrificed.

In August 1998, direct sales and technical support operations began in nine areas of China, including Beijing, Shanghai, Guangzhou and Xiamen. Through these locations, Dell covered over 80 percent of the potential user population. The Company also launched toll-free sales and technical-support telephone numbers to provide immediate local-language assistance to customers. The Xiamen operation employed a little under 500 people. Around 200 were 'outside sales' staff, engaged in door-to-door visits, looking after corporate customers. The rest worked at the CCC and included engineers, production staff as well as 'inside sales' staff. The latter engaged in taking on-line and telephone orders. Staffing was a major challenge for Dell. It was difficult to find experienced direct sales people because direct sales was a new profession in China. Despite this, 96 percent of the workforce were recruited locally, the remainder consisting of management level staff were mostly from Hong Kong. Over 60 percent were university graduates.

Another problem encountered in China was the bureaucracy and red tape involved in securing government contracts, the government and government-owned corporations being major customers in China's PC market. The negotiation process could be extremely lengthy while the terms of the contracts were often one-sided and non-negotiable in any case.

Dell's range of OptiPlex desktops and Latitude notebook computers and PowerEdge network servers were made available to customers in all nine areas [see **Exhibit 10** for a full list of Dell's systems]. Additional products and services were to be introduced in response to market demand and technology advancements. In fact, in April 1999, Dell introduced its award-winning range of Dimension desktops specifically targeted at home and small business customers.

Contrary to popular belief, most of Dell's sales in China and Asia were not to consumers buying over the telephone. While many vendors were targeting the general market, Dell resolved to focus initially on corporate customers. It was, therefore, questionable whether a like-for-like application of the direct model could be achieved in China. This tactic rattled Chinese PC vendors such as Legend and Founder by nibbling into their most valuable client base: state-owned enterprises. Unlike the US market, where two in ten PCs sold by Dell were to consumers, the consumer segment in China was very different. The price of a PC could cost the equivalent of three months of a person's wages. The average consumer could not afford the investment and very few had a bank account, let alone a credit card. If consumers wanted to buy a Dell PC, they would often visit the nearest Dell office to see one first. Alternatively, they could refer to Dell's Website or newspaper advertisements. Although Dell had stopped using distributors, retailers were purchasing direct from Dell and selling systems on to consumers at marked-up prices.

Dell's customer groups were divided into three segments as follows:

❑ Large Corporate Accounts (LCA): companies with 1,500-plus employees.
❑ Preferred Accounts Division (PAD): companies with 500–1,500 employees.
❑ Home and Small Businesses (HSB): establishments with fewer than 500 employees.

The segment in which Dell was seeing some repeat buyers was in the corporate accounts. Initially, resources were mobilised towards maximising face-to-face contact, establishing good customer relations and promoting the Dell brand on a personal level. This 'relationship sales' strategy was required for the LCA and PAD segments to hone business deals. Some business deals were made through customer relationships and recommendations, while others were made purely through pricing advantages. Once trust and confidence were established, Dell expected that these segments would require less face-to-face contact and that more orders would be placed through the telephone or even through the Net, thus reducing Dell's operating costs. Within corporations, Dell targeted the IT managers who seemed to have some knowledge of the latest PC technology and knew what specifications were required for their companies.

Within the LCA segment, four main industries or sectors accounted for 50 percent of Dell's business: government, education, telecommunications and power, and finance/banking. Two-thirds of Dell's corporate customers in China were state-owned enterprises. Dell Asia Pacific had targeted for revenues in China to constitute approximately ten percent of global sales (representing 50 percent of sales for the region) by 2002, making it the second-largest PC vendor (in terms of volume) and possibly the largest supplier to LCAs. But to achieve this target, senior managers at the CCC debated the need to further segment the market to better serve their customers.

In 1999, Dell ranked seventh in China [see **Exhibit 11** for rankings in China's PC market in 1999]. Dell saw orders coming in from nearly 100 of the Mainland's biggest cities via the telephone, the Internet and from the sales staff, which was still the most common method of selling. In the fourth quarter of 1998, Dell's sales in the Mainland grew by 100 percent, albeit from a small base. In the second quarter of 1999, Dell recorded year-on-year unit growth of 561 percent. If Dell could sustain that pace of growth, it was anticipated that it would achieve sales of more than US$100 million in 1999.

China On-line?

However, just as Dell had been careful to identify the timeliness of making the transition from using distributors to using the direct model, so the timing and market readiness for electronic commerce had to be assessed from country to country. Dell anticipated that, whereas 50 percent of its business (by volume) in the US would be conducted on-line within one to two years, this same target would be achieved in two to three years in the Asia-Pacific. [See **Exhibit 12** for details of Internet usage in the US and Asia-Pacific.] The majority of Dell's business in the Asia-Pacific came from large- and medium-sized corporations. Dell's Website supported 16 country-specific sites for the Asia-Pacific, using three languages, including Chinese and Japanese.

Part of the problem was that the Chinese were uncomfortable with credit card sales, especially of high-price-ticket products that could not be viewed before purchase. Many resources had therefore been invested in door-to-door sales calls to corporations. The operating costs were obviously higher for Dell in China than in, say, Europe or the US, where the majority of sales were placed through the telephone or on-line. Until China caught up with the West in terms of Internet penetration and credit card usage, the costs of enforcing the direct model would continue to take a tidy chunk out of Dell's earnings. Furthermore, these limitations would restrict the potential reach of the direct model.

Some large corporations in China had Premier Pages. These preferred to buy through the Net as it was convenient and fast. While the majority of customers could buy through www.dell.com, there were limitations. Payment had to be made by credit card, cheque or telegraphic transfer. Apart from large corporations who were given credit facilities, other customers had to pay upfront. This created complications and delayed the ordering process. Also, access to the Internet was expensive, and only senior executives were granted usage.

In 1999, Internet sales accounted for less than two percent of total sales in China, compared to 25 percent worldwide. Undoubtedly, the future potential for Internet growth was huge. However, the timing remained uncertain. So far, only Premier Pages and DellWare had been launched on the Net.

COPY-CATS

Yes, we're using Dell's direct-selling model when we target Chinese government compa-nies or multinationals in China.
        – Mary Ma, Chief Financial Officer, Legend[20]

Competition in the Mainland PC market was intense. Legend, the government-backed company, remained in number one position and looked set to remain there for a while yet. All the major vendors, such as IBM, Hewlett-Packard and Compaq, were vying for the position, while a growing number had established manufacturing plants in China. Still others felt the best way to do business in China was to form joint ventures with local companies (e.g., Digital and Founder).

Dell was hoping that its experience and knowledge with the direct model, par-ticularly with the leadership it had in on-line direct selling, would give them a clear run in the medium term at least. However, with the insignificant volume of on-line sales in China and the simplicity of the direct model, it was only a matter of time before the competition would try to beat them at their own game. Legend announced to *Fortune Magazine* that it was rapidly adopting the just-in-time delivery model, sell-ing directly to its corporate customers and being able to cut costs and reduce inven-tory holdings in the process. [See **Exhibit 13** for details of Legend's sales growth.]

Compaq, on the other hand, opted to selectively adopt the direct model. In May 1999, the company announced that it had slashed its US distributors from 40 to four to cut costs, in an attempt to better manage inventory and as a positive step towards applying the direct model. In China, however, Compaq continued to sell through distributors and value-added resellers.

The US is a whole different market and it requires a different model to be efficient. Here in Greater China, we will continue to be committed to our channel partners.
        – Tony Leung, Marketing Director – Greater China, Compaq[21]

However, in June, Compaq cut its list of resellers in Greater China from 30 to ten. In July 1999, Mr. Leung conceded that "The trend to go direct is inevitable…".[22] But

---

[20] Chowdhury, N. (1999).

[21] Ong, C. (1999), "Compaq Axes US Retail Outlets, But Keeps China Plan", *South China Morning Post*, 11 May.

[22] Ong, C. (1999), "Crunch Time for Resellers As Direct PC Selling Grows", *South China Morning Post*, 20 April.

unlike the Dell direct model, Compaq chose not to bypass its resellers. Instead, the 'partner-direct' model linked Compaq to its partners' systems so that orders could be input from its customers on-line. In this way, access to customers would not be limited, said Compaq's chief executive.

In June 1999, IBM announced that it would open a new assembly plant in Shekou at the end of 2000. This was a joint venture between IBM and Great Wall. Being the second-largest PC vendor after Legend, IBM hoped that the new facility would help to reduce inventory holdings to less than four days. While IBM had announced that it would apply the direct model to its North American market, company officials commented that it would take some time before the direct model would be adopted in Asia, where 80 percent of its PCs were sold through traditional channels.

Talking about the potential for taking their business on-line, an IBM official said:

> We have to look at market readiness. The environment here is different from the one in the US. And Asia-Pacific is not as comfortable right now with e-commerce the way the US is.[23]

IBM reported Internet sales of US$3.3 billion in 1998 and the company anticipated that this figure would grow to US$10 billion for 1999.

In the midst of a tense PC market in China and bearing in mind that Dell's three golden rules (disdain inventory, listen to the customers and never sell indirectly) were not to be broken, Aaron Loke was to report to the Asia-Pacific regional head office on the strategy for expansion. Could the direct model take Dell to the number two position? Was the target for on-line sales realistic and how could this be achieved? Was Dell to be a box-seller in China or was there a demand for services and support? How should Dell pursue its on-line global strategy?

---

[23] Ong, C. (1999), "Asia Not Affected By IBM Direct-sales Plan", *South China Morning Post*, 13 April.

Exhibit 1:   US and worldwide PC shipments second quarter, 1998

Top five vendors, US PC shipments

Rank	Vendor	Units (000's)	Market share
1	Compaq	1,157	14.4%
2	Dell	1,143	14.3%
3	IBM	511	6.4%
4	Gateway	623	7.8%
5	Hewlett-Packard	628	7.8%
	Others	3,952	49.3%
	All vendors	8,014	100.0%

Top five vendors, worldwide PC shipments

Rank	Vendor	Units (000's)	Market share
1	Compaq	2,819	14.0%
2	Dell	1,818	9.1%
3	IBM	1,573	7.8%
4	Hewlett-Packard	1,239	6.2%
5	NEC/PBNEC	1,295	6.5%
	Others	11,333	56.4%
	All vendors	20,077	100.0%

Notes:
- Shipments are branded shipments and exclude OEM sales for all vendors.
- Data for NEC/PBNEC includes shipments for Packard Bell, NEC, NEC Japan, NEC China and ZDS.
- Data for Compaq includes shipments for Compaq, Digital Equipment and Tandem.

Source: International Data Corporation, Hong Kong, Q3 1999.

Exhibit 2: Dell's build-to-customer order

Start Here with the Customer
Dell customers communicate and buy from Dell in three ways.

www.dell.com   **Voice-to-voice**   Face-to-face

↓

Just-in-time Inventory
Dell receives only the material it is immediately ready to use and only those specified as desirable to that particular customer.

↓

Custom-designed Computers
The Traveler is a sheet that contains all of the customer's unique configuration information. This document travels with the system throughout its assembly and shipping.

↓

Kitting
Based on the Traveler, all internal parts and components required to make the system are picked and placed into a tote.

↓

Build-to-order
A team of workers uses the kit to assemble and initially test the entire system.

↓

Testing and System Integration
Systems are then extensively tested using Dell diagnostics. Standard or custom hardware and software is factory installed and tested.

↓

Boxing, Shipping and Delivery
The build-to-order cycle takes less than five hours from start to finish.

Exhibit 3:   Dell Computer Corporation financial years 1995–98

	Financial year ended				
	29 Jan 1999	1 Feb 1998	1 Feb 1997	28 Jan 1996	29 Jan 1995
Operating results (US$ million)					
Net revenue	18,243	12,327	7,759	5,296	3,475
Gross margin	4,106	2,722	1,666	1,067	738
Operating income	2,046	1,316	714	377	249
Net income	1,460	944	518	272	149
Net revenue by product line					
– Desktops	64%	71%	78%	81%	87%
– Enterprise	13%	9%	4%	3%	5%
– Portables	23%	20%	18%	16%	8%
Non-system net revenue, percentage of total system net revenue	7%	9%	10%	11%	12%

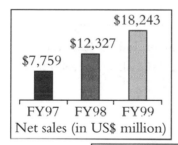
Net sales (in US$ million)

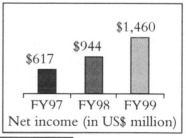
Net income (in US$ million)

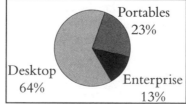

Net revenue by product line for year ended 29 January 1999.

Source: URL: http://www.dell.com/...financials/financialSummReport.htm, August 1999.

Exhibit 4: Dell Computer Corporation revenue by region

	Financial year ended				
	29 Jan 1999	1 Feb 1998	1 Feb 1997	28 Jan 1996	29 Jan 1995
Net revenue					
– Americas	68%	69%	68%	66%	69%
– Europe	26%	24%	26%	28%	27%
– Asia-Pacific & Japan	6%	7%	6%	6%	4%

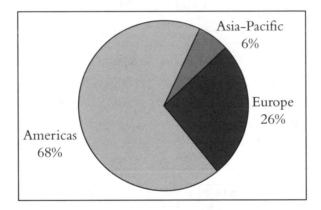

Net revenue by region for year ended 29 January 1999.

Source: URL: http://www.dell.com/...financials/financialSummReport.htm, August 1999.

Exhibit 5:   Dell's rankings and achievements

Dell's ranking

- ❏ No. 1 supplier of PCs to the US corporate market segment (Q2 1997)
- ❏ No. 1 supplier of PCs to the US federal, state and government market segment (Q2 1997)
- ❏ No. 2 for shipment of PCs to large and medium businesses worldwide (Q2 1997)
- ❏ No. 3 supplier of notebooks in the US (June 1998)
- ❏ No. 3 supplier of servers worldwide (1998)
- ❏ No. 2 supplier of servers in the US (1998)
- ❏ No. 1 supplier of workstations in the US (1998)
- ❏ No. 1 supplier of PCs in the UK (1999)

Dell's accolades of industry and business awards

- ❏ The 'Readers' Choice' award for Overall Service and Reliability, *Fortune Technology Buyer's Guide*
- ❏ The 'Readers' Choice' award for Service and Reliability for both desktops and notebooks, *PC Magazine*
- ❏ No. 1 in Web-based support, *ComputerWorld*
- ❏ The 'Reliability and Service Award' for work PCs, home PCs and notebooks, *PC World*
- ❏ Highest customer satisfaction rating for servers, desktops and notebooks from industry analyst firm, Technology Business Research
- ❏ 'Delivering the Best Return on Investment to Shareholders' award among the Fortune 500 (1994)
- ❏ The 'Most Admired Companies' award since 1995, *Fortune*
- ❏ The 'Best Performing Information Technology Company' in the world award, 1998, *Business Week*
- ❏ Top performing stock among the Standard & Poor's 500 and Nasdaq 100 in 1996 and 1997, and top performing US stock on the Dow Jones World Stock Index

Note: This list is not conclusive.

Sources: "Dell Redefines the Low-cost Consumer PC Market", 15 June 1999, URL: http://www.dell.com/corporate/media/newsreleases/99/9906/15.htm, August 1999; "Major Publications, Independent Surveys Declare Dell a Winner", 16 December 1998, URL: http://www.dell.com/corporate/media/newsreleases/98/9812/16.htm, August 1999; Dell DirectWorld – Access: Dell Management (M. Dell), URL: http://www.dell.com/corporate/acce…1mgnt/offcceo/mdell/mdellbiojr.htm, August 1999.

Exhibit 6: Dell's daily on-line sales and weekly technical support volumes 1997

	Q1	Q2	Q3	Q4
Sales per day	US$1 m	US$2 m	US$3 m	US$3 m++
Tech. support/queries per week	30,000	45,000	60,000	120,000
Visitors per week	213,000	225,000	250,000	400,000
Sales outside the US	0%	5%	10%	17%

Source: US Department of Commerce (1998), "The Emerging Digital Economy", 15 April, URL: http://www.ecommerce.gov/emerging.htm, August 1999.

Exhibit 7: www.dell.com

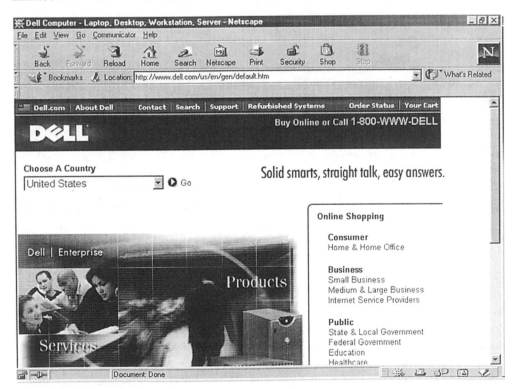

Exhibit 8A: Dell Computer Corporation e-Support services

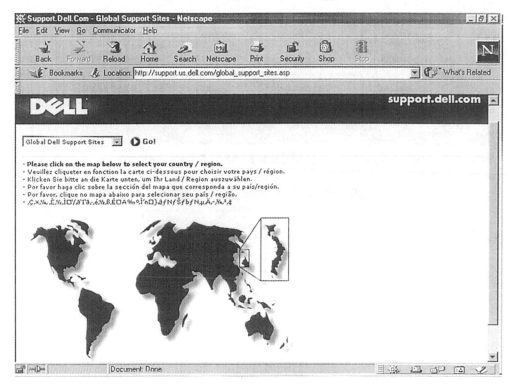

Exhibit 8B: Dell Computer Corporation e–Support services

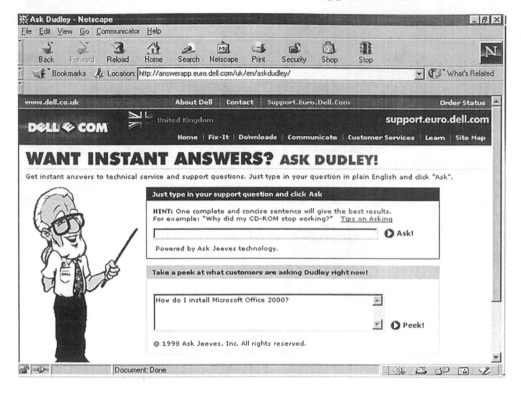

Exhibit 8C: Dell Computer Corporation e-Support services

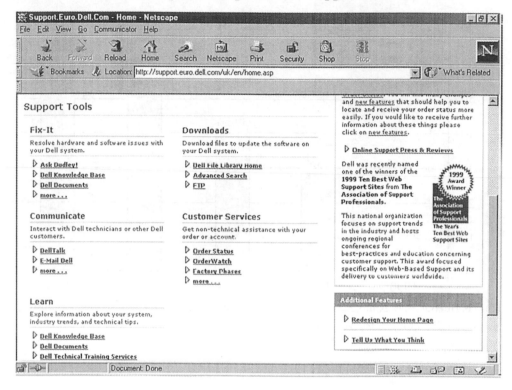

Exhibit 9: Growth of China's computer industry between 1990–96

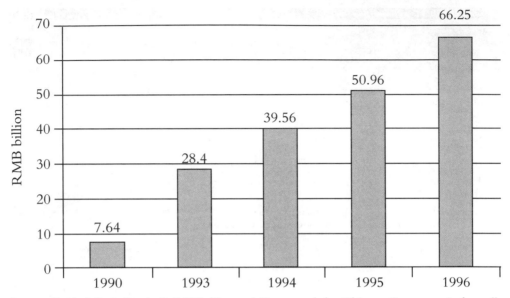

Source: Buchel, B. & Raub, S. (1999), "Legend Group and the Chinese Computer Industry", *Asian Case Research Journal*, Vol. 3, Issue 1, May, p. 51.

Exhibit 10:   Dell Computer Corporation product list

 **DELL PRODUCTS**

DIMENSION®

Performance and value come standard with these versatile desktops for the home and the office.

OPTIPLEX®

Industry-standard, dependable managed PCs designed for reliability and compatibility in networked environments.

INSPIRON™

Inspiron Notebooks deliver All-in-one Multimedia Performance, and power-packed Intel Pentium II mobile processors – all in a mobile package you can afford.

LATITUDE™

Durable notebooks that incorporate easy network connectivity, and managed transitions for a low total cost of ownership.

DELL PRECISION WORKSTATIONS™

A perfect partner for the professional who needs high-end video and amazing 2D and 3D graphics.

POWERVAULT™

A high-performance storage solution for business-critical environments. (SCSI subsystems, fibre channel & tape backup)

DELLWARE ™

From software and printers to monitors, networking products, and nearly everything in between, we've got you covered.

POWEREDGE®

Let a PowerEdge server service your network needs.

Exhibit 11: Rankings in China's PC industry in 1999

	Ranking	Q2 1999	Market share (%)
1	Legend	208,841	17.3
2	IBM	82,330	6.8
3	Hewlett–Packard	71,287	5.9
4	Founder	67,920	5.6
5	Great Wall	38,755	3.2
7	Dell	27,955	2.3
	Others	706,863	58.7
	Total	*1,203,951*	*100.0*

	Ranking	Q2 1998	Market share (%)
1	Legend	117,468	11.5
2	IBM	66,944	6.5
3	Hewlett–Packard	61,500	6.0
4	Compaq	56,045	5.5
5	Tontru	42,379	4.1
11	Dell	7,340	0.7
	Others	671,875	65.6
	Total	*1,023,551*	*100.0*

Source: International Data Corporation, Hong Kong.

Exhibit 12: Internet usage in the US and Asia–Pacific

Country	Internet hosts (1997)	Hosts/1,000 people	Number of Internet users (1997*)	Users/1,000 people
United States	11,829,141	45.8	54,680,000	212.0
Japan	955,688	7.7	7,970,000	64.0
Australia	707,611	40.2	3,350,000	190.3
New Zealand	155,678	44.5	210,000	60.0
Korea	123,370	2.8	155,000	3.5
Taiwan	40,706	1.9	590,000	27.6
Singapore	60,674	21.7	150,000	53.6
Hong Kong	48,660	8.4	200,000	34.5
Malaysia	40,533	2.1	90,000	4.7
Indonesia	10,861	0.06	60,000	0.3
Thailand	12,794	0.22	80,000	1.4
Philippines	4,309	0.07	40,000	0.6
India	4,794	0.005	40,000	0.04
China	25,594	0.02	70,000	0.06

* 1996 for New Zealand, Korea, Taiwan, Singapore, Hong Kong, Malaysia, Indonesia, Thailand, the Philippines, India and China

Source: Dedrick, J. & Kraemer, K.L. (1998), "Competing in Computers in the Network Era", *Asia's Computer Challenge: Threat or Opportunity for the United States and the World?* Oxford University Press, p. 288.

Exhibit 13: Legend's sales growth

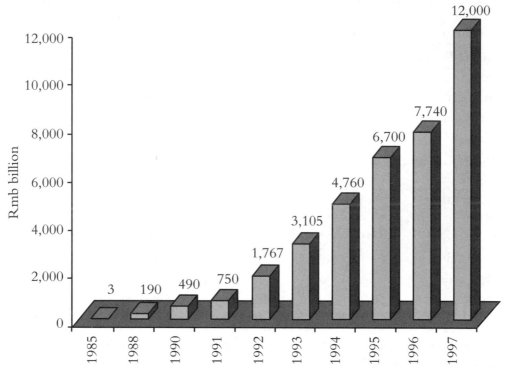

Source: Buchel, B. & Raub, S. (1999), "Legend Group and the Chinese Computer Industry", *Asian Case Research Journal*, Vol. 3, Iss. 1, May, p. 59.

CHAPTER

5

Business-to-Consumer e-Commerce

OBJECTIVES

- To study the reasons behind the growth of business-to-consumer (B2C) e-commerce.
- To differentiate between various types of B2C business models.
- To learn about on-line banking and entertainment.
- To examine the forces that are changing the on-line shopping landscape.

On-line retailers began to emerge between 1994 and 1995. During this period, Web-based start-ups such as amazon.com, CDNow (www.cdnow.com), Peapod (www.peapod.com) and Virtual Vineyards (www.virtualvin.com) seized the opportunity to become the first on-line retailers in their own specialty market segments of books, music, groceries and wine. They invested heavily to build brand awareness and gain market share before super retailers such as Walmart (www.walmart.com), Barnes and Noble (www.barnesandnoble.com) and J.C. Penney (www.jcpenney.com) established their own Websites a year or two later. 'Cybermalls' also started to emerge in 1994. Large information technology companies such as IBM and MCI, and media companies, such as Time Warner, launched on-line shopping malls and attempted to rent virtual retail space to on-line retailers. These early attempts of operating on-line shopping malls were however not very successful. Consumer acceptance and technical problems were the main obstacles. While IBM's Prodigy still struggles for profitability, MCI's MarketplaceMCI was closed down in 1996. Latecomers such as Yahoo!Shopping (www.shopping.yahoo.com) and America Online's on-line shopping mall (www.aol.com/shopping) are much more successful.

B2C e-commerce can be broadly classified into two categories: the retailing of tangible and intangible goods. Before 1997, goods that were retailed on-line were mainly computer hardware and software.[1] Since then, interests of on-line shoppers have shifted to mainstream items. A study conducted by Forrester Research in October 1997 revealed that the most popular items sold on the Internet were, in descending order, computer products, books, travel, clothing, music, subscriptions, gifts and investments.

In the late 1990s, intangible products and services that are sold and distributed on-line include software, music, magazine articles, news broadcasts, securities brokerage, airline tickets and insurance policies. The advent of the Internet has revolutionised the way business transactions are conducted in industries such as entertainment, banking, travel and insurance.

DRIVERS OF GROWTH

According to Forrester Research, B2C e-commerce has left the experimental phase and is moving into the mainstream. Broadened consumer acceptance together with innovative and ambitious strategies adopted by on-line retailers will lead to a rapid growth in on-line retail sales. Forrester Research predicts that by the year 2003, more than 40 million US households will shop on-line. On-line retail transactions will account for six percent of total consumer retail spending in the US and produce total revenue of US$108 billion.[2] The rapid ascent of B2C e-commerce can be explained by several factors.

New Sales Opportunities

The Internet provides an interactive, 24-hours-a-day, 7-days-a-week shopping venue

---

[1] US Department of Commerce (1998), "The Emerging Digital Economy".

[2] Forrester Research (1998).

that is unrestricted by geographical boundaries. It offers a cost-effective means for companies to reach overseas markets without the need to incur extra costs on staffing, travelling and printing of promotional materials. By establishing an on-line presence, even small companies can reach out to potential customers located all over the world. 1-800-FLOWERS, a florist based in the US, is able to use its Website (www.1800flowers.com) to reach an international group of customers it could not reach in the past. About 15 to 20 percent of 1-800-FLOWERS' on-line business come from Americans working overseas who send flowers to friends and families back home.

Consumer Preference

On-line shopping appeals the most to shoppers who lack the patience to shop in physical stores, live in remote areas, cannot adjust their schedules around store hours and like to be well-informed before making purchases. Access to greater amounts of dynamic information to support queries for decision making is considered an important benefit enjoyed by on-line shoppers.[3] Detailed product information along with images of products is usually offered on the on-line shopping Websites. It is also easy for shoppers to conduct on-line price comparison as other on-line stores are just a 'click' away.

Content Websites, such as on-line newspapers and magazines, are well received by Internet users. On-line content is not subject to the same technical restrictions imposed upon print publications. It can be updated frequently. In 1997, nearly 90 percent of Internet users in the US visited news and informational Websites. The US Department of Commerce predicts that as technology becomes more advance and search tools become more sophisticated and user-friendly, individuals will frequent the Internet's content sites even more often to conduct research and to access news and magazine articles.

Lower Capital and Operating Costs

By getting rid of brick-and-mortar storefronts, virtual retailers can avoid almost all the costs of supporting a physical store, i.e., rent, depreciation, labour, utilities and other miscellaneous expenses. Profits are thus increased. Customers of 1-800-FLOWERS may purchase flowers through the company's Website by calling a toll-free telephone number or by visiting the company's retail stores. 1-800-FLOWERS' store-based busi-

---

[3] Kalakota & Whinston (1997), p. 33.

ness and on-line business generate 20 percent and 10 percent of its total revenue respectively. The profit contribution from on-line sales is nearly the same as that of the store-based business because the operating costs are much lower.

As publishers of on-line newspapers and magazines do not need to equip themselves with expensive printing presses, their capital investments are much lower than those of print publishers. The barrier to entry is also lowered. Also, by distributing contents on-line, physical distribution costs, which often account for 30 to 40 percent of a print publisher's operating costs, can be avoided. An electronic publisher's distribution costs come from the investment in Web servers and the technology it employs to deliver the content on-line. As most of these costs are fixed, once the content is created and stored, the cost of delivering it to one reader or 100,000 readers is more or less the same.

New Products and New Sources of Revenue

The Internet provides a new medium in which business transactions are conducted. There are no hard-and-fast rules as to how on-line businesses should be conducted. Innovative enterprises are attracted to the Internet because of its global reach and interactivity. They design new products and services to utilise these characteristics and thus create new sources of revenue. Internet search engines such as Yahoo! and Excite are examples of such companies.

BUSINESS-TO-CONSUMER E-COMMERCE BUSINESS MODELS

Web-based businesses employ various business models to generate revenues and to earn profits. The B2C e-commerce business models discussed by Kalakota & Whinston (1997, p. 43), Timmers (1998) and Mitchell (1999) are summarised and classified into six categories.

e-Shops

e-Shops are on-line stores that sell and support products and services. Web-based start-ups such as amazon.com and Virtual Vineyards are pioneers in setting up specialty stores in cyberspace. Websites of established companies like Walmart were initially used as a means to promote their products and services and to build brand awareness. These Websites were gradually transformed into e-shops when the added capability of processing sales transactions and payments were added. Through on-line storefronts, companies are able to enhance their sales and marketing efforts cost effectively and reach a global audience. By conducting marketing and selling through Websites, companies seek to reduce costs of promotion and sales. On-line customers, on the other hand, are able to enjoy a wider selection of goods and services because displays on electronic storefronts are not restricted by physical store space. Customers also benefit from having more and better information prior to making a purchasing decision and can enjoy the convenience of shopping at any time of the day.

e-Malls

An e-mall consists of a number of e-shops, usually enhanced by a common umbrella, such as a well-known brand. It serves as a gateway through which a visitor can access other e-shops. An e-mall may be generalised or specialised depending on the products offered by the e-shops it hosts.[4] Revenues for e-mall operators include membership fees from participating e-shops and customers, advertising and possibly a fee on each transaction if the e-mall operator also processes payments. e-Shops, on the other hand, benefit from brand reinforcement and increased traffic as visiting one shop on the e-mall often leads to visits to 'neighbouring' shops. When a brand name is used to host the e-mall, the level of trust and readiness to purchase is generally raised among consumers. In addition, participating e-shops are able to access sophisticated hosting facilities such as electronic payments. Visitors to e-malls benefit from the convenience of easy access to other e-shops and ease of use through a common user interface.

e-Mall operators can be on-line service providers, such as America Online (AOL), search engines, such as Yahoo! and Excite, content providers, such as Time Warner's Pathfinder, telecommunications companies and niche marketers. Financial benefits conferred on successful e-mall operators are substantial. In the exclusive advertising partnerships AOL offers to retailers, AOL reserves shopping space in particular product categories on the AOL Shopping Channel (www.aol.com/shopping/home.html) for these partners, advertises and markets their products on AOL's on-line services and participates with them in joint technical development and research. These multi-year advertising partnerships cost advertisers up to tens of millions of dollars.

e-Auctions

An e-auction is an electronic implementation of the bidding mechanism on the Internet.

---

[4] Timmers (1998).

The on-line bidding process may be integrated with contracting, payment and delivery. Revenues for auction providers come from the selling of the technology platform, transaction fees from on-line bids and advertising sales. Due to cost efficiency, e-auctions of surplus goods that are in small quantities and of relatively low value can be conducted feasibly. Both sellers and buyers can benefit from the increased efficiency and timesavings offered by e-auctions. Added benefits to sellers include reduction of excess stock and better utilisation of production capacity. Consumers, on the other hand, may have the opportunity of buying goods at costs that are below market.

In the past, items that were auctioned on-line were mostly computer products and consumer electronics. The range has since been extended to include golf clubs, jewellery, clothing and a variety of other products. First Auction, eBay, ONSALE (www.onsale.com) and Priceline.com (www.priceline.com) are examples of on-line auction Websites for consumers.

First Auction: e-Auction of Consumer Goods

First Auction (www.firstauction.com) was launched in July 1997 by the US-based Internet Shopping Network. It takes advantage of the interactive nature of the Web, allowing people from all over the world to bid against each other for consumer goods in real time. First Auction's target customers are Internet users who are adventurous, looking to be entertained and seeking a bargain. Auctions are conducted 24 hours a day. Thousands of items, including golf clubs, CD players, television sets, jewellery, etc., are auctioned off each week. Only registered users who have submitted their credit card information, among other things, to First Auction can bid. First Auction buys end-of-life, close-out merchandise at large discounts from distributors. With large transaction volumes, First Auction is able to make money and customers can get bargains.

Source: US Department of Commerce (1998).

Virtual Communities

The value of virtual communities comes from their members who add information to an environment provided by the organisers of virtual communities. Revenues for the community organiser mostly come from membership fees as well as advertising. If the organiser is successful in attracting a large membership, vendors that want to do business with members of that community will be eager to join that community. A virtual community can also be a valuable add-on to other marketing schemes in order to build customer loyalty and receive customer feedback. amazon.com's 'Write Your Own Review' is an example of such an add-on service.

---

eCircles.com: The Family On-line Clubhouse

Prescott Lee founded eCircles (www.ecircles.com) in June 1998 out of the need for a central, private forum on the Web that all families could visit to exchange travel plans, calendars, contact information, among others. Today, eCircles is one of the most popular on-line services for building a private, shared Web presence. It provides more than a simple Webpage, it allows users to set up an entire digital hangout for family and friends, school reunions, sport teams, study groups, work contacts and the like. The service allows users to set up multiple 'circles'. Once a circle is set up, a user informs eCircle of those he wishes to invite to join and eCircles sends invitations via e-mail. Access to the 'circle' group is by invitation only. Once they sign up, the invited members can add their own material to the site. These created intimate 'circles' allow members to share photos, discussions, calendars, music, files, games and more. To date, eCircles is host to over a million members in thousands of on-line 'circles'.

According to Lee, the value proposition for eCircles.com is three-fold: (1) advertising — eCircles knows the types of circles the users visit and basic demographics about the members and is thus able to target ads more effectively; (2) 'gifting' — users can enter gift lists and can pick a gift from a gift registry entered in an eCirlce (the company receives a commission); and (3) circles can provide a medium for advice — for example, a user looking for a CPA might be more likely to seek recommendations from an eCircle than from a Website that shows the recommendations of total strangers.

Sources: Dukart (1999); eCircles; Mossberg (2000).

Search Engines/Internet Portals

Yahoo!, Excite, Infoseek, Lycos and AltaVista started off as organisers of the vast resources available on the Internet. They group the information into useful categories. These categories become directories that serve as search and navigation devices that help Internet users locate the on-line information they need. These companies become known as Internet search engines. Search engines initially function as 'portals', i.e., doorways through which Internet users pass through on their way to other destinations. The main source of income for search engines is advertising. The business models of well-known Internet search engines have changed drastically since their early days. They begin to emerge as informational 'hubs'. In addition to being search and navigation devices, they also incorporate informational content, communication and personalisation tools, homepage building devices, virtual community and on-line shopping services into their product offerings. With this expanded role, they seek to attract an even larger audience, thus generating bigger advertising revenues, and new sources of income from e-commerce transactions.

Content Providers

There are two types of Web-based content providers: Web-based database hosts and electronic publishers of newspapers and magazines. Web-based database hosts, such as The Dialog Corporation (www.dialog.com) and Lexis-Nexis (www.lexis-nexis.com), gather a variety of information, such as articles from newspapers, magazines and trade journals, and organise them into electronic databases. They then offer on-line access to these databases to users, such as librarians, students and businesses, who are interested in conducting research on-line. The main source of revenue for Web-based database hosts come from subscription fees paid by users.

Conversely, publishers of on-line newspapers and magazines seldom charge readers for access to the general content. About two thousand on-line newspapers are published around the world. On-line newspapers typically feature the day's news stories from their printed editions, some special Web-only sections, searchable on-line archives, as well as reviews of books or movies. Access to the general content is usually free of charge. Small fees are charged for archived news and other Web-based special services. From the readers' point of view, the advantages of accessing on-line content are choice, convenience, savings, and timely and personalised news.

Most on-line newspapers are still attempting to break even. Electronic publishers are weighing the trade-off between attracting traffic and charging for content. To boost advertising income, they need to gather as large an audience as possible. Imposing a fee to access the content could result in greater revenue in the near term, but may limit the ultimate audience size. On-line publishers generally believe that without an on-line presence, they will eventually lose market share. They, therefore, are keen on establishing an on-line presence despite the lack of immediate profits.

ON-LINE BANKING AND ENTERTAINMENT

There are two areas in the B2C e-commerce arena that shows a rapid rate of growth. They are on-line banking and on-line entertainment.

On-line Banking

In 1995, according to Jupiter Communications, fewer than a million households in the US banked on-line. By the end of 1998, this number has increased to 7 million. There were more than 150 banks that offered on-line services to customers.[5] GartnerGroup predicts that this number will increase further to more than 24.2 million by 2004. The most common banking transactions conducted over the Web are checking balances on savings, checking and loan accounts, transferring money among accounts and paying bills. Other on-line banking services offered include checking balances on credit card accounts, linking banking and brokerage accounts, securities trading and obtaining free stock quotes.

Bank of Bermuda Rolls Out Secure Clients Access Service On-line

Bank of Bermuda (www.bankofbermuda.com) launched its Secure Clients Access service in August 1999 to offer international customers trusted on-line banking. Gavin Grounds, the Bank's Vice President for Global Internetworking expressed: "We needed to be able to provide on-line access for our clients anywhere in the world to their portfolios electronically and be confident it was secure and encrypted." The service utilises PKI technology provided by Entrust Technologies. Bermuda's agreement with Entrust allows the Bank to offer digital signatures and e-mail encryption for file transfers and provide authentication and encryption for on-line access to and management of portfolios. Customers can access their portfolios, transfer funds or process credit card transactions electronically by way of a global private corporate network built around Cisco's secure PIX Firewall technology. The Secure Clients Access service further allows the Bank of Bermuda to authenticate customers using its cash management, client-server software application, Bankline II, and establish an encrypted connection

---

[5] Stark (1998).

over the VPN linking the customer's PC and the Bank's server. The PKI solutions of Entrust also enabled the Bank to offer its services through the Equant network (a provider of end-to-end managed data network services for international businesses), which extends to key business centres in over 220 countries and territories. Equant provides the Bank of Bermuda services such as Global Dial, PPP Dial, X.28 and Remote LAN Access. The Service Clients Access project has rolled out 150 internal users, but will eventually involve 10,000 users worldwide.

Established in 1889, the Bank of Bermuda has now become one of a few international financial institutions to operate as an independent certificate authority, offering digital certificates to its customers. It has offices in 14 countries, including most of the world's key financial and offshore centres.

Sources: Bank of Bermuda; Beale (1999); Entrust Technologies (1999).

On-line banking customers can conduct banking transactions 24 hours a day in the comfort of their own homes or offices without the need to wait in lines. They have a better idea of how much they have in their bank accounts and a diminished need to write cheques. If their bill paying and bank account information is linked to personal finance software, they can easily create household budgets and monitor spending. To banks, on-line banking transactions can be processed at costs much lower than those conducted at branches. Also, an on-line banking service is not subject to the constraint of physical capacity of branches. Once a bank's Website is established, the cost of handling one inquiry and one thousand inquiries is more or less the same. Furthermore, traces left by on-line banking customers provide banks with valuable information on their banking habits and preferences.

Entertainment

Other than being a venue for conducting business transactions, the World Wide Web also acts as a source of entertainment for consumers. The fastest-growing entertainment Websites are those that offer on-line computer games, gambling and adult contents.

❑ *Gaming.* Websites, such as America Online's Games Channel (www.aol.com/Webcenters/games/home.adp), allow players to participate in computer games on-line. In addition to running their own independent Websites, many on-line gaming operators also syndicate their games to other portal and content providers. Total Entertainment Network (T.E.N.), for example, operates its own Website (www.pogo.com) and syndicates its games to 15 major portal and content sites including Excite and Sony Online Entertainment.[6] There are two types of games offered in cyberspace: the male-oriented search and destroy games, and the family card and board games. Revenues of on-line gaming Websites are mainly derived from advertising and pay-to-play fees. These Websites turn out to be strong drivers of Website traffic and user registration. The outlook for this business segment is positive. Forrester Research predicted that on-line gaming revenues would reach US$555 million in 1999 and US$1.16 billion by 2000. Furthermore, 32 percent of US households that have access to the Internet were expected to participate in on-line games by 2000, up from 22 percent in 1999.[7]

❑ *Gambling*. Some studies predict that the revenue from on-line gambling will reach US$100 million by 2006. Although this predicted revenue amount is not as large as other on-line entertainment businesses, the number of on-line gambling Websites are nevertheless growing at a rapid rate. There were about 60 on-line gambling Websites in late 1997. By early 1999, this number has increased to 260.[8] There are two types of on-line gambling: sports booking, i.e., betting on the outcomes of sporting events, and casino-type gambling, such as the virtual slot machines, roulette and blackjack. The modest revenues predicted for on-line gambling could be attributed to the fact that it is difficult to replicate the excitement of gambling off-line. Although on-line gambling is not expected to become a big business in the near future, the associated legal and social issues raised, such as the problem of compulsive and underage gambling, the potential for fraud and the complexity of law enforcement in cyberspace nevertheless warrant special attention.

❑ *Adult content*. The estimated revenue generated by adult on-line entertainment Websites was about US$185 million in 1998, up from US$101 million in 1996, and US$137 million in 1997. Forrester Research forecasts that adult entertainment will generate annual revenue of US$296 million by 2000. As at mid-1998, there are about 28,000 Websites offering adult entertainment to a wide range of audiences.[9] Adult content providers are the most profitable content

---

[6] "Bingo! Online Games Start Paying Off in Stickiness, Registration, Community", *Min's New Media Report*, 10 May 1999.

[7] Tedesco (1999).

[8] Baker (1999).

[9] Franson (1998).

providers on the Web. As a result, they are able and willing to invest in the newest and most sophisticated computer equipment and pioneered most of the technology now commonly used, such as video and audio.[10] The majority of the adult content Websites are subscription-based Websites and the rest are free-access ones. The revenues for free-access Websites come from advertising and the selling of merchandise such as CD-ROMs, videos and garments. Like gambling, on-line adult entertainment also causes heated debates on various legal and social issues, such as free speech versus child protection, free enterprise versus social good, and free market versus fair business practices.[11]

BUSINESS-TO-CONSUMER E-COMMERCE IN THE 21ST CENTURY

Shifting of Power to Consumers

Comparison shopping on the Internet is made much easier with the advent of 'intelligent software shopping agents'. These software products search the entire Internet for products and services based on pre-defined criteria, the most popular one being pricing. With the help of these products, shoppers can easily shop for the best deals in cyberspace. Competition among on-line retailers is thus intensified.[12] The widespread use of 'intelligent software shopping agents' implies that on-line merchants either have to position themselves as the genuine lowest cost providers of goods and services or they have to successfully differentiate themselves from their competitors through non-price attributes such as branding, specialising in niche markets, offering a wide selection of products or providing extensive sales services.

Adoption of One-to-one Marketing

One-to-one marketing is expected to become a popular marketing tool among on-line marketers to differentiate themselves from their competitors. Through mechanisms built into the Websites, customers can personalise the services offered, automate product selection and comparison, and communicate instantly with a sales representative. Based on the information collected upon user registration and the sales history of

---

[10] Vinas (1998).

[11] Franson (1998).

[12] Judson & Kelly (1999).

customers, companies are able to target on-line alerts of new products and services or special offers towards a particular customer or a group of customers. The retail banking industry is one of the industries that practises one-to-one marketing.

Specialized Bicycle: Applying Web's Scalability and Immediacy to Customer Service and Support

Specialized Bicycle (www.specialized.com) is a supplier of mountain bikes, bike components and accessories. Although the 24-year-old company is growing by about 26 percent annually and has a global distribution channel and strong brand awareness, Specialized realised early on that a Web self-service application is strategically important. Thus, in November 1999 it began selling products on the Internet. "Web-based customer interaction is the killer app for branding," according to Mike Regan, senior global e-marketing manager for Specialized Bicycle. Regan comments that branding is important for the Specialized Bicycle 'lifestyle product' – as the company competes against other manufacturers of premium bikes, but more importantly against other commodities the customers are willing to buy. Through the deployment of multi-faceted on-line customer-service facilities, Specialized.com was able to sell over US$300 million worth of high-end mountain bikes and accessories in 1998, making its brand name better known.

Specialized.com attracts more than 12,000 visitors every day and interacting with the customers was a challenge. To interact more effectively with customers on-line, Specialized.com decided to look for a system that would provide an easy-to-navigate list of FAQ based on customer needs and for handling e-mail queries. Specialized.com selected Right Now Web, a Linux application from Right Now Technologies Inc. Using this new system, Specialized.com was able to create and refine the content of its FAQ, automatically put upfront the frequently searched topics, and help track e-mail queries using a trouble-ticket system and on-line content to answer questions quickly. The Right Now Web system provides HTML content generation, knowledge-based management, and helpdesk ticket tracking. For Specialized, the Right Now application seems to be a powerful tool for customer bonding and branding.

Sources: Liebmann (1999); Specialized; Whiting (2000).

Prevalence of Mass Customisation

Mass customisation is the production of goods on a personalised basis.[13] Mass customisation helps businesses attract and retain customers by offering a better fit between the goods or services purchased and customer requirements. The prerequisites for mass customisation are flexible manufacturing processes and informational tools that can profile the usage patterns of customers. The Internet aids mass customisation by providing a two-way communication channel that enables sellers to customise products according to the interactive input of customers. Successful attempts of mass customisation yield substantial profits. A study shows that if ten percent of the manufacturing output is devoted to mass customisation, it would produce 30 percent of company profits.[14] Mass customisation is expected to become more prevalent as more companies equip themselves with the required informational tools and re-engineer their manufacturing processes to accommodate this new way of doing business.

Emergence of a New Breed of Intermediary

Although the advent of e-commerce has caused a disintermediation of components in a traditional supply-chain, the one-to-one marketing model has nevertheless created the need for a new category of middlemen. As manufacturers are traditionally equipped to ship bulk orders to wholesalers and distributors instead of small orders to end users, they need to restructure their logistics system and order fulfilment processes to facilitate this new way of conducting businesses. When their restructuring efforts are hindered by the limitations of their legacy systems, they would need to outsource their fulfilment operations to third parties.

Proliferation of Affiliate Programmes

Affiliate programmes are revenue-sharing agreements among Websites. Under such an agreement, links are set up between the Websites of the host and members of an affiliate programme. When a visitor comes to one of the member Websites, or the referring site, and buys an item from the host through one of these links, the owner of the referring site will receive some credit from the host, redeemable either in the form of cash or credits towards merchandise. The purpose of affiliate programmes is to create

---

[13] Alexander (1999).

[14] Alexander (1999).

a large virtual community to capture visitor traffic and customer loyalty.[15] Hosts of affiliate programmes seek to increase their on-line exposures while smaller Websites hope to earn additional revenues by joining these programmes. Many well-known on-line retailers, such as amazon.com, Barnes and Nobles, CDNow, Reel.com (www.reel.com) and Virtual Vineyards, have launched their own affiliate programmes. Each of these programmes has amassed a large number of affiliates. The use of affiliate programmes has become a popular retailing strategy on the Web.

High Entry Barriers for Small and Medium Businesses

During the early days of e-commerce, the Internet, which offers a low-cost means of reaching a global audience, was expected to level the playing field by enabling smaller businesses to compete with well-established players. However, by the late 1990s, it appeared that the entry barriers for smaller enterprises to participate in e-commerce were becoming higher and higher because of the prevalence of established companies on the Web and the high cost of acquiring customers on-line.

As large companies that have name-brand recognition and an established customer base, such as Walmart and Toys 'R' Us, enter the realm of e-commerce, sales of small- to medium-sized Web-based companies are under pressure. As most consumers are still wary of privacy and security issues, they incline to purchase from large companies that have an established reputation. Consumers also begin to use brands as filtering mechanisms as they are gradually faced with information overload while shopping on-line.[16]

As the Internet begins to prove its effectiveness as an advertising medium, the costs of advertising on-line, especially on popular Websites such as Yahoo! and AOL, have become very high. Established businesses with plenty of funding often combine on-line advertising efforts with multi-million dollar cross-media advertising campaigns to promote their on-line business. It is difficult for smaller companies that have a limited marketing budget to launch advertising campaigns that are of a similar scale.

A CUSTOMER-CENTRIC MODEL

As the world is rapidly moving towards e-commerce, it is no longer a question of

---

[15] Andrews (1999).

[16] Trommer (1998).

whether a company should participate in e-commerce. The question has become: "How should a business survive and flourish in the world of e-commerce?" As Craig Barrett, the CEO and President of Intel, said, "In five years, there won't be any Internet-specific companies because they will all be Internet companies." e-Commerce is expected to move from a vendor-centric model towards a customer-centric model.[17]

It, however, takes a lot more than simply establishing a Web presence for an on-line consumer business to succeed. An on-line consumer business must be able to build brand awareness through advertising and marketing in order to survive in this highly competitive business environment in which customers have the choice of spending their time and money at tens of thousands of Websites. A well-recognised brand name alone is not enough to guarantee success on the Web either. A successful B2C on-line business also needs to have a large customer base, an understanding of information technology, high-value products and services, an appreciation for merchandising and customer service, banking capabilities and powerful logistics. Once a business has all these essentials in place, its chance of standing out among a big crowd of B2C e-commerce merchants increases considerably. The ultimate payoff can be substantial.

SUMMARY

❑ There are many concerns regarding the viability of some of the business models currently used in the marketspace, primarily because many on-line retailers tried to increase their market share at the expense of profitability. The shakeout of late, however, has brought certain sensibility into the market.

❑ On-line shopping provides lower prices, enhanced customisation and increased convenience. Because B2C entities generally have lower operating costs than traditional stores and also because of their ability to bypass one or more layers of intermediaries, they are able to offer their products and services at attractive prices. Moreover, as the case of Dell Computer has successfully shown, companies can increase their revenues and market share by allowing consumers to customise the product and services they are looking for. Finally, since B2C is available 24-hours-a-day, 7-days-a-week, it increasingly fits the busy schedules of many people. If the statistics of the last few years are any indication to go by, we should expect to see a gradual shift from brick-and-mortar shopping to on-line shopping in the future.

❑ B2C will continue to increase the power of consumers through enhanced comparison shopping (the competition is only one click away!). The ability to adopt

---

[17] Markowitz (1999).

one-to-one marketing schemes and to mass customise products and services bring along a host of new challenges and opportunities to companies.

REFERENCES

Alexander, S. (1999), "Mass Customization", *Computerworld*, 6 September, Vol. 33, Iss. 36, p. 54.

Andrews, W. (1997), "Affiliate Programs Grow As Stores Pay for Referrals", 17 November, *Internet World*, URL: http://www.internetworld.com/, June 2000.

Baker, D. (1999), "Betting on Cyberspace", *ABA Journal*, Vol. 85, pp. 54–57.

Bank of Bermuda (2000), URL: http://www.bankofbermuda.com, 23 August.

Beale, M.W. (1999), "Bank of Bermuda Enlists Entrust to Offer Secure On-line Banking", *E-Commerce Times*, 10 August, URL: http://www.ecommercetimes.com/news/articles/990810-4.shtml, 23 August 2000.

Blundon B. & Bonde, A. (1998), "Beyond the Transaction", *Information Week*, 16 November, URL: http://www.informationweek.com/709/09iuss2.htm, June 2000.

Clemmer, K. (1998), "On-line Banking Reality Check", *The Forrester Brief*, 29 December, URL: http://www.forester.com/ER/Research/Brief/0,1317,5157,FF.html/, February 1999.

Computer Retail Week (1999), "CEO Shares Company Strategies, Thoughts on e-Commerce – Buy.Com Exec Speaks Out", 22 March, p. 12.

Computers Today (1998), "Let the Portal Games Begin", 31 October, p. 74.

Drucker, D. (1999), "Wells Fargo: Virtual Bank", *Internet Week*, CMP Media Inc., 23 August.

Dukart, J.R. (1999), "eCircles.com Builds Thriving On-line Communities", 29 November, URL: http://www.office.com/global, 24 August 2000.

eCircles (2000), "The eCircles Story", URL: http://wwwld-00-03-ec.ecircles.com/magic/products/x/view.cgi?page=company/story/index.html, 24 August 2000.

Electronic Commerce News (1999), "Vertical Marketplaces to Rise as e-Commerce Powerhouses", Vol. 4, No. 23, 7 June.

Entrust Technologies (1999), "Bank of Bermuda Chooses Entrust Technologies' e-Business Solutions to Further Expand Global Reach", 3 August, URL: http://www.entrust.com/news/files/ 08_03_99.htm, 23 August 2000.

Entrust Technologies (2000), "Entrust Helps Bank of Bermuda Become First International Bank to Run Its Own CA", URL: http://www.entrust.com/success/bermuda.htm, 23 August.

Forrester Research (1998), "Growth Spiral in On-line Retail Sales Will Generate $108 Billion in Revenues by 2003" (press release), 19 November, URL: http://www.forrester.com/ER/Research/Report/0,1338,2642,FF.html, March 2000.

Franson, P. (1998), "The Net's Dirty Little Secret: Sex Sells", *Upside*, Vol. 10, Iss. 4, pp. 78–82.

Galarza, P. (1999), "The Search Engine That Could", *Money*, Vol. 28, Iss. 4, pp. 48–50.

Gallaugher, J. (1999), "Challenging the New Conventional Wisdom of Net Commerce Strategies", *Communications of the Association for Computing Machinery*, Vol. 42, Iss. 7, pp. 27–29.

Garcia, A. (1999), "Business-to-Business e-Commerce: The Killer App", e-*Business Advisor*, October, Editor's View, p. 8. URL: http://www.advisor.com/articles, August 2000.

GartnerGroup (1999), "GartnerGroup's Dataquest Forecasts Three-fold Increase in Online Banking Over Next Five Years" (press release), 10 August, URL: http://www.gartnerWeb.com/dq/static/about/press/pr-b9945.html/, February 2000.

Harrison, A. (1999), "Web's New Come-on: Giveaways", *Computerworld*, Vol. 33, Iss. 27, 5 July, p. 85.

Judson, B. & Kelly, K. (1999), *Hyperwares: Eleven Strategies for Survival and Profit in the Era of Online Business*, New York, NY: Scribner, p. 35.

Kalakota, R. & Whinston, A.B. (1997), *Electronic Commerce: A Manager's Guide*, Reading, MA: Addison-Wesley, p. 76.

Kalakota, R. & Whinston, A.B. (eds) (1997), *Readings in Electronic Commerce*, Reading, MA: Addison-Wesley.

Karpinski, R. (1999), "The Logistics of e-Business – Web Commerce Demands New Approach to Inventory, Shipping", *Internetweek*, Iss. 767, 31 May, p. 1.

Liebmann, L. (1999), "E-Service at Hub of On-line Push", *InformationWeek*, Iss. 754, 27 September, pp. 373–374.

Markowitz, E. (1999), "Intel CEO Pushes e-Business World", *TechWeb News*, CMP Media, Inc., 20 July.

Melcher, R.A. (1999), "Will PCs and TV Get Playboy Hopping?" *BusinessWeek*, Iss. 3635, 28 June, p. 60.

Min's New Media Report (1999), "Big Media, Big Money Make Portal Plays", Vol. 4, No. 20, 28 September.

Min's New Media Report (1999), "Bingo! Online Games Start Paying Off in Stickiness, Registration, Community", Vol. 5, No. 10, 10 May.

Mitchel, A. (1999), "Internet Zoo Spawns New Business Models", *Marketing Week*, Vol. 21, Iss. 45, 12 January, pp. 24–25.

Morrisette, S., Clemmer, K., & Bluestein, W.M. (1998), "The Forrester Report", Boston, MA: Forrester Research, April.

Mossberg, W.S. (2000), "Services Help You Create Shared Pages on the Web", *Wall Street Journal*, Brussells, 7 January, p. 4.

PR Newswire (1999), "PC Data Announces June Sales Figures from e-Tail Web Sites", Financial News, 28 July.

Rosenoer, J., Armstrong, D., & Gates, J.R. (1999), *The Clickable Corporation: Successful Strategies for Capturing the Internet Advantage*, Arthur Andersen LLP, New York, NY: The Free Press, pp. 104–108.

Specialized (2000), "Backgrounder: Humble Origins Set Customer Service Standards", URL: http://www.specialized.com/who_we_are/press_releases/backgrounder. ehtml?id=2, 23 August.

Stark, E. (1998), "Banking from Home", *Money*, Vol. 1, Iss. 1, Summer, pp. 63–64.

Stewart, T.R. (1998), "Doing Business in Cyberspace", *The e-Business Tidal Wave: Perspectives on Business in Cyberspace*, USA: Deloitte Touche Tohmatsu, p. 15.

Tedesco, R. (1999), "Online Games Gain Ground Slowly", *Broadcasting & Cable*, Vol. 129, Iss. 1, 4 January, p. 75.

Timmers, P. (1998), "Business Models for Electronic Markets", *EM-Electronic Markets*, Vol. 8, No. 2.

Trommer, D. (1998), "Net Levels Playing Field, But Raises Bar", *Electronic Buyers' News*, CMP Media Inc., 13 July.

US Department of Commerce (1998), "The Emerging Digital Economy", 15 April, Washington, DC, URL: http://www.ecommerce.gov/emerging.htm/, June 2000.

Vinas, T. (1998), "X-rated and on the A-list", *Industry Week*, Vol. 247, Iss. 17, 21 September, pp. 11–12.

Wagner, M. (1997), "Online Retailers Buddy Up", *Computerworld*, 15 September.

Walsh, B. (1999), "Electronic Commerce – e-Commerce Seeks Wider Audience", *Network Computing*, CMP Media Inc., 17 May.

Whiting, R. (2000), "Getting to Know You", 16 March, URL: http://www. Planetit.com/techcenters/docs/e_business-e_commerce/product_review/ PIT20000320S0013/1, 23 August.

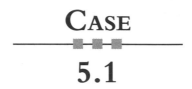

CASE

5.1

Charles Schwab Inc.: Creating an International Marketspace*

By the year 2000, on-line trading was one of the most popular investment methods and its popularity was increasing as the number of Internet users surged. Having pioneered the on-line broking market in 1996, Schwab retained its dominance through a mixture of successful product strategies and technological edge. By late 1998, the Internet had become a crucial channel for Schwab to execute its sales and marketing strategy.

However, growing on-line investment opportunities and potential profitability increased competition, especially due to low entry barriers for electronic service providers. Schwab realised the need to increase its market base since margins would continue to face a downward pressure as the number of market entrants increased. Instead of relying on margins as its core revenue base, Schwab focused on providing an array of investment tools and services to its clients through the convenience of the Internet. In addition, the management was focusing on international expansion as a means of growing its customer base. Schwab's strategy team wondered whether it could replicate its North American on-line success in overseas markets, using its technology advantage. Could it

---

* Maria J. Cascales prepared this case under the supervision of Dr. Ali Farhoomand and P. Lovelock. *Copyright © 2000 The University of Hong Kong. Ref. 99/52C*

maintain its dominance at home while using resources to expand overseas? What market entry strategies would it pursue to build its international markets? These were critical strategic questions surfacing at board meetings, and time, as always, was running out.

EVOLUTION OF THE BROKERAGE INDUSTRY

Before the 1970s, full-service firms had traditionally controlled much of the US brokerage industry. Investors placed all security transaction orders through brokers who charged high commissions to route an average stock trade to the marketplace. Apart from having the ability to trade, brokerage firms monopolised access to information. News and research necessary to make investment decisions were strictly controlled. Brokers were paid for attaining the maximum number of trades possible, while investors were charged for financial advice, asset allocation, investment selection and a host of other services. Traditionally, customers tended to be affluent professionals in their late 30s or early 40s, typically earning more than US$50,000 a year.[1] As commission rates were strictly regulated, firms could only compete on image and reputation, not cost.

But with the dismantling of fixed commission rates in the mid–1970s and rapid technological progress in subsequent years, the landscape began to change. A strong bull run throughout most of the 1980s and 1990s, in addition to rapidly deregulating markets, captured a growing number of investors and brokerages into the market.[2] By unbundling their services, new firms were able to target specific investor groups and charge lower fees. Some firms focused exclusively on providing research data, while others, called discounters, concentrated on the buying and selling process.

The proliferation of electronic hardware and software created a variety of computer based systems that essentially meant that a new player could directly reach out to its customers without establishing physical presence or face-to-face contact. Investors also began questioning whether their brokers' advice and expertise were as valuable as they had been led to believe. Savvy investors who wanted to play a more active role in their investments were on the increase, and therefore, business volumes of specialised brokerages increased simultaneously.

---

[1] CNET.com (1998), URL: http://www.news.com/Special Features/0,5,1870,00.html, January.

[2] Bull run: a prolonged period of rising prices, usually by 20 percent or more.

The Internet culture accelerated the downfall of full-service equity commission brokers; previously privileged information was accessible to investors for free on the Internet, including news stories, press releases, stock charts, earnings projections, even analysts' reports. All investors needed was an on-line service provider to execute their trades. As a result, several roles that full-service brokers traditionally played, as asset allocators, investment selectors and information providers, were bypassed. The chain between trader and stock market had become disintermediated. The appeal of the Web was undeniable for the customer as buying and selling stocks became convenient, private, instantaneous and cost-effective. According to one on-line investor:

> *The colour, the graphics, the thrill of feeling connected to the beating heart of capitalism is amazing! Place an order for 100 shares of General Motors, click, and seconds later it's yours – owning a piece of the means of production has never been easier.*[3]

COMPANY BACKGROUND

One of the first people to capitalise on the rise of specialised brokerages was Charles Schwab. Schwab came from a modest family background and was dyslexic. Although he never excelled academically and struggled through Stanford, he was a gifted stock market player. He made his first investment at the age of 13 and two decades later, in 1971, founded his own full-service brokerage. In 1974, Charles Schwab Corp. began to differentiate itself by offering efficient transactional and custody services at low fees. Schwab was the first firm to enable investors to buy and sell stocks at minimum commission rates. As a result, its name became synonymous with the discount brokerage business.

In 1982, Mr. Schwab sold the company to Bank of America for US$55 million, but bought it back in a leveraged buyout five years later for US$280 million. It went public in 1987, but the market crash that year badly affected earnings; Schwab lost millions of dollars. As trading volumes collapsed, Schwab realised it could compete as a transaction-based firm since it faced increased competition from other discount brokerages.

In order to differentiate itself from the new breed of discounters, Schwab decided to broaden the array of products it offered. Previously, the effort was focused on attracting new investors by lowering commission rates while offering a simple service;

---

[3] Whitford, D. (1998), "Trade Fast, Trade Cheap", *Fortune*, 2 February.

the new strategy was to attract more sophisticated customers. It wanted to emphasise service and enhance client support by providing strategic information and expert advice so that its investors could individually manage their portfolios.

PRODUCTS/SERVICES

Schwab expanded its services into different areas within the financial service spectrum: retail brokerage, mutual funds and support services for independent investment managers. In the late 1980s, Schwab began offering money market funds, and by 1990, as mutual funds gained popularity, it enhanced its portfolio by creating its own in-house funds called SchwabFunds. Two years later Schwab officially launched Mutual Fund OneSource, the first mutual fund supermarket offering clients access to hundreds of funds – including no-load ones – from renowned third parties such as Templeton, Morgan Stanley, Goldman Sachs and Guinness Flight. In addition, in 1996, Schwab introduced the following:

- 401 (k) retirement plans: a bundled package under which Schwab planned and managed the administration of the scheme for employers.
- An unbundled service that offered investment vehicles to third-party administrators.[4]
- Variable annuities and life insurance to its range of products. In 1997, Schwab struck deals with Credit Suisse First Boston, Hambrecht & Quist, and J.P. Morgan that enabled its customers to invest directly in initial public offerings (IPOs).

However, Schwab did not aim at being a niche player. Like other big players, it was becoming a one stop shop. The next logical step was to add more banking-type services to its product list, such as direct deposits and automatic bill paying. Schwab had, in effect, come full circle. Once again it was offering the types of services a full-service firm would provide but at a much lower price.

---

[4] 401(k) plan: A tax-deferred investment device for employees in the US. 401(k) plans allow employees to invest pre-tax dollars into individual accounts. Employers may also match employee investments in the 401(k).

We don't have one target market. That would be an oversimplification of today's market. We may have started out as a business with a narrow range of customers ... but that has evolved dramatically over the years.

– Charles Schwab, co-CEO[5]

Schwab provided a broad array of financial services to individual investors, independent investment managers and institutional investors through a local (US) network of more than 291 branch offices, regional telephone service centres and automated telephone systems. However, it had planned market expansion through another marketing channel.

LEVERAGING TECHNOLOGY

...We're a financial services company on the outside, but a technology company on the inside.

– James Chong, Vice President of
transaction processing technology[6]

Technology was a critical force in Schwab's ability to offer a variety of investment options and it played a central role in Schwab's core business strategy. A survey conducted in 1997 found that of all the large financial houses, Schwab used technology most effectively [see **Exhibit 1**].

From the beginning, we have benefited from our Silicon Valley roots by applying technology to pursue our mission.... The nature of the financial services business we are in creates tremendous opportunities to use technology to create real value that customers see and use.

– Arthur Shaw, Senior Vice President of electronic brokerage[7]

A particular example of Schwab's cutting-edge technology was 'Pocketerm'; this was a hand-held device, launched in 1982, which enabled clients to download stock quotes through an FM receiver. Next, an experiment was conducted with 'Schwabline',

---

[5] McReynolds, R. (1998), "Doing It the Schwab Way", *US Banker*, July.

[6] URL: http://www.chess.ibm/learn/html/e.5.html, April, 1999.

[7] Shaw, A. V. (1998), "Schwab Creates Customer Value By Leveraging the Web – and Other Channels", *Journal of Retail Banking Services*, Spring.

a terminal that gathered market data over a telephone line and printed it out on a roll of adding-machine paper.

But it was only in the mid–1980s that the real technological push began. Recognising the potential impact of the personal computer, Schwab was first to offer investors the option of managing their accounts on-line. In 1985, using the DOS-based Equalizer software, clients could connect to Schwab and make changes to their portfolios. Subsequent upgrades to graphical user interfaces (GUI) with enhanced services arrived with the Windows-based StreetSmart software. By late 1995, some 336,000 Schwab clients were able to access individual accounts from personal computers.

The electronic brokerage site it launched in March 1996 began as a Web-based stock trading programme. The game was designed such that:

1. It enabled a Schwab server to take an order from a Web browser on a personal computer.
2. It routed it through back-end systems and mainframes.
3. It executed it.
4. It sent a confirmation back to the PC from which the order originated.

Recognising the potential, Schwab assembled an independent team to make Web-based trading a reality for Schwab's clients.

In many ways, technology is the driver and enabler of all we do, and it's been Schwab's hallmark to enable customers to interact directly with technology themselves. Schwab will continue to build additional electronic channels to enable more investors to self-direct their financial affairs.

– Charles Schwab, co-CEO[8]

WWW.SCHWAB.COM

By mid-1996, www.schwab.com was fully operational. Investors only had to send a cheque to open an on-line account with Schwab and then they could trade stocks, bonds and mutual funds by simply logging onto the Website. Customers could also access expert market analysis, news, research information and real-time quotes. Schwab transformed from an on-line brokerage to a sophisticated financial service portal.

---

[8] URL: http://www.chess.ibm.com/learn/html/e.5.html, April 1999.

Customers could access comprehensive information at competitive prices. Whereas traditional fees averaged about US$150 (and increased with larger trades), Schwab's on-line trading commissions were initially only US$39 for any stock up to 1,000 shares and this price was also subsequently lowered to US$29.95 in December 1997.

Schwab had originally planned 25,000 new on-line accounts in the first year. However, by the end of the first two opening weeks, its target had already been reached! By late 1996, there were 617,000 active on-line account holders, and by the beginning of 1998, the figure had soared to 1.3 million.[9] From 1996 to 1997, on-line registrations had quadrupled Schwab's accounts; by late 1998, Schwab had 2.2 million active on-line accounts. In 1996, on-line trades formed 22 percent of the Company's total trades, but by 1998 the comparative figure was 58 percent [see **Exhibit 2**]. This successful selling and distribution strategy created a whole new market and culture, where anyone could play the market.

ON-LINE EXPLOSION

The on-line trading industry was growing rapidly. At the end of 1998, there were 7.3 million active on-line accounts, up 100 percent from the previous year [see **Exhibit 3**].[10] A report by Forrester Research predicted that by 2002, 14 million on-line accounts would exist, holding nearly US$700 billion in assets.

But e-broking formed only a small part of the overall market. On-line equity trade represented 14 percent of the total market activity. By 1997, approximately 80 million accounts were managed by full-service and traditional discounters.[11] Even by 2002, on-line accounts were estimated to make up approximately five percent of the overall market.[12] Institutional investors still dominated trading, not retail investors. However, potential profit gains from the on-line business were still very lucrative. As one commentator put it,

---

[9] In 1985, Schwab had only succeeded in attracting 336,000 investors through PCs.

[10] Franco, C.S. & Klein, M.T. (1999), *Piper Jaffray Equity Research On-line Financial Services Update*, March.

[11] Whitford, D. & Rao, R.R. (1998), "Trade Fast, Trade Cheap", *Fortune*, 2 February.

[12] Whitford, D. & Rao, R.R. (1998).

...On-line trading has gone from a little niche opportunity to the single biggest market share grab in financial services and in the process it redefined the way investors managed their finances.[13]

In September 1995, there were no Web-based brokers. Three years later, there were 96 and the number was growing [see **Exhibit 3**]. Many e-brokerage businesses only involved on-line trading without the expense burdens of building brick-and-mortar facilities. Despite the increasing number of on-line brokers, the nascent industry was largely dominated by established players [see **Exhibit 4**]. In 1998, five brokers accounted for nearly three-quarters of all on-line trades. Schwab controlled 27.6 percent of the daily trading volume, approximately equal to its three competitors combined [see **Table 1**].

Table 1:   On-line market share

Market players	Market share (%)
Schwab	27.6
Waterhouse	12.5
E★Trade	11.9
Datek	10
Fidelity	9.8

Even Merrill Lynch, known for its strong resistance to the Internet, finally relented by offering on-line trading services in June 1999 at the same fee as Schwab. Other competitors, such as Ameritrade, charged as little as US$8 per trade in the hope of gaining market share through price reductions.

EXPANDING THE PIE

The intense price war and heavy advertising costs necessary to grab market share forced most US on-line brokers to lose money. Schwab, however, was determined not to slash its prices as its competitors had done. Instead, its initial strategy was to benefit

---

[13] Woolley, S. (1997), "On-line Trading: Do I Hear Two Bits a Trade?" *Business Week*, 26 November.

from disintermediation. By enabling traders to bypass traditional brokers, Schwab took a larger market share. However, on-line trading profitability attracted competition and put pressure on the already shrinking margins.

Schwab had to reposition itself.

Reintermediation

It did this in two ways. First, it began to reintermediate the chain between customer and stock market by providing innovative on-line tools and services that would help keep old customers and attract new ones. Schwab's services included margin loans, money transfers, a referral programme for those seeking financial advisers, trading options and specialised services for those with large portfolios. Investment tools included free equity report cards; an analyst centre where professional and independent research could be accessed; market highlights; stock research and stock screening; access to real-time quotes; watch lists; charting; asset allocation; as well as phone and local branch support. Schwab also provided planning resources such as a retirement savings planner, an estate tax and probate calculator and a college planner. The new strategy was to shift focus away from price, expand its service and leverage its brand name to position itself as a full-service electronic investment specialist. Once more it managed to reinvent itself as a full-service brokerage with the added convenience of conducting business on-line.

International Focus

Schwab's on-line strategy also included gaining exposure in international markets. "We are building breadth as well as depth," said David Pottruck, the Company's President and co-CEO. [14] For the most part, these markets were largely unexplored, offering promising yet unknown potential. Schwab targeted Hong Kong, the UK, Canada and Latin America [see **Exhibit 5**]. The ultimate Web strategy was to create a borderless business to make it easy for anyone, anywhere in the world to access Schwab and its subsidiaries over the Internet.

Executives at Schwab claimed the Asian take-up far outstripped the mature US market. As of May 1999, more than 80 percent of transactions in Hong Kong were on-

---

[14] Pottruck, D. (1998), "Avoiding Downsizing", *Executive Excellence*, February.

line, while the comparative figure for the US was 65 percent.[15] According to a spokes-person, in the first six months since the Hong Kong branch's inception, total assets hit ten times the level commonly targeted for a new Schwab office in the US.[16] Despite the Asian financial crisis in 1997–98, the number of accounts and assets under management continued to grow. In 1997, there were approximately five to ten million Internet users in Asia.[17] Growth figures for Hong Kong alone were expected to be exponential. According to the Office of the Telecommunications Authority, by early 1999, there were approximately 623,000 Internet subscribers in Hong Kong. The number of Internet users for the whole Asia–Pacific region was predicted to reach 21 million by 2001.[18]

Canada and the UK were also critical markets for Schwab.

Canada is an established market that presents immediate, as well as long-term opportunities to leverage Schwab's brand, technology and service capabilities. The growth of the Internet, as well as individuals' desire to have more control over their financial affairs, have already helped us successfully offer Schwab-style services to investors in the UK and through our subsidiaries in Hong Kong. We believe the same will hold true as we expand into Canada.[19]

— David S. Pottruck, Schwab's President and co-CEO

Schwab planned expansion in other countries as well. It completed an agreement with Tokio Marine and Fire Insurance Co. to establish an on-line brokerage service in Japan. The new service would allow Japanese customers to access the main US securities markets rather than the local Tokyo Stock Exchange. A portfolio of registered Internet domain names such as SchwabArgentina.com, SchwabTaiwan.com, SchwabMexico.com, and SchwabBrazil.com had been collected, but Schwab made no official commitment to do business in these countries.

---

[15] Harrison, S. (1999), "Charles Schwab Expands US On-line Trade Service", *South China Morning Post*, 21 May.

[16] Lucas, L. (1998), "The Broking Revolution", *Asian Business*, September.

[17] URL: http://www.lsilink.com/usage_regions.html, February 1997.

[18] Lemon, S. (1997), "Research Group Confirms China 'Net Boom'", *Computer World Hong Kong*, 4 August.

[19] Schwab Canada (1998), URL: http://www.schwabcanada.com/about_priority/default.html, December.

Indigenous e-Players

Schwab was not the only on-line brokerage to realise the growth potential. Indigenous companies were also catching the Internet fever. Although initially, Asia was slow to respond, Internet use accelerated by 1999 as regional governments encouraged local technology growth.

Very few US-based e-brokers offered local market trading facilities, choosing instead to expand the number of customers buying and selling US stocks. Brokers with local market expertise stepped in to fill the gap and were also gradually branching out into other markets.

As a result, indigenous players were mushrooming. One of Schwab's main competitors in Hong Kong was Boom.com. Boom was found in 1997 by a group of professionals from the finance and technology industries. Its stated mission was to create a centralised financial hub Website for the Asia-Pacific, where in-country and overseas retail investors could effectively access Asian and US equity markets through real-time stock quotes, unbiased real-time news, corporate information, as well as inexpensive and efficient order execution facilities.

Boom's customers could buy and sell securities listed in Hong Kong and the US (pending approval), as well as Hong Kong qualified mutual funds. The company aimed to access as many as ten additional stock markets in Asia.

Firms such as Boom.com had strongholds in their regions. They were competitive in providing local insight and expertise and could pose a significant threat to companies such as Schwab in a local or regional context.

WHAT NEXT?

Each competitor pursued a markedly different strategy. Schwab entered foreign markets through joint ventures or acquisitions. E★Trade essentially chose the franchise model, striking licensing agreements with local partners to use its technology infrastructure. Those partners, in turn, sold services under the E★Trade name. Some industry experts believed E★Trade had pursued a much more aggressive international expansion strategy than Schwab. Apart from the US, E★Trade had established a presence in Australia, Canada, France, Israel, Japan, Scandinavia, South Korea and Germany. Other competitors, such as Ameritrade and DLJdirect, were also increasing their global presence rapidly [see **Exhibit 6**].

However, despite growing competition, Schwab's continued high performance reinforced shareholder confidence, and even competitors attested to its business acumen. The figures spoke for themselves: Schwab's total customer assets amounted to US$491 billion; on-line assets formed 35 percent of this figure (US$174 billion). In 1998, Schwab experienced its ninth consecutive year of record revenues and its eighth consecutive year of record earnings [see **Exhibit 7**]. Its stock price reached a high of US$77.50 on 14 April 1999.

Still, Schwab needed to maintain its lead. Competition was heating up and every on-line broker hoped to dethrone Schwab from its position. Low market entry barriers, easy capital access for hot young 'netrepreneurs' and venture capitalists fuelling the Internet growth was the environment Schwab faced. Could Schwab continue to leverage its brand name to succeed? How would it sustain its on-line dominance? What was the next step?

Schwab's strategy team had to recommend a growth plan to the board within three weeks. The main challenge facing them was to identify what strategies were feasible to retain Schwab's competitive market position in an evolving and turbulent market.

Exhibit 1:   The most respected technologist

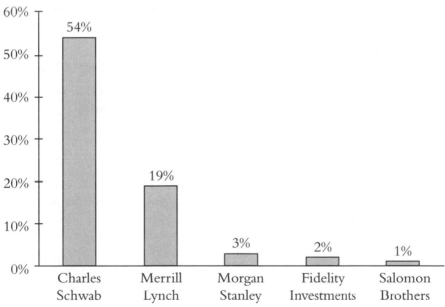

Source: The Tower Group/SIA 1997 Technology Trends in the Securities Industry.

Exhibit 2: Schwab's daily average trades

(in US$ thousands)	1996		1997		1998	
Revenue trades*						
On–line	11.8	*22%*	26.8	*37%*	56.3	*58%*
TeleBroker and VoiceBroker	11.9	*22%*	12.2	*17%*	8.2	*8%*
Regional customer telephone service centres, branch offices and other	30.3	*56%*	32.8	*46%*	32.7	*34%*
Total	*54.0*		*71.8*		*97.2*	
Mutual fund OneSource trades						
On–line	8.4	*31%*	12.8	*37%*	18.0	*45%*
TeleBroker and VoiceBroker	1.2	*4%*	1.3	*4%*	1.0	*2%*
Regional customer telephone service centres, branch offices and other	17.6	*65%*	20.1	*59%*	21.3	*53%*
Total	*27.2*		*34.2*		*40.3*	
Total daily average trades						
On–line	20.2	*25%*	39.6	*37%*	74.3	*54%*
TeleBroker and VoiceBroker	13.1	*16%*	13.5	*13%*	9.2	*7%*
Regional customer telephone service centres, branch offices and other	47.9	*59%*	52.9	*50%*	54.0	*39%*
Total	*81.2*		*106*		*137.5*	

* Revenue trades: Includes all customer trades (both domestic and international) that generate either commission revenue or revenue from principal markets.

Source: Company Annual Report.

Exhibit 3: The on-line explosion

Date	On-line brokers	On-line accounts (million)	On-line equity trades as a percentage of all equity trades	On-line assets (US$ billion)
3/97	15		7.16%	
6/97	24		8.89%	
9/97	33		8.89%	
12/97	51	2.9	9.2%	120
3/98	67	4.6	10.73%	
6/98	84	5.6	11.61%	
9/98	87	6.7	11.44%	
12/98	96	7.3	13.67%	420

Source: Credit Suisse First Boston (URL: http://www.investorguide.com).

Exhibit 4: Average daily on-line trades (June to December 1998)

Brokerage	Q3 1998 Trades/day	Share	Rank	Q4 1998 Trades/day	Share	Rank
Charles Schwab	76,608	30.1%	1	93,000	27.6%	1
Waterhouse	26,500	10.4%	4	42,003	12.5%	2
E*Trade	27,450	10.8%	3	39,990	11.9%	3
Datek	21,272	8.4%	5	33,695	10.0%	4
Fidelity	28,428	11.2%	2	33,100	9.8%	5
Ameritrade	18,246	7.2%	6	25,725	7.6%	6
DLJ Direct	10,448	4.1%	7	13,366	4.0%	7
Discover	9,400	3.7%	8	11,531	3.4%	8
Suretrade	6,900	2.7%	9	9,600	2.9%	9
NDB	3,910	1.5%	10	4,420	1.3%	10
Others	25,462	10.0%		30,306	9.0%	
Total	*254,624*			*336,736*		

Source: Piper Jaffray Inc. and Annual Company Reports.

Exhibit 5: Schwab's on-line products and services

Hong Kong	Charles Schwab Hong Kong

- Charles Schwab Hong Kong. One of Schwab's most successful international ventures was its Hong Kong subsidiary. The office serviced investors from the Asia-Pacific region who wanted access to international markets.
- With a Charles Schwab Hong Kong account, investors could trade in US stocks and options, over 200 Hong Kong authorised mutual funds, American depositary receipts (ADRs), fixed-income investments and ordinary shares of non-US listed securities.
- Trade orders could be placed on-line 24-hours-a-day, 7-days-a-week. Customers could monitor their investment activity on the Web at any time and obtain a wide range of research and information on the Web, including real-time quotes, company reports, comprehensive charting services and a market commentary that was updated every 20 minutes.
- Customer service was available in English, Mandarin and Cantonese. For Chinese-language investors, most of the information on the Website was available in Chinese (although the trading pages were not).

Europe	Charles Schwab Europe

- In 1995, Schwab bought the largest discount broker in the UK to form Charles Schwab Europe. It first began offering on-line trading of British stocks to UK residents in June 1998.
- In 1998, it expanded its service to allow European clients to trade on the main US stock, option, bond and treasury markets.
- In its first year of operation, Schwab's European branch had traded more than 300 million pounds worth of shares and its on-line customers were increasing at a rate of between 500 and 1,000 a week.[20]
- By 2000, 3.6 million people were estimated to be connected to the Internet in the UK and a third were expected to be on-line investors.[21] A number of other players such as Stocktrade and Barclays Stockbrokers also hoped to gain a significant share of the European on-line pie.

[20] Yahoo Finance (1997), URL: http://biz.yahoo.com/rf/990517/xu.html, May.

[21] "Share Dealing: An On-line Revolution", *BBC News*, 15 October 1998.

Exhibit 5 (cont'd)

Canada	Charles Schwab Canada

- In December 1998, Schwab bought Priority Brokerage Inc. and Porthmeor Securities Inc. of Canada to form Charles Schwab Canada. Clients could trade in equities, options, mutual funds, fixed-income securities and a variety of other investment vehicles on both the Canadian and US exchanges through the Internet, touch-tone phone, or person-to-person.
- In Canada, Schwab's main competitors were banks providing on-line trading services, such as Toronto-Dominion Bank and the Bank of Montreal. The latter ran InvestorLine.com, which offered many of the same services as Schwab.

L. America	Charles Schwab Latin America

- Schwab offered Latin American and Caribbean investors the opportunity to trade in the US markets through its Website. Although it did not have physical presence in Latin America, its offices in Miami provided personalised advice via the telephone or e-mail.
- Although its clients could not trade in South American stocks, Schwab planned to make that service available.
- Patagon.com was the first company in Latin America to offer Internet trading facilities for people who wished to buy stock on the Argentine market. Patagon.com was positioning itself to be a regional transaction hub, hoping to enable its clients to invest in Latin American markets such as Brazil, Mexico and Chile.[22]

---

[22] Patagon USA – The Global On-line Brokerage (1998), URL: http://www.patagon.com/services.asp, December.

Exhibit 6: International on-line expansion

Brokerage	International presence	International strategy
Charles Schwab	Internet trading in Europe on the London Exchange, in Canada on Canadian exchanges and in Latin America, the Caribbean, the Asia-Pacific region and Hong Kong on US markets.	Leveraging Schwab brand through development, acquisitions or partnerships, depending on region.
E★Trade	On-line trading in Australia, Canada and France. Partnerships established to form e-trades in Israel, Japan (through relationship with Softbank), Scandinavia, South Korea, Germany and Central Europe.	Partnering with local services to establish e-trade-branded ventures. Long term: Trade anywhere on any exchange at any time.
Ameritrade	Partnership with Cortal, a European discount broker, lets Ameritrade customers trade on the French exchange and Cortal investors trade on US markets.	Extending services through partnerships with local firms, instead of by establishing an international brand.
DLJdirect	A joint venture with Sumitomo Bank in Japan provides on-line trading for Japanese investors. Additional international plans to be funded in part by upcoming IPO proceeds.	Plans to expand either directly or through alliances and joint ventures with local partners.
TD Waterhouse	On-line trading for Canadians and Americans on both countries' exchanges. On-line trading in Australia. Off-line presence in the UK and Hong Kong.	IPO proceeds to help fund international expansion. Toronto Dominion has historically grown through acquisitions.

Source: URL: http/www.thestandard.net, May 1999.

Exhibit 7:   Schwab's financial performance

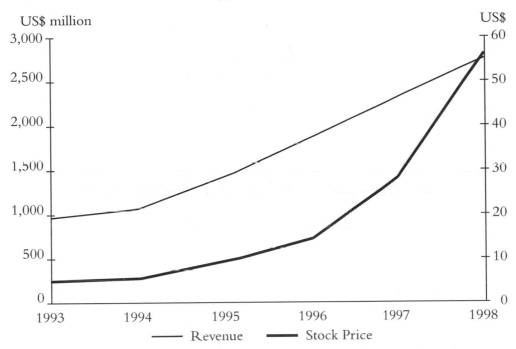

Source: Company Annual Report.

Case

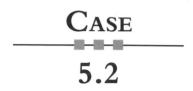

5.2

Seven-Eleven Japan: Venturing into e-Tailing*

Not content with nine million customers per day, Toshifumi Suzuki [see **Exhibit 1**], the Chairman and Chief Executive Officer of Seven-Eleven Japan Co. Ltd., was looking for ways to attract more customers and more sales. Fascinated by the market's optimistic outlook on the growth of business-to-consumer (B2C) e-commerce in Japan, he contacted several prominent Japanese companies to explore the possibility of working together to launch the biggest B2C e-commerce Website in Japan. Suzuki knew that successfully launching and operating a B2C e-commerce business in Japan, known for its citizens' hesitancy to buy on-line, could be a big coup for him. His challenge now was to convince his would-be partners that he had a potentially successful and lucrative business model.

THE E-COMMERCE ENVIRONMENT IN JAPAN

In May 2000, the Economist Intelligence Unit (EIU) surveyed 60 countries and ranked

---

* Deric K.K. Tan prepared this case from public sources under the supervision of Dr. Ali Farhoomand. *Copyright © 2000 The University of Hong Kong. Ref. 99/67C*

them based on their readiness for e-commerce. This was assessed based on the general business environment and connectivity in each country. Factors taken into consideration included local government policies, the state of the existing telephone network and Internet access-related issues such as dial-up costs and literacy rates. Based on these factors, Japan was placed in the 21st position, the lowest among the Group of Seven industrialised countries [see **Exhibit 2**].

Even though Internet usage was high in Japan, the growth of B2C e-commerce was slow compared to other G7 countries. According to a survey conducted jointly by the Ministry of International Trade and Industry (MITI) and Andersen Consulting (AC) in 1999, e-commerce transactions accounted for only 0.02 percent of all the B2C transactions in 1998. This represented only about one thirty-fifth of the level in the US.[1] Numerous surveys were done to determine the reasons for the slow growth. In the March 2000 issue of *Japan Inc.* magazine, the authors of several articles attributed the relatively poor e-commerce environment in Japan to several reasons [see **Appendix 1**]. These included the phobia Japanese consumers had about submitting credit card information over the Internet and a relatively expensive connection charge. Japan had the world's highest combined telecommunication and ISP fees [see **Figure 1**]. In addition, end-fulfilment of on-line orders was a problem for many people. Most consumers were not home during the day to receive parcels they had ordered on-line. Consumers were also doubtful about receiving their parcels from on-line stores, either due to mailing errors or non-fulfilment on the part of the stores.

In a bid to encourage the growth of e-commerce in Japan, the government deregulated stock commissions in 1999, enabling consumers to start trading via the Internet. That year was widely considered as 'the first year of e-commerce' in Japan. The government also attempted to introduce competition into the telecommunications industry by splitting Nippon Telephone & Telegraph, the dominant telecommunication company, into three companies. Several research groups looked favourably upon the efforts taken by the government. For instance, in January 2000, Andersen Consulting projected that the market for B2C e-commerce in Japan would grow from 248 billion yen in 1999 to 3.5 trillion yen in 2003.[2]

---

[1] Ministry of International Trade and Industry (2000), URL: http://www.jipdec.or.jp/chosa/MITIAE/sld013.htm, 4 July.

[2] Andersen Consulting (2000), "Total Consumer Electronic Commerce Market in Japan Estimated at 336 Billion Yen, According to Joint Survey by ECOM and Andersen Consulting", 19 January.

Figure 1: Combined ISP and phone costs

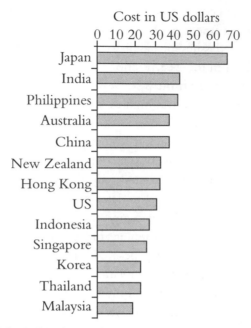

Source: *Japan Inc* (2000), URL: http://www.japaninc.net/mag/comp/2000/06/jun00_unwired_ispgraph.html, 15 November.

Towards the end of 1999, e-commerce in Japan seemed to have evolved into a form that was different from the conventional US-style e-commerce practised in most countries. The focus of e-commerce was on Japan's ubiquitous convenience stores, or *konbinis*, as they were known, each with an average floor space of 100 square metres.[3] The operators of these convenience stores had been racing to introduce e-commerce initiatives to capture the attention and business of the population. The most aggressive so far was Seven-Eleven Japan, with its investments into ambitious e-commerce ventures such as an on-line bookstore that allowed payment and pickup at a 7-Eleven store. Others, such as Lawson Products Inc., the operator of the second-largest chain of convenience stores, were busy announcing e-commerce businesses of their own.[4] Up

---

[3] "Seven-Eleven Japan Takes Two-pronged Net Strategy", *The Nikkei Weekly*, 25 October 1999.

[4] Otsu, T. (2000), "Lawson Plans to Go Online", *China Daily*, New York, 26 February.

until February 2000, Lawson had invested US$60 million installing terminals in its over 7,200 stores nationwide. These terminals allowed customers to browse on-line catalogues, download software or book package tours to overseas destinations, and to pay for their orders at the counter in the store. The reason for the popularity of using convenience stores as a launch pad for e-commerce was that these stores offered a physical location for consumers to pay in cash and to pick up their orders, a method that the Japanese people were familiar and at ease with.

The Japanese would rather pick up their goods and pay for them at a konbini.
— Morihiko Ida, Head of Equities Research, Century Securities, Japan

SEVEN-ELEVEN JAPAN CO., LTD.

Since its establishment in 1973, Seven-Eleven Japan had taken on 'Adapting to Change' as its business slogan, reflecting its focus on adapting to changing consumer trends. As such, its 7-Eleven convenience stores had earned the patronage of much of the population, far outstripping other companies in the convenience store sector as well as in the overall retail industry in terms of growth and profitability. For the fiscal year ended 29 February 2000, while Japan was in the midst of an economic downturn, Seven-Eleven Japan opened an additional 423 stores and recorded the highest profits in the retail industry [see **Table 1**]. This impressive result and its rapid growth was due to its efforts at developing merchandise and services that met customers' needs and requirements. For example, it was the pioneer in providing ready-made meals such as sushi and spaghetti that had become popular among the Japanese population. In addition, the information and distribution systems played an especially large role in placing Seven-Eleven Japan in a leading position.

The Information and Distribution Systems

Since the inception of Seven-Eleven Japan, Suzuki had been preoccupied with the continual application of information technology to capture data so as to better meet customers' needs. Seven-Eleven Japan's first information system was introduced in 1978. The point-of-sale (POS) systems were introduced in 1982 and since then had been continuously upgraded. They formed the backbone of Seven-Eleven Japan's just-in-time ordering system. By showing real-time information such as merchandise sell-out schedules, shelf-stocking methods, the weather and local events, the POS systems

Table 1: Seven-Eleven Japan: Non-consolidated financial information

	Fiscal year				
	2000	1999	1998 (million yen)	1997	1996
Total store sales	1,963,972	1,848,147	1,740,961	1,609,007	1,477,127
Revenue from operations	327,014	297,993	277,186	254,617	231,227
Cost of sales	41,132	33,504	31,036	26,898	23,314
Selling, general and administrative expenses*	148,403	135,155	122,834	111,320	100,329
Operating income	137,477	129,334	123,316	116,399	107,584
Total shareholders' equity	529,822	482,516	439,411	397,744	N/A

* see Table 2
Source: Seven-Eleven Japan Co., Ltd., Annual Reports: 2000, 1999 and 1998.

Table 2: Major elements of selling, general and administrative expenses

	Fiscal year				
	2000	1999	1998 (million yen)	1997	1996
Salaries and bonuses	26,211	23,319	21,712	19,665	17,569
Advertising expenses	19,322	20,073	18,141	14,039	11,630
Depreciation	24,394	22,865	16,234	14,734	14,245
Utilities expenses	20,220	19,144	19,492	17,358	16,612

Source: Seven-Eleven Japan Co., Ltd., Annual Reports: 2000, 1999 and 1998.

allowed the stores to be extremely responsive to consumers' shifting tastes [see **Exhibit 3**].[5] For example, if the weather was predicted to be bad, the systems would remind

---

[5] Earl, M. (1998), "The Right Mind-set for Managing Information Technology", *Harvard Business Review*, September/October.

operators to put umbrellas next to the sales counter. In 1999, Seven-Eleven Japan completed the installation of the Fifth-Generation Total Information System [see **Exhibit 4**], representing a total investment of 60 billion yen. One of the largest information systems in the world, it linked all the 7-Eleven stores via satellite communications and ISDN telephone lines. The system could transmit large volumes of information at high speed and had superior information-processing capability. Using this system, Seven-Eleven Japan was able to provide its stores with useful, easy-to-use data and visual information, enabling reductions in missed sales opportunities and inventory write-offs through precise item-by-item management. As a result, inventory was kept at efficient levels [see **Table 3**].

Table 3:   Inventory levels

	Fiscal year			
	2000	1999	1998	1997
		(million yen)		
Processed food	491	400	346	304
Fast food	0	0	0	1
Daily/fresh food	70	48	42	40
Nonfood	755	596	551	459

Source: Seven-Eleven Japan Co., Ltd., Annual Reports: 2000, 1999 and 1998.

The information system was used in tandem with Seven-Eleven Japan's distribution system, which served its network of stores with over 250 distribution centres, to deliver goods to stores efficiently. In 1999, Seven-Eleven Japan improved on its distribution system by creating one that allowed it to combine products that required the same temperature range control. Within this system, it was able to manage the delivery of temperature-sensitive food products to stores and better preserve their freshness. Cooked rice items and chilled foods, the bulk of total store sales, were delivered to 7-Eleven stores three times a day [see **Figure 2**]. As a result, daily supplies that would have taken 70 trucks to distribute in 1975 were being delivered using 10 trucks.[6]

---

[6]   Seven-Eleven Japan Co., Ltd., Annual Report 2000, p. 8.

Figure 2: Seven-Eleven Japan's distribution system

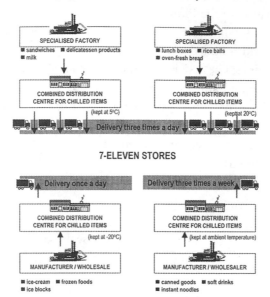

Source: Seven-Eleven Japan Co., Ltd., Annual Report 2000, p. 8.

e-Commerce Ventures

Floor traffic at Seven-Elevens is about 9 million people daily, but basically they're seeing the same people and not generating a lot of new traffic.[7]

– Mike Allen, retail-sector analyst, ING Baring Securities (Japan)

By observing the average monthly sales trend per store and by listening to numerous complaints from franchisees, Suzuki was aware that the level of sales per store had reached a plateau [see **Figure 3**]. In order to increase sales, he recognised the need for Seven-Eleven Japan to venture into other avenues, notably e-commerce. As the operator of the largest chain of convenience stores in Japan, Suzuki was acutely aware of the fact that Seven-Eleven Japan had the distinct advantage of having more than 8,000 convenience stores to act as a payment and end-fulfilment network, both being important factors in e-commerce.

---

[7] Nakada, G. (2000), "Seven-Eleven Japan's Web Dream: On-line Mall Goes Live, Multimedia Kiosks to Come", CBS.MarketWatch.com, 2 July.

Figure 3:   Average daily sales per store

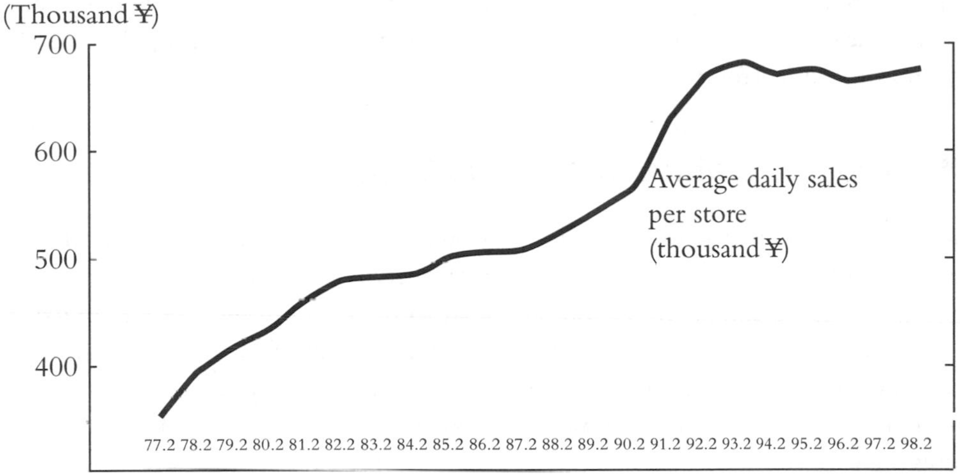

(Thousand ¥)

Source: Seven-Eleven Japan Co., Ltd., Annual Report 1998, p. 6.

Instead of immediately fully diverting resources into a new e-commerce business though, Suzuki thought it was prudent to initially approach e-commerce based on two strategies. The first involved active investment in e-commerce joint ventures. In August 1999, Seven-Eleven Japan established e-Shopping! Books Corp., an on-line bookshop joint venture between Softbank Corp. and Tohan Corp, in which Seven-Eleven Japan held a 30 percent stake. In October 1999, it acquired a 10 percent stake in CarPoint Japan KK, an on-line car broker set up in March 1999 by Softbank Corp., Yahoo Japan Corp. and Microsoft Corp. Seven-Eleven Japan did not deal with the daily operations of these joint ventures, opting instead for a pure investor approach.

The second strategy involved using its chain of stores as a distribution centre for various e-commerce businesses. In September 1999, it announced plans to use its stores as the payment and delivery stations for eight major on-line shop operators, including e-Shopping!, BIGLOBE, @nifty, Curio-city, Plala, Sofmap and So-net. These operators together operated more than 1,200 virtual shops. The premise was simple: the customer makes his purchase at the on-line store, pays at a 7-Eleven store, and a few days later, returns to the store to pick up the item. This service, launched in November 1999, was developed jointly with Nomura Research Institute based on the existing payment acceptance services for utilities.[8] Settlement between the on-line shops and Seven-Eleven Japan was through a settlement software module developed by several leading technology companies – NEC Corp., Hewlett-Packard Japan Ltd., Fujitsu Ltd. and Microsoft Co. Ltd.

A NEW B2C E-COMMERCE VENTURE

Buoyed by the optimistic outlook on the growth of B2C e-commerce in Japan and the success of previous e-commerce participatory-style undertakings, Suzuki decided that the time was ripe for Seven-Eleven Japan to fully venture into e-commerce. A pioneer by nature, he was the first to introduce the concept of a convenience store to Japan, was the first to install an electronic inventory and sales system, and the first to offer fast food. Noting that the obstacles to mainstream e-commerce in Japan were mainly culture-related, he recognised the need to introduce a unique e-commerce model that could entice Japanese people to buy on-line. He began contacting the heads of several major Japanese companies, which included Sony Corp., Sony Marketing (Japan) Inc., NEC Corp., Nomura Research Institute, Mitsui & Co. Ltd., Japan Travel Bureau Ltd. and Kinotrope Inc., to convey his vision and to persuade them to join him into bringing e-commerce to Japanese consumers in a big way [see **Exhibit 5**]. The joint venture, to be named 7dream.com to reflect the brand name of Seven-Eleven Japan, would be aimed at becoming the largest B2C e-commerce site in Japan and help Seven-Eleven Japan to realise its goal of becoming an on-line Japanese shopping behemoth.

Business

Suzuki envisioned that 7dream.com would offer services based on the technical expertise and industry knowledge of each founding member, including Seven-Eleven Japan. As such, he intended 7dream.com to offer services in eight content areas: travel; music; photographs; merchandise, gifts and mobile phones; tickets; books; car-related items; and information [see **Exhibit 6**]. This diverse range of merchandise was specially aimed at the buying pattern of most Japanese consumers and to complement the range of goods offered in the 7-Eleven stores. As the products to be offered on 7dream.com would not usually be found in convenience stores, due to limited space,

---

[8] The use of convenience stores to make utilities and other payments was popular in Japan.

Suzuki expected overall sales for Seven-Eleven Japan to grow. Also, the products to be offered were especially chosen for their ease of handling – if they were not viewable on screen or downloadable, they were small-sized. This was due to Suzuki's plans to utilise the existing Seven-Eleven Japan delivery system as 7dream.com's end-fulfilment system.

The Target Market

Convenience stores resembled centres of community life in Japan: consumers visited *konbinis* to pick up a meal or snack, to pay for their utilities, to socialise with friends and to look at the latest fashion accessories. In addition, the stores were easily accessible as they were located in every conceivable location, at nearly every street corner, in every city or town in the country. Customers of 7-Eleven convenience stores alone numbered almost 10 million per day. Of these, most were mainly young people from their teens through their 30s. Recognising that this represented the portion of society that dictated shopping trends in the country, Suzuki intended to target this group of customers to get them to use 7dream.com to satisfy their shopping needs. In addition, this group represented the generation that had taken to the Internet most enthusiastically. In Suzuki's opinion, these characteristics made this group an ideal target to market an on-line shopping site.[9]

The Payment and Delivery System

Customers of 7dream.com could pay for their purchases by credit card over the Internet. However, recognising that many Japanese consumers were reluctant to reveal their credit card numbers on-line and preferred to settle their transactions by cash, Suzuki planned to give customers of 7dream.com the option of paying for their on-line purchases at a 7-Eleven store of their choice. After making a purchase at the 7dream.com Website, customers could select 'Payment at a 7-Eleven store' as their payment method. Payment slips with barcodes would then be printed out from the customers' printers. Customers could then visit any 7-Eleven store in Japan with these slips to make their payments. Customers without printers could just state their assigned payment reference number to the cashier at the 7-Eleven store. Suzuki was confident that this payment system would work as the 7-Eleven stores were already equipped with the capa-

---

[9] "Seven-Eleven Japan Takes Two-pronged Net Strategy", *The Nikkei Weekly*, 25 October 1999.

bility to accept payments on behalf of other businesses. For example, it was a common sight to see consumers pay their utility bills at convenience stores. Seven-Eleven Japan alone accepted about 70 million payments annually for a total of over 500 billion yen.[10] Besides, Seven-Eleven Japan already had a payment acceptance system with several major Japanese on-line stores in place.

Customers could choose to have their orders delivered to their home or other delivery address. Aware of the problem of end-fulfilment in Japan though, Suzuki planned to allow customers the option to pick up their purchases at a 7-Eleven store. This meant that a customer could pay for his or her purchase and later return to the same store, or another of his or her choice, to collect his or her merchandise. 7dream.com would utilise the existing logistics system that Seven-Eleven Japan employed for the distribution of goods to its network of convenience stores. With over 8,000 stores spread throughout Japan, Suzuki thought that it would be unusual for the customer to have a long walk before seeing the familiar 7-Eleven sign. Furthermore, as the delivery system was already in place, orders on 7dream.com's site would probably only be charged a minimal cost, which would be significantly lower than the shipping and handling charges levied by other e-commerce companies.

> *The Japanese person who doesn't pass a convenience store on the way home from the train station 'doesn't exist'.*[11]
>
> – Makoto Usui, Director, Seven-Eleven Japan

Combining the payment and pickup features offered by 7dream.com, Suzuki envisioned the following scenario:

A customer goes on-line via an Internet-enabled device to make a purchase at 7dream.com's Website and specifies pickup at the 7-Eleven store in his neighbourhood. The order is then processed and shipped by the 7dream.com Order Centre via Seven-Eleven Japan's distribution system to the specified store. The Order Centre then notifies the customer of the pickup date by e-mail. After receiving the e-mail, the customer brings a payment slip that he or she printed out when placing the order to the 7-Eleven store in his or her neighbourhood and picks up the purchased item after payment.

---

[10] Seven-Eleven Japan Co., Ltd. (1999), "Seven-Eleven to Start Payment Acceptance Service for Internet Shopping", 3 September, URL: http://info.sej.co.jp/contents_e/news/index.html.

[11] Kashiwagi, A. (2000).

Marketing 7dream.com

Access to the services of 7dream.com would be initially tailored for consumers with Internet-accessible personal computers. However, the number of homes with personal computers in Japan was considered low. According to eMarketer, the penetration rate of personal computers in Japan was only about 20 percent as opposed to 41 percent in the US.[12] Moreover, getting on-line via wired dial-up was expensive as Japan was considered to have the most expensive Internet dial-up access fee in the world. Space was an issue too. Many Japanese homes were tiny and had no space to accommodate a personal computer.

Recognising that these factors were impediments to people's access to the Website, Suzuki envisioned other channels for consumers to utilise 7dream.com's services. One of the channels under consideration was Internet-enabled multimedia kiosks. Once 7dream.com's Website was enabled, Suzuki planned to start placing these multimedia kiosks in a few participating 7-Eleven stores in October 2000, aiming for a kiosk in all stores by June 2001.[13] The idea was to whet people's appetite for computers and the Internet.[14] These kiosks would enable consumers who did not wish to connect to the Internet at home, or did not have personal computers with Internet access, to access the full services of 7dream.com. Once consumers savoured what 7dream.com had to offer, it was expected that the utility-packed kiosks would offer enough value to attract the consumers into using the kiosks more often to access 7dream.com's services in order to satisfy their shopping needs. The kiosks would be equipped with a screen to access the services of 7dream.com, a digital printer for instant printing and delivery of pictures purchased or photographs taken with the in-built digital camera, and a MiniDisc drive and MemoryStick slot to allow customers to save purchased songs.

Suzuki was also looking ahead to a wireless capability. In Japan, nearly six million of Japan's 17.5 million Internet users, a full 34 percent, were accessing the Web via Internet-enabled cellular phones.[15] This contrasted with the US, where nearly every-

---

[12] Scuka, D. (2000), "Unwired: Japan Has the Future in Its Pocket", *Japan Inc*, June.

[13] Williams, M. (2000), "7-Eleven Japan Embraces E-Commerce", The Standard.com, 6 January.

[14] Moshavi, S. (2000), "Online at the 7-Eleven – Japan Begins Embracing Internet Commerce Its Own Way: At Convenience Stores", *The Boston Globe*, 26 August.

[15] Kashiwagi, A. (2000), "Japanese Going On-line But Leaving PCs Behind", *eMarketer*, 8 February.

one accessed the Internet via a personal computer. One of the reasons for the popularity of wireless access in Japan was because subscribers were given continuous access to the Internet and paid based on the amount of data transmitted or received, not on airtime. This was evidently more advantageous than paying the expensive dial-up fees associated with wired connections. In addition, there were thousands of Websites specially tailored for these phones and many more were being developed. Citing statistical figures that indicated that the number of subscribers to Internet mobile services was on the rise, it seemed certain that wireless devices would be a key factor in promoting e-commerce in Japan. In the future, Suzuki planned to utilise other channels to market 7dream.com, such as digital broadcasting, television and magazines.

Projection of Sales

Convinced of the potential profitability of the 7dream.com model [see **Figure 4**], Suzuki projected 7dream.com to process seven billion yen in e-commerce transactions for the fiscal year ending February 2001, given that the 7dream.com Website could be launched by June 2000.[16] He further projected the amount to increase to 180 billion yen in 2003 and 240 billion yen in 2004. He also highlighted to his would-be partners that since 7dream.com would be dealing with wholesalers, it would be obtaining the goods directly from the warehouses of its suppliers. This meant that it would not have to hold inventory and incur warehousing costs. In addition, the 7dream.com model would be leveraging on an existing delivery system instead of building one from scratch, translating into more savings. As Seven-Eleven Japan was already making deliveries to 7-Eleven stores, the additional cost of delivering 7dream.com's orders to these stores using Seven-Eleven Japan's distribution system would be minimal to Seven-Eleven Japan. The low delivery charges meant that customers would not be charged exorbitant delivery rates, making it all the more attractive to consumers. These factors being two of the more challenging obstacles faced by many e-commerce companies, this meant that the 7dream.com had potentially huge savings in operating costs.

---

[16] "Japan: Seven-Eleven's Success Multiplies", *IDEAadvisor*, 25 October 2000.

Figure 4: Business model of 7dream.com

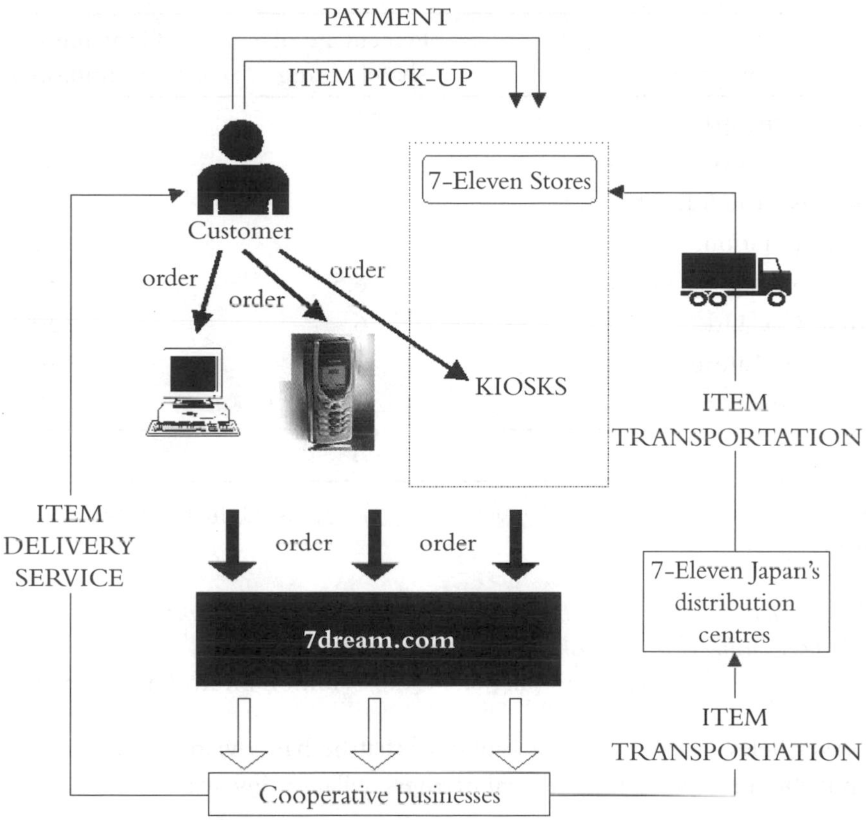

Source: Seven–Eleven Japan Co., Ltd., Annual Report 2000, p. 11.

A BUSINESS DECISION

Suzuki was confident that he had the right business model to penetrate the B2C e-commerce market in Japan. The initial outlay was expected to be five billion yen, with Seven-Eleven Japan taking a 51 percent stake in 7dream.com [see **Table 4**] and the others taking from two to 13 percent. Not surprisingly though, there were critics who believed that the e-commerce model proposed by Suzuki might be short-lived. As technology improved and new products such as debit cards and smart cards were introduced, Japanese consumers were expected to get accustomed to transacting and paying via on-line means. As such, the 7dream.com model, if it did not undergo any structural changes, would be vulnerable to shifts in cultural and shopping habits.

Table 4: Shareholding in 7dream.com

Company	Percentage of shareholding	Contributed capital (million yen)
Seven-Eleven Japan	51	2,550
NEC Corporation	13	650
Nomura Research Institute, Ltd.	13	650
Sony Corporation	6.5	325
Sony Marketing (Japan) Inc.	6.5	325
Mitsui & Co., Ltd.	6	300
Japan Travel Bureau	2	100
Kinotrope Inc.	2	100
Total	*100*	*5,000*

Source: Seven-Eleven Japan Co., Ltd. (2000), "7dream.com Established on February 1, 2000", 1 February.

> *In the short term, they'll be major players because of their networks, but the Japanese will begin using electronic cash and home delivery, like Americans.*[17]
> – Hirokazu Ishii, analyst, Nikko Salomon Smith Barney in Tokyo

Nevertheless, Suzuki was still confident that he had a viable business model. He then put the question to his potential partners: will you invest in 7dream.com?

APPENDIX 1: FACTORS AFFECTING THE E-COMMERCE ENVIRONMENT IN JAPAN

Connection Charges

The state of the communications infrastructure in a country was very important towards e-business. The key to e-commerce was access to the Internet, which was usually through a telephone line and a personal computer. In Japan, the pricing of access charges to the Internet was decided upon by Nippon Telephone & Telegraph (NTT),

---

[17] Kunii, I.M. (2000), "From Convenience Store to Online Behemoth?" *BusinessWeek*, New York, 10 April.

of which the government was a majority shareholder. Through its subsidiaries NTT East and NTT West, NTT controlled 95 percent of Japan's telephone lines. Despite NTT's decision to cut monthly fixed charges by 50 percent from May 2000, the price charged for connection to the Internet was considered to be high. Additionally, connection to the Internet was charged by the minute, deterring many people from browsing the Web, or staying at a Website for very long. In a move aimed at increasing the use of the Internet in Japan, the US government demanded that NTT lower access fees by 22.5 percent over a two-year period starting from 2002, and ultimately by more than 40 percent. The Japan government insisted that the reduction be limited to 22.5 percent over a four-year period instead.[18]

Government Policies

Government policies played a crucial role in the promotion of e-commerce in a country. There was a general consensus among analysts that the system traditionally practised by the government of Japan ultimately cost the B2C e-commerce industry. Under the Japanese system, for the sake of international competitiveness, the government actively intervened in markets to promote producers' interests. In the past, this system was laudable, but in the 1990s, when attention shifted towards satisfying customer requirements, it became evident that the system was maintained at the expense of consumers and could not adapt to the tides of change. For example, under what was termed as the *saihan* system, it was illegal for retailers and e-tailers based in Japan to sell music CDs at a discount because of a law that protected copyright holders.

However, since the mid-1990s, the government had been actively promoting deregulation and e-commerce. Recognising that competition was important in improving the general business environment, the government initiated steps such as splitting the telecom giant NTT into three companies – two regional carriers (NTT East and NTT West) and a long-distance and international one (NTT DoCoMo). Through MITI, the Electronic Commerce Promotion Council of Japan (ECOM) was established in January 1996 in order to develop a common platform to work for the realisation and expansion of e-commerce.

---

[18] Anai, I. (2000), "U.S. Pressure May Give Japan IT Industry Boost", *The Daily Yomiuri*, Tokyo, 1 July, p. 13.

Local Culture

The EIU surmised that even though the Internet was essentially a borderless network that facilitated global operations, the local culture was an important factor that had to be understood for the e-commerce company to survive and succeed.

Japan had traditionally been a cash-based society. It was not unusual to see salaries paid in bank notes. About 90 percent of all mail-order sales were paid for with cash-on-delivery or by bank transfer, which were also the most commonly used methods of payment for on-line shopping. Cheques were not used. Credit card payment, the most common form of payment in e-commerce Websites elsewhere, was not very popular, accounting for just over ten percent. Polls indicated that 70 percent of Japanese disliked using credit cards for on-line purchases, being wary of the ease with which hackers hacked into servers to obtain credit card information and other personal data.[19]

> *It's part of the Japanese culture that people want to buy products, face-to-face.*[20]
> – Minoru Matsumoto, spokesman for Seven-Eleven Japan

Japanese consumers were used to buying off-line. By doing their shopping off-line, they could see and touch the products, and perhaps obtain discounts. For example, if a consumer wanted to buy a personal computer in Tokyo, he could just visit Akihabara, a famous electric town, where all sorts of branded and non-branded systems and parts were offered at ever greater discounts by sales people anxious to outdo their competitors. Furthermore, off-line shopping was very convenient in Japan. There was a long history of mail-order and catalogue shopping. There were also streets packed with stores selling daily necessities. A writer commented that "As long as one doesn't mind walking, which you do a lot of here, there's not much that isn't within 10 minutes."[21] In addition, convenience stores, or *konbinis*, as they were known in Japan, were almost everywhere and, due to their small floor space that allowed them to be exempted from strict government rules requiring regular supermarkets to close by eight o'clock in the evening, most were open all night. Many Japanese consumers, with tiny homes that limited the size of refrigerators and storage space, frequented these stores for their daily necessities.

---

[19] Kunii, I.M. (2000), "From Convenience Store to Online Behemoth?" *BusinessWeek*, 10 April, p. 64.

[20] Zielenziger, M. (2000), "7-Eleven Capitalizes on Japan Market Share with Wide Array of Services", *San Jose Mercury News*, 2 April.

[21] Mollman, S. (2000), "How Convenient to Be a *Konbini*", *J@pan Inc*, March.

Exhibit 1:   Toshifumi Suzuki

The Japanese have Toshifumi Suzuki to thank for snack food at all hours. The name was especially familiar for those in the retailing sector as Suzuki, aged 67, was Chairman and CEO of Seven-Eleven Japan Co., Ltd., the operator of the largest chain of convenience stores in Japan.

A country boy from the Nagano prefecture, Suzuki worked in publishing for a large publication sales agent before joining the Japanese retailer Ito-Yokado Co. in 1963. At Ito-Yokado, he was involved in administration and human resources. In 1973, he led the fight to win a Seven-Eleven franchise in Japan from its US parent, Southland Company. As a result, Seven-Eleven Japan Co., Ltd., was established in 1973 with Ito-Yokado as its major shareholder. Suzuki helped open the first store in 1974, giving him the reputation of being the father of the Japanese convenience store concept. He led the drive to computerise operations and had a reputation of forcefully maintaining his views and ideas through his top-down management style. After becoming the President of Seven-Eleven Japan in 1978, he headed its team merchandising efforts. In 1992, he became the President of Ito-Yokado. Taking advantage of his experience at Seven-Eleven Japan, he tried to make the most of it at Ito-Yokado by implementing a series of reforms. Refuting criticisms that his top-down management style did not allow his staff to make their views reflected in the management of the company, Suzuki maintained that reform could only be done through the top-down line of command.

Sources: "Asian Cover Story – Managers: Toshifumi Suzuki", *Business Week International Editions*, 3 July 2000; "Ito-Yokado Faces Its Limitations", *Nikkei Business*, 30 September 1996, p. 22.

Exhibit 2: The EIU e-business-readiness rankings

Rank	Country	Business environment ranking, 2000–04	Connectivity ranking	e-Business-readiness ranking
1	US	8.69	9	8.8
2	Sweden	8.26	9	8.6
3	Finland	8.21	9	8.6
4	Norway	8.00	9	8.5
5	Netherlands	8.84	8	8.4
6	UK	8.80	8	8.4
7	Canada	8.66	8	8.3
8	Singapore	8.55	8	8.3
9	Hong Kong	8.52	8	8.3
10	Switzerland	8.42	8	8.2
11	Ireland	8.42	8	8.2
12	Denmark	8.41	8	8.2
13	Germany	8.32	8	8.2
14	France	8.17	8	8.1
15	Belgium	8.17	8	8.1
16	Australia	8.14	8	8.1
17	New Zealand	8.10	8	8.1
18	Austria	7.96	8	8.0
19	Italy	7.68	8	7.8
20	Israel	7.61	8	7.8
* 21	**Japan**	**7.43**	**8**	**7.7**
22	Spain	8.01	7	7.5
23	Chile	7.85	7	7.4
24	South Korea	7.30	7	7.2
25	Portugal	7.59	6	6.8
26	Argentina	7.22	6	6.6
27	Taiwan	8.13	5	6.6
28	Thailand	7.27	5	6.1
29	Poland	7.15	5	6.1
30	Hungary	7.09	5	6.0

Source: The EIU ebusiness Forum (2000), "Introducing the EIU's e-Business-readiness Rankings", 4 May.

Exhibit 3:   Examples of point-of-sale data applications

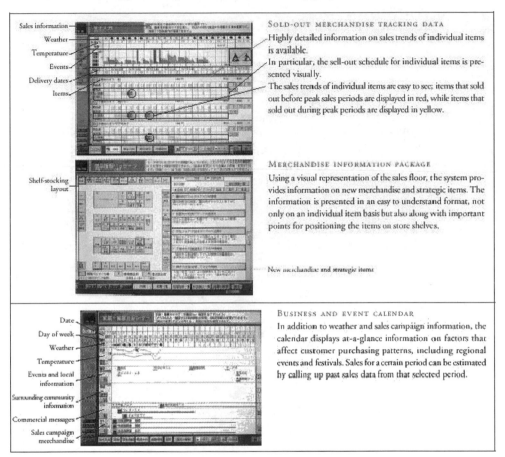

SOLD-OUT MERCHANDISE TRACKING DATA

Highly detailed information on sales trends of individual items is available.

In particular, the sell-out schedule for individual items is presented visually.

The sales trends of individual items are easy to see; items that sold out before peak sales periods are displayed in red, while items that sold out during peak periods are displayed in yellow.

MERCHANDISE INFORMATION PACKAGE

Using a visual representation of the sales floor, the system provides information on new merchandise and strategic items. The information is presented in an easy to understand format, not only on an individual item basis but also along with important points for positioning the items on store shelves.

New merchandise and strategic items

BUSINESS AND EVENT CALENDAR

In addition to weather and sales campaign information, the calendar displays at-a-glance information on factors that affect customer purchasing patterns, including regional events and festivals. Sales for a certain period can be estimated by calling up past sales data from that selected period.

Source: Seven-Eleven Japan Co., Ltd., Annual Report 1999, pp. 9–10.

Exhibit 4: Seven-Eleven Japan's fifth-generation total information system network

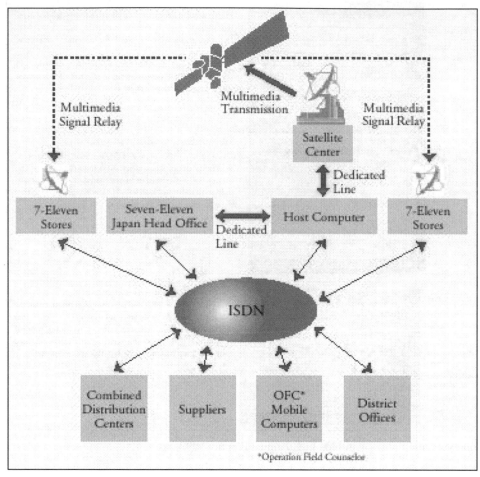

Source: Seven-Eleven Japan Co., Ltd., Annual Report 1998, p. 9.

Exhibit 5:   Business of 7dream.com partners

Company	Business
Seven-Eleven Japan Co., Ltd.	• Operator of the largest chain of convenience store in Japan.
NEC Corporation	• Recognised as a worldwide leader in high technology, NEC was one of the few companies capable of offering a full spectrum of products and systems in semiconductors, electron devices, communications, computer peripherals, imaging and computers.
Nomura Research Institute, Ltd.	• A leading Japanese research and consulting institute specialising in IT-related services.
Sony Corporation	• A leading multinational company specialising in electronics-related items.
Sony Marketing (Japan) Inc.	• The marketing arm of Sony Corp.
Mitsui & Co., Ltd.	• It was Japan's largest general trading company and had two principal roles: to facilitate its clients' international trade-related activities and, making use of its substantial information, human, financial and other resources, to create new trade flows, new enterprises and new industries around the world.
Japan Travel Bureau	• Founded in 1912, JTB was Japan's largest travel company.
Kinotrope Inc.	• Kinotrope was reputed as one of the best independent Website content providers in Japan.

Exhibit 6: Contents and services of 7dream.com

Content area	Service
Travel (about 5,500 items)	• A one-stop service combining an on-line, updated reservation and discount plan, original package tours, event and leisure contents, and hotel, airplane, train and ship tickets.
Music (about 90,000 items)	• Sales of CDs and supply of music-related information.
Photographs	• Sales of celebrity, or special character, photographs.
Merchandise, gifts, mobile phones, etc. (about 1,800 items)	• Sales of lifestyle-enhancing items.
Ticket sales	• Sales of tickets to major events, and regionally oriented services.
Books	• Sales of books via a tie-up with e-Shopping! Books Corp.
Car-related services (about 200 items)	• Acting as agent for requests for automobile inspection, repairs and maintenance, driving school and rent-a-car services.
Information services	• Information on core services, like entertainment and photograph, and referral services for people wishing to take special qualification examinations.

Source: Seven-Eleven Japan Co., Ltd. (2000), "Seven-Eleven Japan Establishes Joint Venture to Undertake Full-scale Development of the Electronic Commerce Market", 6 January.

MODULE

3

Building and Managing e-Relationships

Greater than the tread of mighty armies is an idea whose time has come.

                 –Victor Hugo

Today's information-laden, demand-driven companies function through a loose constellation of relationships built on trust. Trust has taken a more important role in e-commerce than in traditional commerce because of the anonymity of the Internet, on the one hand, and the increasing need for information sharing involved in business transactions, on the other hand. Task-focused project teams within the firm are increasingly becoming autonomous, functioning based on mutual interdependence and contact with outsiders. Because of increasing environmental complexity and uncertainty, companies are more and more relying on each other for information. As such, trust has become a cornerstone of the new organisational form.

So far, e-commerce's full potential has not been exploited because on-line businesses have not been totally able to instil the widespread trust and reliability required to encourage user confidence in the systems and infrastructure underlying e-commerce interactions. As a result, companies operating in the marketspace are constantly under pressure to find ways not only to instil trust to facilitate the acquiring of new customers but also to design and sustain e-relationship with their existing customers and business partners. Instilling customer loyalty has become a business mantra that few companies can afford to ignore.

Building and managing relationships and cultivating trust in the marketspace, however, are difficult tasks. The compression of time and space has indeed created a hyper competitive environment in the marketspace where customers have plenty of options to choose from. For example, even after building initial trust, a small glitch in service quality or any other problem ending in customer dissatisfaction could lead to the loss of customers to the competition.

This module examines the emerging issues associated with building and managing relationships in the marketspace. Chapter 6 covers the important topic of trust. It highlights some of the trust-related impediments that have slowed the adoption and proliferation of e-commerce. It then provides a model of trust that can help companies to design secure systems, build confidence that private information remains private and effectively build customer relationships based on trust.

There are two cases at the end of Chapter 6. The first case – *Case Trust: Building Third-Party e-Tailing Trust* – is the story of an organisation that has developed an accreditation scheme designed to promote consumer confidence in on-line retailers. It seeks to draw out the learning experience as to what builds trust in the B2C marketspace and to apply these globally. The second case – *Cold Storage (Singapore): Establishing Trust Among On-line Consumers* – examines the factors that help a retailer to establish trust with its on-line shoppers in its virtual store. It also outlines the value of being a member of a third-party trust accreditation scheme.

Chapter 7 examines the issues related to Internet marketing and how these differ from traditional marketing concepts. The new tools presented by the Internet enable companies to establish a closer relationship with customers, thus leading to customer loyalty through enhanced mutual trust. At the end of the chapter is a case study – *iTV: Marketing Interactive Services* – that considers the marketing strategy for new interactive multimedia services.

CHAPTER

■-■-■

6

Trust in the Marketspace

OBJECTIVES

- To learn about the importance of trust in the marketspace.
- To examine the factors influencing business trust.
- To differentiate between various types of business trust.
- To study an e-commerce trust model.
- To understand how to alleviate consumer perceived risks of making business transactions in the marketspace.
- To learn how to build and sustain trust in the marketspace.

Trust is stronger than fear. Partners that trust each other generate greater profits, serve customers better and are more adaptable.[1]

The creation and maintenance of trust-based relationships is heralded by many people as a new and necessary strategy for combining cooperation and competition in the networked economy. In reality, trust-based relationships have always been the most

---

[1] Kumar, N. (1996), p. 92.

valuable kind of working business relationships — always have been and always will be. Trust in business development is not a new concept, but rather one with renewed importance, which requires more explicit knowledge and more attention in the virtual market.

What is trust all about anyway? Trust is the very foundation of commerce. It is one of the most salient factors in business commerce, transaction exchanges or trade relationships. e-Commerce does not change trust's role in enabling business development and creating valuable transactional relationships. In fact, establishing trust in the networked economy becomes more difficult, yet more critical than ever. Since e-commerce operates in a more complex environment than traditional business, a higher degree of trust is needed between different stakeholders because of higher interdependency requirements.

The growth of e-commerce is strategically influenced by three main factors: *trust*, *privacy* and *security*. The critical questions to be resolved before e-commerce can reach its potential include, for example, how trust and integrity are built in an on-line space? How trust mechanisms change in a networked economy? What factors affect trust in the virtual market? The unanimous opinion is, while embedding technology facilitates establishing trust in e-commerce to a certain extent, it cannot be built by technology alone. The problem arises because human behaviour and social psychology play critical roles in transactional exchanges and business development; in the end, the degree of real trust between two parties is directly related to how well people know each other.

So far, a major impediment to e-commerce growth in a B2C situation arises from consumers' fear of divulging their personal data to its ultimate commercialisation. On the other hand, e-commerce's full potential has not been exploited because on-line businesses have been unable to instil widespread trust and reliability required to encourage user confidence in the systems and infrastructure underlying e-commerce interactions. Research has shown that overall, trust in e-commerce can increase if users can be convinced of three major factors as follows:[2]

1. Creating the perception that a system is trustworthy and can be used with confidence.
2. Ensuring reliability of systems and processes to manage tasks they are designed to fulfil.
3. Creating trust to provide increased value and return to participants.

---

[2] Keen, Ballance, Chan, & Schrump (2000).

In another words, if firms can manage to design secure systems, build confidence that private information remains private and effectively build customer relationships based on this trust, e-commerce has the potential to transform existing economic foundations.

In this chapter, we will explore trust's role in the traditional business development, factors which influence business trust and introduce the theory of reasoned action model to later build onto a trust and customer relationship model which we discuss in detail. Concepts of third-party trust, privacy and security are also discussed within the context of establishing trust in e-commerce.

DEVELOPMENT OF BUSINESS TRUST

Defining Business Trust

Trust in business relationships is defined as a 'willingness to rely on an exchange partner in whom one has confidence'.[3] A classic view of trust is a generalised expectancy held by an individual that the word of another can be relied on. Both definitions highlight the importance of confidence. Literature on trust suggests that confidence on the part of the trusting party results from the firm belief that the trustworthy party is 'reliable' and has 'high integrity'. Such qualities are associated with consistency, competency, honesty, fairness, responsibility, helpfulness and benevolence.

Trust has also been studied widely in social exchange literature.[4] For example, in strategic alliances, 'the biggest stumbling block to the success of alliances is the lack of trust'. In retailing, 'trust is the basis for loyalty'. In buyer-seller bargaining situations, trust is thought to be central to the process of achieving cooperative problem-solving and constructive dialogue. Therefore, trust is the key to all relational exchanges. These existing notions of trust remain fundamental to the notions of trust on the Internet because the concept of trust remains the same; only the degree and nature of trust changes according to the environment.

Factors Influencing Business Trust

In determining how to build trust, the determination of the factors that influence trust indicates how to develop business trust. Trust literature research produces an exhaus-

---

[3] J.B. Rotter in Morgan & Hunt (1994), p. 4.

[4] Fox (1974); Scanzoni (1979).

tive list of trust antecedents. However, we have selected a list of factors that are commonly attributed to developing trust in transactional relationships in a business setting [see **Table 1**].

Table 1:   Factors affecting trust

Factors	Trust Effects
Reputation	Positive
Willingness to customise	Positive
Expertise	Positive
Frequency of business contact	Positive
Anticipated future interactions	Positive
Intention for future interaction	Positive
Frequent business contact	Positive
Size	Positive
Publicity	Positive
Confidential information sharing	Negative
Length of relationship	Negative
Perceived power	Negative

Types of Business Trust

Trust development relies on the formation of a trustor's expectations about the motives and behaviour of a trustee. Trust literature covers several distinct types and stages of trust that can develop in business relationships.[5]

❑ A calculative trust process involves individuals and organisation assessing costs and/or rewards of another party cheating or staying in the relationship. For example, Rao and Bergen (1992) found that buying firms pay premium prices to suppliers to ensure high levels of quality. Essentially, buyers raise the costs of cheating because suppliers caught acting 'untrustworthy' lose a stream of premium rents from future purchases. This is also known as deterrence-based trust; it emerges from the threat.

---

[5] Doney & Cannon (1997).

- ❏ The prediction process of developing trust relies on one party's ability to fore-cast another party's behaviour. Repeated interaction enables the party to inter-pret prior outcomes better, providing a basis for assessing predictability. For example, through repeatedly making promises and delivering on them, a sales person develops the confidence of a buyer. Extending this line of reasoning, Lewicki and Bunker (1995) suggest that predictability, as a source of trust, re-quires repeated interaction and a long-term relationship.
- ❏ The capability process involves determining another party's ability to meet its obligations, thereby focusing primarily on the credibility component of trust. Knowledge-based trust is based on the knowledge grounded in that of a trad-ing partner, which allows the trustor to understand and predict the behaviour of a trustee or vice versa.
- ❏ Identification-based trust. This trust is based on empathy and common values with the other trading partner's desire and intentions, to the point that one trading partner is able to act as an agent for the other.
- ❏ Finally, trust can develop through a transference process. Strub and Priest (1976) describe the 'extension pattern' of gaining trust as using a "third party's defini tion of another as a basis for defining that other as trustworthy". This suggests that trust can be transferred from one trusted 'proof source' to another person.

DIFFERENTIATING TRUST IN E-COMMERCE

Traditional commerce foundations have been built on the simple principle of trust. Over time, the marketplace has developed many mechanisms, conventions and proc-esses designed to engender and maintain a necessary degree of trust among the trading partners and other marketplace participants.[6] As the marketplace grew in terms of the number of participants, intermediaries, the size nature of transactions and other ele-ments, more *trust enhancers* were needed to maintain user confidence and willingness to participate. These trust enhancers have enabled the development of a large, complex, yet relatively efficient system of commerce, both domestically and internationally. However, establishing trust and building long-term relationships have become more important in e-commerce because of four main reasons: complexity, interdependence, the trust economy and the Internet:[7]

---

[6] Steinauer, Wakid, & Rasberry (1997).

[7] Keen, Ballance, Chan, & Schrump (2000), p. 9.

1. *Complexity*. e-Commerce's environmental complexity makes it important for stakeholders to develop trust among each other because individuals and businesses cannot do everything.

2. *Interdependence*. Successful e-commerce requires tight integration and close relationships with partners and alliances. This creates business relationships that are mutually dependent on each other for growth; trust being the critical element underlying business relationships. The added pressure on virtual firms is user attention which is harder to achieve and retain, and so is the opportunity to build a relationship with them. The slightest transgression of trust can easily switch users to a competitor, and, even worse, could inspire unflattering comments in newsgroups and forums and on mailing lists.

3. *The trust economy*. The concept of trust has always existed in businesses but its form has revolutionised from product trust and trust in service to trust in relationships in the networked economy. For example, features such as physical outlets, size, brand and marketing power provide a measure of trust. In the 1970s, trust was the equivalent of reliable products, product warranties and product guarantees; in the 1980s, trust transpired through service quality and commitment. In an e-commerce environment though, on-line firms need users to put a greater degree of trust in the organisation behind Websites – an organisation that may not exist in the physical world. Users may have no way of learning the firm beyond what appears on the screen.

4. *The Internet*. The Internet, while a valuable tool, increases complexity, coordination and relationship concerns by removing many of the established trust mechanisms, such as physical storefronts, thereby increasing risks to all parties. These concerns need to be addressed by implementing new trust mechanisms and business principles. Trust is harder to build on the Internet simply because the competition is much greater. The fact that the medium is available worldwide, 24-hours-a-day, 7-days-a-week, means there are infinite choices available to meet virtually any conceivable need. The Internet is an anonymous, impersonal medium lacking visual, non-verbal cues we take for granted as a part of off-line communication.

Although the Internet does not change the way firms earn credibility, gain respect or gain trust, building trust is different in e-commerce. e-Commerce is conducted in a different business context. Consider for example the Internet medium's intangibility, the Internet's globalisation affect, increased competitive pressure arising from the ease of establishing an e-commerce business and virtual distribution of certain goods and so on. The structural impact of this transformation from a physical marketplace to a virtual environment requires new trust mechanisms as existing ones become inapplicable in some cases. Emerging trust enhancers include technical methods for protecting the confidentiality and integrity of data, third-party trust (institutional trust), third-party referrals and other trust mechanisms.

This new infrastructure also creates new risks, which are not fully understood by many users. The perception of risk is an aspect of consumer behaviour that is perceived to have two major consequences: uncertainty about outcome and uncertainty about consequences. In the context of the Internet, risk may be defined as a subjective expectation of loss or negative consequences in buying behaviour. Because the Internet is impersonal and distant, the best way to earn trust is to lessen the perceived risks involved in giving trust. It would require far more trust for a customer to purchase a product from an unprofessional, impersonal, low security site than to purchase from an appealing, high security site. Contrary to conventional wisdom, the enabling conditions for giving up information are not product discounts, access to a site or value-added services. Instead, users need to be assured on security, privacy, integrity and systems issues.

The negative consequences associated with on-line buying pertain to the consumer's inability to control the actions of a Web vendor. These perceptions directly affect the consumer's perception of the security of on-line shopping. Control over the secondary use of information reflects consumers' perceived ability to control the use of their personal information for other purposes subsequent to the transaction during which information is collected. On the Web, this lack of trust is manifested by consumers' concern that Web providers will sell their personal information to third parties without their knowledge or permission.[8]

However, these concerns are not limited to on-line consumers. Similar issues also affect many B2B transactional exchanges and relationships. However, the economic incentives of conducting business on the Internet continue to encourage businesses and consumers to find methods to develop system trust. System trust means the extent to which one believes that proper impersonal structures are in place to enable one to anticipate a successful future endeavour. Structural assurances include such safeguards as regulations, guarantees or contracts. These safeguards act as a 'safety net'. Systems can also be designed to reduce uncertainty, to enable security in taking risks with other people. To some extent, security and payment technology has alleviated many of these concerns and continuing efforts are made to embed 'safety' within systems.[9]

---

[8]   Hoffman, Novak, & Peralta (1999).

[9]   Salam, Rao, & Pegels (1997).

In addition, economic incentives play a key role in alleviating perceived risks and highlighting potential gains for all stakeholders in a networked economy. From a firm's perspective, its ability to place itself in the global marketplace and access global markets, achieve greater business opportunities, gain exposure and potential for alliances for low initial investments and low or no inventory costs and low order processing costs, are all economic incentives. The consumers' perceived economic gain might also override the perceived financial loss as they have low costs and convenient access to prices, products and ease of delivery. Such economic incentives increase the potential for gain and, given a certain level of risk, reduce the perceived level of risk.[10]

Despite these economic gains, however, the overriding factor of the Internet threatening security, privacy and information control in new and extreme ways has pushed many users to opt out of various forms of commercial participation in the Internet, including providing personal information to Websites for marketing purposes. The secondary use of information is a source of conflict between commercial Web providers and consumers. Lack of trust arises because consumers feel they *lack control* over personal information during Web navigation processes. A majority of Web users are uninterested in selling their personal data to Websites for financial incentives or access to certain privileges. In other words, consumers do not view their personal data in the context of an economic exchange of information, as many Web providers believe. Therefore, customers remain threatened because of the following risks they perceive:[11]

1. On-line shopping potentially allows commercial Web providers to collect much more detailed consumer behaviour information than they can from most physical shopping trips.
2. Data mining. Data mining is the analysis of data for relationships that have not previously been discovered. For example, the classification or recognition of patterns and a resulting new organisation of data including developing comprehensive customer profiles of customers who make purchases. It also includes clustering, or finding and visualising groups of facts not previously known.[12]
3. Data-warehousing opportunities are being exploited as never before due to the capabilities of the Internet, high-speed networks and terabyte data storage. The data warehouse concept is gaining acceptance due to the possibility of fruitful

---

[10] Salam, Rao, & Pegels (1997).

[11] Hoffman, Novak, & Peralta (1999).

[12] URL: http://www.whatis.com

data mining. A data warehouse refers to a central repository for all or significant parts of data that an enterprise's various business systems can collect. Data from various consumer on-line transaction processing (OLTP) applications and other sources can be selectively extracted and organised; data warehousing emphasises the capture of data from diverse sources for useful analysis and access.[13]

4. Commercial Web providers can collect not only the same information available in most physical transactions – identity, credit history, employment status, legal status – but also such additional information as electronic address, specific history of goods and services searched for and requested, other Internet sites visited, and contents of the consumer's data storage device.

5. Lack of boundaries. Users cannot know how their personal information will be used, shared or disseminated throughout the Internet. In contrast, consumer information in the physical world is stored in a much wider variety of databases and data formats and is much more difficult to combine, analyse and access.

These issues continue to be debated and addressed through increasing macro-regulation and self-regulation methods. However, clear concise policies have yet to emerge on how these issues will be resolved.

APPLICATION OF TRUST IN E-COMMERCE

In the previous section, we discussed how e-commerce threatens existing trust mechanisms and how economic incentives remain unexploited due to a lack of trust developed in managing security, privacy and information control issues. It is evident that managing trust effectively can create real economic value for a firm. It involves effectively managing trust to build long-term mutually beneficial relationships. Mutually trustworthy relationships are formed if parties to a transaction trust each other and trust the infrastructure that makes their transaction possible.

Theory of Reasoned Action

The 'theory of reasoned action' (TRA) is a model developed to predict human behaviours.[14] The theory provides constructs that link individual beliefs, attitudes, intentions and behaviour [refer to **Figure 1**].[15] This model has been widely used in marketing to

---

[13] URL: http://www.whatis.com

[14] Fishbein & Ajzen (1975).

[15] Fishbein, Middlestadt, & Hitchcock (1994).

Figure 1: Classical theory of reasoned action model

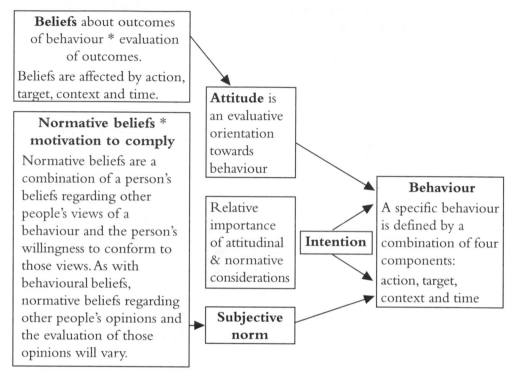

discuss values, beliefs and intentions in consumer behaviour, brand cognisance and so on. We introduce the TRA model and use it as an infrastructure to build an e-commerce trust model later.

The TRA model consists of several constructs following a sequential pattern: beliefs lead to attitudes that lead to intentions and result in a certain behaviour. In the context of building trust, the TRA theory appropriately addresses behavioural *intention* as being a critical facet of trust's conceptualisation because 'if one believes that a partner is trustworthy without being willing to rely on that partner, trust is limited'.[16] Therefore, the willingness to act is implicit in the conceptualisation of trust; one could not label a trading partner as 'trustworthy' if one were not willing to take actions that otherwise would entail risk. More simply, genuine confidence that a partner can rely

---

[16] Moorman, Deshpande, & Zaltman (1993), p. 315.

on another will indeed imply the behavioural intention to rely. Just as behavioural intention is best viewed as an outcome of attitude and not as part of its definition,[17] 'willingness to rely' should be viewed as an outcome (or, alternatively, a potential indicator) of trust and not as a part of how one defines it.

Essentially, the behavioural and normative beliefs – referred to as cognitive structures[18] – influence individual attitudes and subjective norms, respectively. In turn, attitudes and norms shape a person's *intention* to perform behaviour. Finally, *a person's intention remains the best indicator that the desired behaviour will occur.* Overall, the TRA model supports a linear process in which changes in an individual's behavioural and normative beliefs will ultimately affect the individual's actual behaviour. The attitude and norm variables, and their underlying cognitive structures, often exert different degrees of influence over a person's intention. The TRA provides a framework for linking each of the variables together.

In the next section, we will incorporate TRA theory variables and their definitions to evaluate trust's role in e-commerce. Using this human behaviour model, we develop a conceptual framework of how this behaviour leads to developing trust in an e-commerce environment. We begin with describing the e-commerce business environment and identifying what trust mechanisms are beginning to emerge in e-commerce.

e-Commerce Trust Model

To find solutions to address trust issues in e-commerce, we incorporate the TRA theory introduced earlier in the chapter and adopt it into a trust building model in e-commerce [refer to **Figure 2**]. Elaborating on the classical TRA, we incorporate trust building stages and thresholds into the existing TRA theory. We establish three stages of trust: building trust, maintaining trust and confirming trust. The diagram shows that developing trust is a dynamic process which increases over time if the dynamics follow the pattern of transforming beliefs to attitudes, to intentions and trust-based actions which ultimately result in loyalty. The notions of building trust therefore can only deepen over time and through constant reinforcement, reaching a point of loyalty. There are three threshold points, the trial threshold, purchase threshold and habit

---

[17] Fishbein & Ajzen (1975).

[18] Cognitive dissonance theory refers to the concept that people seek consistency in their lives and are sensitive to contradictions and inconsistencies. Dissonance (discomfort, doubt) fosters attitude change (URL: http://www.orst.edu/instruct/comm321/gwalker/influence.htm).

Figure 2:   Trust building TRA model

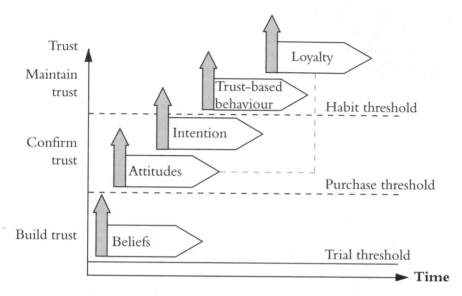

threshold, which are sequential as these levels are reached through a constant increase of trust.

In addition, TRA constructs in the classic model are redefined here to reflect the trust dimension.

❑ Trusting beliefs refer to the extent to which one believes (and feels confident in believing) that the other person is *trustworthy* in the situation. Distinguishing trustworthiness from trust is essential because it relates to the willingness and ability to trust.[19]

❑ Trusting attitude refers to an evaluative orientation towards something. Attitudes do not directly lead to behaviour but attitudes are measured to explain actions.

❑ Trusting intention is the extent to which one party is willing to depend on the other party in a given situation with a feeling of relative security, even though negative consequences are possible. Trusting intention is a situation-specific construct: one is willing to depend on the other party in a specific situation. To understand a behaviour, it is important to understand intentions.

---

[19] Driver, Russell, Cafferty, & Allen (1968); McLain & Hackman (1995).

❑ Trusting-based behaviour. Behaviour is determined by intentions and intentions are explained in terms of attitudes towards the behaviour and subjective norms.
❑ Loyalty.

Building Trust in e-Commerce

The concept of trust affects a number of factors essential to on-line relational exchanges. The difference is that communicating factors that produce a sense of trustworthiness in the e-commerce environment need to be identified in their entirety. Their interactions need to be understood, and their relative importance determined. Understanding the roles of these different factors would allow on-line retailers to ease consumers' concerns and could hasten the maturation of Web retailing. Since time is the key to deepening trust, Internet trust is still relatively shallow. Consequently, beliefs that suggest trustworthiness are main determinants of whether someone will take a chance.

The trusting process begins when an individual perceives indications (or beliefs) that suggest a firm may be trustworthy. According to the Cheskin Research, there are six such forms, which indicate that consumers may be willing to do a transaction with a business.[20] Trust is a requirement, just like quality, for customers to qualify a company to conduct business with. In e-commerce, there are several forms that communicate trust and will influence 'beliefs' which are still in an untrust phase and where users are at a threshold level:

❑ *Seals of approval*. Symbols such as VeriSign and Visa, are designed to ensure the visitor that security has been established. Companies that provide these seals of approval are referred to as 'security brands'.
❑ *Brand*. A corporation's promise to deliver specific attributes and its credibility based on reputation, word-of-mouth or a visitor's previous experience.
❑ *Navigation*. The ease of finding what the visitor seeks on-line.
❑ *Presentation*. Design attributes that connote quality and professionalism.

In the trust building stage, calculus-based trust is the driving motivator for businesses. Where a relationship is economically rooted in the fear of punishment, trust is

---

[20] *Cheskin Research & Studio Archetype/Sapient* (1999).

maintained because of the cost to repair a damaged reputation or relationship. Parties in this relationship understand the binding economics.

Take the example of a user establishing certain beliefs about amazon.com and visiting the Website based on certain dispositions. Trust is affected at the point of navigation entry and built as users go through a process of *browsing, searching and comparing* to confirm or negate their existing beliefs of amazon.com. Where the issue of information control is concerned, there is an inherent conflict of interest, as Websites want as much information as possible to create user profiles but users want to minimise personal information disclosure. Therefore, companies who want to build and maintain trust, for example, will endeavour to provide clear privacy and information use guidelines to build trust with users and perhaps engage users to share this information in the future. Companies that violate consumer trust by using personal information for undisclosed use, lose customers. Thus, at this stage, binding economics is the dominant trust characteristic because it is in the companies' interest and welfare to provide a trustworthy environment. To an extent, the Internet medium instigates a trust by design because unless a company provides certain trust mechanisms, users are unlikely to conduct e-commerce with such businesses and it creates negative results for companies.

If on-line businesses do not deliver on promises, for example, customers are unlikely to go beyond the trial threshold phase. Typically, corporate marketplace purchasers who buy from amazon or CDNow expect at least the same simplicity and quick service on-line when they make purchases in the marketplace. When such expectations are not met, the gap between expectation levels and satisfaction levels widens and creates cognitive dissonance. Users need higher value to use the virtual market than the traditional methods of conducting business because the perceived risks are higher and relatively unknown. Therefore, users need to be given system trust or on-line businesses need to borrow third-party trust to establish the initial trust to further build the relationship.[21]

Confirm Trust

Knowledge-based trust occurs consequent to a history of interactions after a sufficient information base is built so that behaviour can be predicted. This type of relationship is grown and maintained with constant and diverse attention; it is built on past expe-

---

[21] Kaydo (1999).

riences that allow partners to anticipate reliability of the other. The familiarity foundation theory is that trust will be tested repetitively and trust will be confirmed once
established beliefs are reinforced through attitude affirmation. According to Figure 2's
construct, attitudes are reinforced once an on-line experience is *assessed*, *experienced*
and *validated*. Trust building cues are based on both qualitative research and research on
human cognition of how trust develops. It seems that the most important thing for
building trust is keeping promises. However, companies need to build trust prior to a
trust-based action [refer to **Appendix 1** on how to foster trust].

For attitudes to transform into intentions, we highlight as follows some issues
that can help maintain trust, where trust must be simultaneously earned before e-
commerce users will feel comfortable:[22]

- ❑ A clearly stated return policy. Trust in sites including legal rights and user
  control over information and some processes.
- ❑ Stated and authenticated policies of security and encryption.
- ❑ The ability to back out of a transaction.
- ❑ Technology. Appropriate technology to fulfil all functions specified by a
  company and fulfils user expectations.
- ❑ Fulfilment. A system that clearly indicates how orders will be processed and
  provides information and contacts on how to seek recourse if there are any
  problems.

The trust confirming process can also be enhanced by allowing the balance of
power to shift towards a more cooperative interaction between an on-line business and
its interfacers. For example, recognising the consumer's rights to data ownership on
the Internet is an important step. For B2C business models, a more consumer-oriented
information privacy model is likely to encourage commercially valuable relationship
exchanges with important benefits for consumers and companies doing business on
the Internet. A cooperative model promotes the rapid development of e-commerce;
maintaining trust is marked by a collaborative relationship.

As referred to in Figure 2, confirming trust occurs at the purchase threshold level.
At this stage, we hypothesise that issues of security and privacy are the key in the trust
process and can be the shifting factor between a movement from attitude to forming
an intention to act. Privacy, security and return policies act as trust mechanisms to help

---

[22] Urban (1998).

users consider, assess and authenticate a business. As we have mentioned before, on-line commerce potential cannot be exploited unless three main issues are addressed: security, privacy and control over information. The issue of information *control*, therefore, becomes central to privacy and security issues. Typically, when trust is confirmed, it is simply that there is enough knowledge about the other party to make its behaviour predictable. Trust establishment in this stage does not result in a relationship. It only enables a relationship and moves it towards creating a trust-based action.

Maintain Trust

Identification-based trust evolves when deep understanding allows one party to identify with the other's values and goals. At this level, both parties internalise the needs and wants of the other sufficiently to act in each other's best interest. According to Figure 2, at this level of trust, certain beliefs have reinforced attitudes and propelled users into enabling a trust-based action. This trust-based action could be in the form of creating a partnership, a marketing exchange, a transaction or strategic alliance and so on.

By the time stage three emerges, trust should become tractable. Parties respect and trust each other enough to examine the situation and develop an innovative response, rather than stonewall a demand for standard knee-jerk procedures. Basically, it entails pursuing a trust-based action. As we have mentioned before, unless a person has created the intention to act, a trust-based action is unlikely to occur. Ultimately, this trust-based action should result in loyalty; and this is a major objective which firms work towards establishing in e-commerce transactions and relationships. We maintain that loyalty will result from constant reinforcement of the trust-maintaining factors discussed above. Maintaining trust involves an element of customer relationship management; it entails developing a long-term strategy to retain a trust relationship with a customer.

TRUST MECHANISMS IN E-COMMERCE

Consumers see the Web as one of chaos, offering both possibilities and threats. Only after they believe they have secured control over their own personal data within the system are they willing to begin to try out e-commerce.[23] In establishing our trust

---

[23] *Cheskin Research & Studio Archetype/Sapient* (1999).

model, we believe that alleviating consumer perceived risks in an e-commerce environment include managing the following:

- ❏ Third-party trust.
- ❏ Security issues.
- ❏ Privacy policies.
- ❏ Integrity.

Third-party Trust

In e-commerce several intermediaries exist. From the perspective of consumers and businesses, the guarantor's role as an intermediary is an important one because the trustor places trust in the performance capability and integrity of the intermediary.[24] Such institutional trust is beneficial for both consumers and businesses alike as guarantors (intermediaries) can authenticate and validate companies. Financial institutions, such as banks and credit card companies, largely play the role of guarantors in economic exchanges.[25] As trust seems to reside with banks, credit card companies and other financial institutions, and people are comfortable giving these institutions sensitive personal information, their validation can become an asset for on-line firms seeking to establish trust with customers.[26] Financial institutions can also oversee issues concerning security and payments.[27] Therefore, firms seeking to build relationships with customers and move them to the next level on the trust degree sometimes borrow trust from other organisations. Third-party trust is extremely useful for businesses in the trust building stage.

US Postal Service Electronic Postmark: A Third-party Verification

In April 2000, the US Postal Service (www.USPS.gov) announced its new USPS Electronic Postmark (EPM), a service that offers a means of dating and securing

---

[24] Coleman (1990).

[25] Salam, Rao, & Pegels (1998).

[26] Salnoske (1998).

[27] Also, using financial institutions in e-commerce eliminates the need for additional protection from outside entities, such as the regional and national governments which may try to regulate the e-commerce market, hence stifling growth.

e-mail. The service provides on-line communicators "a little peace of mind and add a level of trust and security that Americans have come to expect from sending a regular hard-copy letter," says John Nolan, Deputy US Postmaster General. EPM is a third-party verification of electronic transmission of financial and confidential data, guaranteeing that a document is not tampered during transmission and that a file existed at a specific time and date. The added security includes investigation of illegal interception or tampering with respect to EPM communications, and detection of alterations to postmarked documents. However, EPM does not encrypt documents or identify the sender of recipient of the messages. EPM is not a new e-mail service; it is a feature available through any e-mail service that provides a Postal Service data stamp. The EPM will be available to e-mail providers and will be offered directly to customers. Meantime, PostX is the only company authorised to offer EPM. "EPM combines the integrity and protection of the Postal Service with the speed and convenience of the Internet," says PostX Corporation's founder and CEO, R.C. Venkatraman.

Sources: Enos (2000); *Milwaukee Journal Sentinel* (2000).

Security

To a certain extent, trust can be built through technology as many perceived threats on the Internet, such as security and design, can be embedded within systems. e-Commerce implementation poses numerous technological challenges. However, security is one of the most addressed areas of implementing trust mechanisms. If an appropriate infrastructure is implemented through which merchants' and customers' issues are addressed, e-commerce will be able to grow as concerns with the safety of conducting on-line transactions are reduced. As businesses move towards adapting on-line trading, issues of on-line transaction security become more important.

Overcoming security challenges for e-commerce involves addressing two main issues: to reassure on-line shoppers and merchants that it is safe to conduct on-line transactions and to ensure that appropriate technology is embedded within systems to protect customers, merchants and other players involved. Technology and security protocols, such as Secure Electronic Transaction (SET) and Secure Sockets Layer (SSL), have succeeded in their aim to provide safer and easier use of payment cards on the Internet. In addition to facilitating card payments over the Internet for physical goods, technology companies are developing methods to handle commercial transactions involving electronic merchandise. As the Internet's impact on our lives increases, more goods that require physical mobility will be delivered directly to offices or homes in digital form via the Internet. To take advantage of these new dimensions of service and convenience, there are still no established standards to ensure that sellers of digital merchandise are properly compensated.

Encryption and digital signature technologies can help alleviate those concerns. A robust form of encryption – a key development in securing payments and money transfer mechanisms over the Internet – provides confidentiality by ensuring that information contained in data messages is protected from unauthorised disclosure. Digital signatures can prove that the parties exchanging messages are who they say they are and that they authorised the transaction, and serve as a means of ensuring that an electronic record or document cannot be changed without detection. Digital signatures can also be used to provide evidence of the time at which a message was sent or to verify receipt.

The usefulness and benefits of digital signatures and public/private key encryption systems, however, hinge primarily on the confidence placed in a trusted third party, often called a certificate authority, which is able to confirm the identity of a digital signatory or public/private key user to the satisfaction of other users. Certificate authorities play a central role in the overall regulatory scheme.[28]

VeriSign, Inc.: Providing Security Solutions for e-Commerce Companies

VeriSign, Inc. (www.verisign.com) is a provider of Internet-based trust services – including authentication, validation and payment – that allows trusted and secured electronic commerce and communications over the Internet, intranets and extranets of Websites, enterprises, e-commerce providers and individuals. With its secure on-line infrastructure, VeriSign was able to issue 340,000 Website digital certificates (featuring 128-bit encryption) since the service was launched in July 1995. These include on-line businesses, large enterprises, government agencies and other organisations (over 60 percent of which is responsible for protecting commerce and communications in B2B environments). VeriSign also issued 3.9 million digital certificates to individuals, enhancing trust and security on a far-reaching level. All of the Fortune 500 companies with a Web presence apply

---

[28] Woolford (1999).

VeriSign's Website digital certificate services. RSA Data Security says VeriSign's digital certificates "would take a trillion years to break using today's most sophisticated hacking techniques."

The VeriSign Trust Network has over 28 affiliates globally including Arabtrust (Middle East), Bigon (Poland), British Telecommunications (UK), CIBC, and VPN Tech (Canada), CertiSur (Argentina), Certplus (France), Comsign (Israel), Cybersign (Malaysia), eSign (Australia), HiTrust (Taiwan), IT Trust (Egypt), KPN Telecom, and Roccade (Netherlands), South African Certification Agency (South Africa) and Telefonica (Spain). Using VeriSign's technology, infrastructure and business practices, these affiliate organisations provide interoperable trust services under licensed co-branding relationships for a specific group region or vertical market. VeriSign is based in Mountain View, California.

Sources: Beale (1999); VeriSign; Yahoo!

Privacy

On-line relational exchanges, therefore, are also affected by privacy policy. For a consumer, a firm's privacy policy goes hand-in-hand with what economic value a firm provides to customers in exchange for information; firms that succeed in providing that value will be successful. Information privacy refers to claims of individuals that data about themselves should generally not be available to other individuals and organisations and that where data is possessed by another party, the individual must be able to exercise a substantial degree of control over that data and its use.

An important implication in privacy definition is that privacy has to be balanced against many other, often competing interests of individuals themselves, of other individuals, of groups and of society as a whole. The balancing process is political in nature, involving the exercise of power deriving from authority, markets or any other available source.

Against technology-driven privacy invasion, natural defences have proven inadequate: data is increasingly collected and personalised; storage technology ensures that it remains available; database technologies make it discoverable; and telecommunications enables its rapid reticulation. Organisations have been only partially restrained by professional and industry association codes.[29]

---

[29] Clarke (1999).

Violations of On-line Privacy

IKEA: Breaks privacy breach

Dan Huddle, chief technology officer for Xanga.com, a New York-based Net publisher, tried to order a catalogue on IKEA's (a Swedish furniture company) on-line catalogue site at www.ikea.com on a Monday morning (04/07/00). During the process of personal data submission Dan got an error message that provided him the database file. Dan entered the database file in the URL and was given access to the entire database containing records of tens and thousands of customers who ordered catalogues including names, addresses, telephone numbers and e-mail addresses. Dan expressed, "This is especially concerning to me since I was about to put my own contact info in there. What a spammer's dream!" CNET News.com notified IKEA of the problem. According to Rich D'Amico, IKEA North America's new business development manager, a very high security program was in place for the catalogue database, but speculated that on Sunday night (03/07/00) somebody barraged the site with numerous catalogue requests thus creating the malfunction. The database was accessible until Monday evening, but was shut down on Tuesday (05/07/00) until further notice. An analyst at IDC, Chris Christiansen, said gaffes similar to this were not new. There was a lack of authentication or authorisation on the files, or inadequate firewalls.

Toys 'R' Us: Accused of providing customer data to a third party

The retail store giant is facing a class action complaint filed on 28 July 2000 in a San Francisco Federal Court for allegedly violating its own privacy policy by sharing personal data of its customers to marketers. The class action states Toysrus 'has implemented a sophisticated and covert scheme to wrongfully intercept, transmit, record and compile' personal data. Toysrus.com has another accuser, a Columbus, Ohio-based developer of on-line security and privacy tools, Interhack. Interhack accuses the on-line toys retailer, together with Lucy.com and Fusion.com, of providing customer profiles to Coremetrics, an on-line research firm. Although Toysrus' privacy policy informs customers that personal information may be shared with a third party, the identity of the third party is not provided and no opt-out option is given.

Barclays Bank: On-line service shut down due to security breach

Four of the bank's 1.2 million on-line customers reported a glitch in the bank's 'secure' site when they found that users could gain access to account details of other people. Informed of this confidentiality breach, Barclays immediately shut down its on-line banking service at 3:00 pm, shortly after receiving seven complaints and temporarily terminated all access to accounts. Barclays attributed the glitch to the upgraded system. At 7:00 pm, the service resumed using the old system. The bank reasoned the new system was tested extensively and the security issue had been revealed only when a large number of users logged on at the same time.

Netscape: Challenged with privacy suit

The SmartDownload feature at Netscape Communicator Web browser, along with the cookie information, is alleged to be a tool for tracking file downloads made by individual users, according to a class action lawsuit filed against AOL and Netscape. The suit proposes that Netscape is violating the Electronic Communications Privacy Act of 1986 and the Computer Fraud and Abuse Act of 1986. *Wire News* reported that Chris Specht's protest is that Netscape is aware of all download activity. The "theft of private information", according to Specht, costs either US$100 a day for each day the software has been available or US$10,000 per Netscape user.

Sources: Enos (2000); M2 Communications Ltd. (2000); Merrell & Norfolk (2000); Wolverton (2000).

According to an address by the President of McGraw-Hill, there are four privacy principles firms should implement to build trust:

1. The first principle is *notice*: Tell prospective customers what information you are collecting and what you are planning to do with it. When it comes to collecting information, uncertainty is the enemy. If you keep people in the dark about what is happening to their private information, they will imagine the worst. Building notice into your privacy policy builds confidence in customers.
2. The second principle is *choice*: Adopt a policy with a procedure by which customers can choose not to have their information shared outside your company. It is a way of saying you recognise the information they have shared with you is, in important ways, still theirs.
3. The third principle is *security*: Give the customer confidence that their information is safe from tampering, safe from theft, and safe from misappropriation and misuse.
4. The fourth and final principle is *review and correction*: Give customers a way to see what information has been collected from them, and a means to correct any errors in that data.

Integrity

Integrity is a process that ensures that the information delivered is unbroken and that, where applicable, the information is the same as agreed on by all parties; in other words, integrity implies certainty. Integrity in e-commerce solutions insures information relating to payments, agreed-on-goods and services, can only be changed in a specified and authorised manner. Integrity issues can be addressed through technology and policy.

The integrity of e-commerce data begins with a definition of the business transaction and should result in ensuring transaction consistency. If a customer makes a purchase of X dollars, then merchant, customer and bank should agree that the customer has X fewer dollars and the merchant X more dollars. The underlying fundamental is that all parties to a transaction agree on the original, final and intermediate stages of information and all transformations and modifications should correspond to a legitimate agreed-on business function.[30]

ESTABLISHING TRUST IN THE NEW ECONOMY

Ultimately, the most effective way for e-commerce to grow is by developing profitable exchange relationships earned through trust. Although e-commerce modifies some existing models of traditional business, the long-standing elements of commerce can be replicated on-line. For example, trading partners, goods and services, unit of exchange, transaction infrastructures and trust are mechanisms which have been built over the centuries and these same business principles, including the role of trust, will continue to apply in e-commerce.

As the shift to e-commerce is made, trust mechanisms must be developed such that they allow buyers, sellers and intermediaries to have confidence in the system. The discussion of trust points out the need for mechanisms such as identification and authentication, protection of integrity and confidentiality of information, to facilitate e-commerce growth.

By understanding trust-enhancers, factors which develop trust, and processes that foster trust at the outset of a relationship, e-commerce can become an alternative economic and relational exchange medium. By understanding the dynamics of trust, a

---

[30] Keen, Ballance, Chan, & Schrump (2000), p. 62.

greater understanding of how business relationships grow, change and decline can be understood and applied in the new economy.

While issues of privacy, confidentiality and information use will continue to rage on as issues of unchartered business principles come into the forefront, it will remain critical to remember that existing principles of business trust will remain constant regardless of the business context, whether it is the old economy or the new.

SUMMARY

- ❑ Trust is one of the most important foundations of commerce. However, a host of trust-related issues have adversely affected the diffusion of e-commerce.
- ❑ There are at least four major reasons why establishing trust in the marketspace is difficult:
  - increased environmental complexity forcing companies to outsource bigger parts of their business activities to outside firms;
  - increased interdependence among parties involved in a business transaction;
  - business shift from product-centricity to service-centricity to relationship building;
  - anonymity of the Internet.
- ❑ People's perceptions, biases and cultural habits further exacerbate these difficulties: many people are sceptical about Internet security, while some are not sure how the information they provide on-line will be used and by who.
- ❑ Building trust should be a long-term process through which companies must try to influence their consumers' behaviour so that they will ultimately become loyal customers.
- ❑ In order to build trust in the marketspace, companies can, among other things, rely on their brand, use third-party seals of approval and take a consumer-centric approach in responding to their customers' needs. Companies should also understand that trust is influenced by cultural norms, and thus establishing on-line trust globally requires a full understanding of such cultural specificities.

APPENDIX 1

Nine actions an organisation can take to foster a trusting relationship are:

1. Create an off-line organisation where all relationships – including those with vendors, customers, media, investors and community groups – are based on

frank, fair and honest exchange of information. It is impossible to inspire trust on-line if off-line activities and attitudes undermine it.

2. Create a user-centred Website. A site that allows users to find what they want quickly and easily is indispensable for inspiring trust. Consideration must be given to how Web content is organised, written and presented. The goal should be a site design that is learnable, easy to understand and remember, efficient and pleasant, if not attractive. Even better, the site should allow users to customise their experience.

3. Adopt appropriate Web-writing techniques, including using short blocks or chunks of information; bulleted or numbered lists; and longer articles you know your users will be willing to scroll through. Write from the user's perspective and provide clear, concise information.

4. Include clearly described links to information off your site. This material may include press coverage on your company; third-party organisations with which you have worked; and perhaps even competitor sites. Web users will go looking for this kind of information whether it is there or not; by providing it, you save them time and effort.

5. Regularly update all site information, including photos and biographies of key company personnel, product specifications and financial data. Timely, fresh and accurate data increases familiarity and breeds trust. It shows that you really understand the Internet.

6. If you offer site visitors the option of signing up for a mailing list, tell them what they will be receiving; how often they will receive it; and under what circumstances (if any) they will receive e-mail from companies with whom you share your list. Clearly explain to subscribers how they can opt out of these other mailings, as well as how to unsubscribe from the list. As far as maintaining the privacy of information you receive from Website visitors, it is advisable to post your policy. It is even better if you have independent, third-party verification of this policy. TrustE (URL: http://www.truste.org/) is one such organisation which awards a branded logo or seal to Websites that adhere to its established privacy principles and agree to comply with its oversight and consumer resolution process.

7. If you ask for credit card information, demonstrate that you adhere to the strictest standards of privacy, security and encryption. Seals of approval like that offered by VeriSign (URL: http://www.verisign.com/) offer added assurance to the visitor that controls are in place.

8. Provide a physical street address, phone and fax numbers on your Website so visitors can choose the most convenient means to contact you.

9. Provide multiple e-mail addresses on your Website to connect users directly to different departments. Respond to e-mail promptly. Set a standard and educate and train staff to meet it. Better still, post your policy on the Website for all visitors to see. Internet users expect immediate responses, and companies best equipped to deal with e-mail earn considerable gratitude.

REFERENCES

Beale, M.W. (1999), "VeriSign Puts Clamp on e-Commerce Security", *E-Commerce Times*, 30 June, URL: http://www.ecomm…m/news/articles/990630-2.shtml, 29 August 2000.

Cheskin Research and Studio Archetype/Sapient (1999), eCommerce Trust Study, January.

Clarke, R. (1999), "Internet Privacy Concerns Confirm the Case for Intervention", *Association for Computing Machinery, Communications of the ACM*, Vol. 42, Iss. 2, pp. 60–67.

Coleman, J.S. (1990), *Foundations of Social Theory*, Cambridge, MA: Harvard University Press.

Doney, P.M. & Cannon, J.P. (1997), "An Examination of the Nature of Trust in Buyer-Seller Relationships", *Journal of Marketing*, Vol. 61, Iss. 2, pp. 35–51.

Driver, M.J., Russell, G., Cafferty, T., & Allen, R. (1968), "Studies of the Social and Psychological Aspects of Verification, Inspection and International Assurance", *Technical Report*, No. 4.1, Lafayette, IN: Purdue University.

Enos, L. (2000), "U.S. Postal Service Unveils Electronic Postmark", *E-Commerce Times*, 28 April, URL: http://www.ecommercetimes.com/news/articles2000/000428-6.shtml, 20 September.

Enos, L. (2000), "Toys 'R' Us Sued for Net Privacy Violations", *E-Commerce Times*, 4 August, URL: http://www.ecomm…ws/articles2000/000804-2.shtml, 29 August.

Fishbein, M. & Ajzen, I. (1975), *Belief, Attitude, Intention and Behaviour: An Introduction to Theory and Research*, Reading, MA: Addison-Wesley.

Fishbein, M., Middlestadt, S.E., & Hitchcock, P.J. (1994), "Using Information to Change Sexually Transmitted Disease-related Behaviours", in DiClemente, R.J. & Peterson, J.L. (eds), *Preventing AIDS: Theories and Methods of Behavioral Interventions*, New York, NY: Plenum Press, pp. 61–78.

Fox, A. (1974), *Beyond Contract: Work, Power and Trust Relations*, London: Faber.

Hoffman, D.L., Novak, T.P., & Peralta, M. (1999), "Building Consumer Trust On-line", *Association for Computing Machinery, Communications of the ACM*, Vol. 42, Iss. 4, pp. 80–85.

Kaydo, C. (1999), *Sales and Marketing Management*, Vol. 151, Iss. 10, October, p. 28, URL: http://www.salesandmarket.com/, August 2000.

Keen, P., Ballance, C., Chan, S., & Schrump, S. (2000), *Electronic Commerce Relationships: Trust By Design*, November 1999, New York, NY: Prentice Hall PTR (ECS Professional), pp. 9, 62.

Kumar, N. (1996), "The Power of Trust in Manufacturer–Retailer Relationships", *Harvard Business Review*, Vol. 74, Iss. 6, pp. 92–103.

Lewicki, R.J. & Bunker, B.B. (1995), "Trust in Relationships: A Model of Development and Decline", in Bunker, B.B. & Rubin, J.Z. (eds), *Conflict, Cooperation and Justice*, San Francisco, CA: Jossey-Bass, pp. 133–173.

M2 Communications Ltd. (2000), "Netscape Faces Class Action Privacy", *Internet Business News*, Coventry, 12 July, p. 1.

McLain, D.L. & Hackman, B.K. (1995), "Trust and Risk Taking in Organizations", unpublished working paper, VA: Virginia State University.

Merrell, C. & Norfolk, A. (2000), "Security Lapse Closes Barclays' On-line Bank", *The Times*, London, 1 August, p. 4.

Milwaukee Journal Sentinel (2000), "Postal Service Offers Program to Date e-Mail", *Journal Sentinel* wire reports, 28 April, p. 12A.

Moorman, C., Deshpande, R., & Zaltman, G. (1993), "Factors Affecting Trust in Market Research Relationships", *Journal of Marketing*, Vol. 57, January, pp. 81–101.

Moorman, C., Zaltman, G., & Deshpande, R. (1992), "Relationships Between Providers and Users of Marketing Research: The Dynamics of Trust Within and Between Organisations", *Journal of Marketing Research*, Vol. 29, August, pp. 314–319.

Morgan, R.M. & Hunt, S.D. (1994), "The Commitment-Trust Theory of Relationship Marketing", *Journal of Marketing*, Vol. 58, Iss. 3, pp. 20–38.

Salam, A.F., Rao, H.R., & Pegels, C.C. (1998), "An Investigation of Consumer-perceived Risk on Electronic Commerce Transactions: The Role of Institutional Trust and Economic Incentive in a Social Exchange Framework", Proceedings of the Americas Conference on Information Systems, Baltimore, MD.

Salnoske, K. (1998), "Building Trust in Electronic Commerce", *Business Credit*, January, New York, NY, pp. 24–28.

Scanzoni, J. (1979), "Social Exchange and Behavioral Interdependence", in Burgess, R.L. & Huston, T.L. (eds), *Social Exchange in Developing Relationships*, New York, NY: Academic Press, pp. 61–98.

Steinauer, D.D., Wakid, S.A., & Rasberry, S. (1997), "Trust and Traceability in Electronic Commerce", Information Technology Laboratory, National Institute of Standards and Technology, September.

Strub, P.J. & Priest, T.B. (1976), "Two Patterns of Establishing Trust: The Marijuana User", *Sociological Focus*, Vol. 9, Iss. 4, pp. 399–411.

Urban, G. (1998), "Internet & Trust Based Marketing", Learning Conference, June.

VeriSign (2000), URL: http://www.verisign.com, 29 August.

Wolverton, T. (2000), "IKEA Exposes Customer Information on Catalog Site", CNET News.com, 6 September, URL: http://news.cnet.com/news/0-1007-200-2709867.html, 20 September.

Woolford, D. (1999) "Electronic Commerce: It Is All a Matter of Trust", *Computing Canada*, 7 May.

Yahoo! (2000), "VeriSign, Inc.", URL: http://dir.yahoo.com/Business_and_Economy/ Business_to_Business/Computers/Security_and_Encryption/Software/Encryption/ VeriSign__Inc_/, 20 September.

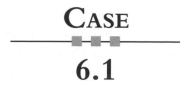

CASE

6.1

CaseTrust: Building Third-party e–Tailing Trust*

The best way for building consumer-retailer relations is for both sides to know upfront the rules of the game.

— Edmund Baker, Executive Director, CaseTrust

In June 2000, CaseTrust, an accreditation scheme designed to promote consumer confidence in Web-based retailing, was into its third year of implementation in Singapore. The scheme was designed to address the three main factors that impinged upon consumer confidence in e-commerce: trust, privacy and security. Edmund Baker, Executive Director of CaseTrust, together with the other two non-executive directors of the scheme, were drawing up plans to extend CaseTrust to other countries in the Asia-Pacific region, notably Japan, Korea, Taiwan, Hong Kong, Malaysia and the Philippines over the next two years. Ultimately, they had plans to take CaseTrust into the US,

---

* Pauline Ng prepared this case in conjunction with Shamza Khan under the supervision of Dr. Ali Farhoomand. *Copyright © 2000 The University of Hong Kong. Ref. 00/95C*

Europe and other parts of the world. However, a number of decisions had to be made that would determine the strategy for CaseTrust. How could CaseTrust establish world-wide recognition among e-tailers and consumers as a reliable and trustworthy scheme that would promote on-line retailing? More specifically, Baker and his colleagues considered the option of incorporating the organisation in the US, which might generate greater appeal for the scheme globally than if it was launched from Singapore. (Privatisation was considered necessary for bringing in the capital funding for the scheme if it was to grow.) They were also considering the appropriateness of the CaseTrust brand name and whether to adopt different brand names in different regions or countries. At the product level, the board contemplated whether to market CaseTrust in its unadulterated form, or to split it into four or five products (such as 'business trust' or 'product trust') and market combinations of these products to suit each country's needs. This would imply that there would be different levels of accreditation and therefore varying degrees of consumer trust in an e-tailer.

Baker thought about his learning curve in Singapore and how he would apply the CaseTrust scheme, or variations of it, to retailers and consumers in other countries. The challenges included the legal jurisdiction/infrastructure, the enforceability of CaseTrust principles over cross-national boundaries, cultural acceptance of a 'foreign' scheme, and whether the administration of the scheme should be licensed through some form of joint-venture agreement or whether CaseTrust should establish a subsidiary body locally to administer the scheme.

ON-LINE E-TAILING TRENDS IN SINGAPORE

For many businesses, the Web served as a channel to provide effective customer service, marketing opportunities, improved customer communication and a means of growth beyond the local market. Singapore had aspirations to become central to international e-commerce activities, building on its strengths as an international trading hub and its business competitiveness. It had the necessary infrastructure to support an international transaction hub. It was well connected with Internet links to the major regional cities and had strong infrastructure to support e-businesses including on-line payment services, security services and bureau services. The legal foundation for e-commerce was also in place with the tabling of the Electronic Transaction Bill, which brought electronically completed contracts into a defined legal framework. Electronic records could be used as evidence in court and contracts formed and signed electronically were given recognition. The Singapore government was committed to making Singapore a competitive place for international e-commerce and had set a target of 50 percent of its businesses using some form of e-commerce by 2003.

Singapore had an IT-literate and Internet-savvy population. By 2000, some 59 percent of Singapore households owned a computer and more than 42 percent (approximately 760,000) of the population subscribed to the Internet. This compared to nine percent in 1996.[1] In fact, Singapore had been recognised as the second-most IT-literate country in the world after the US.[2] A news report in January 2000 revealed the results of a survey by the Infocomm Development Authority of Singapore that suggested Singapore was in the lead in terms of adoption of the Internet at home.[3] With a per capita gross domestic product of S$24,600,[4] Singapore ranked among the world's top 20 richest economies and was therefore ripe for the e-commerce explosion.

Singapore's e-commerce was also advanced, with on-line purchases settled via cashcards or security credit card payment systems, and banks using digital certificates and smart cards to offer secure on-line banking. There were more than 180 on-line retailers on the *Shopping Village* Website (www.shoppingvillage.com.sg). Among the most popular e-tailers were the grocery stores (e.g., NTUC FairPrice, Cold Storage), ticketing services (e.g., Golden Village, SISTIC, TicketCharge) and financial services (e.g., Internet banking, electronic stock trading).

According to official estimates, e-commerce in Singapore in 1999 was worth about S$8.8 million (US$5 million).[5] Electronic goods and clothing were the most popular goods sold on-line, accounting for 52 percent of all on-line purchases. Grocery purchases over the Net represented 11.3 percent.[6] The intention of CaseTrust was to boost sales over the Net by up to 30 percent.[7]

While on-line shopping was expected to grow, there were several factors that seemed to hinder consumers from buying on-line:

---

[1] Tee, E. (2000), "S'pore Beats US, Japan in Internet Use at Home", *The Straits Times*, Singapore, 21 January.

[2] Institute of Management Development (1999), "World Competitiveness Report 1999", Switzerland.

[3] Tee, E. (2000).

[4] US$1 = S$1.72

[5] Yap, E. (1999), "Cybershopping Safer with CaseTrust", *The Straits Times*, Singapore, 2 April.

[6] Wee, A. (2000), "Electronic Goods, Clothes, Most Popular e-Shop Items", *The Business Times*, Singapore, 17 January.

[7] Yap, E. (1999).

❑ Shopping malls were densely planted around the island city. With an efficient public transportation network, consumers were never too far away from a mall. Convenience and the ability to choose, feel and touch before buying did not lend support to on-line shopping.

❑ Singapore's strict credit card issuing requirements impeded the growth of on-line shopping. Credit cards were the main mode of payment for on-line purchases. However, they were not accessible to the younger age group (except for supplementary cards) who were more Net-savvy and had a greater propensity to shop over the Internet.

❑ Consumers and e-tailers were reluctant to make and receive payments through credit cards. In December 1999, Mohamed Mustafa & Samsuddin, retail giants in Singapore who specialised in electronic goods, announced to a local newspaper that they would no longer accept on-line payments by credit card on its www.mustafa.com.sg Website.[8] The company had experienced a series of defaults on on-line payments for goods that its clients denied having purchased. Consequently, the company was denied payment and was unable to recover the goods. Although losses were small in financial terms, the company was quick to put a stop to the auto payment system. On-line sales dropped from S$1 million per month to a mere few thousand dollars a month. For consumers, the considerations for making a purchase on-line went beyond credit card security and privacy of personal information. Unless the retailer was known to be a reputable business with a physical storefront, many consumers were uneasy with the idea of buying from a virtual retailer who may, at best, deliver goods of poor quality or, at worst, not fulfil orders.

❑ The commission that banks charged e-tailers in Singapore started at 12 percent. Unless e-tailers could generate large volumes of sales, the extra cost was a burden to them. While the government was trying to address this problem in an effort to encourage e-tailing, in the short term, this remained a hindrance to e-tailing.

CASETRUST BACKGROUND

The idea is to promote e-commerce, but the focus is on good business practice, good dispute avoidance.

– Dr. Toh See Kiat, President, CASE[9]

---

[8] Koh, E. (1999), "Mustafa Let Down By e-Commerce", *The Straits Times*, Singapore, 13 December.

[9] "Confidence Boost for e-Commerce", *The Straits Times*, Singapore, 15 April 1999.

CaseTrust was a scheme designed to broadly promote trust and credibility in Singapore-based e-commerce. In 1997, CaseTrust was introduced in Singapore to give consumers the assurance needed to encourage e-commerce transactions locally. In the absence of any consumer protection legislation, the scheme was extended to protect the interests of merchants and consumers within the physical retail shopping environment in 1998. Hence, the objectives of CaseTrust addressed the whole retail industry and aimed to:

1. Promote good business practices as a critical component in retailing.
2. Elevate the overall standard of retailing.
3. Promote a Web of trust in a fledgling electronic commerce industry.

Since Singapore did not have an all-encompassing consumer protection act, CaseTrust was designed to ensure that retailers were ethical in their business dealings, promoting a sense of fair play and creating a self-regulatory environment.

The accreditation scheme was to promote good business practices among both store-based and Web-based retailers. It was to enable retailers to gain customers' confidence that would subsequently lead to increased repeat patronage and customer loyalty. For Web-based retailers, the benefits included increased sales once customers gained confidence to trade via a non-personal medium. CaseTrust's certification scheme was, therefore, two-pronged: Web-based and store-based. Both were concerned with ensuring adherence to good business practices that helped to reduce inconvenience, unsatisfied expectations and the risk of loss or fraud. Thus, businesses would reassure their customers about the integrity of their business transactions.

CaseTrust was initiated by the Consumer Association of Singapore (CASE), CommerceNet Singapore Ltd. (CNSG) and the Retail Promotion Centre (RPC). [Refer to **Exhibit 1** for information about these organisations.] Its Board of Directors was made up of three members: Edmund Baker, Executive Director of CASE, the General Manager of RPC and the Chairman of CNSG. Baker was the only executive director of the CaseTrust scheme. As of June 2000, the six staff administering the scheme were employees seconded from the three founder organisations. There was also a committee of volunteers, consisting of nine people who were professionals drawn from business. The committee steered CaseTrust's course and served to balance out the interests of consumers and retailers. It also served as an appeals committee in the case of a dispute.

Being a non-profit-making organisation, CaseTrust was funded by the three founder organisations and received revenues from the joining fees and the annual membership fees charged to its members. As of June 2000, 700 out of 12,000 storefront outlets and 50 out of 600 e-tail sites were registered. In addition, six memorandums of understanding had been signed with the Singapore Jewellers Association, Singapore Furniture Association, Pacific Internet, CyberSource, NTUC Income and ePubliceye.com. By the end of the year, it aimed to have 100 Websites registered.

ACHIEVING ACCREDITATION WITH CASETRUST

The key to accreditation was open declaration of trade practices observed by retailers to create transparency and credibility with consumers. The assessment criteria for applications embodied the principles of good business practice. The criteria for assessing a store-based retailer and a Web-based retailer were different [see **Exhibit 2**]. An e-tailer, for example, had to inform consumers of the resolution process in the event of a dispute, its policy on refunds and its commitment to information security and confidentiality. While shopfront certification required compliance with a code of good business practice endorsed by the trade associations, Web certification required additional assurances on transaction integrity via information security and procedures.

Applicants were graded with a pass or fail on each criterion. The general guideline for grading was that if applicants could satisfy the prerequisites for each criterion, they were granted a 'pass'. [See **Exhibit 3**.] In effect, achieving accreditation meant that retailers and e-tailers were declaring that they were good retailers because they had adhered to the code of practice. Retailers and e-tailers who were accepted as members earned the right to display the CaseTrust logo prominently in-store or on their Websites. It was up to the e-tailer, however, to decide where and on which page on its Website it would put the logo. So the onus was on the shopper to find the logo and it was not immediately obvious to a shopper that an e-tailer was CaseTrusted.

The steps in the application process are summarised in **Figure 1**.

The application fee was S$600 for Web-based retailers and S$100 for store-based retailers. The annual membership fee was S$200 in either case, fixed to the end of 2001. In the first six months of the scheme, a 50 percent discount was offered to all new applicants. In the case of portal registration, the fee structure was different, starting at S$5,000 per annum. Members were required to renew their membership annually to ensure that they adhered to the standards of business practice stipulated by CaseTrust. Renewal forms also required that they declare any changes to their business practices. Membership renewal was subject to approval by the CaseTrust committee.

In addition to the fees, registered members were required to undertake an insur-

Figure 1:   The application process

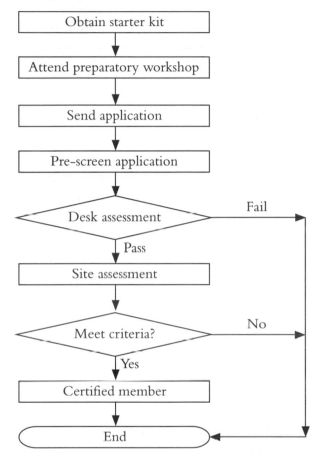

ance bond. In the event of misconduct or breach of agreement, CaseTrust was allowed to use the bond to make good the losses to the consumer. The bond was a fixed amount for all retailers except for certain industries, such as the jewellery trade, where the value of the goods and therefore the risks were greater. CaseTrust experienced great difficulty in finding insurance underwriters that would undertake this kind of cover. Finally, an arrangement was reached with one company based on a ceiling cap assessment to keep the insurance premium low. The last thing CaseTrust wanted to do was to burden businesses with additional costs. For the time being, the insurance bond cost e-tailers S$60 for S$10,000 cover per year.

ANNUAL AUDITS

An audit was conducted upon the initial application for membership using the criteria set out for assessing business practices. An audit could involve a Website and/or shopfront assessment. At other times during the year, members had to allow CaseTrust representatives into their premises for spot checks. Concerning Website security, CaseTrust employed 'Web crawlers' to look into any suspicious activities or transactions. At any time, the committee reserved the right to revoke membership should members fail to adhere to the licence agreement. Penalties were imposed upon breach or infringement of the code of practice. The graded penalty scheme started from a fine, to suspension, to expulsion or blacklisting, depending on the severity of the offence. In Singapore, CaseTrust administered the audits, but with the increasing membership and the limited manpower, it had resorted to reliance on the annual renewal declarations, while spot checks would be conducted throughout the year.

EXECUTING THE CASETRUST SCHEME IN SINGAPORE

The Pilot

The initial pilot launch of CaseTrust involved seven carefully selected established retailers:

- ❑ Franklin Electronics, which sold hand-held electronic reference books, such as dictionaries, by a US brand, Franklin. (www.ecomz.franklin/)
- ❑ The Paint House, a Nippon Paint agent that operated a similar business model to amazon.com. (www.painthouse.com.sg)
- ❑ i nouvi Cosmetics, a Singapore brand. (www.inouvi.com)
- ❑ Prentice Hall offered a wide range of computer books on-line. (www.bookshaw.com.sg)
- ❑ Joaquim Florist and Gifts. (www.joaquim.com.sg)
- ❑ Bee Cheng Hiang sold barbecued pork through its Website, www.bchhc.com.sg.
- ❑ Cold Storage, a grocery store with 30 outlets located around the island. (www.coldstorage.com.sg)

These were picked by CASE to cover the broad range of retailers in Singapore.

Building the Portfolio of Registered Retailers

With limited financial resources to launch advertising and awareness campaigns, or to employ staff to visit every retailer to sell the scheme, CaseTrust resolved to work with various trade associations. By working with, say, the Jewellers Association to introduce a code of practice, uniformity of industry standards could be achieved. The industry code of practice would then become the basis for granting CaseTrust accreditation. CaseTrust signed a Memorandum of Understanding (MOU) with the Singapore Jewellers Association on 16 September 1999, appointing it as the administrator for the Jeweller Trust scheme, the industry accreditation scheme based on the core principles of CaseTrust. More than 60 percent of the jewellery retailers were covered under the scheme, accounting for about 167 out of 223 stores. In early October, a MOU was signed with the Singapore Furniture Association and the Interior Renovations Advisory Committee. This brought on board 36 retailers. However, most of these retailers were trading through physical storefronts.

In late November 1999, CaseTrust signed its first agreement with a portal, Pacific Internet, a local Internet access service provider. Under this MOU, Pacific Internet effectively acted as CaseTrust's agent in ensuring that the accreditation criteria were met by all the retailers on its on-line mall. The MOU also stated clearly what was expected of each party involved. In addition, Pacific Internet was to have an official 'CT administrator' sign on its Website. This arrangement instantaneously brought in 38 new members for CaseTrust.

Then, in March 2000, a MOU was signed with Cybersource, a local company with an international presence covering 480 retail outlets and 35 Websites. Cybersource was one of the largest Asian Internet companies. Its core business included its e-commerce payment gateway to merchants. The company planned to make it a requirement for all its merchants to be CaseTrusted before they could use its payment system.

> *Press tests, poke tests, shake tests (think watermelon) … We all know that they're not really the 'done' thing, but it's the consumer guarantee for high-quality products.*[10]

In spite of CaseTrust's progress in enlisting members, on-line e-tailing in Singapore was still slow to take off. The convenience of off-line shopping in Singapore cancelled out the need to confront the question of trust in on-line shopping. The balance, however, would be different in countries such as Japan or the US, where the

---

[10] "Click for Fish or Go to Tekka?' *The Sunday Times*, Singapore, 30 April 2000.

inconvenience of off-line shopping in some locations could entice consumers to shop on-line and accept the associated risks.

Furthermore, while the larger retailers were beginning to see the benefits of being CaseTrusted in the long term, the main problem was getting the smaller businesses involved, particularly as the costs far outweighed the benefits of membership. CaseTrust portrayed itself as similar to an exclusive club that espoused good business practices. Even so, businesses that were CaseTrusted had not reported any obvious improvements in sales as a result. It appeared that CaseTrust had to work on improving customer and retailer awareness of the CaseTrust cause, and until this happened, its impact, particularly on on-line sales, would be minimal.

ESTABLISHING ON-LINE TRUST AND CREDIBILITY

In on-line sales, credibility is the most important thing. Being 'CaseTrusted' gives us that credibility.
                                                  — Byron Teo, Marketing Manager, i nouvi Cosmetics[11]

The main attraction of CaseTrust, particularly to on-line shoppers, was that it offered redress for consumers who were dissatisfied with their purchase or service quality. In a virtual marketplace where both parties would not come face-to-face to make transactions, the risk of either party defaulting (i.e., problems with the goods or problems with payment) was much greater. The main concern for shoppers was the integrity of cyberstores, particularly as one could not handle, try on or even physically see what one was buying. By giving recognition to retailers with good business practices, CaseTrust aimed to provide a psychological assurance to consumers that they were transacting with an ethical retailer. With the Internet's anonymity and non-accountability, consumers needed greater assurances.

In Singapore, the majority of e-tailing businesses were spun off from the main storefront businesses. Since on-line consumers could physically identify who they were buying from, trust was already established. Where e-tailers did not have a physical storefront, building trust could be a serious problem, especially in the Asian cultural context, where trading standards and consumer rights were immature compared to those in the West. While CaseTrust believed that its role was to give consumers the

---

[11] Yap, E. (1999).

assurance that they were dealing with trustworthy e-tailers, its experience proved that it was playing a more significant role in confirming and maintaining trust. The challenge was to establish trust in e-tailers that did not have a physical face.

Accredited retailers were allowed to display the CaseTrust logo at the storefront or Website. The blue 'C' signified protection of consumers by CASE and the white 'T' signified business being open and transparent. The merging of the two showed the support for the openness of business transparency, or in other words, good business practice.

Despite the connotations of the CT mark, the benefits had not yet been fully realised since few consumers were made aware of the advantages of buying from a CaseTrusted retailer.

The scheme will still need some advertising to generate awareness.
— Kenneth Chee, Managing Director, Joaquim Florist and Gifts[12]

It is difficult to judge whether being 'CaseTrusted' has improved business at this early stage.
— Kenneth Chee[13]

ON-LINE SECURITY AND INTEGRITY

Apart from requiring that members declare that in-house security measures were in place [refer to Section D of **Exhibit 3**], CaseTrust did not certify that retailers' security protocols were safe. The declaration served to enforce a system of self-policing.

THE DISPUTE RESOLUTION PROCESS

Being a neutral body, looking after the interests of both consumers and retailers, the CaseTrust committee acted as the arbitrator in the event of complaints and disputes. This ensured the fairness and integrity of the scheme.

Accredited retailers were obliged to mediate at the company level first to resolve a

---

[12] Dawson, S. (1999), "A Strong Case for Cyber-trust", *The Straits Times*, Singapore, 5 July.
[13] Dawson, S. (1999).

complaint. If, within 14 days, the matter was not resolved, it would be taken up by the relevant trade association, which would have 21 days to resolve the matter. The CaseTrust committee had the power to intervene in the mediation process at any time. The underlying idea behind this was to create a win-win situation for all parties involved. At the last resort, the committee would act as the arbitrator and the decision made would be final. In the process, errant retailers would be penalised for misconduct.

Since the inception of CaseTrust, only two cases of mediation had occurred [refer to **Exhibit 4** for details]. In both instances, the trade associations concerned brought the matters to a satisfactory conclusion and the CaseTrust committee did not have to intervene. On the one hand, this spoke of the success of the scheme in achieving an amicable resolution of disputes and of the process of weeding out errand retailers. On the other hand, the lack of incidences reported and resolved by the CaseTrust committee did not lend support to the benefits of having an independent arbitrator, as it had yet to prove its fairness and authority in making a final decision in the event of a dispute.

ISSUES FACING CASETRUST IN JUNE 2000

Lack of Resources for Building Awareness of CaseTrust

In a project like this where it is important for the consumer to be aware, we have been very limited in what we are able to achieve to promote awareness. There is no conscious effort on the part of the Singapore shopper to physically look for the CaseTrust logo. If they see it, it is more incidental.

– Edmund Baker

Baker identified that the main limitation to CaseTrust was financial. It followed that without the necessary finances, advertising and promotional campaigns were hindered. Additional staff required to administer the scheme, particularly if it was to expand to other countries, could not be employed. Even the printing costs for brochures and information leaflets could not be met. CaseTrust was in desperate need of a capital injection.

The Competition

In Singapore, the competition was only just arriving. [Refer to **Exhibit 5** for details of competitors.] All were US organisations whose schemes had some principles that were addressed by CaseTrust. However, most were simply concerned with privacy issues involved in Internet trading, while CaseTrust embodied other principles of good retail practice. Because CaseTrust applied to physical stores and virtual stores, a retail business simply needed to become CaseTrusted to have his storefront as well as his Website accredited. None of the other schemes incorporated both. From CaseTrust's experience, this was a major advantage since many of the e-tailers had established physical stores, and on-line brand trust was directly associated with off-line brand trust. A consumer would more readily buy on-line from a reputable retailer because he knew who he was dealing with.

The audit procedure was also more stringent than what was required for a privacy type of trust mark. While the latter was a simple declaration that the e-tailer had a satisfactory privacy policy, CaseTrust went beyond privacy to identify, for example, the minimum requirements for Website content and minimum security standards.

CaseTrust felt that it was ahead of the competition in the local market. Having knowledge of the local market was also a competitive advantage. Unlike its US counterparts, who were more used to working in the catalogue-based e-tail environment, CaseTrust understood the Asian way of shopping. Consumers liked to physically see and touch (and maybe smell) the products. Both buyer and seller generally had a concern about 'losing face'. While US consumers may have no qualms about banging on the door of the retailer to demand a refund, CaseTrust preferred to provide a channel for a softer approach in the event of a dispute. By creating a mediation process, both buyer and seller could resolve differences in a win–win context.

PLANS FOR THE IMMEDIATE FUTURE

The only means by which the Board and committee could see CaseTrust growing in the future was through privatisation. The benefits of incorporating the organisation included the extra injection of capital it desperately needed and also public recognition as an independent body. In June 2000, the legal documents for privatisation were in the process of being drafted. Plans were in place for CaseTrust to be incorporated in July. However, in the meantime, a number of decisions had to be made:

- ❑ The place of incorporation: CaseTrust believed that if the company was incorporated in the US, this could give the scheme greater recognition and boost its image as an international scheme.
- ❑ The name of incorporation remained undecided.
- ❑ The CaseTrust brand name: Feedback from various countries indicated the countries interested in the scheme would prefer to have a localised name for

the scheme. They argued that localising the concepts and ideas would make them identifiable to their indigenous groups.

❑ The levels of accreditation (or the product range): Baker considered variations of the CaseTrust concept. He had ideas for breaking the CaseTrust principles into something like a 'product trust' or 'business trust'. By doing so, the advantages included greater flexibility to match the 'products' to the country, particularly where a country was not advanced enough to accept all the principles of CaseTrust. In this way, CaseTrust could be more nimble in dealing with the bureaucracy involved in each country. Bearing in mind that the CaseTrust scheme in its current form was designed for the Singapore market, variations in the packaging of the product had to be considered to make it marketable in other countries.

Following privatisation, several changes would have to take place. CaseTrust would need to transform itself from a non-profit to a profit-making company. The three founder organisations would take a less active role in the management of CaseTrust, although the significance of CaseTrust in promoting Singapore as an e-commerce hub could imply that the government would have an 'invisible hand' in the affairs of CaseTrust. A more formal organisation structure would be necessary, with an executive Board of Directors that would include a Chairman, a CEO and a COO. To be an organisation that was to enforce consumer trust, the management and image of the company itself needed to be trustworthy.

Enforcing e-Trust Outside Singapore

CaseTrust, set to corporatise by the end of the year, aims to raise its profile to become a global standard trademark.[14]

The selection of countries for rolling out the scheme was drawn up by CommerceNet. CommerceNet was part of a global consortium of business partners spread over 22 countries. With these connections, CommerceNet had already sown the seeds for the internationalisation of the CaseTrust scheme. The prioritising of the countries was based on the responses received from each country to the CaseTrust project.

---

[14] Lim, C. (2000), "Case's e-Accreditation System to Go International", *The Straits Times*, Singapore, 14 March.

As Baker pondered on the Singapore experience in implementing CaseTrust and contemplated the internationalisation of the scheme, he realised the scheme was much easier to administer and monitor in Singapore. Locally, CaseTrust could manage the pre-registration and annual audits in-house. In other countries, he felt sure that external agents would have to be appointed to act on CaseTrust's behalf. Policing the scheme would become a major concern. Who would be appointed as the dispute arbitrators and what would be their role?

Could the Singapore scheme be directly replicated in other countries? In Japan, for example, where geographic distance may hinder consumers from frequenting a physical store, consumers may be more ready to accept a scheme such as CaseTrust. While the need for a trust accreditation scheme was identified, several matters had to be overcome. CaseTrust had to understand the legal jurisdiction in Japan and the enforceability of the scheme's principles across national boundaries. This was where the role of the external agent/partnering organisation would be of significance. A further consideration was whether local trust schemes were already in place and whether CaseTrust could negotiate a merging of the schemes. In some countries, internal opposition could come from local consumers and business groups.

There were several options open to CaseTrust when considering the administration of the scheme in other countries. It could form alliances with other organisations in each country. These could be under licence or joint-venture agreements. On the other hand, it could decide to set up subsidiary companies in each country. Baker felt that both methods could be used depending on the regulations imposed by each government.

In my view, schemes like this will take many years to build a level of comfort, where people can say that CaseTrust has proved itself. I don't think it's going to be easy.
— Edmund Baker

Exhibit 1: The organisations behind CaseTrust

CaseTrust is a joint project between the following three organisations:

Consumer Association of Singapore (CASE)

CASE, the only consumer body in Singapore, was set up in August 1971. It was a non-profit-making organisation reliant on membership subscriptions revenue. Other sources of finance included government grants, sponsorship and proceeds from the sale of various consumer publications, seminars and forums. Its purpose was to inform, educate and protect consumer rights (www.case.org.sg).

CommerceNet Singapore Ltd. (CNSG)

CNSG was the first industry-led, non-profit-making consortium in Singapore for promoting e-commerce by making it easy, trusted and ubiquitous. It was incorporated in February 1998 and consisted of 38 member organisations that used, promoted or built e-commerce solutions on the Internet. To achieve this, CNSG tackled issues pertaining to e-commerce from all angles, whether technological, business, legal, regulatory or otherwise. Members participated in discussions and projects. CNSG provided all technical expertise and any strategy or technology was first reviewed by CaseTrust's committee prior to implementation by CNSG. By 2000, CNSG was part of a global consortium with 500 members worldwide and business partners spread over 22 countries.

Retail Promotion Centre (RPC)

An arm of the Singapore Productivity and Standards Board, the RPC was dedicated to helping small- and medium-sized retailers upgrade and modernise.

Exhibit 2: **Summary of the assessment criteria for gaining CaseTrust accreditation**

Processes	Store-based retailers' criteria	Web-based retailers' criteria
Section A		
Browsing	Store policies	Web policies
	Merchandise & services	Webpages
	Pricing	Merchandise & services
	Advertising & promotions	Pricing
	Behaviour of customer support staff	Advertising & promotions
		Behaviour of customer support staff
Section B		
Buying	Deposits	Electronic ordering
	Payment processing	Payment processing
	Receipts/sales slips	Electronic confirmation slips
Section C		
After sales	Delivery	Delivery
	Exchanges & refunds	Cancellation of orders
	Feedback management	Exchanges & refunds
		Feedback management
Section D		
Security/ confidentiality	Customers' particulars	Commitment to information security
		Customers' particulars
		Confidentiality
		Availability of information
		Security activity monitoring

Exhibit 3: CaseTrust assessment criteria (Web-based)

Section A: Browsing

1. Web policies — Applicants shall have a written set of clear and relevant Web policies disclosing their business practices to their customers.

2. Webpages — Applicants shall clearly state products/ services offered and any disclaimers on their Webpages.

3. Merchandise & services — Applicants shall offer services and goods that are of merchandisable condition, i.e., the goods should be fit for their intended functions.

4. Pricing — Applicants shall clearly and prominently display product prices/service rates and any additional charges to their customers without ambiguity.

5. Advertising & promotions — Applicants shall ensure that all marketing communications materials, such as Webpages, advertisements, flyers and menus, are truthful, accurate and not misleading.

6. Behaviour of customer support staff — Applicants shall monitor the behaviour of the customer support staff to ensure that they do not practise any unethical sales tactics.

Section B: Buying

1. Electronic ordering — Applicants shall provide an on-line ordering system such as the 'shopping baskets' to their customers for them to state their purchases. They shall also provide customers information on the status of their orders.

2. Payment processing — Applicants shall ensure accuracy in their billings.

Exhibit 3 (cont'd)

3. Electronic confirmation slips	Applicants shall provide customers with on-line confirmation slip listing the purchase details as proof of purchases.

Section C: After Sales

1. Delivery	Applicants shall deliver orders for merchandise according to the agreed timeframes and conditions.
2. Cancellation of orders	Applicants shall refund customers for payments made in the case of any cancellation of orders due to the company's fault.
3. Exchanges & refunds	Applicants shall declare and honour their exchanges and refund policies. Any exchanges or refunds shall be carried out promptly.
4. Feedback management	Applicants shall maintain an adequate system for monitoring queries, feedback and complaints so that the appropriate remedial action can be taken. They shall also implement service recovery programmes to handle complaints in a prompt manner.

Section D: Security/Confidentiality

1. Commitment to information security	Applicants shall obtain and use customers' particulars only if necessary.
2. Customers' particulars	Applicants shall be committed to maintaining the security of all their information systems.
3. Confidentiality	Applicants shall ensure that customer data is disclosed only to authorised persons and entities.

Exhibit 3 (cont'd)

4. Availability of information	Applicants shall, within their control, ensure that accessibility and usability of all information available on the Website is regularly maintained.
5. Security activity monitoring	Applicants shall ensure that measures are in place to detect and rectify any breach of security.

Exhibit 4: Two cases of mediation

The Jewellery Case

A lady bought a bangle from a jeweller. Six months after the purchase, the gold started to flake off. She demanded a refund from the jeweller, who was a member of the Singapore Jewellers Association (SJA) and was CaseTrusted. During arbitration, the problem was in deciding whether the gold was faulty or whether the gold was flaking off due to normal wear and tear. The case went up to the SJA who decided the lady should be given a partial refund, thus bringing the matter to a satisfactory conclusion for both parties.

The Furniture Case

A piece of furniture was delivered later than the appointed time. The consumer refused to take possession. The case was brought before the Singapore Furniture Association who decided that the transportation fee should be waived and a small percentage discount was given to the consumer to appease him for his inconvenience.

Exhibit 5:   Competitors

The CPA WebTrust

The American Institute of Certified Public Accountants and the Canadian Institute of Chartered Accountants developed the CPA WebTrust program because most people were concerned about security while conducting a financial transaction on-line. The program is a unique assurance for commercial Websites that can enhance consumer confidence in on-line transactions.

BBBOn-line

BBBOn-line is a wholly-owned subsidiary of the Council of Better Business Bureaus. BBBOn-line's mission is to promote trust and confidence on the Internet by encouraging sound and ethical on-line business practices and by providing information to ensure better educated on-line consumers.

BBBOn-line Reliability was launched in April 1997 as a way to help identify on-line businesses with a reliable track record in the marketplace. Companies in BBBOn-line Reliability must be in business for at least one full year, are members of the BBB in their area, agree to BBB advertising standards and dispute resolution procedures, and are visited by a BBB representative at their place of business to confirm adherence to the programme requirements.

BBBOn-line Privacy was launched in March 1999 and awards seals to on-line businesses that have been verified to be following good information practices. Companies that qualify for the seal must post privacy notices telling customers what personal information is being collected and how it will be used.

TRUSTe

TRUSTe is an independent non-profit-making organisation dedicated to building consumer trust and confidence in the Internet. Launched in June 1997, TRUSTe is based in Cupertino, CA, with an office in Washington, DC.

TRUSTe's mission is to build users' trust and confidence in the Internet and in doing so, accelerate the growth of the Internet industry. The TRUSTe programme was designed to ensure the protection of consumer privacy and to empower consumers to make informed choices. The TRUSTe trustmark is awarded only to on-line sites that adhere to established privacy principles and agree to comply with on-going TRUSTe oversight and consumer resolution procedures. Privacy principles embody fair information practices approved by the US Department of Commerce, Federal Trade Commission and prominent industry-represented organisations and associations.

Exhibit 5 (cont'd)

Through extensive consumer and Website research and the support and guidance from many established companies and industry experts, TRUSTe has earned a reputation as the leader in promoting privacy policy disclosure, informed user consent and consumer education. Electronic Frontier Foundation (EFF) and CommerceNet Consortium, who act as independent, unbiased trust entities, founded TRUSTe.

VeriSign

VeriSign, founded in May 1995, headquartered in Mountain View, California, provides Internet trust services needed by Websites, enterprises and e-commerce service providers to conduct trusted and secure e-commerce and communications over IP networks. The company has established strategic relationships with industry leaders to enable widespread utilisation of digital certificate services and to assure interoperability with a variety of applications and network.

SUMMARY

Company	Verifies reliability of business practices	Verifies privacy policy	Sets up complaint resolution procedure
CaseTrust	Yes	Yes	Yes
VeriSign	No	No	No
BBBOn-line	Yes	Yes	Yes
TRUSTe	No	Yes	Yes
CPA WebTrust	Yes	Yes	Yes

Company	Provides technical security	Conducts audits	Re-certification
CaseTrust	No	Yes	N/A
VeriSign	Yes	N/A	N/A
BBBOn-line	No	N/A	N/A
TRUSTe	No	On-going	N/A
CPA WebTrust	No	Yes	Every 90 days

CASE

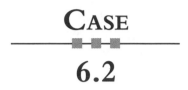

6.2

Cold Storage (Singapore): Establishing Trust Among On-line Consumers*

When it comes to food, when you go to a supermarket, you don't actually buy with your hands. You buy with your eyes; you eat with your eyes. So unless you are an efficient operator and unless you have a strong reputation for selling nothing but the best which means you have the confidence of shoppers, once you run into an on-line service you will have problems.

— Lester Quah, Operations Director, Cold Storage

Cold Storage, which operated a chain of 31 supermarkets located across the city-state of Singapore, was a well-established retail operation renowned for the quality of its fresh food. In June 1998, the Company launched its supermarket services on the Internet in an effort to better serve its customers. By June 2000, on-line shoppers totalled

* Pauline Ng prepared this case under the supervision of Dr. Ali Farhoomand. *Copyright © 2000 The University of Hong Kong. Ref. 00/98C*

15,000, which represented 62 percent of all the orders taken by the Company's Dial-and-Deliver Centre.

Realising that consumer trust was essential for building its on-line services, Cold Storage wasted no time in gaining accreditation with CaseTrust, a local scheme designed to promote consumer confidence in Web-based retailing. Accreditation was granted at the end of 1998. In June 2000, Lester Quah, the Operations Director of Cold Storage, had to evaluate the benefits of being CaseTrusted and other factors that helped establish on-line shoppers' trust in its virtual store.

COLD STORAGE

Cold Storage ('the Company') was a wholly-owned subsidiary company of Dairy Farm International Holdings Ltd., a group that ran nearly 2,000 supermarkets, drugs and convenience stores across the Asia-Pacific region. Registered in Singapore in 1903 as a storage and distribution business for frozen foods and perishable products, the Company opened its first retail outlet in Orchard Road, the central shopping district, in 1905. By 2000, the Company commanded almost 26 percent of the market share and operated 31 stores around the island [see **Exhibit 1**].

Cold Storage had established a reputation not only for the quality of its fresh food, but also for its initiatives in recognising the cultural and demographic diversity of Singapore's population. Within its supermarkets, it offered juice bars, a halal bar grill, a 'spice corner' and an in-store 'wet market'. At the beginning of 1999, the Gourmet food hall was opened to cater for the sophisticated customer, offering an extensive range of international deli products. The Company invested much time and attention in its advertising and marketing initiatives. Its commitment to serving only the best to its customers was reinforced by its campaign: 'We are the Fresh Food People'.

A 'Triple Guarantee Policy' offered assurances to its customers:

- ❏ *Price integrity*: if, at a checkout, a product was scanned in at a price that exceeded the shelf price, Cold Storage would waive the price of the product, thus offering it free to the customer.
- ❏ *Freshness*: if a product was not fresh by the time it reached consumers, Cold Storage would replace the purchase with an identical product free of charge and provide a full refund.
- ❏ *Confidence*: if, during a promotion period, an 'on offer' product ran out of stock, Cold Storage would extend the promotion period until the product became available again.

In August 1997, the Company launched the Dial-and-Deliver service that allowed customers to place orders through Singapore ONE's broadband network.

COLD STORAGE ON-LINE

Cold Storage became the first e-commerce business in Singapore to offer supermarket services. Through the National Computer Board, the Singapore government offered a fairly handsome subsidy to cover set-up and development costs. The on-line business model operated as follows:

- ❑ Consumers wanting to make use of the Dial-and-Deliver service had to complete a registration form giving personal particulars. The application would be approved immediately upon receipt.
- ❑ Upon registration, the consumer was assigned an account number that was physically posted to them and notified to them via e-mail, if the consumer had an e-mail address.
- ❑ Registered consumers would receive a Dial-and-Deliver catalogue that included 2,000 of the 10,000 product items found in-store. These represented the basic lines that could be found in the supermarkets.
- ❑ Orders could then be made through Cold Storage's Website (www.coldstorage.com.sg).
- ❑ Consumers would quote their account number when placing an order. With this, Cold Storage was able to track customers' orders, identify habitual purchases and feed that information through to an on-line prompting service that effectively notified customers that they had not ordered the usual goods at certain intervals of time. On-line customers paid by cash or cheque on delivery, or by Cold Storage in-house card (the equivalent of a credit card).
- ❑ Upon receipt of orders, Cold Storage would confirm orders to consumers on-line.
- ❑ Orders were delivered within 24 hours.

Initially, the on-line product range consisted of mainly dry grocery items. This was later expanded to include fresh fruit juices, hardy fruits and vegetables. In-store promotions were also offered to on-line consumers.

The Cold Storage Website opened new opportunities for the Company. New services were added, such as party catering. The Website also included information about current events in Cold Storage, the history of the Company, how business was conducted in the Company and how the Company dealt with its staff. In this way

Cold Storage used its Website as a tool for deploying its marketing strategy, thus building on the customer loyalty that was already established through its stores.

GETTING CASETRUSTED

CaseTrust

CaseTrust was an accreditation scheme designed to promote consumer confidence in Web-based retailing in Singapore. Introduced in 1997, the scheme aimed to address three main factors that impinged upon consumer confidence in e-commerce: trust, privacy and security. The objectives of CaseTrust were as follows:

1. Promote good business practices as a critical component in retailing.
2. Elevate the overall standard of retailing.
3. Promote a Web of trust in a fledgling e-commerce industry.

For Web-based retailers, the benefits of achieving accreditation included increased sales once customers gained the confidence to trade on a non-personal medium. Accreditation ensured that retailers adhered to good business practices, and acted as an assurance to customers of the integrity of their business transactions.

CaseTrust was initiated by the Consumer Association of Singapore (CASE), CommerceNet Singapore Ltd. (CNSG) and the Retail Promotion Centre (RPC). The three organisations commanded significant status in Singapore as they acted as the voice of consumers and retailers. Being a non-profit-making organisation, CaseTrust was funded by the three founder organisations and received revenues from the joining fees and the annual membership fees charged to its members.

It was during the pilot launch of CaseTrust that Cold Storage was invited, together with six other carefully selected established retailers, to be a pioneer member.

Achieving Accreditation with CaseTrust

The audit process took approximately four months and followed the assessment criteria as set out in **Exhibit 2**. For Cold Storage, achieving accreditation was a simple process as its business practices were well-established and transparent to consumers. CaseTrust did not dictate the format of Websites or the data security modules in place. However, it did require that certain information be accessible to consumers and be neatly and clearly presented.

Once accreditation was granted, Cold Storage was allowed to display the CaseTrust logo on its Website together with a declaration of confidentiality [see **Figure 1**].

Figure 1:   The CaseTrust logo and confidentiality declaration

At Cold Storage, we protect the confidentiality, integrity and availability of our corporate and customer information against errors, sabotage, fraud and breach of privacy. Disciplinary and/or legal action will be taken against offenders who use or alter the company's information assets without authorisation.

ESTABLISHING TRUST ON-LINE

We have got an established structure for people to look at, for people to shop in and for people to build loyalty on. That is a tangible thing. Developing the on-line business in that context will really enhance what we can offer on the shopfront. So by having a storefront, by having that reputation established over the years, and by gaining people's confidence, an on-line service will definitely be an advantage. And unless you are going to have supply-chain efficiency, you're going to find that quality and reliability will be compromised.... When you don't have the face-to-face contact with customers, service becomes the telling factor. In the physical store, you can sell with a reasonable amount of service. But on-line, the relationship becomes impersonal, and whoever is going to estab-lish better rapport with customers in their on-line business is obviously going to gain.

– Lester Quah

At the outset, Cold Storage extended its Triple Guarantee Policy to its on-line customers. This served to enhance the confidence level of its customers. Furthermore, its in-store business practices policy was easily adaptable to its on-line business.

Understanding the significance of personalised service in the absence of face-to-face contact, Cold Storage had gained a competitive edge in giving its customers that personal touch. The Dial-and-Deliver Centre was operated by a small team consisting of one manager and four or five people staffing incoming calls. Customers who chose to phone in their orders could ask to speak to the person they were used to, to ensure that they received a consistent quality of service. For customers ordering on-line, the Dial-and-Deliver staff were alerted only when there was a customer complaint or problem. In those instances, May Chew, the manager, would personally call up the customer to resolve the problem. So where the Company lacked face-to-face contact with on-line customers, May acted as the face of Cold Storage. There were plans to further personalise this service, which could entail May saying something different on-line every day and offering customers a direct number where she could be contacted.

Given that Cold Storage already had a strong reputation for the quality of its service and goods, the impact of achieving CaseTrust accreditation appeared to be moderate. However, since CaseTrust was based on a national effort and Cold Storage felt that it should be seen as part of that effort, accreditation served to affirm its commitment to CaseTrust's cause. Cold Storage identified itself with the CaseTrust objective in promoting good retailing practices in Singapore. Hence, CaseTrust was seen as a vehicle of goodwill and a voice box for consumers, not least because of the urgency with which CaseTrust dealt with complaints and responded to consumers.

Since launching its on-line business, Cold Storage had encountered no problems with consumers that could not be easily resolved within the Company's customer service framework. There had been minor disgruntles, such as late deliveries, when customers were compensated with a bottle of wine or a bouquet of flowers. However, being CaseTrusted gave them the benefit of meeting with CaseTrust to discuss various issues concerning on-line retailing on an ad-hoc basis. Furthermore, because CaseTrust was an arm of CASE, this made dealing with consumers easier, providing a mediator in the event of a dispute. Other benefits of being CaseTrusted were not easily quantifiable. It was difficult to say whether increased trust and confidence translated into an incremental dollar value as far as on-line sales volumes were concerned. Since Cold Storage operated its own established policy of guarantees, getting CaseTrust accreditation served to reinforce those commitments.

The full benefits of being CaseTrusted were yet to be realised. Most consumers were not aware of the CaseTrust scheme and did not consciously look out for the CaseTrust logo on e-tail Websites. Lester Quah was confident, however, that "Once their marketing effort starts, I think everyone is going to benefit.... Once we have the mass and the publicity, I'm sure that its value will increase."

Exhibit 1: Locations of Cold Storage stores around Singapore

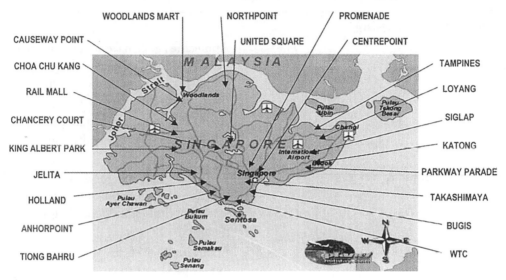

Exhibit 2:   CaseTrust assessment criteria (Web-based)

Section A: Browsing

1. Web policies

    Applicants shall have a written set of clear and relevant Web policies disclosing their business practices to their customers.

2. Webpages

    Applicants shall clearly state products/ services offered and any disclaimers on their Webpages.

3. Merchandise & services

    Applicants shall offer services and goods that are of merchandisable condition, i.e., the goods should be fit for their intended functions.

4. Pricing

    Applicants shall clearly and prominently display product prices/service rates and any additional charges to their customers without ambiguity.

5. Advertising & promotions

    Applicants shall ensure that all marketing communications materials, such as Webpages, advertisements, flyers and menus, are truthful, accurate and not misleading.

6. Behaviour of customer support staff

    Applicants shall monitor the behaviour of the customer support staff to ensure that they do not practise any unethical sales tactics.

Section B: Buying

1. Electronic ordering

    Applicants shall provide an on-line ordering system such as the 'shopping baskets' to their customers for them to state their purchases. They shall also provide customers information on the status of their orders.

2. Payment processing

    Applicants shall ensure accuracy in their billings.

Exhibit 2 (cont'd)

3. Electronic confirmation slips	Applicants shall provide customers with on-line confirmation slip listing the purchase details as proof of purchases.

Section C: After Sales

1. Delivery	Applicants shall deliver orders for merchandise according to the agreed timeframes and conditions.
2. Cancellation of orders	Applicants shall refund customers for payments made in the case of any cancellation of orders due to the company's fault.
3. Exchanges & refunds	Applicants shall declare and honour their exchanges and refund policies. Any exchanges or refunds shall be carried out promptly.
4. Feedback management	Applicants shall maintain an adequate system for monitoring queries, feedback and complaints so that the appropriate remedial action can be taken. They shall also implement service recovery programmes to handle complaints in a prompt manner.

Section D: Security/Confidentiality

1. Commitment to information security	Applicants shall obtain and use customers' particulars only if necessary.
2. Customers' particulars	Applicants shall be committed to maintaining the security of all their information systems.
3. Confidentiality	Applicants shall ensure that customer data is disclosed only to authorised persons and entities.

Exhibit 2 (cont'd)

4. Availability of information	Applicants shall, within their control, ensure that accessibility and usability of all information available on the Website is regularly maintained.
5. Security activity monitoring	Applicants shall ensure that measures are in place to detect and rectify any breach of security.

CHAPTER

■■■

7

Internet Marketing

OBJECTIVES

- To understand the potential of the Internet as a new marketing medium.
- To compare traditional and Internet marketing concepts.
- To understand how to manage customers in the marketspace.
- To describe the promotion and advertising tools available on the Internet.
- To recognise the Web measurement tools and the pros and cons of Internet research.

For decades, traditional marketing has been defined through four essential marketing components: product, price, place and promotion. While conventional marketing still provides useful insight into basic marketing concepts and remains an essential framework, a new business environment has transformed existing marketing paradigms.

A redefinition of some marketing concepts has become essential as a new business environment is emerging through the Internet. Since the Internet has the ability to combine functions and serve multiple tasks (e.g., advertising, public relations, order processing, logistics and distribution, customer service and more), juxtaposing existing marketing applications in the new Internet framework does not create an effective *Internet marketing* strategy. The Internet's uniqueness arises from its ability to act as a *market* and a *medium*. This means, the Internet can efficiently assume a multi–channel role, serving as a *market* for buyers and sellers to access each other in a hypermedia computer-mediated environment and also serving as a *medium* to conduct and execute business functions such as marketing, selling and distribution.

Customer relationships can be built by interaction through the Internet medium and this medium is a powerful tool to acquire detailed customer information. Information can then be organised, profiled and disseminated throughout an organisation with the purpose of developing personal relationships with the customer. Throughout customer relationship management, *trust* needs to be established to gain customer *loyalty*. This view transforms the role of marketing – and marketers – who must rise to the challenge of developing deeper customer relationships, with the assistance of technology in the new hypermedia environment, as a means of developing a successful and sustainable Internet marketing strategy.

In this chapter, we revisit the concept of 'marketspace' introduced in Chapter 1 and discuss the emerging marketing paradigm within the marketspace environment. In addition, we discuss the new Internet marketing concepts and compare key differences between traditional and emerging marketing fundamentals and strategies. Customer relationship management (CRM) and strategy is emphasised in the Internet environment and trust-based relationships are compared to traditional customer relationship approaches. Finally, we assess the Internet marketing and promotion tools and highlight the issues of Web measurement and Internet research.

MARKETING IN THE MARKETSPACE

The Internet presents a fundamentally different environment for marketing activities than the traditional marketing media. Technology is challenging the old paradigms of marketing and inverting them. Virtually every aspect of Internet-based marketing strategy – including advertising, pricing, word-of-mouth influence, distribution channels and product development – differs from the manner in which firms are used to doing business. Consider the following fundamental changes:

❑ The Internet provides a virtual hypermedia environment allowing a diffusion of text, media, icons and audio tools; it has the capability to bring together previously unrelated technologies, products, services and information often from widely disparate sources.
❑ The Internet gives consumers greater control over their search for and acquisition of decision-making information to make purchases.

❑ Consumers can interact with the medium (Net surfing); they become active participants in the marketing process. They can provide product-related content to the medium, freeing them from their traditionally passive role as receivers of marketing communications.[1]

❑ Firms can interact with the medium (B2B marketing as in CommerceNet); businesses and consumers can provide content to the medium.

❑ Businesses can operate without physical market presence.

❑ Consumers can purchase and acquire products and services on the Internet which, in some cases, can be delivered instantaneously.

❑ Leveraging the Internet, businesses can reap the benefits of traditional vertical integration (e.g., economies of scale and scope, low transaction costs) without the ownership of assets.

In Chapter 1 we introduced the transformation of a marketplace to marketspace. Three key elements of change leading this transformation are content, context and infrastructure. The illustration we used to distinguish the physical marketplace from the virtual marketspace was the example of a car auction. In this example, there are three characteristics that differentiate market systems: the content of the transactions, the context in which they occur and the infrastructure that enables them to occur. The main differentiating factor is the radical departure from thinking about 'physical places' to thinking about 'information spaces' instead. Once again, we revisit this notion.

The concept of 'marketspace' where geography, physical interface and time limitations are eradicated, leads to the discussion of the Internet as a *market* and a *medium* where content, context and infrastructure are desegregated. The separation of the three basic elements of the conventional value proposition provides consumers with a rich, interactive platform where they have a great degree of control over their purchasing experience. Similarly, through desegregation of what is being offered (content), how it is being offered (context), and what enables the transaction to occur (infrastructure), companies are able to find new ways to add to consumer value.

The Internet fundamentally changes customers' expectations about convenience, speed, price and service. This shift to customer empowerment must be accompanied with a reformed marketing strategy for firms to capitalise on establishing and leveraging personalised relationships with customers. As a result, the old methods of advertising, merchandising, and providing interface and service no longer fully meet the needs of

---

[1] Hoffman & Novak (1995).

the evolving consumer. For example, unlike radio, television, newspapers and magazines, the Internet is not a one-to-many mass medium. Rather, it is an interactive medium enabling people to personalise their experience by choosing among a huge array of content. Thus, developers and marketers must reconstruct the function for the interactive, many-to-many medium in which consumers actively choose whether or not to approach firms.

As a marketing medium, the Internet promises opportunities for reaching new consumer groups and is an alternative way to offer low-priced and value-added products or services. It is due to these differences, and the fact that marketing is ultimately responsible for customer relationships, that global marketing on the Internet or via the Internet requires new marketing strategies. Increasingly, the emphasis will be in terms of negotiating mutually beneficial relationships with customers, heightening the dependence of buyers and sellers on one another, sharing resources and developing new markets and products together. What this means is that Internet and Internet-based marketing will require an ability to understand the specific requirements and needs of customers who are interacting in the marketspace.

TRADITIONAL MARKETING VS. INTERNET MARKETING

The increasing popularity of the Internet as a business vehicle is due to its current size and future growth prospects, its attractive demographics, and its potential to provide an efficient channel for advertising and marketing, and even the direct distribution of certain goods and information services. Along with these increases in efficiency, Internet marketing proves to be more effective overall than marketing through traditional media [refer to **Table 1**].

One of the most prominent marketing changes is a shift from the passive marketing model, where firms provide content through a medium to a mass market of consumers, to a many-to-many model, in an environment where there is interchange among firms and consumers. Also, the traditional demarcation between advertising, marketing and merchandising has blurred and continues to dissolve over time. As Rayport and Sviokla (1994) have pointed out, marketspace provides a platform to telescope the traditional sequence of market research, market testing, product rollout and product launch into the single activity of selling. In this light, applying old mecha-

Table 1:   Comparison of traditional marketing vs. Internet marketing concepts

Marketing function	Traditional marketing	Internet marketing
PRICE		
Market entry	• Market penetration pricing model. A product is launched with a low initial price to gain rapid market share • Niche pricing model. A product is launched, priced at premium, to create a niche market	• Traditional price models • Zero-based pricing. A company offers a free product (e.g., computer) by either giving customers an *option* or *requiring* them to purchase/subscribe to peripheral services (e.g., subscribe to the affiliated Internet Service Provider for a certain number of hours per month)
PRODUCT		
Physical	• Product-centric environment (focus on 'physical' product attributes)	• Focus on 'bundling' outputs catered to the customer and designed to add value
Search costs	High	Low
Time	• Product availability controlled by companies. Usually, availability is restricted to store timings, etc.	• The Internet is a 24/7 (24-hours, 7-days-a-week) medium • Some products and services can be downloaded immediately, for example, software, information and entertainment
Information	• Information content and accessibility is controlled by the company	• The consumer controls information content and accessibility • Consumers can provide product-related content to the medium • Product reviews can be easily obtained through third-party firms

Table 1 (cont'd)

Marketing function	Traditional marketing	Internet marketing
Information		• Information is an integral part of product support

PROMOTION

Marketing function	Traditional marketing	Internet marketing
Costs	• Traditional marketing is four times more expensive than Internet marketing (Verity and Hoffman, 1994)	• Marketing on the Internet results in ten times as many units sold with one-tenth the advertising budget (Potter, 1994)
Advertising models	• One-to-many advertising model prevalent	• Mass customisation • Personalisation of goods
Mediums	• TV • Radio • Billboard • Magazines • Newspapers • Direct mailing campaigns	• All traditional marketing mediums • Internet sites • Banner ads • Click-throughs • Mailing lists • Usenet groups

DISTRIBUTION

Marketing function	Traditional marketing	Internet marketing
	• Physical storefronts • Physical interactivity • Distribution networks essential to provide access to goods • Vendors extract value from customers	• WWW acts as a distribution channel • Products/services can sometimes be downloaded immediately (e.g., music, information) • Constant accessibility (24/7 concept) • The Internet has established certain characteristics: extremely low entry and exit barriers for firms • Increasing irrelevance of distribution intermediaries; emergence of new intermediaries

nistic marketing paradigms and duplicating physical-world storefronts in electronic settings are not the desirable transformation for businesses.[2]

The existing marketing concepts are no longer enough for the emerging and increasingly diverse, complex and interdependent virtual business environment. Instead, at this stage in the evolution of the Internet as a commercial medium, developers and marketers should develop new systems to permit virtual transactions directly over the network rather than through parallel traditional channels. Marketing innovations should take advantage of the medium's inherent interactivity to 'play value', and attempt to develop stimulating and exciting content-rich environments.

E-RELATIONSHIPS

In contrast to the conventional product-centric, vendor-centric markets, the Internet will shift the advantage to consumers. Markets in which power shifts to the consumer might be called 'reverse markets' – markets in which customers seek out and extract value from vendors, rather than the other way around. In reverse markets, consumers can easily switch vendors.[3] Such consumer empowerment is primarily induced by the profusion of products/services information available on the Internet. As a result of low search costs, customers can easily find the most suitable vendors and extract as much value as possible from them. In **Table 2**, we conduct a detailed analysis of CRM and trust, and how the Internet is capable of transforming some shortcomings of traditional customer relationships.

From the vendors' perspective, a profound shift is also occurring on the basis of competition in the virtual marketspace. Under the milieu of the network economy, competitive advantage for many businesses lies in the ability to capture unique information about customers, in particular, information that is not accessible to other vendors. For example, airlines develop frequent flier profiles that are not accessible to other airlines. Banks use information about account balances and individual funds flow to market various financial products to their customers. Even grocers create loyalty card programmes in order to build and act on the proprietary profiles of their customers. The concept of profiling allows businesses to migrate its target markets through different stages of relationships, both with the consumer and with specific

---

[2] Hoffman & Novak (1995).

[3] Hagel & Singer (1999).

Table 2: CRM and trust in the marketplace vs. marketspace

Type of relationship	Characteristics	Marketing drawbacks	CRM in marketspace
Fiduciary (professional/ legal)	• Trusted relationship with customers • Rich data set on existing customers • Trust may not apply outside a particular business • Data stored in product-centric legacy systems • Generally not risk taking or innovative	• Trust declining, particularly in related industries, i.e., healthcare • Little experience with database marketing • Regulations may restrict the use of data	**Processes** • Developing highly effective means of handling phone and e-mail inquiries in a timely and effective manner is essential in establishing good customer service. It is especially important in high trust relationships. • Integrate database systems with customer service operations to gain customer intelligence and to facilitate the design of an effective customer interface program. • With each acquisition tactic, the database can facilitate the sales process by matching customer needs with tailored promotions and special offers. • Rich information content, for example, URL: http://www.healtheon.com provides medical advice, tips and useful links to other medical Websites. • Ensure internal processes reflect customer service expectations perceived or promoted on the Website; use database to create a personalised approach. **Technology** • Use software to automate processes and queries, i.e., FAQs. • Integrate databases and Internet telephony applications to give customer service representatives the power to capture and utilise customer information.

Table 2 (cont'd)

Type of relationship	Characteristics	Marketing drawbacks	CRM in marketspace
Fiduciary (professional/ legal)			• Either subcontract or create in-house expertise to leverage off database marketing. Can send existing customers newsletter referring to the corporate Website. **Strategy** • In the end, customer-centric brands require an intensely personal relationship between the business and the customer. For example, the traditional family doctor or the local financial adviser exemplifies the kind of relationship required. These relationships begin with a limited request for information from the customer; in exchange, the doctor or adviser quickly turns that information into helpful advice. Ideally, a series of value exchanges creates deep bonds of trust that deliver on the customer-centric brand promise: 'I know more about you than anyone else and can be trusted to use this information and insight in your interest'.
Contractual (B2B)	• Broad set of products sold, thereby creating broad customer profiles	• Typically vendor focused rather than customer focused	**Process** • Implement B2B e-commerce business model to consolidate relationships with vendors and streamline logistic operations. • Shift business with partners on-line, through the support of extranets.

Table 2 (cont'd)

Type of relationship	Characteristics	Marketing drawbacks	CRM in marketspace
Contractual (B2B)	• Skills managing relationships with vendors • Transactional relationship with customers • Quite focused profiles	• Data stored in product–centric information systems	• Design Webpages to deliver customised services site with focus on the customer relationship management process. • Focus on providing product and service information, integrated with other innovative promotions, such as affiliate vendor or merchant marketing. • Use Website to gain customer feedback and use information to decide which e-commerce business model to pursue. Bundling information and products through its multiple vendors may be feasible (aggregator). **Technology** • Focus on providing customer-centric technologies as a way to find new customers and keep new and established ones returning. Shift from a product–centric information system to a customer–centric information system designed to encapsulate customer information and disseminate it for effective utilisation throughout the company. • Use multimedia to create a rich and interactive Website with superior visual support for product presentation and brand building. • Provide easy access to customer information to employees and business partners to leverage when interacting with a customer.

Table 2 (cont'd)

Type of relationship	Characteristics	Marketing drawbacks	CRM in marketspace
Contractual (B2B)			• Use CRM applications in combination with other technology, such as call centres, to allow sales people to focus on establishing customer loyalty through adding value, rather than focusing on processes. CRM technology allows companies to capture exactly what the nature of a customer's transaction and relationship is with the company. • Develop contingency plan in case of systems breakdown. **Strategy** • Use customer profiles to create specific target segments and to differentiate its marketing strategy. • Force customers on-line through an effective marketing strategy and complement the promotion of Website through traditional media. However, establish other communication channels to give customer the choice. • Use the Web to differentiate company, consolidate brand image and differentiate product/service offering.
Mutual (communal)	• Many have sustainable relationships with specific audiences	• Not necessarily a trust-based relationship	**Processes** • Leverage existing relationships and use that information to build a specific customer database. This information can be used to customise a company's marketing strategy. • Sell specific customer profiles to other vendors or create profit-sharing agreement. For example, for every customer purchase through media company, it receives X percent. A long-term strategy with potential for growth through increased sustainability.

Table 2 (cont'd)

Type of relationship	Characteristics	Marketing drawbacks	CRM in marketspace
Mutual (communal)	• Potential to know customers well and to build profiles	• Minimal, if any, profiles kept	• Use traditional media to promote its Website to customers. • Develop strategic alliances with other high-profile companies to improve its image and provide 'deeper' customer value in terms of information and services. • None of these brands says anything about knowing the customer as an individual with unique needs and preferences. This is the challenge and opportunity for customer-centric brands. **Technology** • Use technology to create a personalised customer experience, with the support of existing customer profiles. For example, extranets can be used to sustain and cultivate relationships with existing customers and develop new ones. • Integrated use of the telephone, data and Website. The integration of traditional phone support with Web use allows agents to sell directly to customers viewing goods and services on-line. **Strategy** • Vendors should focus on drawing people to them, rather than intrusively reaching out for them. • Vendors should maximise the value customers receive from the purchase and use of their products and services, by providing tailored help in purchasing and using those products and services.

Table 2 (cont'd)

Type of relationship	Characteristics	Marketing drawbacks	CRM in marketspace
			• Vendors should mobilise the resources of third parties and focus on assembling and packaging these resources to meet the needs of each individual. • Build networking community related to the content. • Allow merchants to access the audience.
Altruistic association relationship	• Strong relationship with constituency • Deep profiles, for examples for fund-raising purposes • Broad, trust-based relationships	• Frequently lack a commercial focus • Likely to lack resources to invest in marketing	**Process** A highly effective marketing force is necessary. Rich content and information on the organisation's core beliefs and issues can be posted on the Website. **Technology** Use discussion groups and chat forum tools to create traffic to the Website through the discussion of related topics. **Strategy** Linking its Website to the right sites is the most important strategic decision, for example, for NGOs. Due to their in-depth customer information and profiles, NGOs can develop very specific and targeted marketing strategies. These strategies can help them implement the most cost-effective electronic solutions.

distribution channels. Technology has facilitated a marketing strategy transformation, from product management to segment management to individual relationship management.[4]

Therefore, regardless of the Internet business model involved (content aggregators, transaction aggregators, virtual communities or portal businesses), the economics depend heavily on the assumption that the company will capture unique information about prospects and customers and will leverage this information to generate advertising revenue. As a result, marketers are shifting marketing expenditures from broad-reach advertising to targeted marketing driven by customers' individual preferences and profiles.

The impact is not limited to traditional, advertising-supported media. Although many retail stores still heavily depend on traditional media to gain exposure for on-line business, the efficiency of this model is questioned as the Internet has the ability to transform all existing multimedia roles. For example, what happens when the infomediary can use the superior targeting capability embedded in its client purchasing profiles to deliver them only to the most receptive customers purchasing competitor products?[5] What happens when the infomediary downloads promotional offers directly into the smart card that customers will one day use to make their purchases in the retail store? By contrast, concentrating solely on advertising or promotional revenue appears rather limited in that it does not exploit the expanding reach and changing roles brought about by the Internet.

These foreseeable changes are expected to cause a reaction among vendors. In an environment of far greater selection and easy access to information, the scarce resource becomes customer attention. As a result, vendors are pursuing a strategy to capture rich information and analyse it and subsequently use the information to deliver personalised products and services cost effectively through integration across multiple business systems. It is deemed that vendors who can successfully 'bundle' related products/

---

[4] The one-to-one advantage, Rometty (1999).

[5] An infomediary is a Website that provides specialised information on behalf of producers of goods and services and their potential customers. The term is a composite of 'information' and 'intermediary'. The advent of the Web has made possible quick 24-hour access to information databases that previously were not available. Gathering these information aggregates and adding services to them is now the business of companies like the Thomas Register of Manufacturers who can bring a base of information from the print medium to the Web. Perhaps more importantly, infomediaries are Websites that gather, organise and link to the new information and services that are being added to the Web (URL: http://www.whatis.com).

services and provide the best value for customers, will reap profits in the future. Such vendors' initial costs will include the expenditure for implementing a business model capable of integrating a 'package' for customers and the costs of accumulating customer profiles. Those who develop these skills early will develop a competitive edge and become harder to compete with in the future. Thus, marketing will evolve to an exercise of identifying, differentiating, interacting and finally customising products and services.

CUSTOMER RELATIONSHIP STRATEGY

Firms are increasingly realising the importance of managing lifelong relationships with their customers and this strategy requires companies to know more about customers and actively anticipate their needs and desires. In **Figure 1**, we introduce the marketing pyramid, which can be used to design a full spectrum CRM strategy.

The pyramid reflects customer segmentation, with the top layer qualifying as the existing customers and inherently the most valuable, while the lower buyers relate to potential prospects. We define visitors as prospective customers, for example, Web surfers who have accessed the company URL to find particular information. Qualified prospects have passed the company's qualification screen. Non-committed customers may be one-time buyers and buyers who have no particular affinity to the company. Loyal customers refer to customers who, all things being equal, would select a particu-

Figure 1:   Marketing pyramid[6]

---

[6] Adapted from Silverstein (1998).

lar company for a purchase. It is every company's goal to gain as many loyal customers as a greater share of its customer portfolio, since the high costs associated with gaining customers can be crippling and the costs of losing existing customers can be even more profound. In **Table 3**, we quote some relevant facts on customer loss.

Table 3:   Customer maintenance facts and figures

- It costs six times more to sell to a new customer than to sell to an existing one.
- A typical dissatisfied customer will tell eight to ten people about his or her experience.
- A company can boost its profits by 85 percent when it increases its annual customer retention by only five percent.
- The odds of selling a product to a new customer are 15 percent, whereas the odds of selling a product to an existing customer are 50 percent.
- Seventy percent of complaining customers will do business with the company again if it quickly takes care of a service snag.
- More than 90 percent of existing companies do not have the necessary sales and service integration to support e-commerce.

Source: Kalakota, R. & Robinson, M. (1999), *e-Business: Roadmap for Success.*

These figures are indicative of potential financial and business damage caused through customer relationship mismanagement. However, this loss can be even more staggering in the marketspace due to the critical importance of building and maintaining long-term client relationships for growth and sustainability. Although traditional marketing theorists have always emphasised customer importance, customer loyalty implementation in the marketplace has neither been widespread nor a critical element of marketing strategy for most enterprises.

Throughout the early 1990s, the emphasis on customer service had been growing in importance and businesses implemented customer management in various forms, but at best, strategies often resulted in fragmented efforts. However, a successful e-business required not only an integrated and full spectrum CRM strategy, but also consistent practical implementation to experience long-term growth and survival. We concede that although classic CRM concepts inherently remain the same, the nature of their implementation will gradually change in the marketspace environment. Well-administered CRM strategies will help with the conversion of inquirers to buyers and increase the purchase frequency of the most valued customers.

At a broad level, CRM strategies need to identify and address value, from both the customer and business perspectives. A strong customer strategy can be built by predicting individual preferences and needs well enough to be anticipatory and proactive in the delivery of the right message to the right customer segment at the right time via the right media. As an enterprise, businesses in the marketspace can put the emphasis on customers, rather than on the product portfolio. It becomes essential to understand who the customers are and their value to the organisation.[7]

Tools, such as CRM, are increasingly vital to building a customer-centric enterprise. When asked to identify the most important benefits their organisation receives from its investment in customer management tools and applications, technology managers at InformationWeek 500 companies mentioned 'customer satisfaction' nine out of ten times. Other benefits noted included the ability to provide faster response to customer inquiries, increased efficiency through automation, having a deeper knowledge of customers, getting more marketing or cross-selling opportunities, identifying the most profitable customers, receiving customer feedback that leads to new and improved products or services, doing more one-to-one marketing, and obtaining information that can be shared with the company's business partners.[8]

When developing a CRM strategy, it is useful to remember that loyal customers are responsible for near-term profits, but qualified prospects contribute to future earnings.

CUSTOMER RELATIONSHIP MANAGEMENT

In the following analysis, we illustrate the processes involved in transforming customer relationships. **Figure 2** illustrates the four stages involved:

- ❑ Stage 1 involves a business attracting 'visitors' to its business site.
- ❑ Stage 2 is the acquisition stage during which a business designates strategies to secure the customer through a unique value proposition, with the purpose of establishing a customer's trust.
- ❑ The retention stage requires a strategy to convert a one-time buyer into a loyal customer, through establishing mutual trust between the firm and the customer.

---

[7] Customer value is typically represented by how much customers have spent with your company and success can be measured in terms of lifetime value/profitability.

[8] Violino (1999).

Figure 2: Customer relationship management model

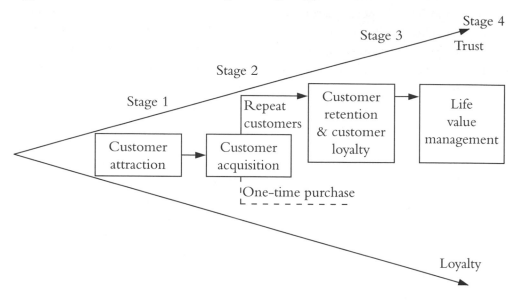

❏ The customer loyalty stage involves a long-term strategy to maintain customer value through established mutual trust.

Attraction

In the information intensive Internet environment, the firm is no longer broadcasting a single communication to many consumers, but tailoring its communications according to consumers' varied interests and needs. This practice involves implementation through the unique process of network navigation in which the consumer chooses what information (if any) to receive from the firm. Thus, marketers must begin to examine the manner in which these more collaborative communication efforts should proceed. Marketers can utilise the opportunities for customer interaction inherent in the Internet in at least three ways as follows:

1. The design of new products.
2. The development of product and marketing strategy.
3. The innovation of content.

These shifts in channel power hold important implications for consumer participation in the marketing process. For example, consumers may collaborate not only in idea generation and product design, but also in the marketing communication effort itself. This is due to the Internet interactivity that gives consumers much greater control of the message. Such control may manifest itself in startlingly new ways. For example, it is feasible for consumers interested in purchasing big-ticket durables, such as cars or appliances, to broadcast their interest and solicit open bids from different firms.[9]

Brands in the traditional market are typically a representation of either the vendor (i.e., P&G) or the products offered by the vendor (K-Mart). Brands have been product-centric, used by customers as benchmarks for quality and price, or service expectations. Marketplace vendors either have a reputation for high-quality products (i.e., Tiffany) or excellent service (Singapore Airlines) or the product itself is a reliable or low-cost product.

However, branding on-line is more challenging than in the off-line environment. Thousands or even millions of people can experience a company's 'brand' simultaneously, when they encounter it on the Internet. Therefore, on-line brand management becomes a component of managing an integrated customer relationship strategy.

Since mistakes are so visible on the Web and switching to competitors is so easy, companies need to ensure that a customer's first 'total on-line experience' (i.e., aesthetic, interactive, speed, service offering, customer service and so on) results in retaining customer attention.

In customer attraction and especially during the customer acquisition processes, brand management plays a critical role in affecting customer perception and behaviour. In an environment where return on attention becomes the key measure of performance, it is important that brands move away from the traditional product-centric approach and evolve into a 'customer-centric' approach. This means the following:

- ❑ Brands assure customers that the vendor knows and understands that individual customer better than anyone else does, and promises to tailor products and services to meet that individual customer's needs better than anyone else. These brands thereby assure customers that they will receive a very high return on any attention they focus on the owner of the brand.
- ❑ Brands offer the promise of increasing returns; the more attention the customer gives to a brand, the more the brand owner will learn about the customer, and the stronger the value of the brand becomes to the customer.

---

[9] Cutler (1990).

amazon.com, for example, has been beating marketing challenges from Barnes and Noble continuously, based on the fact that it has built a respected brand and developed a reputation for superior customer service.

Acquisition[10]

In the process to acquire customers, successful marketers need to learn the following:

- ❏ List themselves effectively in search environments.
- ❏ Engage the consumer at the time of purchase.
- ❏ Tailor products and services in ways that reduce incentives for switching to other vendors.

As the Internet is a source of information overload for customers, there is a very short time span to get a message across and keep it memorable. This is a critical stage in converting the visitor into a qualified prospect. We concede that establishing a higher level of customer trust in the firm seems critical at this stage for the relationship to evolve from a one-time purchase into a longer-term prospect and ultimately a loyal customer. (The issues of trust are covered in detail in Chapter 6.)

Customer acquisition is a critical aspect of an on-line firm's overall marketing strategy. The Internet's ability to integrate value from different businesses becomes apparent when competitors create strategic alliances for mutually beneficial business strategies. For example, there are several ways on-line retailers and media companies can help multiply each other's business. Leading portal players, such as Yahoo! and AOL, have transformed themselves from search engines into media companies in the business of aggregating traffic. There are several ways for businesses to leverage one another to create business advantages:

- ❏ Portals or media companies can make a deal with potential Internet retailers as a way to capitalise on their chief asset – *the eyeballs* they can deliver. The eyeballs refer to the number of guaranteed users that portals will provide exposure to, for example, a retailer's banner.
- ❏ Ideally, media companies want to create alliances with on-line retailers who can bring content that helps the portal player differentiate its services (and potentially increase the number of eyeballs).

---

[10] In 1999, more than 50 percent of consumer marketing expenditure was directed to pre-emptively capturing the attention of the consumer in advance of the purchase.

❑ Portals can enter into revenue–sharing deals, foregoing cash upfront for a profit cut from an on–line retailer's sales.

❑ Affiliate programmes can link a company's site to others to draw customers with a particular interest in the business' product. amazon.com Inc., for example, has more than 200,000 affiliates, who can gain as much as five percent to 15 percent on the sale of items purchased through the amazon.com link. CDNow Inc. garners 25 percent of its customers through its affiliate programmes.

For on-line firms to calculate expected customer value, the retailer must predict the cash flow a new customer will generate over time and discount it to determine the customer's net present value. An economically rational merchant should be willing to pay less than this expected value to acquire the customer. The problem is that this value is much easier to describe than to calculate. Among the uncertainties are average customer expenditures and customer turnover. Also, the retailer must estimate how many new visitors the portal will deliver and how many of those will become customers.[11]

Suppose a fictional firm, Cozmo-opticz (a sunglasses firm) calculates that it would be worth paying US$10 for a customer. A major portal player offers to make Cozmo-opticz the leading sunglasses vendor in its hot new eyewear section for US$100,000. The portal assures Cozmo-opticz that it can drive ten million viewers to the section next year. Cozmo-opticz then calculates that one percent of these viewers will click through to its site, and that two percent of those will actually make a purchase (these are typical industry numbers). This means the company will acquire 2,000 customers for a price of US$50. This is US$40 more than it was willing to pay. Companies cannot rely on any previous trends on which to base their decision. Therefore, each company has to toy with various cost/benefit analyses to determine what CRM strategy is most feasible in its particular business.

Sometimes, firms tend to get carried away with the Internet hype and do not appreciate the value of traditional marketing mediums despite their applicability and significance. Traditional customer acquisition strategies still have much to offer:[12]

---

[11] The following customer acquisition costs were discerned in a few industries by year 2000. Credit card companies paid US$50–75 to acquire customers; long-distance telephone providers typically paid US$100; mortgage lenders paid between US$100 and US$250 to acquire a mortgage, and on-line trading companies, such as E★Trade, paid approximately US$250–700.

[12] Gurley (1998).

❏ *Do the math*. e-Commerce firms should be able to articulate the true cost of customer acquisition and know how much they are willing to pay for each incremental customer.

❏ *Look off-line*. Savvy on-line retailers will also employ traditional media, such as radio and print to gather customers. Before spending millions on on-line distribution, other costs of marketing alternatives should be compared, including TV and direct mail.

❏ *Pick partners carefully*. Not everyone is selling a mass-market product like books. Why spend a lot to reach the widest possible audience? More focused niche distribution players may be better partners than major portal players.

❏ *Focus on brand and services*. If customers are not 'locked-in' with a strong brand or differentiated services, then customers are not being acquired − they are rented. A potential market share loss is possible because firms may have thought they have acquired a certain number of customers, but actually had not.[13]

Retention and Loyalty

"Customer acquisition is six times more expensive than customer retention," says Peter Reville, Vice President of The Willard & Shullman Group, a Greenwich, Connecticut-based market research company. "Keeping that in mind, it makes a heck of a lot of sense to retain your customers."[14] Yet many companies do not adequately address customers' problems. That is a mistake for many reasons: first, customers with problems often stop being customers; second, irate clients tie up a company's servicing function; third, customer complaints often fall on sales people, and if representatives are addressing problems, they are not selling. Also, identifying problems may reveal areas for operational improvement.

A major shift from conventional marketing to Internet marketing has been the change from the concept of 'customer satisfaction' to the principle of 'customer loyalty'. By creating loyal relationships, organisations can enjoy the benefit of up-sell and cross-sell, improve customer retention and reduce the cost of service. Customer loyalty is the driving factor towards developing long-term profitability.

Loyalty has been traditionally defined in terms of its consequences: repurchase intent, referral intent, share of purchase and actual repurchase. For true loyalty, Internet-style, companies must go beyond customer delight and try to address and implement a

---

[13] Swigor (1999).

[14] Rasmusson (1999).

higher level of 'total trust', conceptually similar to 'total' quality. The performance standard is zero 'trust defects'.[15] The companies that are most successful in building and sustaining these relationships tend to do the following four things especially well:

- ❏ First, they make customers feel so comfortable about expressing their views that these customers speak out immediately when, for example, a solution has been created that is workable but irrelevant because it solves a problem that is no longer a pressing need.
- ❏ Second, these companies make it very easy for customers to deliver their views directly to the people developing products.
- ❏ Third, these masters of relationship building demonstrate how well they have listened by quickly delivering products that reflect what they have learned.
- ❏ And finally, they think through the entire lifecycle of the customer's experience with their products, and make it simple and cost-effective to purchase, install, use, manage and upgrade their offerings. While these practices are only common sense, what separates good intentions from consistent results is committing the resources and creating the processes to make them happen.

MyPoints.com: Web-based Loyalty Programme

MyPoints.com is the world's most popular Internet direct marketing services and reward programme and a top-ten shopping site according to PCData On-line. Launched in the US in 1996, the MyPoints Program has attracted over 15 million members, with 25,000 new members signing every day, and a reach of over 12 percent of US Internet users.

MyPoints® is the company's database-driven direct marketing service: enabling businesses to identify, acquire and retain customers, while consumers are able to make the most of the Internet. The programme is free and consumers register on-line by providing a detailed list of their interests, so products or services sent match with their preferences. Reward points are earned by interacting with the programme's advertisers – on-line or off-line – such as reading and responding to e-mail, visiting participating Websites, participating in polls, taking up a trial offer, dining out through MyPoints® Dining! or purchasing through MyPoints® Shopping! Customers can redeem reward points for gift certificates,

---

[15] Hart & Johnson (1999).

prepaid phone cards and travel awards from more than 50 brand-name reward providers. MyPoints is also a leading developer of an Internet loyalty infrastructure – MyPoints® Network – and custom-branded rewards programmes based on the Company's proprietary technology platform – the Digital Loyalty Engine™.

The Company is expanding its reach, launching MyPoints Europe (www.MyPoints.co.uk) on 24 September 2000. MyPoints Europe is a joint venture between MyPoints.com Inc. and The Great Universal Stores PLC (GUS). With over 50 leading brands participating, it expects to attract over five percent of the UK's on-line users within a year of operation. Jupiter Communications predicts household Internet usage will more than double, from 34.2 percent in penetration in 2000 to 71.6 percent in 2005.

Sources: M2 Communications Limited (2000); MyPoints.com Inc. (2000).

In the marketspace environment, not only is it more difficult to keep a customer's attention, but there are fewer barriers keeping them from buying a competitor's product or service. All that a customer has to do to change loyalty is to simply type http://www.anycompetitor.com!

The trick is for companies to figure out how to use e-commerce to make themselves indispensable to their customers. The approach can vary from providing hard-to-find information to simplifying tasks to spending more face time with important clients. But regardless of which tack they take, companies should have specific goals. Loyalty has become a corporate-level strategy whereby firms are geared towards building unbreakable lifetime relationships with their customers. Some of the rules identified to realise these expectations are based on the following four key principles:

1. Proactively identifying a customer's unique situation at any point in time. A firm has to make the effort to get to know their customers one at a time. If a company has up to hundreds of thousands of customers, the cost-effective method is to continuously collect, analyse and use data to create targeted programmes directed to prospects and customers with the greatest profit potential. Personalisation is the key concept here and the first step on the road to personalised customer service is crucial.

2. Creating rules for the actions that need to take place. Through integrating database systems with customer service operations, companies gain increased customer intelligence. The implementation of integrated database and Internet

telephony applications, placed at the fingertips of customer service representatives (CSRs), creates an excellent foundation to effectively capture and utilise customer information. CSRs not only provide the face to the customer, but also obtain and record invaluable information regarding customer history, provide answers to frequently asked questions and offer knowledge about other products or services the customer may buy.

3. Executing those actions across all company access/interaction channels.

4. Reporting the effect of the actions on customer loyalty. Without successfully retaining profitable customers, companies fight an uphill battle to expand the bottom line. A consistently updated, well-managed database is an essential component in helping to monitor satisfaction levels and predicting churn patterns in virtually any industry throughout the customer lifecycle. Once churn candidates are identified, detailed customer information can be displayed for CSRs who can offer incentives to retain profitable customers.

---

eLoyalty.com: Global Specialist in Building Customer Loyalty

Formerly Technology Solution Company's ECM (Enterprise Customer Management) business unit, eLoyalty was launched in June 1999 (www.eloyaltyco.com) as the world's first and only global business/management consulting and systems integration organisation specialising in building customer loyalty. It has over 900 customer relationship experts worldwide in 14 offices throughout North America, Europe and Australia, and has already served hundreds of international industry leaders such as financial services, Internet and telecommunications markets, etc. eLoyalty has already provided loyalty solutions to organisations such as General Motors Corporation, Lucent Technologies, Morgan Stanley Dean Witter, Bank of America, BBC, Deutsche Telecom, Virgin Atlantic Airways, Dow Chemical and Ford Motor Company.

A combination of a focused vision, proven business models, processes, technologies, support methodologies and best practices create eLoyalty's end-to-end loyalty solutions. eLoyalty's eCRM is an expansion of CRM to further include the Internet, e-mail and Web chat across each division of a company. eLoyalty has a unique loyalty process which helps companies identify customer loyalty goals, improve customer retention, increase up-selling and cross-selling opportunities, reduce sales costs and increase customer referrals. It has an array of proficiencies and capabilities that include: Loyalty Strategy, Business Case, Loyalty Process Design, Loyalty Architecture, eBusiness, Systems Integration, Active Change and Learning, Channel Optimisation, Loyalty Support, Loyalty Foundation, Marketing, Sales Force Optimisation, Customer Service, and Field Service and Logistics.

Source: eLoyalty (2000).

CUSTOMER VALUE INTEGRATION

Earlier in this chapter, we highlighted the change from a product-centric market to a market that focuses on information management. According to the marketing pyramid in Figure 1, customers in the three lower segments of the pyramid demand a higher degree of accuracy and service in terms of company background and information on products and services. On the other hand, at this stage companies want to have access to more information about consumers, their needs, habits, and buying behaviour and pattern.

Faced with limited time and unlimited choices, customers have begun to focus their attention on companies that best understand their needs and deliver highly tailored bundles of products and services. To respond to these needs, firms are creating alliances and moving towards an integrated business approach. e-Commerce-based companies are realising that the Internet's universal connectivity has enabled them to create a three-way 'information partnership' with suppliers and customers, by treating them as collaborators who together find ways of improving efficiency across the entire chain of supply and demand, and then sharing the benefits. John Dobbs of Cambridge Technology Partners, a leading systems integrator, helpfully defines value integration as: "A process of collaboration that optimises all internal and external activities involved in delivering greater perceived value to the ultimate customer."

E-MARKETING: PROMOTION AND ADVERTISING TOOLS AND CONCEPTS

What these myriad of changes from the marketplace to the marketspace herald is a metamorphosis of the 'traditional' marketing promotion mix so that 'in a world where traditional marketplace signposts no longer matter, product becomes place becomes promotion'.[16] In the marketspace, a new marketing paradigm is considered necessary

---

[16] Rayport & Sviokla (1994), p. 142.

because the Internet presents a fundamentally different environment for marketing activities than the traditional media.[17] In comparing the traditional marketing communications model for mass media with a new model underlying marketing communications in a hypermedia computer-mediated environment (CME), we consider the following fundamental changes which influence Internet advertising management:

❑ The Internet is both a promotional channel and a distribution channel where advertising and sales can take place concurrently.
❑ Advertising costs on the Internet are lower than in the traditional media.
❑ The Internet provides a higher rate of information dissemination.
❑ The Internet has a worldwide audience not limited by physical boundaries.
❑ The Internet supports interactivity.
❑ The Internet promotes consumer self-selection and offers a level of self-control.
❑ The Internet adds value in terms of providing a rich mix of multimedia, including audio, visual and a computer-mediated environment.

In the process of redefining marketing, marketers need to rethink, for example, the role of brands, and need to redeploy marketing spending. This redeployment will have profound effects on a broad range of businesses that depend on advertising and promotion expenditures from product and service vendors, including television, radio, newspapers and magazines, as well as sports franchises, retailers and agents (i.e., celebrity talent representatives). So far, television networks and advertising-supported cable channels, such as CNN and ESPN, have felt somewhat insulated from competition for their advertising revenue because of the importance of video in communicating brand-oriented advertising.

ADVERTISING HITS!

Given that Internet marketers can now restrict viewers' access to targeted ads and ensure that those targeted ads are seen by exactly the number of people the advertiser purchased, marketers can provide advertisers with detailed statistics on demand.[18] Yet,

---

[17] Hoffman & Novak (1996).

[18] The Internet Advertising Bureau reported that only US$267 million in revenue was generated from Internet ads in 1999, but the rate of growth that this medium is experiencing translated into a 45 percent increase from the third quarter to the last. By the year 2000, ad revenues are expected to reach US$4.8 billion.

in many ways, Internet-based advertising is similar to print advertising. However, certain fundamental differences in the Internet as a communication medium make Internet-based advertising distinct in both terminology and strategy:

1. Internet advertisers frequently refer to 'eyeballs' as they measure the size of an Internet site's audience. These eyeballs translate into the equivalent of a print publication's circulation figures. The number of eyeballs an Internet site attracts is an indication of its potential to deliver customers to advertisers through embedded page links.

2. A potential audience does not guarantee readership of any particular ad, regardless of the medium. For example, the mere fact that someone subscribes to a Sunday newspaper does not mean they read every page, much less scan every ad on those pages. The same is true of the pages in an Internet site.

3. Eyeballs differ from the simple 'hit' statistics that are displayed by the odometer-style counters that proudly disclose the number of times a particular page has been accessed. A person can (and often does) hit a page multiple times during a single visit to an Internet site. A large number of hits can be a misleading indication of the site's popularity.

4. Records maintained on the computer that hosts an Internet site can identify how many different computers 'visited' the site's information pages; hence, a more accurate determination of individuals, or eyeballs. This accounting method is not completely accurate because many people may share a single computer, particularly in a school or office. However, it does give potential advertisers a reasonable basis for comparison among the available Internet sites.

5. Once an ad has been placed, the most important record is a tally of 'impressions' to determine how many times a particular ad may have been viewed. Impressions are similar to the print medium's concepts of reach and exposure. Most Internet sites charge advertisers on the basis of impressions. Impressions differ from hits mainly because of the popularity of rotating ads. Internet-based advertising has become so sophisticated that Internet sites can identify whether a visitor has been exposed to a particular ad and then use that information to determine immediately which ads that person will see the next time a page on that site is selected. In addition, many marketing managers have questioned the usefulness of impression figures and other exposure statistics. The only way to ensure that an ad has been read is to examine its 'click-through' rate. Click-through represents the number of times an ad is selected, indicating that those

readers wanted further information. The print medium equivalents are reply cards, bingo cards and reader service cards.[19]

STICKY TOOLS

Management consultants, industry analysts and big businesses alike have shifted to a renewed corporate focus on 'growth'. As we emphasised earlier in the chapter, the focus no longer remains solely on market share, but on building a loyal and profitable customer base. The on-line environment includes information kiosks, interactive television and the Internet as tools to apply an integrated and tailored on-line customer loyalty strategy. On-line is intimate, interactive and fast. Communication can occur through e-mail (one-to-one), Websites (one-to-many), and newsgroups/forums (many-to-many). However, on-line communication challenges the loyalty of a very fast-moving audience.

The Internet is facilitated through two key communication applications; e-mail, a messaging and information application, and the Web, a multimedia content and network publishing application. e-Mail is a communication medium best suited for direct marketing messages, or calling existing customers to take a very specific action, such as buying an item being offered on-line at a temporary mark-down. So far, the best strategy has been to apply the principals of traditional direct marketing to e-mail. The main objective is to get the right message to the right consumer.

Internet companies continue to realise the importance of customer loyalty as a key sustainable competitive edge. As a result, cultivating customer loyalty is approached through different means as follows:[20]

❏ Many sites have developed single-site loyalty programmes in which a customer can accumulate loyalty points from that site.

❏ Other sites are collaborating to develop 'network awards' – such as partnering airlines – that offer loyalty points to customers who purchase tickets or items from either of these participating sites. This is more valuable since there is higher utility with more retailers. Many single-site programmes are expected to move to network programmes to increase the value. Once a customer has

---

[19] Reply cards and service cards can be used to assess a customer's opinion or feedback on products and services.

[20] Ashworth (1999).

signed up for either a single-site or network programme, on-line businesses can gain a better idea of who their users are. Profiles are valuable because firms can design incentives catered to the individual.

❑ By 2000, eBay Inc. was the 'sticky site' leader, with users averaging 126 minutes on the site. Other sticky sites were Microsoft Corp.'s MoneyCentral (66 minutes); Charles Schwab & Co. (37 minutes) and E★Trade Group Inc. (37 minutes).

❑ Another way for a site to improve its 'stickiness' is to offer more customer services, such as chat, e-mail and auctions. For example, the stickiness model for eBay yields great rewards in user retention and that builds up revenues.

❑ When crafting an e-commerce strategy, firms should provide some kind of enabler, a motivation to move customers off their traditional preference. The incentive should be something that premieres prominently on an Internet site so the value a customer receives can be articulated.

INTERNET MEASUREMENT AND MARKET RESEARCH

The Internet as a medium still remains less measurable than traditional media such as TV and radio since there are no real standards for measurement and no previous models to follow. Advertisers are not comfortable with the flaws of Internet measurement the way they are, for example, with the Nielsen TV ratings. The common problem still remains with the attempt to push square-pegged measurement strategies from traditional media into round-holed Internet platforms! A strategy that measures print will not necessarily have the same applications on-line, where readers behave differently. Although traditional media metaphors help to explain Web concepts to users, they are left equally confounded when off-line measurement strategies deployed in new media environment produce results that are ambiguous and unreliable.

With so many pages, links, links to hyperlinks, and hyperlinks to one another, tracking the activity on the World Wide Web (as well as how other mediums relate to it) can be like visually tracing a single strand of spaghetti through a bowl of pasta!

Web Measuring Parameters

On the other hand, the number of times an advertisement is seen and clicked is not only projected; it is precisely measured.[21] This means that in addition to calculating

---

[21] Zeff & Aronson (1997), p. 65.

Website traffic, it is also possible to measure advertising exposure and response. There are several ways to conduct Web tracking or traffic analysis. This usually includes: assessing the performance of the Website or a specific section of the site; learning about Website visitors and customers; and integrating user profiles and other databases with tracking data, such as what the users are viewing or clicking on. It is not possible or desirable to conduct such analyses manually, therefore, software programs are a valued solution for many enterprises. Marketers should take note however, that the primary benefit of investing time and resources in Web traffic analysis products is to measure the performance of a Website. Website analysis can reveal the following important information to help design target market strategies:

- ❏ Popular pages indicating the appeal of your site.
- ❏ Less popular pages indicating a lack of interest.
- ❏ Length of time spent on pages which shows whether the material is actually read or just skimmed.
- ❏ Starting pages other than your homepage can be reviewed for 'image'.

Hits: Who Knocked? Who Entered? Who Gave Up?

To begin understanding what can be measured and how measurements can help, a re-examination of 'hits' is necessary. The term 'hits' is understood as the successful transfer of a file from a Web server to a Web browser, but a hit is actually a request for a file. A request can either result in a successful transfer, an unsuccessful transfer (an error), or an abort (the person making a request interrupts the transfer).

Likewise, the word 'file' can refer to either a page of text (an HTML page) or an object such as a graphic, a sound or a movie. Here, critics make their strongest point: each graphic on a page counts as a file, so accessing a page with eight graphical elements registers nine hits. Used this way, 'hits' is meaningless, particularly given that the content of many sites changes frequently.

Another criticism of hits, however, applies equally to page transfers. The caching of HTML pages by requesting servers results in undercounting page views. For example, a corporation's internal server may cache the homepage of *The New York Times*. Thus, while 50 of that corporation's employees may view this page, only the first request registers a page transfer on the *Times* server.

Moreover, page transfers broken down by individual pages are among the most helpful of basic reports.[22] This enables a corporation to identify those pages on its site which are most important to people and therefore to focus its resources and attention in those areas.

Visitors: Who Was Here, and How Often?

Two other useful parameters in measuring site traffic are visitors and sessions. Unfortunately, the terms are sometimes used interchangeably. 'Visitors' is the number of unique persons accessing a site. It is not possible to accurately count visitors without requiring registration, and it is a rare site that can successfully demand registration. A 'session' is a series of uninterrupted clicks from a visitor. Any period of inactivity can be defined as an interruption. Thus, if a user is visiting a site, takes a 40-minute lunch, then takes up where he left off, a second session is recorded on the Web server.

Given these definitions, the distinction between the two is clear: a visitor can account for more than one session. As with repeat customers, frequent visitors to a Website are likely to be more valuable than those who visit only once, or once in a great while. Aside from the difficult-to-require registration, four methods are used to estimate visitors and sessions. Each has shortcomings with regard to accuracy. Counting unique IP addresses is the simplest and least accurate way to estimate visitors. IP addresses are the identification numbers (e.g., 168.121.42.127) assigned to computers that directly connect to the Internet.

Matching IP addresses to time stamps is often used to estimate sessions.[23] The above shortcomings apply, but are mitigated by the fact that sessions, not visitors, are being estimated. The accuracy of this method is considered fair to good. Issuing session IDs is the best way to estimate sessions. Issuing cookies (bits of information generated at a Web server, but stored in browsers) is the best way to estimate visitors.[24] The key difference between them is persistence: the ability to identify a specific browser on a specific PC over multiple sessions.

Cookies have the advantage in this regard, but this method has its own shortcoming in that cookies are attached to browsers, not users. For example, if three people in

---

[22] Individual pages refer to a user's access to a particular page of a single site.

[23] Time stamps refer to the timing of the transfer of data.

[24] A cookie is information that a Website puts on your hard disk so that it can remember something about you at a later time. (In other words, it is information for future use that is stored by the server on the client side of a client/server communication.)

Alfred Kahn's office use his desktop to access the Acme Website on the same day, the Acme server counts three visits by one browser, not one visit from three different users. Furthermore, some browsers do not support cookies, and some users – or their office network administrator – turn them off.

But in cases where there is a one-to-one relationship between user and browser, cookies play a very important role for customised Web experiences. For example, if a visitor looked at a specific product at a Website in November, cookies enable the site's server to inform her of newly added information on that product when she revisits the site in December.

Other Useful Measurement Parameters

- ❑ Both session IDs and cookies enable 'clickstream' analysis which details the sequence of page requests made by any group of visitors.[25] Analysing clickstreams helps designers structure sites more effectively, enabling visitors to get the information they want as quickly as possible. For example, if it takes people an average of ten clicks to get to a product page, there is probably a lack of direction in the content.
- ❑ Referring to URLs, or entry points, indicate where visitors are linking to a site from.[26] Knowing this can be of great help in planning site promotion, particularly if Web presence is advertised at other sites.
- ❑ Knowing how users end visits can be useful as well. Users either link out or bail out of a site. For sites offering ad space, link-outs are critical since they are proof of advertising effectiveness. For sites not offering advertising, link-outs indicate which links, among those provided at a site, are most popular. Such data can offer clues to the content that is most interesting to visitors.
- ❑ Page transfers by an individual show what visitors find most interesting. Insight gained from this can help decide where to allocate creative resources, what pages need frequent updates, and where to overhaul or eliminate content. The number of page transfers per session can also serve as a basic indicator of site attractiveness, as it measures how 'deep' visitors are going into a site.

Web Research – A Firm's Perspective

The Internet can be used to collect data about existing customers, as a means to look

---

[25] In Web advertising, a clickstream is the sequence of clicks or pages requested as a visitor explores a Website.

[26] URLs require the use of an extended log format.

for new customers, to conduct market research and to prospect for new customers. The GartnerGroup forecasts that Websites will generate new sources of external data and more than double the data between 1999 and 2004.[27] [See **Appendix 1** for tips on conducting Internet research.]

On-line market research is far less expensive than either mail or telephone surveys and results can be available much faster, literally overnight, rather than in weeks or months, as usually is the case in obtaining the results of phone and mail surveys. However, the accuracy of Web marketing research is still unclear. Do respondents interpret questions sent electronically differently than they do those delivered via other media? Should e-mail responses be weighed equally with those received via other media? How do on-line responses translate into purchase behaviour? More importantly, what is the primary unit of measurement on-line: the individual or the household?

Most of the mathematical models employed in marketing research consider the household to be the primary unit. Are these marketing models sufficient to evaluate the results of Net research? Given the many unknowns about how to interpret electronic survey responses, the Internet is the least favourable choice for marketing research presently, but is likely to increase in popularity over time as researchers gain more experience with the medium. The two major advantages of Internet marketing research are cost and timing, and the major disadvantage is the question of accuracy.

e-Mail and discussion groups are some popular research tools for businesses to interact with consumers (both existing and potential) on a regular basis and find out more information about them. For example, if a user joins an e-mail list about golf and is willing to sign up for daily messages about golf, then chances are they are into golf. This trend indicates that the Web has the ability to bring the fanatics, the influencers, and the early adopters within the reach of the on-line marketer and provide valuable research information through the interaction of all these combining forces.

Many Internet sites include a direct e-mail link for visitors to comment on the site, its contents or just about anything at all! Discussion groups differ however, in that they are usually made up of communities of people with similar interests. Just about anyone, both private individuals and businesses, can subscribe to discussion groups and participate in on-line discussions which might cover a wide array of topics from cars to teddy bears. Companies can use these tools to gain valuable information on trends, customer profiles, costs and demographics. This is useful research for designing a value proposition, for example, catered to a particular group.

---

[27] URL: http://www.thegartnergroup.com

The Internet also enables companies to research the competition. Companies can seek out competitors with similar product offerings, the stages of development for enhancements compared to the competitor's existing products or services, or simply gauge the timing of the release of new offerings in the marketplace and marketspace. By and large, this aspect of market research is dependent on the amount of information that companies post on their Websites.

Web Research – An Individual's Perspective

Customers can conduct on-line market research and reap the following benefits:

❑ Lower search costs.
❑ More product and service information.
❑ Immediate delivery of some products and services.
❑ Control over information access.
❑ Easy interchangeability from one site to another.

However, there are some common complaints as follows:

❑ Conducting research on the Internet solely eliminates data and information available in the form of hard copies; but to ignore hard copies consigns the historical record to oblivion. Also, databases of newspapers and magazines tend to begin at a relatively recent date and go forward from there; prior issues typically remain only on paper or microfilm. By 2000, most information on-line was available only for fees ranging from nominal to high, creating a price discrimination policy and a distinction between 'free Web' and 'fee Web'.
❑ Until the year 2000, some parts of the Web were unreachable. Typically, search engines send out 'spiders' that catalogue Webpages, but a large portion of dataspace is not stored in these pages; to find it, a user must issue a specific request. A site's own software may yield the information being searched, but there is no specific method to go there. Also, search engines for the 'free Web' can rarely receive access past the password-protected tollbooths.
❑ The lapses extend beyond mere text. Images are even more likely to exist only off the Web. The on-line archives of print media (e.g., *Forbes* magazine) typically exclude most photographs and other graphic elements, including advertisements. To help alleviate some of the problems are specialty research software and search engines of search engines, for example, 'Dog Pile'. Instead of having to search through Yahoo!, Excite and InfoSeek separately, a search can be executed in a consolidated way through Dog Pile.

SUMMARY

❑ The Internet provides a significantly different business environment from the marketplace. Therefore, traditional marketing concepts and strategies have to be revised to successfully pursue Internet marketing. The Internet fundamentally changes customer expectations about convenience, speed, price and service. As such, Internet businesses have an opportunity to meet these needs through a hyper-mediated interactive technology environment.

❑ The major shift from traditional marketing to Internet marketing is from the mass marketing of consumers to a many-to-many marketing model. The marketspace environment shifts the advantage in favour of the consumers where businesses compete to capture unique information about consumers and deliver integrated or 'bundled' goods in response to consumer needs.

❑ Internet customer relationship strategies focus on gaining customer loyalty and creating a portfolio of long-term relationships. We define four types of customers: visitors, qualified prospects, non-committed customers and loyal customers. Customer loyalty is attained through four stages: customer attraction, customer acquisition, customer retention, which should lead to customer loyalty, through enhancing mutual trust at each stage.

❑ Promotion and advertising on the Internet is fundamentally different from traditional media since the Internet acts both as a promotional and distribution channel where advertising and sales can take place simultaneously.

❑ Web measurement techniques are still in a nascent stage and marketers still rely heavily on the traditional media for reliable measuring instruments. Research on the Internet is a valuable tool; it benefits consumers in terms of providing more information at lower costs. Businesses have the opportunity to conduct a competitive analysis, interact with consumers to gather personal information and conduct research, and take advantage of low costs and reduced time for conducting on-line market research.

APPENDIX 1: USEFUL TIPS IN CONDUCTING INTERNET RESEARCH

❑ Access helpful sites regularly. Integration is key. In the case of the Internet, it is useful to integrate research with your other favourite sources of information.

❑ Link-up. One good site leads to another. If you find a useful Website, chances that you will find some other good sources on like-minded topics are high.

❑ Bookmark. If you find a useful site, do not let it slip through your fingers. 'Bookmark' it and store its URL (electronic address) in your Web browser so you can find the site again. Periodically update these bookmarks since Website addresses tend to change frequently.

❏ Set time limits. It is possible to spend unlimited hours surfing the Internet looking for information. Set yourself a reasonable time limit, for example, five to ten minutes. Beyond your time limit, you should pursue other methods to find the information.

❏ Cast a net. In addition to Internet sites, you can post questions on a newsgroup specific to the topic you are researching. For example, HR Net, founded by John Boudreau, the professor who teaches the on-line research course at Cornell, acts as a kind of electronic bulletin board for professionals. Search engines like Yahoo! list such newsgroups by subject for your convenience.

❏ Be sceptical. The authenticity of reports and quotations on the Web are questionable. You have to be wary of what is said by whom on the World Wide Web. It is hard to trust some of the information that is posted. Caution is necessary because information can be easily posted by anyone on the Internet. Therefore, there is no guarantee that just because a statement is treated as fact, that it is the truth. Recently, a Website proclaimed that President Clinton and his wife had bought a new VW 'Bug' for their daughter Chelsea. That titbit was written up in newspapers and used by VW dealers in ads; it turned out to be untrue. So do not believe everything that you read on the Web.

❏ Newsgroups can be an interesting source of information, however, you can never know for sure whether someone is who they say they are (people can be impersonated electronically) and whether or not they know what they are talking about.

❏ Data mining and data manufacturing are two techniques that can help companies to devise appropriate marketing strategies.

REFERENCES

Ashworth, J. (1999), "Loyalty Programs Deemed Vital for 'Sticky Sites'", *Report on Electronic Commerce*, 11 May.

Cutler, B. (1990), "The Fifth Medium", *American Demographics*, Vol. 12, Iss. 6, pp. 24–29, URL: http://www.demographics.com/, August 2000.

eLoyalty (2000), URL: http://www.eloyaltyco.com, 27 September.

Gurley, J.W. (1998), "The Soaring Cost of e-Commerce", *Fortune*, 3 August.

Hagel, J., III & Singer, M. (1999), "Shift into Reverse", *Business 2.0*, March, URL: http://www.business2.com/, August 2000.

Hart, C.W. & Johnson, M.D. (1999), "Growing the Trust Relationship", *Marketing Management*, Spring.

Higham, N. (1999), "Amazon Success Story Built on Traditional Marketing Expertise", *Marketing Week*, 14 October.

Hoffman, D. & Novak, T. (1995), *The Challenges of Electronic Commerce*, San Francisco, CA: Wired Ventures Inc.

Hoffman, D. & Novak, T. (1996), "A New Marketing Paradigm for Electronic Commerce", paper submitted for the Special Issue on Electronic Commerce for The Information Society, 19 February.

Lach, J. (1999), "Carrots in Cyberspace", *American Demographics*, May, URL: http://www.demographics.com/, August 2000.

M2 Communications Limited (2000), "MyPoints Launches MyPoints Europe", *M2 Presswire*, Coventry, 22 September.

MyPoints.com Inc (2000), "MyPoints.com Inc. Announces the Launch of MyPoints UK", 25 September, URL: http://www.corp.mypoints.com/investor/index.html, 26 September.

Ramusson, E. (1999), *Sales and Marketing Management*, September, URL: http://www.salesandmarketing.com/, August 2000.

Rayport, J.F. & Sviokla, J.J. (1994), "Managing in the Marketspace", *Harvard Business Review*, Reprint 94608, November–December, pp. 140–150.

Rometty, V. (1999), "Changing at Light Speed", *Best's Review*, April, URL: http://www.bestreview.com/, August 2000.

Silverstein, B. (1998), *Business-to-Business Internet Marketing: Five Proven Strategies for Increasing Profits Through Internet Direct Marketing*, Gulf Breeze, FL: Maximum Press, p. 20.

Singer, M. (1999), "Shelf Life", *Business 2.0*, March, URL: http://www.business2.com/, August 2000.

Swigor, J.T. (1999), *Target Marketing*, October, URL: http://www.targeting.com/, August 2000.

Violino, B. (1999), "Customer at the Core", *Information Week*, 27 September, URL: http://www.informationweek.com/, August 2000.

Wingfield, N. (1999), "Priceline.com Plans to Let Customers Bid for Long-distance Phone Service", *The Wall Street Journal*, 8 November.

Zeff, R. & Aronson, B. (1997), *Advertising on the Internet*, New York, NY: Wiley, p. 65.

CASE

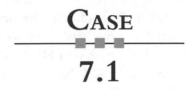

7.1

iTV: Marketing Interactive Services*

iTV (an interactive television service) was commercially launched by the former Cable & Wireless Hong Kong Telecom (HKT) in March 1998.[1] Its performance in the first two years of operations had not lived up to the Company's expectations. The 'killer application' video–on–demand (VOD) did not score a hit and feedback was discouraging. Furthermore, the penetration rate had been slow. It was partly for this reason that Star TV, Asia's largest satellite operator, decided to end the joint venture between the two companies on 2 June 2000.[2] Initially, the joint venture was established to bring in a full range of interactive home entertainment, digital television and Internet services for consumers. The termination of the partnership meant that the chance for iTV to enrich its contents had been jeopardised. In terms of business performance, the Company

---

[1] Pacific Century CyberWorks (PCCW) completed its US$15.7 billion merger takeover deal with the former Cable & Wireless Hong Kong Telecom on 17 August 2000. As a result, iTV became part of PCCW's broadband B2C services unit.

[2] Flagg, M. (2000), "Star Jilts HKT, Hurting the Ambitions of Both – Annulled Alliance Opens Interactive Competition", *The Asian Wall Street Journal*, New York, 5 June.

* Eva Chang prepared this case under the supervision of Dr. Ali Farhoomand. *Copyright © 2000 The University of Hong Kong. Ref. 00/99C*

reported a net loss of HK$2.77 billion (US$355 million)[3] for the six months to 30 September 1999.[4] Allen Ma, HKT's interactive services chief, conceded having to push back the iTV projected break-even date by two years to 2003.[5]

Added to this, on 4 July 2000, the Hong Kong government offered the new pay-television programme service licence to five new operators. Then, on 17 August 2000, Pacific Century CyberWorks (PCCW) took over HKT. In spite of the initial hoopla about the takeover, the stock price of PCCW had fallen from its peak of HK$28.50 (US$3.65) in February 2000 to around HK$6.00 (US$0.77) in early November 2000. To make matters worse, iCable, one of the major TV content providers in Hong Kong, announced that it would terminate its alliance with Network of the World (NOW), a converged service of PCCW that provided interactive digital video viewing and Web access. Faced with mounting pressures from the market, the management of HKT had to decide how best to market iTV; how to leverage PCCW's portfolio of Internet-related businesses to position iTV; and ultimately how to accelerate the push towards profitability.

TELECOMMUNICATIONS AND BROADCASTING INDUSTRIES IN HONG KONG

Telecommunications Industry

By the end of 1998, the Hong Kong Special Administrative Region (HKSAR) had the highest telephone density in Asia and one of the highest in the world, with 71 telephones or 54 exchange lines per 100 population.[6] Such an indicator and others [**Exhibit 1**] demonstrated the importance of the telecommunications services to HKSAR's businesses and residential consumers. Previously, Hong Kong Telecom (HKT) had played a solo role as the dominant player in building up this industry; yet it was all about to change before the end of the 20th century.

---

[3] US$1 = HK$7.80

[4] Hui, Y.M. & Agencies (2000), "HKT Sees Delay in Profit Recovery As Market Deregulation Takes Toll", *South China Morning Post*, 22 January.

[5] Anonymous (1999), "Business: They Have Seen the Future, and They Aren't Very Interested", *The Economist*, London, 13 March.

[6] "Chapter 19: Communications, the Media & Information Technology: Telecommunication", *Hong Kong Yearbook 1999*.

Digital Convergence

In the HKSAR, technological convergence was happening rapidly in the last few years. Digital technology combined three different entities – telephone, computer and broadcasting [**Appendix 1**] – and created new media types and applications never before seen. Integrated information would be delivered via the same piece of wire and a common interface. Consequently, new interactive multimedia services and products emerged and the traditional telecommunications and broadcasting boundaries overlapped. The resultant alliances between the different companies attempted to gain market share at a lower cost.

Broadcasting Industry

There had been rapid development in the broadcasting industry also. Prior to 1991, there were only two free-to-air television operators offering four channels and two radio stations in HKSAR. By the end of 1998, there were 48 domestic and regional television channels, delivered via terrestrial, satellite and cable broadcasters; there were also three radio companies offering a total of 13 different channels. The HKSAR government set an objective to 'create an environment conducive to the flourishing of television market and to the introduction of innovative services using new technologies, and to enhance Hong Kong's position as a leading broadcasting hub in the region'.[7]

Government Initiatives

From 1998, the local government responded to the digital convergence era with the liberalisation of the telecommunications and broadcasting sectors and the removal of all restrictions regarding the forms of service that different types of transmission networks might carry. The government also offered five new pay-television licences in July 2000 [**Exhibit 2**]. As explained by K.C. Kwong, former Secretary for Information Technology and Broadcasting, the government's policy 'to encourage the telecommunication and

---

[7] *Digital21 – IT Strategy* (2000), URL: http://www.info.gov.hk/digital21/eng/strategy/strategy_part31.html, October.

broadcasting sectors to take full advantage of the trend of convergence will create tremendous business opportunities for them in the years to come'.[8]

HKT was one of the first movers to grasp the opportunity to pursue the digital industry.

END OF A MONOPOLY

Linus Cheung, the former chief executive of HKT, told a local newspaper in September 2000 that the "telephone companies have to transform – with liberalisation, with commoditisation of the IDD voice and with a lot of those challenges, a telephone company does not have a very bright future."[9, 10] In fact, he started transforming HKT back in 1998.

In March 1998, HKT gave up its exclusive licence for certain external telecommunication services and circuits eight years ahead of its expiry. This was an important milestone for HKSAR's telecommunications sector, following the deregulation of the Fixed Telecommunication Network Services (FTNS) market in July 1995. Consequently, the company totally relinquished its status as a monopoly in the local telecommunication industry. Instead, HKT shifted its focus to other business areas, including the Internet and the interactive multimedia services. In March 1998, HKT stepped into the broadcasting arena with its launch of the interactive television service (iTV), utilising its broadband network – a big step forward for a traditional telephone company.

---

[8] "Speech by Mr K.C. Kwong, Secretary for Information Technology and Broadcasting at the Luncheon Meeting of the Hong Kong Institute of Directors, 'The Convergence of Telecommunications and Broadcasting'", *Information Technology and Broadcasting Bureau, HKSAR Government*, 11 January 2000.

[9] Hong Kong Telecom changed its name to Cable & Wireless HKT on 16 June 1999. The Company then merged with Pacific Century CyberWorks (PCCW) on 17 August 2000 and became PCCW-HKT. Consequently, Linus Cheung became Deputy Chairman of PCCW and a member of the Company's Executive Committee.

[10] "Broad CyberWorks Responsibilities for Cheung", *South China Morning Post*, Hong Kong, 18 September 2000.

HKT – A Traditional Telephone Company

HKT was one of the largest companies in HKSAR, with about 14,000 employees in 1999. The Company had been under the management of Cable and Wireless plc, a British group, for decades. Its hierarchical, civil service-style line management was deeply rooted until the late Michael Gale, the former chief executive of HKT, took up leadership on 1 February 1988, at the time when the Company went public and began to introduce a more horizontal structure. Under Gale's leadership, the Company advanced technologically and paved the way for the development of its later businesses. Subsequently, Linus Cheung, the successor to Gale, led HKT on the road to 'digital convergence' with the iTV project and its underlying broadband network.

Cheung was awarded the Executive of the Year Award in 1999, organised by DHL/ SCMP Business Awards, for his 'central role in leading HKT into the Internet era'.[11] Before joining the top post in HKT, Cheung spent over 20 years with Cathay Pacific Airways, part of the Swire Group. It was his first job out of university, and he worked his way up the ladder from management trainee to Deputy Managing Director. During his career with HKT, Cheung handled several controversial issues, including the ten percent staff pay-cut in September 1998, the change of corporate identity to 'Cable & Wireless HKT' in June 1999 and the takeover by Pacific Century CyberWorks (PCCW), completed in August 2000. Cheung believed that the takeover would allow HKT to "take on global aspirations and also enter lines of business on a much wider scale."[12]

In terms of business performance, analysts suggested that the Company's net loss of HK$2.77 billion (US$355 million) for the six months to 30 September 1999 was due to "huge exceptional loss of HK$7.1 billion (US$910 million) on equipment write-off, mainly contributed by its interactive multimedia services arm iTV."[13, 14]

PCCW – The New 'Parent'

PCCW's US$15.7 billion takeover of HKT was 'the talk of the town' for many months,

---

[11] Saunier, V. (1999), "HKT Chief Cheung Ready for Challenge", *South China Morning Post*, Hong Kong, 10 December.

[12] "Broad CyberWorks Responsibilities for Cheung", *South China Morning Post*, Hong Kong, 18 September 2000.

[13] US$1 = HK$7.80

[14] Hui, Y.M. & Agencies (2000), "HKT Sees Delay in Profit Recovery As Market Deregulation Takes Toll", *South China Morning Post*, 22 January.

and those within the telecommunications, Internet and financial industries were eager to monitor the new Company's future prospects in the highly competitive environment.[15] PCCW was a young company founded in April 1999 by Richard Li, the son of an influential multibillionaire. In the HKT takeover battle, Li defeated SingTel, Singapore's major telecom operator, which had the backing of the media giant Rupert Murdoch. There was speculation that the Chinese government was behind the scenes deciding the fate of HKT. Francis Yuen, the deputy chairman of PCCW, told the local media that: "Li travelled to Beijing in early February to seek the Chinese government's formal blessing for the [HKT] deal, which he received."[16] Li's response was: "That's bull. I was in Beijing just before Chinese New Year, but I was there for something else."[17] Anson Chan, the HKSAR's Chief Secretary, commented: "It is purely a commercial decision for HKT to make on its own, no doubt in the light of the views of the board of directors and what is the best deal from the shareholders' point of view."[18] The deal eventually went through and with the integration of the two companies, PCCW's new company structure was reorganised into eight business units [**Exhibit 3**]; its head count jumped overnight from 453 to over 14,000.

Company Highlights

When the takeover offer was initially valued at US$36 billion in February 2000, it was based on PCCW's share price of HK$22.15 (US$2.84) at the time.[19] After that, PCCW's share price went into decline, partially due to the global Internet crash that began in April 2000. Other discouraging news included Star TV dropping out of the pay-TV and Internet joint venture in June 2000. On 16 August 2000, the completion day of the takeover from Cable & Wireless, PCCW's share price was HK$15.80 (US$2.03). Then on 22 September 2000, two days after Cable & Wireless' private placement of

---

[15] The quoted result of US$15.7 billion represented a total consideration of US$6.5 million cash and 4.5 billion shares in PCCW at the closing price of HK$15.80 on 16 August 2000, as announced by Cable and Wireless plc on 17 August 2000.

[16] Gilley, B. (2000), "Working Lunch", *Far Eastern Economic Review*, Hong Kong, 30 March.

[17] "The $38-Billion Man", *Asiaweek*, 10 March 2000.

[18] Chung, Y. (2000), "Coming of Age", *Asiaweek*, 10 March.

[19] Wonacott, P. (2000), "HKT Earnings Fall 90% As Competition Grows – Web Strategy, CyberWorks Deal Still on Track", *The Asian Wall Street Journal*, New York, 5 May.

1.04 billion shares at HK$9.88 (US$1.27) each, the Company's stock price continued to slide, closing at HK$8.77 (US$1.12). A local newspaper reported that investors who took up PCCW's shares from the placement had experienced a paper loss of HK$863.2 million (US$110.67 million) in just two days.[20] Also in September, GigaMedia (a leading Taiwan multimedia content provider), decided to terminate the 'would-be Great Ape of Asian interactive networks'[21] deal with PCCW; the deal's original objective was to work together on Chinese content development. The Company's share price continued to drop amid the uncertainties about the fate of PCCW's alliance with Australia's Telstra Corp. in early October. The agreement was eventually signed on 13 October 2000, with Telstra's cash injection into PCCW renegotiated from US$3 billion to US$2.43 billion.[22] Although the joint venture with Telstra helped to reduce PCCW's debt by US$3.56 billion, PCCW still needed to make an effort to improve its financial situation, which was burdened by the outstanding balance of the US$9 billion inherited from taking over HKT.

Richard Li – The New Boss

The PCCW-HKT takeover deal was not Li's first successful story. The 33-year-old Stanford graduate made the headlines back in 1993 when he sold Star TV, Asia's largest satellite television network, which he built up three years earlier, to Rupert Murdoch of News Corporation for US$950 million. In 1999, his Company, PCCW, was awarded the Cyberport contract to build an 'info-tech centre' on 26 hectares of reclaimed land on Hong Kong Island. He led his Company in making alliances and establishing joint ventures with over 50 companies worldwide, including large media, telecommunications, computer and Internet companies such as Intel and CMGI. The HKT deal was originally valued at US$38 billion, the largest takeover in Asia to date.[23] The deal demonstrated

---

[20] Hui, Y.M., Holcombe, C., & Kwok, B. (2000), "CyberWorks Plummets 15pc Cable & Wireless' $10b Placement, Confidence Slide Fuel Fall", *South China Morning Post*, Hong Kong, 22 September.

[21] "The Net: Running with the Big Dogs: Did Taiwan's GigaMedia Diss PCCW's Play?" *Asiaweek*, Hong Kong, 20 October 2000.

[22] Kwok, B. (2000), "CyberWorks Seals US$4.7b deal", *South China Morning Post*, Hong Kong, 6 November.

[23] Spaeth, A. (2000), "The Son Also Surprises", *Time Asia*, 13 March.

his ability to secure a loan of US$13 billion based on the US$1 billion stock, which was raised in 48 hours.

All along, he endeavoured to prove that 'his success was not just a credit to his father's famous name',[24] but that he had achieved it by his own efforts. He once described his feelings prior to the closing of the HKT deal: "The scariest moment was when I decided how much cash to offer. That was the sleepless night. I had five cups of Starbucks and a chocolate bar."[25] Then after the deal went through, he told others that "People say I've done this with my father's help, but I've done it on my own."[26]

Li was a fast mover. He said before: "Now is the time to go out, rather than meandering and relying on existing old models. If there is a vision, you should just go out and do it."[27] His vision was to build a company, a service, that would keep growing long after his retirement, making money and creating value for shareholders, and also providing a good starting block for those who were paying to use the goods and services.[28] One of his close associates commented that: "The people who are close to him get addicted to him, to his charisma of wealth, success and confidence, to the sense that he knows how to be a prince."[29] In contrast, he had been previously described as 'insolent, arrogant and spoiled'[30] and a 'tough taskmaster',[31] though some have said that he has become tamer with age.

At leisure, Li collected watches and enjoyed scuba diving and flying seaplanes. On one occasion, he threw a surprise Millennium Eve party for 2,000 people and invited guests such as Whitney Houston and Bobby Brown. It was an event that society columnists judged as 'the' party to be seen at, since it suggested the marking of 'Li's "coming out" as part of a new generation of Chinese entrepreneurs laying claim to the new century'.[32]

[24] Meyer, M. (2000), "Generation Next", *Newsweek International*, 13 March 2000.

[25] Meyer, M. (2000).

[26] Meyer, M. (2000).

[27] Meyer, M. (2000).

[28] Stirland, S. (2000), "The Chinese Puzzle; Richard Li's Plan for Pacific Century CyberWorks' Interactive Media Juggernaut", *Red Herring*, June.

[29] Meyer, M. (2000).

[30] "Face Value: Asia's Mr Broadband", *The Economist*, London, 8 July 2000.

[31] Stirland, S. (2000).

[32] McKenzie, R. (2000), "Highflier", *HSBC*, Summer.

With his computer engineering degree background, Li's interest was in new technologies. His ambition was to create the world's biggest broadband Internet business. Instead of beating up his rivals, he wanted to 'work together' with competitors since he believed that businesses in the Internet world were all just 'tiny dots' in a rapidly expanding universe.[33]

Li envisaged PCCW as 'a cross between American Online (AOL)-type service and a CMGI or a Softbank'[34] that invested 'in the building blocks, the enabling technologies provided by Internet start-ups'.[35] Analysts believed that Li was attracted to HKT because of its infrastructure. Indeed, Li once said in an interview after the takeover: "We have very stable income from HKT. We want to use this cash cow to invest in projects that have high growth well into the future. Our two engines of growth are broadband connectivity in an Internet backbone company and broadband content and applications.... The fuel is the telephone business."[36] HKT's broadband connectivity engine started with the launch of iTV in 1998.

ITV DELIVERING THE FIRST VOD SERVICE[37]

HKT's Interactive Multimedia Services unit (IMS) launched the world's first commercial video-on-demand (VOD) system as part of its iTV business with much fanfare in March 1998, following a series of failed VOD trials all over the world in the mid-1990s. At the time, the iTV project was HKT's 'star'. In particular, VOD was expected to be a hit.

---

[33] Meyer, M. (2000).

[34] America Online, Inc. was the world's leader in interactive services, Web brands, Internet technologies and e-commerce services. CMGI, Inc., a Nasdaq 100 company, was in the business of managing, developing and investing in a network of 70 Internet companies. Softbank, Inc. (Tokyo Stock Exchange: 9984) was one of the world's Internet leaders, owning more than 300 Internet companies worldwide.

[35] Stirland, S. (2000).

[36] Plott, D. & Gilley, B. (2000), "Interview: Richard Li, Taking a Stand", *Far Eastern Economic Review*, 5 October.

[37] A more detailed account of the initial launch of the iTV services can be found in the business case study "New Technologies, New Markets: The Launch of Hong Kong Telecom's Video-on-Demand", published by the Centre for Asian Business Cases, School of Business, The University of Hong Kong, 1998.

The rolling out of iTV's infrastructure was costly and its implementation took around three years to complete, with various obstacles along the way. It was uncertain at the time whether the business model for service demand and revenue streams existed. Nevertheless, the lack of encouragement did not dampen the enthusiasm of HKT IMS to become the 'first mover' to dominate the future provision of broadband services. The Company also believed that HKSAR was the right place for the innovation; Dr. William Lo once commented that "If [VOD] doesn't work in Hong Kong, it won't work anywhere." [38]

The company initially envisaged the HKSAR as the logical market for launching VOD and other iTV services because the densely packed apartment blocks in the city made the cost of wiring up cheaper than other metropolitan areas. In addition, the HKSAR's consumers were broadly affluent, sophisticated and high-tech savvy. They were always eager to follow new trends so they would most likely be thrilled with the idea of joining a digital society, wherein 24-hour services, shopping and entertainment would be available without the need to leave home.

The similarity in functions between VCR and VOD systems led to assumptions about the future acceptance of VOD. HKT IMS accordingly decided to employ VOD as the first 'killer application' business strategy for its iTV services. With this decision, it was positioning the business on the frontline to compete with video rental stores and cable television networks.

Besides confronting its direct competitors, the promotion of the VOD service led to issues including the strategic relationships with content providers, the unforeseen growth of the World Wide Web, market standards and technology 'lock-in', the Hong Kong government's forthcoming regulations to liberalise the telecommunications industry, and the appropriate marketing strategy for creating demand.

The Company invested HK$2 billion (US$256 million) in the initial development, and at one time planned to invest a further HK$10 billion (US$1.28 billion) within the next decade.[39] Its original target was to attract 250,000 customers by the end of the first year. But the project had not lived up to the company's expectation. The service managed to attract only 90,000 subscribers up to June 2000 and had remained at the same level for the past six months. The number included a 25,000 subscriber-

---

[38] Dr. William Lo pioneered the iTV implementation. He left HKT IMS in September 1998.

[39] Lai, E. (1998), "iTV VOD Launch Gets the 'Oscar' Treatment", *South China Morning Post*, Hong Kong, 31 March.

overlap with its broadband Internet business.[40] Simon Twiston Davies, CEO of Kagan Asia Media pointed out that "the iTV service has been an economic and marketing failure. The perception is [that] the technology doesn't work and there isn't a great deal of content there."[41]

Initial Marketing Effort

Selecting the market ■ From the early days, HKT introduced iTV to the lower-income group living in high-rise apartment complexes because they were more tightly packed and thus cheaper to target. This was the same group targeted by i-Cable Communications (i-Cable), the local cable television provider, which had a head start several years earlier. These less affluent customers were cautious in making their choice of pay-entertainment. It would take a great deal of motivation for these customers to fully appreciate the value of VOD and related services and to deviate from the accustomed alternatives [**Exhibit 4**].

Product strategy ■ Branding was not a problem for HKT, but as a new innovation, iTV needed more than a strong branding strategy to succeed. A reporter commented that "the battle for the multimedia services market will be largely won or lost on content, rather than the technical merits of their networks".[42]

In terms of content, iTV stuck to the original plan to focus on its first 'killer application' – VOD – and passively developed the other services such as the interactive banking and news-on-demand [**Exhibit 5**]. The VOD service was not flawless. Customers were unhappy about the quality of the movies, despite the HKT investment in building a Digital Media Centre with state-of-the-art facilities for its own digital post-production work. Also, some consumers perceived that the VOD channel was only of value for its pornographic movies. Without putting extra effort into content development, iTV could not compete effectively.

In November 1999, HKT established a joint venture with Star TV, Asia's largest

---

[40] Kwok, B. (2000), "HKT to Lean on CyberWorks", *South China Morning Post*, Hong Kong, 5 June.

[41] Erickson, J. (1999), "Arts & Sciences: Technology: Marriage of Convenience: Content Is the Dowry in a Hong Kong TV Deal", *Asiaweek*, 26 November.

[42] Johnstone, H. (1999), "Gates Opens New Telecom Horizons", *South China Morning Post*, Hong Kong, 14 March.

satellite operator, aiming to bring in a full range of interactive home entertainment, digital television and Internet services for consumers. This was a good opportunity for iTV to enrich its VOD, music and infotainment contents. However, the joint venture was terminated in June 2000 when Star TV lost faith in iTV. James Murdoch, Rupert Murdoch's youngest son, appointed as Star TV's chairman and chief executive just days before the breakup of the HKT venture, closed the chapter with the comment: "We did not see eye to eye as far as the vision for this thing is concerned. We have been clear that we have concerns about some of the Internet and interactive TV businesses within this joint venture. Ultimately we could not reach agreement on how we could address those concerns."[43]

Pricing strategy ■ The iTV service was offered on a monthly subscription-based pricing plan. Customers had to pay a monthly fee of HK$178 (US$22.80) or HK$238 (US$30.50) [**Exhibit 6**], which allowed them to receive some basic services. For most of the movies and music programmes, they had to pay on average HK$35 (US$4.50) per viewing in addition to the monthly fee.

By contrast, its competitor, i-Cable, was offering the cable television service at a monthly subscription rate of HK$280 (US$35.90), which already included three basic movie channels plus other news, sports and documentary channels. For additional movie choices, customers could pay an extra HK$80 (US$10.30) per month to tune into the HBO channel and another HK$80 (US$10.30) to tune into Cinemax channel, both offering fairly recent movies. There was an additional pay-per-view rate plan for Adult Programme Services.

Furthermore, many video and music stores were renting or selling videos and VCDs for an average price range of HK$20 (US$2.60) to HK$35 (US$4.50). Some street hawkers would even risk facing legal charges by selling pirated VCD movies at prices as low as HK$10 (US$1.30) each.

New competitors were coming in. Randall Cox, president of Yes Television Asia, one of the five new pay-television operators [**Exhibit 2**], announced that its company planned to offer VOD and other broadband Internet services by March 2001 for an initial monthly fee of HK$180 (US$23.10). That subscription would include ten channels with coverage of local and international news, sports, music and movies.[44]

---

[43] Harding, J. (2000), "Murdoch Pulls Out of HK Venture: Media Star TV and C&W HKT End Eight-month Agreement", *The Financial Times*, London, 3 June.

[44] Kwok, B. (2000), "Yes Will Be Answer to 25pc of Viewer Demand", *South China Morning Post*, 6 July.

Under such competitive market conditions and based on HKT's limited iTV service offerings, there was no justification, in terms of content and quality, for iTV to raise its fees in order to increase its revenue. On the other hand, it would be difficult for HKT to lower its iTV pricing plan to attract additional customers because 'steep discounting meant that HKT would lose money with each new customer it signed up, owing to the cost of providing set-top boxes and buying video content'.[45]

Promotional strategy ■ There was a mix of promotional tryouts, including both above-the-line advertising and below-the-line advertising [**Exhibit 7**] to support its marketing strategy. Despite generous marketing expenditure (e.g., HK$6 million (US$769,000) on its second television ad), the Company seemed to 'struggle to find the right identity for its service'[46] as demonstrated by the two television campaigns, which had totally different themes. The first advertisement promoted a techno-style image, trying to appeal to the status-conscious, while the second commercial conveyed to money-conscious consumers that iTV services were value for money. Though the change in focus might have generated additional interest, it was not substantial enough to boost iTV's market share.

In the meantime, publicity over iTV services was dying down, perhaps due to the lack of significant development. Press releases dwindled from early 1999 onwards except for the occasional mention of iTV in the Company's annual report. Bad publicity continued to plague the business. Some unhappy customers even filed complaints with the local Broadcasting Authority [**Exhibit 8**].

Distribution strategy ■ One of the advantages in distributing interactive services via television was the ubiquity of this platform. Yet, it was natural for people to associate interactive services with their personal computers rather than with televisions. As technology convergence matured, home PC penetration increased and more PCs were connected to the Internet via broadband networks, there was concern as to whether television was the best choice of platform for delivering interactive services.

The Company utilised typical marketing channels on two occasions. Both were one-off programmes – promotions with The Hong Kong Jockey Club and Smartcard

---

[45] Mungan, C. (1999), "Entertainment + Technology (A Special Report) – Going Interactive: Hong Kong Telecom Offers Movies, Music and Shopping on Its Video-on-demand Service; Now All It Needs Is Customers and Profits", *The Asian Wall Street Journal*, New York, 29 March.

[46] Slater, J. (1999), "Ad About-face", *Far Eastern Economic Review*, 25 February.

21. Its competitor, i–Cable, increased distribution through existing consumers by offering a referral bonus to attract new customers and retain old ones.

From May 1998, HKT's broadband Internet service, 'NETVIGATOR Ultraline 1.5M'[47] took centrestage while iTV services blended into the background. The Company's shift of focus was inevitable due to the popularisation of the Internet, in particular, the advent of e-commerce. Also, HKT would be imprudent if it did not 'kill two birds with one stone' by fully exploiting its expensive broadband network. In this connection, HKT offered a bundled rate for the two services [**Exhibit 9**].

NETVIGATOR Ultraline 1.5M

'NETVIGATOR Ultraline 1.5M' performed better. Linus Cheung told a local reporter in June 2000 that the subscriber number for its Internet broadband service had reached 110,000 and the expected growth was 20,000 per month.[48] Its success helped to accelerate the local market to move from 'narrowband' to 'broadband'.[49] It played a significant role in promoting the iTV business as well. HKT reported in November 1999 that customer churn was reduced by packaging the iTV services with 'NETVIGATOR Ultraline 1.5M'.[50,51] More than one year on, the Company still kept the bundled package as one of the options for its customers.

FITTING INTO PCCW'S PICTURE

iTV fell into PCCW's 'Broadband B2C' business unit [**Exhibit 3**] as a result of the takeover. Its profile seemed to match one of the Company's mission statements to

---

[47] "Broadband Internet Access Launched in Hong Kong", *Newsbytes News Network*, 6 May 1998.

[48] Kwok, B. (2000).

[49] Narrowband only had a single voice channel for transmission; broadband had a relatively wider bandwidth that could be divided into several narrowbands, hence capable of transmitting voice, video and data concurrently.

[50] Churn means cancellation rate.

[51] "Transforming Cable & Wireless HKT for the 21st Century", Cable & Wireless HKT press release, 5 November 1999.

'deliver innovative services that enhance the lifestyles and businesses of our customers'.[52] Nevertheless, the Company was focusing on its latest 'star' project, Network of the World (NOW), which was launched on 4 July 2000.[53] NOW was touted as 'the world's first fully-converged TV-and-satellite Internet service',[54] providing fully interactive entertainment, game playing and Internet access, via television, personal computers and even mobile phones. Linus Cheung, taking up the post of deputy chairman of PCCW after the takeover, told a local newspaper: "We will rely on NOW, not our pay-TV, to take us beyond Asia."[55] As a precedent for the new era of broadband services in the industry, iTV would still be an asset to the Company as long as its operation harmonised with NOW.

NOW

NOW delivered a 'linear TV experience and streaming video synchronised to Web content'.[56] The project was based on the idea of forming a hybrid between the media of television and the Internet. Seemingly, the Company was attempting to avoid a head-on confrontation with conventional television:

> *We are not competing against TV, we are competing against narrowband content … But people like Rupert Murdoch think we are coming after them. Absolutely not. We have zero interest going after TV.*[57]
>
> — Richard Li

NOW's executives did not want to associate their product with traditional television,

---

[52] "Pacific Century CyberWorks – Mission Statements", URL: http://www.cyberworks.com/about_the_company/index.html, October 2000.

[53] "The Journey Begins Now: Revolutionary New TV-Internet Service Rolls Out on Schedule to the World", Pacific Century CyberWorks press release, 4 July 2000.

[54] "Pacific Century CyberWorks – Company Profile", URL: http://www.cyberworks.com/about_the_company/index.html, October 2000.

[55] Kwok, B. (2000).

[56] "What's iTV", URL: http://www.itvhk.com

[57] Plott, D. & Gilley, B. (2000).

which they considered as 'a commodity and intellectually unchallenging'.[58] NOW would have 'vortals'[59] instead of channels and 'viewers' instead of TV viewers and Internet users. The service was to extend beyond Asia. John Colmey, a senior vice president at NOW, explained that they aimed "to win over the million most active Internet users worldwide – from university students to tech gurus, and would rely on these 'opinion makers' to drive global demand by word-of-mouth".[60] He also told others at the launch that "Right now, the [NOW] service isn't about subscriber revenue. It's focused on advertising and getting our brand established in the region."[61]

Investment for NOW was not cheap. A local newspaper reported that PCCW had already spent over US$128 million on the project, three months after its launch; the Company planned to spend another US$700 million in the near future.[62] PCCW was expecting to acquire most of NOW's initial revenue from Internet advertising and later on from e-business services transacted through its sites. The Company also hoped users would migrate to broadband connections, thus generating revenue from fees for subscriptions to those services.

The Next Phase – Internet Marketing

Seemingly, iTV would gradually converge with the broadband Internet service to form a new generation of VOD and interactive services. The digital convergence would provide more flexibility for the Internet marketers to work on the different marketing media available in order to find the best solution.[63] As with the marketing plans of other new technological innovations, iTV's future marketing strategy had to demonstrate full understanding of its customers' needs in terms of performance and psychological expectations, in order to succeed.

[58] Stein, P. & Levander, M. (2000), "Richard Li Makes a Bet on Future of Entertainment – His New Network Promises Interactivity, But May Deliver Less – Event-o-Drome and MP3TV; Will 'Viewers' Tune In?" *The Asian Wall Street Journal*, 29 June.

[59] Vortals – vertical portal focused on one subject.

[60] Bolande, H.A. (2000), "Broadband Services Are Launching in Asia. But Will Anyone Sign Up?" *Technology Journal Asia, The Wall Street Journal*, 26 June.

[61] Couto, V. (2000), "Cable & Satellite", *Asia World*, August.

[62] *MingPao Newspaper*, Hong Kong, 3 October 2000.

[63] Hanson, W. (2000), "Chapter 2: The Digital World", *Principles of Internet Marketing*, Cincinnati, Ohio: South-Western College Publishing, p. 48.

New Image Under PCCW

While "the next-generation interactive entertainment is uncharted territory and nobody knows how to do it",[64] as stated by Richard Li, iTV could exploit the advantages brought about by being part of PCCW. For example, the Company's new image and Li's personal image could initiate new ideas for iTV's branding strategy. In comparison with HKT, Francis Yuen described PCCW as a young company that "focused a little bit less on bureaucracy, more on imagination, flexibility".[65] Li's image was that of an Internet celebrity, with his 'new economy' look: crew cut and open-necked shirt. To his staff, he was an energetic leader. His influential family background and his personal academic and career track records helped to raise consumers' confidence in the Company.

The Company's existing iTV, broadband Internet and mobile phone subscribers grouped to form a ready distribution channel for NOW. The service was aired on iTV from June 2000. The Company also tried out other distribution channels such as Cable TV, which already had a substantial subscriber base in the HKSAR, to extend NOW's coverage; although the trial, which ended in November 2000, lasted only three months.

THE ROAD AHEAD

> *We're operators, but we're also a totally integrated Internet play, with an infrastructure side, a service platform and an incubator, all of which converge to make each other more valuable.*[66]
>
> – Richard Li

Whether or not PCCW could fulfil its goal in becoming the 'largest broadband Internet business in the world' remained to be seen. Many still recognised iTV as a pay-television service rather than an interactive multimedia service. The Company would also need to improve on its financials and assess its business portfolio in order to compete in the more complex business environment brought about by the digital

---

[64] Stein, P. & Levander, M. (2000).

[65] "CyberWorks Sets Sights on Becoming Global New Media Colossus As It Completes Asia's Biggest Merger with HKT Giant Leap for PCCW", *South China Morning Post*, 6 August 2000.

[66] Beal, T. (2000), "Integrated Circuit: Pacific Century CyberWorks Casts Wide Net Over Asia", *The Asian Wall Street Journal*, New York, 1 February.

convergence. Those with a similar vision to PCCW, such as the joint venture between Star TV and GigaMedia established in early October 2000, were already entering the arena with high profiles:

> *Many companies make a lot of promises about delivering the next generation of television, but at News Corp, we have actually delivered on it.*[67]
>
> — James Murdoch, Chairman and Chief Executive, Star TV

Some would argue that 'successful high-technology companies do not necessarily have the best product, but they do have the best marketing strategy'.[68] But for PCCW, its challenge would stretch beyond developing a good marketing strategy. Li's management's ability to lead the Company through the new age of digital convergence and his perseverance in making the dream come true might carry significant weight in deciding how the Company would move forward.

APPENDIX 1: CONVERGING DIGITAL INDUSTRIES

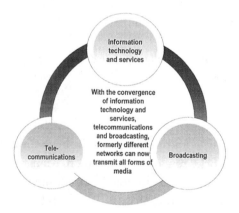

Source: *Digital21 – IT Strategy*, URL: http://www.info.gov.hk/digital21/eng/strategy/strategy_part12.html

---

[67] Hui, Y.M. (2000), "Star-GigaMedia Unveils Region's First Interactive TV Platform", *South China Morning Post*, Hong Kong, 5 October.

[68] Viardot, E. (1998), "Introduction", *Successful Marketing Strategy for High-tech Firms* (Second Edition), Boston: Artech House Publishers, p. xiii.

Exhibit 1:   Telecommunication indications in Hong Kong

The following information was submitted to the International Telecommunication Union (ITU) for the fiscal year ending 31 March 2000.

Indicator		Definition adopted by ITU
DEMOGRAPHY, ECONOMY		The indicators are generally obtained from international organisations or nation statistical offices.
Population	6.721 million	The data for population are based on the mid-year estimates for the calendar year ending 31 December 1999. They typically refer to the *de facto* population within the present boundaries.
Households	2.115 million	The data for households refer to the number of housing units consisting of persons who live together or a person living alone. Estimates are based on growth rates between censuses.
TELEPHONE NETWORK		The indicators in this category refer to the fixed–telephone network.
Main telephone lines in operation	3.869 million	The number of telephone lines connecting the subscriber's terminal equipment to the public switched network and which have a dedicated port in the telephone exchange equipment.
Digital main lines	100% since 1993	Refers to the percent of main lines connected to digital exchanges. This percentage is obtained by dividing the number of main lines connected to digital telephone exchanges by the total number of main lines.
Residential main lines	56.80%	Refers to the percent of main lines in residences. This percentage is obtained by dividing the number of main lines serving households (e.g., lines which are not used for business, government or other professional purposes or as public telephone stations) by the total number of main lines.

Exhibit 1 (cont'd)

Indicator		Definition adopted by ITU
Public payphones	11,710	The total number of all types of public telephones, including coin and card operated and public telephones in call offices. Public phones installed in private places should also be included as should mobile public telephones. All public telephones regardless of capability (e.g., local calls or national only) should be counted.
MOBILE SERVICES		The indicators in this category refer to mobile (wireless) networks.
Cellular mobile telephone subscribers	4.275 million	Refers to users of portable telephones subscribing to an automatic public mobile telephone service which provides access to the Public Switched Telephone Network (PSTN) using cellular technology. This can include analogue and digital cellular systems (including micro-cellular systems such as DCS-1800, Personal Handyphone System (PHS) and others) but should not include non-cellular systems. Subscribers to fixed wireless (e.g., Wireless Local Loop (WLL)), public mobile data services, or radio paging services are not included.
Digital cellular subscribers	4.275 million	The number of mobile cellular subscribers who use a digital cellular service (e.g., GSM, CDMA, D-AMPS).
Coverage of population	63.2%	Mobile cellular coverage of population in percent.
OTHER SERVICE		The indicators in this category refer to text and data communications and value-added network services.
Estimated facsimile machines	390,435	Estimated facsimile machines refer to the total number of facsimile machines.

Exhibit 1 (cont'd)

Indicator		Definition adopted by ITU
OTHER SERVICE		The indicators in this category refer to text and data communications and value–added network services.
ISDN subscribers	9,744	The number of subscribers to the Integrated Services Digital Network (ISDN). It includes both basic rate and primary rate subscribers.
ISDN B channel equivalents	73,156	Converts the number of ISDN subscriber lines into their equivalent voice channels. The number of basic rate subscribers is multiplied by two and the number of primary rate subscribers is multiplied by 23 or 30 depending on the standard implemented.
Telex subscribers	3,011	A telex subscriber line is a line connecting the subscriber's terminal equipment to the public telex network and which has a dedicated port in the telex exchange equipment.
TRAFFIC		The indicators in this category refer to the volume of traffic carried over the Public Switched Telephone Network.
International outgoing telephone (minutes)	2.720 billion	Effective (completed) traffic originating in a given country to destinations outside that country.
International incoming telephone (minutes)	1.747 billion	Effective (completed) traffic originating outside the country with a destination inside the country.
International bothway telephone (minutes)	4.467 billion	The total international traffic handled in the country, which is equal to the sum of the incoming and outgoing traffic. However, some countries also include transit traffic in this figure.

Exhibit 1 (cont'd)

Indicator		Definition adopted by ITU
STAFF		The indicator in this category refers to the number of staff in the telecommunications service sector.
Full-time telecommunication staff	36,453	Full-time staff employed by telecommunication network operators in the country for the provision of public telecommunication services. Part-time staff are generally expressed in terms of full-time staff equivalents.
TARIFFS		Tariffs are expressed in local currency and include any relevant taxes unless otherwise noted.
Connection fee for residential telephone service	HK$475 (US$60.90)	The one-time charge involved in applying for residential telephone service. Where there are different charges for different exchange areas, the charge is generally for the largest urban area unless otherwise noted.
Connection fee for business telephone service	HK$475 (US$60.90)	Same as above but applied to business users.
Monthly subscription for residential telephone service	HK$90 (US$11.50)	Refers to the recurring fixed charge for a residential subscriber to the PSTN. The charge covers the rental of the line but not the rental of the terminal (e.g., telephone set).
Monthly subscription for business telephone service	HK$109 (US$14)	Same as above but applied to business subscribers.

Exhibit 1 (cont'd)

Indicator		Definition adopted by ITU
BROADCASTING		The indicators in this category refer to television broadcasting equipment and networks.
Cable TV subscribers	0.457 million	The number of cable television subscribers. Refers to households that subscribe to a multi-channel television service delivered by a fixed-line connection. However some countries report subscribers to pay television using wireless technology (e.g., Microwave Multi-point Distribution systems (MMDS)). Other countries include the number of households that are cabled to community antenna systems even though the antennas are simply rebroadcasting free-to-air channels because of poor reception.
Home satellite antennas	1,775	The number of home satellite antennas that can receive television broadcasting directly from satellites (i.e., Direct-To-Home (DTH)).

Source: *Telecom Facts, Data & Statistics, The Office of the Telecommunications Authority (OFTA)*, URL: http://www.ofta.gov.hk/datastat/hktelecom-indicators.html

Exhibit 2:   New pay-TV operations

The HKSAR government announced on 4 July 2000 that the following five companies would be offered the domestic pay-television programme service licences. The proposed services would bring in additional 149 television programme channels starting from early 2001.

- ❑ Hong Kong Network TV Limited (owned by Sino-i.com, HKSAR-listed Internet content provider) – the company is a new venture and it plans to have 65 channels, providing 24-hour local news, documentaries and foreign films, with home shopping between programmes. The channels will include local contents and those from Greater China, India, Korea, the Philippines and Japan.
- ❑ Elmsdale Limited (Founder of Britian's Yes TV) – plans to offer ten channels with entertainment, news and education package and services such as VOD, enhanced Internet and e-mail. Seventy-five percent of the programmes will be in Chinese. A large part of the business will focus on e-commerce. The Company has previous experience in operating an interactive channel for British viewers to do home shopping, banking and e-mail using the television remote control.
- ❑ Pacific Digital Media (HK) Corp. Limited (Taiwan-based) – plans to offer 20 channels split into three areas: local and foreign news, pay-per-view films and serials, and educational content linked to a university open-learning channel.
- ❑ Hong Kong DTV Company Limited (owned by Star TV, Asia's largest satellite television operator) – plans to offer 14 channels focusing mainly on big sporting events and news. Some of the overseas channels with phone-in chat shows may also be available.
- ❑ Galaxy Satellite Broadcasting Limited (owned by TVB, a dominant local television broadcaster) – plans to have 40 channels, some would be 'radio' channels with sound only, others would provide information on finance, weather and traffic. There will be 24-hour Cantonese channels with family entertainment and drama, channels for pre-school children and channels with local and foreign films. Viewers will also be able to check e-mail, do shopping, do home banking and play games.

Sources: "Five Applications for Television Broadcasting Licences Approved", Broadcasting Authority press release, HKSAR government, 4 July 2000; Bowman, J. (2000), "Pay-TV Revolution Begins", *South China Morning Post*, Hong Kong, 9 July.

Exhibit 3:   Pacific Century CyberWorks' new company structure

The new PCCW utilised an innovative '8 × 3' model that operated eight business units via three operating sectors, operating on the principles of accessibility, accountability and transparency.

Operating sectors	Business units
Telecommunications Services	Telecommunications Services
Global Communications Services	Connectivity Services
	Mobility Services
Net Enterprises	Broadband B2C Services
	B2B Services
	Data Centres/Web Hosting Services
	CyberWorks Venture
	Infrastructure Services*

* Infrastructure Services directly support all three sectors.

The Company adopts a Strategic Integration Process (SIP) that functions as a communication conduit throughout the new organisation. The SIP is intended to link strategies and ensure coordination within and among sectors and business units without adding a level of bureaucracy. While addressing tasks most central to value creation, the SIP will provide the Company Chairman with direct access to sector Managing Directors and Business Unit Presidents.

Source: "'New' Pacific Century CyberWorks Unveils Strategy '8 × 3' Structure Geared to Capture Global Opportunities", Pacific Century CyberWorks press release, 17 August 2000.

Exhibit 4: Competition – Other options available to iTV's target customers

iTV service	Alternatives
Video-on-demand	• Free local television channels • Cable television channels • Satellite television channels • Video and VCDs for rental • Licensed and pirated VCDs for purchase • 65 local cinemas, some with multi-screens
Home banking	• Hundreds of branches available nearby • Thousands of self-service machines (ATM, deposit machine, balance machine, passbook update machine) • Phone banking • Mobile banking via mobile phone • On-line banking via the Internet
Music-on-demand & karaoke-on-demand	• Radio • Television channels • CD stores • Karaoke restaurants • Home karaoke systems • The Internet
News-on-demand	• Television channels • Radio • Newspapers • Internet
Shopping	• Hundreds of supermarkets and convenient stores available nearby • The Internet

Exhibit 5:   List of iTV products as at 25 September 2000

Entertainment

- ❏ 'Movie' and 'Hollywood extravaGANZA' categories – there were 159 movies on offer. The films were on offer for a period of two to four weeks. Some were co-released with the cinema. Their pay-per-view prices (in addition to the monthly subscription fee) ranged from HK$10 to HK$35.
- ❏ 'Adult' category – there were 186 films on offer. The programmes in this category contained indecent material and viewing was restricted to persons above the age of 18. The films were on offer for a period of two to four weeks. Their pay-per-view prices (in addition to the monthly subscription fee) ranged from HK$10 to HK$30.
- ❏ 'Kiddieland' – there were 54 films on offer. All of them were free for viewing.
- ❏ 'Music' – there were 24 concerts on offer. Their pay-per-view prices (in addition to the monthly subscription fee) ranged from HK$20 to HK$30.

Infotainment

- ❏ This channel provided contents from NOW, documentary programmes, talk shows, sports video, games magazine and Japanese films series. Some programmes were free for viewing, some were offered on pay-per-view prices ranging from HK$10 to HK$35.

Banking News & Finance

- ❏ This channel provided a home banking facility in association with the Bank of China Group, Foreign Exchange Rate, news reported by ATV, financial information from Reuters, talk shows on current affairs and government information.

Shopping

- ❏ Round the clock home shopping services provided by Wellcome Supermarket and City'super. There were also miscellaneous electrical appliances on offer.

Source: iTV (2000), URL: http://www.itvhk.com, September.

Exhibit 6: iTV pricing plan as at 22 September 2000

Interactive TV Package

Offer Details

Service Package	Monthly Subscription Fee	Programmes Include
Basic Plan	#$178	Entertainment which includes Kiddieland, Music Video & Karaoke and Freebies Corner; Shopping; Banking, News & Finance and My iTV.
Family Plan	#$238## #50% off monthly fee for 3 months (for the 1st, 3rd, 5th month only) plus total 300 cash points FREE###	Programmes of Basic Plan and Movie in Entertainment* *Except Hollywood Extravaganza, Adult, Specials which include programmes such as co-release movies and special music programmes.

\# Smart Box installation fee of ($350) will be charged in the first monthly bill.
\#\# Promotion starts from now on till 31st December, 2000, subscribers must complete installation on or before 15th January, 2001.
\#\#\# Customers can enjoy 50% off monthly fee ($119) for the 1st, 3rd and 5th month only. Cash Points can be used for viewing Movies (except Hollywood Extravaganza), Adult and Specials. 1 cash point equals to $1. 50 free cash points will be credited to the subscriber's account on a monthly basis for the first 6 months after installation. Cash points are valid during the credited month only and cannot be transferred to other users and subsequent month. Unused cash points cannot be redeemed for cash.

Notes:
1. Smart Box rental fee is included in the above subscription fee.
2. The above unlimited viewing package incorporates 200,000 cash points where 1 cash point equals to $1. Cash points can be used for viewing the corresponding pay per view programmes.
3. The interactive TV service is available at designated areas.
4. Cable & Wireless HKT Limited reserves the right to amend the content of the offer.

Source: iTV (2000), URL: http://www.itvhk.com, September.

Exhibit 7: Examples of iTV's promotion activities

Above-the-line advertising:

- ❏ Newspapers – printed ads were run monthly in local papers until summer 2000 to promote the video-on-demand contents (e.g., co-release movies).
- ❏ Television – advertisements were done twice, the first time around the time of the launch and the second time in early 1999.
- ❏ Radio – commercial spots were placed quarterly selling the video-on-demand feature and its contents (e.g., co-release movies).

Below-the-line advertising:

- ❏ Direct door-to-door selling – done on a regular basis.
- ❏ Road shows – held at designated housing estates as iTV rolled out every month.
- ❏ Exhibition – participated in trade shows such as Computer Expo annually.
- ❏ Joint promotion – ran one-off referral programmes with the Jockey Club and SmartCard 21.
- ❏ Catalogue – placed catalogues in CSL shops and distributed free programme guides through 7-Eleven stores.

Exhibit 8: Examples of complaints about iTV

The following complaints were filed with the local Broadcasting Authority, but were considered as 'outside of the remit of the Broadcasting Authority':

A member of the public complained that it was disturbing for the Cable & Wireless HKT VOD Limited's staff to promote the iTV's service at her residence late at night on 25.1.2000 at 10:50 pm. – February 2000

A subscriber complained about the poor picture quality and frequent interruptions during the reception of iTV's programme service. – March 2000

A subscriber complained against iTV's practice of delivering the adult programme guide together with its monthly programme guide to its subscribers. The complainant alleged that the free delivery of the adult programme guide would exert an adverse influence to young people. – March 2000

A viewer complained that she was unable to watch iTV programmes since her subscription in April this year. Despite repeated repairs, the technical problem could not be fixed.
– June 2000

Source: Broadcasting Authority (2000), URL: http://www.hkba.org.hk/english/archives.html, September.

Exhibit 9:   NETVIGATOR broadband pricing plan

Services and Details	NETVIGATOR Ultraline 1.5M (iTV subscriber)	NETVIGATOR Ultraline 1.5M (non–iTV subscriber)
Monthly subscription fee	HK$418 (US$54) (bundle price HK$180 (US$23.10) + HK$238 (US$30.50) for iTV subscription)	High Usage Plan: HK$298 (US$38.30) Basic Usage Plan: HK$198 (US$25.40)
Free usage	10:00 am to 10:00 pm every day	High Usage Plan: 1st 100 hours broadband Internet service usage Basic Usage Plan: 1st 20 hours broadband Internet service usage
Additional usage charges	HK$2 (US$0.26) per hour	HK$2 (US$0.26) per hour

Source: Netvigator Member Service Plan (2000), http://www2.netvigator.com/services/index_e.html, September.

MODULE

■ ■ ■

4

Transforming the Enterprise: The Internetworked Enterprise

It is not the strongest of the species that survives, not the most intelligent, but the one most responsive to change.

– Charles Darwin

The new organisational form – the internetworked enterprise – can be regarded as rethinking the way a business uses technology to streamline its operations along its business web – the loose constellation of Web-based relationships. The ultimate objective of such an enterprise is to enhance business value through the seamless integration of its internal information systems and those of its customers and trading partners.

The success of the internetworked enterprise will in the long run rest on its ability to build such an infrastructure and use it to integrate the major business processes involved in its supply-chain and selling-chain: from sourcing to after-market sales, from order acquisition to after sales service. The operative word in this new world is integration: integration from supply-side; integration from demand-side.

In the previous module we discussed how firms leverage the Internet to build and manage their business relationships with their customers, suppliers and partners. In this final module we try to show that sustainability of the emerging business ecosystem depends on enhanced collaboration and communication not only along the firm's external business chain, but also within the enterprise itself. Such collaboration and communication calls for leveraging technology to transform the existing organisational structure into a new form, a new design.

The new organisational form is based on a secure and scalable technology infrastructure capable of providing performance-on-demand. Chapter 8 discusses the components of such techno-business architecture, including the Internet, intranet and extranet. The two cases at the end of the chapter – *EIU's ViewsWire: New Wine in a New Bottle* and *PricewaterhouseCoopers: Building a Global Network* – examine how companies embark on developing and maintaining such an architecture.

Chapter 9 discusses process management through e-business. It introduces the concepts of supply-chain management and selling-chain management. The chapter ends with a case – *Japan Airlines: The Impact of e-Ticketing* – that explores some of the major challenges related to end-to-end processes integration.

The final chapter examines how companies can transform themselves into an internetworked enterprise. The chapter ends with an award-winning case – *FedEx Corp: Structural Transformation Through e-Business* – that discusses the important role of information sharing in enhancing collaboration and communication within and outside organisational bounds.

CHAPTER

8

Techno-business Architecture

OBJECTIVES

■ To recognise the importance of collaboration and communication in the formation of a new form of organisation – the internetworked enterprise.

■ To understand the critical, strategic role of technology in the formation of such an enterprise.

■ To highlight the characteristics of three network types – the Internet, intranet and extranet – that sustain the architecture of an internetworked enterprise.

■ To study emerging technologies, such as the virtual private network and the Extended Markup Language, which underlie such an architecture.

In the last few years a new terminology – e-business – has been used to describe the use of information and telecommunication technologies to automate processes so that business transactions can be conducted in a seamless manner, electronically. Broadly speaking, e-business can be viewed in the realm of integrating processes, systems and business, which together facilitate e-commerce.

In this chapter we focus on the technological infrastructure necessary for e-business. Assuming that the ultimate benefits of e-commerce will be reaped through enhanced communication and coordination between a firm and its business partners, the firm needs to put in place the networks necessary for inter-enterprise interactions. More specifically, to improve the channels for the flow of external information, successful enterprises need to employ inter-organisational Information Systems (IS) to facilitate business transactions with their customers, suppliers and partners. In the same vein, firms need to redesign their internal IS architecture not only to augment the lateral flow of internal information within the organisation, but also to seamlessly capture and integrate such information with information flowing to and from the external systems. The Internet's universal and ubiquitous connectivity makes it a logical platform to create new forms of intra- and inter-organisational space within which all stakeholders of a firm can meet to share information, communicate and collaborate.

Since the survival of most companies in the future will be directly linked to the way they manage both internal and external information, such 'networked intelligence' must transcend organisational boundaries. That is, the IT infrastructure of the internetworked enterprise, based on the following three major interdependent networks, must be flawlessly integrated into those of its strategic partners:

1. Intranets to enhance intra-organisational coordination and collaboration.
2. Extranets to facilitate B2B transactions.
3. The Internet to connect to the public, customers and other organisations.

THE INTERNET

Information is at the heart of decision making. With the emergence of the network economy and gradual removal of geographical and temporal barriers, there is a growing need for fast access to reliable, relevant and up-to-date information. In this light the success of companies in the future will increasingly depend on their ability to access and share business information in a timely fashion within and outside blurring organisational borders. As shown in **Figure 1**, companies traditionally had to make a trade-off between information reach and richness.[1] *Reach* refers to the number of people exchanging information, whereas *richness* includes bandwidth (the amount of information that the network can carry) and the degree to which information is customised and interactive. Richness has usually been compromised at the expense of

---

[1] Evans & Wurster (1997).

reach. However, the Internet provides both a *rich* information infrastructure and a wide, global *reach*. The Internet also provides the bedrock that supports the organisational architecture. At the same time, companies can use such a rich and expansive platform to enhance communication and coordination among the major stakeholders of their internetworked space.

Figure 1:   The traditional economics of information[2]

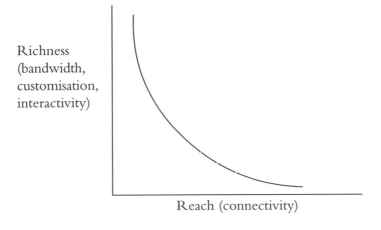

Richness (bandwidth, customisation, interactivity)

Reach (connectivity)

INTRANETS

Companies have tried to link their employees since the early 1980s when client/server networks were introduced. Client/server networks used a proprietary architecture that involved the transmission of information across a private line between the server and the client, through a computer that utilised its own processing capability to run applications. This structure allowed for great flexibility because it permitted the *distribution* of functionality to different PCs.[3] A number of information servers could feed a whole host of active, intelligent processors. Each of these processors, running on different software, could then utilise the information it received to provide a particular service. In this way, one client/server system could offer a whole array of specialised services, each of which was run from different processing nodes in the network.

---

[2] Evans & Wurster (1997).

[3] Wise (1997).

The speed at which information flowed through a client/server network, as well as the array of specialised services that could be provided, facilitated great degrees of collaboration among employees. Sophisticated applications that took advantage of this distributed structure were soon developed, creating networks of shared spaces where employees could meet and work together on projects. The most popular of these early types of applications, IBM's Lotus Notes® entered the market in 1990. It provided discussion databases as well as systems development platforms for the construction of complex database or workflow applications.[4]

But as useful as client/server systems and their groupware are for facilitating group work, certain problems persist. Client/server solutions tend to be costly and complex as they rely on the integration of hardware, software and networking components, rendering such an architecture less reliable and stable than a centralised multi-user architecture.

Moreover, because it is assumed that information should be as close to the client as possible, the system involves distributing masses of information from server to client as well as multiple exchanges of information between the various clients.[5] Another problem is that employees are often insufficiently trained to use the new technologies. Instead of grasping their potential, they see them as offering little more than an extension of e-mail. Indeed, despite all the facilities that early client/server groupware packages offered, and despite all the beneficial effects that they were believed to unleash on a company, the reality often proved to be a disappointment. A study conducted in 1996 of an organisation in which more than two thousand employees had access to Lotus Notes® concluded that 'the introduction of Notes® resulted in general satisfaction but no increase in collaboration'.[6]

It has only been since the surge in the popularity of the Internet in the early 1990s that a more effective kind of network technology has emerged. Intranet is a single and widely accessible (authorised users only) network that integrates the information and communication facilities of a company. It is based on Internet technologies, such as e-mail, bulletin boards and WWW. Because Web-based technologies provide common user interface, intranets can be used to develop cross-platform applications, enabling the integration of the existing legacy applications and databases. In other words, intranet

---

[4] Vandenbosch & Ginzberg (1997).

[5] Babcock (1996).

[6] Vandenbosch & Ginzberg (1997), p. 75.

is a private and secure (through a firewall) Web, which is based on HTTP and TCP/IP protocols and common interface made possible by HTML and XML.[7] As such, an intranet can easily be scaled throughout a company, across departmental divisions, and between branches in different cities or countries, creating a large and powerful corporate network.[8] Such an open client system dismantles the boundaries established by incompatible protocols and proprietary lines, and successfully creates the shared intra-organisational space that is needed for group collaboration.

Major Functions

Intranet networks themselves have two main functions as follows:

- ❏ They enable information to be freely disseminated throughout an organisation.
- ❏ They facilitate greater degrees of communication and collaboration among the organisation's employees, suppliers, customers and other business partners.

Because scaling such a network throughout an organisation is a simple and relatively inexpensive process, traditional groupware packages have already begun to introduce the non-proprietary protocols of the Internet alongside their proprietary structures.[9]

Product catalogues, statements of company policies, customer and employee directories, company newsletters, annual reports, electronic databases and any other information that an individual in the organisation wishes to distribute can be posted on the intranet so that employees can easily retrieve the information they want. Because information plays such an important role in society, an intranet in this way becomes an

---

[7] Extensible Markup Language (XML) is a World Wide Web Consortium (W3C) standard that translates a company's business documents into a format understandable by another company. It is the universal format for structured documents and data on the Web (W3C, 2000). XML is intended for open computer-to-computer communications as it permits the efficient integration of e-commerce solutions across both the Internet and private B2B network. It is a way of enriching Web documents with structured content. Prior to XML, Websites supported only human-to-computer interaction. Under XML, sites can begin talking to each other, opening up the possibility for Web automation.

[8] Babcock (1996).

[9] Pompili (1997).

essential part of running a business. In general, an intranet could provide the following advantages to companies:

❏ Easy access to up-to-date information means that employees are able to make better-informed decisions and to react to industry and market changes more swiftly.
❏ The time that is saved in the hunt for relevant information means that an employee's productivity is increased.
❏ Team members can share research data, designs and job schedules in order to get feedback in the early stages of a project.
❏ Virtual newsgroups can be used to discuss ideas and solutions.
❏ Training courses can be distributed and conducted over the intranet.
❏ Teleconferences over the intranet can be established, enabling participants to share materials in the form of text, video and audio.
❏ Because all documents can be posted on the intranet, printing, photocopying and distribution costs can be significantly reduced.

In spite of these benefits, companies need to be mindful of certain pitfalls associated with the use of intranets. The ease with which anyone can publish anything they wish on the corporate intranet could burden companies with non-essential information. Companies therefore need to pay attention to how the mass of information is catalogued and how it can be retrieved. Alongside this there is the chaos that may result when the use of intranets extends beyond simple information sharing to traditional groupware applications. An effective intranet must integrate systems that were traditionally separate: print servers, e-mail systems, groupware applications and so on. These systems need to share security services, navigational services and user desktop software. Installing a planned architecture becomes a necessary task if chaos is to be avoided.[10]

Firewalls

An intranet's boundaries are enforced by firewalls – security mechanisms that allow limited access to a Webster from the Internet. The most common type of firewall is a screening router that is placed between the secure network of an intranet and the wider network of the Internet. A router screens packets of information from the Internet by comparing information in the packet's header with screening rules that have been established for the network. These rules normally refer to restrictions based on the

---

[10] Cullen (1999).

type of protocol being used, the type of application being accessed or the IP address that the packet is being sent from.

Hospital Intranet Saves Time and Unburdens Staff

A simple intranet built at the Savannah (Ga.) Memorial Health has helped unburden staff duties, streamlining processes, saving time while containing costs. The integrated delivery system which costs about US$125,000 has helped employees gain work efficiencies and cost savings while laying the foundation for even more change. Merely putting information on-line has provided the groundwork for on-line transactions including submitting employee forms and signing documents. When launched in July 1999, corporate policies and phone directories were the first items posted. Benefit services, hospital policies, physician phone numbers, on-call schedules are among the information posted on the intranet. The decision to put information on the intranet is paying off as it centralises information and gives staff easy access to documents and information that require immediate attention. "The biggest savings from using the intranet has been time," says Steve Stanic, Vice President and CIO at Savannah Memorial. The read-only network is connected to each of the delivery system's 2,100 desktop computers with the intranet residing on the existing local area network. Using Web browser software, all staff members can access the network. The network is also accessible from employees' home PCs through one of the system's 48 dial-in lines, making the intranet available anytime, anywhere.

Source: Kelly (2000).

Users access is controlled by an authentication process. When a user logs onto the network, he or she will be asked to enter a user name and password. Based on this information, the server will check to see which files, drives, servers or directories, if any, he or she is permitted to access.[11] Moreover, the privacy of the data is ensured based on encryption and decryption algorithms and schemes.

---

[11] Greer (1998).

EXTRANETS

To fully realise the benefits of e-commerce, there is a need for integrated and seamless interaction between a company and its suppliers, customers and other parties (e.g., distributors). Such interaction is possible only if a company's stakeholders have selective access not only to that company's corporate data, but also to each other's databases. For example, as a customer of an on-line retailer you may want to track the shipment of your order. An alternative is for the retailer to provide you with a shipment number so that you can track your order on the Website of the package delivery company. To do so, you need to start a new on-line session, go to the delivery company's site and type in the shipment number. Alternatively, the company could take your request and directly track your order, without you knowing that the actual information is being retrieved from the delivery company's database. In this example, the secure network that connects the intranet of the retailer and database of the delivery company is an extranet. In other words, an extranet is an extension of a corporate intranet that connects to suppliers, distributors and customers, enabling certain parties outside of the corporation to have access through the Internet to certain information on the corporate intranet. As with intranets, firewalls and user authentication are important aspects of an extranet's structure.

Because extranets are based on open Internet standards, they have many advantages over traditional client/servers. An extranet application runs within a standard browser and is scalable, as you can expand it without major investment over time. The major significance of an extranet is that it allows for an efficient management of a company's supply-chain (see Chapter 9: Process Management Through e-Business). In place of the traditional, costly EDI infrastructure, an extranet works across the standard platform and protocols of the Internet, and makes it easier and quicker for supply-chain partners to communicate with each other and share critical information. This brings about both operational and marketing benefits for a company.[12]

---

[12] Anandarajan *et al.* (1998).

Goodyear Tire & Rubber Company: Connects with Dealers Through Xplor Extranet

Goodyear Tire & Rubber Company (www.goodyear.com) has made corporate ordering easy and accessible to dealers through its extranet system, Xplor. The old order-entry system involving faxes, phone calls and manual tracking is replaced by the Xplor system, providing dealers access to information 24 × 7, enabling on-line ordering and status checking of orders. Goodyear's Customer Sales and Service Centre resources have been re-deployed to other areas as dealers no longer call to request brochures or product information. Xplor also allows Goodyear to save on printing costs for promotions and marketing documents that are distributed monthly to dealers.

Source: Chan & Davis (2000).

The operational benefits are as follows:

❑ A reduction in costs since processes involving paper are no longer undertaken.
❑ An improvement in demand forecasting which will enable partners to more effectively manage inventory.
❑ A reduction in time taken to bring products to market that is made possible by a tighter supply-chain and an improved cash flow.

The marketing benefits include the following:

❑ An improvement in knowledge about customers.
❑ A competitive edge.
❑ Improved relationships between partners.

This third advantage in marketing is perhaps the most important. When the barriers that separate companies from each other are dissolved, what emerges is a huge virtual corporation consisting of a number of traditional companies joined together. Instead of the hierarchical, slow-moving organisation of the traditional corporate world, this virtual company has a distributed structure that takes the form of a network of networks. No one nodal company is always in control; rather, various groups assume leadership at certain stages in the production and distribution process. Collaboration needs no longer only occur among employees of the same company; instead, people from different companies can meet within the shared spaces of the extranet to work together temporarily on a project. Human minds that have been influenced by the ethos and procedures of very different corporations can meet to share knowledge and ideas and work together towards common goals.

VIRTUAL PRIVATE NETWORKS (VPN)

Public networks, such as the Internet, are vulnerable to electronic eavesdropping by hackers. Despite the success that firewalls have had at securing corporate networks, they are not totally impenetrable. In 1994, hackers broke through General Electric's Internet firewalls and gained access to proprietary information, causing serious damage and leading GE to shut down its Internet access for three days.[13] Given the wealth of corporate information that an intranet should carry, the importance of preventing such breaches of security is obvious. The dangers are significantly increased with extranets that allow access by third parties, such as suppliers and distributors. Security issues are therefore a particularly serious concern for the internetworked enterprises.

Companies rely on VPNs to establish secure links with their strategic partners, extend communication among their distributed offices, and provide network access to their remote and mobile employees. A VPN is a network that uses a shared wide area network infrastructure that acts as its transport backbone to connect across a corporate intranet, extranet and the Internet. A VPN design architecture should integrate authentication, encryption, firewalling and tunnelling.[14] **Figure 2** shows the configuration of such a network.

One of the main advantages of VPNs over the traditional remote access methods, such as leased lines, is that VPNs are relatively inexpensive to implement.[15] VPNs are typically implemented as (1) an intranet, (2) an extranet or (3) a remote-access between a corporate network and its mobile employees (Checkpoint, 2000). The full benefits of interconnectivity, however, are achieved only if a VPN can securely inte-

---

[13] Kalakota & Whinston (1997).

[14] A VPN tunnel is an on-demand virtual point-to-point connection made through a public network (e.g., the Internet). Once connected, a remote user can utilise the tunnel to exchange information and access servers and services on the corporate network (URL: http://www.compatible.com/vpn_now/intraport.html/, 2 February 2000).

[15] Derfler (1999).

Figure 2: Network configuration of the internetworked enterprise

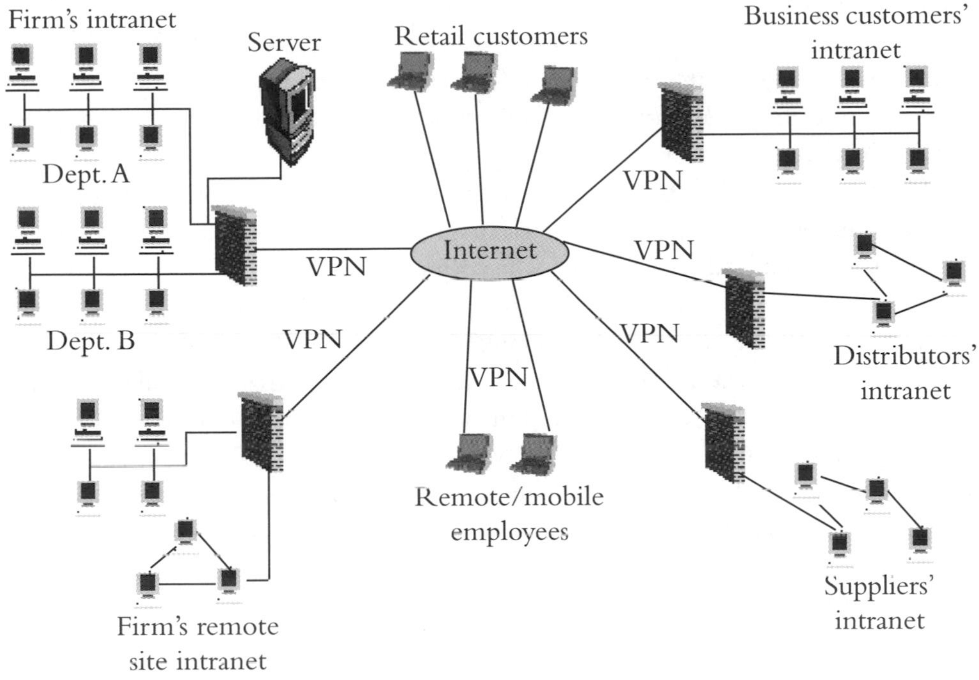

Firm's intranet

Server

Retail customers

Business customers' intranet

Dept. A

VPN

Internet

VPN

VPN

Dept. B

VPN

VPN

VPN

Distributors' intranet

Remote/mobile employees

Suppliers' intranet

Firm's remote site intranet

grate all these three types of application: to connect various parts of the company, to extend reach to strategic partners and to link an increasingly mobile workforce.

In a recent survey by Lucent Technology, the most important networking objectives driving the VPN strategy were cited as follows:[16]

- ❏ Improved remote-access networking capabilities.
- ❏ Reduced wide area networking costs.
- ❏ Improved remote-access security.
- ❏ Improved systems security to external partners.
- ❏ Enhanced data confidentiality.
- ❏ Improved internal systems security.
- ❏ Greater management control.

---

[16] URL: http://www.ins.com/news/events/vpn, 2 February 2000.

THE ARCHITECTURE OF AN INTERNETWORKED ENTERPRISE

As the common role of the Internet, intranets and extranets is to be both a source and a depository of information for all members of a business ecosystem, managing that information becomes a critical task.

By disseminating information throughout an organisation, and by creating a shared space in which employees can collaborate, intranets succeed in transcending the boundaries that have traditionally separated the departments and the people within an organisation.[17] They dismantle the vertical boundaries of an organisation – those that separate and determine different levels and ranks of people – by allowing even those who are in low positions within a company to have access to corporate information and to post their ideas for all to see. They also dismantle the horizontal boundaries, those that separate functions and disciplines by allowing people within different offices, departments, divisions and branches to share information and collaborate on projects. Steve Jobs, the CEO and co-founder of Apple Computer who played an instrumental role in ushering in the era of computer networks, puts it thus: "The intranet has broken down the walls within corporations."[18]

The promises of integrating the Internet, intranets and extranets are even more encouraging. Through the unprecedented extent to which they allow people and their computers to inform, communicate and collaborate with each other, the Internet, intranets and extranets give birth to the superintelligence of a vast network that transcends the vertical, horizontal and external boundaries of the traditional corporate world.

In the face of increased chaos and complexity, however, companies must overcome significant technological and organisational challenges before they can fully realise the potential of e-business. Popular literature abounds with cases of business disasters caused by inadequate or failed technology infrastructure. It is conventional wisdom that e-business is about business, not technology. Such is the case, but without proper planning for and managing the enabling technologies capable of providing high-performance, scalable solutions, there would be little chance of building a viable e-business. In this context, technology infrastructure is a strategic business factor without

---

[17] Ashkenas (1995).

[18] Cortese (1996), p. 2.

which the internetworked enterprise will not survive. Consider true e-businesses such as Dell Computer, Cisco Systems and amazon.com in the absence of their technological backbone. It is hard to conceive that such seamlessly internetworked enterprises can conduct their business without having access to their sophisticated technological infrastructure. Just look at the stock market reaction to the network failure of any company, such as amazon.com or Charles Schwab, to see that technology is a strategic necessity for such enterprises. In other words, technology is increasingly becoming the driving force behind internetworked enterprises, something which they cannot survive without.

Having a solid technology infrastructure by itself, however, will not necessarily lead to success in the marketspace. For the internetworked enterprise to be successful: (1) it needs to fully *integrate* its front-end and back-end processes with those of its customers and suppliers and (2) it must go through massive, and difficult, *structural transformation*. In the next chapter we will discuss the issues relating to process integration through e-business. In Chapter 10, we will show how today's firms need to go through a metamorphosis before they can successfully transform themselves into an internetworked enterprise.

SUMMARY

- ❑ The Internet is providing firms with an information infrastructure that is rich in terms of capacity and capability, and has a wide, global reach.
- ❑ Intranets are becoming the bedrock for integrating information required within and outside the internetworked enterprise.
- ❑ Extranets allow major suppliers and customers to access corporate databases, thus facilitating the integration of various activities of the value-chain.
- ❑ Virtual private networks provide a secure and economical way to link a firm with its partners.
- ❑ Building e-business requires solid technology infrastructure, process integration within and across organisational bounds and structural transformation of business.

REFERENCES

Anandarajan, M., Anandarajan, A., & Wen, J.H. (1998), "Extranets: A Tool for Cost Control in a Value Chain Framework", *Industrial Management & Data Systems*, March, pp. 120–128.

Ashkenas, R. *et al.* (1995), *The Boundaryless Organization: Breaking the Chains of Organizational Structure*, San Francisco, CA: Jossey-Bass Publishers.

Babcock, C. (1996), "Client/Server Is Dead; Long Live the Intranet", *Computerworld*, 11 March, URL: http://www.computerworld.com/, July 1999.

Chan, S. & Davis, T.R.V. (2000), "Partnering on Extranets for Strategic Advantage", *Information Systems Management*, Winter, pp. 58–64.

Checkpoint (2000), "Redefining the Virtual Private Network (VPN)", URL: http://www.checkpoint.com/, January.

Cortese, A. (1996), "Here Comes the Intranet", *BusinessWeek*, 26 February, URL: http://www.businessweek.com/1996/09/b34641.htm, August 2000.

Cullen, A. (1999), "Avoiding Intranet Chaos", *Intranet Journal*, URL: http://www.intranetjournal.earthweb.com/, July.

Derfler, F. (1999), "VPNs Analysis", *PC Magazine*, URL: http://www.zdnet.com/pcmag/stories/reviews/0,6755,2400740,00.html, August 2000.

Evans P.B. & Wurster, T.S. (1997), "Strategy and the New Economics of Information", *Harvard Business Review*, September–October.

Frook, J.E. (1998), "Boeing's Big Intranet Bet", *Internetweek*, Iss. 740, 9 November.

Greer, T. (1998), *Understanding Intranets*, Redmond, Washington: Microsoft Press.

Isidore, C. (1998), "e-Shoppers Choose Cheaper Shipping Over Speedy Delivery", *The Journal of Commerce Online*, URL: http://www.joc.com/issues/980112/page1/e32259.htm/, August 2000.

Kalakota, R. & Whinston, A.B. (1997), *Electronic Commerce: A Manager's Guide*, Reading, MA: Addison-Wesley.

Kelly, B. (2000), "Simple Network Unburdens Staff", *Health Data Management*, Vol. 8, Iss. 4, April, pp. 80–82.

Lheureux, B. (2000), *Monthly Research Review*, GartnerGroup, 1 January.

Pompili, T. (1997), "Multiple Personalities", *PC Magazine*, Vol. 16, No. 10, pp. 117–120.

Vandenbosch, B. & Ginzberg, M.J. (1996–97), "Lotus Notes® and Collaboration: Plus Ça Change...", *Journal of Management Information Systems*, Vol. 13, No. 3, Winter, pp. 65–81.

W3C (2000), "Extensible Markup Language (XML)", URL: http://www.w3.org/XML/, August.

Wilkerson, R. (1996), "Intranet Experiment Pays Off in the Lab", *PC Week Online*, 4 April, URL: http://www.zdnet.com/eweek/, July 1999.

Wise, S. (1997), *Client/Server Performance Tuning*, New York: McGraw-Hill.

CASE

■-■-■

8.1

EIU's Views *Wire*: New Wine in a New Bottle*

Until now, most publishers have offered old wine in new bottles – print sources, published according to print schedules, and simply converted into electronic formats. With the EIU Views Wire, our users also get new wine in new bottles – a truly digital service with content created, updated and analysed specifically for executives using the Web. We call it 'plug-and-play' executive intelligence.

— Lou Celi, Managing Director, EIU Electronic

On 1 May 1998, the Economist Intelligence Unit (EIU) launched its new Web-based information service, Views *Wire*. Views *Wire* was an attempt to take advantage of the Internet by combining the resources of the Economist Group's information services and publishing skills with cutting-edge search-and-retrieval technology and a proprietary database system. By linking related stories, articles and briefings together, the aim

---

* P. Lovelock prepared this case under the supervision of Dr. Ali Farhoomand. *Copyright © 2000 The University of Hong Kong. Ref. 99/56C*

was to allow Views *Wire* users to create their own 'personalised decision-support profiles'.

Moreover, global executives – the service's target audience – would be able to log onto Views *Wire* via the Internet from their desktops, their home PCs or their laptops, to demand and retrieve the information that they needed – background briefings or up-to-date news – *anytime, anywhere*. In other words, Views *Wire* promised to be a publishing service that did away with publishing schedules.

To successfully produce Views *Wire*, however, required the EIU to re-engineer how it organised information internally, and how it coordinated that process across more than 500 editors and analysts in more than 100 countries, working to a variety of different formats and timelines. Was it possible to create a new information product for the Web, based on a global intranet and a worldwide resource of information gatherers? What was the best means of implementing the new structure, and how could it be integrated into the existing work practices? How could a publishing company do away with publishing schedules and deliver information in Internet time?

A NEW BOTTLE

One of the reasons for the 'old wine in new bottles' apophthegm was a general failure to recognise the Internet and, latterly, the World Wide Web as a *new* medium of communication. Despite a great deal of hyperbole that the Net allowed for personalised marketing, and that the Web would have an impact on mass communications similar to the introduction of television in the 1950s, the initial use of the new medium had revolved around old-style billboard (i.e., banner) advertising or information dumps.

For most large media organisations, early attempts through the mid-1990s to exploit the new media opportunity instead proved frustrating, if not altogether fruitless. Limited bandwidth, leading to severe congestion, and disenchanted advertisers, meant that the traditional economics for *mass* commercial communication were ineffective. By July 1996, more than 70 percent of the commercial providers of original content on the Web – including virtually all of the large high-profile mass media sites – had either disappeared or radically scaled back their operations [see **Exhibit 1**]. This prompted Time Inc. President, Don Logan to re-title the World Wide Web 'The Great Black Hole'.[1]

But in many ways, the impact of the Web upon the mass communications world *was* similar to the initial impact of television earlier in the century. Just as at that time producers had tried to repackage successful studio programmes for the new pictures and sound world (with actors standing and reading their lines to the camera), the contemporary content providers of the Web moved in a similar fashion, placing passive text on an interactive medium.

The problem for the media organisations was two-fold. First, most information providers were simply rechurning old content, 'a wrong-headed entry into the digital marketplace'. Operating largely at the expense of their own print operations, hundreds of [for example] newspaper Websites beg the question: "What is a sustainable business model?"[2] This was the problem of 'old wine'. However, intimately tied to this problem of repackaging old content was the failure to recognise the new medium as different. The second problem, therefore, was that most information suppliers failed to utilise the interactive aspect of the new medium, preferring instead to see the Web as a tool for mass communications as they already understood it – i.e., mass distribution. There was also the problem therefore of using the new bottle as an old bottle.

The Web had the feel of radio and television and cable broadcasting. Certainly the Web seemed to mirror the competing interests and the lack of clear business models of early broadcasting.

Even 'dial-twisting', the practice in the early days of radio of sampling and seeking, was regarded at both Time *and* Wired *as the equivalent of Web surfing. And the assumption was that on the Web, as happened in radio by the 1940s, users would settle*

---

[1]   Bayers, C. (1996), "The Great Web Wipeout", *Wired*, Vol. 4, No. 4. "Across the Internet, publishers of the largest Websites are drowning in a sea of red ink. Beginning in 1995, the Web lured mainstream media companies who poured in big money – despite the lack of a sound business model." There were some significant exceptions. *The Wall Street Journal*'s Interactive Journal delivered original, service-oriented news to a global business audience that allowed it to successfully pursue on-line subscriptions such that it was projected to turn a profit in 1999. The *Financial Times* interactive edition was profitable since it launched in 1997. See Lovelock, P. and Clark, T. (1997), "*The Financial Times* Syndication Services: Making Money on the Web", Harvard Business Case Study.

[2]   Davis, J. (ed.) (1999), "Are You Next? 20 Industries That Must Change", *Business 2.0*, Vol. 2, No. 3, p. 52.

into specific habits and favour specific content selections. In other words, the Web would become a predictable world for advertisers — and there is no more important virtue for an advertiser than predictability.

Oddly, I don't remember anyone asking, "What if the Web doesn't become a mass medium?" Or "What if people use it differently from television or radio?" Or "What if advertising doesn't deliver an economical return?" Or "What is it that really makes media, as we know it?" The shared faith that the medium would outlast its own infancy allowed everyone to overlook, or avoid, the most taxing and interesting, questions.

— Michael Wolff (1998), *Burn Rate*, Orion Books, p. 158

Recognising the New Medium

By 1996, the first attempts to innovatively make use of the new media were beginning to emerge. In early 1997, *Wired* magazine proclaimed that the future was all about 'push' technology [see **Exhibit 2**]. Instead of waiting for the customer to purchase, media companies would push out a constantly updatable stream of information on anything from news headlines, to stock prices, to traffic updates.[3] When 'push' failed to take hold by mid-1997, it was replaced by 'portals': all-encompassing information gateways that provided customers with a 'one-stop' solution to their information and en-

---

[3] Push technologies were technologies designed to send content to the client without the client specifically requesting it at a certain point in time. Television and radio broadcasting were classic examples of push technology. Traditionally, the World Wide Web had been based on 'pull' technologies; the user sought out the content he or she wanted and downloaded it to the client machine. In the Internet context, in order for a push technology to work, the user had to have a 'push client' (software designed to receive and display new content) installed on his or her computer. Push technologies ranged in their degree of 'pushiness' from simple notifications that new content was available (whether via e-mail or other means) to automated content delivery. In every instance, however, the user would only receive content if the appropriate push client had been installed on his or her computer. Push technology generated substantial early interest among Internet developers. Push clients such as Pointcast, which would start automatically any time the user's computer was turned on, were launched with great fanfare. Anticipating a demand for push technology, Microsoft used a broadcast or 'Webcast' metaphor in developing Active Channels, a push client/server technology that was integrated into the Microsoft Internet Explorer Web browser and later versions of the Windows desktop. Netscape, in turn, developed Netcaster, a channels-based push client for Netscape's Navigator Web browser. However, push technology proved far less popular than anticipated, and Microsoft subsequently made the enabling of Active Channels (the push technology built into Internet Explorer) optional.

tertainment needs.[4] Portals, in turn, were replaced in 1999 with 'virtual communities', naturally discrete groups to which marketers could deliver a mass message technology [see **Exhibit 3**].[5] None of these attempts managed to deliver on the promise of the new medium, but each was an attempt to exploit the interactive potential.

What this meant for the EIU was that, by 1995, although management recognised that they were coming late to the Web as a major media publisher, they also recognised that this need not yet be a major problem as the medium itself had yet to find its niche. Two aspects of Internet business development made the EIU's comparatively late entry onto the Web seem palatable. First, many media companies had been doing poorly on the Web and many were in active retreat by 1995/96. Second, the lack of strategic use of the Web – as outlined earlier – meant that while other information providers and publishers certainly did have a competitive lead, that lead was far from unassailable.

Through 1995, the EIU management began charting a strategic outlook for using the Internet and the Web to complement and benefit the Company's growth, by addressing two questions as follows:

1. How can we move, strategically, from print publication to electronic distribution?
2. How can we exploit the interactive potential of the new medium so as to build a relationship with the audience?

As they progressed, what became obvious was that capturing the Web's potential meant more than a marketing drive; success would require restructuring the Company's internal coordination.

THE ECONOMIST INTELLIGENCE UNIT (EIU)

The EIU was established in 1948 in London to provide information on business developments, economic and political trends, government regulations and corporate prac-

---

[4] Lombardo, D. (1999), "The Unbearable Attractiveness of Portals", *Inside GartnerGroup This Week*, GartnerGroup Research Products, January.

[5] Hagel, J. & Armstrong, A.G. (eds) (1997), *net.gain: Expanding Markets Through Virtual Communities*, Boston: Harvard Business School Press; Bradley, S.P. & Nolan, R.L. (1998), *Sense & Respond: Capturing Value in the Network Era*. Boston, MA: Harvard Business School Press.

tice worldwide. By the 1990s, the EIU had a worldwide network of offices in London, New York, Hong Kong, Vienna, Singapore and Tokyo.

The target audience for the EIU's core products were multinational companies, exporters and importers, direct and portfolio investors, financial institutions, governments, business schools and any group that needed to know about political, economic and business developments across a number of countries. Within this group, the core services of the EIU were aimed at companies establishing and managing operations across national borders anywhere in the world and, therefore, specifically senior executives, their support staff and the managers responsible for international operations.

The Company's editorial focus was centred on country analyses and regional information provision, covering some 150 countries across five continental regions [see **Exhibit 4**]. To this end, the EIU output its information services in a range of formats and frequencies. They also encompassed an expanding industry portfolio, including information dedicated to the automotive and telecommunications industries. In 1996, for example, the EIU acquired Pyramid Research, a specialist research unit focused on telecommunications in emerging markets [see **Exhibit 5**]. More recently, a healthcare division was created with the launch of Healthcare International and Healthcare Asia.

However, even with its strong growth over 50 years, the EIU was perhaps still best known as the business information division of The Economist Group.

The Economist Group

The Economist Group successfully established itself as an authoritative source of information and opinion on international business and politics. The core of the Group was its flagship newspaper, *The Economist*, a weekly magazine of international news and business. Founded in 1843, *The Economist* garnered a position as one of the most high-profile current affairs periodicals in the world. It reported and analysed world affairs, politics and government, business and finance, economics, science and technology, the arts and multimedia.[6]

Other specialist magazines, newspapers, information services and conferences within the Group catered to more focused communities of interest in commerce and government, the professions, and the trade and transport industries. These included *The Journal of Commerce, CFO Magazine, Treasury and Risk Management* and *Information Strategy* [see

---

[6] Through 1997/98, the circulation of *The Economist* averaged 654,214 per issue, an increase of six percent on 1996/97.

Exhibit 6]. Together, the Group's information activities all centred – at least in part – on world commerce and politics.

In 1998, the Group grew by six percent in revenues, while profit before exceptional items and interest increased by 12 percent to UK£30.5 million and generated a net cash flow from operating activities of UK£37.3 million [see **Exhibit 7**].[7] By comparison, the EIU grew in profits to UK£6.2 million, an increase of 19 percent over 1996/97, with revenues to UK£46 million, an increase of 17 percent.

Given the Group's focus on the executive and multinational market, electronic delivery, especially via the Internet, had become central to the Company's future by the late 1990s, as customers increasingly moved towards the networking of business information. As a result, a team dedicated to electronic delivery, sales and marketing, was created to guide strategy and investment in the area.

THE NEW WINE: EIU GOES ELECTRONIC

> *The digital future is crucial for us.*
>
> – The Economist Group Annual Report

Phase 1 – From Print to Electronic

By the mid-1990s there was a growing recognition within the management of the EIU that electronic distribution was important. What exactly this meant in terms of the Web and the use of the Internet, however, was less clear. So a number of individuals were asked to look at which groups were successful on the Web (and why), and what other major print media were doing electronically.

> *... it was wonderful, revolutionary even, that a major media company would embrace the view of the Web as a profoundly important new publishing tool, but also odd. In the on-line services, you had a functional, understandable business model. People paid to get access to the information and entertainment that was being provided. The Web, so far, had no economic model ... All other major media and software companies who had the foresight to be involved in on-line delivery – Ziff-Davis, Apple, AT&T, and Microsoft,*

---

[7] On the other hand, earnings per share were down by six percent from the previous year. The Group was able to declare a final dividend of 24.5 pence per share, giving a total dividend of 34 pence per share for the year – an overall increase of 13 percent on 1996/97.

for instance – were thinking about closed on-line services rather than the Internet. (Each of those efforts – Ziff's Interchange, which was sold to AT&T; Apple's e-World; the first several versions of Microsoft's MSN; and the AT&T-backed Europe On-line – would die agonizing but quick deaths.) Nor were the existing on-line services giving much thought to the Internet… except to dismiss it.
         – Michael Wolff (1998), *Burn Rate*, Orion Books, p. 152

The first set of results were surprising; although a lot of activity had been undertaken on the Web, there were no (or at least, very few) distinctive publishing strategies emerging. However, there was a growing sense that customers expected to have the *option* to access or receive EIU's material electronically [see **Exhibit 8**]. Together, these two issues suggested to the EIU management that while they needed to develop an Internet presence rather rapidly, they were not yet being required to react defensively; the market was still wide open for developing an aggressive strategy and exploiting the possibilities inherent in the new medium.

Traditionally, the EIU had worked to a series of set publishing formats. Unlike the news media, the EIU did not let latest events determine its focus. It attempted to provide a balanced and well-researched supply of intelligence and foresight on the operating environment of each country along with developments in management thinking. To achieve this, regular contributions from a global network of more than 500 information gatherers were edited into common formats and then published according to specified, regular timeframes. This material was then distributed as printed reports, newsletters and customised briefings. By the mid-1990s, several deals had also been struck with on-line information providers, such as Reuters and Dow Jones, for the distribution of EIU content.

The EIU's first response to the new media was to make sure that their existing group of reports and information services was available on-line.

EIU.com

In February 1996, the EIU launched its first comprehensive Web play with EIU.com. EIU.com was, simply, an initial strategy for offering the EIU's research information services via the Web. Services offered included the same reports, newsletters and customised briefings that had previously been offered, along with archived research material and a set of e-briefings [see **Exhibit 9**]. Customers of the EIU could directly access and download reports and could also search through the archived material for reports up to two years old (using simple boolean searches).

Effectively, this could have been viewed as a marketing drive with the Website being used as a virtual storefront to attract off-line interest. Users were able to enter and 'wander around' the site. If they were interested in what they saw they could register to trial the material, and purchasers would be signed up off-line.[8] However, several abstract features distinguished the strategic orientation of EIU.com from its publishing competitors.

First, the site was not being used to drive new business as much as it was to service the existing customer base. In other words, the EIU's initial Web strategy was to increase the convenience for existing off-line customers (i.e., a strategy to make sure that they did not *lose* sales), rather than attempting to increase sales. Second, there was no price incentive offered to bring people on-line. (Given that the incremental cost of each on-line report was effectively zero, the savings in the publication and distribution of the digital copy are often cited as resources for offering discounts for on-line editions.[9]) Third, the analogy used by the EIU was not that of a storefront, but of an iceberg. By accessing their subscription material on-line, customers saw 'the tip of the iceberg'.[10] Below the waterline lay the rest of the iceberg composed of an ever-increasing array of products and databased material. And this led to the fourth distinction: EIU.com was not the EIU's strategy *per se*. Rather, this was *one* aspect of the EIU's on-line representation.

The strategic, technological and concomitant organisational focus was yet to come.

Phase 2 – Views*Wire*: The Product

Thanks to the Internet we can, for the first time, offer our business customers the intelligence they need in a Web service that draws on the full resources of The Economist Group – from The Economist *newspaper and* The Journal of Commerce, *to the EIU's country reports and newsletters.*

– Helen Alexander, C.E., The Economist Group
commenting on Views*Wire*.

---

[8] In the initial stage, customers were restricted to those buying at least US$7,500 worth of material.

[9] It needs to be borne in mind, however, that the ease with which these reports can then be reproduced and circulated has also often induced copyright holders to charge *more* for a digital edition.

[10] Interview with Clyde McConaghy, Director of Publishing – Asia, 12 May 1999.

On 1 May 1998, the EIU launched Views*Wire*, or what they called "a decision-support tool designed for corporate executives on the Web" [see **Exhibit 10**]. As with its traditional approach, Views*Wire* was compiled from the contributions of more than 500 EIU analysts and editors based in over 100 countries. However, Views*Wire* represented publications across the Economist Group's portfolio, including *The Economist*, *CFO Magazine*, *The Journal of Commerce*, *Oxford Analytica* and the *Financial Times*. Moreover, unlike its existing approach which eschewed a 'latest events' focus, Views*Wire* was compiled on a daily basis. The content of Views*Wire* was divided into three main sections as follows:

- ❑ *Briefings.* EIU's expert perspective on the economic, political and business impacts of recent global events.
- ❑ *Forecast.* From tables of macroeconomic forecasts to summaries of the EIU's expectations, a systematic look at future international trends.
- ❑ *Background.* Factual economic data and a look at regulations that help put current global events and expected trends into context.

The aim of Views*Wire* was to provide the analytical depth required for executives to make informed decisions about the countries in which they were doing business or were going to be doing business. As a comprehensive Web strategy, this approach was more attuned to the medium itself. With 100–150 new articles being added to the site each day, the analogy of the 'iceberg' became more apt. Users could navigate through the system by country, by subject and by addressing facilities that allowed the user to set up a range of personal profiles.

To complement the approach, a much more aggressive pricing system was introduced whereby the more users that accessed the system, the more cost-effective for a company or organisation the service became [see **Exhibit 11**]. In other words, the EIU was encouraging organisations, once they had signed on, to have as many people as possible within their organisation registered as users so that they received the most use that they could from the service.

To make Views*Wire* work, the EIU was looking to sell its information-networking resources directly into the networks of other organisations. In other words, this was not mass, indiscriminate broadcasting, but nor was it individually personalised delivery. This was – if successful – a combining of the information services and internal networking resources of the EIU, sold onto the internal networking resources of its target client base.

As a global professional services company we have relied on the EIU's analysis and forecasts for the countries where we serve clients. With the EIU ViewsWire we can effectively share this information throughout our organisation, empowering our professionals to make informed, effective decisions.
    – Shehan Dissanayake, Director, e-Commerce Services, Arthur Andersen

From a 'macro', strategic perspective, the Views*Wire* service could provide a distinctive edge in presenting commentary and analysis (i.e., 'views') – and not simply news – from the EIU and Economist Group resources. It was also an electronic only service that was completely Web-based – in other words, it would become effectively an interactive 'Web paper'.

However, to produce Views*Wire*, the EIU needed to re-engineer how the Company itself organised and developed its own information internally. There were several elements to this intra-networking reorganisation.

VIEWS*WIRE*: THE IMPACT ON INTERNAL PROCESSES

All firms need to develop their own corporate culture. This was particularly true for a firm that employed a common methodology and an 'intuitive' approach to work practices and needed to come out with a common voice within its newsletter products and information services. Furthermore, the EIU viewed a part of its competitive advantage as being able to 'leverage its collective knowledge through replication and/or new application of knowledge'. To create knowledge required being able to tap into its own expertise, wherever that resided, and at any given time.

To build knowledge by accumulating a company's individual experiences is one of the principal reasons for building databases and corporate intranets. However, building such 'knowledge and information networks' requires significantly greater internal co-ordination of work schedules, constant system maintenance, and a different marketing approach. That the EIU possessed an internal knowledge resource that, if properly exploited, was of benefit to its clients, was not doubted by anyone in the Company. Successful implementation, however, presented a range of structural problems to the Group's existing work practices.

First, Views*Wire* placed the EIU specialists on alert to provide country analysis and forecasts in response to fast-changing events. Second, the production of Views*Wire* required a certain quota of submissions from analysts and editors so that the output of Views*Wire* – 100 to 150 new stories each day – could be met. Third, coordination across the Group now had to be consistent and effective on a daily basis.

Individually, each of these elements appeared relatively straightforward. But to work, the model required a significant degree of flexibility and this represented a marked change for an organisation set up as individual (and largely autonomous) units, working to strict deadlines and timeframes. To confuse the picture even further, Views*Wire* promised subscribers interactive access to Views*Wire* analysts, as part of their anytime, anywhere access.

Addressing and coordinating each of these issues would mean the difference between success and failure for the new service.

Network Reporting – Not a Wire Service

The EIU had no intention of changing its basic strengths in providing the new service. Indeed, the basic belief, as outlined above, was that by networking the internal expertise of the EIU's editors and correspondents, a value-added service could be provided wherein the total was greater than the sum of its parts.

The problem here, however, was that EIU editors did not themselves undertake the vast majority of the writing that appeared in the various newsletters. Their primary job was to locate and solicit expert analysis in a timely manner. A requirement of daily contributions threatened to subvert this basic model. Even more so, responding to client requests implied a level of expertise that the Company neither had, nor wished to acquire. When, for example, important news broke about financial constraints in Mexico or telecommunications developments in China, it was expected that Views*Wire* would be the pre-eminent source of information, analysis and understanding for the corporate business world. However, the EIU was not purporting to be a wire service and simply replicate stories as they happened. Rather, they needed to rely on a greater degree of expertise and understanding of the specific country's operating environment.

This meant that judgement calls had to be made as to which stories were to be chased at any given time on the basis of existing knowledge and resource allocation. As a result, the Group quickly realised that to be effective they had to educate both the editors, who were the principal contributors to the system, and the clients, who were the principal users of the service. Editors had to be taught to break out of the publishing timeframes that they were working towards and to simultaneously adopt a daily perspective in their outlook. They also had to be taught to look inwards to the network itself. Where previously they had looked outwards for expertise to provide analysis and commentary in a traditional publishing manner, now they also had to look inwards to the knowledge *within* the Group, in responding to immediate requests for information and analysis.

Users, on the other hand, had to be taught how to use the system so that: (a) they were not disappointed through unfulfilled expectations and (b) they knew how to 'drill down' into the wealth of information that existed to provide the background and understanding they might be looking for on any given subject.

Setting Quotas – Expecting the Unexpected

Quotas for the new service could not be administered too dogmatically, as it could not be pre-ordained where news would break. In response, loose guidelines were established, which identified 'objectives', rather than requirements. Each newsletter editor was expected to supply approximately two additional stories for the Views*Wire* service each week, more or less depending on whether they were in a 'hot news' area.

It was soon recognised that a networked knowledge product is a significantly different proposition than a simple collection of information. With most editors producing in excess of 16 pages (some six to ten stories) every two weeks, it could be assumed that filling a quota of two stories per week would be a rather straightforward affair. However, each product (the newsletters and Views*Wire*) had a different focus. The EIU newsletters largely eschewed a day-to-day focus, whereas the Views*Wire* was a daily service. Moreover, if all that was being provided was material straight from the newsletters service, then prospective users could simply have subscribed to the relevant newsletters and employed a search function over the on-line archives.[11] Or they could have subscribed to one of the on-line news aggregators (such as Reuters) to whom EIU onsold a certain percentage of its newsletter stories.

Again, this meant teaching contributors how to 'view' the Views*Wire* service and to provide the most value to the network. As with any change in corporate mindset, this took time to implement, as the habits of many years of time scheduling had to be broken and reset.

Micro-management – Coordinating the Network

The EIU management saw that they had several options in implementing the Views*Wire* service and in attempting to tie the network itself together. One was to impose rules –

---

[11] Admittedly, to be required to subscribe to *all* of the EIU's newsletters would not be a particularly value-oriented alternative. But very few subscribers were likely to fall into this category.

albeit flexibly – to achieve the above criteria. Another was to allow the service to grow organically; to set a structure in place and then to encourage both contributors and subscribers to make the most of the potential allowed by the network. Somewhat experimentally, they chose the latter.

The existing individual country and/or regional focuses of the newsletter and information services were retained, but they were now expected to fit into an overarching structure that sought to build the new product from the cumulative strengths of the Group's individual resources. No full-time editor was assigned to oversee the resulting product. A small managerial team in New York was given the coordination responsibility. However, they tended only to undertake minor cosmetic changes to the material; all editing was expected to be done by the contributing editors who had better understanding of the material.

As the service grew, it was expected that a dedicated managerial team would evolve. By late 1998, the date foreseen for such a development was approximately 2000. However, as the service took off through 1999, this projection was increasingly brought forward. Similarly, on the marketing side: at the outset of the service, one person was assigned part-time to develop the product. Within three months, this had become three full-time staff, with many more involved as a part of their existing responsibilities. To some degree, this reflected the general trend that had given rise to the concept of Views*Wire* in the first place: growth in the demand for electronic media and electronic services was far outstripping the demand for traditional delivery. If the EIU were to survive they had to successfully capitalise on these trends.

At the network level, Views*Wire* took advantage of cutting-edge search-and-retrieval technology with an intelligent database designed by eLogic Inc. (www.elogic.com), a California-based Internet software development company. Being Web-based the service was easily and readily accessible, and the cross-linking of material was intuitively simple given the hypertext linkages that comprised the Web. However, the EIU management had decided that placing intelligence within their networked service was important if they were to distinguish themselves from the simple search services offered by various news organisations. By linking related stories, articles and briefings together, Views*Wire* allowed users to create their own personalised decision-support profiles.

VIEWS*WIRE*: A WEB PAPER?

The move to daily electronic delivery of country analysis marked a significant turning point in publishing strategy for the group. Effectively, the EIU was producing a new product by tying together the internal networking capacity of the Company's diverse information resources *with* its external output. In doing so, they were attempting to create a concept of 'anything, anytime' publishing; the antithesis of print journalism with its set time schedules.

However, as with many large groups, the size of the EIU (and of The Economist Group) was both its strength and challenge, requiring phenomenal coordination. The organisation as a whole needed to be able to respond to requests and then to quickly identify individuals with the required skills. It also needed to be able to access its own resources and database knowledge rapidly and efficiently. A further objective of its 'timeliness in delivering solutions' and 'dramatically shortened development time' was the ability to present subscribers with a précis of 'up-to-date commentary and analysis'. Again, this required immediate access to information and knowledge.

Exhibit 1:   The great Web wipeout, 1996

Winners	Losers
PLAYBOY:	PATHFINDER:
"Sex always sells."	"Even Time Warner gets burned."
ALTAVISTA:	C/NET:
"Best of the index services."	"Turning back into a TV network."
FEDEX:	STARWAVE:
"Surprisingly useful Website."	"A Paul Allen tax write-off."
INFOSEEK:	HOTWIRED:
"No. 2 on our search list."	"Hanging on by its nails."
DATAQUEST:	CYBERCASH
"Now the Web authority."	"Retail sales? What retail sales?"

Source: *Wired*, Vol. 4, No. 4, 1996, p. 127.

Exhibit 2: The future is 'push'

Source: *Wired* (1997).

Exhibit 3:   Infomediary potential for Internet-based business

Type	Advantages	Disadvantages
Portal	• High traffic generated by good marketing skills • Frequent visits by customers • Broad range of topics, which provides potential for broad profile • Strength in building partnerships • Innovative and risk taking	• Little experience building trust-based relationships • Lots of trial, not much loyalty • Little to no experience managing profiles • Historically vendor-focused versus customer-focused
Virtual community	• Customer-focused rather than vendor-focused • Strong trust-based relationships • Innovative and risk taking	• Small traffic flows • Depending on scope, may be too narrow to build adequate profiles • Unproven database-driven marketing and relationship-building skills
Transaction aggregator	• Profiles include transaction data • Skilled at building partnerships • Skilled at handling transactions • Innovative and risk taking	• Many are not broad enough • Although trusted to enable transactions, not necessarily a trust-based relationship • Profiles show transaction history only • Unproven database-driven marketing and relationship-building skills
Advertising network	• Understanding of tools and skills required to capture customer information • The infrastructure to capture information across Websites • Broad perspective on consumer behaviour • Experience managing networks of business relationships • Innovative and risk taking	• Profiles contain usage data only, no transaction data • Completely vendor-focused rather than customer-focused • Not a trust-based relationship – no brand-name recognition or awareness

Source: *Business 2.0* (1999).

Exhibit 4: EIU's global coverage

E·I·U

**The Economist
Intelligence Unit**

REGIONAL ANALYSIS

Subscription products

Business Africa
Business Asia
Business China
Business Eastern Europe
Business Europe
Business Latin America
Business Middle East
Business operations report
Business Russia
China Hand
Country Forecasts
Country Profiles

Country Reports
Country Risk Service
Country Monitor
European Policy Analyst
Financing Operations
Global Outlook
Business India Intelligence
Investing, Licensing & Trading
Risk Ratings Review
World Commodity Forecasts
World Outlook
Worldwide Regulatory Update

Research reports
Africa/Middle East Research Reports
Americas Research Reports
Asia Research Reports
Europe and the former Soviet Union Research Reports
Global Research Projects

AUTOMOTIVE

Subscription products
Components Business Europe
Components Business International
Motor Business Asia-Pacific
Motor Business International
Rubber Trends

Research products
Automotive Research Reports

HEALTHCARE

Subscription products
Healthcare International
Healthcare Asia
Healthcare Europe

TELECOMS

Pyramid Research
Newsletters
Market reports
Advisory services

FINANCIAL SERVICES

Subscription products
Strategic finance

Research reports
Research reports Motor Business Japan

MANAGEMENT

Research reports

CORPORATE FINANCE

Research reports

HUMAN RESOURCES

Subscription products
Worldwide Cost of Living Survey

Research reports
Research reports

Source: The Economist Intelligence Unit (1999), URL: http://store.eiu.com/titles, October.

Exhibit 5:   EIU's telecommunications information unit – Pyramid Research

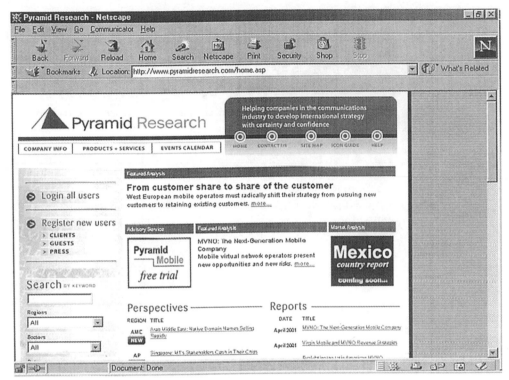

Source: Pyramid Research (1999), URL: http://www.pyr.com, October.

Exhibit 6: The Economist Group's information services portfolio

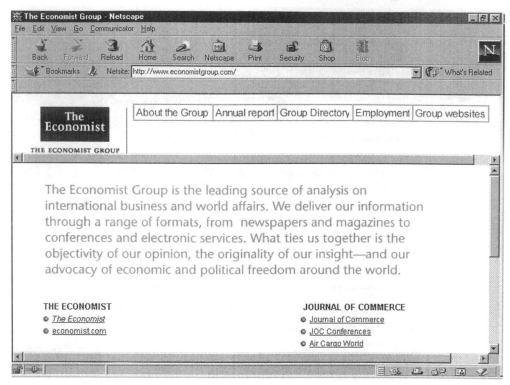

Source: The Economist Group (1999), URL: http//www.economistgroup.com/mainframe, October.

Exhibit 7:   The Economist Group's financial performance

Profit and loss	1998 £'000	1997 £'000	1996 £'000	1995 £'000
Turnover	205,024	193,515	188,659	137,489
Operating profit	28,261	25,599	23,762	17,990
Net interest	(232)	(1,143)	(1,725)	1,775
Profit before taxation	25,076	26,722	23,997	19,765
Profit after taxation	18,884	20,077	17,682	13,420
Balance sheet				
Intangible assets	–	370	658	–
Fixed assets	33,575	35,342	36,398	32,518
Investments	–	–	133	122
Net current (liabilities)/assets	(17,051)	(12,769)	(13,872)	2,850
Long-term creditors and provisions	(29,131)	(47,764)	(56,629)	(9,024)
Net (liabilities)/assets	(12,607)	(24,821)	(33,312)	26,466
Ratios				
Operating profit to turnover	13.8%	13.2%	12.6%	13.1%
Taxation	24.7%	24.9%	26.3%	32.1%
Earnings per share	74.9p	79.7p	70.2p	53.3p
Dividends				
Dividends per share	34p	30p	26p	20p
Times covered	2.2	2.7	2.7	2.7
Net cash from operating activities	37,263	34,669	30,129	29,720

Source: The Economist Group (1999), URL: http://www.economistgroup.com/mainframe, October.

Exhibit 8:   Media publishers target the Web

On-line title	Established	Access	Advertising rates	Claimed reach	Publication time	Content
REGIONAL WEEKLIES						
BusinessWeek *businessweek.com*	Dec 1994	Free for limited content, paid subscription for full content, free to mag subs	US$40–65 CPM depending on quantity	200,000 registered views/mth	Simultaneously with print edition, updated daily	All print content goes on-line for subs. Limited content for non-subs
Far Eastern Economic Review *Feer.com*	1996	Free	US$5,250/wk on homepage; US$3,675 other pages	Not disclosed	One day after print edition hits newsstand	Fee.com has 30% of print content
Newsweek *newsweek.com*	Relaunched on the Net, Oct 1998	Free	US$40/CPM. Packages across print media and washingtonpost.com	5 million views in first mth	Simultaneously with print edition, updated daily	Whole content of print edition posted, longer versions of some stories, breaking news updated daily
The Economist *economist.com*	Jun 1997	Free to mag subs: US$48 for on-line subs.	US$65–80/CPM depending on size (25,000–74,999 hits)	330,000 registered users worldwide	Simultaneously with print edition	All of print content plus surveys from past issues. Archive back to 1990

Exhibit 8 (cont'd)

On-line title	Established	Access	Advertising rates	Claimed reach	Publication time	Content
Time Inc [Time Warner media accessed through umbrella site *Pathfinder.com*]		Free	Rational banners US$40 CPM; homepage sponsorship US$6,500/mth	*pathfinder.com* 90 million views/mth	Posted a few days after the print edition hits the newsstand	Not all content from print editions goes on site. Daily news updates if there is a breaking story
Asiaweek *asiaweek.com*	Aug 1995	Free		600,000 views/mth		
Time.com/asia	Jan 1998	Free		500,000 views/mth		
DAILY NEWSPAPERS						
AWSJ part of *wsj.com*	Apr 1996	Paid sub	*wsj.com* US$28–76/CPM	250,000 + paying subs	Posted and updated daily	Content of all *wsj* editions and other Dow publications
Financial Times *ft.com*	Oct 1998	Subscription is free	US$57–98/CPM	7 million hits/mth	Posted daily and updated at least 3 times daily	50% paper content 50% Web-only content
International Herald Tribune *iht.com*	Jan 1996	Free	US$40/CPM	1.2 million hits/mth	Updated daily at 5:00 am (HK time)	Same as print edition

Exhibit 8 (cont'd)

On-line title	Established	Access	Advertising rates	Claimed reach	Publication time	Content
HongKong Standard *hkstandard.com*	Oct 1995	Free	US$2,838 full banner/mth on homepage US$1,935 for section page	160,000–180,000 hits daily	Posted daily and updated 2–6 times daily	Content different from print edition
South China Morning Post *SCMP.com*	Dec 1996	Free (pay-per-view archives)	US$20–45/CPM	2.5 million page views per week	Posted daily at 11:00 am. Breaking news updated throughout day	About 90% of print edition content posted and more
Straits Times Interactive	Dec 1995	Free	US$193–903/mth	Asia1.com claims one million views per day	Posted noon daily	Virtually all print content goes on-line
Business Times On-line	Jun 1995	Free	US$129–580/mth		Posted noon daily	

Source: *Adweek Asia* (15 January 1999), p. 6.

Exhibit 9:   EIU.com

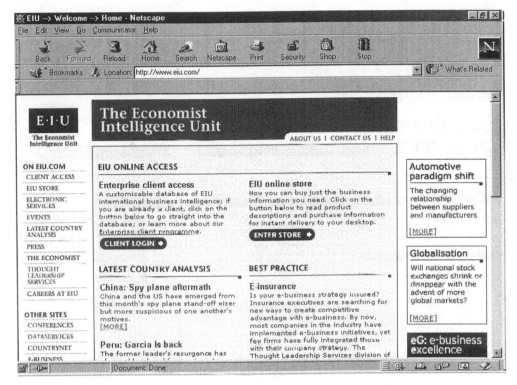

Source: The Economist Intelligence Unit (1999), URL: http://www.eiu.com, October.

Exhibit 10:   Views*Wire*

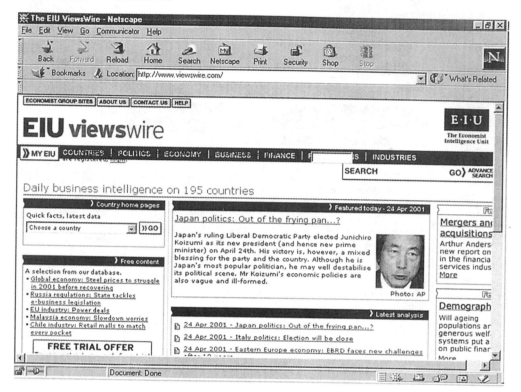

Source: The Economist Intelligence Unit Views*Wire* (1999), URL: http://www.viewswire.com, October.

Exhibit 11: Views*Wire* pricing scheme

Network pricing for the Views*Wire* service is based on the number of authorised users as follows:

Authorised users	£ Price	US$ price
1 user	4,600	7,500
Up to 5 users	6,000	9,500
Up to 10 users	8,500	12,750
Up to 25 users	11,250	17,000
Up to 50 users	14,250	21,250
Up to 100 users	17,000	25,500
Up to 250 users	19,750	29,750
Up to 500 users	21,750	32,500
Up to 750 users	24,250	36,500
Up to 1,000 users	26,000	39,000
Up to 2,500 users	30,000	45,000
Up to 5,000 users	34,000	50,700
Up to 7,500 users	38,000	56,250
Up to 10,000 users	41,000	61,900
Up to 25,000 users	44,000	67,500
Up to 50,000 users	47,000	73,200
Up to 75,000 users	50,000	78,800
Up to 100,000 users	53,000	84,400
Over 100,000 users	55,000	90,000

Source: EIU.

CASE

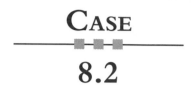

8.2

PricewaterhouseCoopers: Building a Global Network*

On 1 July 1998, Price Waterhouse and Coopers & Lybrand merged to form PricewaterhouseCoopers (PwC), creating one of the world's largest full-service professional organisations. The move was an attempt to meet the increasing client needs for scale and global presence. As a result of the merger, PwC engaged in six lines of business across 24 industries in over 152 countries worldwide, with over 150,000 representatives.[1]

As service professional organisations, the companies had two major assets: their personnel, and the knowledge base of those personnel. Before the merger, both firms were already established information specialists, focused on developing efficient internal networking practices as a competitive advantage. For the new company to be successful, PwC required a system that would enable them to fully utilise their extended resources. Thus, the challenge faced by PwC in the wake of the merger was

---

[1] URL: http://www.pwcglobal.com, 14 January 2000.

* Marissa McCauley prepared this case in conjunction with Minako Fukagata and Peter Lovelock, under the supervision of Dr. Ali Farhoomand. *Copyright © 2000 The University of Hong Kong. Ref. 99/46C*

how to create a global organisation that could fully integrate and add value to the new assets it had acquired. The key to this challenge was how to successfully integrate the internal networks of the firms into one network for the new, larger entity that would incorporate and build on the strengths of the two merging firms.

PricewaterhouseCoopers' ultimate goal was to establish a common global knowledge base: a networked information service that would be available to the PwC workforce and its clients. To achieve this, however, PwC had to consider size – about 150,000 partners and staff with a geographical coverage in 152 countries and territories – in integrating and linking them together. Prior to the merger, PW and C&L operated from different IT platforms. In addition, there were thousands of databases in different types of servers that had to be rationalised for a global knowledge database to be put into effect. How could such a knowledge-intensive firm go about creating an intranet on a global scale? How could it create a new information product based on a global intranet and worldwide resources of information and professional practice? What was the best means to implement the new structure such that both the PwC workforce and its clients would be able to access it?

THE INDUSTRY TREND TOWARDS CONSOLIDATION

For over 30 years since the mid-1950s, the professional services industry consisted of eight major players, known as the 'Big Eight'. This picture changed when the first move towards consolidation took place in the late 1980s, when Deloitte Haskins & Sells coupled with Touche Ross & Co. to create Deloitte & Touche, and Ernst & Whinney joined with Arthur Young & Co. to form Ernst & Young. In 1989, the 'Big Eight' was reduced to the 'Big Six'.

The second wave of industry consolidation took place in September 1997, when Price Waterhouse (PW) announced its merger with Coopers & Lybrand (C&L).[2] In October 1997, Ernst & Young and KPMG Peat Marwick followed suit. The planned E&Y/KPMG merger, however, dissolved in February 1998 due to regulatory issues, client disruption and some cultural issues. On the PW/C&L side, they quietly continued to see their merger through.[3] The industry reduced to the 'Big Five' when Price

---

[2] Law, G. (1998), "And Then There Were Four…", *Management*, Vol. 45, Iss. 1, Auckland, February, pp. 68–70.

[3] Anonymous (1998), "Big 6 Firm Mergers: On, Off and In Court", *Bowman's Accounting Report*, Vol. 12, Iss. 2, Atlanta, February, pp. 10–12.

Waterhouse and Coopers & Lybrand confirmed the merger on 8 July 1998. All of the 'Big Five' – PricewaterhouseCoopers, KPMG Peat Marwick, Ernst & Young, Anderson Worldwide and Deloitte Touche Tomatsu – offered consulting services ranging from taxation consulting through to change management, IT and legal consultancy.

Consolidation was considered the most effective way for companies of this nature to expand their range of services, global capabilities, market share and intellectual capital. As clients expanded their business globally, it became necessary for professional services companies to likewise expand their global presence. Clients wanted the same application to be applied simultaneously to their respective offices worldwide, which meant professional services firms were required to have a matching (and therefore global) presence in order to be able to respond to such demands.

The merger announcement made by Price Waterhouse and Coopers & Lybrand was spurred by this growing need for global scale and presence. The size of the new company as a result of the merger gave both the firm and its clients the advantages of scope and economies of scale. In the light of increasing competition, achieving global presence in terms of scale and scope was one way to gain an advantage over competitors. Achieving organisational economies of scale became important, especially as business became more technology-oriented. In a business environment where speed was one of the important elements for success, companies required new technologies that would enable them to provide better ways to conduct business. Keeping the company at the cutting edge of technology required vast capital investments, and consolidation was a solution to boost capital as well as to utilise the capital in the most efficient manner.

Scale also enabled the company to respond to requests from certain market segments (such as the growing emerging markets) that were not fully covered prior to consolidation. Expanding the scope of business was important as it enabled clients to be provided with more comprehensive services and solutions, and at the same time, it differentiated the company from its competitors. The use of technology, including intranets, and the ability to share information fundamentally improved communication between PwC clients, its workforce and business clients, particularly across an increasing platform (global as well as organisational). The focus of PwC on the knowledge management system would bring value to PwC clients such that it would ensure access to greater resources, with faster deployment of specialists and of new products and services through more efficient management of a larger investment pool.

PRICEWATERHOUSECOOPERS: THE FIRM

The origins of Price Waterhouse and Coopers & Lybrand date back to the mid–1800s, when both companies started as accounting firms based in London. Each company gradually expanded its business through business partnerships, and by the late 1980s–1990s, they had both grown to become global companies offering professional services well beyond accounting. At the time of the merger, both companies were offering services in Assurance and Business Advisory Services (Auditing), Management Consulting, Human Resource Management, Tax and Legal Services, Financial Advisory, and Business Process Outsourcing. [Refer to **Exhibit 1** for PwC industries with old company equivalents and to **Exhibit 2** for PwC's chronological history before the 1998 merger.]

The two companies merged on 1 July 1998, to create one of the world's largest full-service professional organisations. As a result of the merger, the new company, PricewaterhouseCoopers (PwC), surpassed Arthur Andersen, which had previously been considered the industry giant in terms of asset size. PwC had more than 150,000 people in 152 countries and annual revenues pushing US$16 billion.[4,5]

> *The merger brings together complementary capabilities to add value to our clients of all sizes throughout the world. Clients in the United States will benefit from Coopers & Lybrand's strengths in strategy and human resource consulting and Price Waterhouse's equally strong packaged software and global IT implementation practices. Combined, the two organisations offer clients a powerful consulting resource.*
> — Cees G. van Lujik, Chairman, Coopers & Lybrand Europe, and Jermyn Brooks, Chairman, Price Waterhouse[6]

PwC provided unprecedented service to global, national and local companies in markets worldwide; offering a comprehensive range of business assurance, business advisory, tax, management, IT and human resource consulting services and a commitment to helping clients formulate and implement strategic solutions that drive growth and improve business performance. The two firms were similar in terms of business

---

[4] US$1 = HK$8

[5] Anonymous (1998), "Top 100 People: Moore, Schiro: 'We Changed the Competitive Landscape'", *Accounting Today*, 28 September to 11 October.

[6] URL: http://www.colybrand.com/news/091897.html, 19 January 2000.

lines and geographical coverage, however they were not necessarily similar in terms of industry coverage. The uniting of the various practices offered by Price Waterhouse and Coopers & Lybrand was expected to bring significant benefits to clients, particularly in those industries that were rapidly converging and in which sector distinctions were becoming less pronounced and competition more intense.

For example, Coopers & Lybrand's strength in telecommunications could be combined with Price Waterhouse's global expertise in the media and entertainment sectors, creating a powerful industry specialists' group. This was also in accordance with the converging trend between these industries. Within the telecommunications industry, Coopers & Lybrand's strength was in consulting, while Price Waterhouse's strength was in auditing. Combining the two companies therefore enabled the new entity to provide clients with comprehensive and extended services. In the products sector, Price Waterhouse had significant presence in chemicals, while Coopers & Lybrand was strong in consumer products, and they were both strong in the pharmaceutical sector. In the energy sector, there were complementary strengths in oil and gas, mining and utilities. In the financial services sector, the two organisations combined offered unmatched worldwide capabilities in banking, insurance and brokerage and mutual funds. [Refer to **Exhibit 3** for the specific industry strengths of PW and C&L.]

Corporate Structure

We are global, and because we are global, we are local – there to serve you wherever you are.

– PricewaterhouseCoopers Website homepage[7]

There was no formal headquarters for PwC, but the global leadership was based in New York, Frankfurt and London. Headquarters would be wherever services were delivered, which could be anywhere in the world.[8] PwC also split the structure into three 'theatres' namely: the Americas; Europe, the Middle East and Africa; and the Asia-Pacific. The Global Executive Team was composed of eight executives including the Chairman, CEO and six Global Leaders in-charge in Industries, Geography, Service Line, Human Resources, Operations and Risk Management.

There was some overlap on the support side of business that required rationalisa-

---

[7] URL: http://www.pwcglobal.com/gx/eng/about/main/index.html, 29 May 2000.

[8] URL: http://www.pwcglobal.com/extweb/nc…, 14 January 2000.

tion as tasks performed by support staff from both companies were basically the same; downsizing was inevitable for the new organisation to function in an efficient manner. This was not an easy task and it created some tension during the consolidation process. However, overall integration was achieved relatively smoothly as PW and C&L started working together in October 1997, nine months before the merger announcement, to put the heads of the business function in place at an accelerated fashion to minimise the transition time.

As with many of the other companies in the professional services industry, both Price Waterhouse and Coopers & Lybrand were organised in a matrix structure by region, with lines of service running in one direction and industry running across in the other direction. Traditionally, both PW and C&L were very line-of-service-oriented organisations, as being more industry-focused was a relatively new phenomenon in professional services. According to David Lambert, Marketing Communications Director of PwC, "the tilt is towards line of service, but the impetus is towards industry."[9] The line of service was the historical model in which most of the PwC people were well versed. The PwC workforce was being pushed in the direction of the line of service, focusing on a particular industry in a certain geography. For PwC, there was the focus in the industry, but the history was with the line of service.

PwC consisted of six lines of business and 24 market sectors clustered into five groups. The six business lines were: Audit; Assurance and Business Advisory Services; Business Process Outsourcing; Financial Advisory Services; Global Human Resource Solutions; Management Consulting Services; and Global Tax Services. The five-industry group consisted of: Financial Services Industry; Service Industry; Global Energy and Mining Industry; Consumer and Industrial Products; and Technology, Information/Communications and Entertainment.

PwC had an annual revenue of US$17.3 billion worldwide for fiscal 30 June 1999, a record US$2 billion increase in earnings or up 16 percent over 1998. Since announcing its merger in September 1997, global revenues at PwC increased by more than US$4.5 billion. Significant growth was seen in the Management Consulting Services and Global Human Resource Solutions, up 27 percent and 28 percent respectively. On a geographical basis, North America and South/Central America showed the strongest growth patterns, with growth rates of 28 percent and 19 percent respectively. About PwC's robust growth in 1999 PwC Chairman Nicholas Moore said: "Companies

---

[9] Interview with David Lambert (Marketing Communications Director) and Stephen Langley (Global Technology Solutions Director), PwC, Hong Kong, 1 February 2000.

around the world clearly recognise the significant advantages of our breadth and depth of expertise. Equally important, we have already begun to capitalise on the synergies we expected our merger to produce, and have not fallen victim to the internal distractions that frequently plague organisations immediately following a merger."[10] The year 1999 was also a significant one for PwC as it experienced significant achievements, including the acquisition of other consulting firms and citations from various publications.

THE INTEGRATION PROCESS

Nine months before the planned announcement of the merger (in October 1997), the PW and C&L teams had already begun working to plan the structure of the new organisation. Both firms managed the transition to a global, integrated organisation and had it up and running as a global operation by 1 July 1998. Obviously, however, full integration took some time. Overall, PwC went through the integration process in an accelerated fashion.

The planning of the corporate-wide integration was done by the headquarters-based Global Team that reviewed the overall firm and gave guidance to each local office as to how the integration should be done. GTS was the technology team responsible for the planning and implementation of the IT systems within the firm. Overall, it took the IT team one year to completely unify, standardise and simplify both the PCs and the network infrastructure. First, the team created a bridge between the networks to facilitate communication. The next step was standardising the way LOS was connected to the network and the applications being used.

The partnership structure of PwC enabled it to give more independence to each of its offices around the globe, in terms of their respective decisions regarding the integration process. As a global entity, there were people at headquarters level who were responsible for outlining the big picture as to how the new company should look. The partnership structure, however, meant that individual offices had more flexibility in decision making, so people could be more pragmatic about how things were done. The Global Team provided guidance, but the final decision was made at each

---

[10] URL: http://www.pwcglobal.com/extweb/nc...D/CCA2BEF3DF2DCC148525686 C0074296E, 11 February 2000.

office level at its own discretion. This allowed the GTS team at each office level to modify the original guideline and take a more realistic approach.

PWC INTRANET: THE KNOWLEDGE CURVE

Knowledge management was to play an important role in the merger process, as the ability to share knowledge and intellectual capital across the two firms was to become the key to successfully achieving rapid integration with continued client service. The head of the PwC Global Knowledge Management Team explained why knowledge was so important in a professional services firm such as PwC:

> *To a great extent it is all we have, and all we share and sell. It is the basis of what we do. We sell to clients the knowledge our consultants have and have access to. So managing the resources effectively and making sure we can share it across the consultancy is vital to us. It is the lifeblood of the organisation.*
> — Julia Collins, Head, PwC Global Knowledge Group[11]

Technical evolution has enabled cost-effective methods of capturing, updating and distributing knowledge throughout PwC by way of an intranet. The intranet was the entry point to capture firm wide knowledge and make it accessible to the organisation. It was the foundation for stored knowledge, which was the core asset for a knowledge-intensive organisation such as PwC.

Knowledge Curve (KC) was the name of the intranet introduced to PwC. Originally developed by the IT team from C&L, the KC was the core of the PwC intranet system. The KC was the PwC's knowledge management system that incorporated all the assets (knowledge and people skills) of the company to be utilised by the entire firm. To achieve the scale and scope expected from the merger, such a knowledge management system was to play an important role. With careful structuring, this knowledge base could become a powerful tool that could be used as PwC's competitive advantage. Simplicity in usage was important for this knowledge base to be effective, as well as the firm's ability to capture, package and deliver the knowledge.

The KC was advanced in that it enabled extensive profiling from three dimensions: geography, industry and line of business. As a start, the KC was structured on two

---

[11] Thomson, S. (2000), "Focus: Keeping Pace with Knowledge", *Information Week Review*, Vol. 155, Oxford, February, pp. 23–24.

levels: (1) Knowledge Curve Global and (2) Knowledge Curve at each office level. PwC's ultimate goal was to have all the knowledge base centralised under Knowledge Curve Global, which would require significant time to be fully accomplished. Thus, at the global level, priorities were given to topics that were more common firm-wide, which meant that there were limitations as to what the central global site could do. In order to complement the limitations of the global site, each office had its own KC homepage that incorporated the knowledge base and the information that was important at the local level. Depending on how much a particular knowledge base could be shared firm-wide, a knowledge base at office level was incorporated into the Global knowledge base. Information that was important at the local level but did not have to be 'shared', such as personal memos and reminders, was kept at the office level.

One of the GTS' main projects under the GTS Development Team was to build a Website within a local KC. The local portal was designed to complement what the KC Global had not been able to cover, and to customise the KC Global to local needs with added features. The content page would provide the users with office-specific knowledge that would not be incorporated under the global content. As the KC Global developed, some of the contents from the local page would shift to the global page. [Refer to **Exhibit 5** for the Hong Kong Portal and Hong Kong Knowledge Curve diagram as an example.]

'The Bridge' and the GTS Channel

Prior to the Knowledge Curve, PwC had a global database called 'The Bridge'.[12] It was a merger product and the first internal communications product. It assumed correctly that everyone had access to Lotus Notes, but that not everyone had access to the Internet or intranet. The Bridge was very effective in that it provided a lot of information that could be accessed by everyone.

Likewise, a global database called GTS Channel, which was initially developed for the IT people (about 3,000 personnel), was put in place relatively quickly. After the merger, the GTS Channel was made available to everyone. The GTS Channel had been working well: this integrated focus enabled anyone to walk into any PwC office

---

[12] In telecommunications networks, a Bridge is a product that connects a local area network to another local area network that uses the same protocol. Bridging networks are generally always interconnected local area networks since broadcasting every message to all possible destinations would flood a larger network with unnecessary traffic. (See URL: wysiwyg://def.133/http://www.whatiscom.bridge.htm, 31 May 2000.)

worldwide, plug in the computer and get to work. The fundamental base-level requirement was TCP/IP, TACP servers and DNS. PwC was able to implement this project quickly, driven to a large degree by what the business was doing globally. As an organisation, PwC recognised that to capture the market space equally all of its systems and IT had to fit together.

The Knowledge Team

As at February 2000, there were about 300 Knowledge Workers internationally. London-based Julia Collins managed the knowledge resources that served 32,000 fee-earning consultants internationally. Collins supervised 25 staff in the UK, while another 40 worked within PwC's industry and service groups. They included consultants, former consultants, information professionals and technical experts. These intra-industry group knowledge workers had a brief that included:

- ❑ conduct research for the consultants in their teams
- ❑ 'harvest' knowledge inwards by working with consultants to get knowledge from their assignments into the internal repositories kept by PwC
- ❑ help manage content in the central repositories
- ❑ ensure an open communication channel between knowledge headquarters and their industry group at the local level

PwC's focus was on making the firm a global entity, and since the merger the KC team had been moving towards global repositories rather than small databases. The industry group knowledge workers managed the content that belonged to their industry group within the global repositories. There were also central groups based in London, Dallas and Sydney. PwC was also organised into theatres: the Americas; Europe, the Middle East and Africa; and Asia-Pacific. The UK was the leader for Europe, but there were also large groups in Utrecht, Frankfurt, Paris and Brussels.

One of the strengths of the function was the involvement of all the different industry and service groups; it was however difficult to coordinate it. PwC was moving quickly to an intranet platform that would provide a greater chance to integrate everything, eventually eliminating the standard way of informing people, for example, about which database to use. The limitations of the function were mainly related to the team's ability to create awareness about the KC, specifically in terms of how the team would go about educating the consultants on the available information in the KC so that they could understand its capabilities and its applications. It was a big challenge to go after the 32,000 consultants and communicate with each one of them and change over to using the KC Global, a task that the KC team was still working on as at February 2000. The goal of the team was, by year 2005, to ensure that consultants understood more fully what the KC was and how they could contribute to it. PwC was still building its knowledge base and had yet to hit upon a method to capture the knowledge that existed in people's heads. Collins said that the consultants' perception of the KC varied according to how long the knowledge resources had been established in a specific country or area. A more established knowledge function was well-regarded and well-used, while there was more variance in those countries where it was in the process of being established.

The Manager of Communications at PwC had full-time responsibility for promoting the Knowledge Curve. This was a big task as it involved informing the 150,000 PwC workforce scattered throughout 152 different countries about what the PwC intranet had to offer. Campaigns to increase awareness of the Knowledge Curve included visiting various offices and scheduling presentations throughout the day, spending time teaching people (one-on-one) how to use the system, and distributing literature, give-aways, boomerangs, little wallet cards, posters and flyers. There were also specific professional sessions that helped spur interest. For example, accountants were taught to use the intranet to do research and prepare taxes for clients.[13]

Use of the KC was a massive change for PwC people, thus it was important for the staff to understand where to access help once the networks of PW and C&L were merged. Feedback from the PwC workforce was elicited through the Knowledge Point helpdesk. There was also a staff satisfaction survey (covering the whole of an employee's level of satisfaction with working with PwC) that contained questions related to the KC. The KC tracked, year-on-year, whether the team was getting better or not.

PwC consultants could access the knowledge resources mainly through their own computers – either through Lotus Notes or on the intranet. Once logged-on, the consultants could have access to and direct use of the following:

- ❏ all the main information repositories
- ❏ general business tools such as Dow Jones Interactive and Harvard Business School resources
- ❏ alliance databases that were more specific to the field in which people worked, such as Gartner and Forrester

---

[13] Leong, K.C. (1999), "Marketing Gets Innovative", *Internetweek*, Vol. 763, 3 May, p. 27.

Knowledge Point, the PwC global knowledge helpdesk, was another way for users to request searches or access resources. Knowledge Point received about 1,000 calls a month.

The Difference Between Lotus Notes and Knowledge Curve

Lotus Notes allowed users to conduct searches across some or all of the domains. It also allowed users to search against all documents opened over a certain period. However, on Notes, information on a client was stored by industry and by the line of business, which limited its search capability for a particular item of information. The Knowledge Curve was different in that it was possible to search for a particular information by looking down the business development tree. The Knowledge Curve was introduced to facilitate the search process at a global level. However, there was another issue to be solved. The Knowledge Curve lacked an effective search engine that would allow the knowledge base to function effectively.[14] It was necessary to have a search engine that would enable people to search across databases without knowing that a particular database even existed.

According to Stephen Langley, PwC GTS Director, it would be very effective to be able to properly implement a search engine. In September 1998, the issue of implementing a search engine was discussed in a GTS global meeting in Switzerland and a task force was created to look into this. PwC went through a long process of re-evaluating it, and finally signed a global deal with Verity as the search engine. Verity was the search engine within the Knowledge Curve. As at February 2000 this was not fully implemented.

The Global Knowledge Centre

PwC opened its Global Knowledge Centre on 28 July 1998. The Knowledge Centre was an integrated facility for knowledge sharing, training and data warehousing project support. Based in Rosemont, Illinois, the centre was the first of a number of Knowledge Centres planned around the world. Europe was the next site.[15] Through the Global Knowledge Centre, companies would:

---

[14] Larger corporate sites may use a search engine to index and retrieve the content of just their own site.

[15] URL: http://www.pwcglobal.com/extweb/nc...D/100A24F2676A85C385256657006373E0, 30 May 2000.

❑ receive hands-on training in many of the leading data warehousing technologies

❑ have access to continuous market information

❑ view extensive state-of-the-art product evaluations

❑ provide an environment where clients could work with PwC consultants to design and develop strategic knowledge-based solutions

At the global level, the Global Knowledge Group worked closely with the GTS, looking into ways that could effectively leverage their knowledge assets to respond to clients' needs in a more innovative manner. At each office level, however, Knowledge Managers had been appointed only on a part-time basis by line of business. This was expected to change as knowledge management began to gain more recognition within the firm.

ISSUES AND CHALLENGES IN BUILDING THE PWC KNOWLEDGE BASE

When we merged, we also became a global practice, as we had been country-based before. We faced big change and big challenges in getting people up to speed with how to use things, and how to use the technology which changed when our networks merged.
— Julia Collins, Head, PwC Global Knowledge Group[16]

Integration on a global scale was not an easy task. One of the things that made the integration process complex was the way the original systems were developed by each of the firms. Prior to the merger, both PW and C&L had developed their systems around their line-of-business focus and were independent systems. The problem was that this enabled only limited access to the knowledge base by the people within the entire PwC. The new integrated system aimed to eliminate such an inefficient use of assets. Breaking up the closed structure of the original system and creating a system that would enable everyone in PwC to have access to all the knowledge base was the major goal for the new corporate IT system. This required preparation and time to be completed. Other challenges that PwC encountered included:

---

[16] Thomson, S. (2000), "Focus: Keeping Pace With Knowledge", *Information Week Review*, Vol. 155, Oxford, February, pp. 23–24.

❏ differences in IT systems and organisational structure
❏ e-mail networking and intranet using Lotus Notes
❏ integration of databases and servers

Pragmatism was driving the essential forward planning and business culture at PwC. The coordination process was streamlined and there were fewer bureaucratic procedures. According to Lambert, pragmatism seemed to be coming from a very small group of people who actually made the decisions. There was a shift at PwC because of the information technology evolution and all of the business pressures that the firm was going through. In service organisations such as PwC, senior people (in age and experience) propelled the business, whereas people in support functions would do what they were told to. This was the case in 1995. As at year 2000, the senior people were still in control of certain parts of the business (profitability and setting high-level strategies); however, they were less involved in decision making in the day-to-day business. Most of the decisions were down to the 'younger' partners and directors, the 'older' generation recognising that they were less in touch with what was going on.

Another major change was there was less corporate politics than in 1995, when there were a number of 'egos' clashing. As at year 2000, the people below the hierarchy were younger and had the initiative to get things done quickly, so more work was accomplished within a shorter period of time. Although there seemed to be a flatter structure at PwC, there was still a management board that made the policy decisions and approved projects.

Differences in IT Systems and Organisational Structure

There were distinctive differences between PW and C&L in the way the companies operated. Integration was easier on the PW side of the system since its IT team had been working together on a regional basis before the merger. PW used the same software, Novell, and had worked in setting up some of the standards. Though this was rather a loose standard, PW had 70 to 80 percent of the system in common at the time of the merger, which facilitated the integration of the systems on the PW side. Having two IT Directors from each side also added some conflict in the earlier stage of the integration process, especially regarding the issue of rationalising the IT personnel.

On the other hand, C&L's IT team was more independent of the others, so there was less coordination among the IT teams around the world. C&L's IT team was autonomous in terms of personnel and the technology used. In addition to such a fragmented IT structure, C&L's IT level was outdated. C&L had their own Novell server version 3.0, set up in 1995, which they were using until the merger. This was the case with C&L's Lotus Notes; it was not the updated version. There was no TCP/IP on the network, which was a basic communication language or protocol of the Internet or in private networks such as intranets and/or extranets. C&L, however, was more advanced in its Audit group, where they used electronic working papers.

There were strong global IT directions at PwC that had not happened on either side before. On the scale of the merger, things happened on a global level and a strong leadership emerged and started work on planning. Two major things were achieved: (1) the global wide area network (GWAN), which was to link the wide area networks of PW and C&L and (2) integration of the Lotus Notes domain.[17]

e–Mail Networking and Intranet Using Lotus Notes

Linking the e-mail system was the first focus of integration. From prior merger examples, PW and C&L were aware that establishing a solid internal communications system would be a key factor for the new company to run smoothly. This part of the integration was facilitated by both firms using Lotus Notes for their e-mail and intranet systems.[18] Still, it took the IT team one whole year of thorough planning to have the integrated e-mail system running in time with the operation of PwC in July 1999. As at February 2000, this work was still on-going.

When the Global Team announced the global e-mail networking plan, the IT officers at the office level were sceptical, as the structure and routing were so complex and impractical. In one structure, the e-mail messages between the two offices in the same geographical location were routed via distant servers, causing hours of delivery delays. For example, the global networking plan in Hong Kong required messages from PW to C&L offices to be routed via Sydney, causing two hours of delivery delay.

---

[17] Interview with Lambert and Langley of PwC, Hong Kong, 1 February 2000.

[18] Notes is a sophisticated groupware application from the Lotus Corporation, a subsidiary of IBM. Notes lets a corporation and its workers develop communications- and database-oriented applications so that users in different geographic locations can share files with each other, comment on them publicly or privately (to groups with special access), keep track of development schedules, work projects, guidelines and procedures, plans, white papers and many other documents, including multimedia files. Notes keeps track of changes and makes updates to replications of all databases in use at any site. Changes are made at the field level to minimise network traffic. (Definition of Notes from URL: wysiwyg://def.71/http://www.whatiscom/notes.htm, 30 May 2000.)

This was addressed immediately by the IT team, who were not obligated to follow the global executives, but instead opted for the most practical solution.

The most complicated part of the e-mail integration was the restructuring of the topology of Lotus Notes domain. The domain restructuring for PwC was said to have been one of the most complicated restructuring tasks ever done. For example, PW had 115 domains that were to be reduced to seven; while C&L had some 100 domains in Hong Kong alone, while each country had its own domain that also had to be reduced.

The Notes topology also required restructuring. As PW was one of the earliest companies to implement the system, what they had in place was a flat structure type of Notes. C&L used the latter version of Notes, which had a hierarchical structure, and PwC was to implement the hierarchical structure. There were a number of technical issues that had to be dealt with when trying to merge the two Notes versions. One of the difficulties in getting everything hierarchical had to do with the security structure of Notes. To remedy this situation required drilling down to the database level and sometimes even to the document level.

Internal and External Communication: Hong Kong and Sydney Offices as an Illustration

Before the merger, PW had a couple of mail servers, a major database server and Reuters. These all went via Sydney. On the CL side, they had a hub server, a database server, separate mail server lines of service and an audit electronic working paper, which were also routed via Sydney. The difficulty was that the link in Sydney was slow, the replication time and the Notes structure on one side was not optimal. [Refer to **Figure 1** for the old model flow of information between PW to C&L. Refer to **Exhibit 4** for the Hong Kong Notes Topology effective September 1999.] As at September 1999, PwC had only one link to Sydney, which was being upgraded every other month. The number of servers, although being reduced, had yet to be rationalised as there were not that many changes done; PwC kept all the mail and audit servers.

PwC's external communication would still go through a hub. Again, the external communication systems of both PW and C&L were different prior to the merger. C&L had its own domain and its own Internet link and had to push Internet e-mail directly out from Hong Kong. PW did it through global gateways, which went through via the US. After the merger, PwC was able to quickly switch everybody onto a PwC Internet address, thus even though the two firms were 'PW' and 'C&L' to the outside

Figure 1: Information flow between PW and C&L

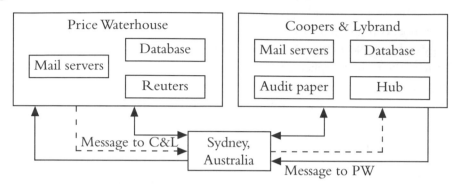

world on the Internet, the Internet address was www.pwcglobal.com. This meant the hub went via the US. Only in February 1999 was PwC able to install a third Internet gateway, and was therefore hubbed into Sydney.

The remaining tasks for the Notes would be the re-certification of the Notes IDs to a global standard and getting them into a hierarchical structure, a project that would be done on a regional basis. Under the change, each Notes name would include line of service, city and country. This would be a big process, as it would affect all of the underlying security within Lotus Notes. In addition, standardisation of the Notes templates and upgrading the entire Lotus Notes infrastructure would take place. The project started in February 2000 in Asia.

PwC had an elaborate process of setting up a dedicated, private link into the client's system, such as BAT, the purpose being to secure communication with the client. The system, however, was never fully utilised because of the complexity in its use. For example, Hong Kong set up a separate Notes domain in Asia-Pacific for external clients using three gateways – Australia, New Zealand and Hong Kong – which enabled access into and out of whichever local gateway was required.

There was strong coordination and communication between the IT workforce in Hong Kong and in Sydney that helped in the integration and standardisation of the PwC techno-infrastructure. Langley said, "Sydney had, traditionally, a competent IT team and the Hong Kong office, which was the largest office in Asia, benefited from that strong interaction."[19] For example, Sydney would run the main consolidation and

---

[19] Interview with Lambert and Langley, PwC Hong Kong, 1 February 2000.

re-certification of the Notes on a regional basis. Sydney also managed the wide area network in Asia–Pacific. Because of Sydney's strong IT team and willingness to do work for other PwC people around the region, those who were relatively autonomous would choose to use the products produced by Sydney.

Database and Server Integration

Duplication of the database ■ There were many duplications of the database that, together with the servers, required rationalisation. Rationalisation took place starting at the office level. The database problem was typified by the fact that there were hundreds of databases in one country location alone. To rationalise, the content of each database had to be checked and re-evaluated by those responsible for those databases. Such a task was beyond what the IT workforce could do, so the task was delegated to the respective line of service. The process included the following steps:

1. Identification of the data owner – a complicated and time-consuming process, but it was completed in a relatively smooth manner.
2. The identified owner was given the responsibility for updating the database on a regular basis.

If the owner could not be identified, data was sent into an archive database. PwC's key to data management was to make sure that every record had an owner who could update the content on a regular basis. Preventing the data from becoming obsolete gave the data more value.

Closed vs. open database ■ Historically, there was no one officially assigned to manage a certain database, and many of the databases were merely stored without being accessed or updated. For example, the contacts databases in the pre-merger were different. In the C&L firm, the contacts database was relatively closed – partners put their contacts in a central database and they were the only people who could view and update details on their contacts. On the PW side, there was an open database – anybody could see anybody's contacts, but only the data owners could edit it. PwC decided to have an open database as it was seen to be counterproductive to maintain a closed one.

Data transfer ■ The next step in rationalising the database was to categorise it and eliminate any duplication. This, again, was a time-consuming process. However, it was a process that had to be done to create an efficient, powerful knowledge base. In January 2000, PwC experienced technical problems in transferring data. There were 25,000 records, of which about 5,000 were duplicates in the contacts database. The IT team had to go through the records and take the duplicates out; a process that was done manually. (There were instances, for example, where an old C&L partner had a PW contact in his database. In February 2000, PwC was able to develop a system where a hard copy of the data list was sent out to various partners, with every record allocated to partners. PwC had implemented a program that facilitated updating the data: every couple of months the marketing functions prompt the data owners by sending a memo to update their contacts list.)

Generally, information in the PwC's Lotus Notes was in the form of documents. PW was not using SQL as it was more focused on using Notes before the merger, whereas C&L had a strong development team using SQL. This made the two systems compatible when brought together during the merger.

Plans to Improve the PwC Technical Infrastructure

At the beginning of year 2000, GTS' main focus was on the GTS itself: its internal policies and procedures. The GTS was reviewing its administrative systems and how it could communicate better with PwC's customers.

❑ *Development Team* – Projects included building the local level KC, the 'Executive Dimension' (a multi-dimensional data analysis tool that would be used for analysing Power data and many other types of data), and numerous other systems, including leave management, tax management, executive recruitment, CA Pacific and document management.

❑ *Network Team* – This team would continue to consolidate servers, starting with ABAS. A new application server was implemented on-line to be used firm-wide for applications and data-sharing, which facilitated the delivery of applications and systems updates across the firm. The two servers ran on NetWare 5 and were Fibre Channel servers.[20] Other concerns included network management, monitoring, security and Internet service. The Virtual Private Network (VPN) was also part of the Network team's responsibility. Notes, voicemail and (with NetWare 5) network files would be available via VPN.

❑ *Notes Team* – Year 2000 would be dedicated to re-certification of Notes IDs. Everyone's official Notes name would change to include line of service, city and country: a global standard within PwC. Other projects included: enabling

---

[20] Fibre Channel servers use fibre-optic technology between the server and the discs and have very high data-transfer rates.

Notes addressing via initials for everyone, standardising the Notes mail templates, and upgrading all of the Lotus Notes infrastructure to Notes version 5.

❑ *Projects Team* – Maintenance and upgrade of the POWER system to the testing and implementation of the new systems and technology, such as Office 2000, would be key projects. Also, the team would test and evaluate new and emerging technology such as voice recognition software.

❑ *Helpdesk Team* – The staffing level was at an appropriate level to be able to provide the service levels that PwC required. The major effort was focusing on how calls were answered, improving first call resolution, speedy response and utilising tools such as remote control software.

PwC had resources that other service professional organisations lack. Fully integrating all the resources at a global as well as organisational level to create a knowledge base was the main challenge. This would mean successfully integrating the internal networks and the *use* of the network. Therefore, PwC had to effectively manage and share the knowledge base across the firm. After all, knowledge was the 'lifeblood' of PwC and it was all PwC had to 'share and sell'.

Exhibit 1: PWC industries with old company equivalents

PricewaterhouseCoopers industries	Price Waterhouse	Coopers & Lybrand
Financial services industry • Banking • Capital markets • Investment management • Insurance • Real estate	Financial services (FSIP) • Banking • Investment Management • Insurance • Management healthcare • Real estate • Securities	Financial services • Banking • Capital markets • Insurance • Investment management Real estate & hospitality
Services industry • Government • Healthcare • Education & not-for-profit • Transport • Hospitality • Engineering & construction • Posts		Engineering & construction Government contracting Integrated healthcare • Healthcare • Pharmaceutical • Health information Management- (HIM) related services Higher education & not-for-profit State & local government Transportation
Global energy & mining industry (GEM) • Oil & gas • Utilities • Mining	World energy group • Oil • Natural gas • Chemicals • Independent power • Mining • Utility	Energy, utilities & natural resources • Oil & gas • Utilities • Mining

Exhibit 1 (cont'd)

PricewaterhouseCoopers Industries	Price Waterhouse	Coopers & Lybrand
Consumer & industrial products (CIP) • Consumer packaged goods • Pharmaceutical • Retail • Automotive • Industrial products	Products	Manufacturing • Automotive • Consumer & industrial Retail
Technology, info/comm & entertainment (TICE) • Technology • Information/ communications • Media & entertainment	Entertainment, media & communications (EMC) Technology industry group • Computers & peripherals • Life sciences • Networking & communications • Semiconductors & semiconductor equipment • Software	High technology • Life sciences (biotechnology & medical technology) • New media • Computer software, computing & electronic • Venture capital Information & entertainment Media & entertainment

Exhibit 2: PWC history

Year	Event
1849	• Samuel Lowell Price sets up business in London
1854	• William Cooper establishes his own practice in London, which seven years later becomes Cooper Brothers
1865	• Price, Holyland and Waterhouse join forces in partnership
1874	• Name changes to Price, Waterhouse and Co.
1898	• Robert H. Montgomery, William M. Lybrand, Adam A. Ross, Jr. and his brother T. Edward Ross form Lybrand, Ross Brothers and Montgomery
1957	• Cooper Brothers & Co (UK), McDonald, Currie and Co (Canada) and Lybrand, Ross Bros & Montgomery (US) merge to form Coopers & Lybrand
1982	• Price Waterhouse World Firm formed
1990	• Coopers & Lybrand merges with Deloitte Haskins & Sells in a number of countries around the world
1998	• Worldwide merger of Price Waterhouse and Coopers & Lybrand to create PricewaterhouseCoopers

Source: URL:http://www.pwcglobal.com/gx/eng/about/press-rm/fact.html, 29 May 2000.

Exhibit 3: Industry strengths of Price Waterhouse and Coopers & Lybrand

Price Waterhouse	Coopers & Lybrand
• Packaged software and global IT implementation practices	• Strategy and human resource consulting
• Global expertise in the media and entertainment sectors	• Telecommunications
• Auditing in the telecommunications industry	• Consulting in the telecommunications industry
• Expertise in chemicals	• Expertise in consumer products and manufacturing

• Strong in pharmaceutical sectors

• Energy sector (oil and gas, mining and utilities)

• Financial services sector (banking, insurance and brokerage and mutual funds)

Exhibit 4:   Hong Kong Notes Topology

Hong Kong Notes Topology Effective 01/09/99

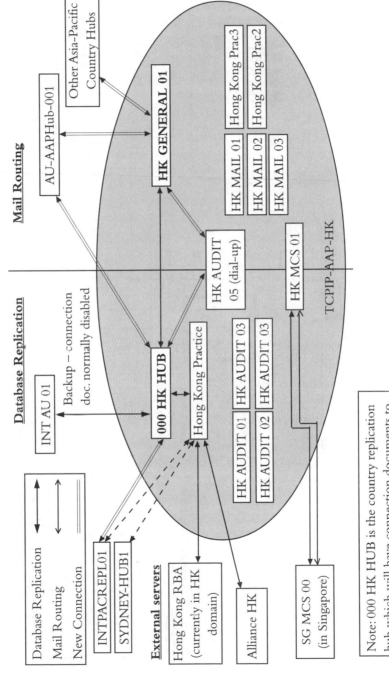

Exhibit 5: Hong Kong Portal and Knowledge Curve

HONG KONG PORTAL AND KNOWLEDEGE CURVE

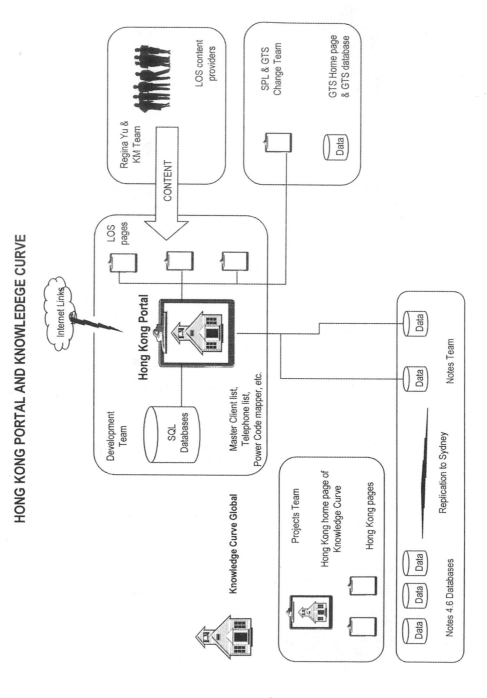

CHAPTER

■–■–■

9

Process Management
Through e-Business

OBJECTIVES

- To understand the concept of process management in an e-business.
- To introduce the selling-chain management concept.
- To understand supply-chain management.
- To discuss process integration through e-business.
- To discuss integration challenges.

In the previous chapter, we discussed various technologies that facilitate e-commerce activities. We noted that technology is an enabler of e-commerce. We also discussed that technology can be used to re-engineer many business processes. In this chapter we show how the success of e-commerce has become contingent on the deployment of an effective e-business strategy. Such a strategy is based on a competitive and integrated infrastructure that allows firms to fundamentally re-engineer their businesses with an eye for long-term growth in the e-commerce environment. In the coming years we will see an increasing number of firms aligning their business strategy with their e-business strategy through redesigning and reconfiguring their business processes.

Since new terminology may bring about confusion, let us first define 'e-business'. In a nutshell, the concept of e-business refers to a complex fusion of business processes, enterprise applications and organisational structure necessary to create a high-performance business model.[1] e-Business requires an integrated technology, process and business strategy. It refers to the implementation of an integrated business management philosophy with a process methodology that takes into consideration every aspect of a firm and its environment. Therefore, the backbone of e-business process management becomes the integration and management of the supply-chain and the selling-chain. This means managing end-to-end business processes from the time a customer orders a product/service to the time a customer receives the product/service. This customer-centric business model requires an e-business design that can integrate the supply- and selling-chains. Through such an integration, companies can in turn streamline their buying and selling processes, improve interactions with their customers and suppliers, and force flexible outsourcing alliances with their partners.

In this chapter, we focus on discussing the process management and process integration aspects of an e-business. First, we introduce the selling-chain and the importance of front-end process integration to create single entry points for customers. Then we discuss back-end processes and supply-chain management to highlight how various links in a supply-chain are interlinked and need to be tightly integrated. The next section provides an overview of the selling- and supply-chains by focusing on how streamlined and integrated processes are adding value to customers and suppliers. Finally, we end the chapter by discussing the challenges related to process integration.

SELLING-CHAIN MANAGEMENT

In the new economy, power has shifted to buyers where delivering superior customer service through long-term customer relationship management has become the ultimate priority for many firms. As a result, business process flows must be studied in reverse, beginning from customer demand and ending with the sourcing of that product.[2] An organisation's major focus should be to *add value* internally and externally

---

[1] Kalakota & Whinston (1996), p. 16.

[2] Kalakota & Whinston (1996).

through the seamless integration of back-end and front-end processes to deliver superior customer service.

By adopting customer satisfaction as the primary goal, firms can work backwards through every link in their supply- and selling-chains, from marketing to shipping to order processing to manufacturing and all the way to raw materials acquisition. In the following sections, we focus on understanding the selling-chain and subsequently discuss the supply-chain and challenges of integrating the two chains.

Selling-chain management refers to an integrated customer order acquisition strategy. An integrated selling-chain mechanism has become critical to an e-business' ability to execute its sales function successfully. The growing focus on an integrated strategy can be attributed to one major factor: rise in customer power. Customers demand shorter order processes, effective systems to manage feedback to their enquiries and sales orders, and efficient delivery infrastructure. In essence, customers are demanding more value and companies are reacting by providing solutions catered to individual customers. However, such a strategy can only be achieved through integrating, automating and managing sales interactions throughout an enterprise.

GM BuyPower's Auto Website

General Motors, the world's largest manufacturer of cars and trucks, is evolving its business model in new ways to capitalise on the Web. With the help of Sun Microsystems, GM is tapping new high-growth Internet markets with solutions that can scale to meet unpredictable levels of demand.

After two years of consumer research and a pilot programme in four Western states, GM launched its GM BuyPower on a national basis on 10 March 1999. Located at www.gmbuypower.com, GM's Website gives on-line shoppers instant access to details about every GM make and model available, including direct access to participating dealers' new vehicle inventory and the ability to apply on-line for GMAC financing. By providing on-line shoppers with third-party competitive comparisons, model availability, GM BuyPower dealer locations and easy access to financing, GM hopes to transform the typical 'haggling' car buying experience into a convenient and satisfying one. Leo Drew, operations manager for the GM BuyPower Website explains, "We learned that many people were very frustrated with the negotiation process. The whole car buying process for them was very difficult." GM BuyPower responded by designing a Website that would give consumers what they were asking for in terms of the kind of information that they would like to have in the shopping and buying experience.

GM BuyPower helps its dealerships automatically track consumer messages through a fax server and via a Lotus Notes message. "From a business perspective, we are able to send this front-line customer information upstream in a timely manner, which is important for us to remain competitive going forward," Drew says. "Our purpose is to distribute information to the appropriate areas of the organisation – in essence to respond more rapidly to the consumer's needs." By committing to specific customer treatment standards, dealers are dedicated to streamlining the customer's purchase process in the most efficient way possible. So, in fact, on-line shoppers are rewarded for the research they have conducted.

Sources: Sun Microsystems; GM BuyPower.

In the pre-Internet business era, sellers and intermediaries derived some advantage by knowing more than their buyers about products, costs and the availability of raw materials. e-Commerce has undermined traditional sources of advantage based on such information asymmetry. As a result, companies have been forced to reassess what value they offer to customers in the Internet's competitive environment. On the Internet, where 'stickiness' is prized, seamlessly connecting Websites and back-office services, such as shipping, is a strategic necessity. Through interactive Web-based applications, firms can rely on integrated supply- and selling-chain to provide customers access to such information as pricing options, customer history, real-time order tracking, etc. Interactive exchange of information, design requirements, component specifications, cost tracking, logistics supervision, service requests and trouble-shooting advice, are all areas which permit an unprecedented level of mass customisation, thus added value to customers.[3]

The selling-chain process integration has impacted many businesses, especially those engaging in B2B e-commerce where most routine aspects of sales processes are moving to the Internet: selling commodity and repeat-purchase products via e-commerce programmes, putting catalogues and product information on-line, tracking orders and even negotiating prices for some deals. Many tasks, such as handling customer questions and taking orders or reorders, can now be done over the Internet by clients themselves. As a result, sales teams can now spend much less time doing mun-

---

[3] Desmarais (2000).

dane account maintenance tasks and spend more time delivering high-level service to customers.

In sum, the rise of e-business has made possible a tight relationship between both back-end and front-end operations. Integrating processes within the selling-chain streamlines the front-end operations of a business. In order to reap the full benefits of e-business, back-end processes must also be well-integrated within the supply-chain.

SUPPLY-CHAIN MANAGEMENT (SCM)

Supply-chain management (SCM) refers to the complex network of relationships that organisations maintain with trading partners to source, manufacture and deliver products. It is the coordination of material, information and financial flows between and among the participating enterprises. To achieve customer satisfaction, it is important to integrate both front-end processes and back-end processes within the selling- and supply-chains.

The supply-chain can be descibed as '... the network of facilities and activities that perform the functions of product development, the procurement of material from vendors, the movement of materials between facilities, the manufacturing of products, the distribution of finished goods to customers, and after-market support for sustainment'.[4] **Figure 1** exhibits a model of SCM that includes the five major stages as shown.

By taking a holistic view, SCM emerges as a comprehensive methodology for handling logistics activities when integrated with the production and marketing aspects of a business cycle. Such an integrative approach is considered essential for firms that wish to gain competitive advantage through streamlined operations and achieve quick market response.

The traditional supply-chain adheres to dedicated private networks, shared information as feasible within the company, customised intra-company collaboration and

Figure 1: Stages in SCM

1. Sourcing → 2. Inbound logistics → 3. Manufacturing → 4. Outbound logistics → 5. After-market service

---

[4] Mabert & Venkataramanan (1998), p. 538.

controlled connection and access to internal corporate network. The traditional SCM has evolved to what is popularly known as e-business CRM. An e-business supply-chain relies heavily on shared global networks, shared information and mutual collaboration among all parties along the chain.

"Mastery of logistics is as vital to success in the digital economy as it was to the extraordinary success of the Roman Empire," explains Fredrick W. Smith, Chairman and CEO, FedEx Corporation.[5] To illustrate the efficiencies that firms may gain from optimising the supply-chain, we take the example of General Motors Co. (GM). GM aims to use the Internet to create an on-line marketplace through which to execute its multi-billion procurement operations. GM has 30,000 suppliers, ten percent of whom are considered core suppliers; it buys goods and services in over 30 countries and manufactures in 107 countries. Given this mammoth operation, compressing its procurement operations translates into better profit margins, greater efficiency and integrated business functions. By creating an on-line marketplace, GM cuts costs by streamlining the supply-chain and can derive major savings from being able to aggregate purchases across their global operations.[6] SCM benefits GM, its suppliers and customers because integrated supply-chains create value in several areas for all parties involved:

❑ *Enhanced market efficiency.* Streamlined processes facilitated by the Internet lead to reduced operational costs for GM and its suppliers. For example, take the process of a GM manager finding a seat supplier. Through the Internet, GM can establish a bidding process for seats where various suppliers submit their bids which include prices, schedules, specifications and so on. GM selects the most cost-efficient supplier for its required seats, the specifications and delivery schedules catered to its needs. This bidding process creates a dynamic and efficient marketplace by allowing pricing transparency, choice and catered solutions.

❑ *Enhanced integration.* By creating an electronic exchange (TradeXchange), GM enhances all aspects of SCM. It can aggregate its procurement functions, negotiate contract terms and execute sales transactions. Meanwhile, suppliers gain access to the marketplace, access to timely information and have the ability to

[5] Jones (1998), p. 221.

[6] In the long term, GM wants to develop trading exchanges into profitable e-commerce portals that will become major sites for B2B Internet transactions.

conduct business 24-hours, 7-days-a-week through self-service capabilities on GM's Websites.

❑ *Improved customer service.* GM customers can order on-line, pay on-line, track car delivery status and receive post-purchase service on-line, through an agent or company representative. On the other hand, suppliers have a single point of contact with GM and have the opportunity to provide process improvement suggestions to GM.

As e-commerce has affected the flow of information between firms, it has become easier for firms to outsource some or all parts of their logistics: 'the logistics function is the underpinning of outsourcing'.[7] Many organisations leverage the existing infrastructure, such as the Internet, to subcontract certain or all operations to a third party, thus focusing exclusively on their core competencies. Successful outsourcing usually results in reduction in lead time, ultimately leading to improved customer service.[8]

In recent years, third-party logistics firms (commonly known as 3PLs) have become more important. Some of these firms have been forced to expand their service from simple warehousing and transportation to monitoring shipments, managing distribution centre operations, selecting route carriers, receiving and paying bills, and monitoring carrier performance.[9] The burgeoning proliferation of Applications Service Providers (ASPs) is another indication that an increasing number of firms will oursource the development and maintenance of their e-business activities to third party, expert companies.

There are several examples of total outsourcing, where a third-party logistics firm (or a group of third-party logistic firms) handles a firm's entire backroom operations. The third-party logistics firm receives goods from vendors based on Internet orders. The third-party logistic firm then performs warehousing, order picking, assembly, packaging, shipping, as well as the huge job of handling returns.

PROCESS INTEGRATION THROUGH E-BUSINESS

Globalisation and the increase in e-commerce activities have boosted competitive pres-

---

[7] Jones (1998), p. 228.

[8] UPS had the third-highest revenue among all private US companies for 1998 (*Forbes*, 1999a), while FedEx was listed as the 85th largest public company in the US in 1999 (*Forbes*, 1999b).

[9] Mele (1999).

sures on businesses. Specifically, higher customer expectations and cost pressures have forced companies to adopt strategies that allow them to deliver customised customer service cost effectively. Such strategies usually require the transformation of business processes and the development of an integrated supply- and selling-chain that can allow firms to do the following:

❑ Conduct their business on a global basis.
❑ React quickly to market demands.
❑ Provide differentiated and customised products and services with a view to winning customer loyalty.

These objectives can best be achieved through an integrated global e-business strategy. Through e-business, companies can accomplish operational excellence by streamlining and integrating their supply- and selling-chains. The upshot of such a process integration is that all business units can work in tandem with one another in terms of goals, processes and customer relations. The critical factor is to maintain a tightly integrated supply- and selling-chain within which each process is designed and to add value to customers. Because interweaving the selling- and supply-chains requires the management of many complex and interrelated links, interactions and partnerships, it is perhaps the most difficult part of formulating and implementing an e-business strategy.

Figure 2 illustrates a tightly integrated supply- and selling-chain. We cover three major process areas and highlight more salient factors through which supplier and customer value is emerging: market discovery, transaction management and service management. We should note that since companies cannot achieve excellence in all areas of business internally, they increasingly focus on pulling together requisite skills and expertise through partnerships and alliances to achieve quality across a full spectrum of business processes.

Market Discovery

Internet e-procurement is the hottest area of e-commerce. That's because of the dramatic cost savings and bottom-line impact it is now offering to companies.
— Stephanie Vargo, Sun Alliance Group Product Manager[10]

---

[10] "Riding the Storm", *The Economist*, 6 November 1999.

Figure 2: An integrated supply-chain and selling-chain

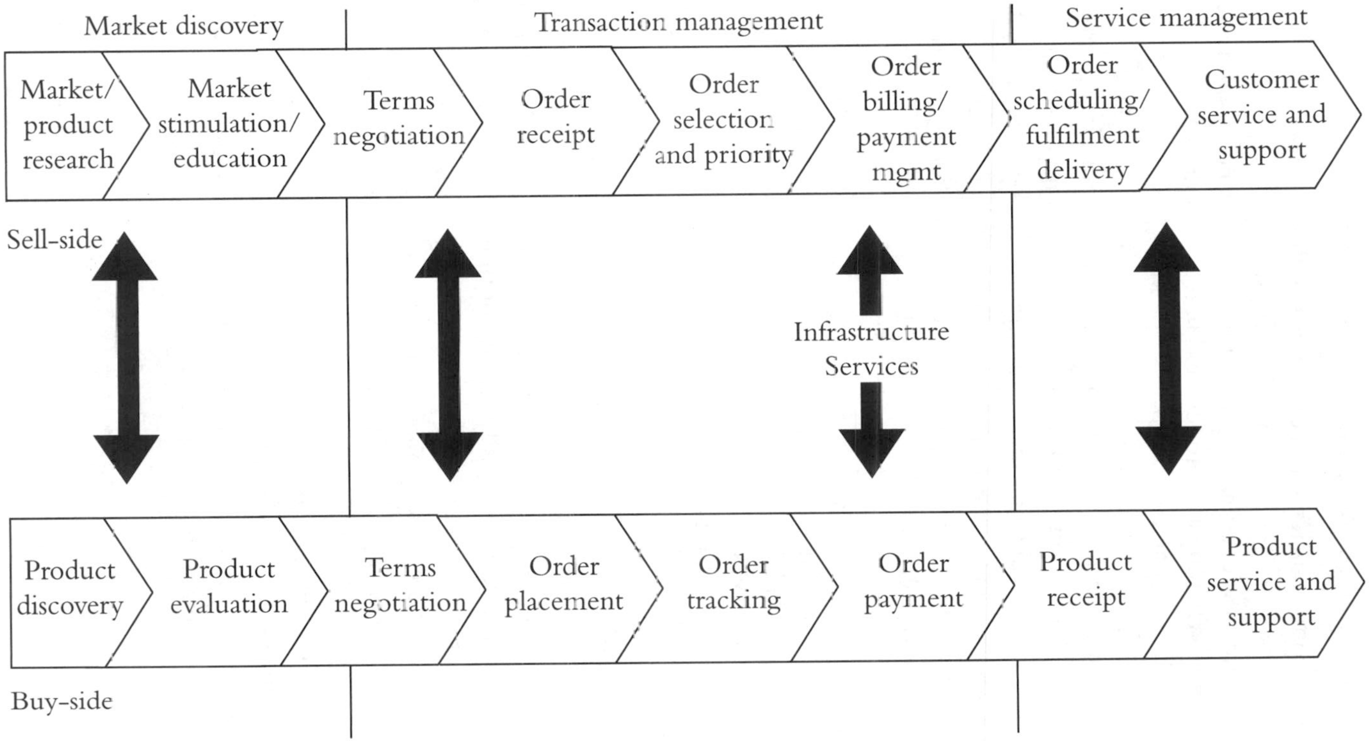

Source: Fellenstein & Wood (2000), p. 28.

Companies are increasingly under pressure to do as follows:

1. Focus on core competencies and technologies with the outsourcing of non-core requirements.
2. Innovate and improve continuously in critical performance areas, including quality, delivery, cycle time and product and process technology.
3. Cut costs in order to be able to compete worldwide.[11]

The Internet's open standards and its global reach make it an ideal platform to achieve these objectives. Firms using the Internet can connect into each other's business processes, flexibly and cheaply. This means, the Internet has become an invaluable sourcing tool that saves time and redirects human resources to focus on more strategic management issues. In fact, firms have begun to use the Internet for a wide variety of sourcing-related tasks as follows:

- ❑ Finding new sources of supply.
- ❑ Looking for product information, including prices.
- ❑ Finding delivery information and tracking orders.
- ❑ Seeking out sales contacts.
- ❑ Negotiating terms and conditions.
- ❑ Receiving technical advice.

By leveraging the Internet, companies can increase their profitability through efficient sourcing. For example, electronic purchasing reduces costs, produces more complete data for both buyers and sellers, saves time and enhances security. A recent study found that procurement departments spend the bulk of time on operational support activities, such as requisition and purchase order processing, supplier selection and material receipts processing. Technology allows the automation of these lower-value processes and the relocation of valuable human resources to higher value-added decision support.[12]

Based on an e-business strategy, streamlining market discovery processes, such as sourcing, can help firms trim costs and improve their overall strategies for the procurement of materials and parts. Such cost savings are relatively easy to achieve through consolidated and improved purchase processes.

---

[11] Trent & Monczka (1999).

[12] McKendrick (1999).

SourcingLink.net: Vertical Community for Home Improvement Retailers and Suppliers

Founded in 1993, SourcingLink.net (www.sourcinglink.net) is a B2B Internet merchandise sourcing company for the home improvement market worldwide. In cooperation with The Home Improvement Industry, over 60 retailers have been invited to join the trading community and 4,000 suppliers have been pre-registered. SourcingLink.net e-commerce solutions enable retailers to organise, automate and significantly reduce the cost of their merchandise sourcing activities. The Company's MySourcingCenter™ for Home Improvement is the first global B2B e-marketplace that allows industry buyers to search and identify products to purchase, and suppliers to broadcast and sell their products on-line. Sourcing applications could be done in an open community model or privately on a one-to-one basis, without having to change any existing business processes. The on-line trading community has developed application tools specifically for retail merchandise sourcing. Buyers send out request for quotes (RFQs) to their supplier base, and suppliers respond with Offer Sheets. Suppliers may also create on-line private catalogues to store and organise product information for the items that they plan to offer retailers.

Source: SourcingLink.net

Transaction Management

The effective use of technology has also allowed firms to streamline their transaction process management. As shown in Figure 2, transaction processes include order receipt, order selection and priority, and order billing/payment. e-Business has greatly facilitated transaction management in terms of allowing efficient and effective transfers of information to and from customers.

e-Business supply-chain has allowed companies to configure products to customer orders, confirm availability and track orders and delivery schedules in real time. Improved technology and enhanced process management systems have also dramatically reduced the costs of creating and processing purchase orders and keeping inventory. In addition to contracting process chains and improving customer relationship management, technology and process improvements have also created a new dynamic e-marketplace for conducting B2B e-commerce.

IBM's Continuous Replenishment Service

Because the demand for a product drives the entire supply-chain, many retailers, distributors and consumer goods manufacturers are implementing accurate forecasting tools in a vendor-managed inventory (VMI) environment that predict how their markets will respond to a wide variety of influences, including seasons, product lifecycle, pricing and promotions. IBM's Continuous Replenishment Service (CRP) links suppliers of consumer goods with their customers/vendor partners, speeding replenishment of these customers' inventories 'just-in-time' while reducing supplier/customer costs. The system efficiently moves EDI documents, allows companies to know what has been sold, and recommends how to replenish (by truckloads). CRP helps to speed up the inventory cycle, reduce inventory levels, decrease stock outs, improve customer service levels, boost warehouse efficiency, and enhance trading partners' perception of value. IBM's CRP is the leading vendor-managed inventory solution on the market and has links with over 60 customers and 100 trading partners.

Source: IBM.

Service Management

Service management refers to the delivery fulfilment and customer service and support. e-Business service management requires a solid infrastructure capable of delivering the right product/service, at the right time, to the right place, while keeping customers informed along the way. As the Internet has forced a fundamental shift in consumer buying behaviour and customer service expectations, order fulfilment has taken centrestage in e-commerce.

The increasing pressure from customers for information transparency and order processing efficiency is pushing firms to provide customers with real-time visibility on product inventory, the processing time required and delivery schedules. However, this is contingent on an organisation's ability to translate information into accurate order status and delivery information for customers.[13] Information visibility as a marketing advantage has helped firms win and retain customers. As companies shorten their supply-chain and rely upon more frequent shipments from their trading partners, information on the components' whereabouts becomes even more crucial. As inventory

---

[13] Hill (1999).

management becomes more of a joint venture, both partners need up-to-the-minute information on goods in production or in transit. Information visibility provides great value to both firms and customers; firms can contract supply-chains by effectively disseminating information throughout each chain link, creating logistics value. Providing customers information on their order status or promising delivery dates can be a firm's competitive advantage and adds value to customers.

Firms must be able to effectively manage customer information from all contact points, including the toll-free call service centre, the voice response system and all sales channels. In order to make on-line transactions work, e-retailers have to accurately capture orders, move goods from warehouses to far-flung customers, track changing inventory levels, capture payment information and make sure that customer enquiries are handled appropriately and in a timely manner. In addition to these demands, companies now have to be concerned about customers in other countries. Receiving an order from abroad, which a firm cannot efficiently process, means the loss of a potential customer and resulting marketing drawbacks.

In implementing an on-line business, firms must be prepared to meet the logistics challenges of the global market. [Refer to **Figure 3** to compare the retail and e-tail supply-chains.) With retailing, the main logistics function is the transportation of products in large batches from manufacturer to wholesaler to retailer; the movement of large batches of goods to a rather small number of places. With on-line retail (e-tail), the product is often delivered directly from the place of manufacture or assembly to the customer; a single good is moved to a large number of places. In the emerging business environment, the customer does not go to the product; the product goes to the customer. This significantly shakes up the traditional supply-chain, as nodes within the network of partnerships become redundant.

To create a successful e-business, companies need to re-evaluate their traditional strategies, not only on back-end, but also front-end processes, such as marketing and customer service, and focus on the integration of both functions. The key to integration is to adopt a process model which links the supply-chain with the selling-chain.

Establishing a reliable distribution system and efficient delivery of goods/services has created great opportunities for shipping businesses. Not only are shipping companies transporting more on-line-purchased goods, they are becoming critical links in customers' supply-chains.[14] By creating extranet links with customers and gathering logistics data, customers can use that data to improve their business operations.

---

[14] CMP Media Inc., 25 October 1999.

Figure 3:   Retail vs. e-tail supply-chain

Retail supply-chain

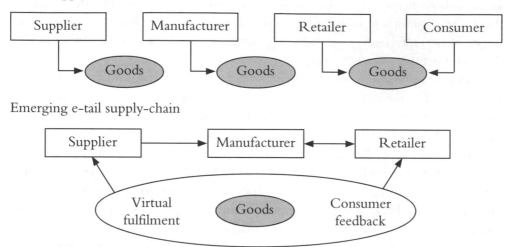

Emerging e-tail supply-chain

Source: King, E. (2000), "e-Commerce to e-Business", *Enterprise Systems Journal* (Dallas), Vol. 15, Iss. 1, January, p. 16.

e-Businesses are also putting enormous pressure on package carriers to participate fully in the just-in-time processes that enable manufacturers to fill orders as swiftly as possible while keeping inventory to a minimum. Package delivery companies are moving rapidly to reshape themselves as masters of logistics, SCM and even warehousing. Federal Express, for example, offers supply-chain and logistics software and consulting services to customers. The growing variety of offerings from shipping and logistics companies is also forcing firms to make some hard decisions about the role that each carrier should play in their supply-chains.

THE INTEGRATION CHALLENGE

Automating inter-corporate transactional processes in the past has been difficult because each firm has treated these processes as an internal matter, thus causing inter-organisational incompatibility. This problem was ameliorated to a certain degree through the use of standardised EDI transaction sets. However, the widespread adoption of EDI was retarded, among other things, by high costs and the proprietary nature of most value-added networks. The Internet, intranets and extranets largely changed that by allowing companies to design common interfaces embedded in an open techno-business architecture. By building their e-business on such an open architecture, companies have been able to closely integrate their business processes with those of their trading partners, thus extending their market reach, increasing sales and improving customer service.

Not only has e-business allowed firms to cut costs by automating their transactional processes, it has also led to improved customer services through rapid response time. However, companies can reap the benefits of e-business only if they can successfully re-engineer their internal processes so that these processes are in sync with those involved in the selling- and supply-chains of their trading partners. Such an integration is perhaps one of the most difficult and challenging jobs facing businesses today.

Designing an e-business strategy based on the philosophy of inter-corporate integration is much easier for start-ups than for existing companies. The new companies build their networking technologies ground up from scratch, without having to accommodate any unnecessary legacy systems, entrenched ways of doing business and a resistant workforce. Such firms are in a better position to design an e-business that is based on closely integrated end-to-end operations. For example, on-line businesses, such as Chemdex, MetalSite and eBay, have designed their e-businesses by continually integrating customer requirements into internal operations, and using their knowledge of their customers to drive their relationships with suppliers and other partners.

In contrast, it has been more difficult for existing businesses to incorporate integrated systems than to reinvent themselves. For most firms, perhaps the most difficult barrier is to overcome the traditional view that various functions involved in the business cycle are separate entities. Adopting an integrated organisational method represents a holistic perspective from which a business is seen as part of an ecosystem — a network of firms. By seeing each firm within the supply-chain as an interdependent partner, and by regarding logistics as an integrated part of the entire business system, a company can move closer to its ultimate purpose: enhancing customer service through the flawless delivery of customised service. Management commitment and education is needed to espouse the idea that the supply-chain and the selling-chain are indeed interdependent and that the whole business cycle, from procurement, through production, distribution and marketing, to selling and payment, must be regarded as an integrated system.

This level of integration requires organisational flexibility which cannot be achieved through traditional structures or business models. The on-going market challenges require a flexible organisational structure that allows firms to work with their partners in unison, in an integrative fashion. We discuss the emergence of such an organisation form – the internetworked enterprise – in the next chapter.

SUMMARY

- ❏ Business designs are being affected by pressures from the e-commerce activity and companies are responding by re-engineering their business processes to conduct e-commerce effectively. Businesses are focusing on building competitive and integrated infrastructures to respond and to align themselves with the new economic structure.
- ❏ Selling-chain management refers to an integrated customer order acquisition strategy. As consumer power has been growing, there is increased demand for customisation, efficiency and value. As a result, firms are integrating various links in the front-end chains to create integrated processes to deliver value to customers. Customers are also demanding increased information visibility; for example, they want to track an order status. This means firms have to link front-end management with back-end processes.
- ❏ Back-end processes are also known as the supply-chain which includes inventory management, manufacturing and production, distribution and after-market service. These are links which constitute a supply-chain and need to be tightly integrated with the front-end process to create value for a firm and its customers.
- ❏ Back-end and front-end process integration creates a lot of value for businesses, its suppliers, customers and employees. The three main strategic processes in an integrated selling- and supply-chains are market discovery, transaction management and service management. In an e-business, these three processes work in tandem to create efficiency, customisation, integration and an interweaved process management system.
- ❏ There are many integration challenges in an e-business. Firms need to address technology, management, process integration and strategy issues. One of the biggest organisation challenges is to adopt e-business at a strategic level and view processes with a 'holistic' and integrated vision.

REFERENCES

Atkinson, H. (1998a), "Companies Face Choice: Net or EDI", *The Journal of Commerce Online*, URL: http://www.joc.com/issues/981217/p1age1/e43083.htm/, August 2000.

Atkinson, H. (1998b), "Swift Logistics Entrepreneurs Combine Forces to Ride Software Wave", *The Journal of Commerce Online*, URL: http://www.joc.com/issues/980827/p1age1/e20011/, August 2000.

Atkinson, H. (1999), "FDX, UPS Broaden Internet Services: FedEx and Netscape in e-Commerce Pact", *The Journal of Commerce Online*, URL: http://www.joc.com/issues/990409/t1ransp/e38920.htm/, August 2000.

Ballou, R.H. (1992), *Business Logistics Management* (Third Edition), Englewoods Cliffs, NJ: Prentice Hall.

Bendor-Samuel, P. (1999), "Redefining Outsourcing: The Value Model", *Everest*, URL: http://www.outsourcing-mgmt.com/html/redefining-overview.html/, May.

Bowersox, D.J. (1969), "Physical Distribution in Semi maturity", in Daniel, N.E. & Jones, J.R. (eds), *Business Logistics: Concepts and Viewpoints*, Boston, MA: Allyn and Bacon, pp. 9–15.

Calza, F. & Passaro, R. (1997), "Case Study: EDI Network and Logistics Management at Unilever-Sagit", *SCM*, Vol. 2, No. 4, pp. 158–170.

Chelsom, J.V. (1998), "Getting Equipped for the Twenty-first Century", *Logistics Information Management*, Vol. 11, No. 2.

CMP Media Inc. (1999), URL: http://www.cmpmedia.com/, January 2000.

Cooke, J.A. (1999), "Web Commerce: Not Ready for Prime Time", *Logistics Management & Distribution Report*, URL: http://www.manufacturing.net/, August 2000.

Crowley, J.A. (1998), "Virtual Logistics: Transport in the Marketspace", *International Journal of Physical Distribution & Logistics Management*, Vol. 28, No. 7.

Daniel, N.E. & Jones, J.R. (1969), "The Nature and Scope of Business Logistics", in Daniel, N.E. & Jones, J.R. (eds), *Business Logistics: Concepts and Viewpoints*, Boston, MA: Allyn and Bacon, pp. 1–8.

Desmarais, S. (2000), "Business-to-Business Potential Unlimited", *The Bangkok Post*, Bangkok, 31 January, p. 1.

Dignan, L. (1998), "US Report: AT&T Buys IBM Networking Unit for $5 Billion", *ZD Net: UK*, URL: http://www.zdnet.co.uk/news/1998/48/ns-6317.html/, May 1999.

Drucker, P.F. (1962), "The Economy's Dark Continent", *Fortune*, Vol. LXV, No. 4, April, pp. 103, 265, 266, 268, 270.

Drucker, P.F. (1989), *The New Realities in Government and Politics/in Economics and Business/in Society and World View*, London: Mandarin.

Fellenstein, C. & Wood, R. (2000), *Exploring e-Commerce, Global e-Business, and e-Societies*, Upper Saddle River, NJ: Prentice Hall PTR, p. 28.

Forbes (1999a), "Forbes: The 500 Top Private Companies: 1998", URL: http://www.forbes.com/, December.

Forbes (1999b), "Forbes 500s Annual Directory: 1999", URL: http://www.forbes.com/, February 2000.

GM BuyPower (2000), URL: http://www.gmbuypower.com, 4 October.

Hill, S. (1999), "e-Tailing: The Internet Meets SCM", *Apparel Industry Magazine*, October.

Hof, R.D. (1999), "What Every CEO Needs to Know About Electronic Business: A Survival Guide", *BusinessWeek: E.biz*, 22 March, pp. 6–9.

IBM (1997), "IBM Lead Story: Outsourcing – Why More UK Companies Seek IT Partnership", URL: http://www-5.ibm.com/uk/stories/uk159.htm/, May 1999.

IBM (2000), "Continuous Replenishment Service", URL: http://www2.clearlake.ibm.com/cpg/discrp.htm, 9 October.

Irish Times (1999), "Delivering the Goods", Dublin, 17 December, p. 74.

Irish Times (2000), "Blarney's Winning Charm", Dublin, 11 January, p. 51.

Isidore, C. (1998), "e-Shoppers Choose Cheaper Shipping over Speedy Delivery", *The Journal of Commerce Online*, URL: http://www.joc.com/issues/980112/p1age1/e32259.htm/, May 1999.

Johnson, J.C. & Wood, D.F. (1990), *Contemporary Logistics* (Fourth Edition), New York, NY: Macmillan; London, England: Collier Macmillan.

Jones, D.H. (1998), "The New Logistics: Shaping the New Economy", in D. Tapsott *et al.* (eds), *Blueprint to the Digital Economy: Creating Wealth in the Era of e-Business*, New York, NY: McGraw-Hill, pp. 221–235.

Kalakota, R. & Whinston, A.B. (1996), *Frontiers of Electronic Commerce*, Reading, MA: Addison-Wesley.

Kalakota, R. & Whinston, A.B. (1997), *Electronic Commerce: A Manager's Guide*, Reading, MA: Addison-Wesley.

Kelly, K. (1994), *Out of Control: The Rise of Neo-biological Civilization*, Reading, MA: Addison-Wesley.

King, E. (2000), "e-Commerce to e-Business", *Enterprise Systems Journal* (Dallas), January, Vol. 15, Iss. 1, p. 16.

Langley, C.J., Jr. & Holcomb, M.C. (1992), "Creating Logistics Customer Value", *FedEx: Worldwide Logistics*, URL: http://www.fedex.com/, May 1999.

Mabert, V.A. & Venkataramanan, M.A. (1998), "Special Research Focus on Supply Chain Linkages: Challenges for Design and Management in the 21st Century", *Decision Sciences*, Vol. 29, No. 3, Summer, pp. 537–551.

MacDonald, J. & Tobin, J. (1998), Customer Empowerment in the Digital Economy, *Blueprint to the Digital Economy: Creating Wealth in the Era of e-Business*, New York, NY: McGraw-Hill, pp. 202–220.

McCarthy, S.P. (1998), "Online Middlemen: Separating the Good from the Bad", *Logistics Management & Distribution Report*, URL: http://www.manufacturing.net/, May 1999.

McKendrick, J. (1999), "Procurement: The Next Frontier in e-Business", *Midrange Systems*, Vol. 12, Iss. 11, 19 July, p. 27.

Mele, J. (1999), "Ready or Not", *Fleet Owner* (Overland Park), January, pp. 14–17.

Motwani, J., Larson, L., & Ahuja, S. (1998), "Managing a Global Supply Chain Partnership", *Logistics Information Management*, Vol. 11, No. 6.

M2 Presswire (1998), "Bay Networks: Bay Selects Trilogy and pcOrder as Vendors of Choice for Electronic Commerce Initiative", Coventry, 16 April, p. 1.

Rayport, J.F. & Sviokla, J.J. (1994), "Managing in the Marketspace", *Harvard Business Review*, November–December, pp. 140–150.

SourcingLink.net (2000), URL: http://www.sourcinglink.net/, 4 October.

Sun Microsystems (2000), URL: http://www.sun.com/dot-com/iforce/success/gm.html, 4 October.

The Economist (1999), "Riding the Storm", Vol. 353, Iss. 8144, 6 November, pp. 63–64.

Trent, R. & Monczka, R.M. (1999), "Achieving World-class Supplier Quality", *Total Quality Management*, August, Vol. 10, Iss. 6, pp. 927–938.

CASE

■-■-■

9.1

Japan Airlines: Impact of e-Ticketing*

During the 1990s, Internet usage doubled every 100 days and inspired the 'e-commerce revolution', bringing changes to business fundamentals and sources of competitive advantage. Electronic commerce radically altered the way companies conducted business and provided services to customers. Firms could enter markets globally to expand their customer and supplier base by positioning businesses on-line. e-Commerce, effectively implemented, resulted in lower costs and increased direct interaction between a business and its customers, suppliers, service providers, employees and other parties in the value-chain.

Since privatising in 1987, Japan Airlines (JAL) faced many difficulties including image problems and intense domestic and global competition. In addition to competitive pressures and increased airport charges, fuel taxes increased while the domestic downturn affected JAL's prospects throughout the 1990s. A restructuring strategy achieved some success in JAL's cost-cutting objectives but such savings through traditional means were nearing their potential.

In the meantime, many major international carriers were making headlines with aggressive efforts to achieve the reality of electronic travel services, including elec-

* Amir Hoosain and Shamza Khan prepared this case under the supervision of Dr. Dennis Kira and Dr. Ali Farhoomand. *Copyright © 2000 The University of Hong Kong. Ref. 00/78C*

tronic ticketing (e-ticketing) and smart cards. However, JAL was so busy managing its financial situation that it overlooked competing foreign carriers that were introducing e-ticketing to the Japanese market.

Airlines that had implemented e-ticketing, primarily in North America, experienced considerable savings in distribution costs through Internet sales and by automating many selling processes. The JAL management wondered, to what extent might this success be replicated by a Japanese major and what would be the best approach for pursuing e-ticketing implementation in Japan?

JAL'S GROWTH

The precursor to Japan Airlines (JAL) was the Japan Air Transport Company, the Japanese national airline dissolved by the allies after World War II. During the US occupation, Japan was not permitted to establish its own airline, but in 1951; a group of bankers founded JAL, in essence a revival of the Japan Air Transport Company. Under the Allied Peace Treaty, JAL was forbidden from using Japanese flight crew and therefore, leased pilots and a small fleet of aircraft from Northwest Airlines. By 1953, the fledgling airline had its own aircraft and crew, with government and the public sharing ownership. Under the Japan Air Lines Company Limited Law, JAL was granted special status as the 'flag carrier' and the only domestic airline allowed to operate international routes.

As the airline grew, its operations received heavy scrutiny from the government, its largest stockholder. Government involvement placed certain limitations on managerial independence and created a highly bureaucratic and complex organisational structure.[1]

In the late 1970s, deregulation revolutionised the US airline industry and the movement inevitably forced the Japanese airline sector to abolish the Japan Air Lines Company Limited Law in November 1987; the government relinquished its stake in JAL and divested its shares to the public. JAL became fully privatised and acquired greater freedom to expand into new areas and to exercise autonomy in corporate decision making. In the new environment, Japanese civil aviation companies were better able to respond and adapt to changing market demands and competitor actions. Perhaps due to the legacy of government protectionism, JAL was not known for its

---

[1]   Chatfield, A.T. & Bjorn-Andersen, N. (1997), *Journal of Management Information Systems*, Vol. 14, No. 1, Summer, pp. 13–40.

customer orientation and when surveyed in 1986, domestic travellers rated the company's service as bureaucratic and unfriendly relative to its domestic competitors.[2] Also, as a consequence of privatisation, air transport was no longer nationalised and JAL's chief domestic rival, All Nippon Airways (ANA) was permitted to enter the domain of overseas service.

During the 1990s, JAL experienced a financial downturn due to high labour costs and over expansion of its fleet and facilities, coupled with the slowing Japanese economic growth as a result of over-investments in the late 1980s. In recognition of these problems, JAL announced a US$4.8 billion cost-cutting plan.

The company's restructuring agenda fell under four classifications as follows:

❑ Outsourcing secondary services.
❑ Overall staff reduction/making wages competitive within industry norms.
❑ Disposing of non-core assets.
❑ Creating lower cost subsidiary airlines such as Japan Air Charter (for short-haul international flights) and Japan Express (for short-haul domestic flights).

By 1994, passenger counts for JAL were higher, but the airline had been pressured to cut prices to match the competition's lower fares. In the same year, Osaka's new airport gave a boost to JAL's overseas traffic, but brought intense competition by allowing more flights into Japan. In 1995, JAL and American Airlines (AA) formed an alliance, agreeing to link their computerised reservations systems (AXESS and Sabre respectively) and to serve as agents for each other's cargo businesses. This partnership was the first of several in years to come and characteristic of a rapidly evolving industry where cost-cutting and strategic alliances were critical for sustained growth.

DEVELOPMENTS WITHIN THE TRAVEL INDUSTRY

Throughout the 1990s, major structural changes in the airline industry were instigated through e-commerce. The use of the Internet created several advantages for airlines, including direct access to customers and cost-effective methods of conducting business processes on-line. On the other hand, growing e-commerce activity and the Internet's globalisation effect increased competitive business pressures and created a

---

[2] Wataname, K. (1995), "Challenges for Japanese Airlines", *Nihon Koku no Chosen*, Tokyo: Nohon Noritsu Kyokai Management Center.

rapidly changing business landscape. The airline industry was pressured to transform organisational processes to adapt to the changing environment by becoming more competitive. The Internet provided airlines with the ability to do business on a global basis, to react quickly, differentiate services, monitor changes and customise services with a view to winning customer loyalty. This was only attainable through the implementation of the appropriate mix of technology, process management and corporate strategy.

Disintermediation and Reintermediation

The nature of e-commerce could reap major benefits for Japan, with its bureaucratic tangle of middlemen in a complex market distribution system. In the air travel industry, travel agents were the traditional intermediaries between airlines and travellers, and were compensated for services through commissions paid by airlines. Through the advent of e-commerce, the very survival of the traditional travel agent was threatened by disintermediation through airline direct services and travel cybermediaries.

e-Commerce observers predicted the displacement of the traditional intermediary – the travel agent. This 'disintermediation' process was achieved through direct access to airlines. However, cutting out the middleman caused new problems, ranging from fulfilment of single transactions from individual consumers, to setting up new customer service centres.

Travel agents needed to provide new value. Additional pressure was placed on travel agents with the airlines imposing commission caps. The emergence of e-ticketing weakened the travel agent's role in the distribution chain as their principal role of putting tickets into the travellers' hands could be eliminated by airlines and Websites offering e-ticketing.

Most travel agents, however, demonstrated strong survival skills. According to the American Society of Travel Agents, 49 percent of travel agencies had Websites of their own, compared with 37 percent in 1998. Studies showed that many people who surfed the Internet for deals then turned to travel agents to make their bookings.

Internet travel agents began refocusing on the leisure travel market by offering a variety of broad travel packages at competitive prices. At the same time, airlines in many cases expanded by acquiring travel sites. UA had a minority stake in GetThere.com (formerly Internet Travel Network) and Continental held a stake in Rosenbluth Interactive, owners of Biztravel.com. To some observers, however, airlines failed to fully exploit the potential of the Internet and invest continuously in their Websites. As a result, they lagged behind on-line agents in innovation and the provision of integrated travel services.

Industry experts observed that while there were disintermediation forces, an equally vibrant industry of intermediaries emerged to serve the needs of airlines and customers. These new intermediaries, known as 'cybermediaries', reintermediated services in the airline industry. Cybermediaries competed with the traditional travel agents and an airline's direct services. They staked territory in cyberspace between the airlines and the traveller. Cybermediaries offered several advantages over an airline's direct services:

❏ Permitting travellers to book flights on almost any airline.
❏ Providing features to assist travellers in searching for the lowest prices.
❏ Notifying travellers by e-mail when a discount fare was posted for a particular destination of interest.

The concept of e-ticketing and its impact on the ticketing process was of prime importance in enabling the development of self-service technologies and electronic travel innovations. According to a study by Jupiter Communications, travel had become the number one product purchased on-line, netting US$911 million in 1997.[3] On-line travel sales are expected to account for 35 percent of all on-line sales globally by 2002 and travel purchases are expected to range from US$5 billion to US$30 billion by 2003.[4] Much of these purchases, however, were made through innovative 'virtual travel agencies'.

On one hand, airlines welcomed the creation of new channels to sell and promote their products, especially those that challenged the costly travel agent system. However, these new entrants also pre-empted the airlines' own efforts to implement direct sales and minimise distribution costs. In response, some airlines imposed tighter restrictions on commissions paid through such channels, but these new industry dynamics remained a cause for concern.

Computerised Reservation Systems

With the deregulation of the US airline industry in the late 1970s, American carriers had experienced similar competitive pressures and invested heavily in the innovation

---

[3] "On-line Travel Purchases Steadily Increase; Airlines Position to Get a Piece of the Pie", *World Airline News*, 9 April 1999.

[4] "Web@Work: E Travel Sales on the Rise", *Asia Computer Weekly*, 4 October 1999.

and development of computerised reservation systems (CRS)[5] to seek a competitive advantage. The advent of CRSs revolutionised airline business dynamics and the broader travel industry, elevating the role of information technology (IT). In 1987, JAL formed its newest subsidiary, AXESS International Network Inc., in a bid to develop its own computerised reservation system. JAL's management witnessed increased competitiveness resulting from the development of CRS (Sabre and Apollo) by its American counterparts and felt it necessary to develop a system of their own to seek a competitive advantage in the evolving CRS market.

JAL's CRS project was originally established as a marketing initiative, receiving full managerial support and huge capital and human resource investments. The resulting system – AXESS, was an integrated travel information and reservation system linked to hotel chains as well as other CRSs. The Sabre Group CRS (which had spun off from its originator, AA) bought a 25 percent stake in AXESS. AXESS became a cornerstone of JAL's strategy and was noted for its superior functionality as compared to other domestic reservation systems. This system was tightly integrated with other JAL information systems and offered enhanced services such as Japanese/English bilingual information retrieval. To ensure target users, such that travel agents and corporate in-house travel departments would adopt AXESS, several value-adding features were incorporated, such as back office accounting and customer profile management systems. AXESS also reduced the ticket-processing time from 15 minutes to five seconds.

Introduction of e-Ticketing[6]

Airline deregulation triggered major changes including the privatisation of national carriers and the proliferation of start-ups throughout the airline industry. In 1993, Valujet, an Atlanta-based no-frills carrier, pioneered a revolutionary innovation with low fares, no traditional paper tickets and a proprietary reservation system, its comprehensive route structure and direct sales channel translated into simple accounting needs and made it especially well suited for the 'e-ticketing' initiative [refer to **Appendix 1**

---

[5] Computerised reservation systems facilitate on-line reservations with a variety of suppliers and enable prior bookings up to one year in advance.

[6] Wauthy, Y. (1997), "Business Research Project: Electronic Ticketing in the Airline Industry, History, Implementation, Consequences and Impact for the Future", Concordia University, October.

for an illustration of the e-ticketing process].[7] In the same year, Morris Air, a small carrier based in Salt Lake City, introduced e-ticketing to increase its distribution potential; it was later acquired by Southwest Airlines. Southwest elected to implement the e-ticketing software and systems that came with the purchase, following a dispute with the Apollo/Galileo and System One systems.

Both e-ticketing pioneers, Morris Air and Valujet, gained tremendous value from the implementation. Morris Air's sales through travel agents decreased to around 33 percent and the carrier observed further benefits in check-in time and accounting labour savings; Valujet estimated that e-ticketing had cut costs by around ten percent Soon, major US carriers were rapidly adopting e-ticketing.

Industry experts believed that e-ticketing would inevitably succeed traditional ticketing as the *de facto* standard because of the following obvious benefits for firms:[8]

❏ Acceptance by the airline carrier's target customers because of enhanced customer service and improved travel efficiency.
❏ High proportion of direct sales. By eliminating the middleman, airlines could save on agent commission costs and agency fees.
❏ High proportion of business/corporate customers. Repeat business allowed airlines to monitor travelling trends and offer personalised service.
❏ Existence of advanced credit card payment systems. e-Ticketing could be integrated easily into existing payment systems to provide 'one-stop' shopping.
❏ Prevalence of carry-on baggage. Many customers liked to travel with minimum luggage, making e-ticketing and seamless travel attractive. Business travel was usually restricted to a short timeframe; the elimination of luggage check-in improved efficiency.
❏ Air travel consists primarily of point-to-point passengers. The existence of self-service check-in equipment reduced check-in times, thus improving efficiency and customer service.

---

[7] e-Ticketing is the process when a ticket is booked either via an agent or on-line, the information is transmitted directly to the airline's database and once the information is sent, one can access the database to check, modify or cancel the details of the booking. After making a reservation or booking through an agent or on-line, the customer needs only a confirmation number and itinerary, both of which can be issued immediately over the telephone or through the airline's Website. At the airport all that is needed is the confirmation number, photograph ID and credit card where necessary.

[8] Orla, K. (1996), "Strategic Technology Assessment: Aer Lingus and Electronic Ticketing", December. URL:http//www.cs.tcd.ie/courses/ism/strtechs/ind1/as/msg00011.html

❏ Airlines controlled the check-in environment. A simple network structure without connecting flights and multi-carrier itineraries give rise to 'seamless' travel.

❏ Ability to adapt computer systems. Airlines preferred to use their own systems, equipment and personnel to avoid the need to develop additional interfaces with other systems.

The earlier e-ticketing pioneers approached systems development through in-house innovation. Major US and European airlines also came under pressure to respond and develop their own systems [refer to **Appendix 2** for an overview of the impact of e-ticketing on various airline functions]. Other airlines adopting e-ticketing technology took a 'fast follow' approach by seeking existing technology and customising it to their requirements. Indeed, airlines opting for the 'fast follow' method benefited from the standardisation efforts.

Ron LeRadza, the General Manager of product distribution at Air Canada, conveyed the essence of this approach:

We don't want to be leaders in the field. By waiting to see what problems and successes other carriers experience, we can make good progress with the introduction of our own systems.[9]

e-Ticketing in North America and Asia

Before the introduction of e-ticketing, distribution costs ranging from travel agent commissions to ticket stock, were high across the airline industry. By the mid-1990s, distribution costs represented an average of 24 percent of total costs, ranking even higher than airlines' fuel costs. Although the concept of e-ticketing emerged in 1993, it was only after initiatives by new airline entrants that major airlines overcame reservations concerning adoption and implementation. Improved value through enhanced customer service, personalised information and other integrated travel information, was difficult to resist once e-ticketing benefits for customers and companies were clear. [Refer to **Appendix 3** for an illustration of some advantages and disadvantages of e-ticketing for the various parties in the air travel process.]

The main benefit of e-ticketing for airlines included transferring a portion of the airlines' travel agency sales, rife with commissions and segment booking fees, to direct

---

[9] "Electronic Ticketing Without Frontiers", Airlines International.

sales channels. This opened up the potential for non-traditional channels of distribution that continued to arise with the advances of modern telecommunications.

As a result of these benefits, by early 2000, e-ticketing had become universal in North America and represented over 40 percent of total bookings for main carriers. In May 1999, UA announced that 51 percent of the seven million tickets it sold that month were e-tickets – the first time that e-ticketing use had achieved such a majority. By year's end, UA's e-ticketing service was 100 percent available to all 259 destinations in its worldwide network. Within five years, its e-ticket strategy had gone from conception to setting world standards in implementation.[10] With growing acceptance of e-ticketing, a number of basic interline e-ticketing (described later) implementations were under establishment.

Although e-ticketing was widely adopted by North American carriers, relatively few Asian carriers provided this service. e-Ticketing services in Asia were first experienced in Hong Kong in 1999. By early 2000, only Singapore Airlines had introduced e-ticketing to limited destinations; Cathay Pacific offered e-ticketing to Hong Kong, Australia, Singapore and Manchester and had further plans to include Japan, the US, Canada, Taiwan and London Heathrow. Airline Websites offered features such as direct ticket sales, frequent flier programme administration, flight-tracking, promotional releases and on-line gift catalogues and on-line ticket auctions.[11]

In Japan, American carriers were pulling ahead of JAL and its domestic counterparts; UA and Delta had introduced e-ticketing and Northwest had imminent plans to follow suit. The Australian carrier, Qantas, was also set to extend its e-ticket offering to the Japanese market. A 1999 study commissioned by SITA, the leading provider of integrated telecommunications and information support to the air transport industry, revealed a possible root of this disparity – the average planned IT investment by Asia-Pacific airlines lagged far behind that of American and European carriers.

Interline e-Travel

Interline e-ticketing referred to travelling by an e-ticket with an itinerary spanning multiple carriers; this service provided great value to customers but could pose consid-

---

[10] "United Airline's e-Ticket (SM) Service Now Available Worldwide", *PR Newswire*, 17 November 1999.

[11] On-line ticket auction is where an airline will post a travel offer on its Website which is then open for surfers to bid against each other until the highest price is reached or bidding has closed.

erable complications for airlines offering the service. So far, most airlines that offered on-line e-ticket bookings only facilitated point-to-point tickets between certain stated destinations. On-line booking facilities could not handle fares permitting stopovers and such requests had to be made at appropriate reservation offices either in person or via telephone.

In October 1996, a resolution addressing interline e-ticketing was adopted at the IATA/ATA Joint Passenger Services Conference and was made effective from January 1997.[12] These resolutions contained specifications for the eventual introduction of interline e-ticketing. However, interline e-ticketing development was progressing relatively slowly.

JAL ALLIANCES

In January 1998, an agreement was signed between Japan and the US, granting JAL, Northwest Airlines, United Airlines (UA) and ANA, unlimited flying rights between the two countries. Additionally, new service opportunities were provided to Continental, American, Delta, TWA and USAirways. The agreement was immediately criticised by JAL executives as favouring the American carriers.

However, by 1998, JAL improved profitability with proceeds from the sale of assets and managed to pay dividends for the first time in seven years; economic conditions had also improved. The number of passengers from Japan was expected to pick up, but questions still remained about JAL's ability to compete with its American and European counterparts, particularly with the opening of a new runway at Narita, which could prompt more aggressive pricing. The reduction in labour costs and the disposal of assets were nearing their limits and the airline found it difficult to make further savings in this area.

With the multitude of one-to-one code sharing and collaborative agreements JAL had accumulated, industry observers began to wonder if the airline had eventual plans to be a formal member of one of the increasing number of alliances among the international carriers. The larger American and European airlines had taken leading roles in pushing for alliances centred on code sharing and joint marketing (including shared frequent flier programmes) to benefit from the economies of scale.

Multi-carrier groups were created to address the pressures of heightened compe-

---

[12] Resolution 722f for airlines and 722g for travel agents in neutral ticketing environments.

tition. Other alliances, such as UA's Star Alliance had grown to a considerable prominence. Although JAL had entered individual agreements with several Oneworld alliance members, including AA, British Airways, Cathay Pacific and Iberia Airlines, it insisted on pursuing collaborations on a one-to-one basis. Nonetheless, by mid-1999, JAL announced the introduction of a task force to study the advantages and disadvantages of joining an alliance.

The Japan–US Civil Aviation Agreement (1998)

"The purpose of the negotiations was to narrow the imbalance between Japan and the US, which has favoured the US since 1952 [when the original US–Japan pact was signed]. Instead, the gap has been widened," said JAL president Akira Kondo.

To some industry observers however, the implications of the Japan–US civil aviation agreement were not so bleak – Japanese carriers still had better access to the domestic corporate market and increased competition would boost overall traffic in the region, potentially to the benefit of all carriers serving Japan.

Despite the deregulation of the Japanese aviation industry, US carriers did not enjoy complete freedom to undercut fares offered by Japanese airlines. While the Japanese government offered assurances that demand would determine prices on trans-Pacific routes, it was thought that JAL's fares would serve as a benchmark for other airlines. More worrisome was the threat of excess capacity across the industry and the loss of control at JAL's hubs as a result. Also on the horizon was further cause for concern – the opening of a second runway at Narita, anticipated in 2002. The new runway would dramatically increase the access that foreign carriers had to the Japanese market, with annual slots going up by as much as 70 percent.[13] Another warning came in a Standard & Poor's report on the airline, where it was suggested that with increased competition, any cost savings that would result from JAL's efforts could be offset by a necessary increase in promotional expenses.[14]

One of the more positive terms of the Japan–US civil aviation agreement was the provision permitting JAL to pursue a code-sharing alliance with a major

---

[13] Hayashi, D. *et al.* (1998), *HSBC James Capel Report: Japan Airlines*, 29 May.

[14] Jones, D. (1998), "From One Crisis to Another", *Air Finance Journal*, September.

American airline. Such an alliance was formed with its marketing partner of three years, AA. This alliance provided JAL with access to AA's extensive feeder network within the US, resulting in a vast increase to the booking options available for clients departing to Asia. The partnership with AA also increased JAL's appeal to passengers unfamiliar with the airline, who might otherwise prefer to make arrangements with a US carrier.[15] Over the next year, JAL announced further code-sharing partnerships with Cathay Pacific, Swissair, Alitalia and Iberia Airlines and formed an alliance with Lufthansa and Scandinavian Airlines System for a cargo route between Japan and Northern Europe.

As the competitive environment grew complicated in the area of international service, Japan's domestic market showed signs of change. By the late 1990s, JAL's domestic market share had made some headway against leaders ANA and Japan Air System (JAS). JAL benefited from the abolition of traffic thresholds on internal routes in Japan that had prohibited it from encroaching on ANA's realm of service. With internal expansion, JAL was able to provide a more extensive international feed than the other two majors and the success of its frequent flier programme contributed further to customer loyalty. This is not to say that the domestic market was devoid of developments – a number of up-start airlines, Hokkaido International Airlines (Air Do), Skymark Airlines and Pan Asia Airways were granted operating authority by the Ministry of Transport and were making a modest emergence. While these start-ups were in their infancies, JAL and ANA implemented aggressive pricing on domestic routes in an attempt to stifle the new threat.[16]

In August 1999, JAL and JAS announced an agreement to code share certain international flights for a trial period from October 1999 to March 2000. This was the first such plan announced by Japanese carriers and called for the use of JAL equipment and flight personnel at the JAS arrival and departure berths at Narita. Each airline maintained its own flight number and tickets continued to be sold through their separate marketing channels. At the time, JAS was also in the process of negotiating a code-sharing agreement with ANA. These developments unfolded amid some

---

[15] Jones, D. (1998).

[16] "Japanese Carriers Defend Domestic Pricing Structures", *World Airline News*, 17 December 1999.

speculation that Japan's airlines may one day combine to form a 'super carrier' for cost-saving and competitive purposes.[17]

Process Integration

With deregulation, JAL recognised the pressing need to advance customer service and improve profitability. To some extent, these objectives were attained through traditional modes of restructuring. Management's desire to reduce the volume of paper-based transactions led to the swift development of electronic data interchange (EDI) applications for cost reduction and logistical coordination.[18] A proprietary EDI system provided JAL with accurate and timely information to manage their complex network of relationships and to enable procurement, just-in-time delivery and joint-venture operations. This network, developed by the Multi-Japan Network, was a JAL group member; JAL readily accepted the EDI implementation. The network's proprietary nature gave JAL confidence in information security and accuracy. EDI encouraged cost reduction by facilitating functions ranging from fuel procurement, aircraft maintenance parts delivery as well as improving the overall communication throughout the group.

For a period in 1997, JAL's Website was the second most popular site in Japan, receiving 60,000 visitors a day, second only to *Asahi Shimbun* daily newspaper's Website.[19] A Website was also created to serve the American region, in conjunction with the company's efforts to expand its North American business. JAL had begun accepting reservations via the Internet in July 1996. Travel reservations were implemented through collaboration with the Travelocity system, belonging to the Sabre Group. e-Ticketing was not available, but customers could make travel arrangements through a customised version of Travelocity and traditional tickets were later sent by mail from the Travelocity service centre. Initially, this service was exclusive to domestic flights, but it was ex-

---

[17] Laterman, K. (1999), "Japanese Airlines Need Restructuring to Keep Their Heads Above the Clouds", TheStreet.com, 26 September, URL: http://www.thestreet.com/int/asia/787066.html, January 2000.

[18] Chatfield, A.T. & Bjorn-Andersen, N. (1997), *Journal of Management Information Systems*, Vol. 14, No. 1, Summer, pp. 13–40.

[19] "JAL Internet Site Proves Popular", *Travel Trade Gazette UK & Ireland*, 15 January 1997.

panded to include international service in January 1997. The reservation system generated US$4 million in revenue.[20]

According to JAL spokesman Akihiko Sato, most people who made reservations via the Internet were business passengers using domestic services and the proportion of repeat users was high.[21] The volume of on-line bookings for international travel was considerably smaller because many Japanese travellers purchased package tours for overseas travel. Direct ticket sales saved JAL the high travel agent commissions, ranging from five to nine percent of ticket price.

By the late 1990s, e-ticket sales represented approximately ten percent of all airline tickets worldwide. Many major airlines offered on-line booking with e-ticketing facilities. Websites were user-friendly, self-explanatory, with step-by-step instructions on booking on-line. Some airlines even gave on-line booking rewards in the form of bonus air miles to create customer loyalty. In fact, firms realised that on-line Website management should produce the ultimate goal of creating customer satisfaction and customer loyalty. During this period, there was growing popularity of the integrated front-end management process, which referred to firms creating seamless and tightly integrated management of customer order acquisition strategies. This meant that Websites were points of entry for customers and that a customer visit on-line should result in the purchase of a good/service and in return, firms manage the purchase in an integrated fashion with the use of appropriate technology, process management and strategy to execute all the functions involved.

For some, e-ticketing was seen as a source of competitive advantage, but JAL adopted a more traditional approach in their business re-engineering process rather than radically changing their business strategy. In response to the impending changes in their competitive environment, JAL formed horizontal alliances with other service providers such as car hire companies, hotels and leisure service providers as a means of improving customer service. They also vertically integrated by establishing value-added services to core activities such as:

❏ Provision of airport transportation services.
❏ Provision of airport lounges.

[20] Hirao, S. (1998), "Japan's Electronic Commerce: Companies Learn By Trial and Error to Sell on the Net", *Japan Times Weekly International Edition*, 11 May.

[21] *Japan Times Weekly International Edition*, 11 May 1998.

- ❑ Provision of advance seat selection services.
- ❑ Provision of a baggage delivery service.
- ❑ Provision of priority guest services.
- ❑ Provision of a strong US and European network by forming alliances with other major air carriers.

However, these had become commoditised services which most major airlines provided. In addition, other airline Websites such as UA's provided customers with one-stop services for all airline booking and vacation requirements. All customers had to do was to get on-line, and UA would manage any requirements thereafter. It created customer satisfaction and entrenched customer loyalty. This was a management philosophy most firms were moving towards. However, JAL, while making small innovations, still had a fragmented strategy with regard to managing passengers' on-line bookings. Domestic passengers could only book through traditional travel agents while North American customers could book JAL seats through Travelocity.

With the expanding interconnection of customers and suppliers, e-commerce will facilitate the creation of electronic 'supply Webs' surpassing the capability of a simple supply-chain. As a result, value will be added as transactions pass between participants, while costly human intervention will be kept at a minimum.

UA was one of the first among the major international airlines to implement e-commerce to enhance its value-chain. UA adopted a management philosophy with a process methodology that took into consideration every aspect of the firm and its environment. They focused on the consumer to improve interactions and streamlined operations by adding value internally to deliver superior customer service. UA carried this out by creating a new Website that provided a new look and improved navigation. They added quick-search features that allowed customers to check schedules and flight information from the homepage as well as the ability to check their Mileage Plus account summary. To make navigation easier, the homepage was presented in four categories:

- ❑ *Planning Travel* – view schedules, compare fares, purchase travel, request upgrades, redeem award miles or update customer profile.
- ❑ *Travel Support* – locate information about services, baggage guidelines, onboard entertainment and airport maps.
- ❑ *Mileage Plus* – review frequent flier accounts and the latest promotion updates to earn bonus points.
- ❑ *About United* – product information, alliances and commitment to improving customer satisfaction.

This philosophy of integrated selling–chain management was gaining a lot of popularity among firms because it created added value for them and was touted as becoming a critical facet of conducting on–line business effectively. The idea was to create added value, for example, through information sharing. By sharing information along each link in an airline's process, airlines created value for customers by providing updated information on schedules and personalised customer services. Such integrated chains required firms to re–engineer their fundamental business processes to adapt their line of business to an e–commerce framework.

JAL'S FUTURE

Within a few years, on–line booking volumes skyrocketed and airlines scrambled with competing virtual distribution channels. Airlines offered various incentives to lure customers, and stood at fairly even market share with the on–line agents. Sales in 1999 were predicted to be at least US$8 billion and the market was expected to go up to US$20 billion in 2001.[22]

Japan's economy, however, remained largely under the influence of government ministries and *keiretsu* affiliations, resulting in a general preference for Japanese developed technology rather than the adoption of systems and technologies from abroad.[23]

In the airline industry, smart cards[24] followed on the heels of e–ticketing as a major component in companies' visions of seamless travel. With the full implementation of such technologies, customers would be able to transfer funds from a bank onto the card and make travel purchases on–line by transferring value from the smart card through a smart card reader installed in a personal computer. In addition, a customer's frequent flier information, mileage record as well as seating and meal preferences would already be stored in the card, thus expediting the on–line purchasing process. Once completed, an e–ticket and any necessary legal notices would then be transmitted and stored in the smart card. At the airport, the card would accelerate the check–in process, enable the use of automated kiosks, store other travel documentation and serve as a boarding pass and baggage receipt as well as provide access to club lounges and other benefits. With

---

[22] "Gomez Advisors Release First Internet Airline Scorecard", *Business Wire*, 8 September 1999.

[23] "Smart Cards Come to Japan", *Credit Card Management*, September 1998.

[24] Smart cards are standard plastic cards containing an integrated circuit, systems and applications software and permanent data.

potentially vast linkages to other service partners, the additional functions of the smart card were left to one's imagination.

Using technology as an enabler, airlines were rapidly adopting strategies and re-engineering their businesses to focus on adding more value to customers. Smart card technology, for example, was a vision which companies thought they could soon implement and offer as a service to customers. Airlines were experimenting with new dimensions in ticket distribution technology with the introduction of speech recognition systems capable of performing reservations, sales, and schedule and flight information functions. Some airlines viewed this as a mere supplement to the existing distribution methods, but others felt it would dramatically impact the industry when used in conjunction with e-ticketing and Internet sales.

Japan's traditionally complex bureaucratic organisational structures, coupled with heavy government regulation, seemed to hinder the development of the Japanese airline industry since its infancy and also affected its ability to innovate. JAL's strategy over the past decade focused on cost savings and efficiency improvement; however, changes remained within the realm of traditional business management practices. No major management effort was initiated to capture the opportunities offered by e-commerce and no dramatic business re-engineering processes were undertaken. At best, efforts to grow JAL's business on-line and seek alternative methods of growth remained fragmented; JAL's management philosophy seemed submerged by heavy cultural and regulatory influences.

JAL President and CEO Isao Kaneko could only express 'cautious optimism' for a turnaround in 1999 on the recent news that Japan's economic growth was accelerating. However, JAL was under pressure despite increasing consumer spending and passenger traffic. Was this costly short-sightedness on the part of management, or was it in fact wiser in the long run for Japan's largest airline to consolidate internally and take a 'fast follow' approach to e-ticketing in the light of vast implementation hurdles and uncertainties over eventual standards? Could it catch up with international airlines and compete effectively in the domestic and international market under the current management? What was the appropriate strategy to compete in the globalised and competitive environment that e-commerce posed?

APPENDIX 1: THE E-TICKETING PROCESS

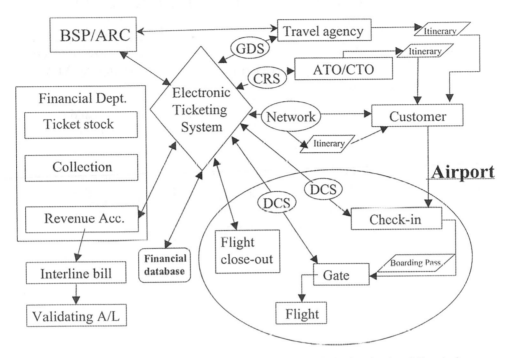

*e–Ticketing process diagram, e.g. Yves Wauthy, Electronic Ticketing in the airline industry.

APPENDIX 2: AN OVERVIEW OF THE IMPACT OF E-TICKETING ON VARIOUS AIRLINE FUNCTIONS

Computerised reservation systems	With the creation of an e-ticket at a CRS terminal, a record is entered into the airline's e-ticketing database according to ATA/IATA standards.
Departure control systems	This system must be adapted to allow airline check-in and gate agents access to the e-ticketing database and enable them to update the passenger's status over the course of passenger handling operations.
Accounting systems	In addition to its function as a travel document, the e-ticket serves a financial function and must be under the auspices of the accounting systems throughout the course of its use. The e-ticket is used for billing and revenue accounting purposes.
Settlement systems	Known as the Airline Reporting Corporation (ARC) in the US and Bank Settlement Plan (BSP) in other countries, settlement systems are in use in travel agencies to expedite ticket and accounting functions. The systems are comprised of a neutral ticket issue to serve travel on multiple providers. The billing function is centralised by ARC/BSP, which then 'settles' the transactions with the airlines. With the advent of e-ticketing, paper ticket settlement systems are no longer applicable, but new settlement systems must be implemented.

APPENDIX 3: THE ADVANTAGES AND DISADVANTAGES OF E-TICKETING FOR VARIOUS PARTIES WITHIN THE TRAVEL INDUSTRY

	Advantages	Disadvantages
Airlines	• Enables new distribution channels • Benefits direct sales over costly intermediaries • Eliminates paper ticket production • Simplifies modification and refunds • Reduction in check-in time and possibility of self-check-in • Eliminates data-entry redundancy • Accelerated revenue processing • Labour savings in terms of sales, passenger handling and accounting functions.	• Uncertainty over acceptance by the travelling public • The matter of implementing interline e-ticketing and similarly, of supporting last minute schedule changes • Display of legal information, such as the Warsaw Convention on liability • Verifying customer identification • Threat of fraud – in terms of unauthorised issuance of e-tickets and fraudulent payment via credit card
Customers	• Greater flexibility in ticket purchasing • Convenience of travelling without physical documentation that can be lost, stolen or destroyed • Ability to modify itinerary and make cancellations without adjusting a paper ticket • Added efficiency with check-in or possibility of self-check-in • Automated access to customer profile/frequent flier information	• Complications resulting from user or system error, such as double booking, neglecting to cancel a ticket • Increased risk of letting tickets go unused, especially by corporate travellers • At the early stages of e-ticket implementation, complications might arise due to system shortcomings – particularly in making last minute changes

	Advantages	Disadvantages
Travel Agents	• Higher productivity resulting from the streamlined ticketing process • Simplified modification of itineraries • Savings on ticket delivery costs • Reduced importance of geographic position of the travel agency – allowing it to cater to a broader clientele and perhaps to experience rental savings	• Large loss of agency fees due to booking by direct channels is a threat to agencies • Initial training required to become familiar with ticketing procedures • Subject to added constraints on CRS as airlines push for e-ticketing standardisation across the board • e-Ticketing still unsuited for complex itineraries and interlining

CHAPTER

■ ■ ■

10

Metamorphosis: The Internetworked Enterprise

OBJECTIVES

- To recognise the importance of collaboration and communication in the formation of a new form of organisation – the internetworked enterprise.
- To examine the effects of disorder and environmental uncertainty on the organisational form.
- To understand the contemporary structural changes affecting organisational architecture.
- To realise the important role that information plays in the new organisational structure.
- To discuss the reinvention of the enterprise.

In the future, conditions of great environmental turbulence will become more and more the rule. The exponential increase in the flow of information will produce an increasingly chaotic temporal behaviour. That is, the external environment will be driven by non-linear laws.... Its short-term behaviour may appear to be predictable, but the longer-term behaviour will be largely unknowable and subject to surprise and shock. It may change spontaneously to a stable state, to a different chaotic state, or to a state of complete instability. The organisation or firm that is embedded in such an environment must be prepared to deal with any and all of those possible conditions.[1]

In recent years we have seen increased debate among organisational theorists about organisational design and form. Such a surge of interest has been prompted, among other things, by the following:

- ❏ Increased environmental complexity.
- ❏ Accelerated rate of mergers and acquisitions in many industries.
- ❏ The proliferation of information technology, particularly the Internet, in business.

In the light of these developments, companies have been grappling with the difficult task of reorganising and restructuring their management and operational processes so that they can respond to market needs more rapidly than before.

In this last chapter we will examine some of the trends that have led to the rethinking of the organisation, as we know it. First, we look at the way environmental complexity and disorder are affecting the organisational form. Then we examine the way the network economy is reshaping the firm's composition in terms of size. Next we look at some of the factors that are influencing the form of organisational architecture. We show how technological developments have played a pivotal role in changing the strategic landscape, thus accelerating the rate by which companies are being forced to adopt new organisational forms that are fluid, flexible and amenable to increased cooperation and collaboration within and outside organisation bounds.

COMPLEXITY, TURBULENCE AND DISORDER

Today's business landscape, characterised by increased complexity, chaos and disorder, is rugged and unstable. Charting through such terrain successfully requires a special form of craft with sophisticated communications and navigational tools. Success also hinges on an unparalleled sense of urgency for adaptability, agility and flexibility. In the

---

[1] Neumann (1997), p. 96.

same vein, for today's organisations to succeed, they need to restructure, reconfigure and reinvent themselves.

Throughout history, companies have devised organisational structures in an attempt to '… meet the demands of the increasingly complex environments within which they found themselves'.[2] The rapidly increasing flow of information in recent years is a manifestation of such environmental complexity within which organisations are subject to unpredictable interactions between their elements whose emergent behaviour borders on stability and chaos. In order to survive in the new business ecosystem, the emerging network organisation, what we refer to as the *internetworked enterprise*, must embed its IT in the macrostructure of its multi-organisational domain.[3] In other words, the internetworked enterprise must be built on a sophisticated IT infrastructure to collect, process and filter information flowing to and from its boundaries so that it can respond quickly to market changes.

Moreover, as firms learn to deal with increased complexity they need to become more self-regulating, self-organising, open and interdependent.[4] Self-regulation and self-organisation for the most part require improved *communication* within the firm, while openness and interdependence entail enhanced *collaboration* with external stakeholders. In the face of increased complexity, self-organisation implies that novel structures will emerge from existing forms, that change is not brought from outside but emerges from within, that departments in an organisation evolve by creating something new from within.[5]

Agile Web, Inc.: An Integrated Source of Manufacturers

Launched in June 1994, Agile Web, Inc. (www.agileweb.com) is a US$310 million integrated multiple source of manufactured assemblies involving electronics or electro-mechanical products. It is a unique corporation composed of 20 manufacturing firms networked together electronically, offering a broad range of services such as electronics, casting, assembly, design and coatings, among others.

---

[2] Neumann (1997), p. 87.

[3] Neumann (1997).

[4] Lewin (1999).

[5] Murphy (1998).

Agile Web provides an infrastructure for member companies to form virtual organisations to respond quickly to specific customer needs, and by retaining a permanent base, also offers a forum for on-going customer relations.

Two significant developments in the manufacturing industry have resulted in the evolution of the concept of Agile Web: (1) the emergence of the agility concept in manufacturing and (2) the trend towards consolidating supplier chains in fabricated products. The widespread trend of companies towards downsizing and consolidating supplier base in the late 1980s alarmed the officials at the Northeast Tier Ben Franklin Technology Center (BFTC) at Lehigh University as the manufacturers in the industrial base of eastern Pennsylvania, mostly small- to medium-sized manufacturers, were under major threat. Competing in the new marketplace involves responding to an opportunity expeditiously, while maintaining close customer relationship. The challenge to the smaller firms were two-pronged: how to rapidly team with other firms in order to respond to opportunities, at the same time being able to maintain customer-supplier relationship continuity.

Thus in 1993, the Agile Web concept emerged as 'a group of companies with complementary capabilities, interwoven in a supply web, functioning as an agile manufacturer, with speed and efficiency in meeting emerging needs for customised output' (www.agileweb.com/bgjun95.htm, 18 August 2000). Meanwhile, the ability of the American industry to compete in the global market and the growing needs of the defence sector, for example the ever-changing need for spare parts and materials of military hardware, have resulted in the development of the Technology Reinvestment Project (TRP). Executives at BFTC scouted for prospective member companies and by August 1993, 19 companies had expressed their interest and commitment to the Web. By October 1993, the government's TRP awarded BFTC a US$2 million grant over two years to study how agility could be applied to small- and medium-sized manufacturing companies. The next 18 months involved numerous meetings to fully define the concept, its implementation strategy and its operating procedures. In June 1994, Agile Web, Inc. was launched. The focus on improving the inter-firm information systems was one of the first tasks implemented by the BFTC – installation of PCs with EDI and electronic mail. The long-term plan was to set up an inter-wide firm system that would allow members to collaborate in real time and provide instant updates on project status to Web management and the interested customer.

Sources: Agile Web; Kunkle (1994); Nagel (1997).

By drawing on evolutionary biology in treating organisations as 'organisms', we can see that in times of relative stability, organisations reinforce the existing dominant organisational form. Such reinforcement is based on *exploitation* of the existing markets and relationships. In contrast, during periods of relative disorder and turbulence, firms are likely to explore new and enhanced capabilities for dealing with higher levels of complexity and disorder. Such *exploration* strategies include mergers and acquisitions, increasing alliances and an increased rate of research and development expenditure.[6] We will discuss some of these issues in the next sections.

ORGANISATION SIZE

The network economy has changed the composition of businesses in terms of size. In 1995, there were over five million non-farm employer firms in the US: 90 percent employed less than 20 people; 9.8 percent had 20 to 500 employees; and a scant 0.2 percent had over 500 employees.[7] In 1998, the Fortune 500 companies employed one in ten US workers compared to one in five 25 years ago.[8]

As these statistics show, small firms have largely been at the centre of economic activity in the last few decades. As shown in **Figure 1**, the Internet will further change the composition of firms in terms of size: (1) it will lead to further increase in the number of small firms and (2) it will also accelerate mergers and acquisitions in certain industries, leading to the creation of some very large firms.

Smaller, Specialised Firms

The new economy has by and large made it easier for smaller firms to compete in marketspace. The internetworked enterprise can increasingly realise the traditional benefits of vertical integration, such as economies of scale and scope, without ownership of all parts of its value-chain. By sourcing various activities involved in the business chain, small companies can transact efficiently and cost effectively throughout the world. As such, the internetworked enterprise, consisting of a web of well-managed relationships, will continue to become smaller than its predecessor (left side of

---

[6] Lewin *et al.* (1999).

[7] Bureau of Census, with funding from SBA, Office of Advocacy.

[8] Malone & Laubacher (1998). Economists point out that firms usually grow in size when it is cheaper to conduct transactions internally, within the bounds of the organisation.

Figure 1). Such firms will leverage their core competencies to develop a niche targeted at particular buyer groups. They will use their expertise to bring specialised, customised products/services to the market. The Internet allows today's small enterprises to gain competitive advantage arising not only from superior cost structure and extended geographical reach, but also from enhanced differentiation accrued from focused marketing and improved customer service.

In addition, the internetworked enterprise will be able to take advantage of technology to diminish the traditional risks associated with the niche strategy – the waning effect of differentiation and the risk of imitation by competitors. Because the effect of differentiation typically fades over time (due to buyers' sophistication), the internetworked enterprises can use market data to continuously improve their existing product line and innovate new products and services. For example, through data mining of their existing and potential customers' preferences, companies can quickly react to changes in the market to customise their products and improve their services, thus defending and sustaining the competitive advantage engendered from differentiation.

Figure 1:   The changing composition of firms based on size

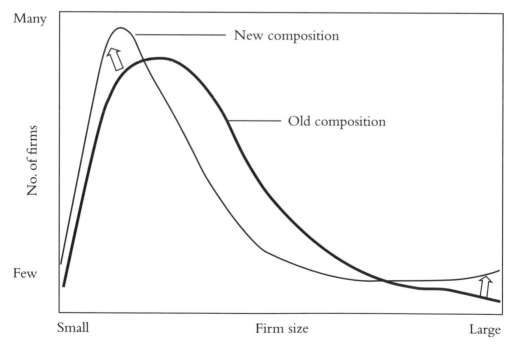

Larger Firms with Aggregated Products/Services

Even though the general trend has been towards the shrinkage of organisation size, we have also seen the emergence of some very large firms created through mergers and acquisitions (the lower right side of Figure 1). In the new economy, epitomised by the increasing environmental uncertainty and disorder, firms are more likely to accelerate their exploration adaptation strategies to respond more rapidly to the changing market forces.[9] One such strategy would be the amalgamation of firms through mergers and acquisitions, particularly in certain burgeoning industries. Recent examples include mergers in the financial industry (Citi Bank/Travel Group), in media (AOL and Time Warner) and in telecommunications (MCI and Worldcom, Vodafone and Mannesmann).

Industry consolidation in the network economy is primarily prompted by an increased market power engendered by a firm's ability (1) to aggregate bundled branded goods and services and (2) to use its brand name to expand into new markets. In the former case, certain companies can accrue added value through vertical consolidation along their main product/service line. The AOL/Time Warner merger was prompted because of the potential synergy resulting from the integration of access (AOL) and content (Time Warner). Such an amalgamation allows the merging companies to further increase their market power by expanding along their traditional business chain by selling a larger number of related products and services.

In the latter case, companies can leverage their brand to expand their reach horizontally by entering markets entirely new to them. As discussed in Chapter 7, branding is a critical success factor for conducting business in marketspace, especially in B2C e-commerce. The effect of branding is so powerful that some of these companies can even expand into different lines of business by acquiring or investing heavily in smaller firms (for example, amazon.com has acquired, invested in or made strategic alliances with other e-tailers such as drugstore.com and Tool Crib of the North).

DESIGNING THE NEW ORGANISATIONAL ARCHITECTURE

The traditional hierarchical form and its associated planning and control, which were geared towards predicting and managing events, are no longer capable of effectively

---

[9] Lewin *et al.* (1999).

dealing with the environmental complexity and uncertainty. The new form of organisation, the internetworked enterprise, relies heavily on IT to adapt quickly to the environment and to exploit uncertainty, rather than to reduce it.[10]

In recent years there has been much debate about the form of the new organisation. Because organisational structure directly affects the way a firm conducts its business, much attention of late has centred on structural changes affecting the organisational design.

In response to the increased environmental complexity, companies have gone through massive structural changes in order to facilitate and expedite decision-making processes in the organisation. In the old days, one of the major functions of management was to filter information that was flowing between the different layers in the organisation. In this context, the majority of managers acted as 'information processors', controlling the direction and quantity of information that was flowing to them from their subordinates and superiors. Not only was such a hierarchical structure expensive,[11] the excessive layers in fact impeded the information flows and slowed down the speed by which companies could respond to market conditions.[12]

In tandem with delayering, we have seen operational decentralisation in areas such as product design and marketing, as well as strategic decentralisation, allowing managers to make strategic decisions in accord with the needs of the units within which they work.[13] For example, a salesperson no longer needs to contact the head office to enquire about production schedules and get authorisation for a particular sale. Such information is readily available through on-line access to corporate databases.

Because of the diminishing role of the 'command-and-control' structure, organisations are now based on a more decentralised power structure and have fewer layers. With less hierarchy, information can flow rapidly both horizontally and vertically. In a recent study of several hundred European firms, Whittington et al. (1999) found that 30 percent of firms took out organisational layers between 1992–96. They also found that during the same period, almost half of the firms reported an increase in operational decentralisation (in such areas as supplier policy and production processes), while 41 percent reported increased strategic decentralisation in such areas as long-term planning.

---

[10] Applegate et al. (1999).

[11] Geroski & Gregg (1994).

[12] Nohria (1996).

[13] Whittington et al. (1999).

Pillsbury: Lotus Notes/Domino-based Intranet

The Pillsbury Company (www.diageo.com/pillsbury) offers consumers the Pillsbury Doughboy, Jolly Green Giant vegetables, Haagen-Dazs ice cream, Progresso soups, and Old Paso Tacos and sauce products. The Company developed its intranet and has fully utilised it to disperse information from its research and development laboratories, resulting in cost savings and providing a faster time to market for its products. With the use of Lotus Notes/Domino-based intranet, researchers enter the information directly into a Notes-based workflow application called Doc-It, by which the documents are accessible to other people responsible for reviewing and approving it. Once approved, the information is automatically diverted to a database called the Tech-Know-Bank. With a Notes client or browser, other employees can access the information from the database. Since 1997, the Tech-Know-Bank database enabled Pillsbury's R&D to develop 150 applications. For example, the Doc-It application and the Tech-Know-Bank database facilitated a reduction in the time needed to approve a food label from an average of 43 days to eight days. Pillsbury plans to leverage its success in its R&D laboratories to launch more widespread usage.

Sources: Pillsbury; Schwartz (1999).

With the introduction of intranet-based tools, it is no longer possible to know which tools and which information each person uses. In fact, management has lost the ability to know exactly how a process is carried out. A person in any position in a company can start to use the information and the tools that he or she finds convenient and start to change his or her role in the company. If this is handled properly, it might be a major advantage for an organisation, giving rise to shorter lead times and more flexibility. It is usually necessary to let the organisation develop in the same direction as the IT support. A typical step that can be taken is to introduce performance and quality indicators that focus on the added value of a unit or a person, rather than measuring whether tasks are carried out in line with fixed process descriptions. A change process like this in an organisation cannot easily be reversed, and it is a typical example of a spontaneous organisation.

The new organisational form is fluid, flexible and information-based. Such a dynamic structure is made possible through task–focused clusters[14] or project teams[15] that are formed and disbanded as required.[16] Each member of the team contributes through her expertise and specialisation as well as through what Tom Peters calls peripheral vision – a feel for the task, the ability to adapt quickly and work with other team members. Because the success of any given project is primarily dependent on the knowledge and expertise of the project team members, such teams are more heavily dependent on one another than employees working within traditional hierarchical structures. "The key role for many individuals – whether they are managers or not – will be to play their parts in shaping a network that neither they nor anyone else controls."[17]

As project teams become increasingly autonomous through mutual interdependence and contact with outsiders, trust becomes a cornerstone of the new organisational form. 'Trust is the foundation of commerce',[18] but as we discussed in Chapter 6, it is an indispensable part of the network economy: Without trust there will be no e-commerce!

In designing the new form of organisation, companies need to strike a balance between the competing forces to match the organisational structure with the external environment. For example, traditional hierarchical structures were adopted to increase certainty in the face of environmental uncertainty. As business environments became more complex, hierarchical structures failed because their capability to process increasing amounts of information reached a maximum.[19]

Figure 2 shows the new organisational structure needed to match today's complex business environment. On the horizontal axis, increased environmental uncertainty calls for dynamism usually found in entrepreneurial firms. Such firms usually rely on loosely coupled, self-organising and self-adjusting teams who can react to environmental changes swiftly, to cut order fulfilment cycles drastically and bring prod-

---

[14] Mills (1991).

[15] Peters (1992).

[16] Whittington *et al.* (1999) also found that slightly over half of the firms in their survey placed greater emphasis on project-based structures between 1992 and 1996.

[17] Malone & Laubacher (1998), p. 152.

[18] Keen *et al.* (2000), p. 1.

[19] Neumann (1997).

Figure 2:   New organisational structure

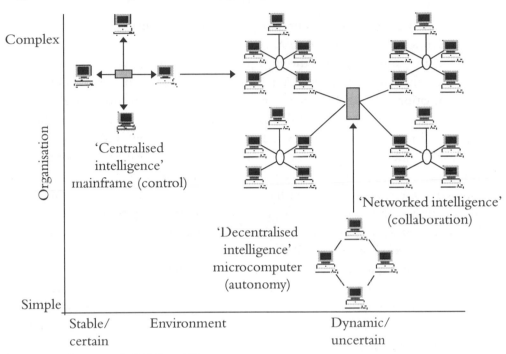

'Centralised
intelligence'
mainframe (control)

'Networked intelligence'
(collaboration)

'Decentralised
intelligence'
microcomputer
(autonomy)

Source: Applegate *et al.* (1999), p. 177.

ucts to market quickly. At the same time, an increased organisational complexity (vertical axis) necessitates tight controls to monitor management and operational processes.[20]

The emerging organisational structure – the network organisation – must simultaneously blend autonomy and control. To this end, firms rely heavily on IT to foster collaboration and enhance communication within and between their boundaries. As such, the internetworked enterprise will increasingly be dependent on information to organise and regulate its internal activities and to facilitate and solidify its external relationships.

---

[20] Applegate *et al.* (1999).

REINVENTING THE ENTERPRISE

We conclude this book with some thoughts on how the major forces behind the network economy are driving companies to adopt new forms of organisational structure so that they can compete in the emerging global business ecosystem where transactions are conducted with an increasing degree of speed, openness and transparency.

Organisations are dissipative in nature: they consume information in order to survive. As such, the very survival of the firm, in the face of an increasingly turbulent, complex and information-laden environment, depends on how well it processes and uses massive amounts of information within and outside its organisational bounds. The new organisation is structured so that its information systems architecture mirrors the complex interdependence between the firm and its partners. Such an architecture, embedded in the Internet, is based on a constellation of loosely connected networks. When nodes within such a supra-network are brought together, the result is a synergetic unleashing of a kind of superintelligence that is not found in any one computer or user but emerges from the interconnections between them. As we have seen in Chapter 2, by adding new points of connection, we exponentially increase the power of the network. The non-proprietary network structure of the Internet, intranets and extranets allow for radical reinvention of the enterprise, letting loose the power that emerges when people, technology and companies are connected to one another.

Formula One

Yes, speed is of the essence in network computing. It also comes in handy for Formula One racing. Sun and McLaren have built a network that is now used for every aspect of race operations. The team uses Sun workstations for the CAD/CAM design of its race cars, airflow analysis and aerodynamics testing, trackside performance monitoring, and even control and management of the race strategy during each contest.

Each West McLaren Mercedes car is extensively monitored as it races. Vital statistics, such as steering response, oil temperature and engine temperature, are all recorded. The data is continuously transmitted in real time to the pit crew, who analyses it using a self-contained network of workstations, which are placed on the pit wall and in the garage, and remain in constant contact with the car. The data is also fed back to the team's factory in real time via a high-speed digital link, giving specialist staff fast access to the information they need. "What this means," explains Kevin Masterson, McLaren's technical computer manager, "is that the engineers often know when a car is going to have problems before the driver does. They also know how serious a problem is, so they're able to make intelligent decisions about how to respond to it."

Source: URL: http://www.sun.com

Like cars on a Formula One race, the organisation of tomorrow – the internetworked enterprise – will also be operating on the fast tracks of the network economy, where speed is god and time the devil.[21] Information is at the heart of such a fast-moving enterprise, where environmental conditions are often difficult to predict, reliance on different stakeholders is a must and self-discipline is vital to success. The key challenge facing the internetworked enterprise will be to successfully use the emerging technologies to manage the increasing chaos and complexity inherent in the network economy. Success will depend on self-organisation and self-regulation within the enterprise, as well as environmental adaptation facilitated through enhanced coordination and collaboration among the nodes of the loosely coupled networks comprising the internetworked enterprise.

SUMMARY

- ❏ Environmental complexity has necessitated the increasing need for communication and collaboration between a firm and its partners. Such complexity has led to the emergence of a new form of organisation – the internetworked enterprise.
- ❏ The internetworked enterprise is decentralised, consisting of a loose cluster of task-focused or project teams that are formed and disbanded as required.
- ❏ The members of such teams, because of mutual interdependence, increasingly function on the basis of trust.
- ❏ The internetworked enterprise relies on a web of well-managed relationships rather than size to achieve economies of scale and scope.
- ❏ In order to succeed, the internetworked enterprise must constantly reinvent itself in order to adapt to an increasingly information-laden, turbulent environment.

---

[21] McKenna (1997).

REFERENCES

AgileWeb (2000),"The Evolution of AgileWeb, Inc.", URL: http://www.agileweb.com/bgjun95.htm, 18 August.

Anandarajan, M., Anandarajan, A., & Wen, J.H. (1998), "Extranets: A Tool for Cost Control in a Value Chain Framework", *Industrial Management & Data Systems*, March, pp. 120–128.

Applegate, L. *et al.* (1999), *Corporate Information Systems Management: Text and Cases* (Fifth Edition), New York, NY: Irwin McGraw-Hill.

Ashkenas, R. *et al.* (1995), *The Boundaryless Organization: Breaking the Chains of Organizational Structure*, San Francisco, CA: Jossey-Bass Publishers.

Babcock, C. (1996), "Client/Server Is Dead; Long Live the Intranet", *Computerworld*, 11 March, URL: http://www.computerworld.com/, July 1999.

Bullock, D. *et al.* (1997), "The Emergence of the Extranet in the Era of e-Commerce", *Project 2000*, URL: http://www2000.ogsm.vanderbilt.edu/Student.Projects/Extranet/extranet.html/, August 2000.

Checkpoint (2000), "Redefining the Virtual Private Network (VPN)", URL: http://www.checkpoint.com/, January.

Cortese, A. (1996), "Here Comes the Intranet", *BusinessWeek*, 26 February, URL: http://www.businessweek.com/1996/09/b34641.htm, August 2000.

Cullen, A. (1999), "Avoiding Intranet Chaos", *Intranet Journal*, URL: http://www.intranetjournal.earthweb.com/, July.

Derfler, F. (1999), "VPNs Analysis", *PC Magazine*, URL: http://www.zdnet.com/pcmag/stories/reviews/0,6755,2400740,00.html/, August 2000.

Frook, J.E. (1998), "Boeing's Big Intranet Bet", *Internetweek*, Iss. 740, 9 November.

Evans, P.B. & Wurster, T.S. (1997), "Strategy and the New Economics of Information", *Harvard Business Review*, September–October.

Geroski, P. & Gregg, P. (1994), "Corporate Restructuring in the UK During the Recession", *Business Strategy Review*, Vol. 5, Iss. 2, pp. 1–19.

Gove, A. (1997), "Client/Server Redux", *The Red Herring*, October, pp. 56, 58, 60.

Greer, T. (1998), *Understanding Intranets*, Redmond, Washington: Microsoft Press.

Hammer, M. & Champy, J. (1993), *Reengineering the Corporation: A Manifesto of Business Revolution*, London: Nicholas Brearley.

Isidore, C. (1998), "e-Shoppers Choose Cheaper Shipping over Speedy Delivery", *The Journal of Commerce Online*, URL: http://www.joc.com/issues/980112/p1age1/e32259.htm/, August 2000.

James, G. (1998a), "Intranets Give New Life to BPR", *Intranet Journal*, 8 September, URL: http://www.intranetjournal.earthweb/com/, July 1999.

James, G. (1998b), "Intranets Rescue Reengineering", *Intranet Journal*, 4 September, URL: http://www.intranetjournal.earthweb.com/, July 1999.

Jarvenpaa, S.L. & Ives, B. (1994), "The Global Network of the Future", *Journal of Management Information Systems*, Vol. 10, No. 4, Spring.

Kalakota, R. & Whinston, A.B. (1996), *Frontiers of Electronic Commerce*, Reading, MA: Addison-Wesley.

Kalakota, R. & Whinston, A.B. (1997), *Electronic Commerce: A Manager's Guide*, Reading, MA: Addison-Wesley.

Keen, P. *et al.* (2000), *Electronic Commerce Relationships: Trust By Design*, New York, NY: Prentice Hall.

Kelly, K. (1997), "New Rules for the New Economy: Twelve Dependable Principles for Thriving in a Turbulent World", *PandaPartners*, URL: http://www.pandapartners.com/, July 1999.

Kunkle, G.C. (1994), "Agility Through Incorporation? A Case Study of the Agile Web Pilot Project", URL: http://www.agileweb.com/incorp.htm, 18 August 2000.

Larsson, M. & Lundberg, D. (1998), *The Transparent Market: Management Challenge in the Electronic Age*, New York, NY: St. Martin's Press.

Lewin, A. (1999), "Application of Complexity Theory to Organization Science", *Organization Science*, Vol. 10, No. 3, May–June.

Lewin, A. *et al.* (1999), "The Coevolution of the New Organizational Forms", *Organization Science*, Vol. 10, No. 5, September–October, pp. 535–550.

Lipnack, J. & Stamps, J. (1997), *Virtual Teams: Reaching Across Space, Time, and Organizations with Technology*, New York, NY: John Wiley & Sons.

LPI Software Funding Group (1998), "The Dominance of the Intranet", URL: http://www.1pilease.com/, July 1999.

Malone, T.W. & Laubacher, R.J. (1998), "The Dawn of the e-Lane Economy", *Harvard Business Review*, September–October.

McKenna, R. (1997), *Real Time*, Boston, MA: Harvard Business School Press.

McQueen, H. & DeMattco, J.E. (1999), "Intranets: New Opportunities for Information Professionals", *Online*, January/February, pp. 14–18, 20, 22.

Mills, Q.D. (1991), *Rebirth of the Corporation*, New York, NY: John Wiley & Sons.

Murphy, W.J. (1998), "Making Intranets Obsolete", in Tapscott, D. *et al.*, *The Blueprint to the Digital Economy*, New York, NY: McGraw-Hill.

Nagel, R.N. (1997), "Scratching the Surface", *Industry Week*, Vol. 246, Iss. 13, p. 54.

Neumann, F.X. (1997), "Organizational Structure to Match the New Information-rich Environment: Lessons from the Study of Chaos", *Public Productivity & Management Review*, September.

Nohria, N. (1996), "From the M-Form to the N-Form: Taking Stock of Changes in the Large Industrial Corporations", Harvard Business School Working Paper, No. 96–054.

Peters, T. (1992), "Blow Up the Organization", *Adweek*, Vol. 42, Iss. 40, 5 October, pp. 26–31.

Pillsbury (2000), "Packaged Food", URL: http://www.diageo.com/pillsbury.html, 17 August.

Pompili, T. (1997), "Multiple Personalities", *PC Magazine*, Vol. 16, No. 10, pp. 117–120.

Schrage, M. (1997), *Shared Minds*, New York, NY: Random House.

Schwartz, J. (1999), "Collaboration: More Hype Than Reality", *Internetweek*, Iss. 786, 25 October, p. 64.

Sprout, A.L. (1995), "The Internet Inside Your Company", *Fortune*, 27 November, pp. 91–94.

USWeb/CKS (1999), "50 Ways to Put an Intranet to Work", URL: http://www.uswebcks.com/, July.

Vandenbosch, B. & Ginzberg, M.J. (1996–97), "Lotus Notes® and Collaboration: Plus Ça Change ...", *Journal of Management Information Systems*, Vol. 13, No. 3, Winter, pp. 65–81.

W3C (2000), "Extensible Markup Language (XML)", URL: http://www.w3.org/XML/, August.

Whittingtton, R. *et al.* (1999), "Change and Complementarities in the New Competitive Landscape: A European Panel Study, 1992-1996", *Organization Science*, Vol. 10, No. 5, September–October, pp. 583–600.

Wilkerson, R. (1996), "Intranet Experiment Pays Off in the Lab", *PC Week Online*, 4 April, URL: http://www.zdnet.com/pcweek/sr/0401/01esper.html/, August 2000.

Wise, S. (1997), *Client/Server Performance Tuning*, New York, NY: McGraw-Hill.

Wong, B.K. & Lee J.S. (1998), "Lotus Notes®: An Exploratory Study of Its Organizational Implications", *International Journal of Management*, Vol. 15, No. 4, December, pp. 469–475.

CASE

■ ■ ■

10.1

FedEx Corp.: Structural Transformation Through e-Business*

[FedEx] has built superior physical, virtual and people networks not just to prepare for change, but to shape change on a global scale: to change the way we all connect with each other in the new Network Economy.[1]

[FedEx] is not only reorganizing its internal operations around a more flexible network computing architecture, but it's also pulling in and in many cases locking in customers with an unprecedented level of technological integration.[2]

Since its inception in 1973, Federal Express Corporation (FedEx) had transformed itself from an express delivery company to a global logistics and supply-chain manage-

---

[1] 1999 Annual Report.

[2] Janah, M. & Wilder, C. (1997), "Special Delivery", *Information Week*, URL: http://www. FedExcorp.com/media/infowktop100.html.

* Pauline Ng prepared this case under the supervision of Dr. Ali Farhoomand. *Copyright © 2000 The University of Hong Kong. Ref. 99/57C*

ment company. Over the years, the Company had invested heavily in IT systems, and with the launch of the Internet in 1994, the potential for further integration of systems to provide services throughout its customers' supply-chains became enormous. With all the investment in the systems infrastructure over the years and the US$88 million acquisition of Caliber Systems, Inc., in 1998, the Company had built a powerful technical architecture that had the potential to pioneer in Internet commerce. However, despite having all the ingredients for the makings of a successful e-business, the Company's logistics and supply-chain operations were struggling to shine through the historical image of the Company as simply an express delivery business. Furthermore, competition in the transportation/express delivery industry was intense and there were reports that FedEx's transportation volume growth was slowing down, even though they were poised to take advantage of the surge in traffic that e-tailing and electronic commerce were supposed to generate. Hence, on 19 January 2000, FedEx announced major reorganisations in the Group's operations in the hope of making it easier to do business with the entire FedEx family. The mode of operation for the five subsidiary companies was to function independently but to compete collectively. In addition to streamlining many functions, the Group announced that it would pool its sales, marketing and customer services functions, such that customers would have a single point of access to the whole Group. The reorganisation was expected to cost US$100 million over three years. Was this simply a new branding strategy or did FedEx have the right solution to leverage its cross-company synergies and its information and logistics infrastructure to create e-business solutions for its customers?

THE EXPRESS TRANSPORTATION AND LOGISTICS INDUSTRY

FedEx invented the air/ground express industry in 1973. Although UPS was founded in 1907 and became America's largest transportation company, it did not compete with FedEx directly in the overnight delivery market until 1982. Competition began with a focus on customer segmentation, pricing and quality of service. For most businesses, physical distribution costs often accounted for 10–30 percent of sales or more. As competition put pressure on pricing, businesses began to look at ways to cut costs yet improve customer service. The solution was to have a well-managed logistics operation to reduce the length of the order cycle and thus generate a positive effect on cash flow.

The growth of the express transportation and logistics industry was brought about by three main trends: the globalisation of businesses, advances in information technology (IT) and the application of new technology to generate process efficiencies, and the changing market demand for more value-added services. As businesses expanded beyond national boundaries and extended their global reach to take advantage of new markets and cheaper resources, so the movement of goods created new demands for the transportation and logistics industry. With this, the competitiveness of transportation companies depended upon their global network of distribution centres and their ability to deliver to wherever their customers conducted business. Speed became of significance to achieve competitiveness, not only for the transportation companies but also for their customers. The ability to deliver goods quickly shortened the order-to-payment cycle, improved cash flow and created customer satisfaction.

Advances in IT promoted the globalisation of commerce. The ability to share information between operations/departments within a company and between organisations to generate operational efficiencies, reduce costs and improve customer services was a major breakthrough for the express transportation industry. However, of even greater significance was the way in which new technology redefined logistics. At a time when competition within the transportation industry was tough and transportation companies were seeking to achieve competitive advantages through value-added services, many of these companies expanded into logistics management services. Up until the 1980s, logistics was merely the handling, warehousing and transportation of goods. By combining the functions of materials management and physical distribution, logistics took on a new and broader meaning. It was concerned with inbound as well as outbound material flow, within companies as well as the movement of finished goods from dock-to-dock. With this, the transportation industry responded by placing emphasis not only on the physical transportation, but also on the coordination and control of storage and movement of parts and finished goods. Logistics came to include value-added activities such as order processing, distribution centre operations, inventory control, purchasing, production and customer and sales services. Interconnectivity through the Internet and intranets and the integration of systems enabled businesses to redefine themselves and to re-engineer their selling and supply-chains. Information came to replace inventory. Just-in-time inventory management helped to reduce costs and improve efficiency. With the advent of IT, express transportation became an aggregation of two main functions: the physical delivery of parcels, and the management and utilisation of the flow of information pertaining to the physical delivery (i.e., control over the movement of goods).

FEDEX CORP.

FedEx was the pioneer of the express transportation and logistics industry. Throughout the 27 years of its operation, FedEx's investment in IT had earned the Company a myriad of accolades. Since 1973, FedEx had won over 194 awards for operational excellence. Fundamental to the success of the FedEx business was the vision of its founder.

The Visionary Behind the Business

If we're all operating in a day-to-day environment, we're thinking one to two years out. Fred's thinking five, ten, 15 years out.
— William Conley, VP, FedEx Logistics, Managing Director Europe

Fred Smith, Chairman, President and Chief Executive Officer of FedEx Corporation, invented the express distribution industry in March 1973. By capitalising on the needs of businesses for speed and reliability of deliveries, FedEx shortened lead times for companies. Its next-day delivery service revolutionised the distribution industry. The success of FedEx's distribution business in those early days rested on Smith's commitment to his belief that the opportunities open to a company that could provide reliable overnight delivery of time-sensitive documents and packages were excellent. Despite losses in the first three years of operation due to high capital investments in the physical transportation infrastructure of the business, FedEx began to see profits from 1976 onwards. To compete on a global basis, the key components of the physical infrastructure had to be in place to connect the world's GDP. The underlying philosophy was that wherever business was conducted, there was going to have to be the movement of physical goods.

Under Smith's leadership, the Company had set a few records with breakthrough technology. In the 1980s, FedEx gave away more than 100,000 sets of PCs loaded with FedEx software, designed to link and log customers onto FedEx's ordering and tracking systems. FedEx was also the first to issue hand-held scanners to its drivers that alerted customers of when packages were picked up or delivered. Then in 1994, FedEx became the first big transportation company to launch a Website that included tracking and tracing capabilities. Very early on, Smith could foresee that the Internet was going to change the way businesses would operate and the way people would interact. By applying IT to the business, FedEx leapfrogged the rest of the industry. Smith was the visionary who forced his company and other companies to think outside of the proverbial one. The core of FedEx's corporate strategy was to 'use IT to help customers take advantage of international markets'.[3] By 1998, FedEx was a US$10 billion company spending US$1 billion annually on IT developments plus millions more on capital expenditure. It had an IT workforce of 5,000 people.

Building the Transportation and Logistics Infrastructure

In the early years of the FedEx transportation business, Smith insisted that the Company should acquire its own transportation fleet, while competitors were buying space on commercial airlines and subcontracting their shipments to third parties. The strategy of expanding through acquiring more trucks and planes continued. By the tenth year of operation FedEx earned the accolade of being the first US company to achieve the US$1 billion revenues mark within a decade without corporate acquisitions and mergers.

FedEx was quoted as being the inventor of customer logistics management.[4] As early as 1974, FedEx started logistics operations with the Parts Bank. In those days, a few small set-ups approached FedEx with their warehousing problems and decided on the idea of overnight distribution of parts. With those propositions, FedEx built a small warehouse on the end of its sorting facilities at Memphis. This was FedEx's first attempt at multiple-client warehousing. Customers would call up and order the despatch of parts and the order would be picked up on the same day. That was also FedEx's first value-added service beyond basic transportation. From there, the logistics side of the business snowballed.

Throughout the next three decades, FedEx's transportation business growth was attributable to a number of external factors that FedEx was quick to capitalise on. These included:

❑ Government deregulation of the airline industry, which permitted the landing of larger freight planes, thus reducing operating costs for FedEx.
❑ Deregulation of the trucking industry, which allowed FedEx to establish a regional trucking system to lower costs further on short-haul trips.

---

[3] Garten, J.E. (1998).

[4] Bruner, R.F. & Bulkley, D. (1995), "The Battle for Value: Federal Express Corporation Versus United Parcel Service of America, Inc. (Abridged)", University of Virginia Darden School Foundation.

❑ Trade deregulation in Asia–Pacific, which opened new markets for FedEx. Expanding globally became a priority for FedEx.

❑ Technological breakthroughs and applications innovations promoted significant advances for customer ordering, package tracking and process monitoring.

❑ Rising inflation and global competition gave rise to greater pressures on businesses to minimise the costs of operation, including the implementation of just-in-time inventory management systems, etc. This also created demands for speed and accuracy in all aspects of business.

As of January 2000, FedEx served 210 countries (making up more than 90 percent of the world's GDP), operated 34,000 drop-off locations and managed over ten million square feet of warehouse space worldwide. It had a fleet of 648 aircraft and more than 60,000 vehicles, with a staff of nearly 200,000. It was the world's largest overnight package carrier, with about 30 percent of the market share.

Building the Virtual Information Infrastructure

We are really becoming a technology company enabled by transportation.
 – David Edmonds, VP, Worldwide Services Group, FedEx[5]

Even as early as 1979, a centralised computer system – Customer, Operations, Service, Master On-line System (COSMOS) – kept track of all packages handled by the Company. This computer network relayed data on package movement, pickup, invoicing and delivery to a central database at Memphis headquarters. This was made possible by placing a barcode on each parcel at the point of pickup and scanning the barcode at each stage of the delivery cycle.

In 1984, FedEx started to launch a series of technological systems, the PowerShip programme, aimed at improving efficiency and control, which provided the most active customers (over 100,000) with proprietary on-line services [see **Exhibit 1** for a chronological list of FedEx systems]. In summary, these PowerShip systems provided additional services to the customer, including storing of frequently used addresses, label printing, on-line package pickup requests, package tracking, and much more.

The emergence of electronic data interchange (EDI) and the Internet allowed

---

[5] Krause, K. (1999), "Not UPS with a Purple Tint", *Traffic World*, URL: http:// www.trafficworld.com/reg/news/special/s101899.html, October.

companies to build one-to-one relationships with their customers. This was the perfect scenario for many manufacturers: the ability to match supply to demand without wastage. FedEx took advantage of such new technologies and started to track back along the supply-chain to the point of raw materials. As they did so, they identified points along the supply-chain where they could provide management services. Often, these services included transportation, order processing and related distribution centre operations, fulfilment, inventory control, purchasing, production and customer and sales services. The ability to interconnect and distribute information to all the players in a supply-chain became the focus of FedEx's attention. For many of its customers, logistics was viewed as a key means for differentiating their products or services from those of their competitors [see **Exhibit 2** for examples of some customer solutions]. In other words, logistics became a key part of strategy formulation. As businesses were placing more emphasis on the order cycle as the basis for evaluating customer service levels, FedEx's role in providing integrated logistics systems formed the basis of many partnership arrangements. By helping them to redefine sources and procurement strategies so as to link in with other parties in the supply-chain, such as raw materials suppliers, customers were outsourcing their supply-chain management functions to FedEx, functions that were seen as peripheral to the core of their business [see **Exhibits 3** and **4** for FedEx's coverage of the supply-chain through integrated systems]. By improving, tightening and synchronising the various parts to the supply-chain, customers saw the benefits of squeezing time and inventory out of the system. Tighter supply-chain management was no longer viewed as a competitive advantage but a competitive imperative.

Businesses sought ways to improve their return on investment and became interested in any business process that could be integrated and automatically triggered (e.g., proof of delivery and payment) as opposed to being separately invoked. So not only was FedEx pushing its customers for integration, but its innovative customers were also demanding greater integration. Some customers had even jumped ahead of FedEx. Cisco, for example, had developed an extranet that allowed its customers to order FedEx services without leaving the Cisco Website. By integrating its services within the supply-chain of its customers, and thus generating increases in customer loyalty and in customers' switching costs, FedEx managed to effectively raise the barriers to entry for competitors.

The Internet refined the COSMOS system. Whenever new information was entered into the system by FedEx or by customers through the Internet, all related files and databases were automatically updated. For example, when a FedEx customer placed an order through fedex.com, the information would find its way to COSMOS, FedEx's global package-tracking system. The courier's Route Planner – an electronic mapping toll – would facilitate the pickup and delivery of the order from the customer. A product movement planner would schedule the order through the Company's global air and courier operations. The customer would be able to track the status of the shipment through PowerShip or FedEx Ship. The COSMOS system handled 54 million transactions per day in 1999.

In 1998, FedEx decided to overhaul its internal IT infrastructure under Project GRID (Global Resources for Information Distribution). The project involved replacing 60,000 terminals and some PCs with over 75,000 network systems. The decision to go with network computers was made to avoid the 'desktop churn' found with PCs.[6] The network computers linked over a global Internet Protocol network aimed to enhance the quality and quantity of services FedEx could deliver to its customers. For example, FedEx employees at any location at any time could track a package through the various steps in the FedEx chain. Other applications planned to be launched included COSMOS Squared, which allowed Non-Event Tracking, a feature that triggered alerts when scheduled events, such as the arrival of a package, did not occur. Through a 24-hour, seven-day operation called the Global Operations Command Centre, the central nervous system of FedEx's worldwide system in Memphis, FedEx was able to provide efficient gathering and dissemination of real-time data. The operation housed huge screens covering the walls that tracked world events, weather patterns and the real-time movement of FedEx trucks and aircraft. New systems were also introduced to predict with greater accuracy the amount of inbound traffic. This system allowed FedEx to prioritise the hundreds of variables involved in the successful pickup, processing and delivery of a parcel. Senior managers at FedEx believed that having current and accurate information helped them to reduce failure in the business.

As well as the data centre in Memphis, FedEx operated other centres in Colorado Springs, Orlando, Dallas-Fort Worth, Singapore, Brussels and Miami.

Also in 1999, FedEx signed an agreement with Netscape to adopt Netscape software as the primary technology for accessing its corporate intranet sites. FedEx's intranet included more than 60 Websites, created for its end users and in some cases by its end users. Customers could build integrated Websites using FedEx Applications Program-

---

[6] 'Desktop churn' refers to the rapid obsolescence of PCs as new applications eat up processing power.

ming Interfaces (API) or FedEx intraNetShip (free downloads from fedex.com) and incorporate a link that would allow them to track packages directly from their own site. Over 5,000 Websites fed hundreds of thousands of tracking requests through to the fedex.com site.

> *Our API solutions are designed to give global visibility and access across the supply-chain, from manufacturing to customer service to invoicing. We've managed to wipe out those irritating WISMO (Where Is My Order) calls because we've seamlessly linked our customers to their customers.*
>
> — Mike Janes, former VP, Electronic Commerce & Logistics Marketing, FedEx[7]

At the beginning of 1999, FedEx launched an enhancement to its package-tracking service. Customers could query and receive package status information for up to 25 shipments simultaneously, and forward this information on to up to three e-mail recipients. Furthermore, users in France, Japan, Italy, Germany, the Netherlands and Portuguese- and Spanish-speaking countries could access this information on-line in their native languages through fedex.com.

FedEx claimed to have the largest on-line client server network in the world that operated in real time. Information became an extremely critical part of its business.

> *We're in the express transportation business, but we've discovered how to lock up a lot of value in the information that we have.*
>
> — Mark Dickens, VP, Electronic Commerce & Customer Services[8]

> *...even when on the physical side of the business, we outsource, for instance, the pickup or the delivery or the warehousing activity for a customer, we have never outsourced the information. Protecting the brand has always been very, very critical for us.*
>
> — William Conley

The benefits of these services were not limited to FedEx's customers. For FedEx, its on-line services, which in 1999 handled 60 million transactions per day, saved FedEx the cost of 200,000 customer service employees. In turn, the Company reported spend-

---

[7] Gentry, C. (1998), "FedEx API's Create Cinderella Success Stories", October, Federal Express Corporation, URL: http://www.fedex.com/us/about/api.html, February 2000.

[8] Janah, M. & Wilder, C. (1997), "Special Delivery", *Information Week*, URL: http://www.FedExcorp.com/media/infowktop100.html.

ing ten percent of its US$17 billion annual revenue on IT in 1999. Information had allowed FedEx to lower its costs such that the cost to customers of using FedEx in 1999 was lower than it was 25 years ago.

Going beyond delivery services, FedEx aimed to fully integrate its corporate partners every step of the way along the supply-chain. Fundamental to FedEx's strategy for establishing its e-business and logistics operations was how well it could forge technology links with customers.

> *It's all about integration, whether it's inside FedEx, with our technology partners or with our customers.*
> – Laurie Tucker, Senior VP, Logistics Electronic Commerce & Catalog[9]

> *Integration of Internet services with our transportation offerings is not an addition to our core business; it is our core business.*
> – Dennis Jones, CIO[10]

> *When it comes to managing synergies across businesses, we've found that seamless information integration is a critical component.*[11]

MANAGEMENT AND OPERATIONS ISSUES

Branding and Business Structure Up Until 19 January 2000

In the first 21 years of business, FedEx operated under the corporate name of Federal Express Corporation. Its customers came to recognise it as 'FedEx' in short and the brand took off as the Company grew and expanded its service offerings under the purple and orange flag. Hence in 1994, it seemed natural that the Company should change its brand name to 'FedEx'.

The Parts Bank was given official recognition when it became a division of FedEx Corp. in 1988 and became known as Business Logistics Services (BLS). It operated as a separate and independent company. In line with the express transportation side of the business, BLS developed expertise in the high-value, high-tech industries. It was

---

[9] Janah, M. & Wilder, C. (1997).

[10] Cone, E. & Duvall, M. (1999), "UPS Keeps Truckin'; FedEx: A Documented Success", *Inter@ctive Week*, 16 November.

[11] 1999 Annual Report.

involved in the express inbound, outbound and redistribution of goods. However, it focused mainly on the small parcel business. FedEx based its solutions on just-in-time logistics. As the business grew, concern was raised that the logistics business was not generating revenue for the express transportation business, but rather feeding this through to other carriers. Hence in 1994, BLS was renamed FedEx Logistics, and it became mandatory for the logistics business to include FedEx transportation as part of its solution to customers. In 1996, the division changed its name yet again, to FedEx Logistics and Electronic Commerce (FLEC). The Company started to focus its resources on doing business on the Internet, and the name change was to reflect the changes in the marketplace.

Following the acquisition of Caliber Systems, Inc. in 1998, five separate subsidiary companies were formed: Federal Express, RPS, Roberts Express, Viking Freight and FDX Logistics. The latter four were Caliber businesses. Each subsidiary was managed independently and was responsible for its own accounts [see **Exhibit 5**]. However, Caliber and FedEx's logistics operations were fundamentally different in that they had completely distinct customer bases and service offerings. Caliber developed expertise in moving raw materials, plates of steel and steel bars and managing work-in-progress. It would manage the manufacturing of cars and fork-lift trucks. Caliber provided an elaborate logistics operation concentrating mainly on high-priced goods industries, and it provided a fuller supply-chain solution than FLEC did, whereas FLEC was primarily focused on finished goods, transportation logistics and reverse logistics (i.e., handling returns). One was concentrating its business at the front-end of the supply-chain (e.g., receiving, work-in-progress) while the other was more involved in the back-end operations of the supply-chain (i.e., warehousing, transportation). Hence the two operations continued to operate independently of each other. Logistics systems and applications were also developed independently. Caliber Logistics became a subsidiary company under FDX Logistics, while FLEC continued as a division within Federal Express, the express transportation arm.

The acquisition served to reinforce FedEx's commitment to becoming more than just an express delivery company. Yet commentators and customers continued to associate the FedEx brand with transportation, and FedEx fought to transform the image of the Company outside of this mould. One solution was to rename the Company. With the acquisition, the Company created a holding company, 'FDX Corporation'. However, FedEx did very little to promote its new FDX corporate brand. Furthermore, its transportation subsidiary continued to operate under the Federal Express name with the purple and orange FedEx brand on its trucks and vans. The FedEx brand lived on, but with no advertising or aggressive promotion of FDX, the name did not resonate in the marketplace. While the likes of UPS had the advantage of promoting just one brand – UPS – to sell the entire company and its many service offerings, FedEx was trying to promote five different subsidiary companies with completely unrelated names and business logos under the FDX banner through distinctly separate sales and customer service teams. Furthermore, with two separate logistics businesses within the Group, separate sales forces selling services offered by different parts of the company, separate customer services staff to deal with different queries and IT resources spread across the Group, customers were confused and resources were duplicated.

Despite the confusion, by 1999, FedEx purported to offer companies 'total one-stop shopping' for solutions at all levels of the supply-chain. Each subsidiary continued to operate independently, with separate accounting systems and customer service staff, while competing collectively. However, while maintaining the autonomy of each subsidiary company, the challenge for FedEx was how to bring the companies closer together to create those synergies. Providing customers with a single point of access to the whole Group was the ultimate goal. In practical terms, the task was to decide how each of the subsidiary companies should leverage its skills and services to a broader audience.

EVENTS LEADING UP TO THE JANUARY 2000 REORGANISATION

FedEx needed to address a number of factors that would affect the prospects of the Company.

FedEx's Performance

In the year ending 31 May 1999, the Company had outperformed analyst expectations, posting record earnings of 73 percent, an increase of 28 percent over the previous year.[12] Net income had risen 30 percent to US$221 million. However, results took a downturn in the following financial year. For the first quarter ended 31 August 1999,

---

[12] Gelsi, S. (1999), "FDX Posts Stronger-than-expected Profit", CBS MarketWatch, 30 June, URL: http://cbs.marketwatch.com/archive.../current/fdx.htm?source=&dist=srch, February 2000.

FedEx announced that rising fuel prices had severely impacted upon the Company's net income, causing it to miss its first-quarter target. With no sign of improvements in fuel prices and with the US domestic market growth slowing down, FedEx warned that earnings for the second quarter and the full fiscal year may fall below analyst expectations. Bearing in mind that the express transportation business (mainly Federal Express and RPS) accounted for over 80 percent of the Group's revenue, and that the US market accounted for approximately US$10 billion of the Group's revenue, both trends had a significant negative impact on net income.

Sure enough, FedEx reported that for the quarter ended 30 November 1999, operating income was down by ten percent on the previous year and net income was down by six percent. The Company was not achieving the level of US domestic growth as expected. Rising fuel prices continued to erode operating income. However, operations other than express transportation (i.e., Viking Freight, Roberts Express, FDX Logistics and Caribbean Transportation Services) achieved revenue and operating income increases of 27 percent and 12 percent respectively in the second quarter. With the adverse fuel prices alone, the Company anticipated that operating income could be down by more than US$150 million for the year ending 31 May 2000. This called for some immediate remedial action.

Other trends within the express transportation and logistics market were also putting pressure on the Company to rethink its business strategy.

The Internet Market and e-Tailing

The Internet changed the basis for competition for most businesses. Its low cost and diversity of applications made it appealing and accessible. The Internet levelled the playing field such that, once a company was on-line, as long as it fulfilled its orders to the expectations of its customers, the size of the company was of no significance. The impact of the Internet on FedEx was two-fold. Firstly, it opened up opportunities in logistics management for FedEx as businesses were using the Internet to re-engineer their supply-chains. So long as customers were satisfied, it really did not matter whether the goods were warehoused or not, whether the goods came directly from a factory in some distant location or whether the goods had been made to order. Integration with customer supply-chains was the key.

Secondly, the express transportation needs associated with the growth in e-tailing (expected to reach US$7 billion in 2000) and B2B e-commerce (expected to reach

US$327 billion by 2002) presented enormous opportunities for companies such as FedEx.[13, 14]

FedEx was sure that it had the right business model to take advantage of these opportunities.

> We're right at the centre of the new economy.... Businesses are utilising the Internet to re-engineer the supply-chain. In the new economy, the Internet is the neural system. We're the skeleton – we make the body move.
>
> – Fred Smith[15]

But so were its competitors.

The Competition

In January 2000, CBS MarketWatch Live reported that FedEx's express delivery business was maturing and was not growing as fast as it used to.[16] Furthermore, the industry was loaded with companies, local and global, that provided a myriad of transportation services to a wide range of businesses. Competition was fierce. All major transportation and delivery companies were betting big on technology. Although FedEx pioneered the Web-based package-tracking system, such systems became the industry norm rather than a competitive advantage.

The four leading companies in the international courier business were DHL, FedEx, UPS and TNT. Between them they held more than 90 percent of the worldwide market.[17]

UPS ■ Since 1986, UPS had spent US$9 billion on IT and had formed five alliances in 1997 to disseminate its logistics software to e-commerce users. However, while FedEx developed all its IS software in-house, UPS made a point in stating that it

[13] Lappin, T. (1996), "The Airline of the Internet", *Wired*, Vol. 4, No. 12, December, URL: http://www.wired.com/wired/4.12/features/ffedex.html, February 2000.

[14] Erwin, B., Modahl, M.A., & Johnson, J. (1997), "Sizing Intercompany Commerce", *Business Trade & Technology Strategies*, Vol. 1, No. 1, Forrester Research, Cambridge, MA.

[15] Collingwood, H. (1999).

[16] Adamson, D. (2000), "FDX Corp. Changes Name to FedEx", CBS MarketWatch Live, 19 January.

[17] Murphy, D. & Hernly, K. (1999), "Air Couriers Soar Despite Mainland Gloom", *South China Morning Post*, 30 May.

was not a software developer and that companies taking that route were "trying to go a bridge too far".[18]

In early 1998, UPS formed a strategic alliance with Open Market, Inc., a US-based provider of Internet software, to deliver a complete Internet commerce solution providing integrated logistics and fulfilment. They were also working with IBM and Lotus to standardise formats on their Website.

In 1999, UPS raised US$5.47 billion through its initial public offering, the largest in the US IPO history. The company shipped more than 55 percent of goods ordered over the Internet and offered the full range of logistics solutions to its customers.

DHL ■ In 1993, DHL announced a four-year US$1.25 billion worldwide capital spending programme aimed at investing in handling systems, automation, facilities and computer technology. The company launched its Website in 1995. It was 25 percent owned by Deutsche Post and 25 percent owned by Lufthansa Airlines. Plans were underway for an initial public offering in the first half of 2001. Though the company dominated the UK market, it projected an increase in worldwide turnover of 18 percent to US$5.26 billion.[19]

TNT ■ In 1998, TNT launched a Web Collection facility on the Internet. Later the same year, TNT launched the world's first global Price Checker service on its Website that allowed customers to calculate the price of sending a consignment from one place to another anywhere in the world. Other applications were under development that would allow customers to integrate with TNT's on-line services. Then in 1999, TNT launched QuickShipper, a one-stop on-line access to TNT's entire range of distribution services, from pricing to delivery. This new service was to be integrated with existing on-line tools such as Web Collection and Price Checker.

Also in March 1999, TNT launched the express industry's first dedicated customer extranet, Customised Services environment. This offered regular customers easy access to detailed and personalised shipment information through the use of user IDs and passwords. With this came a host of service offerings.

While FedEx had pioneered many logistics solutions that had helped it to achieve

---

[18] Blackmon, D.A. (1999), "Ante Up! Big Gambles in the New Economy: Overnight Everything Changed for FedEx", *The Wall Street Journal Interactive Edition*, URL: http://www.djreprints.com/jitarticles/trx0001272701443.html, 4 November.

[19] Exelby, J. (2000), "Interview – DHL UK Foresees Tough Market", Yahoo Finance, URL: http://biz.yahoo.com/rf/000117/mq.html, 17 January.

economies of scale faster than its competitors, the advantages were quickly eroding as newer technologies became even more powerful and less expensive.

THE JANUARY 2000 ANNOUNCEMENT

All of your transportation and logistics needs can now be met by one organisation – FedEx Corporation.[20]

On 19 January 2000, FedEx announced three major strategic initiatives:

❑ A new branding strategy that involved changing the Company's name to 'FedEx Corporation', and extending the 'FedEx' brand to four of its five subsidiary companies. The subsidiary companies became:
   • FedEx Express (formerly Federal Express)
   • FedEx Ground (formerly RPS)
   • FedEx Custom Critical (formerly Roberts Express)
   • FedEx Logistics (formerly Caliber Logistics)
   • Viking Freight (no change)
   [See **Exhibit 6**.]
❑ Major reorganisations such that there would be one point of access to sales, customer services, billing and automation systems. With these consolidations, the Company announced intentions to form a sixth subsidiary called FedEx Corporate Services Corp. in June 2000 [see **Exhibit 7** for new Group structure]. The new subsidiary would pool together the marketing, sales, customer services, information technology and electronic commerce resources of the Group. The invoicing functions would also be combined for all the companies.
❑ Introduction of a new low-cost residential delivery service, FedEx Home Delivery, to be launched in the US.

Of significance was the merging of the two logistics operations (Caliber Logistics and FLEC) into FedEx Logistics. The two companies seemed to complement each other in terms of their service offerings and customer base. Both had a few of the same customers but many different ones. Furthermore, Caliber's presence was mainly in North America and Europe, while FLEC had expanded into other continents. FedEx

---

[20] Federal Express Corporation (2000), "Corporate Overview", URL: http://www.fedexcorp.com/aboutfdx/corporateoverview.html, 20 January.

Logistics brought together all the splintered operations of logistics in all the subsidiary companies, streamlining costs, presenting one menu of logistics service offerings to customers, and aligning R&D of systems upon common, agreed platforms. This reorganisation also brought about another major change in operations. It was no longer mandatory for the logistics business to use FedEx transportation as part of its solutions to customers. Being 'carrier-agnostic' meant that FedEx Logistics would use FedEx transportation where it fitted, both in terms of cost and in terms of geographic coverage. The decision would also rest on customer preference and the kind of goods being transported. For example, Caliber was transporting fork-lift trucks, cars and steel plates that FedEx did not have the physical capacity to handle.

Combining the two operations brought together the IT expertise and the knowhow of the logistics business. Under one CIO, standards were set for the development of systems on a worldwide basis, including vendor selection. In the past, regions developed their own solutions and operated in isolation. However, the Internet forced the Company to consolidate its systems and solutions as customers demanded global solutions. Through the IT groups located in Memphis, Leiden (Holland) and Singapore, the Company resolved to develop global systems for worldwide implementation, with functions such as multiple currencies and multiple languages. FedEx Logistics forecast a 70 percent growth rate in the year ending 31 May 2000. However, the business so far failed to generate any profit. The company aimed to build on its expertise in the five market segments: healthcare, industrial, high-tech, automotive and consumer.

The Company anticipated having to spend US$100 million on these changes over three years. The intention was to take advantage of one of its greatest assets, the FedEx brand name; the name that customers could count on for 'absolutely, positively' reliable service and cutting-edge innovation. The value of the brand had been ignored, particularly when the Company decided to change its corporate name to FDX in 1998. Realising its mistake, the renaming of the Company as FedEx Corporation and the extension of the brand to its subsidiaries fell in line with its intention to provide customers with an integrated set of business solutions. Customers wanted to deal with one company to meet their transportation and logistics needs.

Each subsidiary company was to continue operating independently, but collectively the Group would provide a wide range of business solutions. It was this collective synergy of solutions that FedEx believed would form the competitive advantage of the Company in the future. For customers, the benefits included easier means of doing business with FedEx. There was to be one toll-free telephone number, one Website, one invoice and account number, one sales team, one customer service team and a streamlined customer automation platform to handle electronic transactions for small and large businesses [see **Exhibits 6** and **7** for details of the changes following the reorganisation]. The new organisation was aimed at helping businesses of all sizes to achieve their shipping, logistics, supply-chain and e-business objectives. However, analysts questioned whether the new Group structure would work, given that there would still be different teams of delivery and pickup staff for the different operations. Hence, one person could pick up one package sent by ground and another person could pick up another package sent by express from the same company. Companies such as UPS, on the other hand, would have one person pick up both types of packages.

In addition to these changes, FedEx anticipated growth in consumer e-commerce and planned to start a new service called FedEx Home Delivery (within the FedEx Ground subsidiary company) to meet the needs of businesses specialising in B2C e-tailing. FedEx had been successful in providing services to the B2B e-commerce market. Now it aimed to achieve the same leadership status in the B2C e-commerce market. However, expanding the residential delivery business was one segment that FedEx consciously made a decision not to pursue throughout the 1990s. This gave UPS the opportunity to lead in residential delivery services.

In late 1997, Smith was quoted as saying,

We've made huge investments in our networks, and now that bow wave has passed. We think we have a good chance of harvesting a lot of that investment.[21]

In the two years that followed, the results of the Company showed little signs of a harvest. Was the January restructuring going to bring in the harvest? The announcement certainly served to tell investors that they were making some major changes to address some competitive issues. However, analysts took a pragmatic view to the announcement, saying that, 'the proof is in the pudding'.[22]

Our biggest challenge is to correctly manage everything that's on our plate.

– Fred Smith[23]

[21] Grant, L. (1997), "Why FedEx Is Flying High", 10 November, *Fortune Text Edition*, URL: http://pathfinder.com/fortune/1997/971110/fed.html, February 2000.

[22] Bazdarich, C. (2000), "What's in a Name?: Traders Swayed by Nominal Changes", CBS MarketWatch, 21 January, URL: http://cbs.marketwatch.com/archive...st.htx?source=htx/http2_mw&dist=na, February.

[23] Collingwood, H. (1999).

Was the reorganisation going to leverage the power of the networks and the information and logistics infrastructures that FedEx had built? Did it provide the right ingredients to achieve the objectives of creating value for FedEx customers while at the same time improving profitability for FedEx? Given the speed at which technology and the marketplace were changing, would the new organisation structure be adaptable to the changing business environment? Were there better alternative solutions that the company could have considered?

Exhibit 1: FedEx's record of systems innovations

1979   COSMOS (Customer Oriented Services and Management Operating System), a global shipment tracking network based on a centralised computer system to manage vehicles, people, packages, routes and weather scenarios on a real-time basis. COSMOS integrated two essential information systems: information about goods being shipped and information about the mode of transportation.

1980   DADS (Digitally Assisted Dispatch System) coordinated on-call pickups for customers. It allowed couriers to manage their time and routes through communication via a computer in their vans.

1984   FedEx introduces the first PC-based automated shipping system, later named FedEx PowerShip; a standalone DOS-based system for customers with five or more packages per day. The customer base was immediately transformed into a network that allowed customers to interact with the FedEx system and download software and shipping information.

1984   PowerShip Plus, a DOS-based shipping system integrated with customers' order-entry, inventory-control and accounting systems, for customers who ship more than 100 packages per day.

1985   FedEx was the first to introduce barcode labelling to the ground transportation industry.

1986   The SuperTracker, a hand-held barcode scanner system that captures detailed package information.

1989   FedEx launches an onboard communications system that uses satellite tracking to pinpoint vehicle location.

1991   Rite Routing demonstrates the value of a nationwide, centralised transportation management service.

Exhibit 1 (cont'd)

1991   PowerShip PassPort, a Pentium-class PC system that combines the best of PowerShip and PowerShip Plus for customers who ship more than 100 packages a day (1,500 users).

1993   MultiShip, the first carrier-supplied customer automation system to process packages shipped by other transportation providers.

1993   FedEx ExpressClear Electronic Customs Clearance System expedites regulatory clearance while cargo is en route.

1993   PowerShip 3, a client-server shipping system for customers who ship three or more packages per day.

1994   The FedEx Website debuts at www.fedex.com, the first to offer on-line package status tracking so that customers can actually conduct business via the Internet.

1994   DirectLink, a software that lets customers receive, manage and remit payments of FedEx invoices electronically.

1995   FedEx Ship, a Windows-based shipping and tracking software allows customers to process and manage shipping from their desktop (650,000 users). It extended the benefits of PowerShip to all FedEx's customers, providing software and toll-free dial-up to the FedEx network.

1995   FedEx launches the AsiaOne network, a transportation routing system.

1996   FedEx became the first company to allow customers to process shipments on the Internet with FedEx interNetShip, available through www.fedex.com. (65,000 users). This allowed customers to create shipping labels, request courier pickups and send e-mail notifications to recipients of the shipments, all from the FedEx Website.

1996   FedEx VirtualOrder, a software that links Internet ordering with FedEx delivery and on-line tracking. It also puts customers' catalogues on their Websites for them.

1997   FedEx introduces e-Business Tools for easier connection with FedEx shipping and tracking applications.

1998   FedEx Ship for Workgroups, a Windows-based software housed on a server that lets users share information, such as address-book information, access to shipping logs and a tracking database. The server can be connected to FedEx via either modem or the Internet.

1998   PowerShip mc, a multi-carrier electronic shipping system.

Exhibit 1 (cont'd)

1999   The FedEx Marketplace debuts at www.fedex.com, providing easy access to on-line merchants that offer fast, reliable FedEx express shipping.

1999   The EuroOne network was launched to link 16 cities to FedEx's Paris hub by air and another 21 cities by road-air. Like AsiaOne, this was a transportation routing system.

1999   FedEx MarketPlace, a convenient link to on-line shopping. Through this new portal, shoppers had one-click access to several top on-line merchants that utilised FedEx's delivery services, including Value America, L.L. Bean and HP Shopping Village (Hewlett-Packard's consumer e-commerce Website).

1999   FedEx made a deal with Netscape to offer a suite of delivery services at its Netcenter portal. This entailed automatically integrating Netscape with the FedEx site. Although customers of Netscape could choose not to use FedEx, the use of an alternative shipper meant that they would not benefit from the efficiencies of the integrated systems. Considering that Netscape Netcenter had more than 13 million members, the deal was a winner for FedEx.

Note: PowerShip had 850,000 on-line customers worldwide; PowerShip, PowerShip 3 and PowerShip PassPort were hardware-based products.

Exhibit 2:   Examples of some customer solutions

Dell Computers pioneered the direct selling model in the computer industry and succeeded because it was able to keep inventory very low. FedEx provided the system to track and monitor the assembly of each PC on order. Because the assembly line could be in any one of five manufacturing locations around the world, however, FedEx described itself as the conveyor belt for that manufacturing line. FedEx was a key partner for Dell, allowing customised, built-to-order products to be delivered within days of a customer placing an order, a huge advantage in an industry whose components become obsolete at the rate of two percent per month.

Five years ago, **National Semiconductor Corp.** (NatSemi) decided to outsource its warehousing and distribution to FedEx. By 1999, virtually all of NatSemi's products, manufactured by six factories (three being subcontractors) were shipped directly to FedEx's distribution warehouse in Singapore. Hence, FedEx had control over the goods, the warehouse and the despatch of orders (via FedEx transportation, of course).

Exhibit 2 (cont'd)

Having complete visibility of NatSemi's order systems allowed FedEx to reduce the average customer delivery cycle from four weeks to two days, and distribution costs from 2.9 percent of sales to 1.2 percent. FedEx could pack and fulfil orders without NatSemi having to notify them. In effect, it became the logistics department of NatSemi. Furthermore, this arrangement enabled NatSemi to dispense with seven regional warehouses in the US, Asia and Europe. NatSemi reported savings in the region of US$8 million over the five-year period [see **Exhibit 4**].

For **Omaha Steaks**, when orders were received, they would be relayed from Omaha Steaks' IBM AS/400 to its warehouse and simultaneously to FedEx by a dedicated line. FedEx would generate the tracking and shipping labels and the orders would be delivered to one of FedEx's regional hubs for onward delivery.

Cisco Systems was a Silicon Valley Internet hardware maker that transacted 80 percent of its business over the Web. At the end of 1999, FedEx had signed an agreement with Cisco to coordinate all of Cisco's shipping over the next two years, and to gradually eliminate Cisco's warehousing over the following three years. How could this be possible? Cisco had factories in the US, Mexico, Scotland, Taiwan and Malaysia. The finished parts were stored in warehouses near the factories awaiting completion of the whole order before it was despatched to the customer. But Cisco did not want to build more warehouses, pay for reshipping and hold massive volumes of inventory in transit. So the solution was to merge the orders in transit. As soon as parts were manufactured, they would be shipped to customers. Once all the parts had arrived at the customer's site, assembly would take place, thus doing away with warehousing. (This was known as the 'merge-in-transit' programme offered to companies such as Micron Computers.) FedEx created a unique system for Cisco that would automatically select routes and pick the most effective and economical mode of transportation, which included carriers other than FedEx's fleet of trucks and planes. Just as critical, however, was that the real-time information status of the synchronisation operation was constantly available on the Internet.

Exhibit 3:   FedEx solutions for the entire supply-chain

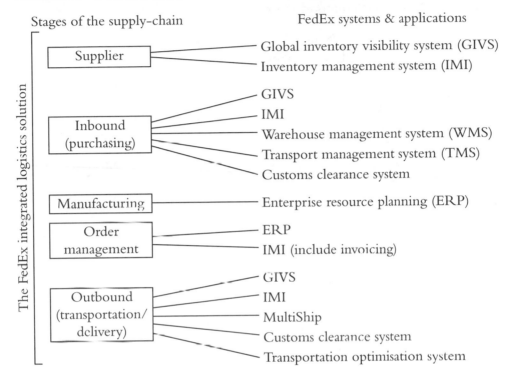

Exhibit 4: **Example of integrated customer order process management: National Semiconductor**

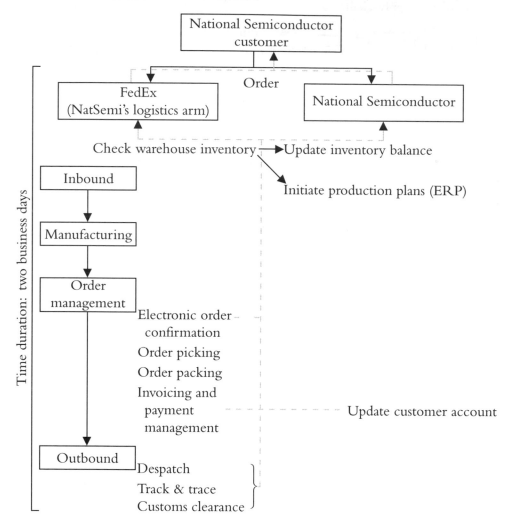

– – – – – – – The information flow value of integrated services to NatSemi's customer

Exhibit 5: **Subsidiary companies of FedEx following the acquisition of Caliber Systems, Inc. in 1998**

- ❏ **Federal Express** was the world leader in global express distribution, offering 24–48-hour delivery to 211 countries that comprised 90 percent of the world's GDP. In 1998, FedEx was the undisputed leader in the overnight package delivery business. It had a fleet of 44,500 ground vehicles and 648 planes that gave support to the US$14 plus billion business. It had 34,000 drop-off locations, and 67 percent of its US domestic shipping transactions were generated electronically. Goods shipped ranged from flowers to lobsters to computer components. This company was constantly running in crisis mode, seeking to move packages through all weather and conditions to fulfil shipments overnight. The underlying philosophy that ensured high service levels was that every package handled could make a difference to someone's life. The company handled nearly three million shipments per day in 1998.

- ❏ **RPS** was North America's second-largest provider of B2B ground small-package delivery. It was a low-cost, non-union, technology-savvy company acquired with the Caliber purchase. The company specialised in B2B shipments in one to three days, a service that FedEx could not attract because it was unable to offer prices low enough to attract enough volume. Being a 15-year-old company, RPS prized itself on having one of the lowest cost models in the transportation industry. It employed only owner-operators to deliver its packages. In terms of volume and revenue growth, RPS outperformed FedEx. For the future, plans were to grow RPS' B2C delivery service to take advantage of the growth of e-commerce, thus carving a niche in the burgeoning residential delivery market. In 2000, the company owned 8,600 vehicles, achieved annual revenues of US$1.9 billion and employed 35,000 people, including independent contractors. It handled 1.5 million packages per day.

- ❏ **Viking Freight** was the first less-than-truckload freight carrier in the western United States. The company employed 5,000 people, managed a fleet of 7,660 vehicles and 64 service centres, and shipped 13,000 packages per day.

- ❏ **Roberts Express** was the world's leading surface-expedited carrier for non-stop, time-critical and special-handling shipments. The service offered by Roberts Express has been likened to a limousine service for freight. In 1999, the company handled more than 1,000 shipments per day. It was the smallest company within the FedEx Group. Urgent shipments could be loaded onto trucks within 90 minutes of a call and shipments would arrive within 15 minutes of the promised time 96 percent of the time. Once loaded, shipments could be tracked by satellite every step of the way. Goods such as works of art or critical manufacturing components often

Exhibit 5 (cont'd)

required exclusive-use truck services. Exclusivity allowed customers greater control but at a price. This service was an infrequent necessity for most customers. Roberts had exclusive use of a handful of FedEx aircrafts, but the company still had to pay for use and for crew time.

❑ **Caliber Logistics** was a pioneer in providing customised, integrated logistics and warehousing solutions worldwide. The acquisition of Caliber in January 1998 brought with it over-the-road transportation and warehousing capabilities. Since the acquisition, FedEx had tried to move away from traditional logistics offerings to providing total supply-chain management solutions, and Caliber Logistics was renamed FDX Logistics. To the customer, this meant that FedEx could provide warehousing services, but only if this was part of a bigger deal. In September 1999, FedEx bought its first freight forwarder, Caribbean Transport Services (formerly GeoLogistics Air Services). Caribbean had a strong overseas network. FDX Logistics was the parent company of FedEx Supply-Chain Services and Caribbean Transportation Services.

Exhibit 6: Before and after the reorganisation

Before	After
Multiple brands under FDX umbrella	A single branding system leveraging the power of the FedEx brand so more customers can use FedEx reliability as a strategic competitive advantage
Separate sales force with directed cooperation	A single, expanded sales force especially targeting small- and medium-sized businesses, cross-selling a wide portfolio of services and pricing schemes
Multiple invoices and account numbers	A single invoice and single account number from FedEx
Multiple automation platforms offering all FDX services	Streamlined customer automation systems to handle electronic transactions and database management needs for small and large businesses
Separate customer service, claims trace functions	Single customer service, claims and trace functions by calling 1–800–Go–FedEx® (800–463–3339) or visiting its Website at www.fedex.com

Exhibit 7: Group structure

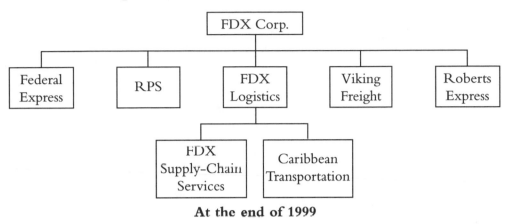

At the end of 1999

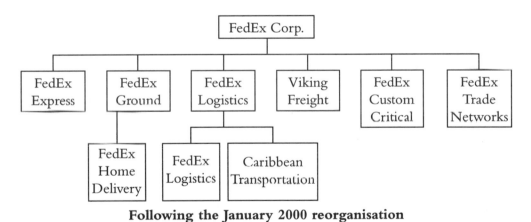

Following the January 2000 reorganisation

NAME INDEX

Company Index

SUBJECT INDEX